ENCYCLOPEDIA OF
PRACTICAL GASTRONOMY

ENCYCLOPEDIA OF PRACTICAL GASTRONOMY

BY ALI-BAB

Translated by Elizabeth Benson

McGraw-Hill Book Company
New York • St. Louis • San Francisco • Toronto

Originally published in French under the title *Gastronomie Pratique, Etudes Culinaires* by Ernest Flammarion, Editeur, Paris.

Design by Robert L. Mitchell
Illustrated by Bill Goldsmith

123456789 MUBP 7987654

Library of Congress Cataloging in Publication Data

Babinski, Henri, 1885–1931
The encyclopedia of practical gastronomy.

Translation of Gastronomie pratique.
1. Cookery, French. 2. Gastronomy. I. Title.
TX719-B313 641.5'944 74-7289
ISBN 0-07-001062-5

CONTENTS

PUBLISHER'S NOTE

Readers of this book—here translated into English for the first time ever—are reminded that Ali-Bab wrote this classic treatise on gastronomy in his native French nearly seventy years ago. He was a mining engineer and in the course of his work traveled all over the world—successfully combining his profession with what, thanks to his own refined tastes and unlimited curiosity about food, made his fame as a gourmet longer-lasting than his engineering skills.

Translator Elizabeth Benson has faithfully recorded recipes and theories, as closely as possible to the way Ali-Bab originally set them down. If you quarrel with the opening sections of the book which sketch food history, cooking utensils, and furnishings back to Stone Age man, keep in mind that the author was neither historian nor archeologist nor anthropologist. He was a keen observer with an excellent palate and a delightful sense of humor who sketched in backgrounds which generations of French cooks have delighted in. Discoveries during and after his lifetime make some of his judgments in fields outside the kitchen invalid. Since he has been dead for many years, it seemed to us unfair to "polish" or "update" the work of a man who isn't around to defend himself. What you will read is what Ali-Bab wrote in 1906 or for a subsequent edition of his book a bit later.

If you've had dinner in a big-chain hotel restaurant in the United States lately, or in run-of-the-mill British eateries, you'll know that Ali-Bab, in the early 1900s, knew exactly what he was talking about when it came to *food*, and that nothing much has improved. Good cooking is a science—sometimes sophisticated, sometimes not—which depends on the best of ingredients and the utmost care in their preparation, whether you're cooking for two or 500. The *science* of cooking is what this book is all about. Its basic principles haven't changed much in hundreds of years.

GASTRONOMY THROUGH THE AGES

HISTORICAL SKETCH

Man did not really rise above animals until he learned how to use fire.

The first representatives of our species lived on fruit, grasses, and roots. Later on, their descendants began to taste insects and shellfish, then meat, which they ate raw, as it came from the animal, or tenderized it by primitive means, some of which survive to this day.[1]

It is conceivable that after a forest fire, presumably ignited by lightning, the bodies of animals were found roasted and the first man who ate cooked meat no doubt enjoyed it despite the charred flavor. From then on fire was hallowed, and for as long as man did not know how to produce it at will[2] it remained the exclusive monopoly of priests, who appointed themselves its custodians. It was to them that the faithful brought victims to be offered to the gods in holocausts. The priests cooked . . . and ate them. They were therefore the first cooks and the first gourmets. Their spiritual descendants owe them a real debt.

As in all the arts, culinary art, whose history parallels that of man, has had its periods of glory and periods of decline. Most wars and great political events have had a notable influence on its development.

Primitive and simple among pastoral and warrior civilizations, luxurious and often vulgar among conquerors of all kinds, lately come to fortune, culinary art only becomes subtle and refined among those peoples who have long been civilized.

Its general development follows a sinuous curve. It will only find its final formula when all the laws governing it have been discovered. Until then, condemned to highs and lows, it will be at the mercy of chance and circumstance—always threatened with reversal.

Prehistoric Times

Prehistoric times. Most historians resist going back as far as the Deluge. I will have to go back even farther. The Deluge of the Scriptures only dates back 6000 years from our time, whereas man's antiquity is far greater, and, even though it is difficult to pinpoint, we can probably state that our species has existed for some thousands of centuries. Be that as it may, Quaternary man of the Paleolithic period, contemporary of the mammoth, already lived by hunting and fishing and knew the use of fire.[3] We are certain of this because of the human bone fragments[4] and calcined animal bones found in caves of that period and by the *kjoekkenmoeddings*,[5] ancient vestiges of human settlements, containing flint instruments, crude pottery shards, coal, ashes, cracked and calcined bones, seashells, fishbones, etc.

The first domesticated animals seem to have been the dog, the reindeer, the goat, the pig, and the chicken.

It is also to the end of the Stone Age (Neolithic phase) and from the age of the Lakedwellers that cattle raising, grain cultivation, weaving, the use of honey, and the use of salt[6] date back.

Antiquity

The Egyptians

The Egyptians. Under the IVth Dynasty, 3000 years before our time, in Egypt, cradle of civilization, wheat, barley, millet, and grapevines were already being cultivated. Bread, wine, hydromel (mead), and beer were being made.

A thousand years later, under the XVIIIth Dynasty, that of the great Pharaohs, the period in which Egypt reached her apogee, the conquest of Syria, Phoenicia, Canaan, Nubia, and Ethiopia augmented the culinary resources of the Egyptians. At this period, there were: red meat, fowl, game, fish oysters, eggs,[7] starchy vegetables such as lentils, peas, beans, etc., various fruits such as olives, figs, dates, apples, pomegranates, apricots, etc., and almonds. The Egyptians knew about garlic and parsley. They loved the onion and not only ate it but worshipped it. Thebes of the four hundred portals had its poultry breeders, short-order food shops, confectioners and pastry shops. For the table of the Pharaohs there existed marvelous truffles of unbelievable size; they weighed as much as eighteen pounds. This variety seems to have disappeared today.

The Hebrews

The Hebrews. Originally the Hebrews lived very frugally. Later on they had the life style of patriarchs. They nourished themselves on cereals such as wheat and barley, certain legumes such as lentils and favas. They also had meat from the animals of their herds.

During their stay in Egypt their food supply grew to encompass all the products available in that country. Twenty centuries before our time, they knew how to make butter.

Then, during the forty years in which they wandered the desert (1420–1380 B.C.), they suffered greatly, but their greatest privation came from not having been able to bring, on their flight from Egypt, either onion seeds or leavening. From this era stems the use of azymous bread (unleavened bread) which the Orthodox Jews still eat at Passover in commemoration both of the ancient Feast of the Azymes and of the Hebrews' wanderings in the desert.

After their entry into the land of Canaan, the Hebrews' food became modified. In order to obey the laws of Moses, they rejected from their diet many of the animal meats which they had previously eaten and butter gave way to other fats and oils when meat was being served. Jewish cooking originated at this time.

Under the proverbially luxurious reign of Solomon, however, the Hebrews transgressed all the principles of their religion. The richness and sumptuousness of their table was such that the prophet Isaiah became troubled and indignant.

Assyrians, Chaldeans

Assyrians, Chaldeans. The Assyrians were not agriculturally minded. They harvested a few wild foods, but mostly they depended upon neighboring peoples.

The Chaldeans, on the other hand, were an agricultural people—witness the lush hanging gardens of Babylon. In Assyria, the poor ate coarse bread, wild vegetables, crabs, fish, and grasshoppers. The rich set a very abundant table. The meats were the same as those in Egypt. Of fish, the most prized was the carp, and they also had barbel, eel, and marine eel. They also had pot herbs, various vegetables such as beans, favas, lentils, chickpeas, okra, cucumbers, squash, eggplant, etc. Fruits they ate included raisins, dates, pineapples, blackberries, almonds, pistachios, nuts, figs, pomegranates, lemons, oranges, plums, and apricots.

After every victory in battle the Assyrians launched themselves into wild orgies, but it was only about the seventh century before Jesus Christ, under the reign of Ashurbanipal, that Nineveh and Babylon reached the high point of their splendor. Love of luxury and material pleasures reached its peak. In the sixth century, under the reign of the ignominious Belshazzar, the Assyrians wallowed in their final and most repulsive debauchery.

Hindus

Hindus. In India, where we get rice and exotic condiments, culinary art was highly developed from earliest antiquity as is evidenced by the *Ramayana* (the ancient Hindu epic poem glorifying the hero Rama).

Persians

Persians. The Persians, who, like the Hindus, were of Aryan origin, had been an agricultural people from very ancient times.

In the ninth century B.C. their food consisted of cereals, legumes, pot herbs, fruits such as raisins, olives, lemons, cherries, plums, and peaches, and nuts. The meats which they ate were deer, wild donkey, beef, mutton, pork, ostrich, and sea turtle.

After the victories which they won over Nebuchadnezzar and Belshazzar and after the conquest of the Median empire, of Assyria, of Chaldea, of Lydia, of India, etc., the Persians, as a result of contact with the vanquished peoples, acquired habits of luxury and intemperance. At the tables of the kings and of the wealthy there were often whole roasted animals, a camel, a beef, a donkey, etc. The poor people had to be content with smaller cuts.

During the fifth century, after the Median wars, during which they often abandoned to the Greek conquerors riches of incredible worth in the form of dishes and furnishings of gold and silver, the Persians followed the example of the Egyptians, the Assyrians, and the Hebrews, by falling into habits of luxury and indulgence. Debauchery was rampant. Decadence began.

Greeks

Greeks. In the year 1582 B.C., Cecrops, founder of Athens, brought from Egypt olives and the art of making oil from them. At about the same time, the Phoenician Cadmus, cook to the King of Sedon, settled in Greece and introduced the principles of culinary art there.

During Homer's time the people's food consisted almost exclusively of boiled cereals, fish, vegetables, and native fruits.

The prosperous classes had, in addition to the above, beef, mutton, goat, and pork. They roasted animals and basted them with fat,[8] and ate them accompanied by fortified wines. Gastronomy, evolving parallel to civilization, was beginning to develop when the Doric invasion put a stop to all progress. It was then that Lycurgus, who wanted to turn the Spartans into an exclusively military people, tried, by allowing each individual only limited pleasure, to inculcate in them an inordinate love of arms and a disdain for all the arts. In order to atrophy their sense of taste he could find nothing better than his famous *brouet*,[9] which he had the gall to force them to eat. This was too much. Stomachs revolted and Lycurgus did not survive the upheaval. After his death the Laecedemonians, feeling that their enforced diet had lasted long enough, started the Messenian wars with the express purpose of seizing the flocks and the harvests of their neighbors. As a result of these conquests, Greek cooking improved. This improvement was also due in part to the influence of Archestratus, the immortal author of *Gastrology*, a work which he wrote after having traveled throughout the whole of the known world, searching for the best of everything to eat and drink. Food supplies were notably enriched through the use of rye, rice, and oats.

It was in vain that the vegetarian Pythagoras preached, using metempsychosis (transmigration of souls) as a pretext for abstinence from meat. Gastronomy, stifled for several centuries, triumphed over philosophy and with new impetus took off irresistibly.

The Medic wars occurred during the fifth century before our era. The principal result of these wars was the introduction into Greece of culinary knowledge which, in the case of the Medes and the Persians, was well advanced.

During the age of Pericles the menus consisted of soups, fish, either roasted, fried, or boiled, the last accompanied by an oil-base sauce (with vinegar, egg yolks, and *fines herbes*), the forerunner of our remoulade; red meats and pork; fowl, particularly the white goose, fattened with fresh figs and much prized for its flesh, liver, fat,[10] and eggs; game, either roasted, braised, or in ragoût; and everything was complemented with appropriate sauces, either sweet ones with honey or spiced ones made with vinegar. There were vegetables, various desserts, all sorts of fruits, cheeses,[11] pastries—and among the pastries were found certain cakes sprinkled with salt which we still make today. Finally there were sweet desserts, some of which were the precursors of pudding.

As beverages, the Greeks used milk, local or foreign wines, either natural or fortified, hydromel (mead), *cervoise*,[12] beer, and herb teas. The most highly esteemed native wines were those of Corinth, Acanthos, and the Ionian Isles. The most sought-after foreign wines were from Syracuse, Falernum, Smyrna, Phoenicia, and Egypt. Of the Egyptian wines those from Thebes were particularly in favor.

The morning and noon meals were light. Dinner, on the other hand, was copious and consisted of several courses. During the evening meals, before the dessert, slaves brought the diners water, perfume, and crowns of leaves and flowers. It was only then that the drinks were poured. During the dessert course there was entertainment provided by mimes, readings, chants, and dances. Musicians played, and the guests, excited by drink, carried on animated conversations peppered with flashes of Attic wit.

These dinners were, above everything else, a delight for the spirit; the food itself left much to be desired, and it must be said that the Greeks—during this period, which marked the pinnacle of their civilization—had not made as much progress in gastronomy[13] as they had in the other arts.

Symptoms of decadence had also been evident for some time. The Greeks had learned from the Libyans the deplorable habit of eating lying down, a prime gastronomic error. They subsequently fell into an even more grievous habit, that of living only to eat. In vain Hippocrates, in the name of health, and Socrates, in the name of morals, battled against encroaching national gluttony. Greece was declining, and one century after Pericles, in 146 B.C., she was subjugated by Rome.

Romans

Romans. The early Romans, like all primitive peoples, led a hard life. Numa Pompilius borrowed from the Sabines, who themselves had borrowed from the Persians, through the intermediary of the Pelagians, the cult of Vesta, goddess of fire. The birth of culinary art in Rome dates from this era, the seventh century B.C.

At first the Romans scarcely ate meat except on feast days. Their everyday food consisted mainly of vegetables—garlic, onions, shelled legumes, turnips, parsnips, leeks, etc., etc. Boiled spelt[14] served as bread.

Originally they castrated their bulls, mainly in order to tame them more easily. But soon they realized that this procedure improved the quality of the meat markedly, and that led them to the caponization of roosters. This was the beginning of animal husbandry for them.

They learned about grapes from the Phocaeans, who brought it to them from Persia.

The Samnium wars put the Romans in contact with the Greeks, who were allies of the Samnites. It was from the Greeks that they learned the principles of culinary art. However, it was only during the time of the Punic wars[15] that gastronomy made really serious progress.

The first war gave them Sicily, whose cooks (*quantum mutati*) were at that time the finest in the world.[16]

The second brought them the Balearic Isles, where they discovered the rabbit, which they hastened to acclimate to their own country.

It is well known how the third war, the one which ended in the destruction of Carthage, was provoked by Cato the Ancient. During the deliberations several senators hesitated. Cato pulled some African figs from his toga and cried out, "It is the conquest of the country which produces these fruits that I ask." The argument was irresistible.

The introduction of the pomegranate also dates from this period.

Later on, the annexation of Greece brought the Romans new gastronomical conquests. In that country they found pheasant, which the Argonauts had brought back from their expedition to the shores of the Phasis. In Greece the Romans also found the woodcock and other game of which we have already spoken; various vegetables, among which we can cite, in addition to those already mentioned, asparagus, carrots, chervil, mushrooms, lettuce, dandelions, and truffles (which originated in Libya); and certain fruits, such as nuts and peaches, both of which came from Persia.

From Asia they brought the cherry,[17] the apricot,[18] the cucumber, the lemon,[19] and the peacock.[20] The Parthians had taught them how to manufacture light (that is, raised) bread.

From Africa they received the large-ribbed melon, which they started cultivating near the village of Cantalupo, whence the name cantaloupe.

In their two oceans and in their rivers they fished for bleak, anchovy, bass, barbel, gilthead, sturgeon, herring, mullet, marine eel, turbot, frogs, and gathered mussels, oysters, sea urchins, and cockles. Neither did they lack for game. They raised furred game in parks and feathered game in aviaries, the first of which was constructed by Marcus Loenius Strato.

It was Sergius Orata who first had the idea of penning oysters and the enclosures in Lake Lucrine furnished mature shellfish. Fluvius Lippinus invented the fattening of snails with a porridge made from flour and wine-must; he thus obtained magnificent specimens. The consul Scipio Metellus, promoter of the forcefeeding of geese in the dark, had invented foie gras. The Romans, very adept at the art of *charcuterie*, or pork butchery, raised sows with very succulent flesh by nourishing them with figs,[21] and they prepared hams, sausages, and so on. Salads were made of watercress, lettuce, sorrel, lamb's-lettuce, and rue. They made a kind of cheese which contained powdered thyme.[22] As a matter of course they made whipped cream, wafers, pies, cakes, puddings, cheesecakes, and sherbets. They also had a great variety of fruits, such as apples, pears, prunes, chestnuts, quinces,[23] raisins, and pistachios.[24]

As to wines, they had those known to the Greeks, their own, and those of the Rhine.[25]

Their considerable gastronomical resources and their relatively broad culinary knowledge had enabled them to create a more refined cuisine than that of the Greeks.[26] Unfortunately, they ended up by becoming too carnivorous and they made the mistake of underrating the value of vegetables, which they found tasteless.[27] The more refined Greeks had known how to appreciate these. The Roman repasts were very sumptuous and were enlivened by theatrical and musical performances,[28] but, contrary to Greek habit, the guests remained the passive spectators of these divertisements.

In summary, the Romans enjoyed great material well-being but the ease with which they had enriched themselves through the pillage of the lands which they conquered led them—eventually fatally—to all sorts of excesses. They took great strides toward decadence and they ended up by living only to satisfy their gluttony. The introduction of the use of the vomitorium marks the end of Roman gastronomy. A veritable wind of folly then blew over Rome. It became a contest as to who could spend the most. Romans rivaled one another as to who could present the rarest and most exotic dishes, most of them completely senseless.[29] They served camel heels, elephant trunks, parrot heads, ragoûts made from nightingale livers and peacock brains and pâtés made from the tongues of talking birds, all of which (of course) cost enormous sums. Lucullus spent small fortunes on one meal alone.[30] During the reign of Tiberius, Marcus Apicius, possessor of a fabulous fortune, found a way to squander away three-fourths of it on orgies and ended by committing suicide when he realized that he did not have enough left to live decently.[31] Vitellius, who only stopped eating in order to vomit, squandered millions in the eight months of his reign. Heliogabalus, hardly eighteen years old, surpassed in debauchery and prodigality all the Caesars who had preceded him. So as to appear to posterity in his true light, he had a personal historian by his side at all times to chronicle his orgies. He gave feasts which consisted of as many as twenty-two courses, and in order to increase the cost he had pearls, gold, and precious stones mixed into the dishes served to his guests. So much for Rome!

Barbarian Invasions

The odor of the Roman orgies spread far and wide and finally attracted the barbarians, whose invasions lasted nearly three centuries and plunged ancient civilization—which was already dying of indigestion—into darkness.

Crushed under the feet of the barbarians, truffles disappeared beneath the surface, not to reappear until the Renaissance.

The scholars, the thinkers, the artists, hounded by the invaders, took refuge in monasteries, which were then regarded as inviolable.

Christianity

Under the influence of Christianity, culinary art as practiced in the monasteries became simpler, and, after a phase of rigorous asceticism, it again became that which it should never have ceased to be: the art of preparing food in a digestible and appetizing way. The development of gardening, favored by monastic orders, added fruits and vegetables to the diet. The healthful practice of fast days was instituted. Fasts and abstinences rested the stomach and allowed it to appreciate the simple cooking which followed.

In all the monasteries, the monks, following the principle of equality, took turns preparing meals. This was the origin of much gastronomical progress, since among the monks there were many who had excellent taste and who were led, quite naturally, to the perfecting of ancient recipes. The cooking was always good, thanks to the excellence of the raw materials used and to the care taken in their preparation. It is unquestionable that it is to the monasteries that we owe the preservation and development of the sensible principles of the science of gastronomy.

Gaul

Before going further, let us retrace our steps a little and say a word about the Gauls.

During the period which preceded the Roman conquests, the Gauls lived on bread,[32] berry products, eggs, vegetables, onions cooked in ashes, red meat and pork, fowl, game, fish seasoned with salt, saffron, honey, vinegar, and nutmeats. They drank hydromel, beer, and wine.[33]

The various invasions modified their cooking greatly. After the Roman conquest, the number of courses increased. Luxury became more apparent through the variety of dishes, spicy seasonings, etc. The invasions of the Huns, however, who ate their meat half raw and almost rotten, stopped this upsurge, and we must go to the period of the Franks before once more finding food which is more or less properly prepared.

Frankish Gaul

During the time of the Merovingians new culinary creations appeared. Some dishes had sauces made with stock or wine and aromatic plants. Many vegetables were prepared with meat broth—such was the case with peas, favas, lentils, beans, red cabbage, and green cabbage. Cheeses were often speckled with fennel seeds. The peach was the most popular fruit, and for dessert there were jams made of roses and violets. In his works, Grégoire de Tours mentions a soup made of fowl which was served to him at the table of Chilperic I.

As was the case with the Romans, the meals were enlivened by concerts.

Under the Carolingians the art of cooking made more progress. Lettuce, watercress, garden cress, chicory, carrots, turnips, and chervil augmented their resources. In the monasteries, on feast days, there appeared for the first time *pâtés* made with eggs, *pâtés* made with fish, and meat pasties which were the precursors of flan and vol-au-vent.

Dishware, already luxurious during the period of the Merovingians, became more and more so. So much effort went into the elegance of the table that the Council of Frankfort became offended and proclaimed severe penalties against those members of the clergy who strayed from the prescribed rules of sobriety and simplicity.

Our first sumptuary laws stem from this period.

France

Middle Ages

Middle Ages. After Charlemagne's death, civil wars and the Norman invasions and brigandage plunged France into poverty. During the ninth, tenth, and eleventh centuries famines and epidemics raged all over the land. As anthropophagy reappeared children disappeared as if by magic!

Luxury returned gradually and reigned until the first Crusade, when trumpeting to saddle tore the knights away from the pleasures of the table.

During the twelfth and thirteenth centuries, when eight successive Crusades were undertaken, gastronomy was more or less neglected. These wars, however, were not without influence on its development. By putting Occidental Europe in touch with the Orient, they gave us buckwheat, sugar, anise, cumin, cinnamon, pepper, ginger, nutmeg, saffron, shallots (from Ascalon), prunes (from Syria), and so forth.

In the thirteenth century, Saint Louis had two sauce cooks, and the taste for highly seasoned food spread so far and wide that merchants dealing in vinegar, mustard, and sauces made from various other spices grew into trade companies.

It was around this time that Gaston Phoebus, Lord of Béarn, created the *lièvre au chaudron* (jugged hare), that the *haricot*[34] *de mouton* or *ragoût de mouton* (lamb stew), copied from an Arab dish, first appeared on menus, and that the artichoke was imported from Venice.

A little later (1421) the lemon, native of China, and rice, native of India, were imported into France.

The French cultivated the appletree, the peartree, the plumtree, the walnut tree, the hazel nut tree, the chestnut tree, the medlar tree. They made wafers, puffs, *darioles* (almond pastries), cheesecakes, fritters, crêpes, tarts, custards. The *pains d'épice* (honey-spice breads) from Paris and Reims were very popular.

Nevertheless, the cuisine of the Middle Ages was still relatively mediocre. There were banquets, and lavish dishes were served; but in truth more weight was given to the luxury of the accessories than to the food and its preparation. For one thing, foods were heavily overspiced. We must note, however, that French wines were already famous.

Modern Times

Only at the beginning of the Renaissance can we note real progress in culinary art.

Under Charles VII, rice soup was very popular. Taillevent, the king's chef, author of the *Viandier*, whose first edition goes back to 1490, created several soups: onion, mustard, fava bean, and fish. He invented various ways of preparing game, several sauces, and the *galimafrée* (chicken stew) which was the ancestor of chicken Marengo. For her part, Agnès Sorel conjured up the *salmis de bécasses* (salmis of woodcock).

Under Charles VIII, butter from Vanves was much sought after. Cheeses from Brie, Champagne, and from the Grande-Chartreuse were considered excellent. Italian cheeses were beginning to be imported. It was during his reign that the melon was imported into France.

During Rabelais's time there already existed fifteen or so French sauces, among which were white sauces, green sauces, sauces made with black butter, mustard sauces, and sauce Robert. Sixty ways of preparing eggs were known, and Gauthier d'Andernach, doctor to Francis I, in less than ten years invented seven *coulis* (*coulis* being a type of meat extract or juice which can be thick or thin and is really an ancestor of our modern sauce), nine ragoûts, thirty-one sauces, and thirty-one soups. The bisque and soups with Italian pasta, with stuffed onions, and with lemon juice appeared at that time. Delicate dishes were not lacking at the table of that gallant king. One of the best known at the time was made from the livers of eelpout stewed in Spanish wine.

Things had been set in motion.

Under Henry II came marine eel cut in chunks, partridges *à la tonnelette*, sunbursts of white meat of capon, oriflammes (colored banners) of jelly. These led to eel *à la tartare*, *chartreuse de perdrix* (a molded partridge dish), and breast of fowl and to aspics. Spinach, which originated in Asia, was first imported into Holland, and at this time acclimated to France. Served as a ragoût it was very much in vogue during Lent.

During the reign of Charles IX corn and turkey were imported from America, the former by the Portuguese and the latter by the Jesuits.

French cuisine, which from this moment had unquestionably attained top place among Western cuisines, received new impetus thanks to the arrival of Italian cooks, after the fashion of Marie de Medici. They helped maintain the Roman culinary traditions and spread the taste for sweets and iced desserts. During this same period they began distilling grape, cider and pear juices, and they manufactured the first alcoholic liqueurs.

Under Louis XIII, Richelieu, well aware of the importance of the services that could be rendered to a wise diplomat by a good steward, encouraged culinary artists. In point of fact, the great personages of that era were not disdainful of doing some cooking themselves. The Marquise de Sablé prepared with her own rosy fingers soups, ragoûts, and desserts of her own creation, and the king himself had the reputation of being an excellent cook.

The *croquante* (a huge mounted pastry piece) was created under the reign of Louis XIII, and it was at this same period that Claude Gelée, known as the Lorrain, who, before becoming the Raphael of the landscape, was a pastry chef of genius, invented *feuilletage* (puff pastry). It was also at this time that the Jerusalem artichoke was introduced in France.

Louis XIV was a gourmand who was more voracious than discriminating. His appetite was incredible. The meals at court consisted of eight courses, in each one of which there were twenty or thirty subcourses. On the occasion of the banquet honoring the engagement of the Infanta Maria Theresa, the sauce known as *espagnole* (Spanish) first appeared. During his reign, green peas became a staple, *potage* Saint Germain was created, and coffee, chocolate, and tea were imported into France. Coffee by the Venetians, chocolate by the Spaniards, and tea by the Siamese. It was at that time that a Sicilian by the name of Procope founded, in Paris, the first *café-glacier* (ice cream parlor).[35] Wines from Champagne were also becoming popular at that time.

Among the most popular foods of the time (in seasoning which they generally overdid the nutmeg[36]), one can list fricassee of chicken and pigeon, the *galimafrée*, rissoles (a sort of fried turnover), chops in *papillotes* which were created by Madame de Maintenon and her brother the Baron d'Aubigné, and, finally, several desserts dedicated to Cardinal Mazarin.

Being fond of gardens, the great king favored the cultivation of orchards and kitchen gardens. Thanks to his influence a great number of fruits and vegetables were improved, notably the peach from Montreuil developed by Girardot.

The *great* French cuisine, however, only dates back to the time of the Regent.

A grandson of Louis XIII who had inherited the gastronomical tastes of his grandfather, the Regent was a true innovator in this field. He invented the small dinner party, which consisted of very subtle dishes he prepared himself, aided by his fops. His kitchen utensils were of silver and the contents of his saucepans were worthy of their containers. His *matelotes* (a type of fish stew) were renowned. From this period on, light and nourishing stocks or juices were extracted from meats in order to use them as a base for other dishes and for sauces. Seasonings began to be used judiciously and flavors were harmoniously blended. New gustatory sensations were created by combining basic stocks one with another.

Louis XV, like the Regent, was not only a gourmet but also a cook. He excelled particularly at the preparation of *pâtés* and coffee, which he would not allow anyone to prepare for him.

It was during his reign that the following foods appeared on court menus: the pineapple, from Surinam; the strawberry, from Chile, which was imported in 1716 by Monsieur Frezier; the *sagou*, a type of palm flour which originated in India; and pepper from Cochin China, which was acclimated to the Ile-de-France.

The cheeses most favored were those from Brie, Roquefort, Cantal, Berry, Livarot, Pont-l'Évêque, Maroilles, Vanves, Clamart, and Gournay.

On the long list of creations in the food line of that time, one finds bread made in the Orléans way, created by the Regent, truffled game *pâtés*, sautéed *animelles*,[37] and the following omelets: *à la royale* with cocks' combs, with chicken testicles, with breasts of ortolans. There appeared also filets of baby rabbit *à la Berry*, attributed to the Regent's daughter, breasts of chicken and filets of young lamb *à la Bellevue*, prepared for the first time in honor of the king, at the Château de Bellevue, and inspired by the Marquise de Pompadour. There were rissolettes *à la Pompadour*, vol-au-vent *à la Nesle*, chartreuse *à la Mauconseil*, chicken *à la Villeroi*, quail with mirepoix (a mixture of diced vegetables used for flavoring), veal sweetbreads *à la d'Artois*, *coulis* of crayfish, *coulis* of game, President Hénault's bisque, Sénac de Meilhan's chestnut *garbure* (soup). The list also included the consommé, bouchées (puff-pastry cases), and chicken *à la Reine*, originated by Maria Leszezynska, boudins (blood sausages) *à la Richelieu*, the cream sauce known as Béchamel, which we owe to the financier Béchameil (later on a marquis), Soubise sauce, and mayonnaise sauce (which, according to some, may have first been called Bayonnaise from the name of Bayonne, where it could have originated. Others say it first may have been called Mahonnaise and should be attributed to the Duc de Richelieu—they claim he may have had the idea for it during the siege of Port-Mahon.

The preparation called d'Uxel (the modern *duxelles*—a sort of mushroom hash) also appeared at this time.

On the sweet list we find strawberries with oranges from the Count de Laplace, *échaudés* (poached, then baked, dough pastry) created by Favart, madeleines from Commercy, crêpes of the Cardinal de Bernis, the baba (liqueur-soaked spongecake) of King Stanislas, creams, mousses, frozen cheeses, etc. Even with this long list I have skipped many—some of the best.

The wines of Bordeaux in general and wines of Burgundy, in particular the Chambertin and Clos Vougeot, gained the well-deserved reputation for excellence at this time.

Finally, in 1765, a well-to-do gentleman whose name must not be forgotten, Monsieur Boulanger, founded in Paris, in the ancient rue des Poulies, the first restaurant.[38] This new venture, banal as it may appear on the surface, inaugurated a new era for gastronomy. Up until this time fine cuisine was, so to speak, monopolized by the nobility, the clergy, the magistracy, and financiers—in a general manner of speaking, by the wealthy classes. The creation of restaurants, quite apart from a purely utilitarian aspect, made it possible for anyone who had several *louis* in his pocket to treat himself and his friends, without any embarrassment, to a superb meal. Gastronomy thereby gained many more adept cooks. A number of new vocations arose and an absolutely unforeseen phenomenon occurred: culinary art became more refined as it became more democratic.

Louis XVI suffered from bulimia (an abnormal and constant craving for food) and this was at least the indirect cause of his death. At the time of his flight, despite the queen's objurgations, he could not resist the charms of a copious luncheon offered to him at Étoges at the home of Monsieur de Chamilly, his first master of the bedchamber. Unwilling to leave the table, he delayed there for sometime; this made him arrive late at Varennes, where the horsemen who were to escort him from there to the frontier had left, convinced after a long wait that he would never arrive. Although he had effectively calmed his hunger pangs, he and his family paid with their heads for this fleeting pleasure.

During his reign, the white potato native to South America, which had been brought into Europe in 1565 by Hawkins, became a staple, thanks to the perseverance of Parmentier. This fact may be considered as fundamental in the history of gastronomy.

Provincial cuisine did not take second place to that of the capital. To it we owe the *garbure béarnaise* (a substantial soup), *escargots en coquilles* (snails in their shells), *bouillabaisse* and *paquets de Marseilles* (fish stews), *bourride de Cette* (fish stew), *brandade de morue* (purée of salt cod), *ailloli* (garlic mayonnaise), *meurette comtoise* (freshwater fish soup from Comtoise), *sole normande*, *civet de lamproie gascon* (lamprey eel stew from Gascony), *tripes à la mode de Caen* (in existence since the end of the fifteenth century), *gras-double* (tripe) and *quenelles de brochet à la lyonnaise* (pike quenelles Lyonnaise), *cassoulet de Castelnaudary* (bean and meat casserole from Castelnaudary), *lièvre à la royale* (hare "royal style"), *gratins dauphinois* (potato casserole with golden crust), *quenelles à la Nantua* (fish quenelles Nantua style), *canard rouennais au sang* (duck from Rouen cooked in blood). Provincial cuisine went on to give us the *pâtés de foie gras truffés de Strasbourg, de Nancy*, and *de Cahors* (truffled goose pâtés from those towns), *terrine de Nérac* (terrines from Nérac), *pâtés de perdreaux de Chartres* (partridge pâtés from Chartres), *pâtés de canard d'Amiens* (duck pâtés from Amiens), *pâtés d'alouettes de Pithiviers* (lark pâtés from Pithiviers), etc.

It was during the reign of Louis XVI that Dutfoy took to replacing some of the silver table decorations with large pastry creations shaped into architectural forms.

1789 to 1907

The French Revolution brought a new element to power. A few of the revolutionaries, among others the conservative Camille Barrère and the General Paul François Barras, knew how to eat, but they were really bourgeois who had been caught up in the turmoil.

The cooks of the emigrants and the victims of the Terror, with no place to go, founded restaurants, laid the groundwork for good eating, and thus paved the way for the arrival of the modern bourgeoisie. At the same time, more than one emigrant, in order to survive, used his gastronomical talents abroad and thus helped to spread the reputation of French cuisine.[39]

The principal creations of that era include *bifteck à la Châteaubriant, tourtes aux rognons* (kidney pies), *godiveaux* and *pâtés de ris de veau de Toutain à la Toulouse* (forcemeat and sweetbread *pâtés* from Toutain in the Toulouse manner), *langues fourrées* (stuffed tongues), *andouilles de fraise de veau au ris de veau* (sausages made with the covering of veal intestines stuffed with veal sweetbreads), *boudins blancs aux truffes, aux pistaches*, and *aux écrevisses* (white sausages made with truffles, with pistachios, and with crayfish, which were all attributed to Mouniot), and so on.

Finally, during the last year of the eighteenth century, a pastry cook from Paris, Monsieur Appert, invented preserving (canning), which today plays a considerable part in our nutrition.

Napoleon I was a great strategist but a sorry eater. He was completely indifferent to the charms of cuisine. Eating seemed to be nothing but a chore for him. The only time that he is known to have expressed a culinary wish was to request some flat sausages, reminiscent of his days as a sublieutenant. The head maître d'hôtel, judging the dish unworthy of His Majesty, substituted instead a partridge hash wrapped in caul fat which the Emperor swallowed without realizing the difference. The Imperial table was, however, very abundantly and luxuriously supplied, because the Emperor always knew how to surround himself with the best specialists in all fields. The kitchens of the Tuileries were veritable schools of cuisine from which a whole galaxy of culinary artists emerged.

It was only at the end of his career, when he was living on Saint Helena, when he was for a time deprived of the services of his chefs, that he recognized the usefulness of gastronomy. Without his having had the slightest inkling of it, they had performed veritable *tours de force* in order to render the available ingredients palatable. Now to his many other regrets he added the belated regret of not having enjoyed this knowledge all his life.

Louis XVIII was a gourmand as well as a gourmet. He had great knowledge of fruits, and even with his eyes closed he could distinguish the difference between very similar varieties simply by tasting. To him we owe several soups, among which I shall mention a purée of lentils with croûtons and a soup with light custard, copied from an Austrian soup. No doubt he had tasted and enjoyed this during the emigration. The paternity of the chop known as *à la victime* is also attributed to him.[40]

His brother Charles X, who had already shown himself to be a gastronome when he was Duc d'Artois, was a great connoisseur. Habitually cold and reserved, he became gracious and warm when he was at table with a carefully prepared menu in front of him.

The beginning of the nineteenth century saw a number of noted gastronomes. Among them was Talleyrand, who, thanks to the excellence of his table, obtained from the allies *inter pocula* certain mitigations in the clauses of the capitulation of 1814. There was also the Marquis de Cussy to whom we owe asparagus au gratin, the Marquis d'Aigrefeuille, Grimod de la Reynière, and Jean Anthelme Brillat-Savarin, the reknowned author of *La Physiologie du Goût* (*The Physiology of Taste*).

The greatest cuisinier of that era was Antonin Carême, who shone above all for his cold dishes, meatless dishes, and desserts. Consummate technician, very erudite in all the branches of his art, Carême, who has left many works, knew how to prepare three hundred types of soups. He is the creator of the modern *vol-au-vent*, and this alone would suffice to perpetuate his name.

From the middle of the nineteenth century French cuisine is essentially that of our own day.

Among the many outstanding culinary creations we can name the following: *potage Camerani*, made with livers Mornay, from the Grand Véfour restaurant; *homard à l'américaine* (lobster "American style"), from the restaurant Bonnefoy; *sauce Mornay*, from the Grand Véfour; *filets de caneton aux oranges* (duck filets with oranges); *poulet braisé financière* (braised chicken *financière*), from the Maison Dorée, created by Casimir; *macaroni* and *tournedos Rossini*; *poulet sauté Archiduc* (sautéed chicken Archduke); *canard à la presse* (pressed duck); *soufflé de homard* (lobster soufflé); *langouste farcie gratinée* (stuffed spiny lobster); *pommes de terre soufflées* (souffléed potatoes); *pommes de terre Anna*; *pommes de terre au jus* (potatoes with meat broth juices), of Maître Blau; *salade japonaise* (Japanese salad), described by Alexandre Dumas fils in *Francillon*; *pudding à la diplomate*, the masterpiece of Montmirel; *le savarin de Julien* (Julien's sponge cake); *l'omelette soufflée en surprise* (souffléed omelet). Let us also mention the following remarkable chefs who left legacies in the form of manuscripts: Urbain Dubois, Émile Bernard, Jules Gouffé, Joseph Vuillemot, and Joseph Fabre. Among famous gastronomes are the following: Alexandre Dumas, Rossini, Jules Janin, Dr. Véron, the Baron Brisse et Monselet, the last more glutton than gourmet. Among restaurants in Paris which have disappeared but which saw the fine days of the second empire were Bignon, the Café Anglais, and the Maison Dorée on the right bank and Magny on the left bank.

French culinary art seemed at that time to have reached its high point. Its superiority may be seen in all its phases—in the perfection of the dishes themselves, the composition of the menus, the setting of the table and the serving. This superiority is due to several things: the richness of the earth, whose products are exquisite; the competence of the agriculturists, the gardeners, and the farmers who created, in the vegetable as well as in the animal kingdom specialized varieties; the art of the cheese manufacturers and the manufacturers of preserved foods; the extremely careful preparation of the broths and sauces which are the fundamental bases of good cuisine; and, finally, our wines, unique in the world, which complement the whole.

The majority of French chefs have, so to speak, suckled along with their milk good culinary principles, and this fact alone suffices to insure them an incontestable mastery.

Paris, center of the world, attracting lovers of the arts from everywhere who come in search of new sensations, is particularly favorable to the development of all the arts; and therefore it is no surprise that, thanks to the whole range of the country's exceptional conditions, French culinary art, which for more than two centuries was at the top of the worldwide gastronomic movement, has arrived at an absolutely incomparable delicacy and finesse.

However, just because our cuisine and our baking are the first in the world, one must not conclude that nothing else good exists in other countries.

Unfortunately, we have a pronounced tendency toward exclusivity. Just as in the time of the Greeks and the Romans all strangers were considered barbarians, we also tend to see in foreigners only savages, unless through exaggeration (which is just as absurd) we turn them into heros or demigods. In everything there is a happy medium, so we must be impartial and eclectic.

It is unquestionable that abroad there are dishes which are entirely different from those to which we are accustomed and which nevertheless deserve attention. I therefore think that it is only just that we glance at the principal types of foreign cuisine.

Foreign Cuisines

Italy

Italy. The triumph of Italian cuisine are the pastas and the fact that the Italians have an infinite number of ways of preparing them. They also have other original dishes such as *polenta*, a very nutritious corn meal porridge, which when prepared with meat is excellent; *risotto*, which has numerous variations; *minestrone*, a Milanese soup with vegetables, rice, macaroni, ham, sausage, and cheese, the whole seasoned with herbs. Among these I will mention basil, whose use is very extensive in the north of Italy. Other specialties are *grisini*, made in Turino, which are a biscuit-type bread in the shape of sticks, prepared with a mixture of manioc flour and oatmeal; *agnoloti*, fritters made from chopped meat, formerly prepared exclusively with lamb (hence their name) but which are now also made with chicken and other meats; and finally ravioli, which are chopped meats or vegetables encased in dough.

The fowl and red meats of Italy, with the possible exception of veal and lamb, are frankly mediocre. As a result they make frequent use of chopped meats. One of the most common preparations for veal and chicken is the one known as "*à la viennoise*" ("Viennese style"), imported by the Austrians.

Fish, notably that from the Adriatic, is excellent. Italian fried foods—without being as good as the French—are good nevertheless. In the way of *charcuterie* I do not find anything worth mentioning other than Parma ham and the *mortadella* (sausage) from Bologna. The most commonly used vegetables are broccoli[41] and *finnochio*[42] (fennel), little known in France, and the tomato, which is absolutely perfect. As to cheeses, I will mention the Parmesan, which is a remarkable seasoning cheese, and the Gorgonzola, which pretends to rival the Roquefort but with which it has very little in common except for the marbling mold. Italian butter unfortunately leaves much to be desired.

(Those who have not been to Italy cannot imagine all the things that one can do with pasta, corn meal, rice, tomatoes, and Parmesan.)

Italian pastry is not famous. I will, however, mention the *millefeuille*, a flaky pastry cake which is served most often garnished with cream, cottage cheese, or jams and which resembles the strudel from Bavaria or Vienna, and *pasta frolla*, a Neapolitan almond cake. One of the great defects in Italian pastry is the use of too much sugar; in certain regions this reaches incredible proportions. In Sicily I saw cakes whose ingredients included at least one-half sugar.

The wines from Vesuvius and those of Sicily are fairly good. The chianti is a good table wine and the asti is a little sweet wine which is not disagreeable to wash down pastry with.

To sum up, Italian cuisine does not lack certain good qualities, and its faults are mostly due to the inferiority of the meats and the butter—inferiorities for which the cooks cannot be held responsible.

Spain

Spain. Spain is a very lovely country but, as for its cuisine, the less said the better. Except in Barcelona, where I was able to live in the French manner, I only remember having eaten more or less properly once in Madrid at the home of friends and another time in Seville.[43]

In truth, it is only pork which is good in Spain. The butter is terrible. The oil is rarely well manufactured and the wine, which is transported in leather bottles, often smells of goat.

The best known dishes of Spanish cuisine—acceptable if they are well prepared—are the *puchero,* a pot-au-feu (stew) the base of which is beef and pork with vegetables such as garbanzos (chickpeas); cod *à la biscayenne* with peppers and tomatoes; *albundigas,* which are small meat balls made with chopped braised beef and which are simmered in broth and tomato juice; fried *criadillas* or testicles; the *olla podrida,* a potpourri of red meats, pork, fowl, and game with the inevitable garbanzos and a *macédoine* of various vegetables; the *chorizo,* which is a sausage made of beef, veal, and pork. Other dishes include chicken *à la valencienne,* which is a chicken with rice and sausages, stuffed tomatoes, artichoke hearts, etc. They also have a sweet ham from Asturias cooked in sherry; *escabeche,* which is a sort of hash made of fish and game and which is most popular when made with partridge; and, finally, *gazpacho.*

As to Spanish wines, let us mention Alicante, Malaga, and sherry.

Portugal

Portugal. Portuguese cuisine is no better than the Spanish. Great quantities of chickpeas are eaten in Portugal and most of the sauces are seasoned with tomato. They even put tomato in the Portuguese pot-au-feu called *cucido,* which is certainly the best thing one can eat in that country. *Tripes à la mode de Porto,* which are a reminder of *tripes à la mode de Caen,* are served with manioc flour.

The best known wines of Portugal are port and madeira.[44]

Great Britain

Great Britain. English cooking remained backward for a long time. Up until barely three centuries ago no vegetables were cultivated in England, and the diet consisted almost exclusively of animals. Today, apart from potatoes, the most common vegetables are celery, Jerusalem artichokes, cabbage, and the sweet onion.

England is essentially a country for meat and fish. Beef, mutton, and pork are superb. Their sole, salmon, and turbot are exquisite. Their whitebait[45] or *Coregonus albus,* which are fished for at the mouth of the Thames, provide a fried dish unknown to us, and the English oysters are perfect. A very tasty type of game which we do not have in France is the heather grouse, which is abundant in Scotland and Ireland and whose flesh, seasoned with wild thyme, is somewhat akin to that of the heath cock and the hazel grouse.

Sea turtle soup, which is an English national dish, enjoys a well-deserved reputation. Mulligatawny, Indian in origin, is a pork broth seasoned with curry and thickened with cream and starch and served with rice. It is very pleasant. Oxtail soup is not without merit, and porridge, a Scotch soup boiled with oat flour generally served at breakfast, is popular. Haddocks,[46] smoked English herrings, flood the continental markets. English roast beef is exquisite. Mutton chops, sandwiches (invented during the eighteenth century by Lord Sandwich), fried eggs and bacon, puddings, and English biscuits are all classics.

As to cheeses, Stilton is well known and Chester is very popular. Welsh rabbit or Welsh rarebit are buttered toasts on which one spreads melted Gloucester cheese mixed with cream and seasoned to taste with mustard.

As to beverages, English beers are well known.

The inferiority of English cooking manifests itself in its sauces and ragoûts. The English use too many aromatic herbs, condiments, and pickles. Under the pretext of cooking simply they often use, instead of our sauce bases made from broths or our simmered sauces, very strong industrially prepared sauces such as ketchup, soy sauce, Worcestershire sauce, and Harvey sauce. Englishmen use them in such quantities that they end up by completely smothering the taste of the original preparation. However, lately—thanks to the influence of King Edward VII, who was a fine gourmet, and because of the French culinary artists who governed the kitchens of many of the great English houses—gastronomy has made considerable progress on the other side of the Channel; and English cuisine today is feeling the effects of the perfectionism which has been brought over by our compatriots.

Germany

Germany. German cuisine, which is derived from German inspiration, lacks lightness and finesse. It can only suit those stomachs which are used to drinking great quantities of beer. One of its characteristics is the combination of salt and sweet; but this alone does not suffice to condemn it *a priori*. Don't we often put a little salt in sweet dishes? Why, conversely, could we not sometimes put a little sugar in salted dishes? It is a question of proportion.

One should mention a certain number of the country's dishes. Culinary artists will find in the composition of these German dishes certain ideas, which, applied with taste, could give interesting results.

Beer soup, for instance, would really not be anything prepared with our beer or with German export beers; but prepared on the spot with the local beers, which are white, frothy, and slightly bitter, it is acceptable and original. There are also oysters rolled in grated Parmesan, breaded, and fried; a fricassee of pike with crayfish and morels; salted beef from Hamburg; *boeuf à la berlinoise*, marinated in bitter white beer and cooked in its marinade with pork fat and vegetables. The beef is served in its reduced broth, which has been strained, thickened, and seasoned with a zest of orange, lemon pulp, and sweetened with a little currant jelly. Other specialties include *Pfannenkuchen gefüllt mit* (etc.), which are omelets made with flour and stuffed with a cooked hash made from veal, ham, and chicken livers, the whole sprinkled with Parmesan and cooked again in a saucepan with butter. They also have *Hammelragoût*, which is ragoût of mutton with sausages and potatoes; Hamburg hens stuffed with bread which has been mashed with butter; goose Mecklenburg style, stuffed with apples and raisins, braised and then served with red cabbage; Bavarian hare with Rhine wine; filets of hare German style, with a sauce sweetened by adding currant jelly and Corinth raisins; Silesian pheasant with sauerkraut; *pâté* of hare Saxony style, layered with sauerkraut; salted herring salad with potatoes, beets, pickles, and salted cucumbers. Salad made with asparagus and crayfish tails with oil and vinegar and a purée of hard-boiled eggyolks is popular. *Nampfkuchen*, a type of *baba*, is often served for dessert. Bavarian *Schmarr* is an omelet made with flour, cooked in a skillet, and cut into pieces which are then cooked again. *Dampfnudel* is a dessert made with noodles. Finally, apple charlottes and cherry custards are the best sweets the country has to offer.

German beers are famous.

Rhine wines have a very original flavor. The best known are

Johannesberg, Rudesheimerberg, Schloss Volrathser, Rosengarden, and Liebfraumilch (milk of a beloved woman!).

The Low Countries

The Low Countries. Among the interesting dishes from the cuisine of the Low Countries let us mention, from Belgium, the *waterzooi*, a sort of bouillabaisse of fresh-water fish, and *paupiettes de sole à la flamande*, garnished with salted herring roe. There is also *ragoût de boeuf à la flamande*, made with onions and beer; a ragoût made with oxtail, beef kidneys, sweetbreads, lamb fores, mushrooms, and beer. In Holland they have *kalbspolet*, a pot-au-feu of veal and rice with lettuce and peas; an excellent codfish from the North Sea, which is simply poached in salted water and served with steamed potatoes and melted butter; quenelles of pickled pork; and, finally, the beef from Dutch pastures, which is prepared in all sorts of ways and which is truly incomparable.

Scandinavian Countries

Scandinavian Countries. Danish cuisine is somewhat like the German. Swedish cuisine is nearer to the Russian. As to Norwegian cuisine, it simply does not exist. In Norway one hardly ever finds, except in Christiania and Bergen, anything else but fish—and then mostly salmon. Salmon boiled, grilled, or smoked is excellent, but one soon tires of it. To give an idea of Norwegian cooking I will mention the salmon in aspic which is prepared in the following manner: coat slices of boiled salmon with a thick, sweet gelatin. This is served with potatoes which are barely parboiled and accompanied by sweet clabbered milk! As a dessert there is only a jam made of whortleberries. For cheese they have reindeer cheese. For bread, there is a very poor spongy spice bread. It is dreadful!

Poland

Poland. Polish cuisine deserves to be studied. Their soup is not, as in France, an unimportant entrée. Polish soups are generally very hearty. They are really a whole course in themselves, comparable to our bouillabaisse, but they never contain bread. When the base is meat broth they almost always contain meat in some form or another, either in pieces, in chunks, or chopped, or in the form of quenelles, or wrapped in dough. The soups are very rarely strained and are generally thickened with cream. There exist in Poland three varieties of soup which are unknown in France. The first is characterized by a sourish flavor which is obtained by the addition of sour cream or by some kind of pickle juice. The second group consists of iced soups, and the third group consists of sweetened soups containing almonds and fruit, which we consider a type of dessert.

Polish sauces are prepared with either a base of meat broth or cream. They are seasoned with horseradish, fennel, salted cucumbers, chives, mushrooms, lemon juice, etc. They sometimes also contain sweet substances, such as dried raisins.

Fowl and red meats are rarely tender, and meats are therefore generally braised or chopped. Pork is fairly good, as it is in most of the poorer countries, and the sausages from Warsaw (*sardelki*) are famous. Game is excellent, but it always has a gamey taste. The very special savor of partridge and pheasant which have been nourished in French game preserves is unknown in Poland.

As to culinary preparations, let us name the following: *barszcz*, which is a type of sourish soup with fermented beet juice; *krupnik*, a soup made with pearl barley; *czernina*, a soup made with blood from either duck, goose, hare, or pork; a crayfish soup made with cream; and *chlodniki*, which are chilled soups. There is also pike in white wine with a sauce made of cream and horseradish; carp with hydromel and with a blood sauce; tripe and blood sausage cooked with buckwheat; a *chaud-froid* of stuffed calf's head with horseradish sauce; *zrazy*, which are slices of braised red meat; and *zrazy zawijane*, which are braised or roasted paupiettes. They also prepare chopped filet of beef, which they serve with cream and horseradish; *bigos*, a stew made with game, red meat, and pork, which is served with cabbage and sour apples mixed; stuffed chicken which is barded and steamed; saddle of hare in cream; *pierogi*, which are pasties of meat, vegetables, or groats; and *kluski*, which are cheese pasties.

Polish pastry, without approaching the finesse of French pastry, unique in the world, is agreeable. I will mention only the Polish crêpes made with flour and buckwheat which are known as *nalesniki*; the *baba* and certain other cakes such as *placki*, made with almonds, and *paczki*, made with jam; the spice bread from Toruń (Thorn in German).[47] There are other pastries prepared with alternate layers of flaky pastry and soft fillings which deserve attention.

During the sixteenth century Princess Bona Sforza, having married King Sigismond the Elder, brought with her to Poland a whole retinue of Italian artists. Some built monuments in the purest Renaissance style, beautiful specimens of which remain today, notably in Krakow. Other Italians brought the tomato, which is called in that country by a name characteristic of its origin, *pomidor*; and they also taught the Poles the art of working dough and the use of Parmesan cheese.

As a result of the various invasions which Poland underwent, many foreign elements blended with the national cuisine.

Thus did the Tartars import the *kolduny* into Lithuania. These were stuffed with raw beef and were the precursors of the Italian ravioli. Rice, oats, semolina, and *kasza* (kasha), which is used so much in the couscous of the Moslem countries, were put into common usage by the Turks. The Austrians brought their breaded and fried meats and their sweet dishes. The Germans brought certain combinations of sweetened meats and fruits, some of which, among these the stuffed roast goose with apples, are far less incredible than they may seem. The Muscovite invasions were of value to the Poles in that they introduced caviar,[48] among other things.

The only thing we can reproach Polish cuisine with is that, although it is savory and succulent, it requires a good stomach. This is truly a fault. It does, however, have certain culinary combinations which are little known in France and which could doubtless, by using superior ingredients and making slight modifications, develop into first-rate dishes.

Russia *Russia.* History tells us that in 1815 the Cossacks camping on the Champs Elysées ate candles. More recently, on a trip that I made to Siberia, I surprised certain of their Cossack descendants drinking the contents of my lamps. One must not, however, conclude from these undeniable facts that this is the whole diet of the Muscovites.

Russian cuisine has certain qualities which deserve notice. There are, in Russia, many edible animals which we do not find at home. Some of these are the sterlet from the Volga, a fat and delicate fish; the sturgeon; the *soudac*[49]; the *sigui*[50]; the *riapushka*[51] from Lake Ladoga; the *kilkis*[52] from Revel; the *navaga*[53]; and a type of grouse different from that of the Pyrenees. This last has been commonly imported into France for the past few years. There are also the *élan*, which is akin to the deer but less delicate, and the bear, which in our country is still a rather unusual food and whose flavor we are not really familiar with since the siege of 1870. At that time we were ungrateful enough to devour our favorite bear, Martin, from the Jardin des Plantes.

Butcher's meat is inferior in quality. As a result, in Russian cuisine there exist many types of hash which are dubbed either steaks or chops according to the shape into which they are formed. Exceptions to generally poor meats are beef and mutton from Circassia, which are passable, and veal from Moscow, which is nourished on milk and nuts and which has a very good flavor.

Russian table service is very original. It is characterized by the presentation of food which has been pre-carved and by a multitude of hors-d'oeuvres. Among these we find all types of fish (salted, smoked, marinated), and caviar canapés. There are sandwiches spread with various butters, with pastes made from fish, shellfish, crayfish tails, and shrimp. There are *bouchées* (small *croustades*), small *pâtés* made with meat and game and coated with the proper glaze, etc. These are set out on a table in a room adjoining the dining room and, preceding the actual meal, are eaten standing up, accompanied by *aquavit* or liqueurs. Such hors-d'oeuvres are known as *zakuski* and always precede an important dinner.

Russian soups are in general much like Polish soups. The most unusual are the *shchi*, which contains vegetables, sauerkraut, and meats such as duck, chicken, beef, or sausages. There is also a meatless *shchi*, in which, instead of meat broth, mushroom broth is used; a soup called *botwina*[54]; and sturgeon soup, which is acidified with pickled cucumbers and contains crayfish, sorrel, and spinach and is served chilled. *Ouka*, made with sterlet, is a soup which is very popular among Russian gourmets.

As to original dishes, we can mention the *kulibiaks*, which are *pâtés* prepared in various ways. The best known of these is the *kulibiak* of salmon and *lavaret* made with *vesiga*[55] and buckwheat. There are also *blinis*, a type of crêpes, either thick or thin, which are generally served with caviar, sour cream, and melted butter. These are eaten especially at the time of Carnival.

Let us also make note of the meat extracts which are manufactured in Siberia, where fowl and game are abundant. These are used in the preparation of many sauces. As to desserts, there are different blancs-mange.

In summary, Russian cuisine, which has certain points in common with Polish cuisine from which we have borrowed a great deal, has a curious and unusual quality. Certain restaurants in Paris have, for some time, served Russian dishes, or what passes for them.

Balkan Peninsula

Balkan Peninsula. In the Balkan Peninsula one finds ancient Byzantine cuisine, based on vegetables, mutton, and oil.

In Turkey, mutton is prepared in various ways. It is either roasted, after being cut into small pieces and impaled on sticks, or served in pilaf with rice (which the Turks imported from Persia); in ragoûts with various vegetables such as diced pumpkin and spinach, and in rissoles. It is also served in the form of highly seasoned hashes, with or without rice, which are sometimes rolled in grape leaves, fig leaves, or cabbage leaves, or even stuffed into eggplants and then braised in broth. The last are known as *dolma*, a name which is given to the various stuffed leaves or to eggplant stuffed with rice and chopped onions and cooked in olive oil. As to other dishes, I will mention mackerel stuffed with a hash consisting of mackerel flesh, onions, rice, and Corinth raisins, and also fried mussels, mussels stuffed with a hash made from onions, rice, and raisins, stuffed eggplant, squash, or green peppers. There is *beurek,* a flaky pastry with Turkish cheese known as *cacher* and *misitra*, also stuffed with chopped beef. *Kataïf* is a type of sweetened vermicelli. *Kurabis* is a sort of vanilla cookie. *Kaïmak* is a cream which may be served accompanied by various ingredients such as quinces.

Mahaleli is a dessert made from rice flour, milk, and cinnamon and flavored with rose water. Lastly there is *locum*[56], a gummy paste, perfumed, from the famous Hadji-Bekir of Istanbul, which is world renowned.

As to modern Greek cuisine, we can mention the pilaf of lamb with peppers, okra,[57] and Smyrna raisins, as well as the ragoût of mutton and tomatoes and the ravioli made with lamb hash.

Austria-Hungary

Austria-Hungary. Austria-Hungary was, before 1918, a heterogeneous aggregation of countries or parts of countries of very different origin, most of which retained the imprint of the past. The people of ancient Austria-Hungary were German, Hungarian, Slav, Italian, and Turkish. It is therefore not surprising that the cuisine of the country should be highly varied.

Austrian cuisine—or, properly speaking, Viennese cuisine—is characterized by the use of light meats, which are breaded and fried. There are various types of *charcuterie*—pork products—and sweet, farinaceous desserts, which are generally quite good, thanks to the excellent hard-wheat flour from Hungary which goes into their preparation.

The dominant quality of Hungarian cuisine is the flavor of paprika, a pepper from that country upon which a great many seasonings depend. We can mention the following interesting dishes: soup with fluid pasta; *wiener Schnitzel,* which are Viennese-style veal scallops; and *wiener Rostbraten,* which are Viennese beefsteaks steamed with butter and onions and served accompanied by a sauce containing meat extract and sour cream. There are Hungarian-style quenelles, served with a tomato and paprika sauce; *Gulyas* or goulash, prepared with beef or veal; *Porkel,* which is a goulash made with chicken and bacon and served with rice; calf's feet with anchovies and paprika; chicken with bacon, sour cream, and paprika; Bohemian-style pheasant stuffed with woodcock and bacon; stuffed sauerkraut made with whole cabbage leaves steeped in brine (as is sauerkraut) then filled with a hash made of meat and rice. For sweets they have *croustades* with fruit, apple flans, and chestnut bread.

We cannot overlook the small Viennese rolls which are enjoyed around the world or the Viennese coffee served with whipped cream; and of course we must make special mention of Prague ham. In the regions bathed by the Danube we can mention the *fogoch,*[58] the sturgeon, the sterlet—and, consequently, caviar.

In Austria-Hungary there are also very agreeable wines. In Hungary the most reknowed is Tokay, certain types of which may be stored for a very long time and which acquire, as they age, some extraordinary qualities.

Pilsen (Bohemia) beer is enjoyed all over the world.

In summary, Austro-Hungarian cuisine synthesizes almost all European cuisine except French.

United States

United States. The kitchens in the United States of North America are unquestionably the largest and most comfortable in the world. But what can be said for American cuisine?

Certainly we cannot accuse the inhabitants of the United States of living to eat. The majority hardly take the time to swallow their food. Under such conditions it is extremely difficult for a country to develop any kind of culinary art.

The newcomers are absorbed with their struggle for survival, and those who have "arrived" are busy protecting their interests; and very rarely, in this new world, are there to be found philosophers who take the trouble to have a good time. I have known certain ones who are charming companions and fine gourmets, but these are the exception.

During stock market hours I have seen millionaires standing up to a meal which consisted of corned beef and pickles in a sandwich. I pity them! Out West I saw the following: A customer comes into a restaurant and sits down. A waitress immediately arrives and reels off a long list of dishes, all of them more or less alike. The menu generally starts with roast beef, boiled beef, corned beef, and ends with corn, ice cream, and cheese. The customer, knowing the list by heart, doesn't listen, never bothers to answer, and keeps reading his newspaper. He is then served several small dishes containing various items on the menu. These are placed around him. He spears his fork haphazardly into one of them, without looking, and continues reading his newspaper. He then mechanically brings his fork to his mouth and swallows what is on the end of it, washing it down with whatever liquid is at hand. This could be local beer, which is generally fairly good; a California wine, some of which, like the Zinfandel, is very drinkable; gin, whiskey and soda, or tea, everything chilled. The whole procedure lasts five minutes. Lamentable!

I can say nothing laudatory about the cooking in the great hotels, which is all alike. It is a fact that American hotels are the hugest in the world, that their dining rooms are the most spacious in the universe; but all this does nothing for the menus.

There are, however, in the United States, certain dishes which are quite original. These include turtle soup; oyster stew with cream; Penobscot soup with okra, oysters, and soft-shell crabs; chowder, which is a sort of bouillabaisse with clams,[59] cod, bacon, onions, potatoes, and milk. There are oysters breaded and grilled, seasoned with lemon juice; oyster fritters; soft-shell crabs either broiled or fried; lobster Newburg, an excellent New York dish; terrapin stew; corned beef and cabbage; pigeon stew with rice, tomatoes, and okra.

The exclusive use of chilled beverages is a terrific abuse which many stomachs cannot withstand. As a result, one of the most lucrative medical specialities is that of treating stomach ailments. Those who have overdone the ice end up by drinking lukewarm water with their meals. This is perhaps very healthy but hardly appetizing.

The passion Americans have for iced drinks has developed into a considerable art in the preparation of these beverages in the United States. America unquestionably takes the lead over old Europe when it comes to the preparation of cocktails.[60]

It is curious that there are many temperance societies in that country. Certain states even have strict laws against the use of alcoholic beverages, which, if the truth were known, are not always observed.[61]

Jewish Cuisine

Jewish Cuisine. Let us say a word about jewish cooking.

Of all the ancient cuisines it is the only one that has perpetuated itself along its general lines, down through the ages.[62] It seems to have been founded around certain rules of hygiene and domestic economy, which developed into religious principles so as to insure their observance. This was the opinion of the philosophers of the eighteenth century and it was also that of Renan. Salomon Reinach in his *Orpheus*[63] maintains that alimentary prohibitions, for reasons of hygiene today, have to be a sign of ignorance. He claims that, if religious Jews abstain from eating pork, it is because their remote ancestors held the boar as a totem—their clan protector. The reason that they do not eat certain fish, he says, is strictly because of superstition. If they do not work on Saturday, it is because they consider it an unlucky day in the same way that certain people think of Friday, especially if it falls on the thirteenth, as being unlucky.

Whatever the reason, the prohibition of meats other than ruminants with cloven hooves has resulted in game being taboo. As to pork, it was often riddled with trichinae, and trichinosis was thought to bring on leprosy. As to the principle of kosher meat which dictates that the animal to be sacrificed for food has to be bled and the the nerves and arteries removed, this insures better preservation of the meat.[64] It was written in the sacred books "Thou shalt not cook the lamb in its mother's milk," and this had the salutary effect of leaving the ewe's milk for her lamb—and the lamb was healthier. This commandment, observed to the letter by the Karaite Jews,[65] was generalized by the Talmudic Jews,[66] who only use milk, cream, and butter for the preparation of fish in meals not containing red meat and in pastry which is to be eaten a certain number of hours before or after the ingestion of meat. They even push this to extreme lengths, to avoid all pollution, by using special pots for cooking. Shellfish and fish without scales—which were believed to cause skin diseases, to which the Jewish race is particularly prone—are equally forbidden.

It is hard not to see in all these interdictions some remarkable coincidences between the rules of health and hygiene and religious scruples.

In any case, the result is that Jewish cooking has certain special characteristics, such as no rare meat, no duck Rouen style, no stews, no blood sausage, and very few roasts. Indeed, meat that has been bled white can scarcely be prepared other than by braising or in stew. These would be stews made with beef suet or oil in poorer homes and with goose fat in the wealthier ones. These stews are always highly seasoned. Pepper, cayenne, black pepper, ginger, garlic, and especially onion are dominant in all Jewish dishes.

Vegetables are also prepared as is the meat, in beef suet, oil, or goose fat.

Fish dishes are often seasoned with ginger and saffron.

Last, among sweet desserts served at the end of the meals we can mention the *matrosh kugel*, which is unleavened bread pudding. It contains dairy products only in meatless meals.

Primitive Jewish cuisine seems to be preserved in its entirety only on the Sabbath. These meals would consist of ragoûts with meat and greens, among these purslane, spinach, and chickpeas, hashes made with goose grease, and onions stuffed into the skin of a goose neck and served with carrots. These are known as *zimmes*. There are also sausages made with beef and rice, hashes made of meat and eggs, beef trotters cooked with lentils, dried beans, etc. All these foods are cooked very slowly in covered pots equipped with woolen covers. They are put on the fire Friday night so that they will be ready the next day, which is the day of rest on which work is formally forbidden.[67]

The majority of practicing Jews, scattered over the earth, have adapted their ritual principles to the cooking of the country in which they have pitched their tents. Because of this, they have given birth to the various types of Jewish cuisines, such as the Russian, German, Alsatian, Algerian, etc. There are really as many as there are countries, but all have a certain quality in common.

In Alsatian Jewish cuisine we find a *choucroute garnie* (sauerkraut with meats) made with beef. In Spanish Jewish cuisine there is *quesada*, a *pâté* made with *cacciocavallo* cheese and roasted eggplant or with cottage cheese. There is also *boreka*, a *pâté* made with *cacciocavallo* cheese and spinach. Among the Sabbath dishes of Algerian Jewish cuisine we find the *tefina*; the *bobinet*, a steamed beef sausage; the *meguina*, a steamed beef and egg hash; and beef trotters cooked with vegetables such as rice, dried beans, etc.

Exotic Cuisines

Exotic Cuisines. I shall mention only briefly cuisines which are by far too bizarre to be encountered often. For lack of thrush one eats crow, and it is true that certain dishes which seem unbelievable are only the result of lack of resources. During the siege of Paris in 1870, did we not eat certain very unappetizing substances which were not even nourishing? I am not speaking about the eaters of larvae, worms, and insects, nor of the geophagists (earth-eaters). I shall be content to point out certain taste analogies which are of interest and I will mention certain curious exotic dishes. These are either personal memories or recounted to me by friends who, like myself, have covered the world traveling off the beaten path.

In the way of taste analogies we can mention dog flesh as being somewhat similar to lamb. In China, dogs of a very special breed, who are hairless or have very little hair, are fattened for the butcher shops, and their flesh is much prized. Of all the edible monkeys (there are certain breeds which are too musky), the best, in my opinion, is the macaque,[68] whose flesh is similar in taste to that of the squirrel. This, after all, is not surprising when one considers that both these animals live largely on grains and berries. Kangaroo tastes like rabbit. The agouti,[69] the *acushi*,[70] and the *pac*[71] have a flavor somewhere between that of the hare and the boar. The *patira*[72] tastes somewhat like boar. The camel tastes like beef and smells like goat. The meat of the alpaca is akin to that of donkey or lamb. The *hocco*[73] reminds one of turkey. The flesh of the iguana[74] is similar to chicken. The bison is analogous to deer, and the muscle meat of the larger deer furnish a tough meat with a strong odor.

Iguana eggs, which come in chaplets of forty or fifty, are enveloped in a soft covering, do not seem to have any whites, and are very delicate.

Land turtle eggs are of a grainy consistency, as large as walnuts, and are excellent in curries. As to ostrich eggs, which are very large[75] and quite edible, they lack any delicacy at all.

The *igname*[76] and the *patate*[77] remind one of the potato with a sweetish flavor. Hearts-of-palm,[78] excellent in salad, taste somewhat like artichoke hearts with a walnut flavor, and the palm worms (*Rhynchophorus*) are highly prized by gourmets because they have the same flavor.

The most interesting dishes of South America are, among the Creole dishes: the *pimentade*, the meat soup with fresh okra, the meatless soup with dried okra; *wara* broth, which is prepared with smoked dried fish, salted cod, crabs, and the red grains from the *wara* palm. There is also *agami*,[79] braised with rice; *kalalou*, which is an okra stew made with Caribbean cabbage leaves, purslane, and small cucumbers; creamed okra; steamed okra and salt pork, hearts-of-palm salad; avocado omelet[80]; avocado salad; and fried bananas. Other dishes include the *casuela*, which is a soup made with chicken or lamb broth, vegetables, and sliced ears of corn; and *seviche*, which is an excellent Peruvian hors-d'oeuvre prepared with Pacific fish called *corbina*. This fish has very few bones and is eaten raw, cut into small pieces, and seasoned with hot peppers and onions after having been marinated for twenty-four hours in the juice of sour oranges. *Carna* is a salad made with Peruvian potatoes[81] which have been boiled, mashed, and garnished with crayfish, lettuce leaves, sliced hard-boiled eggs, and seasoned with oil. *Mazamorra* is a unique Peruvian dessert which has a gelatinous consistency. It is made with red corn, milk, and eggs and is sprinkled with cinnamon. *Humita* is a corn-meal croquette wrapped in a fresh corn husk and then fried in butter. *Empanadas* are a sort of rissole prepared with meat and hard-boiled eggs which are very popular in Argentina and Bolivia. *Feijoada* is a type of cassoulet prepared with red beans and smoke-dried meats and is the national dish of Brazil.

Asia, the land of rice and spices, gives us Indian curry and Persian rice with butter and lemon, which is commonly served at our own tables today. There is also Persian ragoût of mutton with prunes, almonds, and lemon; and Persian *kelap*, which is roasted mutton, sliced and skewered on sticks, each piece separated from the other by fresh mint, basil, and bay leaves, the whole basted in mutton fat. In Persia they also prepare a mutton sausage. Syrian *koubbé* is a *pâté* made with minced mutton and cracked wheat. Carrots stuffed with chopped mutton, rice, or fried piñon nuts, the whole seasoned with onion, garlic, tomato, lemon juice, mint, salt, and pepper are very popular in Syria.

Chinese soup made with swallows' nests is now readily available in Paris. One-hundred-year-old eggs[82] are very popular among the sons of the Celestial Empire. In Korea there is a soup made with *cantjang*.[83] Fried shark fins are very popular in Indochina. Kedgeree is an Indian stew with fish and curry.

Africa has given us the *couscous* and the *meshoui*, which are Algerian.

Australia gave us kangaroo-tail soup.

The Present State of Gastronomy

Last of all, let us say a word about gastronomy today and let us try and predict its future.

While trying to avoid overpraising the past—a pit into which one can easily fall—frankly it seems to me that in gastronomy, as well as in other fields, we are going through a crisis.

Animal husbandry, modern agricultural practices, and modern methods of food preservation have all certainly increased the available food supply. The development of new means of transportation and the use of refrigeration make it possible to distribute these foodstuffs. Famine, that horrible scourge, thereby becomes impossible in civilized countries except in case of unanticipated catastrophe. But if, in a general way, these new conditions have unquestionably had a beneficial influence on everyday life, is this equally true purely from the gastronomical standpoint?

By overfeeding their stock, animal breeders of today regularly produce meats which are too fatty. Intensive agriculture often unfavorably modifies the quality of the products of the soil. It would suffice to mention as an example the potato, which can only achieve perfection when it is left to grow on its own, without cultivation in sandy soil, as was done in the past. Cold frames and greenhouses furnish, all year long, vegetables and fruits which look lovely but are absolutely tasteless. It has not yet been possible to replace the sun. The canning industry buys natural foodstuffs just at the moments when they are the cheapest. The railroads drain what is finest from every region at the expense of the inhabitants of those regions that have produced them. Among these people we originally recruited some of the finest gourmets. Foods are picked before maturity in order to be able to transport them long distances, so that now very few people are able to eat fruits and vegetables when they are at the peak of perfection. There is no more milk available in the countryside. It is difficult to obtain fish at the seashore. It is almost impossible to get a good beefsteak in the cattle country. In a word, we live somewhat as one did in the manorial days, only in reverse.

The adulteration of food is truly a very ancient art, since even the ancient Romans complained about it. But long ago it was only practiced on a very small scale. Today, as a result of chemical progress, it is considered a branch of industry. The procedures used to adulterate are discussed at conventions and their inventors, instead of being hung, are decorated!

Unquestionably, it has become difficult to eat well. It is still possible, however, but it is more important than ever to take a very personal interest in one's own food. In the country, in certain regions where there is no lack of interest in this question, they still know how to eat well. One thinks about cuisine. One discusses the menus ahead of time. One acquires each product from a supplier who is known and who knows one. And, finally, the preparation of each dish is done with extreme care.

In Paris, however, where everyone lives too fast, where everyone is always in a hurry, few people are willing to give much time to the question of food. As a result, culinary art is manifestly in decadance there. Yet it seems as though eating well ought to interest everybody, because nobody would willingly admit that he was indifferent to whether what he ate was poorly or well prepared. Gastronomy affects all classes of society, and it is not at all necessary to be rich in order to eat well. The simplest, most modest meal can be better than an expensive one. If food is of good quality and carefully prepared, one will always have eaten well.

Unfortunately, people today want show. The modest *bourgeois* of yesterday received his friends at his table and didn't serve them more than three simple dishes—but those three were carefully prepared under the guidance of the mistress of the house. The *bourgeois* of today would consider himself dishonored if he didn't present his guests with sumptuous menus (at least in appearance), which would be impossible to create at home. Company meals are therefore ordered from caterers who send them in all prepared with the waiters to serve them.

Now anyone can give a dinner party in an empty apartment hired for the occasion. Caterers furnish the food, the beverages, the dishware, the linen, and the waiters if necessary. And for a small supplement they will even furnish decorative and decorated guests, for the benefit of those who are impressed by a show of wealth. Appearances are everything!

As to the parvenus, they rival one another with false luxury. To give the impression that they care nothing about the expense, they have their dishes loaded with truffles and foie gras to such an extent that in the end everything tastes the same. Many dinners in homes where one ought to be able to eat decently become as odious as public banquets—which they greatly resemble with their motley assemblage of guests.

One of the most flourishing industries today is that of pre-cooked foods. Everywhere one can purchase prepared dishes, so women have a tendency to become disinterested in their households. Some use the excuse of having to work outside the home. Others spend their day shopping or gossiping at the five-o'clocks, in search of happiness. The ideal for many of them would be to have an "up-to-date" house with water, gas, and food on every floor. This would make it possible for them to eliminate the kitchens, while awaiting the discovery of that famous synthetic-food pill predicted by scientists.

As to the public establishments, one notices the appearance of more and more of those cheap eating houses with *prix-fixe* menus. The good restaurants either change or close their doors one after another, and I would be hard put to name more than four or five restaurants in Paris where one can be assured of being well treated in all respects.

Internationalism has its drawbacks. Its progress, deplorable from certain points of view, is disastrous where gastronomy is concerned. If we are not careful, the cuisine of all countries will be dragged down to the same low level.

At the beginning of the last century, a great professor at the University was proud of being able to state that "Today, at this hour, every student in all the tenth grades of every *lycée* in France is working on the same Greek composition." The international syndicates of innkeepers who feed the travelers of the two hemispheres, paraphrasing the words of the professor, may also state that "From the Far West to the extreme Orient, from the North Pole to the South Pole, and from the first of January to St. Sylvester's Day, all our customers will eat the same meals."

And in truth—whether it be on a boat, on a train, or in a hotel—everywhere these poor souls are condemned to the same incredible *barbue* (brill) with hollandaise sauce, the same braised sirloin of beef jardinière (and what a sirloin and what a jardinière!), to the same inevitable chicken (from Bresse, naturally). When one considers that some rather sensible-seeming people who claim to travel for pleasure are willing to ingest those dreadful atrocities, one despairs of the human race. I would like to believe, however, that this is only a temporary crisis, and I am hoping for—if not a general awakening of taste (which is too much to ask)—at least a little stomach heaving as in the time of Lycurgus.

While awaiting this peaceful revolution, gastronomers should not get discouraged. Their efforts shall not be in vain. Methodically, their perseverance will end by making of culinary art, which is today purely experimental, an exact science. By writing down very precise formulas of the knowledge we possess, we do more than perpetuate recipes; we accumulate material from which the laws of gastronomy will emerge and which will form the basis of the Science of All that Is Good.

NOTES

1. The Huns, who are practically our contemporaries considering the time which separates us from the first men, tenderized their meat by sitting on it, on the ground, or better yet on horseback. In the latter case, they put it between the saddle and the animal's back. The Hungarian Hussards of Kosuth, who are descendants of the Huns, were still using the same procedure during the 1848 revolution.

2. It is conceivable that the inhabitants of isolated regions may well not have learned about fire for a very long time. This was true in the case of the Mariana Islands, for instance, whose people only learned about fire in 1521 at the time Magellan discovered the country.

Today most primitive peoples know how to produce fire. I've seen Hottentots strike a light. I've seen Indians in the interior of South America ignite a piece of dry tree pith between their hands, against a piece of dried wood, a procedure which, incidentally, requires some dexterity to be successful.

There still exist, nevertheless, some very backward civilizations for whom the making of fire constitutes a very real problem. Among these are the natives of Tierra del Fuego. It's a fact that intellectually there are scarcely any human people inferior to the Fuegians. I have seen some who were trembling with cold at a temperature of five degrees Fahrenheit, carrying on their heads bales of hides which they were going to the coast to exchange for baubles or alcohol, without it ever occurring to them to cover their bodies with some of their load.

These wretched representatives of our species do, however, know about fire. They value it and use it, but they don't know how to light it. Their intelligence is limited to the maintenance of it, and it is in this respect that they show their superiority over monkeys. (I have seen bands of monkeys warming themselves at the fires left by travelers but they would let the fires go out even though there was ready-cut wood nearby.) Therefore, in each canoe (and each family on the coast has one, which is indispensable for fishing) there is a compartment lined with tamped earth in which a fire is maintained. If the fire goes out for lack of fuel or for any other reason, the Fuegian canoers can do nothing but await the passage of another canoe to borrow some flame. In the interior villages, however, fires are kept alight continually.

I used to believe, as many do, before going to Tierra del Fuego ("land of fire"), that it owed its name to volcanoes, which are visible in the distance. Since then, however, I've changed my mind and I firmly believe that it actually owes its name to the canoe fires which ring the island like will-o'-the-wisps and must have astonished the first navigators who rounded the Horn.

3. At that time, meat was generally cooked on preheated stones. Several years ago I witnessed the use of this same primitive cooking method on the South American Pampas. In that region the first things offered to a traveler arriving at a farm are a cup of *maté* (an infusion made with the leaves of a bush of the Illicinae family) and an *asado con cuero*, that is, meat roasted in its hide. This is prepared in the following manner: first, one lassos a steer, cuts off his head and legs, and immediately sews up the openings to avoid too great a loss of blood; then the animal is laid on a bed of stones which have been heated red-hot on a wood fire. The roasting-cook turns the animal on its bed of stones in such a way as to cook the tenderloin suitably; the rest of the meat is pretty much sacrificed and a good many parts are charred. I don't know whether it is because I ate these *asados* after hours on horseback and was famished, but I remember them with delight. I shall never forget the sight of the gush of hot blood which spurted out when I first plunged my

knife into an *asado* to carve it, nor the delicious taste of the roasted meat. It truly seems to me that I have never eaten a Châteaubriand so juicy and perfectly cooked.

4. A word on anthropophagy. Man, having acquired a taste for meat, became cannibalistic the day he lacked for animals.

"Wolves do not eat each other," it is said. If this were true it would be humiliating for man. Fortunately it is not. When wolves are starving they are perfectly willing to eat each other. I was able to ascertain this for myself *de visu* on one of my voyages to Siberia.

Homo hominis lupus.

If it is correct that "the corpse of an enemy always tastes good," the first victim of cannibalism must have been an enemy of the first cannibal. Whatever the value of this mitigating circumstance, it is likely that man became anthropophagous through *gourmandise*. He remained so for the same reason, as well as for others: out of superstition, thinking that he would inherit the virtues of his victim; out of vengeance; and even sometimes out of respect for the dead, for whom he thought he was providing the most honorable of burials.

The development of morality on the one hand, and the raising of cattle on the other, have amended man's ways, but man is ready to return to cannibalism as soon as his existence is jeopardized—the history of Medusa's raft repeats itself from time to time.

Despite the progress of civilization, there still exist a number of cannibalistic tribes.

Natives of the coast of Kru, in Africa, who had eaten prisoners taken in wars between savage tribes, which were often started purely in order to procure food, told me that they remembered it with pleasure. "It tastes like pork," they claimed. Actually, it is fairly natural that these two omnivores should be analogous in taste. One day one of these Krumen, in a confidential mood, returned to the subject and elucidated his impressions. He said to me laughingly, showing all his strong, white teeth: "White no good, me better like neg." It seems, in actual fact, that the meat of whites is rather bland. This also seems to be the opinion of the Bengal tiger, who has a certain expertise in the matter, and who, having a choice between a white man and a Hindu, never hesitates to take the latter. This is one reason why Europeans always take Hindus along with them on tiger hunts.

I must confess I understood anthropophagy better on one of my voyages when, after having spent twenty-four hours without eating because of the loss of all my provisions while crossing a waterfall, I ate monkey for the first time. This animal, as large as a human roasted on a spit, gave me the impression that I was going to eat one of my own kind.

5. *Kjoekkenmoeddings* were found for the first time on the

seashore in Denmark. From this stems their Danish name signifying "cooking residue." They were later found more or less everywhere in Europe: in France, in Belgium, in Germany, in England, in Portugal. They were also found in Asia, in Japan, and in both Americas.

The various *kjoekkenmoeddings* do not date from the same period. My learned companion and friend, de Morgan, in his authoritative work *The First Civilizations*, dates the Danish *kjoekkenmoeddings* back to the Mesolithic period—the transitional period between the Paleolithic and Neolithic Stone Age, whereas, the Portuguese *kjoekkenmoeddings*, for instance, are distinctly Neolithic.

6. The discovery of salt is one of the most precious from the gastronomical point of view. The properties of this condiment are numerous: it stimulates the appetite, brings on salivation, activates blood circulation in the mucous membranes of the stomach, and facilitates digestion by producing, as it decomposes, the hydrochloric acid necessary to the gastric juices. Thus, in a general way, it contributes to our chemical balance. Moreover, it promotes the oxygenation of the blood, colors the blood cells, is antiseptic, etc., etc.

Indispensable to animal life, it is found in its natural state in most of our foodstuffs but in insufficient quantities, at least for our present organism. Lack of salt is one of the most unpleasant physical deprivations. People who are put on a salt-free diet can only have a fair idea, because expedients of our present gastronomy allow for the use of substitutes and the use of other condiments. In order to realize exactly what it would be like, one would, as has happened to me, have to be deprived of it for a long time without having any substitute. It is thus that, after the canoe accident which I mentioned previously, I lived for a whole month in the forests of Guiana, on game and fish, roasted, plain, without any seasoning whatsoever. The lack of salt made me develop such a disgust for food that I hardly ate anything at all. Also, on this diet, I became anemic to the point that I became dizzy and had to lie down when I had the first tiny glass of wine, at the end of my enforced fast. My appetite revived after the first seasoned meal, and several days later I had regained my strength.

7. At this period the Egyptians already knew how to incubate.

8. This method of cooking is still used nowadays on the Balkan Peninsula. The eviscerated animal, perfumed with a bunch of thyme and spitted on a hazelnut branch, is roasted over a huge wood fire. During the cooking the palikar (soldier of the Greek militia) roasting-cook from time to time dips a small cloth flag into melted fat seasoned with herbs and lemon juice; with this he gently

caresses the roast, more and more frequently as the meat begins to take on color to prevent softening of the meat and give the skin an agreeable crustiness.

The Arab *meshoui* is prepared in a similar manner.

9. Black *brouet* is a ragoût or stew made with vinegar and meats which have been more or less charred, accompanied by aromatic and bitter plants.

10. The Greeks came to know butter rather late, from the Scythians, who had manufactured it since early antiquity.

11. Notably those of Sicily and those from the town of Tromilee, in Arcadia.

12. A beverage similar to beer, and made from barley.

13. In Aristophanes' works one finds mentioned many food substances which were used during his time. I think it is interesting to list them. They include: the lamb, the donkey, the goat, the suckling pig, and the sow. As to *charcuterie* (pork products) and offal, they had: pork sausage, blood sausage, regular sausage, and tripe. In the line of fowl he mentions: chicken, duck, goose, and pigeon. For game he lists: hare, lark, bec-figue (beccafico), quail, thrush, partridge, pheasant, waterfowl, teal, and ostrich. In the fish line they had: eel, loach, mackerel, mullet, plaice, raie, red mullet, sardine, tuna, and turbot. As to shellfish there were: crab, shrimp, crayfish, and oysters. They even ate insects such as grasshoppers, and reptiles like the turtle. For grains they had wheat and barley, and for dried legumes there were favas, beans, lentils, peas, and chickpeas. They grew fresh vegetables and herbs such as: garlic, anis, beets, sugar beets, cardoons, chives, pumpkins, cucumbers, coriander, watercress, beechnut, onion, olive, parsley, leek, horseradish, celery root, sesame, and thyme. He lists the following fruits: figs, grenadines, oranges, pears, apples, and raisins.

Let us add that Aristotle in his *Ethics* mentions twenty varieties of Cullis. (Cullis or coulis in those days was used as we use the word sauces today. In point of fact it does refer to meat juices which are extracted in a natural way, such as the juices which run off a roast as it cooks.)

14. A type of wheat which grows in arid terrain.

15. Flaubert, in the first chapter of *Salammbo*, gives precise details of this period. I believe it is interesting to cite *in extenso* the description he gives of the feast given in the gardens of Hamilcar to celebrate the anniversary of the battle of Eryx.

> The kitchens of Hamilcar not being sufficiently equipped, the council had sent slaves, dishware, and beds. In the middle of the gardens could be seen, as on a battlefield when the dead are being burned, great bright fires on which oxen were being roasted. Breads sprinkled with anis, along with cheeses which were larger and heavier than discuses, were set here and there.

There were craters full of wine and canthars filled with water and golden filigree baskets containing flowers. The joy of finally being able to gorge themselves at will dilated all eyes. Here and there the singing was beginning.

First they were served birds with green sauce, in dishes made of red argyle glazed with black designs. Then they had all sorts of shellfish, which can be gathered on the Punic coasts. Porridges made from wheat, fava beans and barley, and snails spiced with cumin were served on yellow amber plates.

Subsequently, the tables were covered with meats: antelope with their horns, peacocks with their feathers, whole lambs cooked in sweet wine, legs of she-camels and buffalo, porcupines with garum (a condiment used as we would mustard, made with dried and pounded fish), fried grasshoppers, and dormice. In huge porringers, made of wood from Tamrapanni, there floated amid the saffron great blobs of grease. Everything was bathed in brine, covered with truffles and asafetida (an umbelliferous herb with a strong fetid odor). Pyramids of fruits tumbled over cakes made with honey; and not forgotten were several of those tiny dogs with fat stomachs and pink coats that were fattened on olive pulp–a Carthaginian delicacy, which was an abomination to other cultures.

16. Sicilian cooks, the first of whom were originally Greek, played a considerable role in the history of Rome. Hannibal imprudently took them on campaigns with him. During the second Punic war, they fed him so many delicacies that he tarried and was late arriving with his army, and ended up by being beaten. Whereas had he acted swiftly, he could, it is said, have taken over Rome, which was within inches of falling.

17. The cherry was imported by Lucullus from Cerasonte, the town of Pont.

18. The apricot was imported from Armenia.

19. The lemon does not seem to have been introduced into Rome until after Pliny's time.

20. The peacock was imported from Samoa by Hortensius.

21. It is perfectly conceivable that animals thus nourished must have tasted delicious. In Spain, in the province of Seville, pigs are fed on acorns and olives and their flesh is excellent.

22. In his works, Martial mentions some of the cheeses of his day as being those of Luna in Etruria; those of Velabre, which were hardened in fire; and those of Toulouse.

23. Imported from Syria during the time of Galen.

24. Imported from Syria by Vitellius.

25. Martial mentions the wines of Campania, Cecube, Cere; the honeyed wines of Crete; the wines of Falernum, Fondi, Mammerte,

Marseilles, Mares, Nomentanum, Sabina, Sitia, Sigui, Sorrento, Spoleto, Tarragona, and Tuscany. The Romans gladly used iced water as a beverage, either pure or diluted with wine, the water having previously been boiled. Through some sort of curious prescience of asepsis, perhaps founded on an old adage which states that "fire purifies all," they boiled their water.

26. Like the Greeks, the Romans only learned about butter quite late. They learned of it from the Germans. They cooked mainly with oil and fat, as they still do today in the south. Among the most reknowned dishes of the time, one must mention sow udder, tuna fish brine, *pâtés* of fowl, thrush with asparagus, pork à *la Troyenne* stuffed with beccaficos and oysters and the whole bathed in wine and aromatic broth.

27. The upper class Romans only liked rare or unusual vegetables such as huge asparagus, Brussels sprouts, mushrooms, and hearts of lettuce, which they ate dipped in cream or in mackerel garum.

28. On this subject, Martial wrote, "You ask me which is the best banquet. It is the one where there is no flautist." Nowadays, those who write on their bill of fare "*Great attraction*: No gypsies" probably belong to the Martial school.

29. In his *Satyricon*, Petronius mentions several dishes in this category when he describes an orgy at Trimalchio's, which seems to be a criticism of Nero's famous orgy which Nebuchadnezzar gave on Agrippa's pond. Let us mention, among others, a wild sow presented "*en surprise*"—an unbelievable creation consisting of an enormous wild sow with its hide on, from each of whose tusks hung a basket woven of small palm branches, one containing Syrian dates and the other Theban dates, the whole surrounded by small wild suckling pigs made of pastry, one for each guest. When the slave steward opened the sow, out flew a bevy of thrushes which the slaves captured with fowler's rods. Each guest was proffered a pastry suckling pig, live thrushes, and dates. Another surprise dish was a fat-bellied sow, stuffed with regular and blood sausages which the cook brought in, excusing himself for having forgotten to gut it. Let us mention also a hen pheasant in full plumage sitting on pastry eggs stuffed with roasted beccaficos (fig eaters—a type of garden warbler) enrobed in a purée of hard-boiled eggyolks. Modern "surprises" are in good deal better taste, to say the least. Suffice it for me to mention the recipe for Ortolans in Sarcophagi (garden warblers in caskets), which are prepared by stuffing hollowed truffles with roasted ortolans, masked with foie gras. This leaves the aforementioned pheasant eggs far behind.

30. Lucullus, who had scandalously enriched himself during his campaigns in Cappadocia against Mithridates, literally flung

money out the window. He paid enormous sums per year to his squires. At the Bay of Naples alone he had three castles, surrounded by parks and aviaries, which were filled with game and fowl, fish hatcheries for fresh-water fish and still others for salt-water fish. In order to stock his fish hatcheries with fresh water, he had an entire chain of small mountains pierced through, which in that day and age was a colossal undertaking.

31. It was he who had the idea of drowning red gurnet—a variety of the family of spiny fishes called gurnards—in garum and preparing them subsequently with a sauce made of their own livers. The principle of the sauce has survived. Today, red gurnets are served grilled and masked with a purée made of their own livers and butter.

32. It was the Phoenicians who first brought wheat to Marseilles.

33. The grapevine was imported into Marseilles by a Tuscan who had been banished from his homeland.

34. This comes from the ancient word *harigoter*, which means "to cut into pieces."

35. This café was located in front of the Comédie Française, which was then on the rue Mazarine. Procope subsequently moved to the rue des Fossés-Saint-Germain, today called the rue de l'Ancienne Comédie, where a sign still bears its name.

36. "Do you like nutmeg, they've put it everywhere." (Boileau, *Satire III.*)

37. These are split and flattened ram testicles.

38. The fundamental difference between restaurants and cabarets which, as we have seen, already existed in ancient times, was that in cabarets there was no menu. For the most part the cabaret owner only cooked the food brought in by the clients, and, in order to get a meal in a cabaret, one had to order it ahead of time.

Pieds de mouton à la poulette (lamb fores *à la poulette*) were the specialty of the restaurant Boulanger.

39. Monsieur d'Albignac rebuilt his fortune in London by giving consultations on the art of salad making.

40. *"Cotelettes à la victime"* is prepared in the following manner: using three chops, tie them together putting the best one between the other two. The whole is broiled on a grill and turned frequently in such a way as to concentrate the juice in the middle chop, which alone is served.

41. Broccoli is a vegetable of the cauliflower type; it grows in separate branches, either yellow or purple in color. It loses its color almost entirely after cooking.

42. *Finocchios* are shoots of the fennel, an odoriferous plant of the Umbelliferae family.

43. Since these lines have been written, the living conditions

have changed for the better in Spain. Today one finds in several towns, notably in Madrid, Granada, and Algeciras, comfortable lodgings and a meticulous cuisine.

44. Authentic Madeira from ancient vineyards is only a memory today. I remember having had some for the very last time, in Madeira, at the home of the son of one of its last producers, around 1895. As early as that it was difficult to get together a hundred bottles on the entire island.

45. I had the opportunity of eating excellent fried whitebait in Sicily. I note this because many people falsely believe that this fish is only found in England.

46. Haddock or *églefin*, which is still sometimes called *aigrefin* or *merluche* in France, is a type of cod which is mostly found in the North Sea.

47. Copernicus's homeland.

48. In its true terminology, caviar is an excellent hors-d'oeuvre, which consists of sterlet or sturgeon eggs which have been salted in varying degrees. Figuratively speaking, this word designates the spots of printer's ink which the Russian censors use to hide those passages which they consider subversive either in local or foreign publications. The abysmal ignorance of these civil servants often leads them into the commission of tragi-comic errors. In a museum in Galicia I saw a logarithm table, which, after having been extensively caviared, had finally been confiscated. The censors were convinced that they had detected in the arrangement of numbers a secret cabalistic and revolutionary correspondence. The owner, after being hounded for the key to the secret code, was finally hung, just like that. Gentle country!

49. The *soudac*, also known as *sandre*, is a large river fish of the *Lucioperca sandra* type. The taste resembles perch.

50. The *sigui* or *lavaret*, *Coregonus lavaretus*, is a type of coregonoid salmon.

51. The *riapushka* is a small fish which is mostly eaten smoked.

52. The *kilkis* is a small fish which is prepared in oil, like the sardine.

53. A type of cod which is sent deep frozen from Archangel.

54. The *botwina* is actually a type of *chlodnik*.

55. *Vesiga* is a gelatinous substance which comes from the spinal cord of the sturgeon or sterlet.

56. This is a corruption of the Turkish words *rabat el-halkum*, which means "relaxation and well-being of the gullet."

57. Mucilaginous fruit of the *Hibiscus esculente*, a plant of the mallow family, which is served as a vegetable.

58. The *fogoch* or *sandre*, or pike-perch, is a beautiful river fish which can attain a length of four feet. It is found in Central and Eastern Europe, especially in the Danube. It has been acclimated in

certain lakes, especially in Lake Constance in Germany and Lake Balaton in Hungary.

59. This is the *Mya arenaria*, a bivalve mollusk of the Myidae family.

60. Here is a good example of the influence of environment. Although the European chefs generally tend to lose their skills in the United States, barmen are extraordinary there and seem to crop up from under every rock, like generals in France under Napoleon I. In Omaha, Nebraska, I knew the Prince of Barmen. He was a Frenchman who had come to the United States without a job; but, inspired and driven by his environment, he had in less than a year created at least fifty new cocktails, each one more remarkable than the other. His reputation was colossal from the Atlantic to the Pacific.

61. About forty-five years ago I went to the Far West. As I was eating my lunch one day, after I had been on the train about forty-eight hours, the dining car waiter refused to bring me the beer I had ordered; he claimed that we were traveling through a very puritanical state in which the temperance laws were extremely severe. He could, he said, get into serious trouble if he served any kind of alcoholic beverages during the whole time that the train was passing through that state. When I protested, he whispered in my ear, smiling, "Order some tea, out loud." This "out loud" intrigued me. I did what he suggested and a few minutes later he brought me a cup on a tray, an empty sugar bowl and a teapot full of beer. Casting a glance around at my neighbors, I noticed that all my traveling companions were drinking, straight-faced, out of cups, beer which had been served to them in teapots. All right!

62. The Jews, a Semitic tribe from Arabia, whose history goes back more than three thousand years, have better than any other people preserved the purity of their race, their customs, and their morals.

63. *Orpheus, Histoire générale des religions,* by Salomon Reinach.

64. The strict practitioners still salt the meat and soak it in water in order to remove every bit of the blood.

65. A sect which exists mostly in Russia and which follows the sacred writings to the letter.

66. The Talmud is the thesaurus of sacred writings. The Talmudic Jews, who make up the large majority of the practicing Jews, accept and apply the principles of the Talmud.

67. Certain Jews even go as far as eating on Saturday only those foods which were prepared before midnight; or they eat raw foods.

68. The macaque is a type of monkey of the Cercopithecidae family.

69. 70. and 71. Rodents.

72. The *patira* is a South American wild pig.

73. Large gallinaceous bird of the Cracidae family. From the heavy breast area thick slices of meat can be carved.

74. A type of lizard of the Iguanidae family, which sometimes attains six feet in length. It feeds on vegetables and insects.

75. During a trip to Patagonia, eight of us found it difficult to eat up an omelet made with a single one of these eggs, which weighed more than three pounds.

76. Edible starchy tuberous root of the Dioscoreaceae family (yams).

77. Edible starchy tuberous root of the Convolvulaceae family.

78. Shoot of the palm tree belonging to the Arecaceae family.

79. A gallinaceous, wading-type bird.

80. The fruit of the common avocado tree, of the Persea Americana family. The fruit is generally oval in shape, edible, and also known as *beurre végétal* (vegetable butter).

81. The potatoes of Peru, where they originated, are the best in the world.

82. Eggs known as "hundred-year-old eggs" are rarely more than several years old. They are placed in inactive lime with aromatic herbs and left to ripen (never less than six weeks). After a period of time the yolk liquefies and takes on a dark green color. The white coagulates and becomes a light green. This food, which lets off a strong odor of hydrogen sulfide, to which one becomes accustomed, is served as an hors-d'oeuvre. It has a taste reminiscent of lobster.

83. The *cantjang* is a fermented bean curd.

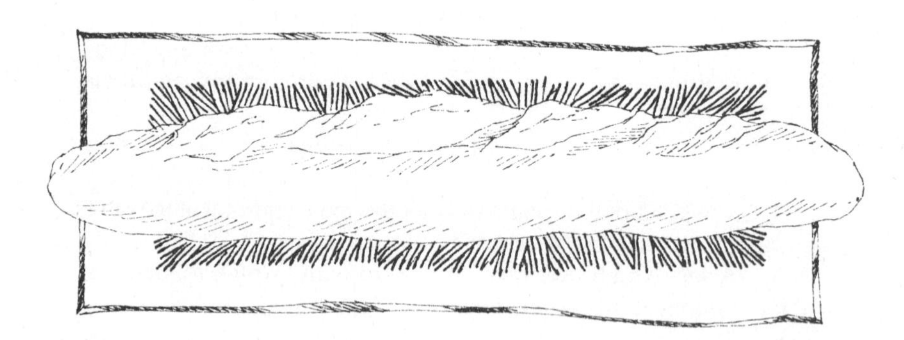

THE SERVICE OF MEALS

The service of meals entails kitchen utensils, furniture, dishware, flatware, silver-plate, and table linen.

In the beginning, the serving of meals was reduced to its most elementary. Prehistoric man ate mostly standing up, in haste, pursued by his peers and by wild animals, both of whom were always ready to snatch away his food. When he felt that he was in a relatively secure spot, he ate crouched or sitting on the ground. His meals, however, were always irregular and generally precarious. When luck put at his disposal any abundance of food, he gorged himself for several days and then, sated, he would lie down to digest,[1] just like the boa constrictor.

Stone Age men cooked their meat on heated stones and used flint axes to cut it up. They drank water from springs or streams, their mouth in the liquid, or from the palms of their hands. They sometimes also used leaves[2] or shells. Later on, at the end of the Stone Age, there appeared some rudimentary pottery and containers made of bone[3] or horn.

The Bronze Age, the lacustrine period, witnessed the birth of the grindstone for milling grain and tools made of bronze and copper.

Afterward came tools made of iron.

Antiquity

Egypt

Egypt. In Egypt, cooking utensils consisted of earthenware and metal pots, frying pans, pastry molds, and ovens, and the tableware consisted of plates, goblets, knives, and spoons.

The lower classes ate their meals crouched around small low round or oval wooden tables on which were earthenware dishes containing the food, which was eaten with the fingers.

Among the wealthy class, the service was quite different. In the room in which meals were served, tables made of wood, stone, or metal, ornately carved or painted, were set up in the middle. Upon them food was placed in dishes made of earthenware or metal, fermented beverages in amphorae, and water[4] in porous earthen crocks similar to *alcarazas* (pitchers of porous earthenware used as water coolers). Stools with either straight or crossed legs and chairs or armchairs for the guests were placed around the room. The lady of the house oversaw all the preparations and presided at meals.

Servants would bring in baskets to each guest the different dishes on the menu. These were served on small plates by means of spoons and metal hooks.

Before beginning a meal, the guests washed their hands in perfumed water and repeated this cleansing procedure after each course.

The beverages were poured into bronze goblets and each person, after having emptied his goblet, wiped his lips with a cloth.

Musicians and singers would perform during the meal.

The Hebrews

The Hebrews. Among the nomadic Hebrews, the dining furnishings consisted almost exclusively of carpets and cushions, leather utensils, and, to hold liquids, goatskins, a very practical material, easily transportable and unbreakable.

When the Hebrews were in Egypt, they replaced leather containers with pottery, glazed inside and, at first, with no other ornamentation.

During the eleventh century B.C., the Hebrews' living quarters were provided with a kitchen with a stove. They used spoons and forks made of wood or bronze but only to serve the food. At meals, which were eaten in groups, the guests sat around a table, and the meal was generally preceded by a prayer. The main meal was at noon. Under the domination of the Persians, they acquired from their conquerors tastes for luxury and indolence. They took to perfuming themselves and eating their meals lying down on more or less sumptuous couches. Those of the very rich were made of carved ivory. The cooking utensils and dishware became elaborate and frequently were made of engraved silver and even of gold. The use of colored glasses, decorated with reliefs of fruit, became very fashionable.

The women, especially those of the upper classes, were generally served separately.

Dances enlivened the banquets, and orchestras, where flute and drum blended with the lute and harp,[5] charmed the music-lovers.

During religious ceremonies, repasts played a very important role. Indeed the luxury of the funerary banquets reached such a point that some people ruined themselves financially by giving, for family funerals, sumptuous feasts to which everyone was invited.[6]

The Assyrians

The Assyrians. The furniture of the poorer classes was very rudimentary. It consisted of stone blocks, woven mattings, primitive stools.

The middle-class Assyrian homes contained chairs and stools, and the kitchen equipment consisted of a bread oven and an open-air hearth with a single kettle on it; the latter served for all culinary preparations.

The wealthy had furniture made of rare woods or of ivory, carved and decorated. For utensils they had kettles, plates, ladles, and goblets of precious metal. During the meals the guests were seated around a table. Only the head of the household was lying down. Women ate separately. Eunuchs served the meals.

The Assyrian kings had extraordinarily luxurious couches covered with embroidery. The legs, backs and armrests of the armchairs were inlaid with ivory, metals, and precious stones. The queens ate their meals sitting in armchairs.

After Diodorus of Sicily, it was the king Ashurbanipal who brought the highest degree of luxury to the dining table.

The Hindus

The Hindus. Table accessories were the object of a great deal of attention in the homes of the rich Hindus, but the common people had only very primitive utensils which, as a matter of fact, they still use today.

The Persians

The Persians. The Persians had great luxury at table. The kitchen and dining utensils were made of precious metals.

At Court, the principal room of the palace, garlanded with flowers and scented with perfumes, which was used both as living and dining room, was paved with marble, porphyry, and alabaster. It was decorated with carpets and wall hangings held up between marble columns with silver rings. The king's couch, the dishware, the bowls, the goblets, the pitchers, the plates, etc., were made of silver and gold.

The king ate alone, lying down. Only on rare occasions did he allow the queen and her sons to join him.

Eunuchs did the serving.

When the king had guests, the guests were grouped in an adjoining room, which was reserved for them and separated by a curtain hung in such a manner that the king could see his guests without being seen by them. However, on certain great feast days, family members—never more than twelve at once—were admitted to the room where he was—but only the monarch would be lying on a couch; the guests who surrounded him crouched on rugs. The king drank a special wine which the royal cupbearers had to taste each time they poured him some. There were other wines for the guests.

The kitchen personnel was numerous. During the reign of Darius, it consisted of 277 cooks and eighty-nine people for the preparation of beverages. To the table servers, over and above the cupbearers and eunuchs, were added forty perfumers, 329 courtesans, musicians, and dancers.

The Greeks

The Greeks. As was the case with all ancient peoples, at first there was no dining room as such. The main hall, which served as living room and kitchen, also was used for meals. This arrangement had the major inconvenience of filling the room with smoke and the odor of burnt fat, because, for the most part, the food was prepared on the home altar. Several centuries went by before the Greeks realized the necessity of having the kitchen in a special room with a chimney, and it was only after the conquest of Macedonia that they began, in each dwelling, to set aside one room to serve as a dining room. This room, generally square, was large enough in size to comfortably hold four tables with three couches each, arranged in horseshoe fashion.

The tableware consisted of plates, oil cruets, bread baskets, vessels which contained liquids, spoons (but only for eating puddings), goblets, bowls, and drinking glasses so numerous that Atheneus describes a hundred or so varieties, of all sizes and shapes.

The kitchenware and utensils consisted of kettles, steam-boilers, pots, saucepans much like our own, chafing dishes, skimmers, skillets and pans for cooking eggs, amphorae, boilers, pottery or metal bowls, spoons, two-pronged forks, knives, and grasping hooks.

The Greeks ate their food with their fingers—those who were afraid of either soiling or burning themselves wore gloves—and others cleaned their fingers after each course with bread pulp which they threw to the dogs.

At special ceremonies, before sitting down at the table, the guests performed numerous ablutions, perfumed themselves and put on white robes and sandals, and adorned themselves with flowers.

The kitchen staff were recruited at first from among the lower classes and slaves. Later, two-year schools trained and graduated professional cooks. Women specialized in the preparation of sweets, and *maîtres d'hôtel* assumed the direction of the table serving and kitchen management. To stimulate artistic zeal, culinary contests were organized. Laureate of the first culinary contests in Athens was one Chiromenes, who presented the jury with spiced truffles, larded with fatback, steamed in wine, and wrapped in a pastry crust. His name deserves to be passed on to posterity.

The towns in ancient Greece which were noted for their sometimes excessively sumptuous tables are: Athens, Corinth, Sybaris, and Syracuse.

The Etruscans

The Etruscans. The Etruscans, who were probably of Phoenician origin and who lived in the north of ancient Italy, enjoyed a very advanced state of civilization. They liked good food, beautiful furnishings, ostentatious tables, sumptuous Oriental-style garments, jewels, and precious ornaments. They excelled in metal crafts. They manufactured vases of black argil depicting busts in the "Canope" style and others in the "Bucchero" style, more simply carved or adorned with reliefs; amphorae; and magnificently decorated dishware.

Their simplest houses, which were square, were constructed of wood, with a porch roof on each side. The more opulent ones were precursors of the Roman houses with an atrium.

The furniture was very luxurious, the most elaborate being adorned with figurines and engraved metal appliqués.

One may get an idea of old Etruscan art in the museums of ancient Etruria and particularly in the one at Volterra. The sculptures of that time depicted feast scenes in elaborately carved and embellished frames, showing richly ornamented furnishings and silverware of enormous value. Frescoes, found in necropolae, showed the guests luxuriously garbed and loaded with jewels, eating and drinking and entertained by musicians and by scantily clad dancers.

Women were admitted to meals and to the entertainment.

The Romans *The Romans.* The early Romans lived very simply in single-room huts covered with reeds or straw. They generally ate on the threshold of the house.

Later they became more civilized, and built, in Rome houses with courtyards and gardens in which the principal hall or atrium served at once as living room, dining room, and kitchen. A square or rectangular hole cut into the ceiling let out smoke and let in the rainwater, which was collected in a hollow cut into the floor exactly beneath the upper opening.

After the conquest of Italy and the first African expedition, Roman houses became more extensive and began to have regular dining rooms, or *tricliniums*, whose floors were paved with mosaic and the walls of which were made of stucco decorated with frescoes. There were ornamental draperies, columns, fountains, basins for the fountains, and climbing vines. There were also kitchens and storerooms for storing food and utensils destined for the dining table.

Torches, which in early days provided light, were replaced by flambeaus made of vegetable fibers coated with pitch or wax, which were placed in candelabra, in wall brackets, or in torch holders. After the conquest of Greece, oil lamps were used.

The Romans did not have plates any more than did the earlier ancient peoples. They served themselves with their hands. Spoons were used only for eating porridges, eggs, snails, custards, and jams. After the meal, or even after each course, they washed their hands. The gourmands licked their fingers. After the meal, the tables were wiped, brushed, and washed. In well-to-do homes one changed tables after each course.

During Caesar's time, the custom of covering the tables with linen, wool, or silk arose. These were the first tablecloths. From tablecloths to napkins was only one step, which was quickly taken. Kitchen equipment and table equipment were the same kind as those used by the Egyptians, the Greeks, and the Etruscans, plus kettles and pails made of bronze, plate-warmers and trivets, trays for serving, various types of spoons, knives, two-pronged forks, which were used in the kitchen and for serving, pastry molds, and tables made of stone for carving food. These tables also had cavities which served as mortars. Finally, hollow stone sinks with drains were used.

Drinking glasses made of clear glass date from the time of Nero.

After the fall of Carthage, incredible luxury invaded Rome. Certain dining room couches brought fabulous prices, and Livius Drusus (to mention only one name) owned ten thousand pounds of silver and gold serving pieces.

In Lucullus's home, twelve richly decorated halls, each named after a divinity—Apollo, Mars, Ceres, etc.—and decorated with their statues in Paros marble, served as living halls and dining rooms.

When the master of the house ordered a meal served in one of these halls, it corresponded to a prescribed cost. A feast ordered for the Apollo hall would be expected to cost fifty thousand drachmas, for instance.

In the Golden Palace of Nero, the dining room ceiling was made of movable ivory panels, allowing for rotation which imitated the movement of the heavens, representing the seasons of the year, which changed with each new dinner course. From this ceiling perfumed essences and flowers showered down upon the guests.

The dining hours were approximately equivalent to ours. The dinner often lasted late into the night and developed into an orgy. Each guest had the right to bring friends. Spongers invited themselves and paid for their share with their wit. Their kind is still with us!

The very numerous staff was well trained and efficient. The kitchen chefs earned a great deal of money, aside from gifts, which doubled or tripled this. The most sought-after were the graduates of the Culinary Academy, which was founded in Rome under Hadrian with its headquarters on the Palatine.

The Gauls, Gallo-Romans, and Franks

The Gauls, Gallo-Romans, and Franks. The inhabitants of independent Gaul lived in caves or in huts made of treetrunks and earth. They ate their meals either in the dwellings or in the open air. They cooked their bread beneath the ashes. They ate sitting down and used a knife, whose sheath hung from the waist, to serve themselves with. They drank from the horns or even the skulls of animals which they had killed, especially those of the bison, mounted on bases of silver and/or gold. They slept on grass pallets or animal hides. Their first kitchen utensils seem to have been grindstones or mortars to grind grain. Then came vessels of baked white clay in elegant shapes and decorated with geometrical designs, in white or in colors, baskets made of very thin wooden strips and sieves made of horsehair. They had no sideboards or closets. The wealthier had only crudely constructed wooden tables, sometimes having small circular excavations, which served as plates and dishes.

Later on the Gauls acquired some dexterity in mining and became very good at metallurgy. They made plates of bronze and vessels and utensils of various metals which they either plated or tinned, and they knew how to work in gold and silver.

They were the inventors of barrels made of staves and circled with iron, used for the transportation of wine.

A half-century before Jesus Christ, the wealthy Gauls owned stone houses which were spacious and furnished with objects which were, if not luxurious, at least comfortable.

After the Roman victory, the country Gauls continued to live the simple existence of independent Gaul, but those of the towns adopted the living style of their conquerors. They built villas, which they decorated sumptuously, much in the manner of those of Rome and Pompei, and these villas were equipped with elegant and artistic dining rooms, beautifully appointed.

The Franks, like all barbarian peoples, were ignorant of any type of comfortable dwellings or furnishings. But after their settlement in Gaul, where they came into contact with the Romans, their existence changed. Rich nobles or landlords owned houses which were generally made of wood and built on hills or on slopes. They had the appearance of feudal châteaux or fortresses, surrounded by moats, fortifications, and sometimes flanked by towers, with outbuildings suitable for serving the needs of the master. Around the manor house were numerous huts and cabins which served as dwellings for the farm workers, the artisans, and the freedmen employed by the Frankish chief, to cultivate his lands, to manufacture everything that was necessary, and to defend him in time of battle. The dining halls, though sparsely furnished, were very spacious. The walls were simply whitewashed and then often decorated with tapestries or embellished with brilliantly hued paintings. Portieres and curtains completed the decoration.

The furniture was simple, unimportant, and poorly made. It consisted of tables mounted on sawhorses or trestles, benches and banquettes, and chests serving as buffets and cupboards. The tableware, however, was very elaborate: dishes made of gold or silver, utensils made of precious metals, silver pieces, and gold serving dishes.

The Franks used spoons, knives, and drinking vessels made of wood, baked clay, glass, marble, and precious metal.

The kitchens generally occupied a separate building. They were very spacious and could serve as refectories for the domestics and slaves.

Each castle had a hand mill and an oven.

In the homes of the Frankish kings the dining hall was divided into three sections by two rows of columns. One section was reserved for the royal family, another for the guests, and the third for the officers of the king's house.

The furniture was neither more important nor more luxurious than that of the landlords—but utensils of gold and silver, great basins made of precious metals, encrusted with jewels, valuable dishes, plates, goblets made of multicolored glass, of marble, of ceramic, made up the table equipment.

During the fifth century, the Frankish lords—the nobles—copying the Roman style, adopted the use of couches grouped around the table.

For feasts, the walls were lined with greenery, the floor was strewn with flowers or covered with rich carpeting, and the table itself looked like a flower bed. The different foods were presented in serving dishes made of various substances: platters of gold or silver, glass, marble, black pottery, painted baskets, and vessels encrusted with precious gems.

Meals were eaten to the tune of flutes and oboes; and mimes, balladeers, singers, and dancers, entertained the guests.

After the banquet, the guests took part in games of chance. Hand-to-hand combat took place between the lords and the Frankish chieftains.

The Middle Ages

The Middle Ages. The dwellings in France during the Middle Ages were more luxurious than comfortable, especially after the Crusades; and they were embellished with all the new equipment and appointments which a flourishing industry could provide.

The more grandiose manor houses had a reception room called the guest hall in which ceremonial dinners and banquets were held, but there was no real dining room per se.

The everyday meals were served, in winter, in the chambers or antechambers, and even in the kitchen. In summer, meals were served out-of-doors in the garden under a bower or in a grove.

Floors in the dwellings were made of beaten earth covered with straw or hay and, later on, with woven mattings. In the homes of the wealthy lords, there were thick woolen rugs instead of straw or hay. The walls were painted with oil or covered with glue.

The lighting was done by means of torches, wax flambeaus, and tiny flat lamps made of copper and filled with oil, placed on the ground or on a table, or supported by chandeliers or crowns.

The furniture consisted of four-footed benches; banquettes (bench–chests with backs and arm rests, covered with slipcovers or cushions); armchairs; richly decorated throne-type chairs; solid tables or ones that could be dismantled, stepping-stools, caskets which were a sort of chest in which valuables were kept; sideboards, dish cupboards, or buffets made of delicate woods, with one or two shelves,[7] artistically carved and destined for the storage of the more beautiful pieces of silver or gold ware. The sideboard played a great part during ceremonies and processions, and it was part of the furniture for all receptions. The luxuriousness of the sideboard reached its peak in the homes of the nobles and prelates. At Court, among certain of the kings, there were buffets made of gold and silver, sideboards of great value covered with tapestries and gold cloth, which supported very rare pieces of silver and magnificent gold dishware.

The kitchens played a very important role in the dwellings of the Middle Ages. They were generally situated in spacious buildings.

In the thirteenth century, they were mostly round and equipped with a chimney, with an air duct in the roof for the evacuation of smoke and odors. In the fourteenth century, the kitchens were square shaped, with two or more chimneys and a central air vent. In the châteaux and palaces, the kitchens were spacious. They had numerous annexes for different types of preparation and services. In the bourgeois homes, the kitchens were small, not separated from the main dwelling, and often were placed in some room or other which then served as dining room, bedroom, and kitchen all at once.

The kitchen furnishings consisted of a dish cupboard or kitchen sideboard, very luxurious in the homes of the princes, rich nobles, and high prelates; of a chest for preserving salted meat; a spice cabinet; a bread-kneading trough; and tables either with legs or on trestles; and benches, banquettes, and stools.

In immense, deep chimneys, tall enough for an adult to stand upright, hung the pothook with its extension made of forged iron and often artfully worked (the one belonging to Charles V was made of silver), on which hung the enormous kettle with a capacity of about twenty quarts. In front of the hearth were two firedogs or cast-iron andirons, on the tails of which were laid enormous logs. The front stems of the firedogs, at least three feet high, were equipped with cramp irons or hooks which served to hang the strainer, the large ladle, and the long two-pronged fork, which were used to plunge into the kettle, as well as tongs, pokers, fire shovels, and several spits.[8] The tops were shaped somewhat like baskets into which was placed some kind of container for heating or cooking certain foods. There were also chafing dishes, which could be placed either close to or far from the hearth.

The display of luxury as far as table accessories were concerned was incredible during the Middle Ages. It reached its apogee between the twelfth and fourteenth centuries. The poor may only have had porringers or plates made of wood or earthenware, and the lower classes only had dishes and bowls and various other containers which were crudely enameled, but the bourgeoisie owned pewter dishes which were real works of art and dishes made of Italian pottery.[9] On the tables of the nobles and the kings, treasures flowered. There was a surfeit of state silverware, dishware, platters, ewers, flagons, spice dishes, sauceboats, forks[10] (extremely rare) for eating fruits, salt cellars of every conceivable shape and size, pinters, chalices, goblets (which were the most elaborate of chalices), marvelous pieces which were precursors of the epergne, made of gold, silver or vermeil, and elaborate crystal utensils.[11]

Sumptuary laws, the first of which goes back to Philippe le Bel, tried to fight this immoderate luxury, but in vain. Juvenal des Ursins, in a long harangue delivered at the États de Tours (1468), said:

"There is hardly anyone left in France who doesn't want to eat on silver plates."

The tableware even included mustard pots made of silver or pewter, perfectly beautiful marmalade pots made of glass, beer mugs with covers, spice graters, pinters made of pewter or crystal, cups, goblets set on trivets, drinking vessels of all sizes and shapes made of precious metals, pewter, copper, rock crystal, glass, marble, baked earthenware, and all types of rare woods, faience spice caddies, large and small knives for carving and boning, and oyster knives. There were Venetian glasses, chalices made out of ostrich eggs and coconuts, wine coolers, sometimes very artistically worked. For the kitchen, there were wooden pitchers girded with iron, vials, jugs, clay pots, three-pronged forks, and funnels made of leather and white metal.

During the fourteenth century, the rich began to acquire whole dinner services in the same pattern.

Table linen, which had fallen into disuse after the fall of Rome, came back into style. The well-to-do had either plain or embroidered cloths and runners, which were narrow cloths which ran around the edge of the table on which the guests used to wipe their fingers. At the end of the fourteenth century there were doilies and napkins.

Despite all this luxury there were still no individual plates[12]; soups, sauces, and all liquid foods were served in porringers. In poor homes, each person dipped his spoon in turn into the porringer containing the soup or other liquid food, and each drank in turn from the same drinking vessel. In well-organized homes, there was a soup porringer and a wine vessel for each two guests, and the tact of the host consisted in grouping his guests into congenial couples.[13] Servants held cloths in front of the ladies as they drank, in order to avoid having them stain their dresses.

Meats and solid ingredients without much liquid, and dry ingredients, were served on slabs of metal or wood, usually round, called trenchers or carvers, on which were arranged, beforehand, one or more slices of stale brown bread,[14] to absorb the juices from the freshly carved meat, so as not to stain the tablecloth. These slices of bread, which were called trencher-bread, were not eaten at the table but were given to the servants or to the poor. There were as many trenchers as guests.

The platters were brought in covered with bell-shaped dish covers (in well-to-do households, these were made of silver), and the goblets which were on the table had covers, a custom which was introduced for fear of poisoning. It is from this custom that the expression *"mettre le couvert"* ("put on the cover," or "set the table" in colloquial English) derives.

Wealth was also evidenced by the number of servants. The bourgeois contented themselves with one domestic or a maid-of-all-work. When, however, they gave dinner parties, they rented valets for ostentation, in order to make others believe that they had a well-staffed household. In the homes of the rich nobles and kings, the dining-room staff was large. Philippe le Bel, promoter of the first sumptuary laws, had a kitchen and dining room staff of fifty-four; Charles V had 158.

Banquets, sumptuous feasts where luxury rivaled eccentricity (reminiscent of the Roman era), were given at the drop of a hat. The nobles gave frequent dinner parties. The halls and tables were garlanded with flowers and crowns of flowers decorated the vessels and drinking chalices. The meals were announced by means of hunting horns.

Before sitting down at table, the guests washed their hands with perfumed water which pages or squires or young ladies brought them in elaborate basins. In the home of the sovereign, this function was reserved for the chamberlain.

The rarest and most varied foods were served in profusion. Poets and troubadours recited stories, poems, fables, and romances. Fiddlers played. Jesters, jugglers, and buffoons displayed animals and did tricks. There were vocal and instrumental concerts, pantomimes, and ballets. Stage plays and mock battles, mythological subjects, and landscapes were depicted. These were the first *entremets*[15] (literally, "inter-courses" or "between courses"). Compartmented "fountains" automatically dispensed the wines.

Among the feasts of that era which were reknowned were: the feast "of the pheasant" given by Philippe le Bon, Duke of Burgundy, to celebrate the expedition which was organized against Mohammed II (1453); and the feast given by Gaston III, Count of Foix, on the occasion of the marriage of the daughter of Charles VII (1458).

The Renaissance

The Renaissance. There were no dining rooms at this period, any more than there were during the Middle Ages. Meals were served in guest halls, in bedrooms, or even in the kitchen, when it was cold. When the weather was fine, they were served out-of-doors. The floors, which were flagged or tiled, were strewn with sweet grasses and flowers in the summer and with woven reed mattings in winter.

During the sixteenth century, the heating consisted of logs continually burning in high, deep fireplaces. But soon stoves made of glazed earthenware, imported from Germany, brought added heat.

The Renaissance placed its stamp on many things. Dining furniture, specimens of which can be seen in our museums, consisted of buffets, cupboards, tables, chairs, and booths, all magnificently carved. There were also extension tables called pull-tables, with small end pieces at each extremity. But this furniture was scattered about in all the rooms, in the halls and even in the kitchens. As styles changed, the sideboards became credenzas, and benches ceded place to stools, which were often very elaborate and even sometimes made of solid silver.

During the Renaissance, table linen was very popular. It was made of linen damask, heavily embroidered. There were even damask aprons. All levels of society, the poor as well as the rich, the aristocracy and the bourgeoisie, had tables covered with cloths, and each diner had a napkin. In high society, the napkins were changed several times during a meal. The table linen was perfumed, and it became a custom to fold the tablecloths and napkins in numerous decorative ways.

The tables were elaborately set and loaded with superb pieces of silverware, goldware, and valuable china.

The serving pieces of the time included: vinegar cruets made of glass, crystal, pewter, and silver; pewter mugs with a cover and a handle; very elegant pitcher-shaped flagons; large drinking glasses; handled mugs, made of earthenware, faience, pewter, and silver; small filigreed baskets of gold and silver, for fruits, cakes, etc.; small baskets of fine wickerwork or gilded wicker, decorated with ribbons and lace; bonbon dishes or pocket candy boxes; pocketknives; silver or gold toothpicks, or toothpicks made of bone and wood; nut crackers; wine or beer pitchers made of earthenware, pewter, or silver; egg cups made of pewter or precious metal; faience dishes; jugs with spouts; vessels and cups with lids, with and without hinges.

Table fountains made of precious metals had almost completely disappeared from the table service except at Court.

An important development during the sixteenth century was the appearance of the individual fork, whose use was popularized by Henry III. However, it was still not in general use. Long-handled spoons saw the light of day out of necessity, since the lords and ladies had taken to wearing large, high, starched, frilly neck ruffs. The kitchens, very spacious in baronial homes and palaces, enjoyed the same luxury as the table. Aside from the silver serving pieces they contained, there were utensils for every conceivable use, made of wood, ivory, pewter, iron, lead, copper, and bronze. These included: hinged bellows, fish pans, basins, pie dishes, skillets, small wooden tubs,[16] kitchen fountains, certain of which were made of copper and extremely beautiful.

At the end of the sixteenth century, rotisseries[17] with hoods appeared, and iceboxes to keep foods and drinks began to come into general use. Despite the new sumptuary laws and the edicts ordering the sale of all valuable dishware to help alleviate the financial penury of the period, the greatest luxury reigned during the Renaissance. Nobody wished to renounce the outward appearance of wealth. During the reign of Francis I, it reached its culmination. To the already existing riches were added the beautiful ceramic pieces of Bernard Palissy and the marvelous chased silver- and goldware of Benvenuto Cellini.

The table service was taken care of, in the wealthy classes, by an enormous staff. In Francis I's household, this meant a staff of ninety-five serving noblemen, to which was attached an army of subordinates.

Meals consisted of several abundant courses. In ceremonial dinners an incredible magnificence was displayed. The taste for cultured pleasures brought from Italy by Marie de Medici had reached all classes: the aristocracy, the bourgeoisie, and even a part of the general populace; but the very poor still ate out of wooden trenchers. During the festivities at Court, wealth was displayed by an abundance of meats of all kinds, and by the sumptuous "*entremets* spectacles" which were given. The lesser banquets were no less luxurious.

The reign of Henry IV put an end to these costly feasts.

Seventeenth and Eighteenth Centuries

Seventeenth and Eighteenth Centuries. During the seventeenth century there was, in many homes—especially in those of the bourgeoisie and in the townhouses—a special room designed for meals. But in the majority of the princely châteaux and manorial dwellings they continued serving meals in any room. Louis XIV and Louis XV were served in their studies. Tables were set up in the antechamber or in the queen's room only during the warm season.

Dwelling floors were covered with brilliantly colored woven mats, which were very elegant and decorative. Then came carpets made of waffled leather for the summer and made of wool for winter. During the seventeenth century, the walls in wealthier homes were covered with multicolored matting or with gilt leather. Later on there were silk tapestries, green hangings from Flanders, and vertical warp tapestries. During the reign of Louis XIV, mural decoration changed. There were now wall ornaments applied directly to the wall, such as moldings, cornices, pier glasses, decorative gingerbread, etc. During the reign of Louis XV, there were white or gilt wood panelings, small tapestry panels, scrolls, artistic medallions painted in oils, and mirrors everywhere.

In bourgeois dwellings, the dining rooms, when they existed, were very simply furnished and the walls were covered with matting. When the matting fashion passed, they were either painted with oil or whitewashed. Later on, they were covered with painted papers.

Heat was insured by wood fires in fireplaces which were of a more restrained size and which very much resembled those we have today. There were also glazed earthenware stoves of various shapes, which were more artistic than they had previously been.

Lighting was supplied by chandeliers and table flambeaus, appliqués, girandoles, lamps, as well as by flambeaus and torches made of copper, bronze, crystal, silver, and vermeil which were held by servants. The nobles kept up this manner of lighting large dinners. It allowed them to show off their large staff and to satisfy their egos and their love of ostentation. Less fortunate citizens used candles and the old oil lamp.

The furniture consisted of carved round or oval tables,[18] extension tables, and mahogany drop-leaf tables. These were covered with table carpets or heavily embroidered materials, which were removed to set the table.

There were also tables and other furniture of inlaid woods, other tables topped with marble slabs set on carved and gilded legs, transformable tables called "machined tables," "flying tables" which rose up, all set, from the floor below, moving buffets and metamorphosing furniture, which were real masterpieces of ingenuity and which were much in style during the reign of Louis XV, especially for small dinner parties. These made it possible to do without valets.[19]

There were also tea tables; various styles of consoles on which the extra dinnerware was placed; small tables with two, three, or four shelves, which were placed alongside the large table and acted as serving tables; massive chairs with backs and armrests; heavy chairs with backs and stools; and folding chairs called *perroquets*.[20]

It was only during the eighteenth century that comfortable chairs, set around the table, finally appeared.

The sideboard became the "dining-room buffet" (in well-to-do homes there were sometimes two or three), and the "dish cupboard" in rustic homes.

Embroidered linen, such as tablecloths, mats, and napkins, was much in favor, and was chosen with great care.

The richness of the silverware and china sometimes reached exaggerated and unbelievable proportions.[21] It was constantly added to according to the current fashion. People offered one another gifts in the form of valuable dishware. The ownership of a large number of these, in silver and gold, was a mark of wealth, nobility, and distinction.[22] Louis XIII, Louis XIV, and Louis XV enacted sumptuary laws against this exorbitant and scandalous luxury, especially since the populace was dying of hunger. Each sent the Court valuables to be melted down: the throne and furniture of silver, precious dishware, which was palace decoration and which was melted down to be minted into money to try to remedy the serious financial crises. The royal family and a few nobles followed this example, but for the most part the people preferred to bury their valuables and await happier times. If it was discovered, however, that which was not willingly given up was seized.

Luxury then leaned toward faience, porcelain, and crystal; faience from Rouen, Nevers, Strasbourg, and Lunéville; porcelains from China, Saxony, Vincennes, Bourg-la-Reine, Sceaux, Sèvres, and Chantilly; glassware from Venice and crystal from Bohemia.

During the reign of Louis XVI, the economic crisis let up for a time. Along with prosperity, the silverware and the luxury reappeared on tables and in furnishings. Everyone wanted dishware and hollowware of silver. Porcelain was allowed at Court, along with dishware of silver and gold. Faience was for the less well-to-do.

The tableware was highly varied. Over and above the sumptuous dishware there were: hollow plates, flat plates, and dessert plates, platters, sauceboats, pitchers, jugs, basins, salt cellars, ewers, sugar bowls and cream pots, *oille* plates,[23] cups, sugar holders, saucers, teapots and coffeepots, chocolate pots, tureens, vegetable dishes, oil cruet stands and mustard stands, trays, epergnes, vases and objects of all kinds, which were made of porcelain and were very beautiful. There were round plate holders made of silver, pewter, or wicker, footed trays for tea, coffee, or chocolate, made of Chinese lacquered wood, metal, faience, lapis lazuli or rock crystal, etc., trays, tea caddies, chocolate boxes made of metal and especially of silver, sugar tongs, marrow-pullers, spoons for coffee, sugar, mustard, olives, servers for stew, ladles,[24] flagons and ewers, made of glass or crystal. There were also bottles, crested earthenware jugs with crook handles, chalices made of rock crystal, engraved and decorated, table liqueur chests, drinking glasses of Venetian glass and of Bohemian crystal, which were chased and engraved. Cooling buckets made of earthenware and of porcelain now replaced the silver and vermeil basins. Fountains of marble, bronze, or molded lead, affixed to the walls of the dining room, replaced the ornate fountains of the preceding century.

In bourgeois homes they used bottles and pitchers; but pots, carafes, ewers, and beakers were only for noblemen's houses.

In the châteaux and manor houses of the wealthy, there existed, near the dining room, a small room furnished with a kitchen stove which served to keep food warm or to reheat it when the kitchen was far away.

All well-to-do homes had a kitchen. Among the bourgeoisie, it was generally relegated to a dark and distant corner of the dwelling, and it was also often poorly kept and dirty. The kitchens of the aristocrats, on the other hand, were spacious, well lit, elegant, clean, and convenient. Nobles and wealthy people took pride in decorating them with kitchenware and luxurious furniture, of which they were inordinately proud and which they showed to their visitors.

In the way of utensils there were, during the seventeenth century: a kitchen stove with several openings to cook the soups and stews; rotisseries; automatic spits; sieves; bellows, some of which were elaborately carved of wood, metal, or earthenware, the air pockets made of hide; corkscrews; small barrels of clay; strainers; big-bellied cauldrons or boilers made of wrought iron; turbot cookers; silver pie dishes; terrines; molds for ices, made of pewter or silver; filtering urns; and portable kitchens.

In the eighteenth century, the kitchens in well-to-do homes changed. The large cumbersome furnishings were eliminated in favor of smaller furniture and the kitchen utensils were added to. Copper and tin took precedence for kitchen utensils; then silver, which had been outlawed by the sumptuary laws, reappeared and was used for the manufacture of kitchenware.

Until the end of the sixteenth century, fingers were used to carry meats and certain vegetables to the mouth. During the seventeenth century, there still was only one porringer for every two guests. During the eighteenth century, each guest had his own individual place setting: personal plate, napkin, spoon, fork, knife, and drinking glass. The glasses were not placed on the table, but remained on a buffet or serving table, lined up in the same order as the guests, and one manservant passed them, being careful that there were no mixups. After each guest had drunk, the domestic rinsed the glass and replaced it on the serving table.

Toward the middle of the eighteenth century, pitchers containing the drinks were placed on the table, knives were pointed and the fork came into general use among the middle classes. At this same period, servers began carving meats in the pantry instead of at the table, as had been done previously, and during meals the plates were changed at least twice—once for each separate dish in the homes of noblemen.

At feasts and large dinner parties during the seventeenth century pyramids of desserts were placed on the table, and porcelain whatnots, often of gigantic proportions, laden with fresh or dried fruits, jams, compotes, sweetmeats, cakes, etc., appeared. There were also large mounted pieces of pastry, vases and supports made of crystal or precious metal, and then large pieces made of silver or vermeil, which were known as "table centers" (centerpieces).

During the eighteenth century, the epergnes were made of porcelain or earthenware, representing in miniature flowers, shrubs, and people, such as shepherds and musicians. Then epergnes made of precious metal with mirrored bases appeared and, for the less wealthy, epergnes made of gilt copper.

Tables were decorated with fresh flowers. Later on, artificial flowers were created. For banquets and feasts at Court, and for the nobles, there were, at all seasons, even in winter, a profusion of flowers placed in baskets, in coffers, in vases made of crystal, gilded copper, or silver. Garlands and festoons of ribboned flowers ran around the table. Over and above these, there were high pyramids of flowers, shrubs constructed of flowers, which were joined by arcades of fruit and garlands of flowers. There were also decorations made of sugar or colored starch and frosted decorations on the green plants and on the mirrors of the epergnes, which; melting in the heat, gave the astonished guests the illusion of melting rivers, or the unfolding of leaves and flowers.

Meals were announced by the ringing of a bell. The guests did not wash their hands in the dining room any more. At Court and among the nobles, this took place in a small corner or in an antechamber. In the bourgeois homes, there was a fountain and a basin affixed to the wall of the dining room. Louis XIV simply had a wet towel placed between two golden plates brought to him at the beginning and end of the meal. The aristocracy followed his example, and the masters, in their own châteaux, were served wet towels between silver or vermeil plates.

The guests recited poetry to one another, as well as literary pieces and proverbs. Epigrams were flung around and were known as "vaudevilles." They were also entertained with "light shows," comedies, music, and dancing.

Etiquette became more relaxed. Only the great banquets retained their ceremonial pomp.

The kitchen staff and the dining room staff were generally very numerous. At Court, during the reign of Louis XIV, these consisted of five hundred people under the guidance of the Great Master of the King's House, who sometimes was a prince of the blood. All the officers of the household associated with dining were nobles and came from illustrious families.

Among the banquets of modern times, where a ridiculous sumptuousness was evident, one must mention those given at Versailles by Louis XIV in 1664, affairs known as the Pleasures of the Enchanted Island. These celebrations went on for seven days and were remarkable because of the profusion of foods, the amount of valuable dishware, the quantity of rare flowers, the sparkle of the girandoles and numerous chandeliers, which was further enhanced by the torches carried by two hundred footmen. Also, there were the festivals of 1668 given on the occasion of the peace of Aix-la-Chapelle, the feasts given by the Prince de Condé in 1688, and finally, the festival of Reims, given in the Archbishop's palace, in honor of the consacration of Louis XV. The king's table, surmounted by a purple velvet dais decorated with fleurs-de-lys, was set up on an elevated platform with four steps leading to it. The Grand-Panetier (Grand Cup Bearer), the Grand Échanson (Grand Equerry), and the Grand Écuyer (Master of the Horse) were all dressed in black velvet and cloth of gold. The Prince de Rohan filled the role of Grand Maître (Major-domo).

The king entered the dining room preceded by the heros and the masters of ceremonies, accompanied by the serving noblemen, and escorted to the sound of the flutes, oboes, and trumpets of his own household.

The various courses of the meal were brought by the *officiers de bouche* (cooks for the king's table), to the sound of trumpet flourishes.

Contemporary Times

Contemporary Times. In the nineteenth century, the dining rooms and kitchens underwent important transformations. The miserably small, dark, airless kitchens were to be found only in the homes of the very poor. Those of the bourgeoisie and of the townhouses were generally very spacious, light, and airy. The walls were covered with oil paint, up to a certain height, and the rest covered above with decorated pottery tiles. The floors were covered with either brick or ceramic tiles. The kitchens were lit either with gas or electricity. The kitchen stove of earlier times disappeared. A cast-iron stove with compartments, decorated with copper and steel, called a *cuisinière* (cooker), heated by coal, coke, gas, or electricity, took its place. In the more important homes, these stoves were equipped with grills, rotisseries, ovens, boilers, steamers, chafing plates, double boilers, plate warmers, etc., allowing for the preparation of the most complicated meals. Large hoods, equipped with traps and ventilators, insured the rapid evacuation of smoke and odors.

Along the walls of the kitchens were affixed copper rods on which were hung saucepans, skillets, lids, strainers, skimmers, ladles, and other utensils of tinned copper or of alloys. Along the walls were also shelves on which were arranged boilers, kettles, basins, molds of all sizes and shapes, platters, teapots, coffee pots, spice caddies, sieves, cooking accessories made of wood, cast iron, wrought iron, nickel, enamelware, tinned copper, earthenware, pottery, porcelain, chinaware, and other articles, either difficult or impossible to hang. As to furniture, there were cupboards containing linens and kitchen china, a sideboard, various tables, some of which had marble tops which serve for different types of operations, with drawers containing spoons, forks, knives, and other utensils necessary for cooking, chairs, iceboxes, and all type of household articles. There was often, adjacent to the kitchen, another room containing a sink, where the kitchen utensils which had been used for food preparation were washed, and where there were receptacles for table scraps and garbage—or, better yet, a trap which allowed for the disposal of garbage directly into the cellar below.

On certain model farms, the kitchens still have a high, deep chimney with its pothook, firedogs, and at the same time a modern stove with pots and other useful utensils. Beautiful kitchen pots and pans and various utensils for food preparation and all other types of household jobs are seen alongside an enormous clock (which is sometimes very beautiful), cupboards, tables, chairs, filtering fountain, sink, etc.

Certain kitchens in very grand townhouses and restaurants are veritable marvels of arrangement and comfort.

Now, everywhere there are dining rooms, even in the smallest of lodgings. Their furnishings and decoration vary with the resources and wealth of the occupant.

In well-to-do homes, the dining rooms are most often very large in size, have high ceilings and are light and airy. The floors are usually waxed parquet, covered with beautiful large woolen carpets or with nailed wall-to-wall carpeting. In summer the carpeting is often replaced with matting. The walls are covered with beautifully painted papers or with gold embossing, waffled leather, or expensive material. They are also decorated with tapestries, paintings, light fixtures, antique porcelain, etc. From the ceiling hangs a light fixture: at the beginning of the era it was modest and held an oil lamp, later on a kerosene one. Nowadays it is often an important piece of artwork, made of forged iron or copper or gilded bronze, sometimes twinkling with crystals and lighted by gas or electricity.

The contemporary dining room is generally very fully furnished. In it may be seen a buffet, sideboard, bread cabinet, dumbwaiter, silverware holder, table, armchairs, and comfortable straight chairs, everything in the style of the epoch. There are sometimes consoles and other small pieces of furniture on which are displayed Chinese vases, ceramics, earthenware objects, pewters, crystals, and other objets-d'art. Near the dining room is another small room, used for serving and known as the *office* (pantry).

In more modest lodgings, the dining room is sometimes used as a living room.

The tableware is extremely varied. It consists of silverware pieces made of "ruolz" (plated metal alloy), dishware services of faience or porcelain, glassware, crystal, whose shapes are prosaic and dull, samples of which can be found in many specialty stores. They are modified, perfected, and others are created according to the tastes of the day.

Our contemporary era marks the complete disappearance of silver plates. One hardly ever sees plates made of silver, except very rarely, in the homes of certain noble families and some of the *nouveaux riches*.

Our era has seen the successive appearance of German silver, white metal alfenide, ruolz, aluminum, and nickel.

The luxury exhibited at table in the preceding centuries does not exist any more. Under Napoleon I, with the exception of a few great banquets, the meals lacked sumptuousness. During the time of Louis XVIII, beautiful dishware reappeared. Under Louis-Philippe, the meals at Court were very bourgeois. The reign of Napoleon III saw the rebirth of these beautiful banquets and splendid feasts. The table was luxurious and elegant. Great silver candelabra, epergnes of the same metal, and some lovely bowls garnished with flowers vied with one another for attention. The plates were of turned silver. On gala days, they were of vermeil or of antique Sèvres porcelain; but many other pieces were of ruolz. The head table steward was dressed in black, the footmen were in brown, as is the custom in France. A superb Negro, magnificently garbed in the Oriental manner, awaited the orders of the Empress exclusively.

The democratic regime, by equalizing the classes, has eliminated all the beautiful pomp. Banquets are now hardly more than public reunions, without any true grandeur or special distinction: commemorative banquets, which prepared the fall of the Bourbons; fraternal banquets of 1848; federation banquets for the Sociétés Mutuelles de France; political banquets, among which one should note the mayors' banquets of 1889, which took place at the Palace of Industry, and that of 1900, which took place in the gardens of the Tuileries. All these banquets are, to the great banquets of the old regime, what today's balls at the Hôtel de Ville, with the singer MacNab, are to the ancient Court balls.

At the end of the nineteenth century and in this first part of the twentieth, table linen is more than ever in style: damask linen, embroidered, hemstitched, and adorned with lace.

There are many ways of serving meals. During large dinners, the table is covered with woolen matting, which is then covered with a tablecloth on which there is a magnificent table runner and matching doilies, to be placed under the carafes. A garland of exotic flowers, discretely scented, links small objects made of porcelain from Sèvres or Saxony, or tiny crystal vases holding flowers and leaves, or a spray of dainty flowers set in arabesque fashion, decorate the table. The table is set with very elaborate porcelain, which is accompanied by drinking glasses of all sizes and shapes, of cut crystal. Pitchers and decanters made of cut crystal with silver mountings, for wines, and decanters or pitchers of cut or blown crystal and silver, for water, lend an elegant touch to the whole. In the middle of the table are low epergnes, silver baskets filled with fruit, porcelain dishes containing desserts and sweetmeats and cakes. Spoons, forks, knives, and menu-holders, knife-holders, and artistically folded napkins complete the decoration. A small nosegay for the corsage or an orchid marks the ladies' places. Green plants are set here and there, and the room is very well lit. The serving is taken care of by domestics in black. In certain more opulent homes, domestics wear black satin knickers or colored velvet knickers with silk stockings, and pumps with silver buckles.

The sight of a dining room, beautifully decorated and cleverly arranged, sparkling with silver and crystal, brilliant with light, is almost like a fairyland. Occasionally the decoration is overdone, and in the presence of a very banal menu, served in a splendid setting, one is tempted to cry out "too many flowers."

The sumptuousness of the dinners and banquets of days gone by has now disappeared. However, the studied refinement and taste which today go into the organization and decoration of kitchens and dining rooms have arrived at such a degree of magnificence that we can affirm that from this point of view, at least, we are not decadent.

NOTES

1. Certain savages still do the same today, and when they are sated, filled to bursting, they have their stomachs stamped on to activate the digestion.

2. In Madagascar, the natives use the leaves of the *ravenala* (a bananalike plant), not only to cover their dwellings, but also to serve as dishes, plates, glasses, tablecloths, and napkins.

3. The use of human skulls as drinking vessels is still found today among savages, generally cannibals. The greatest satisfaction, to an intellectual anthropophage, is derived from drinking from the skull of an enemy whose flesh has provided the feast.

The Eskimos still use cetacean (whale, porpoise, etc.) bones as tableware and—simple household detail!—they have the dishes done by the dogs, who conscientiously lick them clean.

4. Nile water destined for drinking was first allowed to settle before being drunk. From the XVIIIth Dynasty on it was decanted by means of siphons.

5. The invention of stringed instruments is attributed to Jubal, daughter of Laurech.

6. In this vein, today the parents of the deceased may still meet the faithful friends who came to accompany him to his last residence, at the cemetery gate, and offer them a libation at the wine merchant's across the street. His sign usually reads something like this: "One is better here than over there."

7. The number of shelves was proportionate to the nobility of the owner: five for a queen or sovereign prince, four for a prince, three for a count, etc. The untitled gentry had buffets without shelves.

8. The origin of the spit goes back to the fifteenth century. Soon after, dripping pans were added. Spit turning was done at first by young boys and later on by dogs.

9. Manufactured in Faenza, an Italian town.

10. Originally from Byzantium, it would seem.

11. One can conceive of the enormous fortune one had to have to own such tableware when one realizes that gold and silver was valued at that time at least twenty-five times higher than it is today.

12. The use of individual plates dates back to the end of the fifteenth century, and for a long time there was only a single plate for each guest, which he used throughout the entire meal.

13. The guests were generally seated. However, the custom of eating lying down did not completely disappear after the fall of Rome. During the twelfth century, certain elegant banquets were still held in the Roman manner.

14. They also made salt cellars out of brown bread.

15. The word *entremets* originally meant everything that was presented between the meat or fish courses. Then, after having been applied to the entertainment, it began to be applied to the vegetables and sweets, such as sherbets, which separated the courses. Today, the word *entremets* is mostly reserved to designate the sweets served at the end of meals.

16. Small ones were made of silver and gold for the credenzas.

17. These were made of iron and sometimes of silver.

18. There were even some in the shape of a horseshoe.

19. The Marquis de Bouillac was the first to take his meals without his servants, whom he rang for when he wanted them. This type of meal was known as a "bell meal" or "*repas à la clochette.*"

20. At Court, there were for a long time chairs for aristocrats only.

21. The Marquise de Pompadour, at her death, left 687,000 francs' worth of silverware and goldware.

22. Many ruined nobles kept their silverware despite their altered financial standing.

23. *Oille* or *olla* is a ragoût of Spanish origin, made with various kinds of meats and vegetables.

24. The ladle was invented by the Duke of Montausier, who was peculiarly refined and overfastidious.

DISCUSSION OF THE PRINCIPAL METHODS OF COOKING FOODS

THEIR CLASSIFICATION AND SOME DEFINITIONS

The various ways in which food can be cooked may be divided into two main categories: dry cooking and moist cooking.

1. Dry Cooking

Typical of the dry method of cooking I can mention the way ancient man cooked his meat (on hot stones) and also the baking of potatoes in hot ashes. The trouble with completely dry cooking is that inevitably the outside of the food gets somewhat charred. Therefore the idea of greasing food or wrapping it in fat soon evolved.

In modern cooking, roasting, broiling, grilling, and cooking in a pastry crust are typical of the dry method of cooking.

Roasting is done either on a spit or in an open container, in the open air, or in an oven. The best fuel for spit roasting in the open air, or in an oven, is wood. For small game, nothing is as good as grapevine wood. For broiling on a grill, charcoal or wood are the most satisfactory. It is extremely important, however, to avoid the smoke produced by burning grease, which taints the food unpleasantly. Nevertheless, it is essential to brown meat over high heat, at first, without burning it. The rest of the cooking can then be completed at a lower temperature.

Cooking in a pastry crust is done in an oven (hot air).

2. Moist Cooking

Moist cooking involves either boiling, simmering in liquid or in a water bath (*bain-marie*), poaching, stewing, or frying.

(a) Food is called *boiled* when it is placed in a room-temperature liquid, then cooked in the liquid, which is gradually brought to a boil and kept there until the food is cooked. Meat cooked thus is called *boiled*. No matter what kind of food is boiled, the cooking liquid becomes a *bouillon* (broth). A concentrated bouillon becomes a *consommé*.

Courts bouillons[1] are liquids which are generally used for cooking fish, crustaceans, and mollusks.

(b) *Blanching* means to cook food partially (parboil) in a liquid. Foods to be blanched are first washed, soaked in cold water, then plunged into a liquid which is gradually brought to a temperature of 212° Fahrenheit or 100° Centigrade (boiling). The cooking is then completed in some sort of a sauce. This procedure is mainly used for vegetables (to remove any acidity or bitterness), although it may also be used for organ meats and variety meats.

Etymologically speaking, the verb *to poach* means to put in a bag or pouch. In the culinary sense, it is generally used to express the idea of cooking food in a boiling liquid, in order to coagulate the surface albumin, as in poached eggs, where the white envelopes the yolk in a pouch so to speak. Boiled eggs are eggs *poached* in their shells.

Whenever a substance which contains albumin is placed in a hot enough liquid, the albumin coagulates on the surface, thus protecting the inside of the food. The food then acquires a special savor which merits a special designation.

When forcemeats, such as quenelles, mousses, etc., fish, poultry, or filets of poultry, are cooked in a clear, hot liquid (just barely simmering), they are termed *poached*.[2] This term is rarely applied when meats such as beef, pork, lamb, etc., are involved. It seems important to differentiate between the terms boiled and poached. In the former case the food is placed in a cold liquid and gradually brought to a boil, as in the preparation of pot-au-feu; whereas in the latter case, the food is plunged directly into a liquid that is hot enough to coagulate the surface albumin, such as is the case in "English-style" leg of lamb.

In the first instance it is legitimate to call the food *boiled*, but in the second it is more logical to call it *poached*.

(c) *Ragoûts* (stews). These are appetizing dishes in which the solid foods are cooked in a sauce. These may be divided into six categories: real ragoûts, sautés, *salmis*, braised foods, fricassees, and *salpicons*.

In the case of the true *ragoûts*, the meat is first partially cooked—that is, it is heated in an open pan with some type of fat, in order to brown it before cooking it in a sauce in a partially closed kettle or saucepan. Among the true ragoûts, we have *gibelottes* and *civets*, the latter being ragoûts whose sauce is thickened with blood, the best known of which is *civet de lièvre* (civet of hare). Civets may also be made with other types of meat, and even with fish (civet of lamprey eel), and finally *white matelote*, which is a ragoût of fish, whose white sauce is thickened with butter and flour. *Sautés* of meat may also be considered ragoûts by the addition of varying quantities of sauce. These may be prepared with tender meat, naturally small in size or cut into small pieces, which need less cooking time than the other types of ragoûts. Sautés are made with frogs' legs, quenelles, filet mignon, chicken, veal, etc. They are first partially cooked by sautéing them in fat in an open utensil with a long handle, known in France as a *sauteuse* (skillet). The rest of the cooking is then completed in a large or small quantity of liquid, stirring all the while, in order to avoid having the food stick to the bottom of the pan.

Sautéed vegetables are cooked entirely without added liquid.

Salmis are ragoûts in which the meat is partially precooked before finishing off in a sauce.

Braised meats, which are synonymous with meats *en daube*, are ragoûts cooked in a hermetically sealed kettle. In France this type of kettle is called a *braisière* because originally a *braise* (hot coals) was placed on the cover. Food cooked in a *braisière* is cooked by the combined action of the heat of the fuel and the vapor of the juices imprisoned in the pot. Nowadays, braised foods are cooked in an oven.

Fricassees are ragoûts in which the meat is not browned before being placed in the sauce. For example, *blanquettes* are fricassees made with light meats (chicken, veal, spring lamb, young venison), in a cream sauce. Ordinary *matelotes* are also fricassees, but made of fish, with a wine sauce.

Salpicons (hashes) are delicate ragoûts, usually used as garnishes. They are made of tender meats, and choice vegetables, such as truffles, mushrooms, etc., all cooked separately, then diced, and finally bound with a rich sauce. Diced vegetables or cooked or candied fruit mixtures, bound with a suitable sauce, are also sometimes known as *salpicons*.

(d) To *fry* food is to cook it in a bath of one or more types of fat. A cook must realize that all fats do not decompose at the same temperature. Ordinary butter burns at 248° Fahrenheit; if it is clarified, however, it can be heated up to 275° Fahrenheit. Animal fats, the best of which are pork fat, beef or veal kidney suet, and poultry fat (notably goose grease), may be heated up to between 356° Fahrenheit and 410° Fahrenheit before they burn. Last come the vegetable fats, certain ones of which, such as olive oil, can be heated up to 572° Fahrenheit.

To condition a deep-fry-bath, it is essential to begin by clarifying it—that is, by removing any sediments and then straining the liquid through a cloth. This last procedure should be carried out each time the oil or fat is used. A good fry-bath should always be clear. It must also be quite abundant, so that the food to be fried does not lower the temperature perceptibly when it is put in.

Fried foods may be divided into two separate groups: (1) Foods fried in butter, in which the food is cooked relatively slowly, at a lower temperature than 248° Fahrenheit, if ordinary butter is being used, or below 275° Fahrenheit, if clarified butter is being used; (2) foods fried in animal fat or vegetable fat, in which the food is cooked very rapidly, at a temperature of over 284° Fahrenheit, and sometimes even going above 392° Fahrenheit. In my opinion, only the second method may be considered as true deep frying, and this term should apply only to this method of cooking, because frying in butter has quite different characteristics. I would then say that to fry a food is to fry it always at a temperature of over 284° Fahrenheit, in a fry-bath consisting of either animal or vegetable fat.

As far as the temperature goes, fry-baths, generally speaking, are often designated by one of the following expressions: moderate frying, hot frying and very hot frying. These correspond, respectively, to 284° Fahrenheit, 320° Fahrenheit, and 366° Fahrenheit.

Breaded food or food wrapped in pastry must be plunged into *hot* fat, so that the covering cooks immediately without disintegrating.

Fish of a certain size, such as sole, whiting, etc., which need a relatively longer period of cooking, should be put into fat at *moderate* temperature. Tiny fish, on the other hand, to be crisp, must be thrown into a *very hot* fry-bath, so that they cook immediately. Olive oil is excellent in this case, because the cooking time is very short, and the fry-bath does not have time to impart any strong taste to the food.

Vegetables to be fried are often plunged, at the beginning, into a *moderate* temperature fry-bath, in order to dehydrate them. The fat best suited for vegetable frying is a mixture of melted pork fat and beef or veal kidney suet. The cooking is done in two operations, and sometimes in three, as is described in the recipe for *Pommes de*

Terre Soufflées (Souffléed Potatoes). Goose grease may also be used—or oil, if one likes the taste.

It is generally considered that the best type of fat for pastry, fritters, etc., is a mixture of fifty percent goose grease and fifty percent veal kidney suet, or even clarified butter. I prefer melted pork fat.

When frying is not started in very hot oil or fat, it is best to keep increasing the heat until the end of the cooking time.

As an example of frying in butter, I would mention the recipe called *à la meunière,* which is applicable to all delicate fish of medium size, and also those recipes known as *poêlées,* or pan-fries, using meat and poultry, which differ from *rôtis à la poêle,* or pan roasts, because of the amount of butter which they imbibe, which changes the taste.

Gas is the most convenient fuel for all moist cooking methods, as it allows the cook to modify the temperature according to necessity, and it does not impart any taste to the food being cooked when it is used for dry cooking such as broiling.

Gratins and Aspics

Gratins and *aspics* are not dishes which are cooked in a special way. After they have been prepared according to methods indicated above, they just undergo a "finishing" process.

Designated under the term *gratins* are cooked preparations which are sprinkled with grated cheese, with breadcrumbs, or breadcrumbs mixed with grated cheese, and which are then browned (glazed) or *gratinéed* in the oven or under the broiler.

The word *aspic* denotes cooked foodstuffs which are enveloped in jelly and served cold.

In order to complete this introduction to culinary art it would be wise to say a word about *fonds de cuisson, glaces de viandes, essences, fumets,* and *appareils,* which are used for sauces and soups.

NOTES

1. The term thus refers to liquid mixtures with a base of wine and water which are lightly or heavily seasoned with vinegar, seasoned and spiced with salt, pepper, and grains, onions, carrots, parsely, thyme, bay leaves, and so on, and let boil before serving. Later on, the cooked substances—the fish, crustaceans, and mollusks—stayed inside only a short time, for "short boilings" (*courts bouillons*): hence the name of these preparations.

2. In cookery the word "poach" is used to designate cooking in a barely simmering liquid—that is to say, at a low temperature, but one which is as near as possible to the boiling point.

COOKING STOCKS, MEAT EXTRACTS, ESSENCES, FUMETS, AND MIXTURES

Fonds de cuisson

Fonds de cuisson.—(The nearest English equivalent is "cooking stocks.") These are liquid meat juices or meat extracts, seasoned and aromatized with vegetables and condiments.

Glaces de viandes

Glaces de viandes. (The nearest English equivalents seem to be "meat extracts.") These are the result of the slow reduction of very clear stocks, which have been skimmed several times and strained through a fine cloth and subsequently reduced down to a thick paste or even a solid.

Essences

Essences. (In English one can use the same term.) These are veal stocks, saturated with another ingredient, for flavoring, such as "essence of ham," "essence of mushroom," or "essence of truffle."

Fumets *Fumets.* The word fumet (for which there is no English equivalent) designates extracts of game or fish.

Appareils *Appareils.* (The nearest English equivalent seems to be the word "mixtures.") In the culinary sense this term is applied to mixtures, such as the meat glazes or extracts, the fumets, the essences, which serve to season a culinary preparation but which differ from these in that they have no stocks in them. They go into the making of other dishes.

The simplest mixture or appareil is the roux* (mixture of fat and starch).

Another appareil or mixture is the *mirepoix** and still another the duxelle.

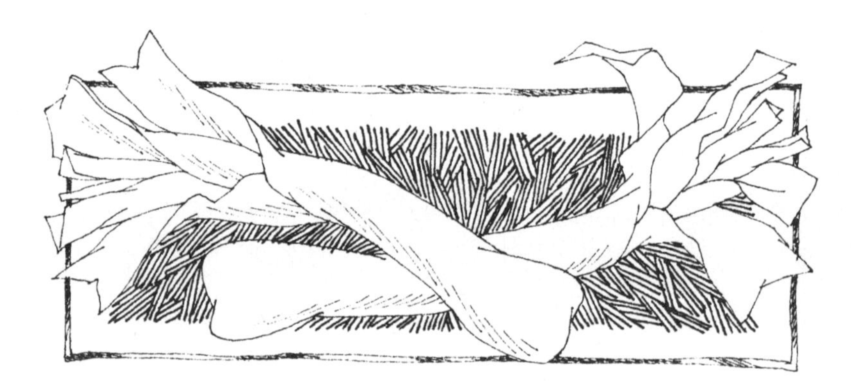

A FEW WORDS ABOUT SAUCES

Sauces are liquid food combinations, either thickened or not, which accompany certain foods.

The thickened sauces are by far the more important. They are made from stocks of varying strength, then seasoned, flavored, and thickened or bound with a liaison of some sort. The number of basic sauce stocks is considerable, and the number of possible flavorings is very great, and there are many ways of thickening the sauce. Therefore, in view of this, it is easy to understand that there are, so to speak, an infinite number of possible combinations. This is a veritable mine for the researcher.

All thickened sauces may be classified under one of the following:

1. Oil-based sauces such as *mayonnaise*.
2. Sauces made with milk or cream such as *béchamel*.
3. Sauces whose base is butter such as *hollandaise*.
4. Sauces made from meat consommés, which are the most numerous.

5. Sauces made from vegetable stocks, used mostly in vegetarian cooking.
6. Mixed sauces, made from two or more of the preceding groups. An example of a nonthickened sauce is *vinaigrette.*

Sauces made with consommés of animal substances may be divided into several groups, according to the type of consommé used: consommé made from meat, fowl, game, shellfish, or fish.

They can also be subdivided, according to color, into two groups: brown or white (light).

An example of the brown sauces is the sauce called *espagnole*[1] ("Spanish"), based on brown stock, bound with a roux. The *sauces civet* (civet sauces), thickened with blood, are part of this group.

The white, or light, or blond, sauces may be subdivided into: *veloutés,* with or without meat, with a light stock base, bound with starch or with cooked flour; sauces called *allemandes* ("German"), with a velouté base, whose thickening is completed with egg yolks; and *sauces suprêmes,* with a velouté base, thickened with both starch or cooked flour and egg yolks, and then enriched with cream and butter. The latter, extremely savory, are the triumph of refined cuisine.[2]

The art of the sauce-maker consists in blending the ingredients at his disposal to make them coalesce into a whole which harmonizes perfectly with the fundamental ingredient of the dish, which the sauce must enhance while still being only an accompaniment.

In important homes, the function of the *saucier* or sauce cook is specialized; his work entails the daily preparation, for his creations, of stocks and mixtures which he will use at the proper time along with the essences and aromatics with which his laboratory is stocked. Just as the artist searching for a hue amalgamates different colors on his palette to arrive at his goal, the artist–*saucier,* delving into the different elementary preparations kept warm, in hot water baths, amalgamates their various flavors to arrive at the dreamed-of result.

But it is rare that a modest amateur can work thus. This is why, in my recipes, rather than speak of complex elements which one rarely has at one's disposal, I have judged it preferable to give for each sauce the amounts of simple ingredients which are easily found everywhere, and then to indicate the proper procedures for obtaining the result desired. This is, I believe, the most practical solution to the complex problem of preparing sauces.

NOTES

1. The sauces known as *espagnole* ("Spanish") and *allemande* ("German") get their names from their color.

2. When one wishes to obtain a sauce *suprême* which is very white, one cuts down on the egg yolks and adds cream to make up the difference.

HOW I ENTERTAIN FRIENDS FOR MEALS

Meals may be divided into general categories: on the one hand the large ceremonial dinners, group meals, and banquets: on the other hand, family meals and meals with friends.

Large ceremonial dinners are organized according to meticulous protocol which would require a very extensive household, including all types of specialists: roasting cooks, *sauciers*, pastry chefs, assisted by a large household staff and directed by a very experienced major-domo. Few private people are in a position to give really large dinners.

As far as meals for large groups and large banquets are concerned, these are generally catered by specialists who have the proper equipment for this type of sport, which has very little to do with true gastronomy, since caterers are principally concerned with providing suitable menus, decorating the tables according to the occasion, and insuring regular and prompt service. Whenever, for one reason or another, one is obliged to attend such an affair, the most sensible thing to do is to eat and drink as little as possible.

Now there remain the family meals and the meals for entertaining friends. I will not go to the former; "John Doe is master at home." But when one entertains friends, one assumes a certain responsibility. One is, so to speak, in charge of souls. Therefore, it might be well to devote a few words to this subject, both from the point of view of choice of guests and choice of menus.

The first consideration for a well-organized dinner for friends, where everyone may speak freely, is a certain general agreement among the guests where fundamental ideas are concerned. This is necessary in order to avoid any sweet-sour discussion, which might trouble the digestion. This is sometimes difficult to avoid, even among the most well-bred people, as soon as certain subjects are broached, tolerance being the rarest of virtues. Therefore, it is essential to gather or bring together people who get along well and are congenial. This, in itself, would be sufficient to limit the number of guests, even if, on top of that, one did not have to take into account the practical difficulty of serving too many people in a normal household with normal equipment. When more than twelve guests are involved, intimacy disappears and general conversation deteriorates. A friendly gathering aims at creating harmonious vibrations among the guests, both of the spirit and of the palate.

It is not enough, however, to gather a certain number of congenial friends in order to have a proper dinner party: there must also be some congeniality insofar as gastronomy is concerned. If their tastes differed too much, one would be obliged, in order to satisfy everyone, to compose pantagruelic menus, which it is certainly best to avoid. In order to do things sensibly, it is important to pick your guests in such a way that of the four or five courses which normally make up an unpretentious meal there will be something to please everyone. When there are only a small number of guests, one can easily find three courses which would suit everyone. In this case the menu is simplified.

Let us now consider the general principles which should be applied to the preparation of a menu.

Repetitions and analogies must be avoided. For example: the same meat should not be served twice in separate guises, nor must one serve two light meats, such as veal and chicken, nor two types of fowl, such as chicken with feathered game, such as pheasant or wild duck. Do not present the same garnishes twice. Interplay foods and sauces for color as well as for taste, in such a way that each course, although having its own special characteristics, complements the preceding one and leads pleasantly to the enjoyment of the following one. Cheese should be chosen with great care, and it is nice to offer at least two different types, one raw and one cooked.

Goat's cheese accentuates the bouquet of a wine. The most aromatic cheeses are generally the most digestible.

As to wine, aside from special considerations of taste, the simplest thing is to serve two Burgundy wines and two Bordeaux, white and red. Wine serving and quality are discussed in the chapter on wine. On the whole, there is no absolute, and sometimes a lesser wine from a good year is superior to a greater wine from a poor year. Among the wines offered, one red and one white wine, at least, should be of respectable age. Contrary to general usage, I believe that all wine should be poured into large glasses, which allows it to be fully savored.

In simple meals, one enjoys greater latitude as to the order of the various courses, as long as one is guided by the preceding general rules, which, in any case, should always be observed. While on this subject, I feel that it is necessary to protest against the custom which consists of offering, at classic dinners: ices, cheese, and fruit, in that order. This, to my mind, is real heresy. In fact, those guests who partake of cheese and fruit are those who have not eaten the ices. In my opinion, cheese must close the meal *per se*. It is while enjoying this that one takes the last few sips of red wine. Then come the fruits, which refresh and perfume the palate, and then the ices, which accentuate the cold sensation, soon to be followed by a goblet of champagne.

Expanding what I have already said about ices (which should always be served with small sweet wafers) to include everything referred to as sweet desserts, in general I believe that all sweets should be presented at the end of the meal, after the cheese and fruit.

Before I finish I should like to say a word regarding the deplorable habit, which is very common nowadays, of waiting indefinitely before sitting down at the table, for latecomers, under the pretext of courtesy. This favors the unprompt people to the detriment of the other guests, which is very unkind and serves only to make your guests eat at incredible hours and to spoil the best meals. Each course must be served when it is ready. Some people must have some very odd notions about cooking if they think that hot dishes can wait indefinitely without being ruined.

It would be very simple to include in all dinner invitations the following sentence: "We will sit down to dinner at such and such an hour" and to make a firm rule never to wait for anyone. I might also seriously consider not letting latecomers into the dining room in the middle of a course. There is such a precedent: During serious concerts, people are not admitted to the hall during a number. Those impossible people, who arrived in this world an hour too late, and who can never be on time anywhere, would end up by staying home, and nobody would be sorry.

POTAGES AND SOUPS

Definition and Classification of Potages

Potages are foods which are either more, or less, liquid, and which we serve generally at the beginning of the evening meal.

These foods are usually based on stock, which is made from either meat, fowl, game, shellfish, fish, or vegetables.

They are either accompanied by a garnish, or not.

When the garnish consists entirely or in part of slices of bread, which are dunked in the broth, the *potage* takes on the name of soup.[1]

Potages, as they are correctly called, may be divided into two large groups, according to whether they are, or are not, thickened.

The *potages* which are not thickened comprise the bouillons and the consommés.

The thickening of *potages* may be done in various ways: by means of a light or dark roux; with egg yolks; with butter; with cream; with some kind of starch, etc. Actually, several of these are often used together, and hence it is difficult to classify these *potages* and soups according to the way they are thickened.

The three most easily differentiated characteristics are: (a) the use of purées; (b) the use of cream without the addition of egg yolks; and (c) the use of cream and egg yolks together. It is on these three that I shall base my attempt at classification of thickened *potages*, which I shall divide into six groups:

1. *Potages* without either purée or cream, which will be designated by their principal ingredients.
2. *Potages* without purée, but with cream and no egg yolks; these will be called *potages à la crème.*
3. *Potages* without purée, but in the thickening of which there is cream and egg yolks; this group I shall designate as the *potages veloutés.*[2]
4. *Potages purée,* without cream or egg yolks.
5. *Potages purée,* in the thickening of which there is cream but no egg yolks; I will call these *potages crème.*[3]
6. *Potages purée* in the thickening of which there are both cream and egg yolks; for these I reserve the name *potages crème veloutée.*

When presenting the recipes, I shall keep to the following general order: (1) nonthickened *potages;* (2) *potages* that are thickened without purée or cream; (3) *potages à la crème;* (4) *potages veloutés;* (5) *potages purée;* (6) *potages crème;* (7) *potages crème veloutée;* (8) soups.

NOTES

1. The term *velouté* is used in the current culinary language in two different senses: it serves on the one hand to denote light sauces (with or without meat stock), well skimmed, with a white stock base, thickened with starch or flour which has been colored in butter; and, on the other hand, cream soups which have been thickened and enriched with egg yolks beaten with cream. Hence the confusion.

To avoid any ambiguity, I have used the term as a *noun* in the classification of sauces, and as an *adjective* in the above discussion on *potages,* to denote those *potages,* without purée, which have been thickened with egg yolks blended in cream.

2. The words *potages crème,* which is quite euphonic, is used in several ways: (a) certain people use this name for simple *potages purée,* in order to make them sound more grandiose; (b) others seem to use the term to denote *potages* thickened with egg yolks and cream; (c) and still others apply this term to *potages* thickened with a roux and cream.

It is therefore essential to specify in each case what one means by this term.

POT-AU-FEU DE FAMILLE

Family Style Pot-au-feu

For eight people, use:

4 lbs. center cut beef brisket (which makes excellent boiled beef)
1 lb. shank and knuckle bones
1 lb. carrots
6 oz. beef liver[1]
2 turnips
4 T. salt
6 dried pea pods[2] (oven dried)
black pepper to taste (optional)
4 qts. water
4 medium leeks (white part only)
2 chicken giblets
2 cloves[3] (stuck into parsnip)
small piece parsnip
small stalk celery
1 small clove garlic
1 onion (optional)
1 small bay leaf
1 sprig parsley

When one prepares pot-au-feu for the family, one generally plans to have both a good broth and a good piece of boiled beef. Here is a recipe which provides both.

Clean and trim the giblets. Peel the vegetables,[4] wash them, and make a *bouquet* with the pea pods, leek, parsnip, celery, thyme, bay leaf, parsley, garlic, and onion (all wrapped in cheesecloth).

Put the meat, the bones, the liver, the water, and the salt and pepper into a heavy pot, either stainless steel or porcelain which can be placed over a burner.[5] Bring these to a simmer and remove the gray scum as it forms but leave the white scum, which will dissolve and flavor the broth. Add the vegetables and the bouquet. Cook this at a simmer without covering the pot too tightly. After three hours, skim off the fat, add the giblets, and cook another hour.

Strain the stock through a colander lined with cheesecloth. Serve with slices of bread, either toasted or not, or with tapioca, pasta, or rice, which has been cooked in the broth; or with potatoes which have been grated raw, rinsed in a colander, dried in a cloth, and cooked in the broth. The broth may also be served accompanied by tiny puff pastry biscuits, which are delicious, or with ravioli, fried croquettes, ham *boulettes* (meatballs), *boulettes* made of cheese pastry, quenelles, profiteroles made with grated Gruyère cheese, etc., etc.

Arrange the boiled beef on a platter, garnish with the giblets and the cooked vegetables, to which other vegetables may be added, such as potatoes, Brussels sprouts, or cauliflower (which has been blanched in salted water, then finished in butter).

Serve with the usual accompaniment of pickles, mustard, and coarse salt or with marinated cucumbers, beets pickled with horseradish, or with a horseradish sauce, which is prepared in the following manner.

For eight people, use:

3/4 C. cream
3/4 C. beef, veal, or chicken stock
3/4 C. grated horseradish
4 T. butter
5 T. flour
lemon juice and sugar
salt and pepper

Make a roux with the butter and the flour. Moisten with the beef juice or veal and chicken broth. Stir and cook until thickened. Remove from fire and add the cream and horseradish. Season with salt, pepper, sugar, and lemon juice, to taste. Heat without allowing it to boil.

A hollandaise sauce into which a little grated horseradish has been incorporated is also excellent with hot boiled beef.

With cold boiled beef, one could serve cold horseradish sauce prepared with cream, which has been soured with lemon juice, grated horseradish, mustard, salt, and pepper to taste; or a vinaigrette sauce with or without horseradish; or a sweet sauce or even a ravigote mayonnaise, or a horseradish mayonnaise.

NOTES

1. The purpose of the beef liver is to clarify the broth.

2. The purpose of the pea pods is to color the broth while flavoring it subtly. For a very dark-colored broth, caramel may be added.

3. Flower buds of the *Eugenia aromatica*, of the Myrtle family.

4. The indicated quantities correspond to winter vegetables.

5. I don't believe in using the classic earthenware pots, which are only serviceable for a certain length of time. At first they smell of earth and toward the end they smell of burnt meat and burnt fat.

6. The simplest way of obtaining meat juice is to cut beef in slices, sear it, then put it through a meat press.

I prefer the following method: Cook some walnut-sized pieces of beef with some minced vegetables, well seasoned, in a double boiler. Cook for six hours, keeping the water in the bottom part at the highest possible level and always boiling. Strain the juices off the meat and put the meat through a press in order to extract every last bit. Three pounds of beef should give about 2 cups of juice. To make a good, strong broth, it is best to use boneless meat without any fat and the same vegetables that I recommend for the *strong* broth, in the following recipe. For sick people and convalescents, it is advisable to use only a few slices of carrot and 1 slice of turnip.

BOUILLON À BOUILLI PERDU

Plain Broth with No Accompanying Meat

A. Light Broth for Invalids

1 lb. beef shank and knuckle bones
1 lb. veal shank
1 T. salt
2½ qts. water
2 chicken giblets
1 medium carrot
1 medium turnip

B. Broth for Convalescents

1 lb. beef shank and knuckle bones
1 lb. veal round
1 T. salt
2½ qts. water
2 chicken giblets
1 medium carrot
1 medium leek (white part only)

C. Strong Broth for Gourmets

1½ lbs. beef round with bone
1 lb. beef shank and knuckle bone
2 T. coarse salt
¼ tsp. pepper
2½ qts. water
3 medium carrots
2 chicken giblets
1 medium turnip
bouquet made up of the following ingredients:
3 oven-dried pea pods
2 leeks (white part only)
small piece parsnip
small piece celery
½ bay leaf
1 sprig parsley
½ small clove garlic
½ onion (optional)

When one does not wish to use the meat, it is very simple to make broths of varying strengths.

Here, for example, are three formulas for making broths of increasing strengths.

This is cooked just like the Family Style Pot-au-feu, but the cooking will be prolonged for an extra four hours. At the end of eight hours, the solid ingredients will have been exhausted. The broth will be strained and only that will be kept. With the above indicated quantities, one will obtain, in all three cases, about 1 quart, which when chilled will form a jelly. Broth A will produce a golden-colored jelly, broth B will be somewhat darker, and broth C will produce a definitely brown jelly.[1]

NOTE

1. Jelly is the result of the cooling of concentrated broth made from substances which are more or less gelatinous. The consistency is elastic. Jellies may be clarified and highly seasoned to taste. Their consistency must be sufficiently soft so that they may be eaten with a spoon.

CONSOMMÉ ET BOUILLI PARFAIT

Perfect Broth and Boiled Beef

In order to obtain both a good sturdy broth and a good piece of boiled meat, one would first prepare a very strong broth (as in formula C of the previous recipe) and discard the meat. In this broth one would put a good piece of beef, such as brisket, flank, top or bottom round, or tongue, according to one's taste for either lean or fatty meat, or even a fowl. The broth would be brought to a boil, skimmed as for the pot-au-feu, and the meat would be cooked for one half hour per pound.

The broth or consommé may be served as is, or garnished either with bread, noodles, rice, or tapioca, and the meat served separately on a platter, surrounded by vegetables cooked in broth.[1]

NOTE

1. The name *croûte au pot* (crust in the pot) is applied to a consommé which is served in a glazed earthenware pot which contains *croûtes* (large croûtons) made of *flutes* (long, thin loaves of French bread) which have been dried in the oven and with minced vegetables which have been cooked in the consommé.

A *petite marmite* (small pot) is the name given to a consommé served in tiny glazed earthenware pots which are served on a napkin-covered platter and which contain cut-up meat (beef, oxtail, fowl) and vegetables, which have been cooked in the consommé. These are accompanied by tiny slices of toasted French bread garnished with beef marrow, seasoned with salt and pepper, and served very hot, or accompanied by tiny slices of *flute*, crisped in the oven, and with grated Gruyère cheese.

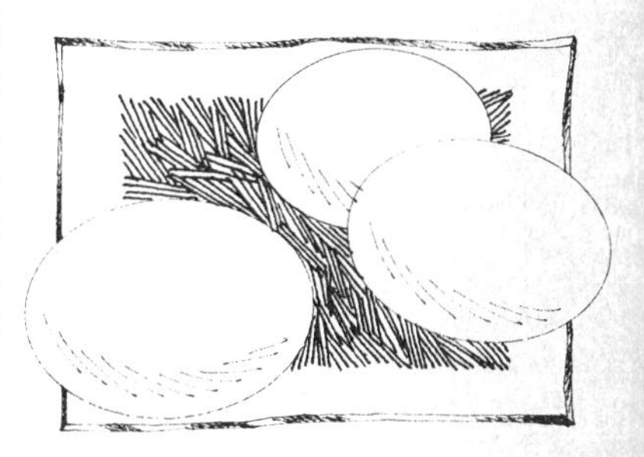

CONSOMMÉ AUX OEUFS POCHÉS ET AU FROMAGE

Consommé with Poached Eggs and Cheese

For six people, use:

1½ C. grated cheese
3 T. good meat glaze[1]
5½ C. good consommé
12 croûtons
6 fresh eggs
butter

Boil the consommé with the meat glaze.[1]

Butter the croûtons and toast them until golden brown in the oven.

Remove them from the oven and place them in a soup tureen.

Break the eggs into the boiling consommé. As soon as they are set, pour the whole contents into the tureen and serve accompanied by grated cheese in a separate bowl. This very invigorating and nourishing soup cannot be too highly recommended for those who are tired and overworked.

This potage may be served also in individual soup tureens. The eggs should be broken directly into each small tureen and the consommé kept at the boiling point.

NOTE

To make two quarts of stock, use:

2 1/2 lbs. beef shank
2 1/2 lbs. veal shin and knuckle bone
1/2 lb. pork bones
4 oz. pork rind
1 medium carrot
1 medium onion
1 sprig parsley
1 tsp. salt
1/2 tsp. thyme
1 bay leaf
1/2 small clove garlic

1. Meat glaze is a syrupy or semi-solid product resulting from the concentration of a brown stock. As the stock is boiled down, it is strained through cheesecloth and poured into smaller and smaller pans. Each time, it is carefully skimmed and cooked at lower and lower temperatures, and the final cooking is done in a moderate oven to avoid burning. The meat glaze is just right when a spoon is dipped into it and it comes out with a shiny coating.

The classic meat glaze, which involves a lengthy procedure, is made in the following manner.

Remove the meat from the bones and break up the bones into small pieces. Brown the latter in a little fat in the oven, then brown the vegetables. Add the 2 quarts of water and the salt, and let this cook very slowly for twelve hours, adding liquid as necessary to maintain the same level of liquid. Strain the stock and skim off the grease. Cut the meat and the pork rind into small pieces and brown them. Pour off the fat and moisten with some of the stock. Let it cook down to a glaze two or three times, adding more stock each time. Deglaze one last time with the remaining stock, bring this to a boil, skim off any impurities and grease, strain through a cloth, and reserve the liquid which must be quite limpid.

Brown veal stock is prepared in the same way.

To obtain a meat glaze which is lighter in color and texture, use brown veal stock.

POTAGE MIMOSA

Cut up some cooked stringbeans.

Push some hard-boiled egg yolks through a coarse sieve.

Heat up some very good stock; then, at serving time, put in the cut-up stringbeans and the little dots of egg yolk. These simulate the leaves and flowers of the mimosa.

POTAGE À LA TORTUE

Turtle Soup

Turtles (*Testudinates*) belong to the reptile family. According to their habitat, they are either marine, terrestrial, or fluvial.

Turtle soup should always be prepared with fresh marine turtle. The best species is the green turtle of the Chelodinae family,[1] whose size may reach as much as four feet and can weigh as much as one thousand pounds. However, because its size and weight make the extraction of the meat difficult, it is almost impossible to prepare it in the home kitchen as it should be.

In England, where turtle soup is very popular, it is prepared by specialists who deliver it and ship it all over the world in cans.

I suggest that those who wish to taste this soup use the canned product. It is sufficient, in order to obtain a delicious soup, to dilute the contents of a can of turtle soup with some good beef consommé which is slightly gelatinous (which can easily be achieved by cooking it with a beef foot). The seasoning should then be corrected to taste and the soup should be flavored with some good old madeira wine.

One can also prepare turtle soup with dried or dehydrated turtle meat, which can be found in English groceries.

Here is a recipe for its preparation.

Soak the turtle meat in fresh water for twenty-four hours.

In a kettle or pan, put the 2 quarts of water, the soaked turtle meat, the salt, leeks, onion, celery, shallots, garlic, and let this cook like a pot-au-feu. After it has cooked for two hours, remove one-third of turtle meat and set it aside. Continue the cooking at a simmer. At the end of seven hours from the start, add the lemon zest, peppercorns, coriander, marjoram, basil, sage, fennel, savory, thyme, bay, and clove, all tied in a cheesecloth bag. Allow this to cook for another hour, at which time you should have about 1 quart of turtle broth. Strain this through a cloth and add the consommé. Taste for seasoning, spice it with cayenne pepper and aromatize it with madeira.

Mince the reserved turtle meat. Add it to the soup, heat it up again, and serve.

By thickening this soup with egg yolks and cream, one would obtain a *Potage Crème Velouté de Tortue*, which one could garnish with toasted slivered almonds or not, according to taste.

One may also, if absolutely necessary, prepare a soup with land

For eight people, use:

1½ lbs. dehydrated marine turtle meat
3 leeks
1 medium onion
1 large stalk celery
⅓ cup shallots
2 T. old madeira
1 T. peppercorns
5 tsp. coriander
3 large cloves garlic
2 tsp. salt
1 piece lemon zest
½ tsp. marjoram
⅛ tsp. basil
⅛ tsp. sage
⅛ tsp. fennel
⅛ tsp. savory
⅛ tsp. thyme
½ small leaf bay leaf
2 qts. water
1 qt. jellied beef consommé
1 clove
cayenne pepper to taste

turtle. Here is the proper way to go about this: cut off the head of a land turtle and collect the blood. Scald the animal in order to extract the meat more easily from the shell, which must be cracked with a hammer and a cold chisel, or with a power tool.

Empty the turtle. Soak the meat in cold water or, better yet, in milk, and then use it as you would sea turtle.

This soup may be thickened with the turtle blood.

Last, in the same vein, and by using the same method, one can make an interesting soup called *Potage Fausse Tortue*, or Mock Turtle Soup, by replacing the turtle meat with a calf's head.

The garnishes for this soup might be, for example, fried *boulettes* or profiteroles, stuffed with cooked calf's brains, slivers of veal tongue, or cooked, diced veal sweetbreads.

NOTE

1. This turtle, which feeds on *Fucus* (brown algae) and *Zostera* (marine grass), is found in all oceans except the Mediterranean. The horny plates of its back shell meet edge to edge and it has two claws on each foot.

BOUILLON DE LÉGUMES

Vegetable Broth

For two quarts of broth, use:

1/2 lb. carrots
1/2 lb. potatoes
1 small turnip
1 leek (white part only)
2 T. dried white beans
2 T. split peas
2 T. lentils
4 tsp. salt
4 qts. water

This broth, either hot or cold, is an excellent beverage, and very healthy for those who have stomach disorders. It may also serve as a base for other dishes and sauces for meatless dishes.

Here is a recipe for which there are many variations:

Add the salt and the vegetables to the water and boil for four hours, reducing the liquid by half.

One may use the liquid plain, but it is preferable to strain it through a coarse sieve and mash the vegetables, in order to have a bouillon which contains some of the vegetable purée.

This soup may also be thickened and garnished according to taste. You may thus make excellent meatless soups.

POTAGE AUX LÉGUMES NOUVEAUX

Soup with New Vegetables

Take some good consommé and cook in it, for the proper length of time, a variety of new vegetables, such as carrots, turnips, potatoes, all cut into julienne pieces, cut-up cauliflower and artichoke hearts, tomatoes, green beans, peas, and asparagus tips.

At the same time, cook some minced mushrooms in butter and add them to the vegetables at the last minute. Heat up again for a minute or two, pour into a soup tureen, and serve.

By thickening this soup with cream, or with egg yolks beaten with cream, one would obtain, in the former case, a *Potage de Légumes Nouveaux à la Crème* (New Vegetable Soup with Cream) and, in the latter, *Potage Velouté de Légumes Nouveaux* (New Vegetable Velouté Soup).

POTAGE AUX GOMBOS[1]

Okra Soup

For four people, use:

½ lb. okra
2½ T. rice
1 qt. chicken broth
2 tomatoes (peeled, seeded, and diced)
cayenne pepper

Wash the rice and blanch the okra several minutes in boiling water, then drain it.

Put the chicken broth in a saucepan and bring it to a boil. Add the okra, cut in two lengthwise, and cook this for ten minutes. Shower in the rice and continue cooking long enough to cook the rice, but still keeping the grains whole. Add the tomatoes and cayenne pepper to taste. Bring to a boil once or twice and serve.

In the French colonies, okra soup is often prepared without adding rice. The rice is cooked separately in the Creole manner—that is, dry. It is then served along with the soup, but apart.

NOTE

1. Okra is the incompletely developed fruit of the *Hibiscus esculentus*, of South American origin.

POTAGE À L'OIGNON

Onion Soup

To prepare an onion soup, one may use sliced onions, either browned or not browned, and add to them water or some kind of meat or meatless stock or even milk. The onion may either be removed or left in the soup.

If one makes a clear soup, it can be served as is or thickened with egg or something else. Other ingredients may be added, such as tomatoes, cheese, etc. Soups may also be prepared with puréed onion, and there are also cream of onion soups and velouté cream

For eight people, use:

1. *For the soup*

1 lb. veal shank
2 T. salt
1/8 tsp. pepper
2 qts. water
3 chicken giblets
3 medium carrots
2 leeks (white part only)
1 medium turnip
1 small piece parsnip
1 small piece celery
1/2 small leaf bay leaf
1 sprig parsley
1/2 medium onion

2. *For the garnish*

1/2 lb. pearl barley
1/2 carrot (red part only, cut into tiny dice)
2 T. butter
1 chicken wing (roasted and cut into julienne pieces)

of onion soup, which could be garnished according to taste, with fried croûtons or Parmesan croûtons.

It is easy to imagine many types of onion soups, each one different from the other.

KRUPNIK

Krupnik is a Polish soup made with pearl barley.

With the first group of ingredients prepare a white stock; strain it and discard the meat.

Put the pearl barley and the butter in a saucepan, cover with broth, and let it simmer for two and a half hours. Stir it occasionally with a wooden spoon, and add more liquid as necessary, to prevent the barley from sticking.

Cook the carrot dice in more of the same broth.

Keep the cut up chicken meat warm.

Just before serving put together the white stock, the barley, the carrot dice, and the chicken.

To vary, one may use, instead of the white stock, a vegetable bouillon; but in this case the soup should be thickened with egg or with heavy cream, to which may be added some lemon juice.

BARSZCZ[1]

Borsht

For four people, use:

2 1/2 C. strong beef and chicken consommé
1 large carrot
2 medium raw beets
2 medium baked beets
1 large slice onion
1/2 oz. dried mushrooms
2 springs parsley
2 T. chopped fennel leaves
2 tsp. granulated sugar
salt to taste
pepper to taste
2 C. pickled beet juice[2]

Barszcz is the Polish version of the sour-type soups which one finds in most Slavic kitchens. There are many ways of preparing it, but the slight sour taste is always achieved by using pickled beet juice.

Here is one of the simpler recipes for this soup.

Peel and mince the carrot and the raw beets, sprinkle on the sugar, and set aside.

Bring the consommé to a boil and add the carrot, raw beets, parsley, onion, mushrooms, salt, and pepper. Bring again to a boil for a few seconds.

Slice the baked beets (which have been peeled); macerate the slices in the pickled beet juice, by heating it up but without allowing it to boil. Add this to the first mixture and bring to a boil. Taste and correct the seasoning if necessary. Correct the acidity[3] and color the soup.[4] Strain and add the chopped fennel, some poached eggs or slices of sausage (which have been cooked and skinned separately); or you may even add some ravioli. Serve very hot.

Five minutes before serving, blend the flour into the softened butter and stir this into the soup to thicken it. Take the pan off the fire and add the cream and enough vinegar[2] to acidify the soup slightly. Taste, add salt if needed, and serve.

NOTES

1. Paprika or Hungarian pepper is really a "sweet pepper."
2. One tablespoon of vinegar is generally sufficient.

One can easily give this soup a more distinguished appearance by straining it through a sieve or vegetable mill and serving it with fried croûtons. One would then have a *Potage Crème de Choux* or Cream of Cabbage Soup.

POTAGE AUX CONCOMBRES ET À LA CRÈME

Cucumber and Cream Soup

In some good consommé, cook some sliced cucumber, which has been salted and drained, until reasonably soft. Remove from the fire and blend in some cream to which has been added a little of the salted cucumber juice. Taste for seasoning and add more of the salted juice or cream according to taste.

This soup must have an agreeably acid flavor.

CONSOMMÉ VELOUTÉ AU PARMESAN

For eight people, use:

1/3 C. cream
6 T. grated Parmesan cheese
4 oz. vermicelli
2 qts. beef consommé
4 egg yolks

Cook the noodles in the beef consommé until tender.

Blend the egg yolks and the cream in a soup tureen. Pour the hot beef consommé with the noodles over them, and serve. Pass the Parmesan separately.

To vary, use chicken broth instead of beef consommé, tapioca instead of noodles, and Swiss cheese or half Swiss and half Parmesan, instead of the Parmesan. This would then be referred to as Chicken Velouté with Cheese or *Velouté de Volaille au Fromage*.

POTAGE VELOUTÉ AUX PETITS POIS

Velouté Soup with Peas

For six people, use:

1 lb. freshly shelled peas
14 T. butter
1/3 C. cream
4 tsp. salt
1 sprig parsley
small leaf chervil
1/8 tsp. freshly ground black pepper
1 1/2 qts. water
3 egg yolks
1 small onion

Boil the water and add the salt, onion, parsley, and the peas and cook until the peas are tender. About half an hour is generally enough.

Cut the bread into small cubes and brown these cubes in 5 tablespoons of the butter.

Chop the chervil and place it in a soup tureen along with the egg yolks, which have been beaten with the cream. A few minutes before serving, remove the onion, the parsley, and some of the peas. Add the rest of the butter and the pepper, and boil up two or three times, then pour into the tureen and mix well. Add the croûtons and serve immediately.

This simple soup, unpretentious as it is, is really excellent.

One may prepare the same soup with fresh favas, but in this case it is best to replace the chervil with some savory.

POTAGE VELOUTÉ AUX PÂTES

Velouté Soup with Pasta

For four people, use:

1 C. cream
1¼ C. grated Parmesan cheese
4 oz. pasta (preferably noodles or lasagne as prepared in pasta section)
4 T. butter
2 T. flour
1 qt. consommé
2 egg yolks
salt and pepper to taste

Cook the pasta in the consommé.

Make a roux with the butter and the flour and add a teaspoon of the grated Parmesan. Let this cook for two minutes, stirring with a wooden spoon; then add the consommé with the pasta. Beat the egg yolks and cream together and blend these into the soup. Heat, complete the seasoning with salt and pepper and serve.

Pass the Parmesan separately.

POTAGE VELOUTÉ À LA SEMOULE

Velouté Soup with Semolina

For four people, use:

¼ C. cream
4 T. butter
⅓ C. semolina
1 qt. chicken consommé (broth)
1 egg yolk
lemon juice to taste

Bring the consommé to a boil, throw in the semolina, and let this cook for about ten minutes.

In a soup tureen, beat the egg yolk with a little of the consommé, the cream, the butter cut up into small pieces, and the lemon juice. Pour the consommé with the semolina over this, and stir to blend thoroughly. Taste and add salt if necessary and serve.

This is a very light soup.

As a variation, one may cook the semolina in the butter before putting it in the consommé, in which case the lemon juice is omitted, and the soup should cook for about twenty minutes.

One may make the same types of velouté soups using buckwheat.

POTAGE PURÉE DE TOMATES

Purée of Tomato Soup

For eight people, use:

1 C. (scant) tomato soup
2 qts. consommé

Mix the tomato purée in the consommé and cook together. Serve this soup with fried croûtons or with rice which has been precooked in the consommé.

By adding sweet cream or cream which has been soured with lemon juice, one would have a Cream of Tomato Soup or *Potage Crème de Tomates*. By enriching this cream of tomato soup with the adding of egg yolks, one would obtain a *Potage Crème Veloutée de Tomates* or Cream of Tomato Velouté Soup.

POTAGE PURÉE DE CAROTTES ET DE TOMATES

Purée of Carrot and Tomato Soup

For eight people, use:

1 lb. carrots *à la Vichy* **(see recipe)**
1 C. tomato purée (see recipe)
4 T. tapioca
4 qts. chicken broth

Put the carrots *à la Vichy* through a food mill and mix this purée with the tomato purée. Cook the tapioca in the chicken broth and mix this with the purées. Taste and correct seasoning if necessary, and serve.

One may, naturally, make in this same way puréed soups or cream of beets and tomatoes. Beets should be baked or boiled in broth. For the cream soups one would use either sweet cream or acidified cream.

POTAGE PURÉE DE POIS SECS

Purée of Dried Pea Soup

Like all the soups made with puréed dried vegetables, purée of dried pea soup may be prepared using plain, salted water, or some sort of a broth, either vegetable, beef, pork, chicken, game, or fish.

The procedure is always the same.

The peas are cooked in the liquid, then they are puréed through a food mill, and the soup is then enriched with butter, and colored green by mixing in some spinach juice. (By adding cream instead of butter, it would become a cream soup.)

Purée of dried pea soup is served with croûtons fried in butter, which is the classic way. It may also be served with blanched green peas, which is known as *Potage St. Germain*, or it may be served with precooked rice.

When a pork broth has been used for cooking the peas, which I consider as the best kind to use in this case, one may serve the soup with some minced pork in it, using the cartilaginous parts, such as the ears, which should be precooked, preferably in a well seasoned broth.

For six people, use:

1 C. dried peas
7 oz. lightly smoked fat bacon
1 1/2 qts. water (or vegetable broth without salt, according to whether you wish to retain the unadulterated taste of the peas)

To vary, I shall give the recipe for *Potage Purée de Pois Secs, au Lard* or Purée of Dried Pea Soup, with Bacon.

Dice the bacon and add it, along with the peas, to the liquid you have chosen. Cook for as long as necessary. Usually this takes about an hour and a half. Put the mixture through a sieve or a food mill. Color it green or not, according to taste. Complete the seasoning, if necessary. Add whatever garnish you prefer and serve.

For six people, use:

1/2 lb. asparagus tips
1/2 C. madeira wine
2 qts. consommé
2 C. chestnuts

POTAGE PURÉE DE MARRONS

Purée of Chestnut Soup

Peel the chestnuts, blanch them in boiling water, and remove the thin skin. Cook them in some of the consommé and put them through a food mill.

Add some consommé to the purée, along with the wine. Skim the soup by heating it very slowly and remove the skin on the surface as it forms.

Cook the asparagus tips for fifteen minutes in the rest of the consommé and pour into the soup just before serving. The total volume of liquid should have reduced to about 1 1/2 quarts.

The cooking and skimming should take about three-quarters of an hour.

It is usually unnecessary to add salt or pepper, as the seasoning of the consommé and the madeira is usually enough to balance the sweetness of the chestnuts.

The asparagus tips give this prosaic soup a little distinction.

For six people, use:

1 lb. trimmed cauliflower
1/2 lb. trimmed Brussels sprouts
2/3 C. cream
4 T. butter
2 T. flour
1 1/2 qts. consommé
salt and pepper

POTAGE CRÈME DE CHOU-FLEUR, AUX CHOUX DE BRUXELLES

Cream of Cauliflower Soup with Brussels Sprouts

Blanch the cauliflower, then cook it in the consommé until tender. Remove it and put through a vegetable mill. Keep the cauliflower purée and the consommé separate. Cook the Brussels sprouts in salted water until they are tender but still keep their shape. Remove them and keep them warm.

Blend the flour with 3 tablespoons of butter and add the consommé. Then add the cauliflower purée and allow this to boil up once. In a soup tureen, put the cream and the rest of the butter cut into small pieces. Pour over the consommé and taste, adding salt and pepper if necessary. Add the hot Brussels sprouts and serve.

POTAGE CRÈME DE TOMATES AUX NOUILLES

Cream of Tomato Soup with Noodles

For six people, use:

1 lb. tomatoes
4 oz. noodles
1/2 C. cream
7 T. butter (cut into tiny pieces)
1/4 C. shredded Parmesan cheese
1 qt. water
1 onion
1 clove
small *bouquet garni*
salt and pepper

Peel and cut up the tomatoes. Cook them very slowly in a saucepan with the clove, the onion, and the *bouquet garni*, for about a half hour. Put through a vegetable mill and set aside.

Cook the noodles in lightly salted water for fifteen minutes. Add the tomato purée; heat up and pour into a soup tureen. Then add the butter, the cream, the Parmesan, and taste. Correct seasoning if necessary.

POTAGE CRÈME DE CHOUCROUTE

Cream of Sauerkraut Soup

For six people, use:

1 lb. pork sausage
1/2 lb. sauerkraut, washed and drained
1/2 lb. peeled potatoes
3 oz. bacon
4 T. cream
1 oz. dried mushrooms
2 qts. beef bouillon
salt and pepper

In the bouillon cook the sauerkraut, bacon, chopped mushrooms, and potatoes for three-quarters of an hour. Put everything through a vegetable mill.

Cook the sausage in the bouillon, then remove it, skin and slice it, and set it aside.

Blend the cream into the soup. Taste and season with salt and pepper if necessary.

Pour the soup into a tureen and add the slices of sausage. Serve.

POTAGE CRÈME DE POIS, AUX PETITS POIS

Cream of Pea Soup with Peas

For six people, use:

3 lbs. fresh, unshelled peas (preferably a starchy variety sometimes known as "telephone")
5 C. chicken broth
1 lb. small, sugar peas
2/3 C. cream
4 T. butter
carrots
onion
lettuce
bouquet garni **(parsley, chervil, thyme)**
salt and pepper

Shell each type of pea separately.

Put 1 quart of the chicken broth in a saucepan along with the telephone peas, carrots, onion, lettuce, and *bouquet garni*. Cook these thoroughly, then remove the carrots, the onion, and the *bouquet*, and put the peas and lettuce through a vegetable mill or press through a fine sieve.

At the same time, in the rest of the broth, cook the smaller peas with a little carrot. As soon as they are just tender remove the carrot.

Put the strained soup and the small peas together, add the cream and the butter, and mix, without allowing it to boil. Taste and add salt and pepper if necessary, and serve in a tureen.

If telephone peas are not available one could use another type of starchy peas. However, one would need a larger quantity in order to obtain the same quantity of purée having a like consistency.

One could also prepare this soup with dried peas which one

would cook with carrots, onion, lettuce, and *bouquet garni.* Fewer peas would be needed than when using the telephone variety, to obtain an equal quantity of purée of the same consistency. To the purée thus obtained, one would add the butter, cream, and some plain canned peas which have been heated up in a double boiler. It is hardly necessary to point out that the soup made with dried peas would be inferior, as far as taste, to the soup made with the fresh vegetables.

The *potage crème de pois aux petits pois* therefore differs from the classic *potage St. Germain* in the following ways: by the addition of carrots, onion, and *bouquet garni* to the peas, and by the addition of cream.

POTAGE CRÈME VELOUTÉE D'ASPERGES

Cream of Asparagus Soup Velouté

For eight people, use:

2/3 C. cream
2 qts. chicken consommé
4 egg yolks
2 lbs. asparagus

Cook the asparagus tips only in boiling, salted water. Make a purée of half the tips, setting aside the best-looking ones.

To this purée add the egg yolks blended with the cream, and heat up without boiling. Pour this soup into a tureen, add the hot consommé, mix well, and garnish the soup with the reserved tips. Serve.

POTAGE CRÈME VELOUTÉE DE TOPINAMBOURS[1]

Cream of Jerusalem Artichoke Soup Velouté

For six people, use:

1 lb. Jerusalem artichokes
1/2 C. cream
3 T. seasoned tomato purée
1/4 C. tapioca
3 T. butter
1 1/2 qts. consommé
2 egg yolks
salt and pepper

Cook the Jerusalem artichokes in the oven, peel them and put them through a vegetable mill or rub them through a fine sieve.[2] Keep the purée warm.

Cook the tapioca in the consommé for twenty minutes, add the hot tomato purée, and the purée of Jerusalem artichokes, and mix well.

In a tureen mix the cream, the egg yolks, and a little of the hot consommé. Add the butter cut into tiny pieces, pour the hot soup over all, and mix well. Taste and correct the seasoning and serve.

NOTES

1. Jerusalem artichokes or *Heliantus tuberosus* is a plant of the Compositae family, whose tubers have a taste reminiscent of the more commonly known artichoke hearts.
2. This procedure can be simplified by using an electric blender.

POTAGE CRÈME VELOUTÉE DE CELERI AUX PETITS POIS

Velouté Cream of Celery Soup with Peas

Cook the celery in some veal stock and some peas in chicken broth. Put the celery through a food mill then through a strainer.[1] Mix the resulting purée with the liquid from the peas, thicken and enrich with the cream beaten with the egg yolks, add the peas, and serve. This is a very nourishing soup.

POTAGE CRÈME VELOUTÉE DE SOJA* AUX PERLES

Cream of Soya Bean Soup Velouté with Tapioca

For six people, use:

2 lbs. soya bean sprouts
7 T. thick heavy cream
3 T. butter
1/4 C. white wine
1/4 C. water
4 tsp. tapioca
1 1/2 qts. chicken broth

Wash the soya bean sprouts and cook them over a very low flame with the butter, white wine, and water, for about twenty minutes. Strain through a sieve or purée in a food mill or electric blender.

At the same time cook the tapioca in the consommé. Add the soya purée.

In a tureen, mix the cream and egg yolks, pour on the consommé and stir, taste, correct the seasoning with salt and pepper, if necessary, and serve. This soup, which is quite delicate and very agreeable, could very well take its place on the menu for an elegant dinner.

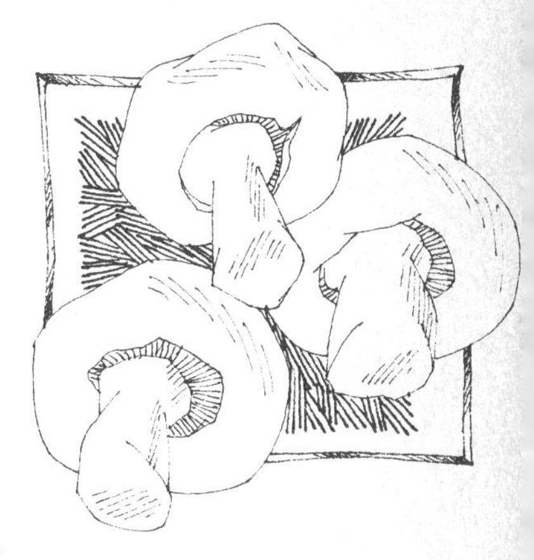

One could also prepare a soup in exactly the same way using Chinese artichokes, regular artichoke hearts, or Jerusalem artichokes, etc.

NOTE

1. *Soja* or *Soya hispida,* which originates in the warm regions of Asia, is still known under the name of *Glycine hispida,* colloquially called Chinese peas. This is a legume of the Phaseolae family. In China and Japan it is used a great deal, especially among the poorer classes. These vegetables are mainly used in the preparation of pasta, sauces, and a type of cheese. Only recently introduced into Europe, only the sprouts are in general use.

BOUILLABAISSE[1]

Bouillabaisse is a Provençal soup made with ocean fish and crustaceans, which is served along with the ingredients used in

*Use an electric blender to purée the celery, then strain out any strings and pulp.

its preparation. There are quite a number of these, and they can be distinguished one from another mainly by the various ingredients used.

To be very tasty, all of them must contain a great variety of different fish, each one adding its own particular flavor and aroma, all blending together so as to produce a harmonious concert of gustatory and olfactory sensations. This fundamental condition hardly allows for the creation of a good bouillabaisse in small quantities. To arrive at a truly satisfactory result, it seems to me that it is indispensable to use at least five or six pounds of fish.

The quality of the bouillabaisse also depends on the freshness and the quality of the ingredients used—which is why it cannot ever be as good anywhere as at the seashore.

The bouillabaisses of France may be divided into three categories: the bouillabaisse from the Mediterranean coast (the mother of all the bouillabaisses), that of the Atlantic, and last, that of the interior, a type of which is known as *bouillabaisse parisienne.*

The ingredients normally used in the making of Mediterranean bouillabaisse are, in alphabetical order, the following: *l'anguille de mer* (sea eel), *la baudroie* (anglerfish), *le congre noir ou murène noire* (conger eel), *la daurade* (sea bream), *la gallina* (gurnard), *la girelle* (girella), *le grondin* (gurnet), *le loup* (sea bass), *le merlan* (whiting), *les mulets* (gray mullets), *la murène* (moray eel), *les rascasses* (hogfish—these are essential), *les rougets* (red mullets), *le sar* (sargo), *le Saint-Pierre* (John Dory), *le turbot* (turbot), and *la vive* (weever). The crustaceans are: *les cigales de mer* (hermit crabs), *les crabes* (crabs), *le homard* (lobster), and *la langouste* (spiny lobsters). Some of these are particularly good along the Algerian coast, which is why one often eats excellent bouillabaisse in Algeria.

For about ten people, use:

10 lbs. assorted fish and crustaceans[2]
12 oz. minced onions
1/2 C. olive oil
3 oz. fish livers from the anglerfish, whiting, hogfish, etc.
6 minced shallots
1/2 green pepper
3 T. parsley
3 T. fennel
4 cloves crushed garlic
large pinch powdered saffron
3 qts. fish broth (or clam juice)
2 sliced, peeled, seeded tomatoes
2 bay leaves
2 cloves
1 piece orange peel
2 sprigs thyme
salt and pepper

Here is a precise recipe for a Mediterranean bouillabaisse prepared with ingredients chosen from among those listed above.

Scale the fish, clean them, and cut off the fins. Then cut the crustaceans and the fish into chunks. Arrange these on two separate platters: on one put the more tender ingredients, such as sea bass, whiting, red mullets, John Dory, etc., and on the other platter the firmer ones, such as the anglerfish, conger eel, hogfish, weever, crabs, lobsters, etc.

Pour a little oil into a heavy pot or kettle and in it gently cook the onions, shallots, garlic, tomatoes, peppers, parsley, fennel, thyme, and bay leaf. Then add the rest of the oil, the cloves, orange peel, fish broth, and the firmer fish and crustaceans. Add salt and pepper and bring to a boil over a high flame. After this has boiled five minutes, add the more tender fish and cook for another five minutes. Remove the pan from the fire, take out the chunks of fish and shellfish. Drain them, clean them off, and keep warm. Strain the broth through a cloth, add the saffron, boil the liquid down to two quarts, taste, and complete the seasoning, which must be quite heavy. Thicken the broth with the mashed fish livers.[3]

In a deep serving dish put some half-inch-thick slices of French bread and pour the fish broth over them.

Arrange the chunks of fish and the shellfish on another platter, sprinkle with blanched, chopped parsley, and serve everything together.

For variation, one should note the "fishermen's" bouillabaisse, in which the aromatic ingredients are not cooked first, and which normally does not contain any saffron.

Atlantic bouillabaisse is prepared with ingredients chosen from among the following: *l'anguille de mer* (sea eel), *la barbue* (brill), *le congre noir* (conger eel), *la daurade* (sea bream), *le grondin* (gurnet), *le lieu* (pollack), *le maquereau* (mackerel), *les rougets* (red mullets), *le Saint-Pierre* (John Dory), *la vieille de roche* (labrus), and *la vive* (weever). Crustaceans and mollusks used would include: *l'araignée* (hermit crab), *le homard* (lobster), *la langouste* (spiny lobster), *les moules* (mussels), *les oursins* (sea urchins), *les palourdes* (clams), *les sauterelles de mer ou chevrettes* (literally, "sea grasshoppers"—members of the shrimp family), *le tourteau* (large edible crab).

This Atlantic bouillabaisse is prepared in the same way as the Mediterranean bouillabaisse, except where the mussels, clams, and sea urchins are concerned. The mussels and clams are opened separately, over a hot fire, and the juices are thoroughly strained and then added to the fish broth; but the mollusks themselves are only added at serving time, or they will toughen. The coral is the only part of the sea urchins which is used and this is put into the soup at the very last minute, without cooking.

In Paris, the ingredients which are most easily found are:

Fish: *l'anguille de mer* (sea eel), *la barbue* (brill), *le colin* (hake), *le congre noir* (conger eel), *la daurade* (sea bream), *le grondin* (gurnet), *la limande* (dab), *le merlan* (whiting), *le maquereau* (mackerel), *la plie* (type of flounder), and *le turbot* (turbot).

Crustaceans and mollusks (shellfish): *les crabes* (crabs), *les crevettes* (shrimp), *le homard* (lobster), *la langouste* (spiny lobster), *les moules* (mussels), *les oursins* (sea urchins), and *les palourdes* (clams).

The preparation remains pretty much the same. However, in Paris, Sauterne wine is often added to the broth, the green pepper is replaced by black pepper, and the consommé is enriched with butter. As to the fish, it is not usually sprinkled with parsely.

For variation we can also mention the bouillabaisse made with fresh-water fish and crayfish, which is not unpleasant but which is not worthy of the preceding ones.

Last, also known under the name bouillabaisse, are analogous preparations made with only one type of fish, which is often accompanied by vegetables, such as bouillabaisse of cod with potatoes. These dishes, however, are bouillabaisses in name only.

NOTES

1. Or *bouille-abaisse*, which means a bouillon (broth) reduced or concentrated by cooking.
2. For instance: a slice of anglerfish, a slice of conger eel, a small sea bream, a gurnard, a sea bass, a hogfish, three red mullets, one John Dory, ten hermit crabs, and one spiny lobster.
3. This procedure is often neglected.

BOURRIDE

A *bourride* is a Provençal fish soup made with salt water fish such as conger eel, sea perch, whiting, gurnard, eelpout, etc.,[1] whose difference from bouillabaisse lies mainly in the absence of shellfish and in the addition of a garlic sauce.

Prepare a fish broth by making bouillabaisse but adding a little more liquid.

Prepare an *ailloli*,[2] that is, a garlic mayonnaise. Set aside half of it and beat the rest into the fish broth, over the fire, without letting it boil.

Place slices of French bread in a tureen, pour the thickened broth over it, and serve. Serve the hot boiled fish on another platter and the rest of the *ailloli* in a sauceboat.

NOTES

1. Other fish which could be used are: sea bass, cod, flounder, grouper, haddock, halibut, pollack, scrod, red snapper, etc.
2. Originally, *ailloli*, which is also called *pommade à l'ail* (garlic paste) and *beurre de Provence* (Provençal butter), was a sauce made with olive oil and mashed garlic, thickened with breadcrumbs and hot mashed potato. Nowadays, it is thickened with egg yolk, and modern *ailloli* is really a garlic-flavored mayonnaise. The proportion of garlic depends on the strength of the garlic and personal taste. In Provence, where the garlic is mild and much enjoyed, they can easily include several garlic cloves per person.

SOUPE À LA MORUE

Codfish Soup

For eight people, use:

- 2 lbs. freshened salt cod
- 1 C. dry white wine
- 1/2 C. olive oil
- 1 1/2 qts. fish stock[1]
- 4 tomatoes
- 4 potatoes
- 2 onions
- 2 garlic cloves
- 1 *bouquet garni* (parsley, chives, thyme, and bay leaf)
- coarsely chopped parsley
- freshly ground black pepper

In a heavy kettle or an earthenware pot which can be set over a flame, put 1/3 cup of the oil, the minced onions, and the garlic, and cook these gently but do not brown. Add the peeled, seeded, and cut-up tomatoes, the peeled, sliced potatoes, and the *bouquet garni*. Pour in the fish stock and white wine. Cook until the potatoes are about half done. At this point add the cod, which has been cut up into domino-sized pieces, along with the rest of the oil. Remove the *bouquet garni*, sprinkle on the parsley, and let this come to a boil. Taste for seasoning and add pepper if desired. Pour the soup into a hot tureen over slices of toasted bread.

This dish is sometimes referred to as "bouillabaisse of cod."

NOTE

1. Canned commercial clam broth or clam juice makes an excellent substitute for fish stock. See index for making home-made fish stock.

SOUPE AU GRAS-DOUBLE

Tripe Soup

For six people, use:

- 1 lb. tripe (which has been blanched and slivered)
- 2 large carrots (peeled and cut into julienne strips)
- 3 stalks celery (peeled and cut into julienne strips)
- 2/3 C. grated Parmesan cheese
- 1 1/2 C. thinly slivered onions
- freshly ground black pepper to taste
- 2 qts. bouillon
- 12 small slices rich bread, toasted

Cook the carrots, celery, and onions in the butter until they are faintly colored. Add the bouillon and bring it to a boil. Then add the tripe and let this all cook slowly for two hours.

Taste for seasoning—a little pepper is usually sufficient.

Pour into a soup tureen into which you have put the twelve slices of toast and serve.

Pass the grated Parmesan separately.

SOUPE À L'OSEILLE

Sorrel Soup

For six people, use:

- 1/2 lb. trimmed sorrel
- 2/3 C. butter
- 5 T. cream
- 4 tsp. salt
- 1 qt. milk
- 2 C. water
- 3 eggs
- bread

Break the eggs and separate yolks and whites. Beat the whites* and put the yolks in a bowl with the cream.

Gently cook the sorrel in the butter and add the boiling water.

Add the beaten egg white and the salt and let this cook for a moment.

*One could omit the egg whites but one should then use 4 yolks.

At the same time boil up the milk.

Arrange some thin slices of French bread in a tureen and pour the boiling sorrel broth with the egg whites over them. Add the milk, thicken with the egg yolks beaten with the cream, cover, and let this soak together for a minute or so. Serve.

One can prepare cream of sorrel soup by replacing the bread with tapioca or pasta.

In the fall and winter, when the sorrel contains a strong proportion of oxalic acid, one should use only half the indicated quantity.

SOUPE AUX POIREAUX ET AUX POMMES DE TERRE

Leek and Potato Soup

For six to eight people, use:

14 oz. peeled potatoes
8 leeks (white part of leek)
1/2 C. butter
6 tsp. salt
pepper
4 qts. water
bread

Cut the leeks and potatoes into large pieces and put them into a saucepan with the water, salt, and pepper. Cook over high heat for about one hour in order to reduce the liquid to about one-half.

Strain the liquid through a coarse sieve,[1] crushing the vegetables more or less, according to whether you want a thick or thin soup. Put the resulting liquid in a pan, add the butter, and boil it up two or three times.

In a soup tureen, put some thin slices of French bread (about 3 ounces); pour the boiling leek and potato soup over it. Cover the tureen and allow this to soak for a moment and serve.

One can also, if desired, prepare the same soup with leeks and potatoes after having cooked the leeks a little bit in butter.

One can also choose to replace the bread with tapioca or pasta which has been cooked in the strained soup before adding butter.

Last, by increasing the quantity of vegetables which are pushed through the strainer, one can obtain a purée of leeks and potatoes. These soups could be served as is, or garnished with fried croûtons.

NOTE

1. An electric blender is ideal for this operation, but more liquid should be used as the vegetables tend to thicken the soup more when run through the blender.

SOUPE AUX CHOUX, À LA PAYSANNE

Peasant-Style Cabbage Soup

For four people, use:

10 oz. pork belly
1/2 lb. carrots
1 medium turnip
3 oz. potato
4 slices bread
3 T. butter
4 tsp. salt
3 qts. water
2 leeks (white part only)
1 curly cabbage
1 onion
pepper

There are a great many ways of preparing cabbage soup. Here is a simple one.

In a saucepan, put the water, salt, pork belly (cut into four pieces), leeks, carrots, turnip, onion, and some pepper. Let this all cook for two hours. Then remove the leeks and the turnip, add the cabbage and the potato, and cook until tender.

Toast the bread and put it into a tureen. Add the butter and pour in the contents of the saucepan. Mix and serve at once.

SOUPE À L'OIGNON

Onion Soup

To make plain onion soup, gently cook some onions in butter or other fat, according to taste. Brown them without burning. Then add either water, some sort of meat or meatless bouillon, or even milk, and season with salt and pepper. Cook this for a moment or two, then either strain or do not strain the soup.

In a tureen arrange thin slices of French bread, either toasted or not, some fried croûtons, or some pieces of *flute* (long thin French bread), and pour the boiling liquid over this and serve.

If you wish you may send along some grated Gruyère cheese separately.

For variation, one can spread the slices of bread, the fried croûtons, or the *flute*, with a purée of onion mixed with a thick Béchamel sauce.

Last, one can make "*gratinéed*" soups by adding to the plain onion soups some grated cheese, and putting them in the oven to brown.

SOUPE À L'OIGNON GRATINÉE

Browned Onion Soup (First Recipe)

For four people, use:

7 slices crumbs from white American bread
1½ C. sliced Gruyère cheese
2 medium thinly sliced onions
4 T. butter
2 T. fat (either from a roast or salt pork)
2 tsp. salt
large pinch powdered sugar
pepper
1½ qts. water

Cook the onions in a saucepan in the fat over a very low fire for about twenty minutes, until the onions begin to take on color. Sprinkle them with the sugar so that they take on a little more color without burning. Remove any excess fat, add the water, salt, and pepper, and let this cook for about ten minutes.

Line a fireproof casserole or soup tureen with slices of French-type bread, about one-half-inch thick. Cover each slice with a thin slice of cheese about the same size. Keep doing this until all the bread is used up. Pour in the broth, either strained or not. The bread will rise to the surface of the liquid. Place a tiny piece of butter on each slice of bread, bake in a slow oven for about twenty minutes, and serve.

This soup—the characteristics of which are (1) the way the onions are cooked, (2) the quality of the bread used, (3) the pieces of very thinly sliced cheese, which insure a creamy coating of cheese on the bread, without lumps—is delicious.

SOUPE À L'OIGNON GRATINÉE

Browned Onion Soup (Second Recipe)

Cut some ordinary French bread into half-inch-thick slices, toast them, let them cool, spread them with fresh butter, and sprinkle them with some grated Emmenthal cheese. The thickness of the cheese and butter layer must be about one-half inch, in the proportions of one-third butter to two-thirds cheese.

Take some medium-sized onions (one per person), slice them very thin, and cook them with butter in a skillet. In a fireproof casserole arrange a layer of bread slices, on which you will spread one-third of the onions, then another layer of bread, the second layer of onions, another of bread. On this last bread layer you spread some tomato pulp (about 4 teaspoons per person). Continue with the next layer of bread which you top with the rest of the onions and a little more tomato pulp. Finally, cover the whole dish with a layer of grated Emmenthal cheese.

The casserole must not be more than two-thirds full, in order to allow for the swelling of the bread without having the soup spill over.

Take a glass funnel, and, placing the tip at the very bottom of the casserole, at the edge, slowly pour some hot, salted water into the casserole so that the liquid rises just to the top layer of cheese without drowning it.

Put the casserole on the fire but do not cover it. Let this simmer for one-half hour, taste, and add salt if necessary; then put it in the oven and continue to cook it for an hour, replacing the water (always using the funnel) as it evaporates. The soup is ready when the surface is baked and looks like a crusty, golden cake, and the inside is unctuous and so well blended that it is impossible to discern either cheese or onion.

Each person is served some of the baked crust and some of the inside, which should be thick but not completely without liquid.

SOUPE À L'OIGNON, AU VIN BLANC

Onion Soup with White Wine

For eight people, take:

1/2 lb. butter
3/4 C. flour
5 T. meat glaze
3 qts. water
1 qt. white wine
8 medium onions
French *flute*-type bread (the loaf is long and thin)
grated Parmesan
salt and pepper

Mince the onions and fry them in 5 teaspoons of the butter.

Make a roux with 10 tablespoons of butter and the flour. Stir in water, wine, and meat glaze, and add the fried onions. Season with salt and pepper and let this all boil up a couple of times, then simmer for thirty minutes in an open pan so as to reduce the liquid to about 3 quarts.

Prepare twenty slices of *flute*, spread them with the rest of the butter, sprinkle on the Parmesan cheese, season with pepper and put them in the oven to brown.

Arrange the slices of bread in a tureen and five minutes before serving pour over the strained or unstrained soup.

This soup, which is slightly acid, is highly recommended after a long day of hunting.

TOURIN TOULOUSAIN

For six people cook about 10 cloves of garlic in 3 tablespoons of goose fat. Add water and let this boil for several minutes.

Break 2 eggs and separate the whites from the yolks. The yolks will serve to thicken the soup. Beat the whites and put them into the boiling liquid and they will form a clabber. Take the pan off the fire and thicken the soup with the yolks (which have been mixed with a little of the hot liquid first). Salt and pepper energetically and pour the whole into a tureen in which you have arranged some slices of French bread.

This soup is not suitable, of course, for a ceremonial banquet—in fact, I wouldn't even recommend it for a small dinner party! However, when all the guests are from the Midi, it proves to be an enormous success. The *méridionaux* are crazy about it and assure us that it smells heavenly!

GARBURE

Classic *garbure* is made with the young shoots of green cabbage, but it may also be made from the tender leaves of other cabbage.

Wash the cabbage and shred it very fine. Put a wing of preserved goose in a hot frying pan in order to remove the fat which surrounds it, then put it in a kettle with some boiling water.

Place the cabbage in a colander over the kettle, pour the hot goose grease over it, then add it to the kettle. Season with salt and pepper to taste, add a clove of garlic, and simmer the soup for an hour in the uncovered kettle.

Arrange some slices of stale French bread in a tureen, spread the cabbage over them, pour the broth over all, and serve very hot.

It is advisable to make only just enough broth to cover the bread as it is tasteless reheated. The goose wing is eaten cold.

SOUPE AUX LÉGUMES À LA PAYSANNE

Peasant Vegetable Soup

Take all kinds of vegetables which you like and some pork belly.*

Peel the vegetables, cut them up, or leave them whole, depending on size.

If you are adding cabbage, start by blanching it in order to remove some of the bitterness.

In a skillet, using a mixture of half pork fat and half goose fat, cook the cut up pork meat; then cook the larger vegetables.

In a saucepan, with the necessary amount of water, put the pork, bring it to a boil, and skim. Then add the blanched cabbage and a little salt and pepper; then add the other vegetables one after another so that they will all be cooked at the same time without falling apart. At the end of the cooking time taste and correct the seasoning with salt and pepper, if necessary. Then add some small pieces of butter, allow these to melt and pour the contents of the saucepan into a tureen over some slices of very crusty bread.

Serve.

This soup is best when the vegetables are young and tender. With freshly picked vegetables it is delicious.

*If fresh pork belly is unavailable you may use freshened bacon as described in the glossary.

GARNISHES FOR SOUPS

BOULETTES FRITES

Fried Boulettes

For six people, soften two thin loaves of French bread or a small loaf of ordinary bread in cold water; then squeeze it in a towel to extract all the water.

In a saucepan, in 2 tablespoons of butter, sauté 1 minced shallot or tiny onion. Add the bread, and season to taste with salt, pepper, and a little ground ginger. Let this cool and add 1 whole raw egg. This will form a dough. Knead or mix it well and add another egg. Mix again until there are no more lumps.

Let this dough rest for an hour; then make small, walnut-sized balls and fry them in deep fat before adding to the soup.

BOULETTES AU JAMBON

Ham Boulettes

For ten people, use:

- 4 slices bread, white or brown, crusts removed
- 2 oz. raw ham
- 5 T. butter
- 1/3 C. milk
- 1 T. herbs (chopped mixture of equal parts of chives, chervil, tarragon, and parsley)
- 1 egg
- flour
- salt and pepper

Scald the milk.

Cut the bread into small cubes and brown these in 3 tablespoons of the butter. Put them in a bowl. Pour the scalded milk over them and let it soak in. Add the egg and work the mixture well so as to obtain a very smooth dough.

In the remaining butter cook the ham and the herb mixture. Mix this well into the dough and season to taste with salt and pepper.

With this dough make small walnut-sized balls, roll them in flour, and poach them in the bouillon in which they are to be served.

In Austrian cookery they serve ham *boulettes* as a dish in itself (see under pork section).

QUENELLES À LA MOELLE

Beef Marrow Quenelles

For six people, use:

- 4 oz. beef marrow
- 1 1/4 C. breadcrumbs
- 3 fresh eggs
- flour
- salt

Mash the marrow, push it through a sieve or vegetable mill, and, one by one, add 3 eggs, mixing well after each addition. Add the breadcrumbs little by little, season with salt, and mix thoroughly.

Roll this dough out onto a floured pastry board and cut into pieces the size of a walnut. Shape these into cylinders (quenelles) and poach them in simmering broth. Remove them with a skimmer and add them to the soup.

PROFITEROLES

For twelve people, use:

- 1 C. water
- 1 1/2 C. flour
- 7 T. butter
- 2 tsp. salt
- 6 eggs

Put the butter and flour in a saucepan, heat gently and stir together to form a paste. Dilute with the water and stir to eliminate any lumps. Let the mixture cook for five minutes, making sure it does not stick.

Remove the pan from the fire and add the eggs one by one, mixing well after each addition. This paste is ready when a spoonful drops of its own weight but does not spread. Put this into a pastry bag and drop small balls of it, one-half to three-fourths of an inch in diameter, onto a baking sheet. Bake these in a hot oven and then turn the heat off and let them dry a little longer in the oven.

Profiteroles intended for soup must be very crisp and crusty.

Serve these with clear soups, either as is, or stuffed with foie gras, caviar, or a purée of sea urchin, for instance, according to whether the soup has meat or not as its base.

PÂTES AU PARMESAN

Parmesan Custard

For six people, use:

2 C. milk
$1/3$ C. grated Parmesan
6 fresh eggs
salt

Beat together the milk, cheese, and eggs. Season with salt to taste. Pour the mixture into a shallow pan and place it, in turn, in another pan containing boiling water. Bake in a moderate oven for twenty minutes.

To test for doneness, insert a piece of straw in the middle of the custard. It should come out clean.

Unmold the custard onto a flat surface and let it cool slightly. Cut it into fancy shapes and put these in the soup.

CROÛTONS AU PARMESAN

For six people, use:

$2/3$ C. grated Parmesan cheese
3 T. flour
2 fresh eggs
pepper
nutmeg

Mix the flour and Parmesan and season to taste with pepper and nutmeg.

Break the eggs and separate the whites from the yolks, removing any visible membrane.

Beat the whites until stiff and fold in the yolks without deflating the whites. Without stirring, fold in, little by little, the flour and Parmesan mixture. The mixture should then have the consistency of well-cooked scrambled eggs.

Spread the paste one-half-inch thick on a baking sheet and bake for about twenty minutes. Then, when it is almost cool, cut it into rounds, ovals, squares, or diamonds, etc.

HORS-D'OEUVRES

Hors-d'oeuvres are unimportant dishes. Their name comes from the premise that, since they are not listed among the principal dishes which make up a meal, one can just as well omit them without affecting in any way the orderly arrangement of the menu. Originally, the hors-d'oeuvres were left on the table so that the guests could nibble at them between courses. They were a form of distraction. Nowadays, they are served at the beginning of a luncheon and after the soup at dinner. It is a preface, an introduction, a curtain-raiser, an operatic overture, a flirt, a bit of sentimentality, a passing love affair. Their role consists in exciting the appetite without filling the stomach. They must therefore be light, delicate, small in size, and very savory tasting.

Hors-d'oeuvres are of two kinds: cold hors-d'oeuvres, used especially for luncheons, and hot hors-d'oeuvres, which are generally served at dinner.

Cold hors-d'oeuvres, which are very handsome when presented

in compartmentalized silverware, but which may also be served very modestly in small dishes, are: butter, radishes, tomatoes, celery, beets, cucumbers, red cabbage, cauliflower, pickles, tiny marinated melons or mushrooms, sour cornichons, artichokes, chutney, horseradish, fennel, pickled hard cherries, green walnuts, olives, fresh figs, melon, snails, shrimp, crayfish, mussels, oysters, shellfish, anchovies, sardines and small mackerel in oil, smoked sardines, herring filets either smoked or marinated, marinated tuna fish, smoked salmon, small marinated trout, eel, *poutargue* (salted fish roe made into sausages), caviar, stuffed hard-boiled eggs, garnished eggs, *rillettes*, *rillons* (pork hashes), sausages of all kinds, *cervelas* (a type of sausage), mortadella, smoked sausages, tongues, ham, beef muzzle and palate, lamb or calf's brains, smoked goose, vegetable salads, salads made with organ meats, *macédoines* (mixtures of raw fruits or vegetables), *barquettes*, croûstades, tartelettes filled with tongue, brains, oysters, foie gras, or with hashes, purées, custards, mousses, aspics made with fish, shellfish, fowl, or game, etc.; canapés, which are small pieces of toast garnished with butter, or with mixed butters, and with purées or hashes made from shellfish, fish, meat, fowl or game; éclairs, puffs, and brioches (sugarless), stuffed with purées or mousses made with foie gras, fowl, or game, and masked with assorted *chaud-froid* sauces, or with jelly; etc., etc.

Melon, oysters, or caviar are always served separately. Oysters are served in special plates and caviar in carved, hollowed out, blocks of ice, the edges of which are decorated with half-lemons.

Hot hors-d'oeuvres are generally served on plates covered with a napkin. The tremendous variety offers the culinary enthusiast a vast field in which to exercise his talents.

There is also a type of minuscule entrée, such as a variety of brochettes made with thin slices of shellfish, tongue, ham, lamb, or veal sweetbreads, veal or chicken livers, brains, truffles, mushrooms, artichoke hearts, foie gras, chicken, and game, covered with various sauces, then breaded and fried; small pastry crusts filled with delicate forcemeats made with fish, chicken, or game, or stuffed with slivers or slices of the same substances, set on suitable forcemeats or dressings; fritters made from the roe of various fishes, with brains, fowl, ham etc.; *bouchées* (small puff pastry patties), garnished with spring vegetables, asparagus tips, mushrooms, truffles, shellfish, fowl, feathered game, tongue, ham, foie gras, dainty hashes, or purées of furred game, various forcemeats, custards, breaded and fried, made of delicate ingredients, *fritots* (fritters); oysters cooked in all kinds of sauces; *barquettes*, *croûstades*, *croûtes*, and tartelettes garnished with tiny slices or fine hashes, purées, or forcemeats of shellfish, fish, foie gras, fowl, and game, with suitable sauces;

oysters, roe, cock's combs, and kidneys; tiny stuffed potatoes; croquettes, tiny soufflés, tiny *pâtés*, tiny timbales, very small in size.

These hot hors-d'oeuvres remind one of the ancient flying entrées of the *service à la française*.* Their passage on the table only lasted long enough for guests to appreciate the excellence of the cuisine and to augur well for the meal.

*In the *service à la française*, each dish is presented to the guests arranged artistically and placed symmetrically.

EGGS

Omelet

It may seem banal to give a recipe for an omelet, because everyone thinks they know how to make one. Actually, there is no lack of people who have never eaten a really good omelet.

Certainly the preparation of an omelet is not complicated; but it is absolutely necessary to take certain precautions, which people often neglect to do. Those cooks who always succeed go about it in a generally similar way—a bit different here and there, but they all have certain guidelines.

I only intend to point out the most important points which will allow anyone to make a savory omelet. I will not waste time by describing the preparation of all the different varieties of omelets, which are innumerable; I will only explain the preparation of the simplest of omelets, a plain omelet. He who can make that one can make them all, with the possible exception of the *omelette soufflée*, which is entirely different from the others, and of which I will speak in the section on sweet desserts.

First of all, it is necessary not to forget that in an omelet, as in all preparations using eggs as a base, the product will reflect the quality of the eggs. Therefore, one must use only the very freshest eggs, and I prefer those with brown shells, rather than those whose shells are sparkling white, which I find tasteless. Needless to say, one must also use top-grade butter. The pan must be spotlessly clean and of a size suitable to the number of eggs one is using. An omelet must never be too thick.

It is difficult to make an omelet with more than a dozen eggs, so it is therefore preferable to make smaller omelets.

To specify, I will describe the procedure for making an omelet with four eggs, each weighing from 2 to 2½ ounces, or from 8 to 10 ounces in all.

In this case one should use a six- or seven-inch frying pan.

For two people, take:

3 T. butter
2 T. milk
1 scant tsp. salt
pepper to taste
4 large eggs

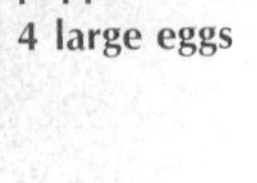

Break the eggs into a bowl; add the milk, salt, and pepper, and beat for about one minute. Melt the butter in the frying pan over a hot fire. When it is at the required temperature, which should take about two minutes, and which can be recognized when the froth on the surface of the melted butter has almost disappeared and the butter has acquired a nut-brown color, pour in the eggs. After about one-half minute the under side of the omelet will have set; then rapidly lift the sides of the omelet all around with a fork by tilting the frying pan and allow the surface liquid to run down where you have lifted it. Repeat this procedure a second time and then let it cook by itself. The entire procedure should take about two minutes. The omelet is ready when one notes steam rising from the edges of the pan. At this precise moment, fold the omelet as you slip it onto a hot platter. Serve.

By following these indications step by step, you will have an omelet with a lovely golden color on the outside which is tender and soft inside.

The milk, which after all could be replaced with water in this mixture, plays a double role. It serves to distribute the seasoning evenly, and it keeps the eggs from setting too rapidly.

The omelets in which one uses hot fillings, either boiled, fried, or grilled, such as omelets with bacon, mushrooms, herring, etc., are cooked in an identical manner. The ingredients which one wishes to incorporate are added only at the moment of pouring the eggs into the pan.

Eggs which are destined for the preparation of omelets aromatized either with raw, or boiled and cooled ingredients, such as omelets with *fines herbes*,[1] chopped meat, shrimp or crayfish tails, morels, or truffles, etc., should be beaten fifteen minutes before cooking and the added ingredients must remain in contact with the eggs during that time in order to have the flavors penetrate. The eggs should then be beaten again, either with a whisk or a fork, just before cooking.

NOTE

1. *To make an omelet with* fines herbes *for two people:*

4 T. butter
3 T. water
1 scant tsp. salt
1 tsp. each chopped parsley, chervil, chives, tarragon
freshly ground black pepper
4 (2 oz. each) fresh eggs

Break the eggs; add the *fines herbes*, salt, pepper, and water. Beat vigorously and let the mixture stand for about a half hour. Beat the eggs again at the last minute and make the omelet as above.

OEUFS BROUILLÉS

Scrambled Eggs

For five people, use:

½ C. butter
½ C. heavy cream
10 fresh eggs
salt and pepper to taste

Scrambled eggs may be prepared plain or, as in the case of omelets, various ingredients may be added. Below is a recipe for plain scrambled eggs.

Break the eggs and strain them to remove any membrane that might spoil the looks of the final dish, but do not beat them.

Using a deep saucepan in which the food will be two or three inches deep, butter it and put in the eggs. Cook them over a very low flame or over boiling water, stirring constantly. As soon as they begin to set, add the cream, then the remaining butter, cut up into small pieces. Add salt and pepper to taste. Complete the cooking and serve immediately, on hot plates.

There are a great many kinds of scrambled eggs; the number of ingredients which may be used is considerable. I will only mention three: scrambled eggs with truffles or mushrooms, scrambled eggs with shrimp, and scrambled eggs with black-pudding (blood sausage).

To make scrambled eggs with truffles or morels (mushrooms) one would add to the ingredients for plain scrambled eggs truffles or morels to taste. This preparation would be served in a ring of puréed fowl or game, prepared with one pound of puréed fowl or game and three eggs, cooked in a buttered ring mold set in a pan of hot water.

For five people, use:

½ lb. live shrimp[1]
½ C. butter
½ C. cream
8 fresh eggs
salt and pepper

To make scrambled eggs with shrimp, the proportions are the following:

Boil the shrimp in a court bouillon made of sea water, or in salted water. When they are cooked, peel them and set aside the tail meat. Crush the shells in a mortar and strain through a sieve or food mill, from which you will get a very tasty juice.

The cooking is carried out in the same way as described in the above recipe. One adds the shrimp tails and the juice from the shells to the eggs, along with the cream.

Scrambled eggs thus prepared make a very delicate dish which pleases everyone.

To prepare scrambled eggs with blood sausage, one simply replaces the shrimp with the inside of a blood sausage which has been freshly broiled.

NOTE

1. In general, the liquid most suitable for cooking shellfish and freshly caught ocean fish which is destined to be eaten plain is sea water.

OEUFS EN COCOTTE

Eggs Cooked in Ramekins or Cocottes

Eggs which are cooked in small porcelain *cocottes* are the nearest thing to eggs boiled in the shell; and this offers the added advantage of lending itself to many different culinary combinations.

To prepare a plain egg in a *cocotte*, which is very digestible and a real dish for dyspeptics, one begins by putting into a *cocotte*, previously heated in hot water, 1 tablespoon of water or broth. Then one breaks an egg into each *cocotte*; and the cooking is carried out in a hot water bath for four to six minutes according to taste. These are served immediately and each guest seasons his own egg according to taste, when he is ready to eat.

One may also prepare eggs in *cocottes* by replacing the water or the broth with some butter or cream. In this case the seasoning is done during the cooking.

A good way of preparing eggs in *cocottes* with cream consists in cooking the eggs as in the preceding recipe, but for only two minutes, in *cocottes* which have been spread with butter or cream. Then add to each *cocotte* a tablespoon or so of cream, seasoned to taste, and complete the cooking in a hot-water bath, in the oven.

Eggs may be prepared in the same manner using meat juice, meat purée, chicken stock, plain veal stock, veal stock with tarragon, with tomato, etc.

One may also line the *cocottes* with different mixtures, such as forcemeat as for chicken quenelles, purée of goose liver, veal broth with or without tomato, Béchamel, ham purée, purée of game with cream, etc.; and the eggs can be masked with a julienne of vegetables, a *salpicon* of morels or truffles, *purée Soubise* (onion), purée of sorrel, purée of spinach, purée of tomatoes, asparagus tips with cream, shrimp or crayfish tails with suitable sauces, etc., by properly blending the two substances which surround the egg. Thus, there are quite a number of combinations, and it is enough just to mention the general principle.

OEUFS POCHÉS EN ASPIC, AU GRAS

Poached Eggs in Meat Stock Aspic

Boil some water in which you have put 1 teaspoon of salt and the juice of 1 lemon per quart. Break the eggs, one at a time, into the boiling water, at the point where the liquid bubbles. Remove the pan from the fire and let the eggs poach for three minutes. Remove them with a skimmer or slotted spoon, run them under cold water to remove any acidity, and trim them.

Take some small molds; pour into each one a little jellied veal broth or, better yet, veal and chicken broth, as indicated in the veal section, or use some game jelly. Let it set and place a poached egg on it, sprinkle on, for example, some minced ham anu truffles, and cover it with more jelly. Let this set in a cold place, or on ice, then unmold and serve on a bed of hearts of lettuce.

These are very cooling.

OEUFS POCHÉS GARNIS EN ASPIC, AU MAIGRE

Poached Eggs in Meatless Aspic

Prepare a meatless aspic.

One prepares a strictly meatless jelly by cooking only with some vegetables, in salted water with or without added wine, either fish or fish trimmings in sufficient quantities to obtain, after reduction of the liquid, a fairly thickish liquid.

When fish is scarce, one may use a semi-meatless jelly made with a mixture of fish and a calf's foot or veal knuckle.

In either case, the broth must be clarified with egg white and strained through a cloth.

Poach some eggs as in the preceding recipe.

Line small molds with jelly and let it set. Place an egg in each, and add one of the following: oysters poached in their own liquid, plain steamed mussels, boiled shrimp or crayfish tails, sea-urchin coral, caviar, small slices of fish filets cooked in court bouillon, asparagus tips in Béchamel, sliced truffles cooked in madeira, etc., according to choice. Cover with the aspic jelly. Place on ice.

Unmold and serve with a vegetable salad.

OEUFS POCHÉS GRATINÉS SUR CANAPÉS

Poached Eggs Baked on Canapes

Meatless.

For four people, use:

1 C. grated Parmesan
1/2 C. butter
7 T. cream
1/2 C. flour
4 T. puréed shrimp or crayfish tails
1/3 C. grated Swiss cheese
3 T. breadcrumbs
1 tsp. salt
to taste freshly ground pepper
1 qt. milk
8 eggs
1 medium onion
1 medium carrot
1 stalk celery
bouquet garni
bread
nutmeg
salt and pepper

This recipe may be prepared with or without meat.

Prepare a meatless Béchamel sauce—that is, in 5 tablespoons of butter lightly cook the minced onion, carrot, and celery. Add the flour and stir for about five minutes without browning. Stir in the boiling milk and add the *bouquet*, salt, and pepper. Let the mixture come to a boil and let it simmer until smooth and thick. Strain the sauce, add the cream, then cook again until the mixture is thick enough to coat the spoon. To the above, add grated Parmesan cheese and you will have a *sauce Mornay.*

Make small two and a half inch canapés: that is, eight squares of crustless bread sautéed until golden brown in 2 tablespoons of butter and spread with a purée of shrimp or crayfish tails; or prepare 8 small sandwiches or patty shells of similar size and garnish them with the same purée.

Poach the eggs lightly.

Butter an ovenware dish with the remaining butter, spoon a layer of *sauce Mornay* on the bottom, arrange the canapés on the sauce, on each canapé set a slightly poached egg, season with salt, pepper, and nutmeg, and coat with more *sauce Mornay*. Sprinkle on the mixed breadcrumbs and grated cheese; put the dish in a hot oven to brown, and serve.

With meat stock.

Using the preceding recipe, substitute for the meatless Béchamel sauce a Béchamel made with meat stock (see recipe for this under the title *Poularde Demi-Deuil*), and instead of using the shrimp or crayfish tail purée use a purée of ham or foie gras with truffles.

OEUFS SUR LE PLAT EN SURPRISE

Shirred Eggs Surprise

Peel the truffles and the mushrooms and roll the latter in lemon juice.

Mince the livers, the truffles, and the mushrooms, and sauté them in a frying pan with clarified butter.

Put this mixture in a shallow fireproof dish and break the eggs onto it. Add the meat glaze dissolved in some stock. Season with salt and pepper and sprinkle on some breadcrumbs and some chopped parsley; then put the dish in the oven for several minutes and serve immediately.

For six people, use:

4 oz. mushrooms
2 oz. truffles
3 T. butter
5 tsp. meat glaze
6 eggs
2 chicken livers
stock
breadcrumbs
lemon juice
parsley
salt and pepper

OEUFS SUR LE PLAT À LA CRÈME

Shirred Eggs with Cream

Cream blends very well with eggs. I have already mentioned its use in scrambled eggs, eggs in ramekins, and eggs gratinéed. I will not list all the preparations in which it can be used; I will only say a few words on its use in shirred eggs.

To prepare shirred eggs with cream, prepare plain shirred eggs in an earthenware or porcelain fireproof dish. Season with salt and pepper to taste and sprinkle with some chopped chives; then cover with heavy cream to which has been added a tiny bit of vinegar. Cover and heat in a slow oven for about ten minutes. Serve in the same dish.

OEUFS SUR LE PLAT GRATINÉS

Oven-Browned Shirred Eggs

Butter a shallow ovenproof dish, sprinkle heavily with Parmesan cheese, add some sour cream which has been thinned with veal stock, and put the dish in the oven to heat. Five minutes before serving break eggs into the dish, leaving them whole, season with salt and pepper, and sprinkle them with Parmesan cheese. Put the dish back in the oven just long enough to set the egg whites.

OEUFS DURS À LA TRIPE

Hard-Boiled Eggs Tripe Style

Start by hard boiling some eggs. Boil some water in a saucepan, add the eggs which have been placed in a wire basket for easier handling, and let them boil for ten minutes. Remove the wire basket from the hot water and plunge it immediately under cold water.

When the eggs are cold, shell them, cut them in half and remove the yolks. Cut the whites into thin strips.

Make a Béchamel sauce (see recipe for *Oeufs Pochés Gratinés sur Canapés*), but increase the quantity of onions.[1] Add the half

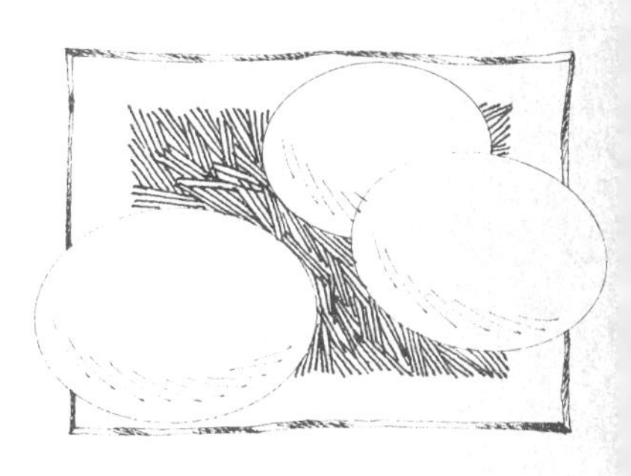

egg yolks, the slivered egg white, decorate with chopped parsley and serve.

For variation, one may sieve the yolks through a wire strainer and fold them into the sauce; or else the sieved yolks may be used just to decorate the dish.

One may substitute a Mornay sauce[2] for the Béchamel sauce, sprinkle the top with a mixture of breadcrumbs and grated Parmesan cheese, and then put the dish in the oven to brown. One would then have *oeufs à la tripe gratinés*.

NOTES

1. Onion lovers sometimes put as much onion as eggs, either leaving them in the dish chopped, or straining them out.
2. Mornay sauce is a Béchamel sauce with cheese.

OEUFS DURS GRATINÉS

Browned Hard-Boiled Eggs

For six people, use:

½ C. Bechamel sauce[1] (made with meat stock)
4 T. butter
4 T. grated Parmesan cheese
10 eggs

Hard boil the eggs, cool them, and cut them in two. Remove the yolks and, using a pestle or wooden spoon, force them through a sieve or wire strainer. Chop the whites. Butter a fireproof dish and put a layer of chopped egg whites on the bottom. Mask these with Béchamel, cover with the sieved egg yolks, sprinkle with cheese, and dot the top with the rest of the butter. Put the dish in the oven to brown for ten minutes, and serve.

NOTE

1. Prepare the Béchamel sauce as in the recipe for *Poularde Demi-Deuil*.

OEUFS DURS AUX POMMES DE TERRE

Hard-Boiled Eggs with Potatoes

For four people, take:

2 lbs. potatoes
¼ lb. butter
1 T. wine vinegar
2 shallots
parsley
4 eggs
salt and pepper

Cook the potatoes in salted water, peel and slice them. At the same time, hard boil the eggs, shell them, and cut them in two.

Put the egg halves and the sliced potatoes on a warm platter and keep them hot. Put the butter in a frying pan along with the chopped shallots and sauté gently until light brown. Add the salt, pepper, and vinegar and heat up. Pour the contents of the pan through a sieve onto the eggs and potatoes. Sprinkle with chopped parsley and serve.

This dish, which I had the opportunity of sampling out in the country, seemed simply delicious after a long walk.

OEUFS FARCIS,[1] À LA CRÈME

Stuffed Eggs with Cream

For five people, take:

1 C. thick cream (heavy enough to be heated without curdling)
4 T. butter
10 eggs
1 shallot
chopped parsley
salt and pepper

Hard boil the eggs,[2] shell them, and cut them in two lengthwise. Remove the yolks and push them through a sieve with a pestle or wooden spoon.

Put the butter and the chopped shallot in a frying pan and cook until the shallot is soft. Add the sieved yolks, and the chopped parsley. Season with salt and pepper and work the mixture until you have a smooth paste. Use this mixture to fill the whites.

Put the stuffed eggs on a fireproof dish, cut side down. Heat the cream, adding a little more salt and pepper and pour it over the eggs. Place the dish in the oven for several minutes and serve.

NOTES

1. In the culinary sense the word *farces* (stuffings) refers to hashed ingredients, suitably seasoned and aromatized, either thickened or not. They are generally used to fill or stuff eggs, fish, meat, fowl, game, *pâtés*, and vegetables. Their role is to add a new note the finished dish, harmonizing with the main ingredient and enhancing it. Stuffings are also sometimes used to fill small patty shell or *bouchées*.
2. In order to avoid any possible sulfur odor, hard boil the eggs the day before preparing the recipe.

OEUFS AU FROMAGE

Eggs with Cheese

Butter a fireproof dish and line the bottom with thin slices of crustless bread. Cover these with a thin layer of grated Gruyère cheese (the lightly salted kind), Parmesan cheese, Chester, or Stilton, according to taste. Break an egg on each slice of bread, add a little more cheese, and cook quickly over a hot fire without any other seasoning.

One may also put some slices of ham between the bread and cheese. In either case one can also cover it all with cream and complete the cooking in the oven.

All these preparations, which are a little out of the ordinary, are generally well received.

SYMPHONIE D'OEUFS

Egg Symphony

For six people use twelve eggs.

Hard boil two of them. Cool and chop them.

Poach six eggs and keep them warm.

In a large skillet, using the four remaining eggs, make a thin omelet, either plain or with additional hot ingredients, according to taste.

As soon as the omelet is cooked, sprinkle on the chopped hard-boiled eggs, then put on the poached eggs. Fold the omelet and slip it onto a platter and serve.

The poached eggs must be placed and served so that each person gets one poached egg for his serving.

This may be accompanied by a tomato sauce, a Béchamel sauce, or some cream slightly acidified with lemon juice, as desired.

A more elegant way of presenting this dish is to prepare individual omelets for each person and place one poached egg in each.

CRÈME AU FROMAGE

Cheese Custard

For four people, use:

3/4 C. grated Gruyère cheese
4 T. heavy cream
2 tsp. butter
6 eggs
salt and pepper

Beat together the eggs, cream, and 2/3 cup of the cheese. Season to taste.

Butter six small molds or ramekins and sprinkle on the rest of the cheese. Pour in the mixture you have just prepared, cover the molds to keep the contents from rising while cooking, and poach them in boiling water for twenty minutes.

Unmold and serve with a tomato hollandaise sauce (hollandaise sauce to which a little tomato purée has been added for color).

Croquettes

Croquettes are preparations which consist of finely minced or ground ingredients, either meatless or with meat (eggs, shellfish, fish, chicken, or game), bound with various sauces.

They are prepared with a main ingredient which gives the name to the croquette. To this may be added auxiliary ingredients: mushrooms, *cèpes* (boletus), truffles, ham, tongue, or foie gras, etc. These hashes are cooked, then cooled on a buttered plate.

Croquettes may be made in different shapes: cork-shaped, round, oval, disk shaped, apricot or pear shaped, etc.

They are then breaded and fried in very hot deep fat.

They are served on a napkin, with fried parsley.

Croquettes are always accompanied by a sauce or a light *coulis*, suitable to the basic ingredient of the croquette.

They are either served as a hot entrée or as a garnish.

CROQUETTES DE CRÈME AU JAMBON ET À LA LANGUE

Croquettes with Cream, Ham, and Tongue

For six people, use:

2 C. milk
4 oz. ham
4 oz. smoked tongue
4 oz. peeled mushrooms
1 medium peeled carrot
3 T. butter
½ medium peeled onion
1 small leek (white part only)
3 T. flour
1 small cleaned truffle
salt and pepper
1 qt. water
6 eggs
1 chicken giblet
bouquet garni **(consisting of parsley, thyme, and bay leaf)**
breadcrumbs
nutmeg
parsley
lemon

Simmer for three hours: the giblet, mushrooms, carrot, onion, leek, *bouquet garni*, in the quart of water until you have about ½ cup of strong stock. Cook, skim off the fat, and strain.

Scald the milk.

Chop the ham, tongue, and truffle.

Beat together 3 whole eggs and 2 yolks.

Put the butter and flour in a saucepan; stir and cook without browning, until smooth. Add the milk and the stock and cook, stirring, for several minutes until smooth and thick. Off the fire add the beaten eggs, the chopped meats, and the truffle. Season with salt, pepper, and nutmeg. Mix everything together well and put the pan back on the fire for a moment or two, then complete the cooking over boiling water, like a custard, until it sets. Let it cool.

Beat the remaining egg and the 2 whites together.

Cut the cooled custard into pieces, mold them into croquettes, then roll them in beaten egg. Coat them thoroughly with the breadcrumbs and fry them as you would fritters, in hot, clear, fat.

Arrange the croquettes on a hot platter and just before serving decorate them with fried parsley and slices of lemon.

This is a very elegant dish.

FONDUE AU FROMAGE

Cheese Fondue

For six people, use:

3 C. grated Gruyère cheese
½ lb. butter
5 oz. black truffles
½ C. meat essence (well skimmed, either from meat or fowl, and preferably from roast turkey)
12 eggs
½ lemon juice
salt and pepper

Wash, brush, and peel the truffles. Cut them into fine dice and sauté them for five minutes in 5 tablespoons of butter, stirring them constantly. Season them to taste with salt and pepper, then set aside on a plate.

Break the eggs, separating the whites and the yolks. Strain each separately through a fine sieve in order to remove any membrane which would mar the looks. Beat the yolks and whites separately. When the whites are stiff but not dry, fold in the yolks little by little. Season with salt and add 8 tablespoons of butter cut into thin slivers, the grated cheese and the truffles. This preparation will be used immediately.

Put 6 tablespoons of the meat juice or essence in a fairly deep non-metal saucepan, bring it to a boil and add the above mixture, whisking everything together. When the mixture begins to thicken, take the pan off the fire and keep beating until you have a very smooth custard. Add the remaining meat essence and the rest of the butter cut into tiny pieces. Season with pepper.

Put the pan back over a very low heat and complete the cooking very slowly and carefully, as you would a custard. Season with lemon juice and serve on hot plates.

This mixture must be absolutely smooth, without any lumps. Prepared in the above manner, it is not far from perfection, it seems to me.

Soufflés

Soufflés are preparations, for entrées or desserts, in which beaten egg whites play a large role.

Their composition may be based on a fine forcemeat, either with or without meat. It can be prepared with either the raw or cooked flesh of fish, shellfish, meat, organ meat, ham, chicken, foie gras, furred or feathered game; or with vegetables, truffles, cheese, etc. It may also contain cream, Béchamel sauce, or egg yolks.

Soufflés can be plain, stuffed or garnished.

They are served in the dish in which they were cooked: molds, deep dishes, timbales, small *cocottes*, small molds, etc.

They are accompanied by a variety of sauces.

Cold soufflés are really mousses which are molded in small round molds, in small *cocottes*, or in small ramekins, the bottoms of which are coated with a layer of jelly, and the sides of which are wrapped in a band of paper which makes it possible to have the contents rise above the top of the mold in order to give the illusion, once the paper band has been removed, that the contents have risen.

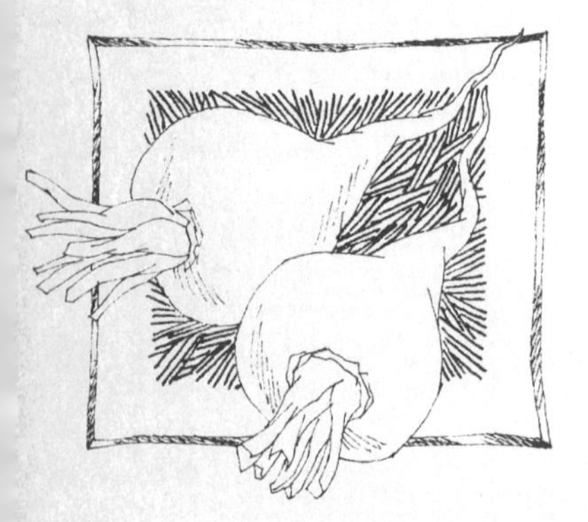

Here are some general indications on the preparation of some eupeptic combinations of soufflés, garnishes, and sauces which give cooking enthusiasts some ideas: shellfish soufflé in a ring of boiled rice, hollandaise sauce made with lobster roe; soufflé of ocean fish in a ring made of mashed potatoes and fresh-water fish, with a sauce based on fish stock; ham soufflé in a ring of macaroni, with tomato demi-glace sauce seasoned with paprika; soufflé of chicken in a ring of rice cooked with beef marrow, velouté sauce or *sauce Regence*; soufflé of duck with olives, stuffed with foie gras, madeira sauce; soufflé of foie gras made with a purée of morels and cream, sauce suprême; soufflé of furred game in a ring of Champs Elysées potatoes with truffles, sauce made with venison stock or *sauce grand veneur*[1]; soufflé of feathered game, such as soufflé of woodcock, with truffle purée, garnished with fried croûtons, covered with the giblets flamed in brandy, and a sauce made with woodcock broth.

One can also make sweet soufflés. These light desserts can be very varied.

Soufflés may be made with cream, chocolate, coffee, vanilla, violet, or pistachio; they also may be made with fresh fruits of all kinds: strawberries, raspberries, cherries, currants, whortleberries, apricots, peaches, prunes, apples, quinces, pomegranates, pineapple, oranges, tangerines, lemons, melons, etc., or with cooked fruits, jams and marmalades, or candied fruits. They can also be made with cookies. They can be flavored with all kinds of liqueurs.

They are generally served in timbales or in special molds which have been buttered and sugared—or even in plates, shells, pastry shells, and in savarins (sponge-cake shells).

In this book there are to be found many precise recipes for soufflés (see recipe index).

NOTE

1. *Sauce grand veneur* (master-of-the-hounds sauce) is a peppery sauce made with venison stock to which is added the blood of furred game which has been diluted in the marinade (seven tablespoons of blood to each quart of sauce), and then added at the last minute. Heat up without boiling and strain through a sieve or cloth.

SOUFFLÉ AU FROMAGE

Cheese Soufflé

For six people, use:

1 C. cream
1½ C. grated Gruyère cheese
2 T. butter
⅓ C. grated Parmesan cheese
3 T. cornstarch or potato starch
6 eggs
nutmeg
salt and freshly ground pepper

Break the eggs and separate the yolks from the whites. In a saucepan put the cream, butter, and starch. Heat and stir constantly until the mixture is smooth and well blended. Season to taste with nutmeg, salt, and pepper. Take the pan off the fire and add the egg yolks, Gruyère, and Parmesan. Mix everything together thoroughly.

Beat 4 egg whites until stiff and very carefully fold them into the above mixture without deflating the egg whites. Pour this mixture into a lightly buttered soufflé dish and bake in a moderate oven. Twenty-five to thirty minutes should be sufficient.

Serve at once.

OEUFS POCHÉS EN SOUFFLÉ

Soufflé with Poached Eggs

For six people, use the same ingredients as for the preceding soufflé, plus 6 more fresh eggs.

Prepare the cheese soufflé exactly as above.

Poach 6 eggs.

Butter a deep casserole and in it place half the soufflé mixture, lay the poached eggs over this, and pour on the rest of the soufflé mixture and cook in the oven as above.

This dish provides a pleasant surprise.

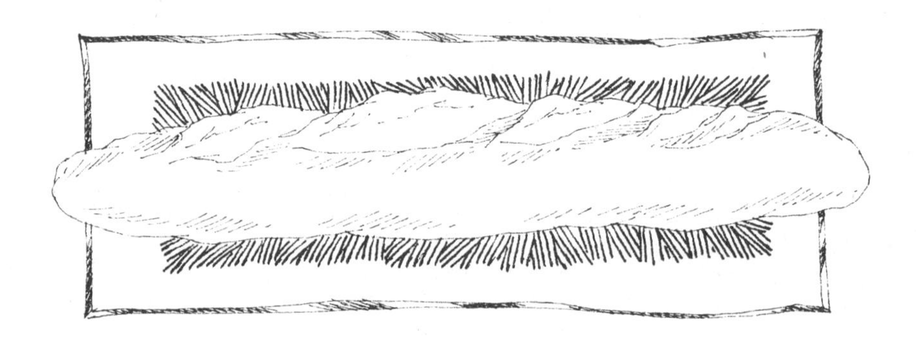

FROGS, CRUSTACEANS, AND MOLLUSKS

Frogs

Frogs, *Rana*, are batrachian reptiles of the *Ranadae* family. The legs, the only edible part, whose taste is reminiscent of squab chicken, is very light, healthy, and agreeable fare.

Commercially frogs are offered for sale already cleaned and without the unedible parts, strung through the hips on flat skewers, legs crossed. Just before preparing them, one removes the feet and trims off the top part of the legs.

Frogs may be prepared in various ways: (1) in soup; (2) fried, either breaded or not, in butter, fat, or oil; *au naturel*, or with parsley, *fines herbes*, etc.; *à la provençal*, with garlic; *à la portuguaise*, with tomatoes; *à l'indienne*, with curry; *à la hongroise*, with paprika; *à l'italienne* with mushrooms; (3) *au blanc*, *à la poulette*; (4) *à la meunière*; (5) fried as in fritters; (6) *au gratin*; (7) in mousses; (8) *en ragoût*; (9) *en chaud-froid*.

I shall give detailed instructions for the preparation of three of the above: breaded sautéed frogs' legs, frogs' legs *au blanc,* and ragoût of frogs' legs. Other preparations are easily imagined.

GRENOUILLES SAUTÉES, PANÉES

Fried Breaded Frogs' Legs

For four people, use:

2/3 C. butter
1 C. fine stale breadcrumbs
2 dozen plump frogs' legs
2 lemons
2 shallots
brandy
flour
parsley
tarragon
chives
salt and pepper

Soak the salted and peppered frogs' legs for one hour in brandy, turning them every now and then. Drain them and roll them in flour. Mix the breadcrumbs with salt, pepper, chopped parsley, tarragon, and chives to taste.

At the same time sauté: on the one hand, the frogs' legs and the shallots in 1/3 cup butter, for six or seven minutes; on the other hand, the mixture of breadcrumbs and herbs in the rest of the butter. The butter should permeate the breadcrumbs and they should turn a golden brown. Remove the shallot and join the breadcrumbs and frogs' legs in one pan and continue to fry them together for a minute or two, mixing them well. Serve with half-lemons.

GRENOUILLES AU BLANC

Fricassee of Frogs' Legs

For eight people, use:

3 C. dry white wine
1 lb. mushrooms
1/2 lb. onions
1 C. cream
1/3 C. milk
4 T. butter
4 tsp. flour
4 dozen plump frogs' legs
2 fresh egg yolks
bouquet garni
lemon juice
salt and pepper

Wash frogs' legs in the milk.

Melt the butter, stir in the flour, and cook them together without browning. Add the wine to the saucepan, along with the sliced onion and the *bouquet garni.* Season the mixture with salt and pepper and cook for about thirty minutes. Strain the sauce and add the mushrooms which have been peeled and washed in lemon juice. After ten minutes add the frogs' legs. Let this all cook for another five minutes and then enrich the sauce with the cream and the egg yolks beaten together. Taste for seasoning and correct if necessary.

RAGOÛT DE GRENOUILLES ET D'ÉCREVISSES

Ragoût of Frogs' Legs and Crayfish

For six people, use:

36 pair frogs' legs
36 crayfish
36 small round mushrooms
chicken or veal broth
egg yolks
truffles
flour
butter
lemon juice
parsley
salt and pepper

Cook the crayfish in court bouillon. Remove the shells and crush them with butter to obtain a crayfish butter.

In a saucepan put the crayfish tails, the peeled mushrooms, and the chopped parsley, and gently sauté all these in butter. Add the frogs' legs, salt, and pepper and continue to cook very slowly for fifteen minutes, shaking the pan now and then.

In another saucepan, melt the butter and add the flour without browning. Stir in the chicken or veal broth, and cook it down to reduce it to a fairly thick sauce. Season with lemon juice to taste and whisk in the egg yolks. Just before serving whisk in the crayfish butter. Spoon the contents of both saucepans into a timbale and garnish the top with a few slices of truffle and some small golden cutouts made from flaky pastry.

This ragoût may also be served in a vol-au-vent crust.

LANGOUSTE AU NATUREL[1]

Plain Lobster

The best method of cooking lobster is to boil it.

Take a plump, live, female lobster, tie it up, and plunge it into a pot of boiling sea water or, instead, plain salted water, using sea salt if possible. Keep it boiling for twenty minutes for a 2-pound lobster.

Let it cook in the water, then drain it.

Cover a platter with a linen napkin or a towel, place the lobster on it, and decorate the platter with parsley. Along with it serve some plain mayonnaise, lemon mayonnaise, lobster roe mayonnaise, mustard or horseradish mayonnaise.

NOTE

1. The term *langouste* refers, in France, to *Palinurus locusta* of the Palinuridae family. In English it is known under the names rock lobster, spiny lobster, sea crawfish. They are readily distinguished from the true lobsters, which form the family Homaridae, by the fact that the first legs are not provided with chelae or pincers, whereas the Homaridae have the first three pairs of legs terminating in chelae. Recipes for *langouste* are perfectly adaptable to the true lobster.

To make a lobster roe mayonnaise, use raw lobster roe, mash it and boil it up in a sauce pan with about ⅓ of its quantity of vinegar. Cook this over boiling water until it has thickened and taken on a lovely red color.

Strain through a sieve and add this purée to regular mayonnaise.

To make horseradish mayonnaise simply mix some grated horseradish into plain mayonnaise, to taste.

Plain lobster may be served as a salad.

One would then decorate the platter with hearts of lettuce and

some quartered hard-boiled eggs. It would then be served with a simple oil and vinegar dressing or with a *sauce douce* (sweet sauce) made as follows: Mash the yolks of 4 hard-boiled eggs with 6 tablespoons of herbs (equal quantities of chives, tarragon, chervil, and parsley, chopped). Then make a plain oil and vinegar dressing adding to it 2 teaspoons of sugar and the mashed yolks and herbs.

One may also serve the lobster sliced. The slices would be arranged semi-upright on the shell, starting from the head, and overlapping them slightly. They may be decorated as desired and then coated with a fish aspic.

The platter can be garnished with hard-boiled eggs, some pastry cases or *barquettes* or artichoke hearts filled with vegetable salad to which has been added the trimmings and the creamy portions of the lobster. This vegetable salad is bound with any of the above-mentioned mayonnaises. This is known as *langouste à la parisienne.*

SALMIS DE HOMARD À LA CRÈME

Salmis of Lobster in Cream

For four people, use:

2 C. dry white wine
1 C. cream
1/3 C. madeira, sherry, or white port
1 carrot
1 onion
4 T. butter
2 1/2 T. coarse salt
1 tsp. table salt
pinch white pepper
paprika to taste
few grains nutmeg
cayenne to taste
40 freshly ground black peppercorns
3 egg yolks
1 live 2-lb. female lobster with roe
bouquet garni
truffles cooked in madeira (optional)
water enough to cover lobster

Cook the lobster for a half hour in a court bouillon prepared with the dry white wine, carrot, onion, coarse salt, peppercorns, *bouquet garni*, and the necessary water. Allow it to cool in the liquid. Remove and slice the tail and claw meat. Set aside any other lobster meat and the stomach meat and roe.

Add the table salt and the spices to half the fortified wine you have chosen.

Mix the leftover lobster meat, stomach meat, and roe with 2 teaspoons of butter. Pound in a mortar and push through a strainer.

In the rest of the butter place the sliced lobster meat and cover with the rest of the fortified wine. Cook very gently for about ten minutes and keep it warm.

In a double boiler blend the strained purée and the spiced wine and heat it up thoroughly, adding, little by little, the cream and egg yolks, and beating constantly in order to obtain a smooth thick sauce.

Arrange the sliced lobster meat on a platter; mask it with the sauce on which you can sprinkle a julienne of truffles which have been cooked separately. Serve at once.

This *salmis* is very pretty as an entrée for an elegant meal.

This *salmis* can also be prepared with rock lobster, langostinos, large prawns, etc.

All these *salmis* may be presented in a timbale.

By straining any of these *salmis* and adding to the purée some fish broth flavored and colored with red shellfish butter, one would get fish soups—absolutely delicious—which would acquire, respectively, the names lobster bisque, langostino bisque, shrimp bisque, etc. They may be decorated with tiny crayfish and pike quenelles and some fried croûtons.

PILAF DE HOMARD

Lobster Pilaf

For four people, use:

2 C. chicken broth or consommé
1¾ C. dry white wine
2 C. rice
4 oz. mushrooms
4 oz. shrimp
½ lb. butter
5 T. diced carrots
⅓ C. heavy cream
⅓ C. chopped onion
4 tsp. brandy or Calvados (apple brandy)
2 T. parsley, chopped
½ tsp. peppercorns
1 pint mussels
12 oysters
2 whiting (weighing about 1 lb. together)
2 soles or any flat fish or trimmings (weighing 1 lb. together)
2 egg yolks
1 live lobster weighing about 2½ to 3 lbs.
bouquet garni
1 bay leaf
few sprigs thyme
flour
lemon juice
quatre épices
salt and pepper

Peel the shrimp; set aside and save the shells.

Peel the mushrooms, save the peelings, and sauté the mushrooms gently in 1 tablespoon butter, adding a few drops of lemon juice, for about three or four minutes.

Scrub and steam the mussels until they open. Strain the broth and save.

Cook the oysters in their own juice just until they open.

Put the mussels, oysters, mushrooms, and shrimp together and keep warm.

In a heavy saucepan put 4 teaspoons of butter, the chopped carrot, parsley, thyme, and bay leaf. Cook these gently in the butter for a minute or two. Then cover the pan and cook until soft. Add the wine and brandy, the liquid from the mussels, oysters, and mushrooms, the mushroom peelings, the whitings, and the soles, and season with a pinch of *quatre épices*. Cook together until everything is well blended. Force this rich stock through a sieve, pressing well with a wooden spoon to extract every last bit of broth.

While the above is cooking, boil the lobster in salted water for about twenty minutes. Remove the tail meat and cut into neat slices. Remove and reserve the roe, coral, and any other meat inside the lobster cavity.

Mash the roe, the insides of the lobster carcass, and the shrimp shells, with 2 tablespoons of butter. Force the butter through a strainer and you will have shellfish butter.

Wash the rice and drain it.

Sauté the chopped onion in 3 tablespoons of butter. Add the rice and the *bouquet garni*, stir a minute or two, and then add the chicken broth or consommé. Season with salt and pepper and cook in the oven twenty to twenty-five minutes, until the liquid is completely absorbed and the grains are still whole and separate.

To finish the sauce, melt the rest of the butter, and add an equal quantity of flour and stir to blend. Then add the broth and cook for several minutes until hot and smooth. Beat the egg yolks and cream together, add a little of the hot sauce to this mixture, then pour it all back into the pan and heat very gradually. Add a few drops of lemon juice, then gently stir in the shellfish butter. Correct the seasoning. You now have an excellent *sauce normande*.

Make a ring of the rice on a hot platter. Pour a little of the sauce over it. Mix the mussels, shrimps, and mushrooms with a little of the hot sauce and spoon into the center of the rice ring. Arrange the sliced lobster tail meat on the rice border and top each with a dab of the coral.

Serve and send along the sauce in a sauceboat.

Naturally, one may add truffles to this dish if desired.
Truffled or not, lobster pilaf is a lovely dish.

CREVETTES À L'AMÉRICAINE

Prawns à l'américaine

For six people, use:

½ lb. tomatoes
¾ C. butter
1 C. sauterne wine
1 C. fish broth
⅔ C. brandy
⅓ C. fish fumet[1] or, alternatively, meat glaze
2 oz. lobster roe
2 T. olive oil
6 shallots
1½ tsp. salt
pinch pepper
pinch *quatre épices*
few grains cayenne
24 large, live shrimp (weighing about 2 lbs. altogether)
3 sweet peppers
parsley
chervil
tarragon
lemon juice

The large Mediterranean shrimp known as *Penoeus caramota*, of the Carididae family, prepared in the following manner, is a dish similar to lobster *à l'américaine*, but much more delicate.

Put the olive oil and 5 tablespoons of the butter in a frying pan; heat these and throw the shrimp into the smoking liquid fat. As soon as they have turned pink, raise the heat, pour on the brandy and flame it, then add the sauterne and the fish broth, and either the fish fumet or the meat glaze, the tomatoes (peeled, seeded, and chopped), the shallots, salt, pepper, *quatre épices*, cayenne, and peppers. Cover and let these cook for ten minutes.

At this point, remove the shrimp and keep them warm in a hot water bath. Boil down the liquid to reduce it and strain.

Mash the lobster eggs and force through a sieve, add them to the liquid, heat it up, taste, complete the seasoning if necessary, then add the chopped parsley, chervil, and tarragon, the rest of the butter and the lemon juice.

Arrange the shrimp on a platter, coat them with the sauce and serve.

One may also peel the shrimp, keep the tail meat warm, then, with the shells and trimmings, make a shrimp butter.

One would then arrange the tails on the platter and coat them with the sauce. This is not as pretty to look at as when the shrimp are whole, but it does have the advantage of not having to be eaten with one's fingers.

One may prepare, in the same way, scallops, prawns, etc., which are also very delicate.

NOTE

1. One prepares fish fumet in a similar manner as white stock. Take the head, bones, and trimmings of soles, whitings, brills, or alternatively some whole common fish; add onions, some parsley, mushrooms, salt, pepper, and lemon juice; then add either water or a good white wine. Let this all boil, skim carefully, and finish cooking at a steady simmer, then strain. Cooking time is about one and a half hours. Essence of fish is obtained in the same way, but the liquid added is fish fumet instead of water. Cooking time is about twenty minutes.

QUEUES D'ÉCREVISSES[1] EN HORS-D'OEUVRE

Crayfish Tail Hors-d'oeuvre

For six people, use:

1 1/3 C. milk
1 1/4 C. dry white wine
1 1/4 C. water
1/4 lb. or 8 T. butter
1/2 C. brandy
1 small carrot (sliced)
1/3 small onion (sliced)
3 T. coarse salt
1 T. tarragon
24 medium-sized shrimp
20 peppercorns (crushed)
bouquet garni **(parsley, thyme, bay leaf and fennel)**

Soak the crayfish in the milk for two hours.

Prepare a court bouillon[2] with the white wine, water, brandy, carrot, onion, salt, pepper, tarragon, *bouquet garni*, and 2 teaspoons of butter. Cook these ingredients together for twenty minutes or so.

Remove the intestinal vein from the crayfish, throw them into the boiling court bouillon, cook them for fifteen minutes, and let them cook in their liquid.

Shell the crayfish, set aside the tails in a deep serving dish, then, with the trimmings and the rest of the butter, make a crayfish butter, which will be used to coat the crayfish.

Crayfish butter is prepared in the following manner:

In a mortar, pound the crayfish trimmings or, better yet, some whole cooked crayfish, and add an equal quantity of butter. Heat this all up in a double boiler, then strain through a fine sieve, over a bowl containing cold water. Skim the butter off the top and drain it well.

Shrimp butter is prepared in the same way. One takes an equal quantity by weight of boiled shrimp and of butter.

NOTES

1. The crayfish of England, Ireland and Europe belong to the genus *Astacus* (*Astacus fluviatilis* and *Astacus leptodactylus*) of the Astadicae family. In North America, west of the Rocky Mountains, the genus *Astacus* reappears, but east of the watershed it is replaced by the genus *Cambarus*, of which numerous species range from the Great Lakes to Mexico.

For ten people, use:

$3^1/_4$ C. milk
$2^1/_3$ C. dry white Bordeaux wine
1 lb. 3 oz. butter
$^3/_4$ C. brandy
$^3/_4$ C. fish fumet[1]
$^3/_4$ C. fish velouté[2]
$^3/_4$ C. thick tomato sauce
2 medium carrots (red part only)
$^1/_3$ lb. onions
4 shallots
several sprigs parsley
tarragon leaves
60 plump live crayfish
thyme
bay leaf
salt, pepper, cayenne to taste

ÉCREVISSES À LA BORDELAISE

Crayfish à la Bordelaise

Soak the crayfish in the milk for two hours.

Chop the carrot, onion, shallot, tarragon, and half of the parsley. Put these in a saucepan with 2 tablespoons of butter, the thyme, bay leaf, salt, and pepper. Cook these together.

Rip out the intestinal vein of the crayfish and throw them alive into the saucepan. Sprinkle a little cayenne pepper over them and toss them until they are very red. Heat, light, and pour the brandy over them.

Remove the crayfish and keep them warm.

Now add the wine and reduce the liquid by about one-third: then add the crayfish, the fish fumet, the fish velouté, and tomato sauce, and let everything cook together for about ten minutes.

Arrange the crayfish in a hot serving dish and keep them warm.

Strain the sauce, boil it down to reduce it, enrich it with the rest of the butter, add the rest of the parsley which has been blanched and chopped, and coat the crayfish with this sauce.

Serve with some well-aged dry Bordeaux wine.

Lobster, spiny rock lobster, or langostinos may be prepared *à la bordelaise.*

The sauce would be prepared as above. The shellfish would be cooked in a court bouillon. The meat would be removed from the shell and added to the sauce along with any bits of flesh and the white creamy parts.

NOTES

1. Fish fumet is prepared in the same way as a white stock. One uses the heads, bones, and trimmings from sole, whiting, brill or some whole ordinary fish. Then one adds onion, parsley, mushrooms, salt, pepper, lemon juice, water, and very good white wine. These ingredients are boiled together and carefully skimmed; then the liquid is simmered for a long time. Cooking time is about one and a half hours.

Essence of fish is prepared in the same way but instead of water one uses fish fumet. Cooking time is twenty minutes.

2. To prepare a seafood velouté, take some fish broth and flavor it with white wine, some aromatic vegetables and herbs, some spices, and mushrooms to taste. Thicken this with *beurre manié* or with a roux. Boil the sauce down and skim it thoroughly.

ÉCREVISSES AU GRATIN

Crayfish au Gratin

For six people, use:

$1/2$ C. heavy cream
$3\,1/2$ T. butter
10 T. Gruyère cheese
10 T. Parmesan cheese
1 oz. in 1 slice lean ham
2 T. flour
$1/4$ C. breadcrumbs
50 crayfish
2 egg yolks
nutmeg
salt and pepper

Cook the crayfish in a court bouillon. Remove the tail and claw meat. Prepare a crayfish butter with the trimmings, shells, and 2 tablespoons of butter.

In the rest of the butter cook the chopped ham and the flour and stir in enough crayfish court bouillon to make a sauce. Add the tail and claw meat, salt, pepper, and nutmeg to taste. Let this simmer a few minutes. Then add the cream, four-fifths of the Gruyère and Parmesan cheese mixed together, and blend everything well together. Heat up without boiling, then thicken with the 2 egg yolks.

Spoon the mixture into an ovenproof serving dish, sprinkle on the rest of the cheeses mixed with the breadcrumbs, and brown rapidly in the oven.

CHAUSSONS AUX ÉCREVISSES

Crayfish Turnovers

Prepare a *demi-feuilleté*[1] (semi-flaky pastry) or buy some commercial prepared pastry. Roll it out to about one-quarter-inch thickness and cut it into circles of about five or six inches in diameter.

Sauté the crayfish as in the Bordelaise recipe. Finish the cooking in some fish fumet to which has been added either Château Yquem wine or some sherry. Reduce the cooking liquid.

Shell the crayfish and slice the tail meat. Pound the trimmings in a mortar with some butter and force through a strainer. Add this purée to the reduced cooking liquid and thicken the sauce with a little bit of roux. Add the sliced crayfish tail meat and you then have a mixture with which to fill the turnovers. On half of each of the circles, add a small quantity of the filling, fold the dough over, wet the edges, and seal; then bake in the oven.

Serve with Château Yquem wine or sherry, according to which has been used in the preparation of the turnovers.

For variation one could purée the crayfish, cooked as above, along with some lobster, which one would then bind with a very thick *sauce suprême*, colored with lobster roe and enriched with shellfish butter.

NOTE

1. Ingredients used to make semi-flaky pastry are the following:

1 lb. of hard wheat flour
13 oz. of firm and elastic butter
2 T. water
2 tsp. salt

The procedure is the same as for regular flaky pastry, but instead of giving six turns one only gives five.

Mousses and Mousselines

Mousses are mixtures of meat or seafood forcemeats, thickened with cream (mousseline forcemeats) and worked with butter, jellies, or veloutés.

One may use either cooked or raw flesh.

Mousses are molded in large molds; mousselines are molded in small, low molds, or shaped with a spoon into ovals, or even shaped with a pastry bag, using either a plain or fluted tip, into meringue shapes.

Mousses and mousselines are generally decorated; the latter may be stuffed or not stuffed. They can be served either hot or cold.

Mousses or mousselines may be accompanied by delicate vegetables: small green peas, asparagus, truffles, morels, Duchesse potatoes, etc.

MOUSSES ET MOUSSELINES DE CRUSTACÉS

Shellfish Mousses and Mousselines

Shellfish mousses are prepared with cooked flesh and they are served cold.

Mousselines of shellfish are always prepared with raw flesh and they are served hot.

MOUSSE DE CREVETTES

Shrimp Mousse

Cook some shrimp with a meatless *mirepoix* made with white wine spiked with a little flaming brandy.

Shell the shrimp and set some of them aside; they will serve as decoration.

Mash together the remaining shrimp, the *mirepoix* in which they were cooked, and a little butter. Force the pounded mixture through a strainer. Weigh the resulting purée, and use one-half its weight of heavy cream.

Put the shrimp purée in a saucepan, add one-fourth of its weight of velouté, and one-fourth its weight of fish jelly. Heat these together, boil it up once and cool.

Half-whip the cream and fold it into the cooled mixture.

Line a chilled mold with a little colorless aspic jelly. On the bottom of the mold arrange the shrimp you set aside, which have been coated with aspic. Fill the mold with the mousse and chill it. At serving time, unmold the mousse onto a serving platter covered with a napkin.

MOUSSE D'ÉCREVISSES

Crayfish Mousse

The preparation of a crayfish mousse is similar to that of a shrimp mousse.

This mousse is decorated with crayfish tails split in two lengthwise. A garnish is added consisting of crayfish shells which have been filled with a little of the mousse mixture.

Crayfish mousse must have a pink color, which is easily obtained by adding some pink-colored shellfish butter or by adding some paprika or, alternatively, some food coloring.

MOUSSE DE HOMARD OU DE LANGOUSTE

Lobster or Spiny Lobster Mousse

Cook a lobster or a rock (spiny) lobster as in the recipe called *à la bordelaise*. Let the animal cool in the liquid. Remove all the meat from the shell, set aside a small amount for decoration, and pound the rest with half its weight of fish velouté. Push the mixture through a sieve. Work the purée thus obtained over ice with several spoonfuls of fish jelly and half its weight of semi-whipped cream. Spike the seasoning with a little cayenne pepper.

Put this mixture into a mold that has been lined with aspic and decorated with some little medallions cut out of the reserved meat, and chill.

Unmold on a napkin.

Shellfish mousselines are always prepared with raw flesh. They are molded in small buttered molds, or made into the shape of an egg, or in small *barquettes*, then poached like quenelles for twelve to fifteen minutes according to their size.

They are served hot with suitable sauces: shrimp, Nantua, *américaine*, lobster, etc.

In the same way one can make mousses or mousselines of prawns, hermit crabs, and crabs.

Oysters

The oyster *Ostra edulis* is a bi-valve, Lamellibranch, acephalous, hermaphrodite mollusk.

Among the edible varieties, the choicest are the oysters from Belon, from Marennes, from Ostend, the *côtes-rouges*, the native oysters from England such as the Burnhams, the Colchesters, and the native oysters of Zeeland. These oysters, which should only be eaten raw and alive, are a delicate, light, luxury food. Other oysters, which are less delicate, may be used for sauces or for garnishing.

How should one eat raw oysters?

Certain people swallow them whole, without chewing. They might as well be taking pills! Others are agreeable to chewing them —but only after having doused them with fiery sauces which completely mask the taste, and whose use I would only understand if I were condemned to eat horses' hooves or *portuguaises*.[1] Others, however, simply add a little lemon juice and eat them along with some buttered brown bread or caviar sandwiches. Each person thinks that his own way is the best. Here is the way of oyster lovers, who feel that a good oyster deserves to be loved for itself.

Have them opened, but only just at serving time. Select your favorite oysters, plump, fleshy ones, and make sure in each case that the oyster is alive, by testing its reflexes. This is an infallible sign which cannot fool you.[2] Then, gently remove it from the shell, bring it immediately to the mouth, all naked, without any other accompaniment, and, at once, with one bite, pierce the liver. If the subject responds in the manner you expect of him, your gums should immediately be bathed and your mouth flooded with juice.[3]

Remain like that a moment and then slowly swallow the juice and continue chewing and swallowing the mollusk. Then spark yourself with a swallow of good dry white wine, eat a mouthful of dark bread, either buttered or not, to neutralize the taste buds of the tongue so that you will be ready to enjoy the next oyster.

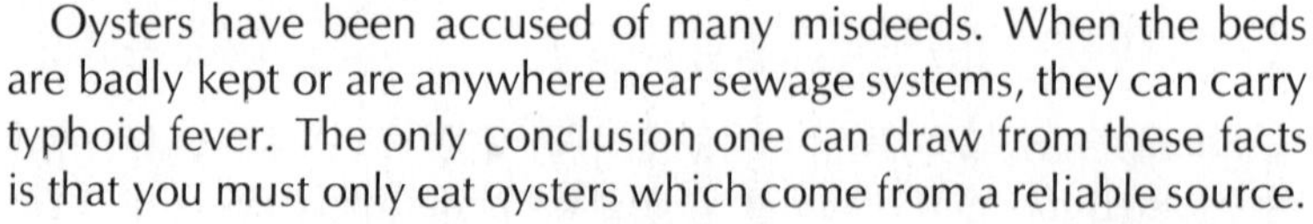
Oysters have been accused of many misdeeds. When the beds are badly kept or are anywhere near sewage systems, they can carry typhoid fever. The only conclusion one can draw from these facts is that you must only eat oysters which come from a reliable source.

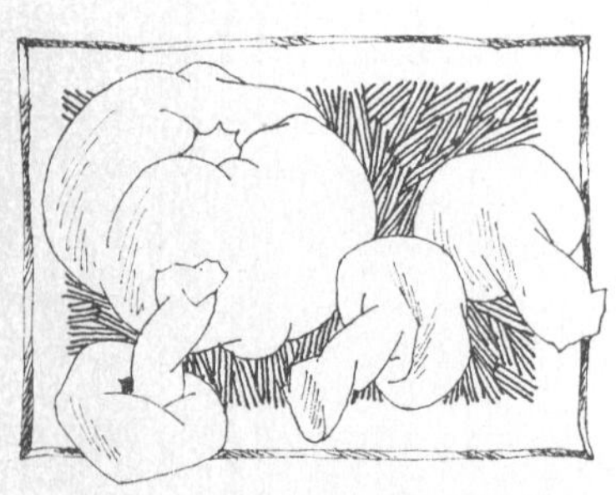

NOTES

1. The *portuguaise* (or Portuguese oyster) is not a true oyster. It is really the *Gryphaea angulata*.

2. Testing the reflex of an oyster is very easily accomplished. One need only touch the edges of the lamellae, which will retract if the animal is alive.

3. This is the real criteria, *a posteriori*, of the perfect oyster.

BOUCHÉES* AUX HUITRES

Oyster Bouchées

For 20 patty shells, use:

2 C. milk
1 lb. mushrooms
1 1/3 C. butter
1 C. cream
1/4 lb. live shrimp
3 T. flour
60 plump Portuguese oysters (or use oysters from Cancale or any ordinary oyster)
lemon juice

Make a flaky pastry, as in the recipe, or, if you have a good bakery in the neighborhood, order some patty shells and prepare the following filling:

Open the oysters; put the mollusks and their juice in a saucepan and bring it to a boil. After it boils up once, remove the blanched oysters. Keep them warm and strain the juices.

Prepare a court bouillon as in the recipe for Crayfish Tail Hors-d'oeuvre, using the oyster juices instead of plain water. In this liquid cook the shrimp, peel them, set aside the tails, crush the trimmings, and add the juice thus obtained to the shrimp cooking water. Strain everything and boil it down until you have about 3/4 cup of liquid. Put the peeled mushrooms in a saucepan along with 2 scant tablespoons of the butter and a little lemon juice. Let this all cook.

Melt 1 cup of butter and stir in the flour. Cook until the flour is lightly browned, then stir in the milk and the concentrated shellfish liquid. Boil these together to reduce again, then add the cream, the rest of the butter, the mushrooms, oysters, and shrimp tails. Keep this mixture warm in a double boiler or a hot water bath until serving time.

At serving time, fill the hot patty shells with the mixture.

Bouchées or patty shells, prepared in this way, are vastly superior to those one buys commercially.

HUITRES FRITES

Fried Oysters

For twelve people, use:

2 C. *velouté maigre*[1]
2 C. fish jelly[2]
48 plump oysters[3]
6 lemons
4 eggs
4 egg yolks
dry, sifted breadcrumbs
cream
flour
parsley

Open the oysters and save the juice.

In a saucepan put the velouté, the fish jelly, and the strained and reduced oyster liquid. Thicken the mixture with the egg yolks and the cream in order to obtain a thick *chaud-froid*.[4]

Beat the four whole eggs.

**Bouchées* are tiny vol-au-vents. One may also use the term *bouchées* for those tiny culinary preparations whose covering is made of dough and which contain animal flesh: fish, chicken, game, etc.

Coat the oysters with the *chaud-froid* sauce, roll them lightly in flour, dip them in the beaten eggs, and finally roll them in bread-crumbs and drop into boiling oil. As soon as the coating is golden brown, remove them.

At serving time, reheat them a second in the hot oil, arrange them on a serving platter, and garnish with some fried parsley and some lemon halves.

NOTES

1. To prepare a *velouté maigre*, take some fish broth (made by boiling in slightly salted, aromatized water, some vegetables, and whiting or conger eel, for instance, along with heads and bones and fish trimmings), flavor it to taste with some white wine, aromatic vegetables, spices, mushrooms, and thicken this with some *beurre manié** or with a roux. Boil the sauce down to strengthen it, and skim it well.

2. To make a fish jelly, use water, white wine, fish and fish trimmings with bones, a calf's foot, vegetables, a *bouquet garni*, onions, shallots, garlic, spices, aromatics, salt, and pepper to taste. Boil these well then strain and clarify.

3. It is not necessary to use the very choicest oysters. Above all they must be plump.

4. In a general way *chaud-froid* sauces are made with equal quantities of either brown or white sauce (based on animal consommés) and with either a brown or white jelly.

For fish, mollusks, and crustaceans (shellfish), one uses either a *velouté*, an *allemande*, or a *suprême* sauce made with seafood and some fish jelly.

Chaud-froid sauces for white meats are made with either a *velouté*, an *allemande*, or a *suprême* sauce and some light-colored jelly.

Chaud-froid sauces for red meats are made with *espagnole* sauce and a brown jelly.

For game, one uses an *espagnole* sauce with game stock and a game jelly.

HUITRES EN ASPIC

Oysters in Aspic

Prepare a good fish aspic jelly by cooking fish or fish trimmings (such as whiting or pike) in some veal broth; clarify it.

Pour a little of this jelly in some small molds, then put in one or several oysters (which have been blanched in their own juices), and top with some mustard mayonnaise flavored or not with lobster eggs. Cover with more jelly and continue these layers until the molds are filled. Let them set in the refrigerator.

Unmold just before serving.

These same aspics may be prepared with shrimp or crayfish tails, sea urchin coral, mussels, etc.

All these aspics make very appetizing hors-d'oeuvre.

One may also use them as a garnish around cold fish in aspic, which will enhance the richness of the dish.

COQUILLES SAINT-JACQUES

Scallops (First Recipe)

For four people, use:

½ lb. mushrooms
1 C. dry white wine
7 T. butter
1 oz. brandy
2 heaping T. flour
4 whole scallops in their shells
1 onion
1 shallot
bouquet garni **(parsley, thyme, bay leaf)**
dry, sifted breadcrumbs
parsley
lemon juice
salt and pepper

Pecten maximus and *Pecten jacobaeus*, popularly known in France as *coquilles Saint-Jacques* and as scallops in England and America, are bi-valve mollusks (Pectinidae family). Their flesh is very delicate.

Here is one of the best ways of preparing them.

Open the shells and save the juices. Wash the scallops several times in cool water. Remove the black parts; set aside, separately, the white part, the coral, and the beards.

Using nine-tenths of the wine and brandy, cook the white part and the coral with the *bouquet garni*, onion, and some salt and pepper. Remove them when they are cooked and add the beards and cook these.

Strain the cooking liquid.

Cut the white and the coral into fairly large pieces.

Set aside the beards.

Cook the mushrooms in part of the butter with a little salt and some lemon juice.

Chop finely or grind the beards, mushrooms, and parsley.

In a saucepan, put some butter, the flour, and the chopped shallot. Let these cook until lightly browned. Add sufficient cooking liquid along with the strained juices from the scallops, then put in the chopped or ground beards, mushrooms, and parsley. This constitutes a stuffing. Using the deeper of the two shells of each scallop, butter them, place one-fourth of the white and the coral in each shell, on top spoon one-fourth of the stuffing, sprinkle with sifted breadcrumbs, and dot the top with butter. Sprinkle on the rest of the mixed wine and brandy.

Brown them in the oven for ten minutes.

COQUILLES SAINT-JACQUES

Scallops (Second Recipe)

For four people, use:

1 C. white wine
5 oz. mushrooms
1/2 C. cream
3 1/2 T. butter
3 1/2 T. flour
8 scallops
3 shallots
breadcrumbs
salt and pepper

Open the shells and detach the scallops. Wash them in several changes of cold water. Remove the black parts and the beards. Set aside, separately, the white muscle and the coral. Cut up the muscles, leave the coral whole, and cook these in 2 tablespoons of the butter. Then add the chopped shallots, the flour, the beards, and the mushrooms which have been peeled and minced. Stir these all together for a moment or two then add the white wine and season with salt and pepper to taste. Let this all cook together for about ten minutes, then reduce the cooking liquid.

Now stir in the cream and simmer the sauce without letting it boil.

Fill the 4 deeper shells with the mixture. Sprinkle with breadcrumbs and dot with the remaining butter. Brown in the oven.

RAGOÛT DE COQUILLES SAINT-JACQUES

Ragoût of Scallops

For four servings, use:

1 C. tomato sauce
4 T. butter
3 T. brandy
1 T. chopped parsley
1/2 clove garlic
8 scallops (whole in the shell) or 1 lb. if using only the muscle
Parmesan or Gruyère cheese
salt and pepper
paprika

Remove the scallops from their shells. Wash them thoroughly under cold running water.

In one-half the above amount of butter gently cook the cut up white muscles and the coral. Flame with the brandy, season to taste with salt and pepper, add the minced garlic and the tomato sauce. Let this all cook for about ten minutes. Then add the chopped parsley and continue cooking for several more minutes. Add paprika to taste.

Fill the shells with the ragoût, sprinkle on the cheese and dot with the remaining butter. Brown in the oven.

COQUILLES SAINT-JACQUES FROIDES

Cold Scallops

Remove the mollusks from their shells, wash them under cold water, then cook the white muscle and the coral in white wine, flavored with shallots and aromatics, and seasoned with salt and pepper. Remove the white and the coral and slice the white flesh. Boil down the cooking liquid to reduce it. Strain and cool.

Fill the deep shells with the white meat, the coral, and some slices of hard-boiled egg; coat with a plain mayonnaise or a mayonnaise to which you have added some of the concentrated cooking liquid.

This is an excellent hors-d'oeuvre.

MOULES[1] AU NATUREL

Plain Mussels

For four people, use:

3 qts. mussels
parsley
salt and pepper

Scrape the mussels thoroughly one by one. Throw away any that will not close, as they are dead. Wash the rest until the water remains absolutely clear. Drain them.

In a saucepan put the mussels, some parsley, and some salt and pepper to taste. Toss everything together so that the mussels cook very rapidly. This should take four or five minutes. Remove the mussels and keep them warm in a covered dish. Strain the water through a cloth and allow it to settle; then pour it off leaving any residue behind.

Serve the mussels in the dish and the juices separately.

This is the simplest way of preparing mussels.

NOTE

1. *Mytilus edulis;* Mytilidae family.

MOULES AU CITRON

Mussels with Lemon

For four people, use:

2 carrots
5 T. butter
6 shallots
3 T. flour
3 qts. mussels
4 lemons
bouquet garni
salt, pepper, *quatre épices**

Clean the mussels as in the preceding recipe.

Cook the minced carrots and shallots in 2 tablespoons of butter along with the *bouquet garni*. Season with salt, pepper, and *quatre épices*.

De-glaze the pan with the lemon juice, then add the mussels and cook them rapidly, tossing them all the while. Keep them warm.

Cook the flour in 2 tablespoons of butter until it is lightly browned. To this add the mussel liquid which has been strained and decanted. Let this mixture cook for a moment or two, and, last of all, enrich it with the rest of the butter.

Arrange the mussels in a deep serving dish after removing the top shell from each one.

Serve the sauce separately in a sauceboat.

Mussels go very well with lemon.

MOULES À LA CRÈME

Mussels with Cream

For four people, use:

1/2 lbs. mushrooms
1 C. cream
1/2 C. butter
1 medium carrot
4 T. flour
3 qts. mussels
vinegar (optional)
bouquet garni
salt and pepper

Clean and scrub the mussels thoroughly.

Peel and chop the mushrooms.

Cook the thinly sliced carrot with the *bouquet garni* in 3 tablespoons of the butter for about one-half hour. Season with salt and pepper, then add the mussels and make them open by tossing the pan for the necessary length of time to cook them. Keep them warm.

In another saucepan put a few tablespoons of butter and add the chopped mushrooms and let them render their water. Stir in the flour without letting it brown, then add the water released from the mussels, which has been strained through a cloth. Let this cook for a few minutes. Last, enrich the sauce with the rest of the butter and the cream, taste and add some vinegar if you like it.

After having removed one shell from each mussel arrange them in a serving dish or in individual plates, coat them with the sauce and serve.

Creamed mussels are delicious and are a good dish for shellfish lovers.

SUÇARELLE DE MOULES

For four people, use:

7 T. cream
7 T. butter
1 1/2 C. dry, sifted breadcrumbs
7 T. tomato purée
1 medium clove minced garlic
3 qts. mussels
4 anchovies
2 egg yolks
1 medium onion
milk
salt, pepper, paprika

Pound the anchovies with 3 1/2 tablespoons of the butter and force them through a sieve.

Scrub the mussels, put them in a saucepan with three-fourths of the garlic and toss them over a hot fire until they open. Remove them from their shells, but set aside a few in their half shells. Slightly reduce the juice given off by the mussels, strain, let it settle, then decant the top part of the clear liquid and set aside.

In some butter cook the minced onion with the rest of the garlic. Add the anchovy butter, the tomato purée, the breadcrumbs (which have been soaked in milk, drained, and pressed dry), salt, pepper, and paprika. Now add enough mussel water to make a fairly thin sauce. Cook this for about fifteen to twenty minutes.

At the last minute thicken it with the cream and the egg yolk, without letting it boil. Add the mussels and the rest of the butter, heat up for an instant and serve on a dish garnished with the mussels on the half shell.

You may prepare another type of *suçarelle* by substituting *ailloli* for the cream and the egg yolks. This is suitable for garlic lovers.

Ailloli is a mayonnaise to which has been added a greater or lesser quantity of garlic, according to taste.

In either case, to vary, one may brown the dish in the oven after having sprinkled it with a mixture of dry, sifted breadcrumbs and grated cheese.

MOULES SAUTÉES PANÉES

Sautéed Breaded Mussels

For four people, use:

2 C. dry, sifted breadcrumbs
2/3 C. butter
7 T. cream
1 very small onion
1 T. chopped parsley
3 qts. mussels
salt and pepper

Put the thoroughly cleaned mussels in a saucepan and make them open up over high heat in a heavy pan. Throw away those that remain closed. Remove the top shell of all the others and keep the mussels hot.

Mince the onion very finely with a knife which has been rubbed on a clove of garlic to flavor it slightly. Cook the onions until golden brown in a frying pan with some butter, then add the breadcrumbs and let them get the same golden color as the onions. Season with salt and pepper, sprinkle on the chopped parsley, then add the mussels and toss everything together for about ten to twelve minutes. Then add the cream and continue tossing until the cream has been absorbed.

All the ingredients must become attached to the inside of the mussel shells.

Serve hot without any sauce.

Breaded, sautéed mussels thus prepared must remain tender under a slightly resistant coating.

MOULES FRITES

Fried Mussels

Use nice large mussels, clean them thoroughly, and open them up over a hot flame in a heavy pan. Remove them from their shells, roll them in flour, and drop them, just like that, into a hot olive-oil bath.

Serve at once, as is, or accompanied by a hollandaise sauce seasoned to taste.

In Constantinople, where I tasted fried mussels for the first time, they are served as an hors-d'oeuvre, along with a glass of *mastic*.[1]

Oysters may be prepared in the same way.

NOTE

1. *Mastic* is the resin of the *Pistachia lentiscus*. The alcoholic infusion of this resin, very choice in the East, has a taste reminiscent of *anisette*.

ORMEAUX

Abalone

The *ormeaux*, or Haliotidae, scientifically known as the *Haliotis tuberculata*, are gastropod mollusks which live in rock crevasses and can rarely be caught except during spring tides. In France they are mainly found on the Brittany coast. (In California, the abalone is represented by various species of "ear shells" or *ormers*, such as *Haliotis splendens, Haliotis rufescens,* and *Haliotis cracherodii*, etc.)

They may be sautéed or prepared in a ragoût.

In either case, they must first be removed from their shells, the intestine must be cut off (which is easily done with a knife), and then they must be washed several times and well brushed to remove any remaining black parts. Last, they are pounded with a wooden mallet to tenderize them.

When one wishes to sauté them, they are first cooked in salted water for one hour, then they are dried and allowed to cool. They are then sautéed in a frying pan with some butter for about fifteen minutes and lightly salted.

When one wishes to prepare them in a ragoût, they are simmered for one and a half to two hours with some butter, onions, carrots, salt, and pepper to taste, in water or, better yet, some fish broth.

Certain people feel that ragoût of abalone is more digestible than the sautéed abalones. Prepared either way, however, abalones are a dish which, in Paris, is not commonplace.

ESCARGOTS EN COQUILLES

Snails in Their Shells

The snail is a gastropod mollusk of the Helicidae family. The choicest species are those large, fat, white snails known as *Helix pomatia.*

Certain people refuse to think of snails as edible because they are often hard and indigestible and they get a feeling similar to that produced by chewing on a piece of rubber. Others declare that the seasoning alone makes them passable. In reality, however, the snail is delicate, which is precisely why it is important to prepare it with care; otherwise it loses its taste very easily. Properly cooked and aromatized with well-chosen condiments in proper quantities, the snail is savory, tender, and digestible. One of my friends who has a delicate stomach, having prepared snails precisely according to the method outlined below, and, having found them delicious, let himself go so far as to eat 4 dozen of them and was surprised to find that he had no ill effects from his imprudence.

Realize, first of all, that it is important to prepare the snails the day before one is going to eat them. They then have a chance to absorb the seasonings and have a much better flavor than when prepared the same day.

For six people, use:

- ½ lb. unsalted butter
- ½ C. dry white wine
- 10 T. coarse salt
- 4 T. chopped parsley
- 3 tsp. table salt
- 1 medium clove garlic
- freshly ground black pepper to taste
- 72 big fat burgundy snails (if possible) (preferably vine snails)
- well-seasoned court bouillon prepared with water, salt, pepper, carrots, parsnips, garlic, thyme, bay leaf, and parsley

If you are preparing them in winter the snails will have fasted and will be covered with a film. Remove this film and soak the snails in coarse salt for one hour, then wash them five or six times in cold water, changing the water each time. If you are preparing them in another season, start off by letting them fast for two days and then proceed as above.

Cook the court bouillon for thirty minutes. Put in the snails and cook them for one hour. Let them cool in the liquid. Remove them from the court bouillon, take the bodies out of the shells, wash the bodies and the shells in hot, salted water, and dry them. If necessary, remove any black portion (which is the intestine), which in summer tends to have an earthy taste.

Mash together the butter, parsley, table salt, garlic, and freshly ground pepper. Mix these well so as to get an absolutely smooth paste.

Put the mollusks back in their shells and pack in the seasoned butter.

At serving time, place the snails, opening up, in an oven-proof dish in which you have placed a little water to avoid having the shells or the dish burn. Sprinkle each snail with a little dry white wine, with a dropper, and heat this over a slow fire until the butter begins to boil in the shells. At this point the garlic is cooked and everything is ready.

Serve at once with special forks and special tongs *ad hoc*, so that your guests will not soil or burn their fingers.

Serve some Chablis in glasses and you will hear praise.

ESCARGOTS EN BROCHETTES

Skewered Snails

Prepare the snails as in the preceding recipe. Let them cool in the court bouillon, remove them from the shells, and remove the intestines.

Thread the snails on skewers alternately with small squares of lean bacon.

Prepare a snail butter as in the preceding recipe. Melt it. Soak the skewers so that everything is well impregnated with the seasoned butter, then roll in some dry, sifted breadcrumbs and broil them under the broiler or on a grill, basting them with the rest of the melted butter.

Serve very hot.

FISH

MATELOTE AU BLANC[1]

Fish Stew

Cut fish up into small chunks.

Make a roux with the butter and flour; add the *bouquet garni* and the whole onions. Stir in the water and the wine and season to taste with salt and pepper. Cook these for one hour.

Then add the fish; warm and light the brandy and pour it over the fish. Cook the fish chunks according to size. Fifteen minutes before serving add the mushrooms and strengthen with the fish broth or the meat glaze.

At the last minute fry some little slices of bread in the rest of the butter.

Remove the *bouquet garni*, strain the sauce if you do not wish to have the onions; arrange the *matelote* in a serving dish, garnish

For six people, use:

2 lbs. fresh-water fish[2]
2 C. dry white wine[3]
1 C. water
1/2 lb. mushrooms
1/2 lbs. fish roe
1/4 lb. butter
2 small onions
1/4 C. brandy
3 T. flour
6 slices white bread cut in half
6 crayfish
fish broth or, alternatively, meat glaze
bouquet garni
salt and pepper

with the croûtons, the crayfish, and the fish roes which have been cooked separately, and serve.

Matelote of pike is made in the same way: it is delicious.

By substituting cider for the white wine and Calvados for the brandy, one would have a *Matelote Normande* or Normandy Fish Stew. One could use other types of fish, such as sole, conger eel, or red gurnet.

NOTES

1. *Matelote* is a fish stew made with either red or white wine and fresh-water fish.
2. Fish such as eel, carp, bass, chub, gar, muskellunge, perch, pickerel, whitefish, etc., or a mixture of several of these.
3. If the wine used is quite bitter or acid, it is advisable to sweeten it with a little sugar.

MATELOTE AU VIN ROUGE

Fish Stew with Red Wine

For six people, use:

2 lbs. fresh-water fish[1]
1 lb. fish heads, bones, trimmings
1 3/4 C. good burgundy wine
1/2 lb. mushrooms
1/2 lb. soft roes and fish eggs
1/4 lb. or 8 T. butter
1 small minced onion
3 T. brandy
2 T. flour
2 C. water
12 small slices bread (French-type long loaf)
6 crayfish
bouquet garni **(parsley, thyme, 1/2 bay leaf)**
garlic to taste
salt and pepper

Clean and peel the mushrooms and set aside the trimmings.

Cut the fish up into chunks.

Prepare a fish stock by cooking together, covered, the fish trimmings, onion, garlic, mushroom peelings, *bouquet garni*, salt, pepper, wine, and water, for about one hour. Strain through a cloth.

Make a roux with some butter and flour. Add the fish stock to this, stirring until smooth; then put in the fish, flame it with the brandy, and cook. Fifteen minutes before serving add the mushrooms.

Arrange the *matelote* in a serving dish, garnish with the slices of bread which have been browned in the rest of the butter, the crayfish, soft roes, and fish eggs which have been cooked separately, and serve.

The *meurette* is a *matelote* made with red wine. The fish are flambéed in a brandy made from grape husks and it is thickened with a white *beurre manie*. It is garnished with croûtons of French bread, cut into squares, dried in the oven, rubbed with garlic, and spread with butter.

NOTE

1. You could use freshwater eel, bream, pike or carp.

FRITURE DE LAITANCES, SAUCE MOUTARDE

Fried Milts (Soft Roes), Mustard Sauce

For twelve people, use:

1.

36 herring milts or 12 carp milts

2. For the batter

1 C. light beer or warm water
1 C. flour
2 T. olive oil or melted butter
½ tsp. salt
2 eggs

3. For the sauce

1¼ C. hot water
6 T. butter
3 T. heavy cream
3 T. wholewheat flour
2½ tsp. table salt
1 T. tarragon or *fines herbes* mustard
1 dash vinegar or lemon juice
½ tsp. dry mustard
freshly ground pepper to taste

Prepare a light batter with the batter ingredients.

Break the eggs and separate yolks from whites. Set whites aside. Mix everything else together so as to obtain a smooth, lumpless batter having the consistency of boiled custard. Let this rest for one hour.

Beat the egg whites until stiff and fold them into the batter just before using.

Dip the milts in the batter and fry them in very hot fat and serve with a hot mustard sauce, which is simply a plain white sauce with mustard added.

Start by making a plain white sauce. In a saucepan put four tablespoons of butter, the flour, salt and pepper. Heat, stirring well, then add the water and cook it for about ten minutes. Add the rest of the butter in small pieces, then the cream and the vinegar or lemon juice, and heat it a little, stirring constantly until the butter is completely melted.

To make a mustard sauce, blend the two types of mustard with the vinegar or lemon juice and add it to the white sauce above.

By substituting, for the plain white, an *allemande* sauce, one would obtain a far superior mustard sauce. Here is how to prepare it: Cook some butter and flour together without browning, add fish fumet or some veal or chicken stock, then thicken with the egg yolks and finish off the sauce with mustard, salt, and cayenne to taste. Strain before serving.

SAUCISSON MAIGRE

Fish Sausage

For twelve people, use:

2 lbs. fresh-water eel
1½ lb. hake
2 ½ C. dry, sifted breadcrumbs (with a little bit of the crust left on)
1 live female lobster weighing about 1¼ lbs.
table salt
freshly ground black pepper

Grind the raw fish separately (eel and hake) after removing the bones. Mix them together and grind again. Mix in the breadcrumbs and grind once more. Season with salt and pepper to taste and work the mixture to a smooth, well-blended paste.

Cook the lobster for ten minutes in a court bouillon made with white wine (see recipe for *Salmis de homard à la Crème*). Let it cool in the liquid, then remove the eggs; and, after having forced them through a fine sieve, mix them with the fish hash. Dice the lobster meat.

Take two sausage casings (beef guts in this case) and fill them with this hash, alternating it with the diced lobster meat. Tie and

cook the sausages for twenty-five minutes in the lobster court bouillon.

Let them cool in the liquid.

As a variation, one may substitute shrimp tails for the lobster meat.

One may also prepare, in the same way, some very small fish sausages to be eaten hot, with or without a garnish.

PIES

Tourtes, which are precursors of the vol-au-vents, are low pastry shells which may be filled with decorated forcemeats, ragoûts, godiveaux (forcemeats made with veal and beef kidney), quenelles, fish, foie gras, morels, etc.

Originally *tourtes* were made of bread dough. Today they are made of plain pastry, as are timbales, and about the same height as timbales with or without a cover or lid; or they are made of puff pastry with a covering lid.

The name *tourtes* is also applied to preparations containing fruit mixtures, fruit jams, and cream served in a pie crust and glazed with syrup.

TOURTE MAIGRE

Seafood Tourte

For six people, use:

1. For the crust

4 C. (1 lb.) sifted flour
1 lb. butter (unsalted)
1 C. water
2 tsp. salt
1 egg yolk

2. For the filling

24 nicely shaped small mushrooms
18 tiny salmon quenelles
8 carp milts
6 scallops
fish stock
butter
lemon juice

3. For the Nantua sauce

1¾ C. milk
1 cup (scant) heavy cream

Preparing the crust. With the first group of ingredients make a puff pastry. Pour the flour out on the table in a cone shape. Make a crater at the point and put in the salt and a little water. Start to mix this with the fingers, adding water little by little. Work the dough quickly, pressing it with the tips of the fingers and pushing it away with the heel of the hand. Fold it over itself and keep work-it with the heel of the hand. When it is smooth but not yet elastic, roll it into a bowl and let it rest and expand. Roll it out with a rolling pin into an eight- or ten-inch-square of even thickness. Spread the butter out onto this (either having softened or cooled it according to the season). The butter must have about the same consistency as the dough. Make sure it is evenly spread over the whole dough, then fold the dough in four by bringing the four sides in toward the center so as to completely enclose the butter.

With the rolling pin, roll the dough to a width of eight inches and a thickness of about one-half inch, making it as long as possible without tearing it. Fold it in thirds along the width, like a napkin: this is the first turn. Fold it again in the other direction: this will be the second turn. You now have nine layers of dough. Let it rest in a cool place for at least ten minutes. Roll it out again, in the same way as before but in the opposite direction from the first time—and give it two more turns. Let it rest another ten minutes. Then roll it out a third time, always in the opposite direction, and give it two more turns. It will now have had six turns. Let it rest ten minutes.

Now roll it out to a thickness of one and one-quarter inches and a length of twenty inches. Cut a one-inch-wide strip. Divide the rest of the dough into two parts. Give each part two turns and roll it out. Cut an eight-inch-diameter circle from each piece. One will be the bottom and one the top.

Arrange one of the circles in a pie plate and wet the rim of the dough. Stick the strip of pastry to the rim, pressing it down firmly so it really adheres. On the bottom place a piece of buttered paper and on top of this a wad of paper to fill the cavity coming to above the rim. Set the cover on the paper and press it against the rim, flattening the rim slightly with the fingers and indenting it lightly. Decorate the cover, brush on some egg yolks beaten with a little water, and bake in a moderate oven.

Preparing the filling: Make some quenelles weighing about one ounce each of salmon forcemeat and also some quenelles of the same size made of mousseline forcemeat using whiting and shrimp.[1]

6 T. butter
1 medium carrot
1/3 C. flour
1/2 small onion
18 crayfish
bouquet garni **(celery, parsley, thyme, bay leaf)**
salt and pepper

NOTE

1. See quenelles recipe in this section.

Cook the first quenelles in the oven, poach the others in salted water.

Open the scallops, wash them several times in cold water, remove the black parts, then cook the mollusks in a good fish stock.

Poach the carp milts in the same broth then boil down the liquid to reduce it drastically.

Cook the peeled mushrooms in some butter with the lemon juice.

Preparing the sauce. Grind or mince the carrot and onion. Put them in a saucepan with 4 tablespoons of butter, the mushroom peelings, the *bouquet garni,* and the salt and pepper. Simmer over a very low fire then stir in the flour and cook several minutes without browning. Add the boiling milk and let the sauce simmer. Add the mushroom liquid (if there is any), the concentrated fish broth, and the cream. Reduce this sauce until it is thick enough to coat a spoon. Taste.

Cook the crayfish as for the Crayfish Hors-d'oeuvres (see recipe) and shell them.

With the rest of the butter and the trimmings make a crayfish butter.

Force half the crayfish tails through a fine sieve and set aside the purée.

Strain the sauce, add the purée to it along with the crayfish butter. Add the rest of the crayfish tails either split in two or sliced.

Presentation. When the pastry case is cooked, unstick the cover and remove all the paper. Now fill it with the quenelles, the scallops, the carp milts, the mushrooms and the Nantua sauce.

Serve hot.

Vol-au-vents

The vol-au-vent is a triumph of French baking. Its creation goes back much more than a century and a half. It consists of a crust of extreme lightness, to which it owes its name ("gone with the wind"), made in a very special way and filled with a *salpicon* (type of hash).

Vol-au-vents are prepared with fish or with meat.

Here is a recipe for a pretty seafood vol-au-vent.

VOL-AU-VENT DE CARÊME

Vol-au-vent for Lent

For eight people, use:

1. For the crust

3½ C. flour
2 C. butter
1 C. water
2 tsp. table salt

2. For the filling

1 oz. raw lobster eggs
24 quenelles made with pike and crayfish (medium-sized, made as in the quenelles recipe)
24 pink shrimp
24 plump oysters
24 mushrooms
1 small lobster
truffles (optional)
champagne
butter
lemon juice
salt and pepper

First prepare a puff pastry as in the recipe before the last.

Roll this pastry out to a one-quarter-inch thickness.

On a baking sheet place a thin layer of plain pastry[1] and brush it lightly with butter. Then, using a round plate or a pan of some sort having a scalloped edge, cut an eight-inch circle of puff pastry with a pointed knife, holding the knife at a slight angle so that the bottom of the pastry will be ever so slightly smaller than the top surface. Lay this circle (smaller surface down) on the protective layer of plain pastry. One can thus obtain a very uniform vol-au-vent.

Brush the top of the puff pastry with egg yolk beaten with water and make a slight incision one-sixteenth of an inch deep, about one-eighth of an inch inside the edge of the dough, to form a cover.

Put it to bake in a hot (425°) oven, then lift out the cover and pluck out the insides of the casing, shoring up the side walls with some of the removed dough if necessary.

At the same time prepare the filling: cook, in a good court bouillon made with wine, the lobster and shrimp. Shell them and set aside the trimmings. Dice the lobster tail meat but keep the shrimps whole. In the same court bouillon cook the lobster eggs.

Blanch the oysters in their own juices, strain the liquid, and boil it down. Set aside.

Peel the mushrooms, rub them with lemon juice, and cook them in butter.

Cook the truffles in the champagne and mince them.

Keep everything warm.

Prepare a Béchamel sauce with fish broth, substituting shellfish butter for the ordinary butter. Spark up the color with the lobster eggs, which have been forced through a sieve with a wooden pestle. Stir in the truffle cooking liquid, the oyster water; taste and complete the seasoning so that you have a fairly spicy seasoning.

Mix the sauce with the quenelles, the shrimp tails, the oysters, the lobster meat, the mushrooms, and the truffles.

Set the vol-au-vent shell quickly in the open hot oven and fill it immediately. Serve hot.

This vol-au-vent, it seems to me, is worthy of a conclave.

To vary, one could prepare, in the same vein, a vol-au-vent whose filling would contain salmon quenelles, filets of sole poached in white wine, mushrooms cooked in butter with lemon juice, sliced or diced rock lobster tails, and sliced lobster—everything mixed with a *sauce suprême* or a lobster sauce.

One can also prepare a much simpler vol-au-vent. For that, all one has to do is to omit some of the preceding ingredients and substitute less expensive ingredients.

NOTE

1. The ingredients for the plain pastry are as follows:

1 C. flour
7 T. butter
4 T. (approximately) water
1 tsp. salt

CAVIAR[1]

For eight people, use:

1/2 lb. caviar
1/2 lb. fresh Dutch cheese
1/2 C. madeira wine
1/4 lb. (8 T.) butter
1/4 C. Curaçao
1 loaf firm sandwich bread, unsliced

Caviar is generally served as an hors-d'oeuvre, either alone or with some lemon juice and buttered bread. It is often presented in a hollowed-out block of ice and garnished with lemon slices. One may also serve it on canapés. Here is such a recipe:

Mash the butter and cheese together. Add the madeira wine and the Curaçao, and blend everything well.

Cut the bread into one-half-inch slices, shape them into squares and diamonds with sides two and a half inches in length. Make twenty-four of them. Spread the prepared butter mixture on them and add the caviar on top. Serve cold.

Oyster canapés can also be made in this same way.

NOTE

1. Caviar, which is imported from Russia and Roumania, consists of the salted eggs of the sturgeon *Acipenser sturio* or of the sterlet *Acipenser ruthenus*, fish of the Acipenseridae family.

BROCHET[1] À LA GELÉE

Jellied Pike

Prepare this dish the day before it is to be eaten; it will only be the better for it.

Scale the pike, gut it, wipe it carefully, and, if you wish to retain all its flavor, do not wash it either inside or out.

Prepare enough wine court bouillon to completely cover the fish (eighty percent good white wine and twenty percent red wine), seasoned and flavored with a *bouquet garni*, onion, carrot, shallot, garlic, spices, and aromatics to taste. Season with salt and peppercorns.

Simmer the fish in this. Remove it to a platter and coat it with the reduced cooking liquid mixed with jelly made from a calf's foot cooked with vegetables and then clarified. Let this set and then decorate with slices of lemon and some nasturtiums.

The quality of the jelly depends primarily on the quality of the wines used. While it is not necessary to use great wines, which would be sacrilegious, I nevertheless recommend using a good quality wine.

Generally, jellied pike is served without a sauce; however, there is no reason why one could not pass a sauceboat of plain cold *rémoulade* sauce or a green *rémoulade* sauce, or a *sauce gribiche*, for example.

Plain cold *rémoulade* sauce is a mayonnaise to which has been added a mixture of minced shallot, chopped pickles, capers and mustard.

To prepare an ordinary mayonnaise (which is an emulsion of oil and egg yolks), put two fresh egg yolks in a bowl and work with a wooden spoon, adding some good olive oil little by little while stirring constantly. Alternate the oil with a few drops of lemon juice or vinegar and salt the mixture as you go. When you have enough sauce, add a few drops of vinegar, mix well, taste, and complete the seasoning to taste with salt, pepper, and lemon juice.

One may also substitute some chopped lemon pulp for the lemon juice.

Sauce gribiche is a *rémoulade* sauce to which one has added some hard-boiled eggs, the yolks of which have been pounded with the oil and the whites cut into fine julienne strips and added at the last.

One obtains variations of the *rémoulade* by adding to the preceding *rémoulade* some garlic, *fines herbes*, anchovies, etc.

Cold green *rémoulade* is an ordinary *rémoulade* colored with spinach juice.

Carps, as well as pike, may be prepared in jelly. The only difference would be in the proportions of wines used in the court bouillon. For carp one would use eighty percent red wine and twenty percent white wine.

Trout may also be prepared in the same way and most particularly salmon trout, char, lavaret,[1] the basses,[2] and salmon. In these cases, however, it is preferable to make the court bouillon with white wine alone and to serve the fish with a green sauce made by coloring mayonnaise with spinach juice.

NOTES

1. *Coregonus lavaretus*, Salmonidae family.
2. *Labrax lupus and Labrax nigrescens*, Percidae family.

BROCHET FARCI, BRAISÉ AU CIDRE

Stuffed Pike, Braised in Cider

For four people, use:

1⅓ C. good cider
1 C. fish stock
1 lb. 7 oz. salmon
¼ lb. mushrooms
1 large carrot
5 T. butter
1 small onion
4 tsp. port wine
1 T. flour
few sprigs parsley
pinch thyme
2 eggs
1 pike, weighing about 2 lbs.
curry
dry, sifted breadcrumbs
fines herbes
salt and pepper

Make a good forcemeat with the fresh boneless and skinless salmon, the peeled mushrooms, *fines herbes*, some dry, sifted breadcrumbs, the port wine, some curry powder to taste, and salt and pepper. Bind the mixture with one egg and one egg yolk.

Scale, gut and trim the pike. Stuff it with the above mixture.

In 4 teaspoons of butter cook the minced carrots and onion, without letting them brown. Add the cider and the fish stock along with the washed mushroom peelings, the salmon trimmings, the aromatics and the parsley. Cook these for a half hour. Strain, cool, and skim the fat off the liquid.

Arrange the pike on the buttered rack of a fish pan or in any type of ovenproof and fireproof pan with a rack in it. Pour the cooled liquid over it and start the cooking on top of the stove over a hot flame. Then put the pan in the oven to braise for another twenty minutes, basting frequently.

When the fish is cooked, remove it, strain the cooking liquid, and reduce it over a high flame.

Blend the flour into 4 teaspoons of butter and cook them together without browning. Blend in some of the reduced cooking liquid, reduce it a little further, and, last of all, enrich the sauce with the rest of the butter.

Arrange the pike on a hot serving platter, coat it with a little of the sauce, garnish the platter with *barquettes* filled with creamed asparagus, some croquettes made with crayfish tails, and fried carp milts.

Serve, passing the sauce separately in a sauceboat.

One may prepare other fish in this same way: whiting, for instance, stuffed with mushrooms, carp milts, shrimp tails and *Panade à la Frangipane.*[1] The sauce would be enriched with a shrimp butter made with the trimmings and finished off the cream.

Carp may also be prepared in this same way.

NOTE

1. The recipe for *Panade à la Frangipane* may be found under the recipe for quenelles.

LES QUENELLES

Quenelles are mixtures of ingredients which are mashed and pounded, forced through a sieve, thickened, then molded.[1] Their weights and shapes are different according to their intended use. The smallest may be the size of a rooster kidney, large ones may be as large as big sausages. Quenelles for filling vol-au-vents weigh about one-third of an ounce. The weight of those used to accompany other dishes may vary from two-thirds of an ounce to an ounce and a half. Last, the large entrée quenelles served by themselves may weigh as much as three ounces.

Quenelles are shaped into cylinders (either smooth or ridged), oblongs, or flattened disks. They are served either plain or stuffed and may be decorated or not.

Classic forcemeats for fish or meat quenelles are made of one basic ingredient: crustaceans, fish, veal, fowl, or game, to which one sometimes adds a little beef kidney suet, either alone or with some veal kidney suet or beef marrow, and which one binds with eggs, *panades*, or cream.

Preparation of panades: Panades may be either based on bread, flour, rice, or potatoes.

1. *Bread panade* is made by soaking 4 ounces of stale white bread in 2/3 cup of boiling milk and 1/2 teaspoon of salt. This paste is dried out over a high flame until it no longer adheres to the spoon. Then it is spread out on a baking sheet or on a buttered platter and allowed to cool.

This *panade* is used primarily for firm forcemeats.

2. *Flour panade* may be made with or without eggs:

a. For the panade without eggs one boils 2/3 cup of water with 5 teaspoons of butter and a pinch of salt. Off the fire add 9 tablespoons of flour. This mixture is dried out over a good flame, as for a *pâte à chou*. Then it is cooled as the above bread *panade*.

This *panade* may be used for all sorts of forcemeats.

b. For the flour *panade* made with eggs, which is a very delicate *panade* known as *panade à la frangipane*, proceed as follows: in a saucepan work together 6 tablespoons of flour with 2 egg yolks, then one adds, while stirring constantly, 3 tablespoons of melted butter, a pinch of salt, a dash of pepper, and a little nutmeg to taste. Then one gently blends into this mixture 1/2 cup of boiling milk. The paste is then thickened over a low flame, while beating constantly, and it is cooked until fairly thick, which would take about eight to ten minutes.

The dough is cooled as above.

This *panade* is used most of all for forcemeats made with shellfish, fish, game, etc.

3. *Rice panade* is prepared as follows: Moisten 3/4 cup of well-washed rice with 1 1/3 cups of white stock, add 2 teaspoons of butter, then cook the rice in the oven without touching it for about forty-five minutes.

After removing it from the oven rapidly and vigorously mash the rice with a spoon; and then allow it to cool.

Rice *panade* is used in many types of forcemeats.

4. *Potato panade*, which is most often used for large white meat quenelles which are to be stuffed, is obtained by mixing 5 ounces of peeled and thinly sliced boiled potato with 1 cup of boiling milk, 4 teaspoons of butter, a pinch of salt, and a few grains of white pepper. One cooks this for fifteen minutes. *Potato panade* is used lukewarm but never cold; otherwise the purée becomes rubbery.

All the indicated quantities for the different *panades* will yield eight ounces of *panade*.

There are five different kinds of quenelle forcemeats:

1. Forcemeats made with suet or *godiveau: godiveau* moistened with meat glaze, *godiveau* with cream, and *godiveau lyonnais*.
2. *Panade* forcemeats made with butter.
3. *Panade* forcemeats made with cream.
4. Fine forcemeats with cream or *mousselines*.
5. Potato forcemeats.

Preparation of Forcemeats.

Whether the basic ingredient is seafood or meat, the proportions of the ingredients and the method of preparation remain the same for all the forcemeats.

1. *Forcemeats made with suet or godiveaux:*

a. *Godiveau made with ice.*

1½ lbs. very dry peeled beef kidney suet
1 lb. veal rump, trimmed, sinews removed
10 oz. clear ice
2½ tsp. salt
pinch white pepper
few grains nutmeg
4 eggs

Grind the veal, season it with salt, pepper, and nutmeg. Grind the beef suet. Mix the two ingredients and pound them together again until they are perfectly blended, then add the eggs one by one, pounding and mashing all the while. Force this mixture through a sieve or food mill. Spread the forcemeat in a thin layer on a platter and chill until the following day.[1]

The next day put the forcemeat back in the mortar or bowl; work it again while adding small quantities of crushed ice until everything is very smooth and blended.

Try out the forcemeat (by either poaching or baking as described further on in this recipe). If the mixture is too firm, soften it by adding a little ice water and if it is too thin give it a little more body by adding some egg white.

b. *Godiveau with cream.*

1 lb. veal rump, very white, trimmed, sinews removed
1 lb. beef kidney suet, very dry, peeled
1½ C. heavy cream
2½ tsp. salt
pinch pepper
few grains nutmeg
2 whole eggs
2 egg yolks

Grind and pound, separately, the veal and the suet. Mix the two together adding the seasoning, the eggs, and the egg yolks, one by one. Vigorously work everything together until it is smooth and well blended. Force the mixture through a sieve. Spread it out on a platter and chill it until the following day.[1]

The following day, put the forcemeat back in the chilled mortar or bowl, set it on ice, pound it again incorporating the cream, little by little. Test the forcemeat as above and rectify the consistency if necessary.

c. *Godiveau lyonnais, seafood godiveau.*

½ lb. shellfish[2] or fish[3] trimmed of skin, bones, shells, etc.
½ lb. beef kidney suet, peeled, or ¼ lb. of suet and ¼ lb. of very white beef marrow
½ lb. *panade à la frangipane* **(see previous recipe)**
1½ tsp. salt
few grains pepper
few grains nutmeg
2 egg whites

First of all pound the diced fish or shellfish, then grind and pound the suet to which you will add, little by little, the chilled *panade à frangipane* and the egg whites. Combine the two mixtures; season with salt, pepper, and nutmeg. Work the mixture vigorously with a wooden pestle and force it through a sieve and chill until ready to use.[1]

If you are using half suet and half marrow proceed in the following manner: Grind and pound the fish or shellfish, add the *panade*, the egg whites, and the seasonings to it. Force the mixture through a sieve, put it back in the mortar or bowl, and pound vigorously while adding the melted suet and the beef marrow. Chill.[1]

Godiveau quenelles are mostly used in vol-au-vents and for *garnitures financières.*

Mince the meat; pound it in a mortar with salt, pepper, and nutmeg. Remove it from the mortar. In its place put the *panade*; pound it; add the butter, the pounded meat, and work it all together until you have completely amalgamated the mixture. Then, one by one, add the eggs and the egg yolks, and force the mixture through a fine sieve into a bowl; then work it again with a spatula until it is quite smooth.

These forcemeats are used for ordinary quenelles and for decorating entrées.

Dice the meat and pound it in a mortar along with the seasonings. Little by little add the egg whites, then the *panade.* Work these vigorously together to make it smooth. Force through a fine sieve, collecting the purée in a bowl. Smooth it with a spatula and chill it for an hour. Then add one-third of the cream. Half-whip the remaining cream and add it to the forcemeat, which must be made very white, well amalgamated, and smooth.[1]

These types of forcemeats are used for very delicate quenelles.

In a mortar, put the diced meat and the salt and pepper and pound together, adding the egg whites, a small quantity at a time. Force through a fine sieve. Spread the paste on a flat dish, smooth it with a spatula, and chill it for two hours. Then gradually beat in the cream, in one bowl, which has been set into another bowl containing ice.[1]

These forcemeats are used for small quenelles, mousses, and mousselines.

Potato forcemeats are rather special and are prepared in the following manner:

Dice the veal and pound it with the seasonings. Remove it from the mortar or bowl and in its place put the lukewarm potato *panade.* Pound it thoroughly, add the veal and the butter, mashing continually. Then add the eggs and yolks, one by one, and, last, add the cold Béchamel. Force this mixture through a strainer into a bowl and work it again with a spoon or spatula until it is very velvety and smooth.[1]

These forcemeats are mainly used to make stuffed quenelles and border garnishes.

Molding quenelles.

Quenelles are molded either with a pastry bag, by hand, with a spoon, or in egg-shaped molds.

Pastry bag: the forcemeat is put into the pastry bag, equipped with either a smooth or a decorator tip, and either a large or small tip according to what size the quenelles are to be.

By hand: the forcemeat is placed on a floured board or table

2. *Forcemeats with* panade *and butter:*

1 lb. raw meat without sinews
1/2 lb. *panade* **(either flour,** *à la frangipane,* **bread or rice)**
1/2 lb. butter
1 tsp. salt
few grains white pepper
4 egg yolks
2 whole eggs
nutmeg to taste

3. *Forcemeats with* panade *and cream.*

2 3/4 C. heavy cream
1 lb. raw meat, trimmed, without sinews
3 oz. *panade à la frangipane* **(see previous recipe)**
1 1/2 tsp. salt
few grains white pepper
few grains nutmeg
2 egg whites

4. *Forcemeats with cream, or mousselines:*

2 3/4 C. heavy cream, very fresh[4]
1 lb. raw meat, trimmed, sinews removed
2 tsp. salt
few grains white pepper
1 or 2 egg whites

5. *Potato forcemeats:*

1 lb. veal rump, skin and sinews removed
1/2 lb. potato *panade* **(see previous recipe)**
10 T. butter
1/3 C. thick cold Béchamel sauce
2 tsp. salt
few grains pepper
few grains nutmeg
4 egg yolks
2 whole eggs

and rolled with the fingers to form cylinders of whatever size you wish, or they are shaped to resemble rooster kidneys.

With a spoon: the quenelles can be molded with a wet teaspoon or a soup spoon.

Large entrée quenelles are sometimes molded in either tartlet or *barquette* molds.

Whichever forcemeat is used, one must always test it before using.

Cooking the Quenelles.

Godiveau quenelles may be poached or baked in the oven. Baking is preferable. In this case one would proceed in the following manner: Put the moistened *godiveau* forcemeat into a pastry bag with a smooth tip. Press out quenelles close to one another lengthwise on buttered paper layed on buttered baking sheets. Bake them in a slow oven. When one notices a few drops of fat glistening on the surface of the quenelles they are ready. One removes them from the oven, turns them upside down on a marble surface or on a baking sheet, and, when they are lukewarm, one gently removes the paper on which they were lying. When they are completely cold they are arranged on a platter or on a wicker screen until serving time.

The other quenelles, after having been dropped into a skillet filled with barely boiling, salted water (2 teaspoons per quart), are kept at a simmer until cooked.

When they have been poached in the salted water, they are drained, then put to simmer for another ten minutes in stock or in a suitable sauce, until they have swelled.

If the quenelles are served with a thickened sauce, one puts them to swell in a closed container in a white stock with which the sauce was made.

Large quenelles, either breaded or not, or wrapped in a truffle hash, which are served as entrées with a suitable sauce, can be cooked in clarified butter.

Aside from these classic preparations one may, according to taste, change the proportion of the different ingredients. There will be other recipes for quenelles in this volume.

NOTES

1. The classic mortar and drum-sieve method for preparing quenelles is a tedious and time-consuming procedure. Nowadays, with the help of modern equipment, they can be prepared in as little as fifteen minutes.

Instead of pounding and sieving boneless fish and meats, one may (a) put them twice or three times through the finest blade of a meat grinder; (b) grind them in the very efficient Moulinex (this takes less than ten seconds per batch); or (c) use an electric blender.

An electric blender is not always satisfactory, as the presence of sinews may clog up the blades, so one of the other two methods should really be used.

In all three methods the resulting purée may be placed in an electric blender and the egg whites and/or cream, butter, etc., may be added to it and blended. Sometimes this is not altogether satisfactory; and in that case one has to revert to the wooden spoon or spatula.

Fish which may leave some remaining bone must be forced through a sieve to make sure that all the bones are carefully strained out.

Those who wish to make quenelles should experiment with the above methods and evolve the most efficient method for the ingredients they are using.

2. Shrimp, crayfish, lobster, spiny lobster.

3. Pike, carp, whiting, perch, red mullet, trout, salmon, etc.

4. The quantity of cream necessary may vary according to the freshness and thickness of the cream. One may even substitute some Béchamel sauce for part of the cream.

QUENELLES DE BROCHET ET D'ÉCREVISSES

Pike and Crayfish Quenelles

Cook the pike and crayfish[1] in a court bouillon.

Shell crayfish and set aside the tails. With some butter and the trimmings, make a crayfish butter.

In a mortar (see explanation for easier procedure under recipe for quenelles in this section) pound separately the pike and the crayfish tails. Combine them and add half of their combined weight of *panade à la frangipane* (see quenelles recipe), the crayfish butter, and four egg yolks, two whole eggs for each two pounds of forcemeat. Pound again to blend the ingredients thoroughly and to obtain a very smooth and velvety homogeneous paste which you may moisten, if necessary, with a tiny bit of the cooking liquid. Rub this mixture through a fine sieve.

With this mixture mold some quenelles, which you will poach in fish broth or salted water.

These quenelles would normally serve as a garnish for seafood dishes, timbales, and vol-au-vents made with seafood.

Pike and shrimp quenelles may be prepared in the same way.

NOTE

1. Shrimp or prawns may be substituted for crayfish; however, it must be noted that in the particular case of pike and fresh-water crayfish, the fresh-water character of the dish would be spoiled if shrimp were used.

PERCHES[1]

Perch may be prepared in various ways according to size: the smaller ones are generally broiled or fried; the medium-sized ones are more often prepared *à la meunière*; large ones are preferably stuffed and braised.

NOTE

1. *Perca fluviatilis* and *Acerina cernus*, Percidae family.

PERCHES AUX ÉCREVISSES

Perch with Crayfish

For six people, use:

½ lb. butter
1¾ C. champagne
2 oz. mushrooms
5 T. heavy cream
2 T. water
30 live crayfish
6 medium-sized perch
4 egg yolks
court bouillon for the crayfish
fish trimmings, bones, and heads
lemon juice or vinegar
salt and pepper

Scale, gut, clean, and wash the perch. Dry them.

Cook the crayfish in court bouillon, shell them, keep the tail meat warm.

Make a crayfish butter with the trimmings and 3 tablespoons of butter.

In a little of the crayfish court bouillon cook the minced mushrooms, the fish heads and bones. Boil down this fish fumet a great deal and strain it.

Spread the crayfish butter in an ovenproof dish, arrange the perch over it; pour over it the fish fumet and the champagne and bake in the oven.

Make a hollandaise sauce with the rest of the butter, the egg yolks, water, lemon juice or vinegar, some salt and pepper to taste. Whip the cream into it and at the last moment add the liquid in which the perch were cooked.

Arrange the fish on a platter, garnish with the crayfish tails, coat the whole with the sauce, and serve without delay.

Prawns or large shrimp may be substituted for the crayfish.

TRUITES[1] AU BEURRE

Trout in Butter

For four people, use:

1 C. butter
2 trout ($^1/_2$ lb. each)
1 lemon
flour
parsley
salt

River trout, and particularly trout that lives in cold water running over a granite soil, is an exceedingly delicate fish. The cooking method which is best suited for retaining its fine flavor is simply to cook it in butter, a method known as *à la meunière*. The following method is particularly suitable for medium-sized trout, weighing about one-half pound.

Clean the trout, roll it in flour. Melt $^3/_4$ cup (6 ounces) of butter without letting it brown. Add the salted trout and the juice of $^1/_4$ lemon. Let this simmer for approximately twenty minutes, turning once.

Just before serving mix the rest of the butter with some chopped parsley; heat and pour the mixture over the trout on a hot platter and garnish with the remaining lemon, sliced.

As a variation, tomato juice may be added to the pan juices. The name of this dish would then become *Truite Meunière Tomatée.*

Other fish of similar size may also be prepared in this way—bass, bream, mullet, mackerel, perch, whiting, etc.

NOTE

1. *Salmo fario,* Salmonidae family.

TRUITES AU BLEU

Trout

For six people, use:

3 C. white wine
$1^1/_3$ C. water
$^1/_4$ C. vinegar
1 small carrot, chopped
1 small onion, chopped
3 T. salt, coarse
6 sprigs parsley
1 parsley root
5 tsp. peppercorns
6 small brook trout, weighing approx. $1^1/_4$ lbs. in all

The cooking method known as *au bleu* (blue style) consists of plunging the fish in a boiling, acidified liquid, which gives it an azure tint.[1] The cooking is then continued in a court bouillon. This method is rarely used except for trout and, preferably, small brook trout, or pickerel, and carp.

Make a court bouillon with the wine, water, carrot, onion, two kinds of parsley, peppercorns, and $2^1/_2$ tablespoons of salt.

Boil this for one hour, strain and reserve liquid.

Put the rest of the salt in the vinegar. Dissolve it and bring it to a boil.

Lift out the live trout from the water by the gills; without touching the body, knock them on the head and gut them without scaling or drying them. Pass a piece of string through the fish from head to

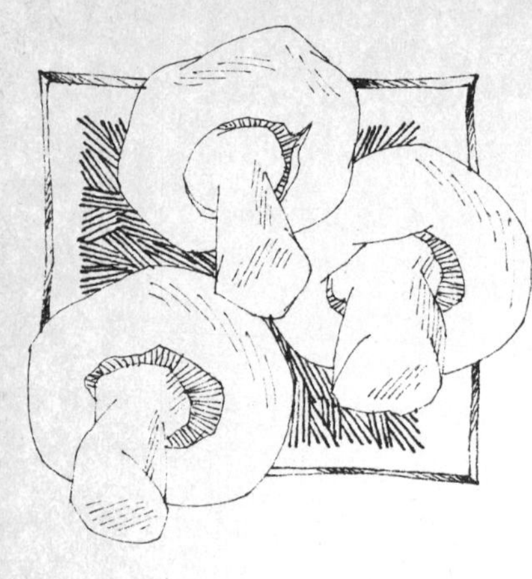

tail, using a large trussing needle, and roll the trout into a circle—head to tail—tying the two ends of the string.[2]

Put the prepared trout in a saucepan, sprinkle them quickly all over with the boiling vinegar. Their skin will immediately take on a blue color. Add the court bouillon and cook over moderate heat for fifteen minutes.

Lift out the trout, remove the string; arrange them on a hot platter and serve immediately.

Along with these, serve melted butter seasoned with lemon juice.

When one prepares a pickerel or carp in this manner, the fish, being large, needs a little more cooking time, and it is not rolled.

Fish cooked *au bleu* may also be served cold. In this case, the court bouillon is prepared exclusively with wine in order to give it more savor. The fish is allowed to cool in the broth. It is then served with a vinaigrette sauce. Below is a recipe for vinaigrette sauce, of which there are many variations.

Use:

1 C. olive oil
1/3 C. wine vinegar
1/2 small onion, minced
5 T. chopped parsley
4 T. chervil, chives, tarragon, chopped
2 T. capers
salt
pepper

Blend the ingredients opposite together thoroughly and serve in a sauceboat.

Red wine may be substituted for the white wine in the court bouillon, but the dish is more appetizing with white wine.

NOTES

1. Where does this blue tint come from? The question has not yet been answered. What is known for sure is that this color only occurs with fish which are alive and still coated with their organic slime.

2. The string is not indispensable for rolling the fish into a circle. The fish will do this of its own accord in the hot court bouillon. The string, however, gives it a more even shape.

TRUITE SAUMONÉE[1] À LA CRÈME

Salmon Trout with Cream

Cook some thick slices of salmon trout gently in butter without browning. Remove the fish to a hot platter, deglaze the pan with cream and lemon juice, and heat this up for a moment or two without allowing it to boil. Serve.

NOTE

1. The common trout, *Salmo fario*, with reddish flesh.

SAUMON[1] GRILLÉ, AU BEURRE D'ANCHOIS

Broiled Salmon with Anchovy Butter

For six people, use:

2 lbs. fresh salmon
$^2/_3$ C. butter
3 oz. salted anchovies[2]

Prepare an anchovy butter as follows: Wash the anchovies, let them soak a little to remove the salt, wipe them, remove any bones, pound the flesh in a mortar[3] with some butter, and force through a fine sieve.

Cut the salmon in three-quarter-inch thick slices and cook them on a greased grill over a hot fire without any seasoning whatsoever, for three to four minutes per side.[4]

Serve on a hot platter accompanied by the hot anchovy butter in a sauceboat.

NOTES

1. *Salmo salmo,* Salmonidae family.
2. *Engraulis encrasicholus,* Clupeidae family.
3. An electric blender may be used but the resulting purée should be sieved in order to remove any fine bones. Commercially prepared anchovy paste may also be used instead of the salted anchovies.
4. Or broil it under a broiler.

GALANTINE DE SAUMON

For twelve people, use:

4 lbs. center cut of salmon
1 lb. 5 oz. hake, whiting, or gurnet, and sole trimmings
$^1/_2$ lb. *panade à la frangipane* **(see under quenelles recipe in this section)**
1 C. dry white wine
1 oz. crushed pistachino nuts
12 crayfish[1]
1 pike weighing about 3 lbs.
butter
bouquet garni
egg whites
lemon juice
*quatre épices**
nutmeg
salt, pepper, and cayenne

Scale the salmon; remove the skin and the bones without damaging the filets. Reserve the trimmings.

Scrape the pickerel; gut it and wipe it. Remove all the meat without any bones and set aside the trimmings.

Split the salmon filets lengthwise. The two larger ones are cut into four strips, the smaller ones into three strips. Season them with salt and pepper.

Preparation of the fish stock. In a saucepan put two quarts of water, the hake, whiting, or gurnet, all cut into pieces, the trimmings from the sole, salmon, and pike, the *bouquet garni,* white wine, salt, pepper, and a little *quatre épices.* Bring this to a boil, skim it, then continue to simmer it for about a half hour. Strain, pressing it firmly through the sieve to extract as much as possible.

In the fish stock cook some crayfish from which the intestinal vein has been removed. Shell them and reserve the tails. With the trimmings and 3 tablespoons of butter make a crayfish butter.

Preparation of the forcemeat. In a mortar[2] pound the cut-up pike flesh; then add the crayfish tails and pound again. Last add the *panade à la frangipane* and the crayfish butter. Season well with salt, pepper, and nutmeg to taste.

Preparation of the galantine. To make a galantine measuring approximately five inches per side, place a piece of buttered parchment paper on the table. The paper should measure about eight inches in length and twenty inches in width. Butter it well and spread on a layer of forcemeat about one-half inch thick covering a surface of five inches by sixteen inches. On this arrange two rows of pistachios set end to end lengthwise. Over these lay three long strips of salmon alternating with the two smaller ones. Cover with forcemeat. Repeat these layers again until all the ingredients are used up, ending with forcemeat. Roll the galantine along its width into a cylinder, making sure that the paper only covers one-fourth of the roll. Fold the edges of the paper over the ends of the roll evenly so as to enclose all the ingredients of the galantine. Wrap this roll in a light piece of cloth without making any pleats. Tie the ends against the paper. Roll the galantine, without squeezing it, over all its length with small bands of cloth[3] in a spiral fashion, edges touching.

Put the prepared galantine, thus wrapped, on a rack in a kettle. Pour the hot fish stock over it. The liquid must come to the top of the cloth. Bring it to a boil; simmer until it is cooked, which should take about forty-five minutes. One can tell it is cooked if, when it is touched with the finger, there is some resistance. Remove the galantine from the liquid, let it cool a little, remove the bands of cloth, and open up the other cloth too. On each side of the galantine arrange some small boards, up-ended, and held back by some kind of weight so as to exert inward pressure on each side. On top put another little board with a two-pound weight on it. Let the galantine cool under pressure for twelve hours.

Preparation of the jelly. Strain the cooking liquid through a cloth. Give it some body, if necessary, with a little veal stock. Clarify it with egg white; spike the seasoning with a little cayenne and some lemon juice. Strain through a cloth.

Presentation. Unwrap the galantine from the cloth and paper. Arrange it on a platter and coat it with some of the softened jelly. Chill it. Finally, decorate it with some of the firm jelly cut into fancy shapes.

As a variation, one could substitute filets of soles for the pike and some carp milts for the crayfish.

One could prepare this galantine from any number of other fishes, such as, for instance, eel.

NOTES

1. Large shrimp or prawns could be used as a substitute for the crayfish.
2. See notes under recipe for quenelles for a quicker modern method.
3. If using old sheeting for this step, be sure to boil the cloth with a little vinegar before using so as to make sure of removing any residue left by bleach.

MOUSSES ET MOUSSELINES DE SAUMON, CHAUDES

Hot Mousses and Mousselines of Salmon

Take a nice thick slice of salmon yielding about one and a half pounds of pure flesh, without skin or bones. Cut a few thin slices to serve as decoration. Cut up the rest of the salmon. Pound it in a mortar[1] with 2 egg whites, 1 teaspoon of salt, and a few grains of white pepper. Force this mixture through a fairly fine-meshed sieve. Add 2 cups of very heavy, half-whipped cream and smooth the paste with a spatula. Butter a mold of suitable size, spoon in the salmon mousse, and bake the mold in a pan of hot water in a moderate oven for a half hour.

Unmold on a serving platter. Decorate the mousse with a few boiled prawn or crayfish tails and with the slices of salmon which have been cooked in the shellfish cooking liquid.

Serve with either a lobster or Nantua sauce.

To prepare mousselines of salmon, pack the mixture in small, low molds, or pipe the mixture into a frying pan with a pastry bag and poach them as you would quenelles. Poach them very slowly in barely simmering salted water for ten to twelve minutes. Drain them, decorate them, and serve with either of the above sauces.

One could prepare, in exactly the same way, hot mousses and mousselines of other fish: pickerel, trout, whiting, red mullet, etc. These could be decorated by using, not only the slices of fish, but sliced milts, mushrooms, truffles, etc. They could be accompanied by any of the following sauces: Mornay, shrimp, *normande*, Béchamel, Régence, etc.

For six people, use:

1¼ lb. raw salmon, without skin or bones
1¼ C. very heavy cream
2½ tsp. salt
few grains pepper
6 egg whites

NOTE

1. See notes under recipe for quenelles for a quicker modern method.

SOUFFLÉ DE SAUMON

Salmon Soufflé

Beat two egg whites until stiff.

In a mortar[1] pound the cut up salmon with the salt and pepper. Add the 2 beaten egg whites, little by little. Force the mixture through a fine-meshed sieve. Place this paste in a shallow pan; smooth it over lightly with a spatula and chill it for two hours.

Beat the remaining 4 egg whites until very stiff. Half-whip the cream.

Little by little incorporate the half-whipped cream into the salmon mixture, working very carefully over a bowl of cracked ice so the paste remains very chilled. Then fold in the egg whites without allowing them to deflate.

Spoon this mixture into a soufflé mold and cook it in a hot water bath in a slow oven for thirty-five to forty minutes.

Serve with a shrimp sauce.

Soufflés of all other types of fish may be prepared in the same way. They should be served with suitable sauces.

Instead of making one large soufflé, one could spoon the mixture into as many individual soufflé molds as there are guests.

NOTE

1. See notes under recipe for quenelles for a quicker modern method.

CIVET DE LAMPROIE[1]

Civet of Lamprey

Take a live eel, cut off its head and tail, collect the blood, then gut it and plunge it into boiling water. Scrape, trim, and cut it up into chunks.

Cook, on the one hand, the chunks of eel with some white part of young leeks for a few minutes in olive oil; on the other hand, prepare a hash made up of bacon, shallots, parsley, hyssop, and bay leaf. Sprinkle the hash with flour, add some good red wine, season with salt and pepper, add to it the eel and the leeks, and let everything cook together for two hours.

At the last minute thicken with the eel blood and some chicken blood, so that the sauce takes on a very dark color. Taste, complete the seasoning, if necessary, with salt, pepper, a little numeg, and some powdered sugar.

Serve with fried croûtons.

This civet is excellent for canning.

To can it, all that is necessary is to put the stew into preserving jars or cans and cook them for three hours in a hot water bath.

To serve, all one has to do is to open the jars or cans, heat up the contents in a double boiler, pour the contents into a hot serving dish, and serve with fried croûtons prepared at the last minute.

This recipe is applicable to conger or marine eel. It is equally good made with salmon.

NOTE

1. *Petromyzon marinus et fluviatilis,* Petromyzonidae family.

MATELOTE D'ANGUILLE AUX RAISINS DE SMYRNE

Eel Stew with Raisins

For four people, use:

1½ lbs. eel
1¾ C. red wine
⅔ C. water
5 oz. mushrooms
7 T. butter
3 oz. small onions
¼ C. fish fumet or meat glaze
2 oz. raisins
1 medium carrot
2 T. brandy
3 T. flour
2 small cloves garlic
12 croûtons
1 clove
bouquet garni
lemon juice
salt and pepper

Cut the eel into chunks.

Cook the pieces of eel with the whole onions and the garlic and sliced carrot in two tablespoons of butter. Remove the fish and keep it warm.

Add the flour to the same pan, stir in the water, wine and brandy. Add the *bouquet garni,* clove, salt, and pepper to taste. Cook for forty-five minutes, then add the eel and continue to cook for another forty-five minutes.

Meanwhile sauté the mushrooms with 2 tablespoons of butter and the juice of ½ lemon.

Scald the raisins.

Fifteen minutes before serving carefully remove the pieces of eel, strain the sauce, put the eel back into the saucepan along with the sauce. Add the fish fumet or the meat glaze, the mushrooms, and the raisins, and finish cooking.

Arrange the chunks of eel on a platter, coat with the sauce, decorate the platter with the mushrooms and the croûtons fried in the rest of the butter. Serve.

This is an excellent dish.

For six people, use:

4 lbs. sorrel
1¼ C. butter
3½ T. cream
3 egg yolks
1 shad, with roe weighing about 2½ lbs.
chopped parsley
lemon juice
mustard
salt and pepper

ALOSE[1] GRILLÉE, À L'OSEILLE

Broiled Shad with Sorrel

Shad is a marine fish which swims up river in the spring. Its flesh is excellent when it is fresh.

One may prepare shad in a number of ways. The classic procedure, which is most highly recommended, consists in broiling it or roasting it on a spit and serving it with sorrel.

Here is a precise recipe.

Trim and wash the sorrel carefully. Blanch it a few minutes in boiling water and drain it well.

Scale, gut, and wipe off the shad. Slash it in several places and spread it with 3 tablespoons of softened butter. Season it with salt and pepper. Then cook it on a preheated broiler rack or grill for fifteen to eighteen minutes per side, basting frequently with the pan juices.

In a saucepan put the blanched sorrel along with ½ cup of butter and some salt and pepper, and continue to cook it until tender. Thicken it with the egg yolks beaten with the cream.

Prepare a mustard maître d'hôtel butter using the rest of the butter, some parsley, lemon juice, mustard, salt, and pepper to taste.

Arrange the shad on a platter and serve it, along with the sorrel, in a vegetable dish and the mustard maître d'hôtel butter in a sauceboat.

For variation one could substitute, for the maître d'hôtel butter, any one of the mixed butters or one of the sauces which accompany broiled sole.

NOTE

1. *Clupea alosa,* Clupeidae family.

ALOSE FARCIE

Stuffed Shad

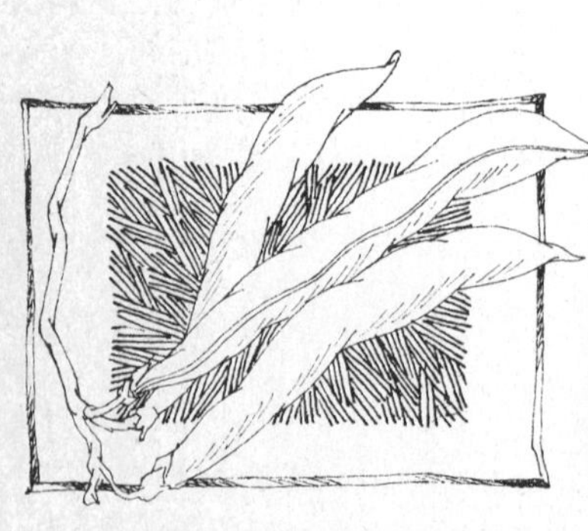

Get a nice shad weighing about 2½ to 3 pounds. Scale it, gut it through the gills, and dry it.

Prepare a small amount of forcemeat stuffing with a small pickeral, a medium-sized whiting, some mushrooms and parsley. Season with salt, pepper, *quatre épices* and cayenne to taste. Bind the stuffing with a little very thick Béchamel sauce made with fish stock. Force the mixture through a sieve or food mill.*

Stuff the fish with this mixture. Slash the fish several times diagonally, wrap it in slices of bacon, and roast it in a moderate oven. This requires from thirty to forty minutes depending upon the size of the fish. Baste it often, as it cooks, with the pan juices.

Remove the bacon slices and arrange the fish on a platter. Serve, sending along some Rubens sauce in a sauceboat.

For six people, use:

1 1/3 C. strong fish fumet
3/4 C. white wine
1/4 lb. shrimp or crayfish
1/2 C. butter
2 small carrots
1 small onion
2 T. madeira
3 T. parsley
1 T. fresh lobster roe
2 egg yolks
thyme
bay leaf
paprika

Rubens sauce is prepared in the following way:

Shell the shrimp and reserve the trimmings.

Pound the shrimp tail meat with the cream in a mortar. Force through a strainer.* Set the purée aside.

Crush the shrimp shells and trimmings with 1 tablespoon of butter; force it through a sieve and set aside the seasoned butter.

In 1 tablespoon of butter, cook the finely minced carrot, onion, and parsley. Add a little thyme and bay leaf. Pour in the white wine and fish fumet and cook for twenty-five minutes. Then, add the mashed lobster roe and continue to cook for another five minutes. Strain this broth through a fairly fine sieve, let it cool somewhat, and completely skim off the fat.

Put the skimmed and degreased broth on the fire and reduce it to about 1/4 cup. Add the madeira and let it cook for a few minutes; then thicken it with the egg yolks. Whisk in the rest of the butter and the shrimp butter, season it with paprika, and enrich it with the shrimp purée.

BAR À LA GELÉE

Bass in Jelly

For six people use a 3-pound bass. Cook it, preferably in some sea water or, alternatively, in water salted with sea salt. It must be cooked at a simmer, and the cooking time should be about forty-five minutes.

Let the fish cool.

Meanwhile prepare a good jelly with water, white wine, fish and fish trimmings, a calf's knuckle, vegetables, a *bouquet garni*, some onion, shallot, garlic, spices, aromatics, and salt and pepper to taste. Strain the jelly and clarify it.

Arrange the fish on a platter, decorate it with a few tarragon leaves, coat it with jelly, and let it set.

One may serve the fish as is, accompanied by a mustard mayonnaise, or by a green mayonnaise known as *sauce verte*.

To make mustard mayonnaise for six people use:

2/3 C. olive oil
few grains pepper
2 egg yolks
mustard, lemon juice, salt to taste

Prepare an ordinary mayonnaise, as described in the recipe for jellied pike (*brochet à la gelée*). Add the mustard and blend thoroughly.

*See notes under the recipe for quenelles for a quicker modern method.

To make 12 barquette *shells,*[1] *use:*

2 C. minus 2 T. flour
7 T. butter
4 T. water
salt

To make a green sauce, one would add, to a very thick ordinary mayonnaise, one-tenth of its weight of colored purée, obtained by mashing, in a mortar, some watercress, spinach, sorrel, chervil, and tarragon, in equal quantities. The vegetables should have been pre-blanched in boiling water and squeezed dry. After these have been pounded the purée should be forced through a sieve, or squeezed in muslin to extract all the color.

An elegant way of presenting bass in jelly consists in surrounding the fish with pastry *barquettes*[1] garnished with vegetable salad or even filled with a mousseline of gray shrimp, either with or without some truffles.

Prepare a smooth dough, roll it out quite thin, and line some small *barquette* molds with it. Fill the inside with dry beans or well-washed pebbles, and bake. Cool them.

Other salt-water fish may be prepared in jelly.

NOTE

1. *Barquettes* are a type of tiny pastry shells or small tartlets, oval in shape, which one fills with purées or *salpicons* (hashes) made of shellfish, fish, fowl, game, vegetables, jams, or fruits. *Barquette* crust is either salty or sweet according to whether the filling is salty or sweet.

ROUGETS[1]

Red Mullet

Red mullets are very delicate fish of the Mullidae family, but they decompose fairly quickly and are therefore only really good at the seashore. The best species seem to be those of the Mediterranean, especially those taken off the Algerian coast.

Two species are worthy of the attention of gastronomes: the *Mullus surmuletus* and the *Mullus barbatus.*

The Romans were very fond of mullets, and they spent enormous sums for the construction of hatcheries and breeding ponds destined to receive them.

NOTE

1. While the European red mullet is known to be far superior to it, the American mullet is the most important food fish in the southern United States.

ROUGETS AUX TOMATES

Red Mullet with Tomatoes

For four people, use:

½ lb. tomatoes
3 T. butter
1½ tsp. table salt
1 small shallot
½ clove garlic
few grains black pepper
pinch *quatre épices**
a grating nutmeg
4 small red mullets, weighing 1 lb. together
1 onion stuck with a clove
1 small *bouquet garni*
flour

As soon as one leaves the seashore this fish is not as fresh; plain cooking in butter, therefore, is not quite satisfactory. It is best to prepare it in the following way, then.

In a saucepan put the tomatoes, the onion, and the *bouquet garni*. Let these cook, then put through a strainer to make a purée.

Melt the butter, and, when it is good and hot but not brown, toss in the minced garlic and shallot. Then add the red mullets, which have been rolled in butter. Season them with salt, pepper, *quatre épices,* and nutmeg. Cook the fish on both sides. This requires fifteen minutes. Add the tomato pureé and continue cooking everything together for another ten minutes. Serve.

One may prepare other fish in this manner, notably tuna steaks.

SOLES[1]

Sole—whose name is derived from the Latin word *solea* (sandal) —by which name they were called in Rome because of their shape —are fish of the family Pleuronectidae.

They are represented in Europe by five or six species, two of which are regularly sold in Paris: the common sole or *Pleuronectes solea,* which has a brownish dorsal skin, and the lascaris sole or *Pleuronectes lascaris,* whose dorsal skin is grayish. The latter is the more delicate.

Sole is unquestionably the queen of the salt-water fishes. Its flesh, white, delicate, light in texture and succulent, pleases everyone: large and small, young and old, healthy or sick, all adore it and delight in it. And, too, cooks have dedicated themselves to the creation of numerous ways of preparing it, and they have deployed all the resources of their art so that its flavor may be appreciated. Because of the physical impossibility of describing them all, which would be boring, I will show that the number of possible combinations is, so to speak, infinite, and that each cook, each aficionado of cooking, may easily create his own personal dish, either using the whole fish or using only the filets.

Methods of cooking sole are:

1. Broiling, grilling.
2. Poaching in water or court bouillon.
3. Cooking in wine, then browning or not.
4. Cooking in butter, in cream, in oil or fat, either followed by browning or not.
5. Frying.

Here are a few general remarks on each of the above methods of cooking:

1. Broiled or Grilled Sole. To prepare broiled sole, one starts by trimming it; then one may detach the filets, which should be slashed. The fish is then coated with melted butter or oil and lemon; it may or may not be rolled in flour or in dry, sifted breadcrumbs. In the former case one bastes it again with melted butter or oil, and then it is slowly broiled and served simply with a few slices of lemon or with a sauce: maître d'hôtel, hollandaise, Béarnaise, *sauce diable*, etc. Or it may be served with a compound butter: watercress, shallot, garlic, ravigote, horseradish, paprika, mustard, anchovy, smoked salmon, shrimp, crayfish, lobster, rock lobster, sea urchin coral, lobster or rock lobster coral, caviar, fried mullet roe, milt butter, truffle, etc. Last, the dish is garnished to taste with oysters or mussels cooked in their own juices, milts poached in a highly seasoned court bouillon, potatoes *noisette, duchesse, marquise, dauphine*, souffléed, chips, or even truffles, etc.

2. Poached Sole. Sole may be simply poached in sea water or in boiling salted water and served with a hollandaise sauce or melted butter and either boiled or steamed potatoes. When it is poached in a court bouillon, seasoned to taste, it is generally served with a sauce made with the reduced court-bouillon and whisked up with butter.

3. Sole with Wine.[2] It is in the preparation of sole with wine that the ingeniousness of cooks has been manifested. It has given birth to numerous combinations, each of which has a special name. I shall only mention here those that are true classics: sole in white wine, *Sole Normande*, Sole Cardinal, *Sole au Gratin*, sole Mornay.

As a general rule, sole in wine is cooked with wine and aromatics in a buttered fireproof dish[3] or, better yet, in an aromatized fish fumet made with wine. The sole, arranged on a platter, is coated with the sauce, then served with or without a garnish. Therefore, just by varying the wine, from the ordinary white wines, to the ordinary red wines, to classified wines, and using only French wines, one already has a number of variations. A certain number of foreign wines may also be used. One can also spike the preparation by adding other spirits, such as brandy or vermouth, and it can be flavored with liqueurs. As to condiments, which may be used in varying proportions, it will be sufficient to mention essence of mushroom or truffle, oyster and mussel juice, different peppers, cayenne, paprika, sweet peppers, nutmeg, spices, tomato, onion, shallot, garlic, mustard, numerous *fines herbes* and other herbs, vinegar, lemon or orange juice, etc.

The sauce is generally based on a seafood velouté. It is thickened with flour, starch, or egg yolks. It is whisked up with cream and plain butter or with one of the numerous blended butters of which we have spoken above. One may also use other sauces, however.

The number of possible garnishes is equally great: slices of lobster meat, anchovy filets, fried smelts, *brandade de morue,*[4] sea urchin coral, lobster or rock lobster roe, caviar, *poutargue,*[5] whole milts or milts made into purées and served in *barquettes* of flaky or puff pastry; certain fish livers, among them anglerfish or *raie* livers; seafood forcemeats and quenelles; seafood such as oysters, mussels, scallops, shrimp, crayfish; fungi such as mushrooms, particularly morels and truffles; vegetables such as tomatoes, spinach, asparagus, eggplant, squash, cucumbers, sweet peppers, artichoke hearts, potatoes, olives, and juliennes of various vegetables; fruits such as lemons and oranges; nuts such as walnuts, almonds, as well as dried raisins; rice made into risotto with white truffles or made into pilaf with or without saffron; fried croûtons, pasta, etc.

It is hardly necessary to mention that one may prepare filets of sole in wine. The latter may also be served cold with a seafood jelly, for instance, with a crayfish mousse, or with a mousse of milts (soft roes) with horseradish. They may also be served in aspic with a crayfish *chaud-froid* sauce, or in salad with a mayonnaise dressing, etc.

4. Sole in Butter.[6] The typical sole in butter is that known as *à la meunière*; it is prepared in the following way:

After having seasoned the sole with salt and pepper and having rolled it in flour, it is cooked with butter in a skillet with a little lemon juice. Then it is salted and peppered again, sprinkled with blanched, minced parsley, moistened with *noisette* butter and served immediately.

Here again, one may vary the three ingredients used in this recipe—for instance, by adding to the pan juices some essence of mushroom, or by substituting for the plain butter some blended butters, seasoned to taste. Last, it can be varied by garnishing the dish with any of the numerous garnishes listed above.

5. Fried Sole. Sole can be fried in fat[7] or in oil, either after it has been soaked in milk and rolled in flour, or after it has been dipped in batter, or after it has been breaded. In all three instances, it is served surrounded with fried parsley and lemon slices.

One can also fry, in the same way, a julienne of sole (strips of sole). One would then achieve somewhat the illusion of having fried whitebait.

Then again, sole can be fried after it has been coated with a sauce, such as *sauce Villeroi,* and then dipped in batter.

The classic preparation known by the name of *sole Colbert* consists in fracturing the spine of the fish before cooking (by bending the fish backward and forward), and then, once the sole is fried, removing the backbone and substituting in its place a maître d'hôtel butter.

As a variation on *sole Colbert*, one could substitute, for the maître d'hôtel butter, a blended butter, garnished with crayfish and truffles, and seasoned with a shrimp purée.

All these methods of preparation may be applied to other fish, notably brill, small turbots, filets of brill, young turbot, and adult turbot.

They are also suitable for filets of trout, lavaret, etc.

I shall now give a number of specific recipes for the preparation of sole.

NOTES

1. The American "sole," although it is not of the same family as the English Dover sole, is nevertheless a member of the flatfish group. The winter flounder, lemon sole, gray sole, and dab, as well as the summer flounder, are excellent food fish and can all be used in any of the recipes calling for sole. (Dover sole, or *Platichthys flesus*, has a related species which appears on the Pacific Coast of North America known as *Platichthys stellatus*.)
2. Sole cooked in cider also belongs to this group.
3. In certain areas oil or fat is used instead of butter.
4. *Brandade de morue* is pounded, salted codfish mixed with oil and garlic.
5. *Poutargue* is the word used to designate dried, salted, and pressed mullet roe.
6. Under this heading we can also include similar preparations for sole with cream, oil, or fat.
7. In the Midi (the South of France), happily, they use goose fat.

For four people, use:

3/4 C. white wine
1/2 C. cream
1/4 lb. mushrooms
6 T. butter
3 minced shallots
2 T. breadcrumbs
1 tsp. salt
2 tsp. chopped parsley
to taste pepper
few grains paprika
4 large crayfish
1 sole, weighing approximately 1 1/2 lbs.
lemon juice

SOLE AU VIN BLANC, SAUCE À LA CRÈME

Sole in White Wine with Cream Sauce

Cook the crayfish.

Peel the mushrooms, dip the caps in lemon juice, and mince the stems.

Butter a flat ovenproof casserole with 2 1/2 tablespoons of butter. Trim and gut the sole, season it with salt, pepper, and paprika, lay it in the buttered casserole, add the parsley, lemon juice, and white wine. Cover the pan with buttered paper to keep the sole from drying out or browning.

Bake it in the oven for about twenty minutes.

In a saucepan, melt the rest of the butter without browning. Cook the shallots in this, then add the mushroom caps and the minced stems and cook for five minutes. Add the breadcrumbs; then spoon everything onto the sole and continue to cook for another ten minutes or so. At the last minute, add the cream and mix it with the other ingredients in the casserole by gently shaking it, to blend. Heat up again without boiling.

Decorate the dish with the mushroom caps and the crayfish and serve.

Other fish may be prepared in this same way, notably pike and bream.

SOLE NORMANDE

For eight people, use:

1¼ C. water
1 C. white wine
10 T. butter
¼ lb. mushrooms
5 T. cream
2 T. Calvados (apple brandy)
1 tsp. peppercorns
1 qt. mussels
32 large shrimp
16 oysters
16 smelts
2 soles, weighing approx. 1 lb. 3 oz. each
2 egg yolks
1 whiting, weighing approx. 11 oz.
bouquet garni
pot-au-feu vegetables
dry, sifted breadcrumbs
1 loaf unsliced bread
flour
lemon juice
oil
nutmeg
salt and pepper

Prepare a court bouillon with the water, wine, Calvados, *bouquet garni*, peppercorns, and some salt. Cook this for twenty minutes, then strain.

Peel the mushrooms and reserve the peelings.

Meanwhile cook the shrimp for several minutes in the court bouillon; and the mushrooms in 4 teaspoons of butter and the lemon juice, for about fifteen minutes.

Poach the oysters in their own juices.

Put the mussels in a heavy-bottomed pan and open them over a hot fire.

Keep the shrimp, mushrooms, oysters, and mussels hot.

Combine the shrimp court bouillon, the oyster juices, and any juices from the mussel pan, add the cut up whiting, the mushroom peelings, a little nutmeg, and cook these together. You will now have a very aromatic fish fumet. Boil it down to reduce it somewhat and strain it through a cloth.

Arrange the soles in a low-sided, ovenproof casserole coated with 2 tablespoons of butter. Add the fish fumet, cover with a piece of buttered paper and bake in the oven for about twenty minutes.

Prepare the *sauce normande* by blending the flour into 2 teaspoons of the butter in a saucepan and adding the sole cooking liquid and any juices from the mushroom pan, thickening this with the egg yolks, and then whisking in 5 tablespoons of butter and the cream. Add a little lemon juice and complete the seasoning, if necessary, with salt and pepper.

Cut the unsliced bread into 8 thin slices. Sauté them in the rest of the butter.

Roll the smelts in the breadcrumbs and fry them in boiling oil.

Coat the soles with the sauce and garnish the dish with the shrimp, oysters, mussels, smelts, mushrooms, and the bread slices. Heat up in the oven for a moment and serve.

Certain people use crayfish and gudgeon for this dish. However, it seems to me that, in order to retain the salt-water character of this dish in all its purity, it is best not to use crayfish but to use fried smelts.

The dish may be made even richer by adding truffles cooked in madeira. Truffle peelings could be used for flavoring the fish fumet, and the madeira used to flavor the sauce. The truffles, whole or minced, can become part of the garnish.

By adding to the *sauce normande* one-eighth of its weight of shrimp and crayfish butter, in equal quantities, one would have a *sauce Joinville*.

Brill, young turbot, and full-grown turbot may be prepared this way.

SOLE SOUFFLÉE, SAUCE HOLLANDAISE VERT-PRÉ

For twelve people, use:

1. For the Sole Soufflée:

1 C. fish broth[1]
1 C. white wine
1/4 C. heavy cream
7 T. butter
1/4 lb. potatoes
1/4 lb. mushrooms
48 mussels
12 crayfish
4 egg yolks
2 egg whites
1 sole, weighing approx. 2 lbs.
1 tiny pickerel, weighing about 4 oz.
1 tiny whiting, weighing approx. 4 oz.
bouquet garni
lemon juice
salt
pepper
nutmeg
cayenne

Split the skin of the sole on the white side, along the backbone. Remove the backbone without damaging the filets. This is a disecting job which takes some care. Save the trimmings.

Remove the head and the backbone of the pickerel and whiting, pound the flesh in a mortar,[2] and strain through a fine sieve.

Beat the egg whites until stiff.

Prepare a forcemeat with the pickerel and whiting purée; season it with salt, pepper, nutmeg, and cayenne. Work this over a bowl of cracked ice and little by little add the 4 egg yolks and the 2 whites.

Stuff the sole with this mixture.

Separately cook: potatoes *à l'anglaise*,[3] the crayfish in a court bouillon, the mussels with a little white wine and a *bouquet garni*. Strain the liquid from the mussels and reserve.

Peel the mushrooms, dip them in lemon juice, and cook them in 2 1/2 tablespoons of butter.

Keep the potatoes, mushrooms, crayfish, and mussels warm.

Combine the fish broth, the wine, and the strained mussel liquid and boil the fish trimmings in this.

Arrange the sole in a low, ovenproof casserole coated with 4 tablespoons of butter. Strain the liquid over the fish and bake in the oven for twenty-five minutes, basting frequently.

Serve in the same dish. Arrange the crayfish, mussels, potatoes, and mushrooms around the fish as a garnish. At the same time send along a sauceboat filled with *sauce hollandaise vert-pré*.

2. For the Sauce:

1 lb. butter
1/2 C. water
2 T. vinegar
8 egg yolks
lemon juice
parsley
chervil
spinach
salt and pepper

Sauce hollandaise vert-pré ("green field") is a colored hollandaise sauce.

To prepare a hollandaise sauce, which is an emulsion of butter and egg yolks, put four tablespoons of water in a small saucepan with 2 tablespoons of vinegar. Reduce this to 2 tablespoons. Now place the saucepan over another pan containing hot water (a double boiler) and add 4 teaspoons of water and the egg yolks. Whisk these together well; then, little by little, whisk in the butter which has been cut into tiny pieces, also adding at the same time another 2 tablespoons of water. The sauce must puff up and thicken as in floating island, but at the same time it must be light and have cohesion. One generally seasons this only with salt, but one may also add a little pepper and some lemon juice to taste. Strain the sauce.

To obtain a *sauce hollandaise vert-pré*, color the preceding plain hollandaise sauce with a mixture of chopped chervil, watercress and spinach, which has been blanched. The color will be lighter if the sauce is colored exclusively with spinach greens.[4]

One can make another type of *hollandaise vert-pré* by using, for twelve people:

1 lb. butter
4 T. cold water
1 oz. watercress
1 oz. spinach
several tarragon leaves
8 egg yolks
6 hard-boiled egg yolks
lemon juice or vinegar
salt and pepper

Chop the watercress, spinach, and tarragon.

Prepare the preceding hollandaise sauce, add the chopped herbs and mashed hard-boiled egg yolks, and season with salt, pepper, and lemon juice or vinegar, to taste. Whisk this all together.

This sauce may also be used with asparagus.

To complete the discussion of hollandaise sauce in general, I will add that if one uses, in its preparation, some shrimp or crayfish butter, or some butter to which has been added some coral either from sea urchin, lobster, or spiny lobster, instead of plain butter, one would have tinted and flavored sauces for which there are many uses.

Any number of fish may be prepared in this way, in particular young turbot and brill.

NOTES

1. If no fish broth is easily available canned or bottled clam juice makes a satisfactory substitute.

2. For a quicker and easier method see notes under the recipe for quenelles.

3. Potatoes *à l'anglaise* are potatoes which have been peeled

and cut into a uniform size and either steamed or boiled in salted water.

4. To obtain green spinach coloring: pound in a mortar (or put through meat grinder) some well-washed and drained spinach. Put this in a cloth and wring it out to extract the juice into the top of a double boiler. Heat this juice up well to reduce it somewhat, strain through another cloth and scrape off the green colored matter which remains on the cloth.

Green butter is obtained by blending together this green spinach pulp with twice its weight in butter.

FILETS DE SOLES AU VIN BLANC

Filets of Sole in White Wine

For four people, use:

- **1 C. water**
- **1 C. white wine**
- **2 oz. mushrooms**
- **3 T. heavy cream**
- **1 T. flour**
- **2 soles, weighing approximately 1½ lbs. together**
- **2 egg yolks**
- **1 medium carrot**
- **1 small onion**
- *bouquet garni* **(parsley, thyme, bay leaf, celery)**
- **1 clove**
- **lemon juice**
- **salt and pepper**

Cut off the sole filets and reserve the trimmings.

Peel and wash the mushrooms.

In a saucepan put the water, wine, mushrooms, sole trimmings, cut-up carrot, onion stuck with a clove, *bouquet garni,* salt, and pepper. Cook so as to obtain a fumet, reduce it by boiling it down, then strain.

Butter a low, fireproof porcelain baking dish with 4 tablespoons of butter. Arrange the filets of sole on this, season with salt and pepper, add several spoonfuls of the fumet and bake in a moderate oven without browning.

Prepare the sauce: melt 5 teaspoons of butter and blend the flour into it without browning, then stir in the rest of the fumet, along with any juices from the pan in which the soles were baked. Thicken with the 2 egg yolks, and then whisk in the rest of the butter and the cream. Add a little lemon juice to taste. Heat this up just to boiling; taste and complete the seasoning, if necessary.

Arrange the filets on a serving platter, coat with the sauce, and serve at once.

FILETS DE SOLES AU VIN ROUGE

Filets of Sole in Red Wine

Cut off the filets of sole and reserve the trimmings.

Peel the vegetables, slice the carrot and the turnip, chop the mushrooms, and stick the cloves into the onion.

In a saucepan put the water, wine, mushrooms, fish heads and bones, the fish trimmings, carrot, turnip, onion, shallot, garlic, *bouquet garni*, salt, pepper, and cayenne. Cook this so as to obtain a very strong, highly seasoned, and concentrated fish fumet. Strain it.

Butter a low, flat, porcelain fireproof baking dish with 4 tablespoons of butter. Arrange the filets of sole on this, season with salt and pepper and moisten with several spoonfuls of the fish fumet. Bake in a moderate oven without letting it brown. Keep the fish warm.

Now prepare the sauce: make a roux with 3 tablespoons of butter and the flour. Stir in the rest of the fish fumet. You now have a fish *velouté*. Add any liquid from the sole cooking dish and thicken the sauce by whisking in the egg yolks; then whisk in the rest of the butter and the anchovy butter, and flavor with a little lemon juice. Heat this up just to a simmer, taste and correct the seasoning if necessary with salt, pepper, and cayenne.

Arrange the filets on a serving platter; coat with the sauce and serve.

For four people, use:

1 C. water
1 C. red wine
1/4 lb. (8 T.) butter
1/4 lb. mushrooms
5 tsp. anchovy butter
2 tsp. flour
2 soles, weighing approximately 1 1/2 lbs. together
2 egg yolks
2 cloves
1 medium carrot
1 small turnip
1 medium onion
1 shallot
1 clove garlic
bouquet garni **(parsley, thyme, bay leaf, chervil, celery)**
fish heads and bones
lemon juice
salt, pepper, cayenne

FILETS DE SOLES, GARNIS

Stuffed Filets of Sole

Cut off the filets and flatten them; then roll them around a cylinder cut from some vegetable such as a potato or a carrot.

Butter a skillet with some shallot-flavored butter. Arrange the rolled filets in the pan, season with salt and pepper, and cover with white wine or some good vermouth and some lemon juice. Cook the fish until just done; remove the vegetable cylinders and set the filets aside to keep warm.

In some butter, sauté some cut-up and seasoned tomatoes. Pour these out onto a platter and arrange the rolled filets, upright, on top. These filets can now be stuffed with your choice of any of the following: a mixture made of shrimp or crayfish tails, mushrooms, lobster coral, oysters poached in white wine, salmon forcemeat, mussels prepared in a thickened sauce, or even with a hollandaise sauce which has been mixed with a goodly amount of sea urchin coral, etc.

Melt some butter in a saucepan, blend in some flour and stir in the cooking liquid from the filets, along with any liquid left from the cooked tomatoes. Boil down rapidly to reduce it and thicken it with fresh egg yolks blended into a little cream.

Top the rolled filets with some truffles or mushroom caps and serve, sending along the rest of the sauce in a sauceboat.

FILETS DE SOLES AU GRATIN

Baked Filets of Sole

To prepare filets of sole *au gratin*, cook them as in the recipe for *filets de soles au vin blanc*. Then arrange the filets on a dish and coat with the cooking juices which have been concentrated and thickened. Sprinkle on some fresh breadcrumbs about 1/4 inch thick, then pour over melted butter, and put the dish in a hot oven to brown.

FILETS DE SOLES MORNAY

Cook the filets of sole as in the recipe for *filets de soles au vin blanc*, keep the fish filets hot, and rapidly boil down the cooking liquid.

Prepare a *sauce Mornay* based on a fish *velouté* as in the recipe for *Oeufs Pochés Gratinés sur Canapés*. Use the above concentrated fish liquid to make the *velouté*.

In a low, porcelain ovenproof baking and serving dish spoon half the sauce and arrange the fish on this. Spoon over the rest of the sauce and set in a hot oven to brown.

FILETS DE SOLES AUX MORILLES, GRATINÉS

Filets of Sole with Morels

For four people, use:

2 C. white wine
1 lb. vegetables (carrots and onions)
1 1/3 C. water
1/2 lb. morels[1]
14 T. butter
2 soles, weighing approximately 1 1/2 lbs. together
fine, dry, sifted breadcrumbs
bouquet garni
lemon juice
salt and pepper

Cut off the filets of sole and reserve the trimmings.

In a saucepan put the wine, water, minced sole trimmings, peeled vegetables, *bouquet garni*, salt, and pepper. Simmer this so as to obtain a sufficient quantity of fish fumet. Strain through a cloth.

Now cook: (1) the filets of sole in the fumet to which you have added 5 teaspoons of butter; and (2) the morels in 3 tablespoons of butter with some lemon juice. Keep the filets of sole and morels warm.

Combine all the cooking liquids and boil them down rapidly to reduce them to a good sauce consistency. Without letting the sauce boil whisk in 5 tablespoons of butter. You should have a smooth, velvety sauce. Taste and complete the seasoning if necessary.

Arrange the filets of sole on an ovenproof serving dish, surround them with the morels, coat everything with the sauce, sprinkle on the dry, sifted breadcrumbs, dot with the rest of the butter, and put in a hot oven to brown.

Serve in the same dish.

This is a remarkable preparation, especially when one uses freshly gathered morels.

NOTES

1. If no morels, either dried or fresh, are available, any other type of mushroom may be used—but of course it will not be exactly the same dish.

TIMBALE DE FILETS DE SOLES AU PORTO, SAUCE NANTUA

Timbale of Filets of Sole with Port Wine, Nantua Sauce

Cut off the filets of sole and roll them on themselves.

Use a thick salmon steak and cook it in court bouillon, using a mixture of eighty percent good white wine and twenty percent white port wine; flavor it with a *bouquet garni*, an onion, a carrot, some shallots, garlic, aromatics to taste, and season with salt and peppercorns. When the fish is cooked remove the skin and bones.

Pound the flesh in a mortar or bowl[1] and rub it through a fine sieve. Add some dry, sifted breadcrumbs and some eggs. Moisten this paste with some of the salmon cooking liquid and work it until you have a fairly thick mixture which you can mold into quenelles.

Prepare a fish stock with port wine as in the recipe below.[2]

Cook some crayfish as usual, shell them, and reserve the tail meat. With the shells and trimmings prepare a crayfish butter.

Combine the fish stock and the rest of the salmon court bouillon. Cook the filets of sole in this liquid, then remove them and boil down the liquid rapidly to reduce it.

Cook some morels or field mushrooms in butter.

Prepare a seafood Béchamel sauce, whisk in some cream, and enrich it with the crayfish butter. To this sauce add the filets of sole, the salmon quenelles, the morels or mushrooms, the crayfish tails, the reduced fish broth. Heat this all up for a minute or two.

Pour everything into a timbale[3] and serve.

1 lb. 7 oz. fish heads, bones, trimmings, from sole, whiting, brill, etc.
6 T. white wine, port, or madeira
2 oz. mushrooms
1/2 medium onion
several sprigs parsley
1 tsp. salt
8 peppercorns
1 qt. water
butter
lemon juice

1. For a quicker way of preparing this see note under recipe for quenelles.

2. For 1 quart of fish stock use ingredients at right.
Put a little butter in a saucepan and add the mushrooms, onions,

parsley, and fish trimmings, and season with salt. Pour in the water and the wine. Bring all this to a boil and skim carefully. Cover the pan tightly and continue to cook at a regular simmer for about one hour. Ten minutes before it is finished add the peppercorns and lemon juice. Strain through a cloth.

3. The term timbale refers to certain containers made of pastry dough, rice, or porcelain, earthenware, or metal, shaped like a drum. The term is also used to designate the culinary preparations which are served in these containers.

PAUPIETTES DE FILETS DE SOLES FRITES

Fried, Rolled, and Stuffed Filets of Sole

For six people, use:

8 filets of sole, weighing 1 1/2 lbs. each
10 oz. filets of whiting
5 oz. gray shrimp
1/4 lb. mushrooms
8 T. butter
3 T. olive oil
1 small onion
4 T. breadcrumbs (soaked in milk and pressed dry)
several sprigs parsley
to taste paprika
4 lemons
3 whole eggs
1 bay leaf
flour
dry, sifted breadcrumbs
salt and pepper

Boil the shrimp as usual.

Sprinkle the filets of sole with 2 teaspoons of salt, some paprika, and put them to marinate[1] for an hour in 2 tablespoons of oil and the minced onion, thyme, bay leaf, parsley, and lemon juice.

Prepare a dressing (forcemeat):

Peel the shrimp; reserve the tail meat and make a shrimp butter using the shells and trimmings and 4 tablespoons of butter. To the shrimp tail meat add the pressed out breadcrumbs, the shrimp butter, some salt and pepper, and pound everything together.[2] Add 2 eggs and pound again so as to obtain a very smooth, velvet-textured paste. Taste and complete the seasoning, if necessary; and, if you do have to, work the paste thoroughly once more to incorporate it well. Force through a fine sieve.

Peel the mushrooms, mince them, add some lemon juice, and cook them in a saucepan with the rest of the butter and a little chopped parsley. Spread this mixture on the filets, then spoon the shrimp dressing over this and roll the filets without tying them.

Coat these paupiettes with flour, then dip them into 1 egg beaten with the rest of the oil, and, last, roll them in dry, sifted breadcrumbs. Plunge these into a moderately hot fry-bath. Cook them for ten minutes, keeping the fry-bath at the same temperature.

Arrange the paupiettes on a platter covered with a napkin, decorate with lemon slices and fried parsley, sprinkle with a little lemon juice and serve.

These paupiettes look elegant and are delicious. The crustiness of the outside of the fried sole, sparked with the lemon juice, contrasts very agreeably with the smoothness of the stuffing, and the two different main elements of this dish retain their individual flavor each enhancing the other.

One can prepare, in this same way, paupiettes of other types of fish and substitute, for the shrimp and shrimp butter dressing, crayfish and crayfish butter or anchovies and anchovy butter. Here one has a whole gamut of dishes with varying nuances of flavors which can be varied according to taste.

NOTES

1. Marinades tend to have a tenderizing effect on animal flesh and may mask the flavor, which could be advantageous in certain cases. They are made of varying ingredients, they may be cooked or uncooked, and the fish or meat remains in the marinade for varying lengths of time according to their quality and the time one has.

In this volume may be found recipes for marinades for fish, meat, and game.

2. For a quicker and easier way of proceeding see the note under recipe for quenelles.

JULIENNE DE FILETS DE SOLES, PANÉE, SAUTÉE

Breaded Sautéed Strips of Filets of Sole

For four people, use:

1 C. white wine
1 C. butter
4 slices of breadcrumbs (fresh)
3/4 C. water
1/4 lb. mushrooms
4 T. heavy cream
1 1/2 T. flour
1 lb. sole filets
2 eggs
1 medium carrot
1 medium onion
bouquet garni
*quatre épices**
salt and pepper

Cut off the filets of sole and save the trimmings.

In a saucepan put the wine, water, sole trimmings, mushrooms, carrot, onion, *bouquet garni*, salt, pepper, and a little *quatre épices*. Cook this together until you have a fairly strong fish fumet in which you will poach the filets of sole. Remove them and cut them into julienne strips.

Cook the breadcrumbs in 3/4 cup of butter; then add the fish julienne and sauté this mixture so that all the small pieces of sole are coated with breadcrumbs.

In a saucepan melt a little butter and stir in the flour; then add the cooking liquid from the filets. Reduce this mixture to thicken it if necessary. Thicken this sauce with egg yolks, then whisk in the rest of the butter and the cream. Heat it up just to a simmer.

Serve the fish on a platter, the sauce in a sauceboat, and the grated cheeses in a separate bowl.

Whiting[1]

Whiting or silver hake may be prepared in many ways: broiled, fried, in white wine, *à la meunière, à la dieppoise, à la maître d'hôtel, à la sauce gratin, à la sauce Colbert, à la sauce Bercy,* in truffle sauce, with *fines herbes,* etc.

They are cooked whole, in either flat or rolled filets, or *en paupiettes*.

NOTES

1. *Gadus merlangus.* The European whiting is a gadoid fish between ten and sixteen inches long. It is caught mainly in the English Channel and the Baltic. Its flesh is fine in texture, flaky, and easy to digest.

Another species of whiting, the pollack, is similar in appearance but yellowish in color and darker. Its flesh, though of good quality, is less delicate than that of the whiting proper.

The American whiting is also known as silver hake and is fished off the coast of New England. The average size is from twelve to fourteen inches, but larger specimens are not uncommon.

MERLANS AU GRATIN

Baked Whiting

Clean the whitings, wipe them off, split them down the back, and remove the backbone.

Prepare a stuffing or forcemeat with some shrimp tails, some cooked prawn meat, some mushrooms, and some *fines herbes*. Season this mixture with salt, pepper, and curry; then bind it with 1 egg and put the stuffing in place of the backbone.

Make a light roux with some butter and flour, add a few slices of carrot, a little thyme, a bay leaf, some minced shallots, and the washed mushroom peelings. Moisten with equal parts of white wine and fish fumet. Cook this for about twenty minutes, skimming well so as to reduce this *sauce gratin* to about one-half its volume. Strain it.

Prepare a shellfish butter using the shrimp and prawn shells and trimmings.

Butter a low porcelain ovenproof baking dish with the shellfish butter. Spoon a few teaspoonfuls of sauce into it and arrange the whitings on this. Surround them with a border of overlapping slices of mushroom. On each whiting put 2 or 3 mushroom caps. Sprinkle a few spoonfuls of white wine on and add the rest of the sauce. Sprinkle the whole surface with breadcrumbs and then with melted butter. Bake this in the oven at a temperature which will be suitable for all three of the following: the cooking of the fish, the reduction of the sauce, and the formation of a brown crust—and having everything finished at the same time as well. The larger the fish, the lower should be the oven heat.

After removing the pan from the oven, sprinkle the surface of the *gratin* (crust) with a little lemon juice and sprinkle on a little blanched, minced parsley.

Carp may be prepared in this same way.

COLINS

Hake

The word *colin* in French serves to denote either a small feathered game bird originating in America, imported frozen into Europe, which one may prepare like partridge, or a rather common fish.

All preparations indicated for whiting and cod are applicable to *colin*.[1]

It may be cooked in a skillet after having been marinated in olive oil with salt, pepper, and *fine herbes*. It may be poached in a court bouillon; it may be roasted, fried, stuffed, or browned whole or in steaks, and accompanied by plain melted butter or maître d'hôtel butter, or Bercy butter, etc., or even *sauce au beurre* (butter sauce).

Butter sauce is prepared as follows.

For four people, use:

1 scant C. boiling water
7 T. butter
4 tsp. clarified butter
2 T. flour
1 T. heavy cream
a pinch salt
2 egg yolks
lemon juice or vinegar

Put the clarified butter in a saucepan and blend in the flour without letting it brown. Stir in the boiling water in which you have dissolved a pinch of salt. Whisk this all together. Remove the saucepan from the fire and thicken the sauce with the egg yolks and the cream beaten together, by pouring a little of the hot sauce over the eggs and cream and then returning all to the pan, whisking constantly. Acidulate the sauce with the lemon juice or vinegar, to taste. Heat it up just to a simmer, strain the sauce, and at the last minute add the butter cut into small pieces. These are just barely allowed to melt.

NOTE

1. *Colin* is the *Gadus carbonarius*, known as *merlan noir* of the Gadidae family. In America the name hake is applied to any of several marine food fishes that are related to the common cod.

Turbot

The turbot, *Rhombus maximus*, and the brill, *Rhombus laevis*, are fish of the Pleuronectidae family. Their flesh is delicate and they appear in the fish course of menus for elegant dinners. If the sole has justly been named queen of the seas, the turbot deserves to be the king.

Turbots, young turbots, and brills are generally cooked and served whole. However, they may also be prepared in steaks or filets.

When the turbot is to be served whole, one starts by scraping it; then, with a sharp, pointed knife, one detaches the filets from the backbone along about two or three inches down the center. Then the fish is folded to crack the backbone and the head is skewered.

Thus handled, the fish will not lose its shape during cooking.

Generally, one cooks the turbot in a court bouillon with a water base, to which ¾ cup of milk, 1 tablespoon of sea salt, and a slice of lemon peel have been added, per quart of water. This is placed in a *turbotière*[1] which is set over the fire. When the liquid comes to a boil, it should be skimmed; then it should be placed over a very low flame to simmer ever so gently. After it has been skimmed, one must count on about five minutes of cooking per pound of fish.

Brush the turbot with melted butter to make it glisten, then arrange it on a platter covered with a napkin and surround it with parsley. It is served accompanied by a vegetable dish containing boiled or steamed potatoes and a sauceboat containing either melted butter, maître d'hôtel butter, or a hollandaise sauce, according to taste.

Turbot filets or steaks, as well as those of young turbot, may be prepared in all the ways applicable to sole.

Turbot may also be served as a *pâté*, in a salad with or without added vegetables, etc.

Turbot, cooked the day before, chopped and mixed with Béchamel sauce, rice, and hard-boiled eggs, the whole seasoned with nutmeg, curry and cayenne, is an Indian dish which is called kedgeree.

All the above recipes are applicable to brill.

NOTE

1. A *turbotière* is a square-shaped saucepan with a removable rack which is used to cook turbot and other flat fish.

ESCALOPES DE TURBOT PANÉES

Breaded Turbot Filets

Clean and gut a turbot, remove the backbone, and slice off the filets. Season them with salt, pepper, and lemon juice, then roll them in flour, dip them in beaten egg, and, last, coat them with fine, dry, sifted breadcrumbs.

Arrange the filets, thus coated, in a low porcelain ovenproof baking and serving casserole which has been buttered. Cook for about ten minutes basting it with the pan juices.

Serve in the same dish.

At the same time, send along a sauceboat with some Italian seafood sauce, *sauce italienne maigre*, which is prepared as follows:

Melt some butter in a saucepan and cook some chopped shallots and mushrooms in it. Allow the mushroom water to evaporate, then add some chopped parsley, some peeled, seeded, and chopped tomatoes, or some tomato purée, and season with salt, pepper, and flavor with fish fumet. Let this cook down so as to have a fairly thick sauce. Strain it and add some chopped *fines herbes*.

Filets of brill, filets of sole, hake, conger eel, whiting, etc., may be prepared in the same way.

BARBUE AUX POINTES D'ASPERGES

Brill with Asparagus Tips

Prepare some asparagus tips in cream sauce as in the recipe.

Poach the brill in court bouillon, well seasoned and flavored with wine. When the fish is cooked, remove it and remove the backbone without damaging the fish. Stuff it with the asparagus tips and arrange it in a low, buttered ovenproof baking and serving dish. Sprinkle it with some grated Gruyère cheese and brown the top quickly in a hot oven. Serve at once.

As a variation, one may use, instead of the asparagus tips, some spinach, blanched whole in salted water and mixed with cream.

Soles and young turbots may be prepared in the same way.

It is very easy to think up a whole series of *gratinéed* (browned) fish dishes with vegetables which would be prepared in this same way.

BARBUE MARINÉE, PANÉE

Breaded, Marinated Brill

Clean and gut the fish, slash it across the back, dip it in lemon juice, then marinate it for three hours in some white wine seasoned with salt, pepper, and an aromatic *bouquet garni*.

Remove it from the marinade, dip it in some melted butter and coat with some fine, dry, sifted breadcrumbs.

Arrange the brill on a buttered ovenproof dish. Season it with salt and pepper and dot it with butter. Bake it in the oven.

Decorate the dish with lemon slices and fried parsley.

Serve, sending along in a sauceboat some hollandaise sauce made with crayfish butter.[1]

Other fish may be prepared in the same way, notably conger eel, sole, and turbot.

Instead of using the whole fish, one could use just the filets. The dish is less presentable but it has the added advantage of not having any bones.

NOTE

1. See recipe for this hollandaise under *Sole Soufflée Sauce Hollandaise Vert-Pré.*

PIMENTADE DE FILETS DE DAURADE[1]

Peppery Sea Bream Ragoût

Pimentade is a ragoût of fish with a liquid pepper sauce which is eaten especially in the Antilles and in Guyana and is served at the beginning of the meal. The best *pimentade* which I have eaten was a *pimentade* made with *aïmara* heads. This is a large Guyana fish, the size of a salmon, which one fishes for at the river mouths. Its cheeks are very delicate and tasty. For the most part, however, one uses less delicate marine fishes, especially the *mâchoiran blanc*, a fish which lives in mud and slime and which would hardly be edible prepared in any other manner.

In the French colonies, *pimentade* is always accompanied by *couac* (a manioc semolina) or by *cassave* (a pancake made of *couac*). It is quite difficult, in France, to make a *pimentade* as in the colonies because of lack of basic ingredients.

However, here is a recipe for *pimentade* prepared with filets of sea bream which should give an idea of the Creole dish. It is interesting from this point of view.

For six people, use:

1 lb. tomatoes
1⅓ C. white wine
½ C. fish broth
4 carrots
7 T. butter
½ small onion
5 tsp. flour
½ tsp. salt
few grains paprika
10 *cacarats* **(small Guyana peppers)**[2]
1 sea bream, weighing 2½ lbs.
1 lemon (if possible a green Antilles lemon)
1 clove garlic
1 *bouquet garni*

Cut off the sea bream filets and put them in a container with salt, paprika, minced garlic and the juice of ½ lemon. Let this marinate for one hour.

Prepare a court bouillon with the white wine, the fish broth, the *bouquet garni*, two-thirds of the onion, the minced carrots, the peppers, the zest of half the lemon. In this cook the bones and head of the sea bream for about ½ hour, then strain.

Reduce the tomatoes to a pulp in a saucepan. Strain them and add the juices to the strained court bouillon and set aside.

In a skillet, melt the butter, blend in the flour, add the rest of the minced onion, and cook this for a few minutes. Now stir in the strained court bouillon and add the sea bream filets and the rest of the lemon juice; simmer gently for thirty minutes.

Arrange the filets in a deep serving dish, pour the sauce over them, and serve. Instead of *couac* pass some dry, boiled rice, separately, in a vegetable dish.

NOTES

1. *Chrysophrys aurata,* a marine fish of the Sparidae family.

2. If these are not available any other type of small, hot pepper could be used.

DORADE[1] FARCIE

Stuffed Fish

Take a nice large *dorade* with roe, with a nice pink or reddish color and silvery belly. Scale it, clean it and wipe it.

Slit the fish along the dorsal side and remove the backbone without damaging the fish.[2]

Prepare a delicate forcemeat stuffing using some mashed, soaked, and desalted anchovies, the fish roe, and some chopped mushrooms cooked in butter and lemon juice. Season this mixture with paprika and bind with an egg. Put the stuffing in place of the backbone.

In order to avoid having the fish lose its shape during the cooking, wrap it in one or two layers of cheesecloth, or some other thin material which can be sown tightly to the fish. Cook it for ten or fifteen minutes in a court bouillon made with white wine. Remove the fish and keep it warm.

Make a purée with the tail meat of some gray shrimp and some heavy cream. This will give you what is known as a *coulis* of shrimp. Make a shrimp butter with the shells and trimmings from the shrimp.

Reduce the fish cooking liquid rapidly and strain it. Thicken it with a little flour or potato starch. Whisk the shrimp butter into it. Arrange the fish, wrapping removed, on a platter, coat it with the sauce and decorate the platter at each end with a little bunch of pink shrimp. Along the sides arrange some large mushrooms filled with capers and some croquettes of souffléed potatoes.

Pour the sauce into a sauceboat after having added the shrimp *coulis* to it.

Serve the fish and sauce at the same time.

Other fish may prepared in this way: bass, brill, bream, trout, young turbot, etc.

NOTES

1. The name *dorade*, in France, is applied to various fishes of the Sparidae family, such as: *Cantherus vulgaris*, not a very choice fish; *Pagellus erithrinus, Pagellus controdontus, Pagrus vulgaris,*

and the *Pagrus orphus*, which are all excellent food fishes. The porgies, scups, and giltheads are related to the *dorade*.

2. Those who find this procedure too difficult may simply fill the stomach cavity of the fish with the stuffing. It will not be as pretty, that's all.

MAQUEREAUX[1] FARCIS, GRILLÉS

Broiled Stuffed Mackerel

For six people, use:

- **1 1/3 C. very thick, highly seasoned Béchamel sauce made with fish broth**
- **1 C. grated Parmesan cheese**
- **2 T. chopped** *fines herbes*
- **9 mackerels with milt, weighing 4 lbs. together**
- **butter**
- **salt and pepper**

Clean and gut the fish and set aside the milts.

Prepare a stuffing with the Béchamel, the Parmesan, the *fines herbes*, and the milts.

Stuff the mackerel with this mixture, season them with salt and pepper, and wrap them in well-buttered parchment paper.

Cook them under the broiler for about twenty minutes.

Remove the wrapping paper and arrange the fish on a platter. Serve, sending along at the same time, in a sauceboat, tomato sauce or some tomato béarnaise,[2] or even some gooseberry sauce.[3]

NOTES

1. *Scomber scomber*, Scomberidae family. A learned gentleman of the eighteenth century, Dr. Louis Lemery, "docteur régent de La Faculté de Médecine de Paris" and member of the Royal Academy of Sciences, in his *Traité des Aliments* (2nd edition, page 387, printed in Paris in 1705 by Pierre Witte at l'Ange Gardien, rue Saint-Jacques), says that "the name [*maquereau*] has been given to this fish because as soon as spring arrives he follows the small shad, collectively referred to as virgins, and leads them to the males." In French *maquereau* means pimp!

2. To make a tomato béarnaise sauce, just add, to plain béarnaise sauce at least one-fourth its volume of very thick tomato purée.

3. Gooseberry sauce is prepared as follows: skin, wash, and blanch some very green gooseberries for five minutes in boiling water. Drain them and finish cooking them in 1/3 cup of sugar dissolved in 1/4 cup of white wine. Strain them through a fine sieve and then add 1 3/4 cups butter sauce (see recipe for *colin*). Mix these together thoroughly.

MAQUEREAUX AUX TOMATES, GRATINÉS

Oven-Browned Mackerel with Tomatoes

For four people, use:

- **1 1/2 lbs. tomatoes**
- **1/4 lb. butter**
- **4 mackerels with roe, weighing about 1 1/4 lb. in all**
- **1 clove garlic**
- **dry sifted breadcrumbs**
- **chopped parsley**
- **salt and pepper**

Scald and skin the tomatoes.

Melt 5 tablespoons of butter in a saucepan. Cook the garlic clove in it without browning and then strain the butter.

Cook the tomatoes in this flavored butter, sprinkle on the parsley, season with salt and pepper, and continue to cook until the liquid has reduced somewhat.

Clean and gut the mackerels, split them down the back, remove the backbones, and cut off the heads. Season the opened fish and then wrap them in buttered paper and broil them.

Grease a low ovenproof casserole with 4 teaspoons of butter and spoon in half the tomatoes. Arrange the unwrapped mackerels on top, cover with the rest of the tomatoes, sprinkle with dry, sifted breadcrumbs, and dot the top with the rest of the butter. Bake this in the oven for about ten minutes.

This method of preparing fish may be adapted to other varieties: fried weever or whiting, baked hake, broiled gurnet, poached sea bream, etc.

NOTE

1. In France the mackerels from Dieppe are the choicest.

MAQUEREAUX À LA CRÈME

Mackerels in Sour Cream

Clean and gut some medium-sized mackerels and put them in a dish. Cover them with coarse salt and leave them for two hours. Shake them to remove the excess salt and cook them in a court bouillon.

Remove the heads, skin and bone the fish, and slice them into filets. Arrange these on a platter and let them cool.

Season them with wine vinegar and coat them with sour cream.[1] Sprinkle them with a few chopped chives.

This is a very pleasant hors-d'oeuvre.

NOTE

1. The French recipe in its original form uses what is known as *crème double*. This is cream which has been extracted by a separator and contains at least thirty percent butterfat. In a great many recipes commercial sour cream makes an interesting substitute, although, naturally, the taste will differ somewhat from the original.

HARENGS[1] À LA POÊLE, MAÎTRE D'HÔTEL

Skillet Herring, Maître d'Hôtel

Clean and gut, wash and wipe the herrings. Slash them in several places and season them with salt and pepper.

In a heavy skillet put as many teaspoonfulls of olive oil as there

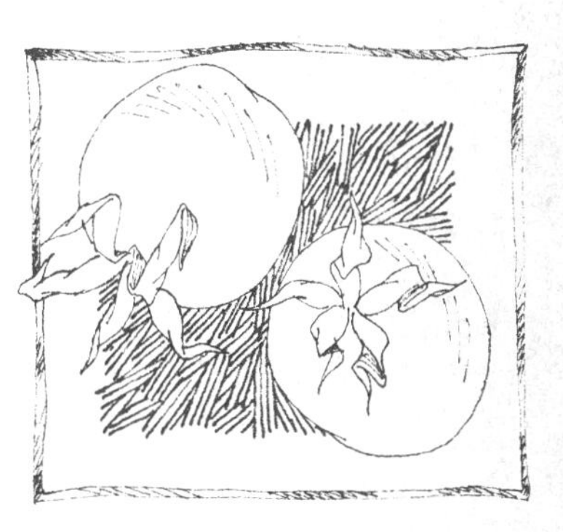

are herrings. When it is very hot put in the fish and let them cook for three or four minutes per side. Then remove and drain them.

Serve the herrings on a platter containing some melted butter, sprinkle some parsley on them, season with salt and pepper, and dribble on either vinegar or lemon juice, to taste.

This method of cooking helps the herrings retain all their flavor.

NOTE

1. *Clupea harengus*, Clupeidae family.

HARENGS FRAIS MARINÉS

Marinated Fresh Herrings

For six people, use:

1 C. white wine
½ C. vinegar
1 carrot
1 small onion
1 T. butter
2 tsp. salt
1 tsp. sugar
2 tsp. flour
1 shallot
few sprigs parsley
1 tsp. white peppercorns
a pinch coriander
a pinch mace
a pinch thyme
½ leaf bay leaf
a pinch cinnamon
2 cloves
a pinch marjoram
few grains cayenne pepper
6 fresh herrings with roe
1 lemon

Clean, gut, wash, and dry the herrings. Cut off their heads.

In a saucepan put the butter, the sliced or julienne of carrot, thyme, bay leaf and peppercorns. Cook these slowly without browning, then sprinkle with flour and let brown lightly. Stir in the wine and vinegar and season with salt, sugar, minced shallot, parsley, coriander, mace, cinnamon, and clove. Bring this all to a boil and let it simmer very slowly for thirty-five to forty minutes so as to reduce the liquid about one-third. Take the marinade off the fire, add the powdered marjoram and the cayenne, and let it cool.

Slice the onions paper thin.

Arrange the herrings on a platter with the raw onion rings. Pour the almost-cool marinade over them. Chill these together, covered, for at least twenty-four hours.

Remove the herrings from the marinade and place in another dish. Arrange 6 thin slices of lemon on top. Boil up the marinade with all the ingredients in it and cook it again for five minutes; then, when it is boiling hot, strain it over the herrings.

When cold, cover the dish and keep in a cool, dry place.

The herrings may be served from the next day on. This is an excellent hors-d'oeuvre.

Small mackerels may be prepared in this way, but it would be best to boil them up twice in the marinade since mackerel flesh is much more compact than that of herring.

FILETS DE HARENGS SAURS MARINÉS

Marinated Salt Herrings

For eight people, use:

3 T. vinegar
3 T. white wine
3 T. olive oil
4 plump salted herrings with roes
2 finely minced shallots
2 cloves
thyme
bay leaf
peppercorns

Soak the herrings for twenty-four hours in water to remove the salt. Skin them, remove the roes, and wash everything in cold water. Mash the roes until they are reduced to a paste and force them through a fine sieve.[1] To this purée add the vinegar, the white wine, and the oil, stirring and beating well. Then add the shallots, cloves, thyme, bay leaf, and peppercorns, and spoon this mixture over the herring to marinate.

These herrings may be served either whole or using just the filets, or even cut into small pieces. This is a very good hors-d'oeuvre.

These herrings, along with their sauce, strained through a fine sieve,[1] may be mixed into a potato salad, to which they add a tasty seasoning.

NOTE

1. An electric blender is useful for this procedure and much quicker.

Cod

The cods *Gadus* of the Gadidae family are large voracious fishes from the Arctic Sea. They rarely come down to Europe below Iceland and the North Sea, or, in America, below Newfoundland.

One designates, under the name of cod, certain fishes of different species. Only two really deserve, gastronomically speaking, any attention: the *Gadus morua*, with a greenish skin, which can attain a length of three or four feet, and is very prized for its flesh and for the oil which is extracted from its liver; and *Gadus aeglefinus*, or the black cod of Saint-Pierre, which only differs from the former by its smaller size and dark gray color.

In France, the name for fresh cod is *cabillaud*. When it is salted, for preservation purposes, it is called *morue verte* (green cod); when it is dried, it is called *merluche* (stockfish).

The *Gadus aeglefinus*, commonly called *églefin* in French, is fished for mostly in the North Sea and also in the Irish Sea and even on the coast of Brittany. It is eaten fresh in the area where it is caught, but quite often it is smoked in order to preserve it.

There are several ways of preparing both species of cod.

They can be cooked in a court bouillon, fried, broiled, boiled or poached. The last three methods of preparation are generally served with boiled or steamed potatoes and everything sprinkled with parsley, which has either been blanched or not, and the dish then coated with melted butter.

It goes without saying that it can also be prepared according to the recipes given below for cod and haddock.

MORUE AUX POMMES DE TERRE

Salt Cod with Potatoes

For six people, use:

1½ lbs. freshened salt cod
1 lb. peeled potatoes
½ lb. butter
2 cloves garlic
2 T. parsley (chopped)
black pepper
lemon juice

Separately, cook the cod in water and steam the potatoes.

Remove the skin and bones from the fish and flake it. Slice the potatoes and keep everything warm.

Cook the garlic in 8 tablespoons of butter for five minutes then strain the flavored butter.

In a large skillet arrange alternate layers of flaked cod and sliced potatoes, pouring a little of the flavored butter on each layer, along with salt, pepper, and parsley. Cook this for a minute or two without browning, adding the rest of the butter, cut up, as it cooks. Sprinkle with lemon juice and serve.

In this recipe the cod and potatoes blend perfectly. The garlic flavors the dish agreeably without overpowering it, and the lemon juice gives a very discreet note of acidity.

Garlic enthusiasts would add even more.

Instead of using the 4 ounces of butter, added at the last, one could use 14 tablespoons of heavy cream and the dish would be smoother and more unctuous.

MORUE AUX HARICOTS

Salt Cod with Beans

For six to eight people, use:

1½ lbs. freshened salt cod
1 lb. dried haricot beans
14 T. butter
⅔ C. cream
3 onions
2 carrots
2 medium leeks
1 clove garlic
bouquet garni (parsley, thyme, bay leaf)
blanched, chopped parsley
salt and pepper

Soak the beans for several hours or overnight, depending on the age of the beans and package directions. They will soften and swell.

At the same time, cook the following: the beans in salted water with the leeks, carrots, one onion, and the *bouquet garni* (drain the beans and save the liquid; keep everything hot); the cod in water, then remove the skin and bones and flake it (keep this hot, too).

Cook the garlic and the 2 remaining onions in 7 tablespoons of butter, without browning. Then add some of the bean cooking liquid, season with salt and pepper, and let this cook to flavor the liquid.

Strain this through a fine sieve and give it some body with a little bean purée, obtained by mashing some of the cooked beans and forcing them through a sieve, ricer, or vegetable mill.

Whisk this sauce up with the rest of the butter and the cream. Heat, taste, and complete the seasoning if necessary, so as to have a fairly highly seasoned sauce.

Put the flaked cod and the beans into a deep serving dish. Sprinkle with the chopped parsley and pour the sauce over everything.

For variation, one could make the same dish by adding to the sauce some thick tomato purée (about 1 cup), which should be added to the sauce at the same time as the bean purée. This should be cooked until the sauce is fairly thick and the butter and cream added at the last.

For another variation, half the beans could be omitted and in their stead a dozen croûtons, fried in butter, could be used.

MORUE À LA CRÈME EN TURBAN DE PILAF AU CURRY

Creamed Salt Cod in a Ring of Curried Rice Pilaf

For six to eight people, use:

1½ lbs. freshened salt cod
2 C. rice
1 C. butter
14 T. cream
2 T. chopped parsley
1 tsp. curry powder
1 small onion (optional)
lemon juice
pepper

Poach the cod in water, remove the skin and bones, flake it, and keep it warm. Save the water.

In a saucepan put half of the butter, the chopped onion, and the rice. Cook this until the rice has turned a golden color. Add some of the cod liquid and the curry. Continue cooking until the water has completely evaporated and the grains of rice are cooked but still separate and not mushy.

Fill a ring mold with this pilaf and keep it warm in a hot water bath.

Cook the cod in the rest of the butter. Season it with salt, pepper, and lemon juice. Sprinkle on the parsley and add the cream. Mix everything well. Heat this up for a minute or two.

Unmold the pilaf ring on a platter and fill the center with the cod and its sauce, and serve.

MORUE À L'ESPAGNOLE

Spanish Style Cod

For six people, use:

1¼ lb. freshened salt cod
1¼ lb. potatoes
1 lb. tomatoes
1 lb. sweet, fresh, red peppers[1]
7 T. olive oil
1 small onion
2 cloves garlic
4 tsp. flour
freshly ground pepper to taste
bouquet garni **(parsley, thyme, bay leaf)**
dry, sifted breadcrumbs
salt

Cook the cod in water, drain it, remove the skin and the bones, and cut it into serving pieces. Reserve 1 cup of the cooking liquid.

Scald and peel the peppers and cut them into strips. Sprinkle the strips with a little freshly ground black pepper.

In the oil cook the peeled, chopped onion, add the cut up tomatoes, garlic, *bouquet garni*, a little pepper, and pour in the reserved cod cooking liquid. Let this all cook together for ten minutes. Thicken with some flour mixed with a little cold water and continue cooking for another few minutes. Complete the seasoning with a little salt, if necessary, and strain the sauce.

At the same time, steam some potatoes, and peel and slice them.

In an ovenproof casserole spread a layer of the sliced potatoes, on top put some pieces of cod, then add a layer of peppers, and spoon on some of the sauce. Repeat this procedure until all the ingredients are used up. Sprinkle the top with breadcrumbs and bake the casserole in a hot oven until the dish has acquired an unctuous consistency, which would require about thirty minutes. The liquid should have almost completely evaporated.

This is an excellent dish.

By substituting, for the salt cod, some fresh cod cooked in a wine court bouillon, the dish would be even nicer.

NOTE

1. Paprika could be used if the fresh peppers are not available.

For six to eight people, use:

1½ lbs. freshened salt cod
½ lb. macaroni
½ lb. mushrooms
1 cup thick tomato purée
14 T. cream
¾ C. (12 T.) butter
½ C. fish fumet
7 T. capers
cayenne
sweet red pepper
lemon juice
salt and pepper

TIMBALE DE MORUE

Timbale of Cod

Peel the mushrooms and dip them in lemon juice.

Cook, at the same time: the cod in water (remove the skin and bones and flake it); the mushrooms in butter; and the macaroni in salted water (drain it).

Keep all these warm.

Dissolve the tomato sauce in the fish fumet and add some chopped red pepper to taste. Heat this up.

Cook the flaked cod in five tablespoons of butter.

Cook the well-drained macaroni in the rest of the butter without letting it brown.

Combine the tomato mixture, the flaked cod, the macaroni, and the mushrooms and their cooking juices. Season with cayenne and add the capers and the cream. Mix these together carefully so as not to break up the macaroni. Heat it up slowly, taste and complete the seasoning, if necessary, with salt and pepper. Spoon the mixture into a porcelain timbale which has been preheated in a hot water bath.

One may make, in a similar way, a vol-au-vent of salt cod, by substituting, for the macaroni, some pike and crayfish quenelles (see recipe), and by adding some chopped truffles cooked in madeira. This mixture would then be spooned into a vol-au-vent shell.

All these recipes are applicable to dried unsalted cod.

For six people, use:

10 oz. salted cod filets
1⅓ C. flour
⅓ C. milk
⅓ C. water
4 tsp. butter
7 eggs
potatoes
tomato sauce
nutmeg
salt and pepper

CROQUETTES DE MORUE, SOUFFLÉES

Souffléed Croquettes of Cod

Soak the cod in cold water changing the water several times. Then poach it in fresh water.

Boil the milk and water together; add the butter and let it melt.

Off the fire, add the flour all at once and then beat the mixture with a wooden spoon over the fire until the mixture comes away from the sides of the pan and the paste is smooth. Take the pan off the fire again and, one by one, add 5 eggs beating well after each one. Cool the paste.

Cook the potatoes in their skins, peel them and purée them in a ricer or food mill, or force them through a sieve.

Little by little mix 7 ounces of this potatoe purée into the cooled *panade,* along with the 2 remaining eggs. Season with salt, pepper, and nutmeg to taste.

Either chop or flake the cod.

Using a wet dessert spoon take up a little of the potato *panade;* on top put a little of the flaked cod, then cover with more *panade.* Smooth croquette with another wet spoon and slip it gently, with a spatula, into a medium-hot fry bath. Repeat this procedure until you have as many croquettes as you need. Let them cook.

Serve on a napkin-covered platter and pass a thick tomato sauce at the same time.

Different types of souffléed croquettes can be made with meat or fish.

SOUFFLÉ DE MORUE AUX POMMES DE TERRE

Cod and Potato Soufflé

For six people, use:

1 lb. 3 oz. freshened salt cod
1 lb. 3 oz. peeled potatoes
7 T. cream
7 T. butter
freshly ground black pepper to taste
a pinch cayenne pepper
a grating nutmeg
4 eggs

Separate the yolks and whites of the eggs.

Separately, cook the cod in water and steam the potatoes.

Remove skin and bones from the cod and either grind or chop it, or make a purée by forcing it through a sieve.

Purée the potatoes and add the cream, 5 tablespoons of butter, salt, pepper, cayenne, nutmeg, and the egg yolks. Mix these together thoroughly; then add the cod and mix again.

Beat the egg whites until stiff, fold in the above mixture, and mix a final time. Spoon everything into a soufflé casserole which has been buttered with the rest of the butter.

Bake this in a hot oven for twenty minutes. The mixture should puff up and brown lightly. Serve it in the same dish.

The soufflé will rise more or less depending on how finely chopped the cod is. However, cod lovers prefer to sacrifice a little of the puffiness and find a few pieces of the cod itself.

BRANDADE DE MORUE

Brandade of Cod

Brandade de Morue is a Provençal dish which has the reputation of being heavy. This is true only when it is prepared carelessly and with inferior ingredients.

For six people use 2 pounds of well-freshened cod. Put it in a saucepan with quite a lot of water and heat it up. When it comes to the first boil, cover the pan and put it on an asbestos mat over a very low flame. Let this poach for about twenty minutes, then bone it and chop it up.

In a saucepan put the chopped or flaked cod along with the skin[1] and 1/2 cup of warm olive oil. *Brandissez* (literally, brandish) it with a spoon. This means to agitate it and work it, first for five minutes over the fire, and then in a double boiler or hot water bath. Continue to work it until the oil has been completely absorbed. Now, add some more oil, in small quantities, always working the mass vigorously with the wooden spoon so as to obtain a very smooth, velvety mixture.

Add the cream, mix it in well, flavor the mixture with crushed garlic, lemon juice, grated lemon peel, and some freshly ground pepper. Taste and complete the seasoning, if necessary, with a little salt.[2] To this mixture add a little minced raw truffle. Heat this all up for a moment and then keep it warm in a hot water bath until serving time.

Spoon the *brandade* into patty shells or in a vol-au-vent crust. Decorate it with slivers of truffle cooked in madeira, and serve.

To vary, one could incorporate some Béchamel sauce or a few steamed, puréed potatoes to the mixture. The real *brandade*, however, is prepared as above.

NOTES

1. One could omit the skin and the *brandade* would be much whiter. However, I prefer to use the skin because it gives flavor and helps to bind it.

2. It is almost impossible to give precise amounts of each ingredient because everything depends upon the quantity of oil absorbed by the cod. The quantity varies with the quality of the fish.

Haddock[1]

Haddock arrives in Paris very lightly salted and very slightly smoked. It therefore must be eaten immediately because it deteriorates rapidly. The choicest is the lightly smoked haddock from Finnan, a small port town in Scotland.

In England haddock is served broiled or boiled with melted butter or with a curry sauce.

In my opinion, it is best to poach it for five to ten minutes according to its size and to serve it like fresh cod or fresh haddock, poached.

NOTE

1. This is the English name for what the French call *églefin*.

HADOCK POCHÉ, AUX POMMES DE TERRE SAUTÉES, SAUCE AUX OEUFS DURS

Poached Haddock with Sautéed Potatoes and Hard-Boiled Egg Sauce

For six to eight people, use:

2 lbs. potatoes
1½ lbs. haddock filets
2 C. milk
14 T. butter
7 T. cream
4 T. flour
2 hard-boiled eggs
1 small carrot
1 small turnip
1 small onion
bouquet garni
chopped parsley
lemon juice
nutmeg
salt and pepper

Boil the potatoes in salted water, peel, slice, then sauté them in 7 tablespoons of butter. Season them with salt.

Poach the haddock filets in a small amount of salted water or milk (the milk used here would be over and above the 2 cups listed above). Finish cooking the fish over a very low flame in a covered pan. Cooking time should be about fifteen minutes in all.

At the same time prepare the sauce.

In 3 tablespoons of butter cook the chopped carrot, turnip, and onion until they are lightly browned. Add the flour and stir around a few minutes without browning. Add the boiled milk, season with the *bouquet garni*, salt, pepper, and nutmeg. Let this all simmer until the sauce is thickened. This should take about one hour. Strain the sauce and whisk in the rest of the butter and the cream. Heat it up. At the last minute put in some chopped parsley and the hard-boiled eggs, either coarsely chopped or pushed through a coarse sieve.

Arrange the haddock filets on a platter, surround with the sautéed potatoes, and serve. Pass the sauce at the same time.

THON[1] GRILLÉ, SAUCE TOMATE

Broiled Tuna Steaks with Tomato Sauce

Cut tuna steaks about three-fourths of an inch thick and broil them over a hot fire. Salt them, and when they are cooked serve them with a tomato sauce, which goes exceedingly well with tuna. Cooking time should be about twenty minutes. The fish is done when the flesh separates easily from the bone.

A word about tomato sauce. During about seven months of the year it is difficult to find fresh tomatoes at a reasonable price. It is then preferable to use home-canned tomato purée[2] or a commercial brand, especially Italian ones.

1 C. tomato purée
4 T. butter
4 tsp. flour
bouillon or meat juices
salt and pepper

In winter, if one wants to have 1 cup of sauce or enough to fill a normal sauceboat, one would use:

One would cook the flour in 3 tablespoons of butter without letting it brown, then add the tomato purée, a small quantity at a time, mixing well. This should be seasoned and thinned, if necessary, with a little bouillon or meat juice, and should cook for fifteen minutes. The rest of the butter should then be added and allowed to melt before stirring the sauce smooth at serving time.

This method has the advantage of helping to retain the distinct character of the sauce and of obtaining, at a time when the fresh fruits are rare, a sauce which seems to have been made with fresh tomatoes.

In summer, it goes without saying, one can make the sauce exactly the same way using fresh fruit, starting out as directed in the recipe for making canned tomato sauce. But there is no reason why one cannot add other ingredients while still preserving the natural supremacy of the tomato.

It is in this spirit that I give the following recipe.

To make a sauceboat full of tomato sauce, use:

2 lbs. fresh ripe tomatoes
1 C. white wine
4 T. butter
4 tsp. flour
2 onions
bouquet garni
meat glaze
clove
salt and pepper

Peel and cut up the tomatoes. Put them in a saucepan with the onion, the *bouquet,* cloves to taste and wine. Let these cook for one hour over a very low flame. Strain.

Cook the flour in 3 tablespoons of butter without browning; then add the tomato purée, the meat glaze, salt, and pepper. Reduce this to the desired consistency, taste, add the rest of the butter. Let it melt, mix, and serve.

NOTES

1. *Thynnus vulgaris,* Scomberidae family.
2. See recipe in vegetable section.

RAIE[1] AU BEURRE

Raie in Butter

For six people, use:

3 lbs. *raie,* **taken from the center**
1 C. butter
2 oz. capers
2 T. coarse salt
2 qts. water
1 carrot
1 onion
bouquet garni
vinegar
lemon juice
chopped parsley
salt and pepper

Wash the *raie* in cold water and trim it.

In a fish pan put the water, the chopped onion and carrot, the *bouquet garni,* salt, some peppercorns and vinegar to taste. Cook this for a half hour then plunge in the *raie.* The boiling will stop immediately. Bring it up once to a boil, reduce the flame, and cook the fish at barely a simmer for about a half hour.

Lift out the *raie,* skin it, trim it, drain it, and keep it hot.

Melt the butter and cook it to a nut-brown color or to black[2] but without letting it burn. Add salt and pepper, chopped parsley, capers, lemon juice and vinegar to taste and pour this over the *raie*. Serve, after having garnished the platter with fried parsley.

One may prepare, using nut-brown or black butter, other types of fish, especially tuna and cod.

NOTES

1. There are different types of *raie*. The best are the *Raia punctata*, which is called *raie douce* in Paris markets, and the *Raia clavata* of the Raiidae family.
2. In my opinion, the *beurre noisette* is the most suitable. Black butter is rather indigestible.

ORGAN AND VARIETY MEATS

GRAS-DOUBLE[2] AU VIN BLANC

Tripe in White Wine

Prepare: on the one hand, two *bouquets garnis* using the leek, celery, thyme and bay leaves; on the other hand, two cheesecloth bags each containing half of the onion, half the peppercorns and half the cloves.

Wash the tripe in hot water. Cut it into three-inch squares.

In a porcelain, fireproof casserole, or *cocotte*, put half the carrots, one of the bouquets, and one cheesecloth bag. Add the tripe, the calf's foot, the rest of the carrots, the second bouquet and the second cheesecloth bag. Season with salt and nutmeg to taste. Now pour in the water, the sauterne, and the brandy. Bake this in a very slow oven, covered, for at least twelve hours.

For ten to twelve people, use:

4 lbs. scraped, blanched tripe
3 C. sauterne wine
1/2 lb. sliced carrots
1/2 lb. onions
1 C. water
1 leek
4 T. coarse salt
3 T. brandy
1 stalk celery
1 T. black peppercorns
1/8 tsp. thyme
2 bay leaves
cloves
1 large calf's foot, boned and cut up
nutmeg

Remove the *bouquets* and the cheesecloth bags. Serve in heated plates.

In the Midi (South) one often adds two cloves of garlic to the ingredients.

One would have *tripe à la périgourdine* by adding to the above ingredients some sliced truffles, which would be cooked with the tripe.

One would have *tripe à la mode de Caen* if one replaced the wine with some pure, fresh apple cider and used Calvados instead of brandy.

Another interesting variation consists in using, as the liquid, 1 1/2 cups of white wine, 1 1/2 cups of cider, 3/4 cup of good bouillon, and 3 tablespoons of *eau-de-vie de Châteauneuf-du-Pape*. One would also add to all the other ingredients 1/4 pound of peeled, chopped, and seeded tomatoes.

NOTES

1. From the gastronomical point of view, meat byproducts, or variety meats and organs, comprise the extremities, the entrails, certain viscera, and certain glands such as the head, tail, feet, tripe, heart, liver, spleen, lungs, kidneys, sweetbreads, udder, etc.
2. In Paris the term *gras-double* is applied to what in other parts are called tripe. Tripe consists of not only the *gras-double* proper, which is the lining of the first stomach of ruminants, but also consists of the second stomach, the third stomach, and the fourth stomach. In the United States tripe, on the market, is usually the first and second stomachs.

GRAS-DOUBLE AUX TOMATES

Tripe with Tomatoes

For six people, use:

3 lbs. tripe
2 1/3 C. good strong consommé
1/2 C. thick tomato purée
3 T. butter
4 tsp. flour
2 marrow bones (4 inches long)
bouquet garni **(parsley and celery)**
breadcrumbs
marjoram
salt and pepper

Wash the tripe in hot water and cut into slivers. Put it in the boiling consommé and let it simmer, very slowly, for enough time to tenderize it. This would probably be at least three hours.

Make a roux with 5 teaspoons of butter and the flour. Add to it the tripe, tomato purée, *bouquet* of parsley and celery, some marjoram to taste. Let this all simmer together for a half hour. Taste and complete the seasoning with salt and pepper, if necessary.

Plug the ends of the marrow bones and poach them in salted water. Slide out the marrow and slice it.

Arrange the tripe on a platter, garnish with the marrow, sprinkle with breadcrumbs, and pour the rest of the melted butter over it. Serve.

FRITURE DE GRAS-DOUBLE

Fried Tripe

For four people, use:

1½ lbs. tripe
2 C. milk
1 small onion
3 tsp. coarse salt
black pepper to taste
2 eggs
2 lemons
bouquet garni
dry, sifted breadcrumbs

Peel and slice the onion.

Cut the tripe into 2½-inch squares and cook it in the milk along with the onion, *bouquet garni*, salt, and pepper, for four hours. Let the tripe cool in the liquid and then remove it. Scrape off any accumulated scum.

Beat the eggs, dip the pieces of tripe into them, then coat them with breadcrumbs and fry in hot fat. After removing them from the fry bath, sprinkle with table salt.

Serve on a napkin-covered platter with some lemon halves.

LANGUE DE BOEUF SALÉE[1]

Salted Beef Tongue

For six people, use:

4 lbs. sea salt
5 tsp. powdered saltpeter
2 T. freshly ground black pepper
2 T. *quatre épices*
5 tsp. paprika
2 T. chopped thyme
½ tsp. sugar
10 medium sliced onions
10 shallots
6 garlic cloves
6 bay leaves
1 tsp. coriander seeds
beef tongue
white wine
curry to taste

Make small incisions in the skin of the tongue.

Rub the tongue with the saltpeter, then place it in a porcelain container with the onions, shallots, garlic, bay leaf, and thyme. Sprinkle on the pepper, curry, *quatre épices*, paprika, sugar, coriander, and cover the whole with coarse salt. Keep this in a cool place, in the open container, for two weeks.

Lift out the tongue, shake off the salt, and cook it for three hours in some white wine. Let it cool in the liquid, then lift it out, wipe it off, and it is ready to serve.

Beef tongue, prepared this way, is far superior to all similar commercial products.

NOTE

1. Salting, which is either done dry or in brine, is a very ancient method of preserving food.

A. Dry Method

The proportions are:
2 lbs. sea salt
10 tsp. saltpeter
1 small bay leaf
1 sprig of thyme

The ingredients to be salted are first pierced fairly deeply beforehand with a large needle. Then they are rubbed with saltpeter and place in a receptacle along with the salt, saltpeter, bay leaf, and thyme, where they will remain varying lengths of time according to size.

B. Brine Method.

The proportions are:
5 lbs. of sea salt
1 cup saltpeter
1 cup brown sugar (firmly packed)
1 tsp. juniper berries
1. tsp. black pepper
6 qts. water
thyme
bay leaf
quatre épices (optional)

Cook everything together and let it cool, then pour this brine over the food to be salted. The food should have been deeply punctured with a large needle and rubbed with salt and saltpeter. A deep glazed earthenware crock is ideal for this procedure.

The food to be salted must rest on a sort of wooden rack placed at the bottom of the crock and the brine must cover everything completely.

The larger pieces to be salted should be injected with the brine using a hypodermic needle, to make sure that the innermost portions get salted.

LANGUE DE BOEUF FUMÉE[1]

Smoked Beef Tongue

Tongue, which has been salted as described above, then dried off, is exposed for eight whole days to the smoke of green juniper branches with berries on. The intensity is increased progressively. Once it is smoked, it must be hung in a dry place. After six weeks of drying, it may be eaten, either raw or cooked, and either hot or cold.

When it is to be served hot, one would cook it in plain water for three hours. But if it is to be served cold, one should use, preferably, as the cooking liquid, a court-bouillon made with wine, in which it should stay until cool.

NOTE

1. Smoking, or the exposure of meats and fish to the action of smoke, is an excellent way of preserving. It allows for the flavor-

ing of the food in a different way, according to its use. The ingredients to be smoked are first salted, then wiped, and, last, exposed, in a chimney, or better yet, in a smokehouse, far enough away from the hearth so that the fire cannot reach them, yet near enough for the smoke to penetrate them thoroughly. Smoking must be progressive and the fuel must be fresh so as to throw off the maximum amount of smoke. The most commonly used woods are: birch, oak, beech, poplar, and larch. However, the choicest fuel consists of green juniper branches with berries.

Smoking is finished off with the burning of aromatics such as bay leaf, rosemary, thyme, dried prunes, licorice wood, cloves, etc.

To be smoked properly, pieces of beef or lamb must not weigh more than six pounds. Smoking requires about seven weeks. One week of intensive smoking with juniper and six weeks of slow smoking with ordinary woods. After six weeks of drying, these smoked meats may be eaten raw. They may also be prepared with vegetables.

Hams are frequently put to macerate in some brandy flavored with juniper berries, for several days, *after* having been removed from the brine and *before* being smoked. The length of time for smoking a medium-sized ham is about two weeks.

The same method may be used for sausages of all kinds.

Certain parts of fowl are smoked, especially goose breast.

Fish is also smoked. The time period goes from twenty-four hours for herring, four days for pike and eel, to three weeks for salmon.

In a general way, the food to be smoked must be suspended during the operation by each end turn and turn about. The smoked foods must be hung in a dry spot to avoid spoilage.

LANGUE À L'ÉCARLATE

Scarlet Pickled Beef Tongue

Get a nice fresh beef tongue, rub it with saltpeter, and put it in brine for eight days. After removing it from the brine, soak it in cold water for four or five hours, changing the water several times. Then, cook it in plain water for three hours.

When it is cooked, remove the skin, wrap the tongue (so that it doesn't darken) in buttered paper and let it cool.

Wrap it in a thin slice of blanched pork belly, which can then be wrapped again in beef casings, reddened with vegetable coloring, or, even better, it can be covered with a good layer of dissolved gelatin (5 ounces of gelatin dissolved in 10½ ounces of water) colored with red food coloring and a little caramel.

TÊTE DE VEAU

Calf's Head

For ten to twelve people, split a calf's head in two, remove the tongue and the brains, and put it to soak in cold water for at least one hour. Blanch the head in boiling water for thirty minutes, then remove it, dry it, and rub it with lemon juice.

In order to keep the head very white, prepare a *blanc* (white broth) in sufficient quantity to cover it completely. To make a *blanc* combine 3 tablespoons flour, 2 tablespoons vinegar, and 1 tablespoon of salt per quart of water. Blend these ingredients together smoothly and cook them. Add a large onion stuck with 1 or 2 cloves, a *bouquet garni,* pepper to taste, and add some ground veal kidney suet.

Wrap the head, minus tongue and brains, in a cloth and plunge it in the boiling *blanc*. Simmer it very slowly for about three hours, as for a *pot-au-feu*. The tongue and brains need less cooking time—an hour and a half for the tongue and twenty-five to thirty minutes for the brains.

Lift out the head, bone it, and arrange it on a napkin covered platter. Garnish it with the sliced tongue and brains. Decorate with parsley.

Serve the calf's head and send along at the same time, in small separate dishes, some chopped onion, chopped parsley, and some capers. Pass around a good vinaigrette sauce in a sauceboat.

For variation, one may serve the calf's head, very hot, without the capers, onion, and parsley, but with a tomato sauce instead.

For another variation one could, after having sliced the head, tongue and brains, place the slices for several minutes in a *sauce poulette* or even in a ravigote sauce made with veal stock and whisked up with ravigote butter. The meat could be arranged on a hot platter with blanched chopped parsley sprinkled over it.

A *financière garniture* in madeira sauce could be added to the sliced calf's head. This would be spooned into a timbale.*

TÊTE DE VEAU EN ASPIC, SAUCE DOUCE

Calf's Head in Aspic, Sweet-Sour Sauce

For ten to twelve people, use:

1 whole calf's head
1 large, 4 small carrots
1 leek
1 onion stuck with 2 cloves
lemon juice
bouquet garni
sea salt

Wash and split the head in two. Remove the tongue and brains and set everything to soak in cold water for two hours. Wipe the head, rub it with lemon juice, and put it in a porcelain kettle with the large carrot, the leek, the onion, cloves, *bouquet garni* and a sufficient quantity of water to cover it completely. Add salt at the rate of 1 tablespoon per quart of water. Bring this to a boil, skim it, and continue to simmer it slowly as for a *pot-au-feu*. The head requires three hours of cooking, the tongue one and a half hours, the brains twenty to thirty minutes.

For one quart of sauce:

1/3 C. equal parts of chopped chives, tarragon, chervil, and parsley
4 hard-boiled eggyolks
oil and vinegar
salt

At leisure, cook the other four carrots in some bouillon without letting them get too soft.

Remove the head from the broth, cut it up into small pieces along with the tongue and brains. Decorate the bottom and sides of a mold with carrot slices, put in the meats mixed together, pour the cooking liquid over all, and let the jelly set.

Prepare a sauce by mashing the hard-boiled egg yolks with the *fines herbes*. Then make a plain sauce with oil, vinegar, and salt, add the sugar, egg yolks, and *fines herbes*. The proportion of sugar indicated above is generally suitable, but it is preferable to depend on one's personal taste and to add it in small quantities, stirring well each time, until the sauce is perfectly blended.

It is the sugar which gives this sauce its special touch. However, one must not notice that it has a sweet taste—it should be hardly noticeable, in fact.

Unmold the aspic and serve it with the sauce.

For variation, one may serve a calf's head in aspic with a cold mustard sauce which would be made as follows: blend egg yolks with lemon juice or vinegar and mustard, then add olive oil, little by little, beating constantly until the consistency is right. Season it with salt, pepper, and chopped tarragon, to taste.

TÊTE DE VEAU FRITE, SAUCE TOMATE

Fried Calf's Head with Tomato Sauce

Six hours ahead of time prepare a very smooth, slightly liquid batter with flour, milk, and salt.

Cook the calf's head as in the preceding recipe. Cut it up, dip each piece in the batter, and deep fry the pieces in a hot fry bath. Remove the pieces as soon as the batter is cooked and serve at once with tomato sauce.

Calf's brains may also be prepared in this way. The only difference would lie in the fact that they should only be poached in the court-bouillon beforehand for twenty minutes.

Slices of cod filet may be prepared this way too.

For six people, use:

5 T. butter
1/4 C. raisins
1/4 C. almonds (chopped)
3 T. flour
4 tsp. meat glaze
1 tsp. granulated sugar
black pepper to taste
1 veal tongue
1 large carrot
1 leek
1 onion stuck with 2 cloves
bouquet garni
salt

LANGUE DE VEAU, SAUCE AUX RAISINS ET AUX AMANDES

Veal Tongue with Raisin and Almond Sauce

Cook the tongue with the vegetables and the *bouquet garni* for an hour and a half as described in the master recipe for *tête de veau*. Keep it hot. Reduce the cooking liquid and skim off the fat.

Blanch, peel, and chop the almonds.

Pick over the raisins and wash them.

Cook the flour in the butter until lightly browned. Stir in a sufficient quantity of the cooking liquid to make a sauce. To this add the meat glaze, sugar, lemon juice, raisins, chopped almonds, and taste for seasoning, adding salt if necessary.

Skin the tongue, slice it, put the slices in the sauce, and let them simmer for an hour over very low heat.

Serve with it some boiled or steamed rice with clarified butter.

Raisin and almond sauce may also accompany certain fish and, in particular, carp poached in court-bouillon.

For six people, use:

7 T. butter
4 T. chopped carrot
4 T. chopped onion
3 T. good meat juice or broth
several large sprigs parsley
1 pair sweetbreads
salt and pepper

RIS DE VEAU AU JUS

Sweet Breads

Skin the sweetbreads and soak for at least 1 hour in water that has been slightly salted with sea salt. Remove them and wipe them off. The classic recipes generally recommend blanching[1] the sweetbreads in water before cooking them. In my opinion this is an error, for their delicate flavor is better preserved if they are not put through that first step.

Here is how I suggest preparing them.

In a saucepan put the butter and the soaked sweetbreads. Cook for about fifteen minutes until they are lightly browned. Remove and put in their place the onions, carrots, *bouquet garni* and the bunch of parsley sprigs. *Pincer*[2] the vegetables for fifteen minutes, put back the sweetbreads, add the meat juice and the salt and pepper, and finish cooking very slowly for a half hour.

Skim the fat off the sauce.

Serve the sweetbreads, coated with the sauce, on a layer of vegetables: peas, spinach, chicory, or sorrel.

NOTES

1. In certain cases people pour boiling water over them; others plunge them into cold water, bring it to a boil, and then remove them.

2. In the culinary sense, the word *pincer* (to pinch) means to attach to the bottom of the pan.

ESCALOPES DE RIS DE VEAU SAUTÉES, AU PIMENT

Sautéed Slices of Sweetbread with Peppers

For six people, use:

1 C. strong veal stock
1 C. tomato purée
¼ lb. mushrooms
½ C. butter
¼ C. white wine
3 sweet red peppers
2 egg yolks
1 pair sweetbreads
salt and pepper

Trim the sweetbreads and soak in cold water.

Slice them. This procedure is somewhat delicate. Therefore, since many people have difficulty slicing raw sweetbreads, one can stiffen them in boiling salted water. They are then cooled under a weight and easily sliced.

Peel the mushrooms, chop them, and cook them in 2 tablespoons of the butter until they have rendered all their water and have browned slightly. Stop the cooking as soon as you smell their very characteristic aroma.

Cook the sweet peppers in the veal broth, cut them into strips, and reserve the cooking liquid.

Heat the tomato purée and add the mushrooms and peppers to it. Keep warm.

Sauté the slices of sweetbread in the rest of the butter; season them with salt and pepper. Remove them and keep them warm in a hot water bath. Deglaze the pan with some good wine, add the pepper cooking liquid and the rest of the veal stock. Boil down quickly to reduce the sauce; then, off the fire, thicken it with the egg yolks.

Put a layer of the tomato mixture on a serving platter, on top of this arrange the slices of sweetbread and coat with the sauce. Serve.

One may increase the proportion of sweet peppers and some crushed hot pepper may also be added if one likes hot food.

This recipe is applicable to many other foods: lamb, lamb sweetbreads, veal, veal kidney, calf's liver, tripe, chicken, filet of brill, turbot, sole, etc.

TIMBALE DE RIS DE VEAU

Timbale of Sweetbreads

For eight people, use:

1. FOR THE CRUST:

3 C. flour
½ C. butter
2 tsp. salt
2 eggs

Timbale cases are generally prepared with regular pastry dough. But they may also be made out of other types of dough. Here is one which has given very good results.

2. FOR THE FILLING:

1 lb. chicken quenelles
1 lb. rooster kidneys
1/2 lb. mushrooms
1 qt. strong veal stock
8 chicken livers
1 pair sweetbreads
truffles to taste
butter
flour
madeira wine
salt and pepper

Make dough with the flour, butter, eggs, salt, and enough water to obtain a smooth dough. Let this rest until the next day.

Trim the sweetbreads and soak in cold, salted water for about an hour.

Roll out the dough, setting aside enough to make a cover. With the rest of it line a timbale mold about five or six inches in diameter and about eight inches high.

With the rest of the dough cut out a circle the diameter of the timbale, decorate it, and brush it with egg yolk.

Fill the timbale with dried beans or well washed pebbles and cook it in the oven along with its cover.

While the crust is cooking prepare the filling.

Peel the mushrooms and dip them in lemon juice. Wash and brush the truffles. Cook the mushrooms in some butter and the truffles in madeira.

Mince the truffles and reserve the cooking wine.

Cook the sweetbreads and chicken livers in butter without browning, then slice them. Cook the sweetbreads and the livers in the veal stock. A few minutes before they are done, add the quenelles and the rooster kidneys, after having blanched the latter. Finish cooking everything together.

Make a roux with the butter and flour in equal quantities, stir in the sweetbread cooking liquid and let it boil up a couple of times.

Into this sauce spoon the sliced sweetbreads, the quenelles, livers, rooster kidneys, mushrooms, truffles, and pour in the reserved madeira wine. Heat, taste for seasoning, then spoon everything into the crust. Cover the timbale and serve at once.

CERVELLES[1] DE VEAU, SAUCE HOLLANDAISE À LA RAVIGOTE

Calf's Brains with Ravigote Hollandaise Sauce

For six people, use:

1/2 lb. equal parts of a mixture of chervil, tarragon, salad burnet, chives and watercress
1/2 lb. butter
2 T. water
2 tsp. olive oil
1 tsp. tarragon vinegar
4 egg yolks
2 calf's brains
turned[2] vegetables
bouillon
salt and pepper

Trim the herbs, wash them, blanch them, drain them and pound them in a mortar or mince them as finely as possible. Slowly add the oil, vinegar and butter. Mash these all together and force through a fine sieve.[3] You now have a ravigote butter.

Blanch the calf's brains in some boiling water to which salt and vinegar has been added. Then, finish cooking them in some good bouillon, letting them simmer very slowly for fifteen minutes. Drain them and keep them warm.

At the same time prepare a sauce with the egg yolks, water, salt, pepper, and the ravigote butter. Whisk this up as for hollandaise.

Serve the brains whole, very hot, and coated with the sauce, on a platter garnished with some turned vegetables such as potatoes, carrots, turnips, etc., which have been boiled or steamed.

NOTES

1. All recipes for calf's brains are applicable to brains from other animals, such as pork.

2. "Turning" vegetables means to peel them and pare them down with a knife to the shape and size of a cork.

3. An electric blender could be used for part of this operation provided the vegetables have been minced beforehand; otherwise they tend to clog the blades.

CERVELLES DE VEAU EN COQUILLES

Calf's Brains in Scallop Shells

Cook the brains in water to which salt and vinegar has been added along with a flavoring of vegetables and onion. Force them through a fine sieve[1] and keep them warm.

Prepare a *sauce suprême,*[2] and to it add some boiled shrimp or crayfish tails, some mushrooms cooked in butter and lemon juice, and slices of black truffle cooked in port wine. Add the calf's brains purée and spoon this mixture into some scallop shells.[3] Sprinkle with a mixture of dry, sifted breadcrumbs and Parmesan cheese. Dot with butter and brown in the oven just before serving.

Serve with lemon slices.

For variation, one may substitute for the *sauce suprême* a Béchamel sauce made with meat stock.[4]

One may also use the above filling to fill *bouchées* or a vol-au-vent case.

One may even use the same mixture, keeping it quite thick, to make croquettes. These should be rolled in beaten egg, then in dry, sifted breadcrumbs and fried in a hot fry bath.

The platter would be decorated at serving time with fried parsley and slices of lemon.

NOTES

1. An electric blender could be used for this procedure.

2. To prepare a *sauce suprême*: cook two tablespoons of butter and two tablespoons of flour together without browning. Stir in some veal stock and some Sauterne wine. Cook this for fifteen minutes, at least, then add 2 teaspoons of butter cut into tiny pieces. Complete the thickening with 2 egg yolks and 7 tablespoons of cream. Stir these together thoroughly, heat without boiling, taste and complete the seasoning, if necessary, with salt, pepper, and lemon juice.

3. If no shells are available small ramekins could be used.

4. This type of Béchamel would be made with any type of meat stock: in 14 tablespoons of butter sauté 1 1/2 pounds of veal rump, 1/2 pound of ham, all cut up into walnut-sized pieces. Add 2 medium chopped carrots and some chopped celery. Add 9 tablespoons of flour and stir these all together for five minutes, then add 1 quart of consommé, 1/4 pound of chopped mushrooms, a *bouquet garni*, some salt and pepper. Bring everything to a boil and simmer over low heat for two hours.

Skim the fat off the surface, strain the sauce, mix it with 10 tablespoons of heavy cream and heat it up without boiling until it thickens enough to coat the spoon.

ROGNONS DE VEAU SAUTÉS, SAUCE À LA CRÈME

Sautéed Veal Kidneys with Cream Sauce

For four people, use:

1/2 C. cream
1/4 lb. mushrooms
7 T. butter
1/3 C. veal stock
1 small chopped onion
2 T. grated horseradish
1 T. chopped parsley
1/2 tsp. salt
1 tsp. paprika
2 trimmed veal kidneys, weighing 1 lb. together
vinegar

Cook the onion in 4 teaspoons of the butter, without browning. Add the veal stock and cook until soft.

Split the kidneys lengthwise, remove the fat and sinews, then cut them into thin slices and season with salt and paprika. Sauté them for five minutes in the rest of the butter. Drain them in a colander and keep them warm.

Peel and chop the mushrooms and sauté them in the butter in which the kidneys were cooked. Set them aside and keep them warm.

To the seasoned veal stock add the butter in which the mushrooms were cooked, the cream mixed with a little bit of vinegar, to taste, and mix well. Now add the parsley, the horseradish, and the kidneys. Heat this all up for a moment or two without allowing it to boil.

Serve with some rice sautéed in butter.[1]

These kidneys in cream are excellent; all the ingredients of the sauce blend perfectly and none dominates.

NOTE

1. See recipe in vegetable section entitled *Riz Sauté au Beurre Noisette.*

ROGNONS DE VEAU SAUTÉES, SAUCE À LA FINE CHAMPAGNE

Sautéed Veal Kidneys with Brandy Sauce

For four people, use:

1/2 lb. morels
1 C. veal stock
7 T. butter
5 T. brandy
4 slices French bread
2 veal kidneys
flour
salt and pepper

Thoroughly clean the morels.

Trim the kidneys, and split and slice them.

Prepare a roux with a little flour and 4 teaspoons of butter. Stir in the veal stock and boil it to reduce.

Cook the morels in 2 tablespoons of butter and add them to the sauce. Keep everything warm.

Quickly sauté the sliced kidneys, for several minutes, in 2 tablespoons of very hot butter. Season with salt and pepper and drain them.

Now put the kidneys in a saucepan and flame them with the warm brandy. Add the ragoût of morels and the rest of the butter. Heat these up for a few minutes.

Toast some slices of bread, arrange them on a platter, and spoon the contents of the saucepan over them. Serve.

For variation, one may substitute, for the brandy, either rum, calvados, gin, etc., and for the morels, some field mushrooms, cultivated mushrooms, boletus, skirrets, truffles, etc.

ROGNONS DE VEAU SAUTÉS, SAUCE INDIENNE

Sautéed Veal Kidneys with Indian Sauce

For six people, use:

2/3 C. veal stock
1/2 lb. mushrooms
1 C. cream
7 T. butter
4 T. flour
mild curry powder to taste
3 medium veal kidneys
2 egg yolks
salt and pepper

Trim the kidneys; remove the skin, fat, and sinews.

Peel the mushrooms and cook them for one hour in 2 tablespoons of butter and 1/4 cup of veal stock. You will then have an essence of mushroom. Strain.

Cook the flour in 3 tablespoons of the butter until light brown. Add the rest of the veal stock and cook this for thirty minutes, skimming frequently as it cooks.

In a frying pan, cook the rest of the butter and the kidneys. Let the kidneys brown on all sides for twelve to fifteen minutes, shaking the pan so they won't stick.

Combine the sauce and the mushroom essence, add the curry, the cream, and the egg yolks. Heat without boiling. Taste and complete the seasoning, if necessary, with salt and pepper.

Arrange the kidneys on a platter, coat them with the sauce and serve, along with some Duchesse potatoes (see recipe), or add the Duchesse potatoes to the sauce at serving time.

ROGNONS DE VEAU FARCIS

Stuffed Veal Kidneys

For four people, use:

2/3 C. rich veal stock
4 oz. bacon
4 oz. mushrooms
5 T. butter
1/4 C. madeira, port, sherry, or malmsey wine
1 T. parsley
4 veal kidneys
1 lamb's brains
1 egg
nutmeg to taste

Chop the bacon, mushrooms, brains, and parsley separately.

Fry the bacon in 3 tablespoons of the butter; to it add the mushrooms, let them brown lightly, and then add the brains and parsley. Heat these together for a few minutes, then remove the pan from the heat and thicken the mixture with the egg. Season with salt, pepper, and a little nutmeg. Stir this all well together so as to have a very smooth stuffing.

Split the kidneys, remove the fat and gristle, spread them out flat, and coat the cut surfaces of two of the kidneys with the stuffing. Cover them with the unstuffed kidneys and tie them together.

Brown the kidneys on all sides in the rest of the butter for fifteen minutes over fairly high heat. Add the veal stock and wine, then finish the cooking over low heat for a half hour, basting frequently. Reduce the sauce.

Remove the strings, arrange the kidneys on a platter, coat them with the sauce, and surround with potato chips.

To vary, one could wrap the kidneys in pork fat and roast them, basting them with the cooking juices, veal stock, and wine. The pork fat should be removed before serving.

OREILLES DE VEAU FARCIES, SAUCE BÉARNAISE[1]

Stuffed Veal Ears with Béarnaise Sauce

For twelve people, use:

1.

14 T. cream
12 T. (3/4 C.) butter
4 oz. truffles cooked in madeira
4 oz. white meat of roast chicken
4 oz. sweetbreads cooked in butter
4 T. flour
2 T. veal stock
freshly ground black pepper to taste
6 veal ears
6 cooked crayfish
3 eggs
1 carrot
1 onion
dry white wine
bouillon
dry, sifted breadcrumbs
bouquet garni
lemon
salt and pepper

2. For the sauce

1/2 lb. butter
7 T. vinegar (medium strength)
2 T. cold water
4 egg yolks
2 shallots
tarragon
salt and pepper

The ears must be prepared several hours beforehand.

Blanch the ears in salted water, then wash them in cold water; rub them with lemon juice and wrap each ear in a white cloth and sew it up.

Prepare a court bouillon with some white wine and some broth, in equal quantities, adding the cut-up carrot and onion, the *bouquet garni*, salt, and pepper.

Cook the ears in this court bouillon and let them cook for three hours, adding wine and bouillon mixture as the liquid evaporates, so that the ears are always completely covered with liquid. Remove the ears from the court-bouillon and remove the cloth.

While the ears are cooking prepare the stuffing.

Mince the chicken meat, the sweetbreads, and the crayfish. Mix them together thoroughly.

Prepare a crayfish butter with 5 tablespoons of butter and the trimmings and shells.

Cook the flour in 3 tablespoons of butter and then add the veal stock, part of the cream, the crayfish butter, the sliced truffles, salt and pepper to taste. Now add the chicken, sweetbread, and crayfish mixture and cook these together for a minute or two.

Remove the pan from the fire and thicken it with the rest of the cream, blended with 2 egg yolks. Let this mixture cool.

When the forcemeat is cold, stuff the ear cavities. Beat the last whole egg and the 2 egg whites together until frothy. Dip the ears in this, then roll them in dry, sifted breadcrumbs. Repeat these steps twice so that the ears are well breaded.

Make a Béarnaise sauce as follows: with the butter, egg yolks, cold water, salt and pepper, make a hollandaise as in the regular recipe (q.v.) to which you will add chopped tarragon to taste. Season this with some vinegar which has been reduced with some shallot in it and strain.

Fifteen minutes before serving, brown the breaded, stuffed ears in the oven in the rest of the butter. Drain them and serve, having arranged them standing up, on a platter. Send the sauce along in a sauceboat.

NOTE

1. Béarnaise sauce is a hollandaise sauce seasoned with vinegar which has been reduced with shallot and flavored with tarragon.

FOIE DE VEAU AU NATUREL

Plain Calf's Liver

Plain calf's liver can either be broiled or sautéed.

To broil it: place on a pre-heated, buttered, or greased grill as many slices of liver as there are guests. Cook them more quickly the thinner they are so that the inside remains pink. Season with salt and pepper.

Arrange the slices on a heated platter, pour over them some maître d'hôtel butter, and serve at once.

To sauté it: coat liver slices with flour. Melt some butter or some fat off a roast beef and brown the slices quickly in this. Cook the thin ones faster. Remove them, drain them, and season with salt and pepper. Arrange them on a hot platter and sprinkle them with maître d'hôtel butter and serve immediately.

To vary, one may substitute for the maître d'hôtel butter a Bercy butter (see recipe) or a *sauce italienne* (see recipe).

Of the vegetables that could accompany plain calf's liver, the best are either potatoes or pasta, especially sautéed potatoes, and breaded, sautéed noodles (see recipe).

A platter of plainly cooked calf's liver, either garnished or not, must never, on any condition, wait.

Veal kidneys may be prepared this same way.

FOIE DE VEAU EN ASPIC

Calf's Liver in Aspic

Season the liver with salt, pepper, and *quatre épices*. Put it to marinate for two hours in the madeira. Then wrap it in the pork fat.

For six people, use:

2 lbs. calf's liver
$^2/_3$ C. white burgundy wine
$^2/_3$ C. madeira wine
1 tsp. salt
few grains black pepper
few grains *quatre épices*
1 qt. strong bouillon to which a calf's foot has been added[1]
bouquet garni
1 thin slice pork belly fat

In a porcelain, fireproof *cocotte* pour the bouillon, white wine, and the madeira from the marinade. Add the *bouquet* and boil this down rapidly to reduce the liquid to 1 quart.

Plunge the wrapped liver in the boiling liquid and put the *cocotte* in the oven for twenty to thirty minutes, according to whether you like liver cooked more or less. Let the liver cool slightly in the broth so that it won't shrivel.

Skim off the fat, reduce and clarify the cooking liquid.

Pour some of the liquid into the bottom of a mold. Let it set, then add the liver and pour the rest of the liquid over it. Let this all cool and set.

Unmold and serve.

Calf's liver cooked this way does not pretend to rival goose liver in aspic (see recipe), but it may honorably accompany a salad for a family meal.

NOTE

1. If a calf's foot or veal knuckle is not available use commercial gelatine. About 1 tablespoon for each 1 $^1/_2$ cups of liquid would be satisfactory.

PIEDS DE VEAU, SAUCE AU SAFRAN

Calf's Feet with Saffron Sauce

Cook the calf's feet in a well-seasoned white wine court bouillon to which you have added some vegetables and some saffron to taste. Remove the feet when they are done, bone them, cut them into pieces, and keep them warm.

Strain the court bouillon through a cloth, boil it down to reduce it, then add some mashed hard-boiled eggs, capers, chopped sour pickles, and a little sugar to taste. Boil this all up once, then acidify it with some lemon juice.

Coat the feet with this sauce and serve.

ROGNONS DE MOUTON, SAUCE AU CITRON ET À LA MOUTARDE[1]

Lamb Kidneys with Lemon and Mustard Sauce

For four people, use:

5 T. butter
8 lamb kidneys
lemon juice
mustard
salt and pepper

Trim the kidneys and split them lengthwise.

In a saucepan heat 3 tablespoons of butter, add the kidneys, and cook them for two minutes per side. Season them with salt and pepper and remove them. Keep them warm.

Deglaze the saucepan with some lemon juice, add mustard, salt and pepper and mix well.

Whisk the rest of the butter into the sauce and pour this over the kidneys. Serve them accompanied by sautéed potatoes in a vegetable dish.

Lemon and mustard sauce is also very suitable for veal kidneys, or veal and lamb sweetbreads, as well as any white meats cooked in butter.

NOTE

1. The proportion of lemon juice and mustard vary according to the main ingredient used. As a general rule I would indicate the proportions of juice from two medium-sized lemons and two teaspoons of tarragon mustard.

PIEDS DE PORC BOUILLIS

Boiled Pig's Feet

Buy some fresh pig's feet, scrape them, scald them, remove the nails, and wash them in cold water.

Prepare a court bouillon with water, white wine, onion, carrot, garlic, shallot, clove, *bouquet garni* (made of thyme, bay leaf, parsley, and sage), peppercorns, and salt.

Cook the pig's feet in this court bouillon for five hours in simmering liquid, as for pot-au-feu, being careful that they are constantly immersed in the liquid.

Remove them and keep them warm.

Strain the cooking liquid, reduce it rapidly, add some cream of rice blended into a little of the cooled liquid; let this cook, then thicken the sauce with fresh egg yolks and pour the sauce over the feet.

Serve on hot plates.

For variation, one could bone the feet, cut them into pieces, dip them in fritter batter or in dry, sifted breadcrumbs and fry them in hot fat.

Boiled pig's feet could be served with any of the following sauces: *sauce Poulette* (using the cooking liquid from the feet); tartar sauce; caper sauce; hollandaise or ravigote sauce; Béarnaise sauce; tomato sauce; sweet sauce; or vinaigrette sauce.

PIEDS DE PORC PANÉS, GRILLÉS

Broiled Breaded Pig's Feet

In Sainte-Menehould, pig's feet which have a world wide reputation are prepared. Here is the recipe:

Scrape and scald the feet, remove the nails, and wash the feet in cold water.

Tie them to boards in order to keep them from losing their shape and put them in brine for forty-eight hours.

Prepare a court bouillon with water, to which has been added dry white wine (one-fifth by volume), some pot-au-feu vegetables, some aromatics, a *bouquet garni*, and some salt.

Put the feet in this, boil them for three-quarters of an hour, then keep them in barely simmering liquid for five hours.

Strain the cooking liquid; let the pig's feet cool in the strained liquid. Split the feet lengthwise, dip them in freshly beaten egg, then in dry, sifted breadcrumbs. Broil them, basting them with melted butter.

Serve them as is, without any other garniture; or serve them accompanied by a sauceboat of *sauce Robert*.

To prepare *sauce Robert*, melt some butter; add some sliced onions and cook them without browning. Add some good strong broth or stock strengthened with meat glaze. Reduce it. Season the sauce with pepper and spike it with mustard, then strain.

BEEF, VEAL, LAMB, AND PORK

GRILLADE DE FILET DE BEEF

Broiled Beef Tenderloin

Broiling is the procedure best suited to preserving the basic taste of red meats.

For four people buy a nice slice of beef filet, at least two inches thick and weighing about 2 pounds.

To cook it, use a broiler with an overhead flame, and preheat it to avoid having the meat stick, or use some appliance which is equipped with a pan to catch the juices.

Put the meat on the broiler rack, brown it quickly under a hot flame, then continue cooking it for eight to ten minutes at a lower temperature. Turn and do the same for the other side. Shortly before it is ready, season it with salt and pepper, to taste. The meat is just right when droplets of blood appear on the surface of the meat.

Broiled filet of beef may be served as is, or with a maître d'hôtel butter, a *marchand de vin* butter,[1] a Bercy butter,[2] an anchovy butter, anchovy oil,[3] a plain *sauce béarnaise*, a Choron sauce,[4] or a *sauce Foyot.*[5]

Accompaniments for broiled filet of beef are: sautéed potatoes, potatoes Anna, potatoes Champs Elysées, straw potatoes, potato chips, souffléed potatoes, Duchesse potatoes, etc.

Sirloin or rib steaks may also be prepared this way.

For four people, use:

1 C. red wine
14 T. butter
7 shallots
2 T. meat glaze
bouillon
lemon juice
chopped parsley
salt and pepper

1. *Marchand de vin* butter is prepared as follows.

Mince the shallots and put in the wine. Cook them; then add the meat glaze dissolved in a little bouillon. Season with salt and pepper, and boil the liquid down rapidly to reduce it. Whisk in the butter, acidify with a little lemon juice, and sprinkle the sauce with chopped parsley.

2. One prepares a Bercy butter by substituting, in the previous recipe, white wine for the red wine and poached, sliced beef marrow for the meat glaze.
3. Anchovy oil is made by mashing some anchovies in a mortar and adding some good olive oil to them, then straining it.
4. Choron sauce is a béarnaise sauce with tomato.
5. Foyot sauce is a béarnaise sauce seasoned with meat glaze.

FILET BOSTON

For six people, buy a slice of filet of beef (beef tenderloin) about two inches thick and weighing about 2 pounds. Also purchase 36 oysters.

Cook the filet as in the preceding recipe.

At the same time prepare an oyster sauce.

Open the oysters; put them, with their juices, in a saucepan. Bring this to a boil, skim off the scum, remove the oysters and keep them warm. Reduce the oyster liquid.

Prepare a hollandaise sauce or a béarnaise sauce or an Allemande sauce (see recipes). Beat the oyster liquid into whichever sauce you have decided on, taste, complete the seasoning with lemon juice, salt, and pepper.

Put a layer of this sauce on a serving platter, on top arrange the broiled filet, surround it with the cooked oysters and garnish the platter with souffléed potatoes. Serve.

Sirloin or rib steaks may be prepared this same way.

Oyster sauce is a good accompaniment for fish poached in court bouillon, especially turbot or brill, lobsters, and prawns, but in these cases it is better to use a fish *velouté* as a base for the sauce.

ENTRECÔTE GRILLÉ, SAUCE À LA MOELLE

Broiled Rib Steak, Marrow Sauce

For six people, use:

- 1 slice, 1 1/2 inches thick, well-marbled rib steak, weighing 2 lbs. 7 oz.
- 1 C. red Bordeaux wine
- 3 oz. beef marrow
- 7 T. meat juice or strong stock
  or
- 5 T. meat glaze in 2 T. meat stock glaze dissolved in stock
- 4 T. butter
- 2 tsp. minced shallot
- 1 tsp. essence of anchovy
  or
- 1 de-salted anchovy mashed with butter and puréed
- 1 tsp. lemon juice
- 1 clove garlic
- 1 1/4 bay leaf
- flour
- olive oil
- chopped parsley
- salt and white pepper
- cayenne pepper

Soak the marrow for several hours in some cold water. Change the water several times. Poach it for thirty minutes in salted water and keep it hot.

Prepare the sauce. Put the garlic, shallot, and bay leaf in the wine. Reduce the volume of liquid to one-fourth. Strain it, add the meat juice, lemon juice, essence of anchovy, salt, pepper, and cayenne to taste. Make a *beurre manié* by blending butter and flour together. Add this to the sauce and let it cook for a moment to thicken it. Taste, add a little more cayenne to give it a little bite. Keep it warm.

Dip the steak in olive oil, put it on the preheated broiler rack, brown it quickly, and continue cooking it for seven or eight minutes. Turn it and cook it the same way on the other side.

Slice the steak and arrange the slices on a hot platter.

Slice the marrow with a knife dipped into hot water and arrange the slices over the meat. Sprinkle with chopped parsley, either blanched or not, as you prefer, and coat everything with the sauce. Serve.

These three procedures—blanching the marrow, preparing the sauce, broiling the steak—are carried on more or less simultaneously. The meat, however, must not wait, so it is important that the other two things be ready when the steak is done.

The vegetables which are most suitable as an accompaniment for broiled steak are souffléed potatoes, Dauphine potatoes, or potato chips.

ENTRECÔTE OU FAUX FILET, SAUCE HONGROISE

Rib or Sirloin Steak with Hungarian Sauce

For six people, use:

- 3 lbs. rib or sirloin steak
- 1 1/2 C. velouté sauce made with meat stock, seasoned with mushrooms or a *sauce espagnole,* according to preference
- 1 C. good white wine
- 2/3 C. thick, soured cream
- 4 oz. fresh pork fat
- paprika
- 1 large onion
- butter
- salt and pepper

First prepare the sauce: Dice the pork fat and sauté in butter. Remove the dice and in their place add the minced onion and let it brown. Put back the fat dice, add the paprika, pour in the wine, and let this reduce almost completely. Skim off the fat. Now add the velouté sauce or the *sauce espagnole* and the cream. Boil it up once or twice, then place the pan over very, very low heat and let the sauce simmer without boiling.

Quickly sauté the steak in some butter. Season it with salt and pepper, then put the meat in a large pan, pour the strained sauce over it, cover the pan and finish cooking the meat in the oven. A few minutes before it is done, add some potato balls so they can cook together.

When the meat is ready, arrange the steak on a long platter, surround it with the potatoes, coat it with the sauce, which should be very flavorful and a little thick. Serve.

Paprika gives this dish a gentle pink color and a characteristically warm taste.

To vary, one could substitute a coarse julienne of vegetables for the potato. Then one would sprinkle the dish with some thin slivers of blanched lemon peel.

FILET DE BOEUF TRUFFÉ RÔTI, SAUCE DEMI-GLACE

Truffled Beef Tenderloin with Demi-glace Sauce

Lard a piece of beef tenderloin with some strips of pork belly fat and stick into it some slivers of truffle. Tie it up neatly and roast it on a spit, keeping the center pink.

Arrange the meat on a platter and garnish it with small slices of foie gras or circles (medallions) of foie gras, cooked *au naturel* (plain), some cock's combs sautéed in butter and some Champs Elysées potatoes with truffles. Serve with a *demi-glace* sauce made with port wine.

Demi-glace sauce is a delicate *sauce espagnole* to which has been added some meat glaze, or chicken glaze or game glaze, according to what it is to be used with. Then the sauce is finished, off the heat, with 7 tablespoons of madeira or port per quart of sauce.

Sauce espagnole is prepared as follows.

For 1 quart of sauce espagnole, *use:*

- **3 oz. salt pork or unsmoked ham**
- **5 T. flour**
- **4 T. clarified butter***
- **1 medium carrot**
- **3 T. white wine**
- **1 small onion**
- **2½ qts. brown stock[1]**
- **thyme, bay leaf**

Prepare a mirepoix:[1] Fry the salt pork or ham, cut into small pieces. Add the carrot, onion, thyme, and bay leaf, to taste. Let these brown lightly. Pour off the fat, add the wine to the pan, and reduce it by half.

Cook the flour slowly in the clarified butter to get a smooth, shiny roux. Pour in 2 cups of brown stock, stirring constantly. Bring this to a boil, add the mirepoix mixture, and let this cook very slowly for three hours, skimming the sauce frequently.

Strain the sauce, pressing the vegetables a little in order to get all the pulp. Add another 1¾ cups of stock and let this simmer very slowly for three more hours. Cool the sauce, stirring it constantly to keep it smooth and to keep a skin from forming.

The next day, put the sauce back in a saucepan with the rest of the stock and 1¾ cups of fresh tomato pulp. Cook it, whisking it frequently and skimming repeatedly, until it has been reduced to 1 quart.

Strain and cool the sauce, stirring it to keep it smooth and to keep scum from forming.

A seafood *sauce espagnole* is made the same way; instead of using brown stock, one uses fish stock, butter is used instead of salt pork, and mushrooms are added.

NOTE

1. The term mirepoix is given to an aromatized mixture, most often based on ham, veal, and vegetables. This was invented by Maréchal de Mirepoix's cook. It is used to season sauces. Those who consider *le mirepoix* (masculine) as an essence use this other term in the feminine—*la mirepoix*.

ALOYAU

Loin

The *aloyau* is the part of the animal located between the hip and the first ribs. It consists of the tenderloin and the sirloin.

In olden days it was served whole, without being boned. Today it is most often boned and rolled.

The *aloyau* is the large, choice piece for a roast or for braising, when there are a large number of guests. It is what is known as the classic English roast beef, which Henry VIII, who was a great meat eater, ennobled and titled "Sir": *Sir loin of beef,*[1] in imitation of Caligula who had elevated his favorite horse to the rank of knight.

Garnishes and sauces of the most varied types are suitable as accompaniments to loin of beef. Here are a few:

Garniture à la Clamart: barquettes of tiny peas and lettuce in thickened meat juice;

Garniture à la du Barry: croustades of cream of cauliflower and potatoes, beaten with butter, either browned or not, with a demi-glace sauce;

Garniture à la forestière: morels sautéed with tiny cubes of bacon; sauce made with *Duxeller* and the juices from the roast;

Garniture à la Godard: a hash of artichoke hearts, sweetbreads, mushrooms, and quenelles; demi-glace sauce;

Garniture Lucullus: large, plain truffles or truffles stuffed with foie gras; madeira sauce;

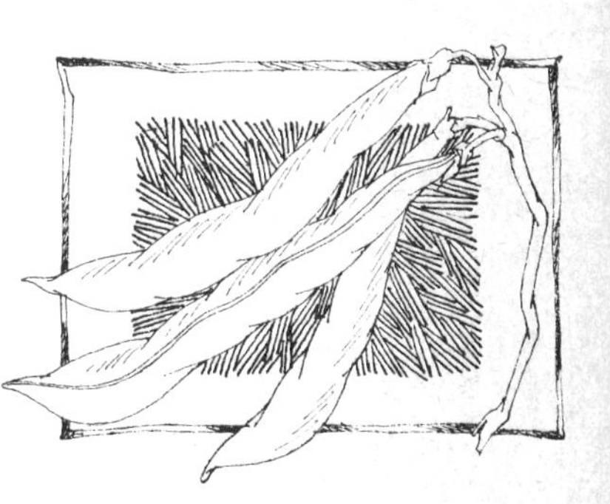

NOTE

1. Today one simply spells it Sirloin of Beef.

Garniture à l'algérienne: croquettes of yams and tomatoes; tomato sauce spiked with chopped peppers;

Garniture à l'anglaise: Yorkshire pudding or boiled potatoes; horseradish sauce;

Garniture à l'andalouse: broiled peppers with rice and fried eggplant; tomato sauce with meat juices;

Garniture à la napolitaine: hash made of spaghetti, ham, and Piemont truffles, with grated Parmesan; tomato sauce with meat juices;

Garniture à la polonaise: stuffed, broiled mushrooms; demiglace sauce enriched with onion purée Soubise.

PAUPIETTES DE BOEUF RÔTIES À LA BROCHE

Spit-Roasted Beef Rolls

For three people, use:

1 lb. trimmed sirloin steaks cut into 3 steaks
4 oz. mushrooms
2 oz. black truffles
3 T. white wine
3 T. butter
1 T. chopped onion
1 tsp. olive oil
3 thin slices of salt pork or bacon
1 raw egg yolk
lemon juice
freshly ground black pepper
salt

Cook the onion in the butter without browning and set aside the butter.

Peel the mushrooms, dip them in lemon juice, cut them up, and cook them in the same butter the onions were cooked in.

Peel the truffles and cut them up.

Mix the onions, mushrooms and truffles; season them with salt and pepper and bind with an egg yolk.

Lay this stuffing on the slices of beef which have been seasoned, and roll them into cylinders (or make little packages). Roll the pork around them and tie securely. Put them to marinate for six hours in the wine mixed with the oil and the pepper.

Last, roast the paupiettes on a spit over a fairly hot fire, basting with the marinade. Twenty minutes of cooking is generally enough. Remove the string and what is left of the pork fat and serve. Send along, at the same time, same sautéed potatoes.

RUMP-STEAK[1] À LA POÊLE, AU RIZ

Skillet Rump Steak with Rice

For four people, use:

1 lb. 10 oz. in a 1-inch-thick slice slice of rump steak
1½ C. rice
10 T. butter
1 tsp. salt
black pepper
chopped parsley

Cook the rice as in the recipe for dry rice and keep it warm.

Put 4 teaspoons of butter in a skillet, heat it up, then add the meat, and let it cook for six minutes per side. Season it with salt and pepper just before it is done.

Sauté the dry rice in a saucepan with 7 tablespoons of butter, without letting it brown. Stir and sauté.

Arrange the meat on a hot platter. Blend the rest of the butter with the chopped parsley, let it melt, and pour it over the meat and serve. Send the rice along in a separate vegetable dish.

NOTE

1. Sometimes, in French, the word is spelled *romsteck*.

FILETS MIGNONS, AU MADÈRE AVEC POMMES DE TERRE À LA CRÈME

Filets Mignons with Madeira and Creamed Potatoes

For six people, use:

2 lbs. potatoes
1¾ C. cream
1 scant C. madeira
4 oz. (8 T.) butter
½ C. consommé
4 oz. mushrooms
3 T. flour
6 filet mignons
1 black truffle from Périgord
nutmeg
salt and pepper

Peel the mushrooms.

Clean the truffle and slice it very thin.

In a saucepan of suitable size, put 5 tablespoons of the butter, stir in the flour, letting it get slightly brown. Now add the madeira and the consommé and let this simmer for a half hour, stirring now and then. Add the chopped mushrooms and the truffle. Continue to cook this, stirring, for another half hour.

At the same time, cook the potatoes in their skins in some salted water. Peel them and cut them into pieces if they are large, but leave them whole if they are small. Put them in a saucepan with the cream, salt, pepper, and nutmeg to taste. Let this simmer for fifteen minutes over very low heat.

Heat the rest of the butter in a frying pan. Put in the filet mignons and cook them for five minutes per side. Arrange them on a platter, coat them with the madeira sauce, and serve.

At the same time, send along the potatoes in a vegetable dish.

This is an excellent dish which usually is received with success.

For variation, one could arrange the filet mignons on canapes of bread sautéed to a golden brown in butter and garnished with foie gras.

FILET DE BOEUF POCHÉ, AUX TOMATES

Poached Beef Tenderloin with Tomatoes

For six to eight people, use:

3 lbs. trimmed beef tenderloin in one piece
6 to 8 C. good bouillon
1 C. seasoned tomato purée
½ C. madeira wine
5 T. butter
3 T. flour
freshly ground white pepper
1 tsp. table salt
12 tomatoes, weighing 2 lbs. together

Scald the tomatoes, peel them, remove the seeds, and season them inside with a little mixed salt and pepper.

Bring the bouillon to a boil and plunge the filet into it and let it cook for fifteen minutes per pound or for forty-five minutes altogether.

At the same time, make a roux with the butter and flour. Stir in the madeira and ½ cup of the filet cooking liquid. Add the tomato purée and boil the sauce rapidly to reduce and thicken it.

As soon as the filet is cooked, remove it and slice it. Season each slice with a mixture of salt and pepper. Arrange the slices on a platter, coat them with the sauce, and keep them hot.

Dip the tomatoes for a moment in the rest of the boiling liquid, arrange them around the filet, and serve.

In this recipe, the meat does not have, as in a roast, certain parts which are more or less hardened. It is juicy. The tomatoes retain all their flavor and the whole dish is one which deserves some attention.

Dauphine potatoes, Marquise potatoes, potatoes *voisin,* potato croquettes, either souffléed or not, gnocchis, potato fritters, or even a potato loaf are very good accompaniments.

DAUBE[1] DE FAUX FILET, AUX POMMES DE TERRE À L'ETUVÉE

Potted Beef Sirloin with Steamed Potatoes

For six people, use:

4 lbs. beef sirloin
1¼ lb. potatoes (peeled and sliced into thick, even slices)
¾ pound butter
¾ lb. mixture of pitted olives, truffles, and peeled mushrooms
bouquet garni
salt and pepper

The utensil which is the most suitable for the preparation of *filet en daube* is a two-part kettle with a cover, the bottom of the top section being perforated with holes.

In the bottom part, put the meat, olives, mushrooms, truffles, butter, and *bouquet garni,* and season with salt and pepper. Put the top section on the pot and over the holes arrange the potatoes seasoned with salt and pepper. Cover the top kettle firmly and let this all cook over a very, very low burner for three hours.

Make a purée by pushing the pan juices, mushrooms, truffles, and olives through a sieve or food mill. Put a layer of this purée on a hot platter, arrange the braised meat on top of this, garnish with the potatoes and serve.

The potatoes, steamed as they have been, and seasoned with the vapors from the butter, flavored by the meat and by the aroma of the mushrooms, truffles, and olives, are excellent.

One could also make the same thing, but a little differently, by putting all the contents of the bottom pan (meat and all) through a press and saving only the juices. One would then serve the potatoes alone in a vegetable dish and the pressed-out juices in a sauceboat.

One would then have a very good vegetable dish which one could designate as steamed potatoes, *au jus.*

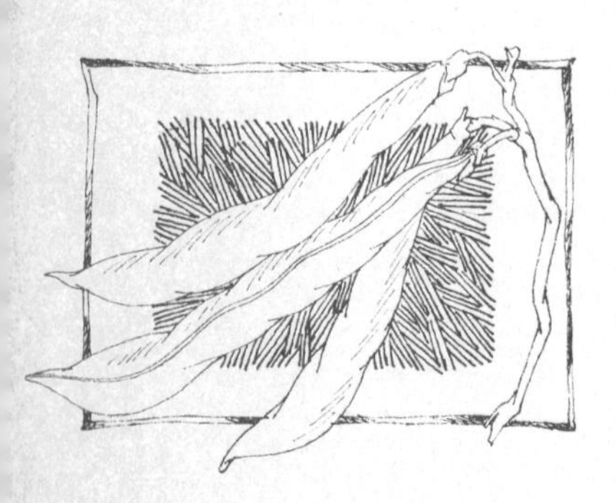

NOTE

1. The word daube is synonymous with the term "braised meat."

In the Midi the cooking is done in wine in a *braisière* (braising kettle) that has been lined with pork rind. The meat is generally larded and the seasoning, which is quite sharp, always has some garlic and orange peel.

One often adds tongue, tripe, pig's feet, chicken. These may be cooked either with the beef or separately.

RUMP-STEAK BRAISÉ, AUX POMMES DE TERRE À LA CRÈME

Braised Rump Steak with Creamed Potatoes

For six people, use:

- 1 lb. 7 oz. rump steak
- 2 lbs. potatoes
- 1½ C. bouillon:

  or
- 5 T. meat glaze dissolved in: 1½ C. water
- 1 C. cream
- 1 C. red wine
- 6 T. butter
- ½ C. breadcrumbs
- 3 T. flour
- 100 capers
- 2 medium onions
- 2 medium carrots
- 2 cloves
- *bouquet garni* (parsley, celery)
- juice ½ lemon
- chopped parsley
- salt and pepper

Sour half of the cream by keeping it in a warm spot and reserve the rest.

Cut the meat into slices, each the thickness of your finger. Beat them to tenderize them. Season them with salt and put them in a pan with 5 tablespoons of butter, the onions, carrots, and *bouquet garni.* Then add the breadcrumbs which have been cooked in the rest of the butter, a few grains of black pepper, and the cloves. Pour in the wine and the bouillon, cover the pan, and let this simmer for an hour and a half, basting frequently with the pan juices.

At the same time, steam the potatoes.

Strain the sauce, add the soured cream, the lemon juice, and the flour (if the sauce is too liquid), and the capers. Cover and simmer for another fifteen minutes.

When the potatoes are cooked, add the rest of the unsoured cream to them, season with salt and pepper, and let them simmer for fifteen minutes.

Arrange the sliced meat on a platter, coat with the sauce, and serve, sending along separately in a vegetable dish the potatoes, which have been sprinkled with parsley.

PAUPIETTES DE BOEUF BRAISÉES, À LA CRÈME

Braised Beef Rolls with Cream

For four people, use:

- 1½ lbs. well-marbled beef loin, trimmed and cut into four slices
- 1 C. veal stock
- 1 C. cream
- 7 T. grated horseradish
- ⅓ C. dry, sifted breadcrumbs
- 3 T. butter
- 2 egg yolks
- lemon juice
- flour
- salt and pepper

Thoroughly mix the horseradish, breadcrumbs, and egg yolks, and season with salt and pepper.

Spread a quarter of the mixture on each slice of meat, roll into packages, tie and sprinkle the rolls with flour. Lightly brown the paupiettes in butter on all sides; then add the veal stock, season with salt and pepper to taste; simmer them over low heat for about an hour.

Fifteen minutes before they are ready add the cream and lemon juice to taste; but do not boil further.

When they are fully cooked, remove the strings and serve the paupiettes, sending along, in a vegetable dish, some sautéed rice, for example.

CÔTE DE BOEUF BRAISÉE AU CHAMPAGNE

Beef Rib Braised in Champagne

For twelve people, use:

10 lbs. untrimmed rib of beef
1 bottle demi-sec champagne
1 calf's foot
bouquet garni
fat from the roast
carrots
onions
bouillon
salt and pepper

Brown the meat on the two surfaces in some of the fat cut off the roast.

Put it in a large kettle with the calf's foot and pour in four-fifths of the champagne. Let these cook for an hour and a half. Now add some bouillon, carrots, onions, and a *bouquet garni*, and let these all simmer very slowly, over very low heat for five or six hours, adding more liquid (wine and bouillon) as the liquid evaporates.

Last, remove the calf's foot, reduce the cooking liquid, skim off the fat, strain, taste for seasoning, and complete if necessary with salt and pepper. Serve.

As an accompaniment serve one of the following: a *macédoine* of vegetables, gourmand potatoes, souffléed, truffled potato croquettes, morels with cream or butter, or a purée of mushrooms or truffles.

CÔTE DE BOEUF GRATINÉE

Browned Beef Rib

For six people, use:

3 lbs, well-marbled rib of beef about 1¾ inch thick
1 C. bouillon
½ C. red wine
3 oz. mushrooms
5 T. grated cheese (equal parts of Gruyère and Parmesan)
2 oz. pork fat
1 small onion
3 T. dry, sifted breadcrumbs
2 tsp. olive oil
2 tsp. salt
1 T. parsley
pepper
1 sliver garlic
few grains *quatre epices*
1 hard-boiled egg
1 slice bacon
bouquet garni **(parsley, thyme and bay leaf)**
butter
pork caul

Bone the meat and brown it in a little butter. Reserve the bones.

Chop together the hard-boiled egg, the mushrooms, the freshened bacon, garlic, parsley, and season with salt, pepper, and *quatre épices*. Add the olive oil and mix well. Coat the meat with this mixture and wrap it in the pork caul.

In the bottom of a saucepan lay the slice of bacon. Place the meat on top and pour in the bouillon and wine. Add the onions, *bouquet garni*, and the reserved bones. Cook these for an hour to an hour and a quarter, then turn the meat and cook it again for the same amount of time.

Arrange the meat on a fireproof serving platter, keep it warm. Reduce the cooking liquids, skim off the fat, and strain it over the meat.

Mix the breadcrumbs and the grated cheese; cover the meat with this mixture and brown it in the oven for a few minutes before serving.

A filet of beef may also be prepared in this way.

BOEUF EN COCOTTE[1]

Cut the steak into two-and-a-half-inch squares. Thinly slice the potatoes, carrot, and marrow. Chop the onion, celery, and parsley.

In the bottom of a thick fireproof porcelain *cocotte* arrange the ingredients in the following order: marrow, meat, salt, pepper, potatoes, carrots, onions, celery, and parsley, and then repeat these layers.

Cover the *cocotte* with its cover, under which you have fitted a piece of buttered paper. Cook this in a slow oven for an hour and a half. Then skim off the fat.

Serve in the *cocotte*.

For four people, use:

1½ lbs. rump steak in a 1-inch slice
10 oz. potatoes
2 medium carrots
¼ lb. beef marrow
1 small onion
1 small stalk celery
1½ tsp. salt
1 T. parsley
black pepper

Beef pie is an English variation of *boeuf en cocotte*. In that recipe, however, one covers the *cocotte* with a layer of flaky pastry which is decorated as for a *pâté* and which has an opening. This opening is sealed after the dish is cooked with a little piece of dough.

When the beef pie is to be eaten cold, pour into it, through the opening, before it is cold, a few spoonfuls of stock, which will set when cold.

One often adds some beef or lamb kidneys to the beef.

NOTE

1. In French the word *cocotte* may be spelled with one or two t's. Generally, a true *cocotte* is almost identical with what we call a Dutch oven and is also made of iron. Here Ali-Bab calls for a porcelain one because of the wine in the recipe which would be altered in taste by the iron. An enameled iron casserole with cover would be ideal, as it could go onto direct heat as well as into the oven.

BOEUF À LA MODE, EN ASPIC

Pot Roast of Beef in Aspic

For ten to twelve people, use:

5 lbs. beef rump, boned and trimmed
4 C. bouillon
2 C. white Sauterne wine
2 C. madeira wine
½ lbs. carrots, red part only, peeled and sliced
½ lb. thin strips of pork fat
1 medium onion, peeled and sliced
3 T. brandy
1½ oz. fat from roast
3 cloves
2 egg whites
1 large calf's foot, washed, cleaned, and cut up
1 inch square pork rind
bouquet garni
quatre épices
salt and pepper

A well-prepared *boeuf à la mode* is an excellent family dish which may be served hot[1] with carrots, or cold in jelly.

Served cold, in aspic, it is very handsome, and it is particularly suitable for country picnics.

Season beef with salt, pepper, and *quatre épices*. Put the beef along with the strips of pork fat, 2 cups of white wine, and 2 cups of madeira in a kettle in which the meat can bathe in the liquid.

After twenty-four hours take out the lardoons, season them, and run them into the meat, parallel to the fibers, with a larding needle or skewer. Melt the roast beef fat in a large skillet and brown the meat on all sides for twenty minutes, then flame it with the brandy.

Place the pork rind in the bottom of a large kettle, arrange the beef on it, add the calf's foot, the carrots, onion, *bouquet garni*, and the cloves, and pour in the bouillon, the rest of the white wine, the rest of the madeira, and the marinade. Salt and pepper lightly, cover, bring everything to a boil, then put it to simmer over very low heat for four and a half hours. Before the cooking is complete, taste and add more seasoning if necessary.

Once the meat is tender, remove the beef and the carrots. Strain the pan liquid, skim it, clarify it with the beaten egg whites and 2 egg shells, heating it over a moderate fire until it comes to a boil, at which time remove the pan from the heat and strain the liquid through a wet cloth.

Cut the beef into slices, perpendicular to the lardoons.

Decorate the sides of a mold with whole carrot slices which have been cooked separately and pour in some of the liquid. Let this set, then arrange a layer of beef slices, on top of these a layer of carrots, cover these with liquid and let it set. Continue these alternating layers, ending with a layer of beef. Chill and unmold.

Serve by slicing this aspic as though it were a *pâté*.

Guests will discover in each mouthful some beef, some of the lardoons, some carrots, and some jelly.

One may also prepare, in this same way, a *canard à la mode*, (duck *à la mode*), either hot, cold, or in aspic.

NOTE

1. *Boeuf à la mode*, hot, may be served without the accompanying carrots but with an onion purée; this would then be called *boeuf Soubise*.

One may also serve it without carrots but with rice: dry rice, rice cooked in meat broth, risotto, or pilaf.

CULOTTE DE BOEUF AUX PÂTES

Beef Rump with Pasta

For ten to twelve people, use:

5 lbs. beef rump or *culotte*, boned and trimmed[1]
1 lb. noodles
1 lb. grated Parmesan cheese
2 C. bouillon
1 C. tomato purée
1/2 lb. freshened salt pork (chopped)
7 oz. pork fat lardoons in 1/4 inch strips
3 medium onions, peeled and chopped
3 T. brandy
3 cloves
1 calf's foot
bouquet garni
1/2 clove garlic
salt and pepper

Season the lardoons with salt and pepper and run them into the meat with a larding needle.

In a heavy-bottomed saucepan, put the chopped pork, render the fat a little, then add the meat and the onions. Brown everything together in the open pan over high heat, for about twenty or thirty minutes, stirring frequently. Flame with brandy, pour in the bouillon, add the calf's foot, garlic, *bouquet garni*, cloves, tomato purée, salt, and pepper. Lay a piece of buttered paper under the pan lid and let this simmer very slowly for six hours. Taste, complete the seasoning if necessary, remove the meat, and skim then strain the cooking liquid (this will be served with the noodles).

Cook the noodles for twenty minutes in bouillon or in salted water. Drain them and arrange them in a vegetable dish in layers, alternating with grated Parmesan and sprinkling the meat juices over them. The top layer should be Parmesan. Serve the noodles along with the beef.

Among the available commercial pasta I prefer the spaghetti from Naples and the vermicelli from Palermo.

I suggest cooking the beef the day before and reheating it the following day just before serving. I find it tastier that way.

Pasta must never be cooked ahead of time.

NOTE

1. The part of the rump known as *culotte* (pants) is the part which starts at the loin and ends at the tail.

GOULACH DE BOEUF

Beef Goulash

For eight people, use:

3 lbs. beef sirloin
2 lbs. potatoes
1¾ C. bouillon
½ lb. pork fat (belly if possible)
½ lb. onions
7 T. meat glaze
paprika
salt

Goulach is a Hungarian ragoût with paprika which may be prepared with red meat, pork, or chicken and which is either accompanied by pasta or potatoes.

Here is a recipe for beef goulash with potatoes.

Dice the pork and render it in a saucepan. Add the thinly sliced onions and cook these in the open pan for five minutes.

Cut the beef up into walnut-sized pieces and brown them in the saucepan. Season with paprika, salt lightly, add the bouillon into which the meat glaze has been dissolved, cover, bring it to a boil, and let it simmer. At the end of one hour add the peeled and diced potatoes and cook until the potatoes are done. This will take about twenty minutes. Taste, complete the seasoning if necessary and serve.

One should not add too much salt at the beginning because it is difficult to judge ahead of time how much salt the bouillon and the meat glaze will contribute.

In Viennese goulash the paprika would be replaced by cumin or marjoram to taste and the liquid could be either broth or cream.

One could also prepare, in this same way, a goulash in which one would use equal parts of eye round of beef, tenderloin of lamb, and pork tenderloin.

MIROTON

The *miroton* is a dish made up of slices of cooked beef, more especially boiled beef, which one reheats in an onion sauce.

Mince some onions, brown them in butter in a skillet; and when they have taken on a light golden color add some wine vinegar and pepper, and let this cook a little. Now add a *bouquet garni*, some tomato sauce, and some meat glaze dissolved in bouillon, and reduce this mixture to a saucelike consistency. Remove the *bouquet*, taste, complete the seasoning (which should be quite pronounced), add the sliced beef, heat, and serve.

To make *miroton gratiné*, sprinkle some breadcrumbs over the *miroton*, prepared as above, dot the top with butter, and brown in the oven.

Cooked lamb may also be prepared in this manner.

GALETTES DE BOEUF

Beef Patties

In France butcher's meat is generally quite tender; therefore one hardly ever uses it in the form of meat patties or meatballs unless they are made from remains of roasted or boiled meat. Abroad (speaking from the French angle), on the contrary, where meat is often tough, raw meat is often used ground up.

Here are two examples of *galettes de boeuf:*

1. Take a piece of beef round and either mince it with a knife[1] into pieces the size of a pinhead or grind it. Add some fine, dry, sifted breadcrumbs which have been soaked in milk and pressed dry, some minced onion sautéed in butter without browning, and some egg yolks. Season with salt and pepper. Knead everything together and shape it into patties. These could be shaped like beefsteaks, for instance, which you will cook in butter in a skillet. Serve these with mashed potatoes.

For variation, these patties could be dipped in egg white, then in dry, sifted breadcrumbs, and then cooked in butter, sprinkled with lemon juice, and served with sautéed potatoes.

One may, it goes without saying, cook these patties in a broiler. However, one should then increase the quantity of egg yolks in order to give them a firmer consistency.

Grated horseradish makes a good accompaniment for these patties, whether they are breaded or not.

2. Either mince or grind the meat as above, add to it one-third of its weight in butter, and a little madeira wine. Season with salt, pepper, and nutmeg, and mix well.

With this mixture make some patties which you will smooth over with the moistened flat side of a knife blade. First roll them in flour, then in beaten egg, and last in some dry, sifted breadcrumbs. Cook them in a frying pan in butter. If you prefer to broil them, first wrap them in a thin layer of pork fat.

At the same time prepare a béarnaise sauce or a sauce made with some meat juice and cream and soured with lemon juice. Heat this up, garnish the top of the patties with some chopped onions cooked in butter, and coat everything with the sauce.

These patties, as well as the ones above, may be accompanied by mashed potatoes, sautéed potatoes or some vegetable or other, according to taste.

One may also make patties using other types of meat. One could, for instance, make: (a) lamb patties with a garnish of dried beans, either sautéed or puréed; (b) pork patties, served with a purée of dried peas or lentils with bacon; (c) chicken patties, which are delicious, made of white meat of chicken, ham, sweetbreads, cream, and served with a Nantua sauce, or a mushroom purée, or even with some morels cooked in meat juice.

All these recipes will be enjoyed by older people and those who have difficulty chewing.

NOTE

1. This method of cutting up the meat is preferable to grinding it, as grinding tends to cause a loss of juices.

FILET DE VEAU RÔTI

Roast Tenderloin of Veal

Trim the tenderloin and remove any sinews or gristle. Lard it with tiny strips of fat pork and slivers of truffle, or some slivers of ham and truffle. Season it, wrap it up completely in a thin sheet of pork fat, and roast it on a spit.

Arrange the meat on a platter and glaze it with the skimmed and reduced cooking juices. Garnish the platter with some tiny tartlets or small *croustades* filled with some kind of hash, or garnish with some tiny timbales filled with noodles, or with macaroni and ham, tongue, and mushrooms, or even with some croquettes made of Duchesse potatoes, etc.

Serve, sending along at the same time some *sauce demi-glace.*

Larded veal tenderloin may also be braised. It should be served with delicate garnishes and suitable sauces.

CARRÉ DE VEAU PIQUÉ, RÔTI

Roast Larded Loin of Veal

Take the top part of the veal loin, saw the rib bones in the middle, trim the top, and lard it with strips of pork fat. Salt and pepper it and cover it with a piece of buttered paper or cover it completely with a thin sheet of leaf lard. Skewer it onto a spit and roast it. A few minutes before it is done remove the paper or the pork fat and let the meat brown lightly.

Arrange the loin on a platter on which you have poured a well-reduced layer of veal and chicken stock.

Serve, sending along at the same time, according to choice, a vegetable dish with either one of the following: chicory, a *macédoine* of vegetables, some spinach, carrots cooked in meat juice or fried, noodles, macaroni, or rice.

ESCALOPES DE VEAU PANÉES

Breaded Veal Cutlets

A. For four people, use:

12 oz. in two thick cutlets, 1/2 inch thick, veal rump (upper, fleshy part of the hind leg)
5 T. butter
1 T. milk
1 egg
flour
dry, sifted breadcrumbs
salt and pepper

B. For four people, use:

12 oz., cut into 4 1/4-inch-thick cutlets, veal rump
7 T. butter
1 T. milk
1 egg
flour
dry, sifted breadcrumbs
lemon juice
salt and pepper

Breaded veal cutlets may be prepared in several ways. Here are two which differ essentially one from the other by the thickness of the cutlets and by the sauce which accompanies them.

Beat the egg with the milk, a pinch of salt, and a few grains of pepper. Dip the cutlets first in the flour, then in the beaten egg, and, last in the breadcrumbs. Repeat this procedure if necessary to make sure that the meat has a good, heavy coating.

Melt the butter in a frying pan, add the cutlets, sprinkle with salt and pepper, and let them cook for twenty to twenty-five minutes over moderate heat.

Serve with a tomato sauce.

Bread and cook the veal cutlets as in the preceding recipe but cook them for only twelve to fifteen minutes. Sprinkle them with lemon juice and serve with a garnish of fried eggplant with cheese.

ESCALOPES DE VEAU AU JAMBON, GRATINÉES

Oven-Browned Veal Cutlets with Ham

For four people, use:

1 lb. veal (cut into 4 thin slices)
1/2 lb. ham or bologna (in 4 thin slices same size as the veal
3 T. butter
grated Parmesan cheese
salt and pepper

Cook the cutlets in the butter in a frying pan, season lightly with salt and pepper, and remove them.

Put the slices of ham, for one minute, in the same butter, barely hot.

Arrange the veal slices in a low, ovenproof casserole, on each slice place a slice of ham, sprinkle with Parmesan, moisten them with the butter in which they were cooked, and brown them in the oven for three or four minutes.

Serve in the same dish and send along, at the same time, but in a separate dish, some gnocchi made with semolina (see recipe index).

This dish, which is a Bolognese specialty, is a pleasant surprise for those who are not familiar with Italian cuisine.

CÔTELETTES DE VEAU GRILLÉES, SAUCE MORNAY

Broiled Veal Chops with Mornay Sauce

Broil the veal chops. A moment before they are done, stop the cooking.

In a low, ovenproof casserole or pie plate put a layer of thick Mornay sauce made with veal and chicken stock. Arrange the chops on top, coat with more of the Mornay sauce, sprinkle with a few fresh breadcrumbs or dry, sifted breadcrumbs, dot with butter, and brown in the oven for ten minutes or so and serve.

For variation, split the partially broiled chops and stuff them with a purée of mushrooms or a *purée Soubise* (onions) before adding the sauce.

CÔTELETTES DE VEAU AU PAPRIKA

Veal Chops with Paprika

For four people, use:

1 1/3 C. thick cream
2 1/4 C. dry, sifted breadcrumbs
1 C. veal stock
4 T. butter
3 T. meat glaze
4 T. flour
paprika
4 veal chops (3/4 inch thick), weighing about 11 oz. each
2 onions
salt

Brown the flour and the minced onions in the butter. Stir in the veal stock in which you have dissolved the meat glaze. Add the salt and paprika to taste. Let these cook.

Roll the chops in the breadcrumbs so that the crumbs adhere thoroughly. Partially cook the chops in the broiler; then finish the cooking for five minutes in the sauce.

At the last minute whisk the cream into the sauce and taste. The seasoning must be a little sharp but not excessively.

Serve, sending along some buttered beets in a vegetable dish.

For four people, use:

2 2/3 C. good white wine
7 T. butter
3/4 C. dry, sifted breadcrumbs
1 C. grated Parmesan
4 veal chops (3/4 inch thick) weighing about 11 oz. each
2 onions
salt and pepper

CÔTELETTES DE VEAU BRAISÉES, AU PARMESAN

Braised Veal Chops with Parmesan

Melt 3 tablespoons of butter in a saucepan and brown the chops. Season with salt and pepper on both sides, remove the chops, and add the minced onions to the pan. Let these brown lightly; then put back the chops and add the wine, which must not cover them. Spread the mixed Parmesan and breadcrumbs over the chops, dot with the rest of the butter, cover and cook over low heat for about one hour. Baste as this cooks and make sure the meat does not stick to the bottom of the pan.

At the last minute reduce the sauce, which must be quite thick.

Arrange the chops on a platter, coat them with the sauce, and serve. Send along, at the same time, in a vegetable dish, some peas, spinach, or noodles, for example.

QUASI[1] DE VEAU BRAISÉ

Braised Veal Round

The veal, seasoned simply with salt and pepper, is braised in butter, on low heat, without any other liquid. It is turned frequently and basted with its own juices.

When it is cooked, it is arranged on a platter with its own juices, which have been skimmed of fat.

All garnishes indicated for the various pieces of veal are perfectly suitable for the round.

Rouelle (a thick slice across the leg) of veal may also be prepared in this way.

NOTE

1. The *quasi* is the piece which surrounds the iliac bone; it is particularly tender.

For six people, use:

4 lbs. veal round in one slice 2 inches thick
2 C. dry white wine
1/3 C. breadcrumbs
1 small sliced carrot
5 tsp. olive oil
1 small sliced onion
2 tsp. salt
pepper
2 cloves
1 clove garlic
1 bay leaf
thyme
butter
parsley

QUASI DE VEAU MARINÉ, GRATINÉ

Bone, trim, and tie up the meat.

Place it for about twelve hours in a marinade made with the white wine, olive oil, carrot, onion, garlic, cloves, bay leaf, thyme, parsley, salt, and pepper. Turn the meat over in the marinade several times.

Melt the butter in a fireproof casserole, put the veal in it, sprinkle it with the breadcrumbs, add the marinade, and cook it in a slow oven for about one and one-half hours, basting often.

Garnishes which go best with veal thus prepared are spinach, chicory, sorrel, peas cooked in butter or cream, creamed beets, carrots, celery, etc.

NOIX DE VEAU BRAISÉE

Braised Rump or Loin of Veal

For eight people, use:

4 lbs. veal loin, trimmed and larded
1/2 C. brandy
7 T. meat glaze
2 T. butter
1 bottle dry, white burgundy wine
carrots
onions
pork rind
bouquet garni
salt and pepper

Put the butter in a *cocotte*, and in it brown the veal, some minced onions, some pork rind, and any veal trimmings. Flame the contents with the brandy, add the wine, the meat glaze, the carrots, a *bouquet garni*, salt, and pepper. Cook in a very slow oven for four hours, basting frequently with the pan liquids.

Arrange the meat on a platter, skim the fat off the sauce, strain it, and send it along in a sauceboat at the same time as the veal.

Noodles with tomatoes or *petit pois* with asparagus are a very good accompaniment for braised veal.

This same recipe can be applied to other cuts of veal.

If you want to make the dish a little more elaborate, garnish the platter with some tiny *flans* (custards) filled with sliced mushrooms sautéed in butter, covered with Mornay sauce, browned in the oven, and topped with a nice slice of poached marrow.

CÔTE DE VEAU BRAISÉE, À LA PURÉE DE TOMATES

Braised Veal Rib with Tomato Purée

For six people, use:

3 lbs. veal rib
1 C. meat juice or broth
2/3 C. seasoned tomato purée
7 T. butter
5 T. brandy
4 tsp. flour
2 tsp. olive oil
1 chopped shallot
bouquet garni
salt and pepper

Grease a saucepan with the oil.[1] Heat it up and then add 4 teaspoons of butter and the veal. Brown the veal for twenty to thirty minutes, flame it with the brandy, sprinkle it with the flour, add the meat juice, shallot, *bouquet garni*, and salt and pepper to taste. Simmer the meat for one and one-half hours.

Fifteen minutes before serving add the tomato purée to the sauce, along with the rest of the butter.

Serve the veal coated with the strained sauce.

NOTE

1. Coating the pan with the oil first keeps the butter from burning.

For four people, use:

1½ lbs. veal rib
1 lb. morels[1]
7 T. butter
3 T. meat glaze
3 T. veal stock
2 T. madeira wine
2 tsp. salt
black pepper
potato starch

CÔTE DE VEAU AUX MORILLES

Veal Rib with Morels

Scrub and wash the morels, dry them in a cloth, and split them in two lengthwise.

Brown the veal in butter for thirty minutes and season with salt and pepper. Add the madeira and the veal stock in which you have dissolved the meat glaze. Add the morels and continue cooking everything together over very low heat for thirty minutes. Reduce the pan liquids if necessary and then thicken with a little potato starch.

Serve the veal coated with the sauce and the morels around the platter as a garnish.

NOTE

1. If no morels, either fresh or dried, are available, one could substitute mushrooms, but the dish would not be as delicate.

For six people, use:

2 lbs. sliced veal in six thin equal slices
1 lb. 3 oz. smoked ham in six equal slices, a little smaller than the veal sliced
1 C. tomato sauce
7 oz. mushrooms
10 T. butter
4 tsp. salt
2 T. flour
6 T. chopped parsley
black pepper
1 large shallot

PAUPIETTES DE VEAU AU JAMBON

Veal Rolls with Ham

Put a slice of ham on each slice of veal, after having trimmed the veal neatly.

Prepare the following stuffing:

Chop the shallot and cook it for two or three minutes in 4 teaspoons of the butter, without browning. Add any ham or veal trimmings, the chopped parsley, mushrooms (peeled and chopped), and 4 tablespoons of tomato sauce. Let this all cook together for about ten minutes, stirring, then put in 2 tablespoons of butter blended with the flour. Continue to cook and stir for ten more minutes; you will then have a fairly thick stuffing.

Spread a layer of stuffing on each ham and veal slice, let it cool, then roll up and tie the meat.

Brown the paupiettes over low heat in the rest of the butter, for about thirty minutes. Add the rest of the tomato sauce, the rest of the stuffing, salt, and pepper, and continue to cook for another thirty minutes.

Remove the paupiettes, arrange them on a platter after having removed the strings. Strain the sauce[1] through a sieve, pushing it through with a masher, or use a vegetable mill. Coat the paupiettes with it. Garnish the platter with tomatoes stuffed with broiled mushrooms and serve.

This is a very delicate dish. The happy blending of all the ingredients with which it is made, and the way it is cooked over low heat, seem to lend a harmony to the dish which produces on the palate of a gourmet the effect that a Beethoven symphony produces on the ears of a music lover.

NOTE

1. By adding some *fines herbes* to this sauce one would have what is known as *sauce italienne*.

PAUPIETTES DE VEAU AU BACON

Veal Rolls with Bacon

For four people, use:

1 lb. top round of veal
1⅓ C. veal stock
10 oz. bacon
1 medium onion
2 T. butter
5 shallots
bouquet garni **(parsley and celery)**
flour
salt and pepper

Cut the veal into four thin slices, trim them, cover three-fourths of their surfaces with thin slices of bacon, season with salt and pepper, and roll them up. Tie them with string and roll them in flour.

In the butter cook the remaining bacon, diced, along with any veal trimming and the onion and shallots. Then add the paupiettes and brown them. Add the veal stock and the *bouquet* and braise everything over very low heat for about one and a half hours.

Arrange the paupiettes, strings removed, on a platter. Strain the sauce over them and serve, sending along, at the same time, some boiled potatoes which have been coarsely mashed and browned under the broiler or in the oven; or serve some plain mashed potatoes.

The bacon, with its smoky taste, gives this dish a pleasant flavor.

PAUPIETTES DE VEAU AU FOIE GRAS

Veal Rolls with Foie Gras

For six people, use:

1 lb. 9 oz. veal slices, cut into 6 very thin, equal slices, without tears
9 oz. foie gras
1⅓ C. hard cider
¼ lb. mushrooms
⅔ C. strong veal stock
½ C. heavy cream
4 T. butter
1 oz. uncooked truffle
1 egg
dry, sifted breadcrumbs
nutmeg, salt, and pepper

Peel and chop the mushrooms and brown them in a little butter.

Prepare a stuffing with the foie gras, chopped truffle, browned mushrooms, and a little of the dry, sifted breadcrumbs. Bind the dressing with the egg and season to taste with nutmeg, salt, and pepper.

On each slice of veal spoon one-sixth of the dressing, roll the paupiettes, and tie them up with string.

Brown the meat in the rest of the butter, add the onion, and let the veal sweat. De-glaze the pan with the veal stock and the cider, and continue cooking over moderate heat.

Remove the paupiettes, keep them hot, boil down the sauce, and thicken it with cream. Taste—the sauce must be slightly acid. If it is not, add a little bit of lemon juice.

Arrange the paupiettes on a platter, coat them with the strained sauce, and serve. Send along, at the same time, a vegetable dish containing some Dauphine potatoes.

For four people, use:

1.

8 small veal steaks
strong veal stock
larding fat
potato starch
salt and pepper

2. For the sauce:

1 cup heavy cream
4 T. butter
4 tsp. flour
milk
salt and pepper

GRENADINS[1] DE VEAU AU JUS, SAUCE À LA CRÈME

Veal Medallions in Meat Juice with Cream Sauce

Run two or three strips of the seasoned pork fat through each little *grenadin* and season them with salt and pepper. Put them in strong veal stock and let them cook slowly, turning them frequently.

At the same time, prepare a cream sauce as follows:

In a saucepan melt the butter, stir in the flour, and cook it without letting it brown. Slowly stir in a little milk; then add the cream in small quantities and season to taste with salt and pepper. Let this sauce simmer until it has acquired the consistency of mayonnaise.

(I do not specify the quantity of milk, because, actually, everything depends on the thickness of the cream. If it is light then there is no need to use milk, but if it is very heavy, which is preferable, putting in a little milk beforehand keeps it from curdling—which could happen to an inexperienced cook, who might add the cream too rapidly.)

Pour the sauce or spoon it onto a platter, arrange the little *grenadins* on it, and keep everything hot. Thicken the cooking juices from the meat with a little potato starch, coat the *grenadins* with it, and serve.

NOTE

1. The term *grenadins* is applied to tiny slices of meat, cut like *escalopes*, but smaller and thicker. They are usually cut from loin of veal which has been sliced away from the bone into 1½-inch-thick medallions.

These can be made out of veal, turkey, chicken, venison, fish, etc.

I know people who have acquired a taste for veal just from eating these.

One may prepare, in this same way, either veal or lamb sweetbreads or slices of chicken. They are all equally delicious.

For four people, use:

1 lb. 9 oz. trimmed veal round
1⅓ C. pure apple cider
⅓ C. cream
4 T. butter
6 T. chopped onion
5 tsp. meat glaze
4 tsp. potato starch
1 egg yolk
larding fat
bouquet garni
salt and pepper

GRENADINS DE VEAU AU CIDRE

Veal Medallions with Cider

Cut the boneless veal round or loin into eight small, equal, fairly thick medallions. Lard them with the seasoned larding fat.

Cook the onions in 5 teaspoons of butter without letting them get too brown. Add the *bouquet garni*, the cider, and meat glaze. Cook for about twenty minutes, strain, and reduce it to thicken the sauce.

Brown the little steaks in the rest of the butter. Add the strained sauce to the pan; complete the seasoning, if necessary, and cook for about fifteen minutes.

Arrange the *grenadins* on a hot platter, thicken the sauce with the potato starch and the egg yolk, and add the cream. Heat this up but do not boil. The sauce must be slightly acid.

Coat the meat with the sauce and serve, sending along, at the same time, some truffled potato croquettes, souffléed (see recipe index).

Kidneys may be prepared this same way.

QUASI DE VEAU BRAISÉ AU LAIT

Veal Round Braised in Milk

For six people, use:

- 3 lbs. boneless veal round
- 3 C. milk
- 3/4 lb. veal bones
- 2 medium carrots
- 1/4 lb. mushrooms
- 6 T. chopped onion
- 6 shallots
- 3 T. flour
- 3 tsp. salt
- several sprigs parsley
- a pinch thyme
- pepper to taste
- 1 bay leaf
- meat glaze
- currant jelly (optional)
- 1/2 C. butter
- 1 T. meat glaze

Peel and chop the carrots, mushrooms, onions, and shallots.

In a large heavy pot or Dutch oven brown the veal and the bones in 1/4 cup of butter. Add the salt, pepper, and the meat glaze and simmer the pot (covered) for one hour.

At the same time, bring the milk to a boil in a separate pan and add the carrots, mushrooms, onions, shallots, bay leaf, thyme, and parsley. Simmer for one hour in order to obtain about 2 cups of herb-seasoned milk. Strain.

Melt the rest of the butter, blend in the flour and add the milk slowly, stirring, to make a smooth, lumpless sauce.

Remove the meat and bones from the kettle. Strain the pan juices, then replace the meat and the strained juice and add the sauce. Cook everything together for thirty minutes.

Just before serving, stir in the currant jelly (no more than a tablespoonful).

This dish, which may seem a little unusual, comes from Danish cuisine. I tasted it in Copenhagen and found it to have a certain charm.

ÉPAULE DE VEAU BRAISÉE AU CHABLIS

Shoulder of Veal Braised in Chablis

For six to eight people, use:

- 5 lbs. white-fleshed, fatty, veal shoulder, boned, rolled, and tied
- 1 1/3 C. chablis
- 3 T. butter
- 4 medium carrots
- 4 medium onions
- 3 medium tomatoes
- 1 bay leaf
- potato starch
- paprika
- salt and pepper

Boned the shoulder, roll and tie it, and set aside the bones and trimmings.

Slowly brown the shoulder, along with the carrots and the onions, in the butter. Season with salt and pepper and put everything in a braising kettle. Add the bones, tomatoes, bay leaf, and pour in the chablis. Let this all braise very slowly in the oven for four hours, tightly covered. Baste from time to time with the pan juices.

Remove the meat, arrange it on a hot platter, and keep it hot. Skim the fat off the pan juices, strain, boil down and thicken with a little potato starch. Boil it up again for a moment or two. Taste and complete the seasoning with a little paprika.

Pour the sauce over the meat and serve, sending along, at the same time, some plain noodles, or noodles with tomato sauce.

One may prepare a stuffed shoulder this same way. A mixture of ground pork, bacon, veal kidney, mushrooms, shallots, and parsley, seasoned with salt and pepper, makes an excellent stuffing.

ÉPAULE DE VEAU FARCIE, BRAISÉE

Braised Stuffed Veal Shoulder

Bone the shoulder, pound the inside surface with a mallet, season and stuff it with a mixture of ground veal kidney, tongue, ham, mushrooms, a large truffle, parsley, and a little chopped chives, all bound with a fresh egg yolk.

Roll and tie the shoulder, brown it in butter, and braise it very slowly in a very little veal and chicken stock, basting frequently as it cooks.

Arrange the shoulder on a platter, skim the fat off the pan liquids, strain and serve the sauce in a sauceboat at the same time as the meat.

Cauliflower, spinach, chicory, mushrooms, *petits pois*, carrots, potatoes, and vegetable *jardinières* are good garnishes for braised veal.

A loin of veal or a stuffed breast of veal may also be prepared in this same way.

JARRET DE VEAU AU JUS

Veal Knuckle au Jus

For four people, use:

3 lbs. veal knuckle or shank cut into 4 2-inch-thick slices
3 C. veal stock
1 lb. tomatoes
1⅓ C. white wine
1 C. chopped onion
4 T. butter
bouquet garni
flour
parsley
lemon
salt and pepper

Roll the pieces of veal shank in flour and brown in butter. Remove them and in their stead put the onions and let them brown. Now add the peeled, seeded, and crushed tomatoes, the browned meat, and *bouquet garni* and grated lemon rind to taste. Pour in the veal stock and the white wine.

Simmer until the sauce becomes fairly thick—two and a half

hours is generally needed. Taste and complete the seasoning with salt, pepper, and lemon juice.

Arrange the slices of veal on a platter, coat them with the strained sauce, sprinkle with blanched, chopped parsley, and serve, sending, along, at the same time, either some boiled rice, some rice sautéed in butter, or even some spinach which has been cooked in meat juice.

Veal shank or knuckle, cooked as above, differs from the Milanese dish known as *ossobuco* only because of the addition of wine and veal stock, which makes it tastier.

By substituting, for the veal shank or knuckle, some veal shoulder, and by using garlic instead of the lemon, one would have the classic dish known as Veal Marengo.

Square pieces of breast of veal may also be prepared as above.

RAGOÛT DE VEAU ET ISSUES DE VEAU AUX CHAMPIGNONS DE COUCHE OU AUX MORILLES

Ragoût of Veal and Veal Organ Meats with Field Mushrooms or Morels

For eight people, use:

2 lbs. veal round
1 lb. field mushrooms or morels
$^1/_4$ lb. butter
3 T. flour
1 qt. veal and chicken stock
$^1/_2$ bottle sauterne wine
8 chicken livers
2 veal kidneys
1 veal sweetbread
carrots
onions
bouquet garni
lemon juice
salt and pepper

Trim the sweetbread; soak it in salted water for one hour. Brown the veal lightly, along with the carrots and onions, in 3 tablespoons of butter. Season with salt and pepper and pour in the sauterne, then the jellied veal and chicken stock and the *bouquet garni*. Simmer these together for about one hour.

Peel the mushrooms and dip them in lemon juice; or carefully clean and scrub the morels.

Brown the sweetbread lightly in some butter for fifteen minutes. Cook the kidneys for a few minutes in the same butter. Add the sweetbread and kidneys to the pan containing the veal. Cook these together for fifteen minutes, then add the mushrooms or morels to the pan and continue to cook them together for another fifteen minutes.

Sauté the chicken livers lightly in the butter used for the kidneys and sweetbreads and add them to the veal pan and cook for another five minutes.

Make a roux with the rest of the butter and flour, stir in the veal cooking liquid, reduce to a fairly good sauce consistency, taste and complete the seasoning, if necessary, with salt, pepper, and lemon juice to taste.

Carve the veal, sweetbread, and kidneys. Arrange the three meats on a serving platter and surround them with the chicken livers,

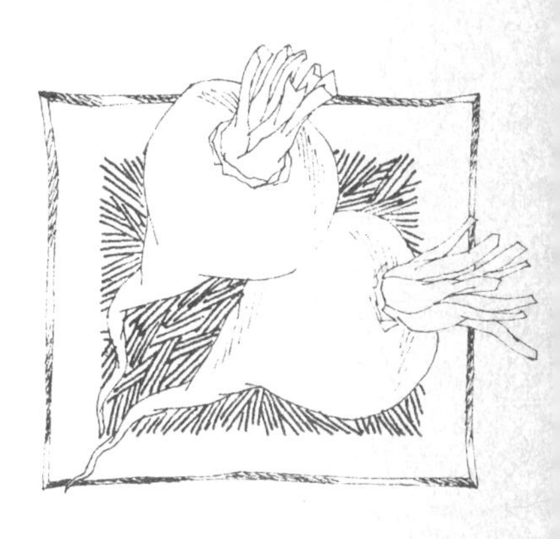

mushrooms, or morels, and coat everything with the sauce and serve.

This is a royal ragoût.

RAGOÛT DE VEAU AUX ÉCREVISSES

Ragoût of Veal with Crayfish

For four people, use:

2 lbs. veal shoulder
½ C. veal stock
6 T. butter
4 tsp. flour
24 crayfish (or prawns)
1 cauliflower
1 large carrot
1 small stalk celery
1 small leek
asparagus tips
lemon peel
parsley
salt and pepper

In 3 tablespoons of butter, brown the veal, along with the cut-up carrot, celery, and leek. Sprinkle with flour, stir in the veal stock, add the lemon rind, some parsley, salt, and pepper. Let this all cook together.

At the same time, cook the crayfish (or prawns) in a court bouillon and the cauliflower and asparagus in salted water.

Shell the crayfish, keep the tail meat warm, prepare a crayfish butter with the remaining butter and the trimmings.

Arrange the meat in the middle of a platter on which you have poured the strained cooking juices. Coat with the crayfish butter, and arrange, around the meat, a garnish of crayfish tails, asparagus tips, and cauliflower. Serve.

BLANQUETTE DE VEAU

Veal Stew

For four people, use:

2 lbs. breast of veal, cut into serving pieces
½ lb mushrooms
7 T. cream
7 T. butter
3 T. flour
4 tsp. salt
freshly ground black pepper to taste
10 small onions
3 egg yolks
bouquet garni
veal stock
lemon juice
parsley

One may prepare *blanquette de veau* with breast of veal or with veal round or loin.

Here is a recipe using breast of veal.

Melt the butter and stir in the flour, cooking until the flour is lightly colored. Add the pieces of veal, onions, *bouquet garni*, salt, pepper, and enough veal stock to cover the meat. Simmer very slowly for one and a half hours. Remove the meat, strain the pan juices, and skim off the fat. Put the meat back in the saucepan, along with the strained sauce, add the peeled mushrooms, and continue cooking for another twenty minutes. Thicken the sauce with the egg yolks beaten with the cream. Season with the lemon juice and heat up without boiling.

Arrange the meat in a deep serving dish, surround it with the mushrooms and pour the sauce over it, sprinkle with chopped parsley and serve.

If you use veal that has already been roasted, it is best, after having browned the flour a little in the butter, instead of regular veal broth, to use white stock,[1] since the meat you are using will not render any juices. One would only add the mushrooms, which would be cooked for twenty minutes. At the last minute, you will add to the saucepan the sliced roast veal, heating just long enough to get it hot without boiling. You would then thicken the sauce with the egg yolks and cream and season with lemon juice. It can then be arranged on a platter and served as above.

Blanquette of veal made with roast veal is more presentable than that made with the breast of veal; however, the breast of veal has a particularly interesting texture as you bite into it and has more charm. Therefore, in order to enjoy both things, I suggest preparing the blanquette partly with breast of veal and partly with the roast veal, combining the two above recipes.

One can make a *blanquette* of baby lamb and also of young deer, but the cooking time would be much shorter.

NOTE

1. To make one quart of white stock, use:

2½ lbs. veal shank and other inexpensive cuts
1 carrot
1 onion
2 T. salt
1 leek
1 small stalk celery
black pepper to taste
1 clove
1 small *bouquet garni* (parsley, thyme, and bay leaf)
butter or other fat
water

Cook the carrot, onion, leek, and celery for a short time in a little butter or fat. Remove the vegetables and add the cut-up veal. Let this brown lightly and pour off the fat. Then add a little water and let this boil down to a glaze. Do this several times, each time adding boiling water as soon as the other becomes a glaze. Last, deglaze the pan with a lot of water, add the vegetables, *bouquet garni*, clove, salt, and pepper, and let this all cook for five or six hours, keeping the liquid at about one quart by adding boiling water as necessary. Skim off the fat and strain the liquid.

To make one quart of chicken stock one would add 3 chicken gizzards to the above recipe for white stock. The rest of the recipe remains the same.

FRICANDEAU

Veal Stew

For six to eight people, use:

3 lbs. veal, rump, sirloin, or round, cut lengthwise along the fibers of the meat
2 C. bouillon
1 C. good white wine
7 oz. pork fat for larding
carrot
onion
butter
salt and pepper

Run some strips of seasoned larding pork fat through the meat with a larding needle. Place the meat in a braising kettle with a

little butter and turn it onto all surfaces for a few minutes without letting it brown. Add some sliced onion and carrot; season with pepper and one-third cup of bouillon and one-third cup of white wine. Boil until the liquids have evaporated but do not allow the meat to stick to the bottom of the pan. When the cooking liquids have become syrupy, add the rest of the bouillon and the rest of the wine, then simmer, in the partially covered kettle, for one and one-quarter to one and one-half hours. Baste as it cooks.

Taste and complete the seasoning with salt and pepper if necessary.

A little before the meat is done, put the pan in the oven and brown the meat, that is, let it take on a brilliant, shiny, golden color. Baste frequently during this last procedure.

Arrange the meat on a platter, strain the sauce over it and serve, passing, at the same time, in a vegetable dish, some cooked sorrel or even spinach or creamed chicory.

For variation, one could serve the *fricandeau* garnished with tartlets filled with creamed morels (or mushrooms), or even stuffed morels or mushrooms.

The *fricandeau* may be served cold, coated with the jellied pan juices.

One can also prepare, in the same way, shad, sturgeon, tuna, etc., with this difference—that one would use fish broth and increase the quantity of wine.

FRICANDEAU AUX CÈPES[1]

Veal Stew with Mushrooms

In a saucepan, put some leeks, carrots, onions, garlic to taste, salt, pepper, a veal bone, and some goose fat. Let these all brown a little and flame with Armagnac. Add some tomato sauce, then pour in enough veal broth to eventually cover the meat.

Cook these together and strain the liquid.

Lard a piece of top round of veal with some fatty ham strips, then cook the meat as in the preceding recipe, but baste it with the above liquid.

Arrange the veal on a platter, coat it with the very reduced sauce, garnish with some tartlets or some small timbales filled with creamed *cèpes*, and serve.

NOTE

1. *Cèpes* are known as "the edible boletus." Regular field or cultivated mushrooms could be used instead.

FRICANDEAU À LA MOUTARDE

Veal Stew with Mustard

For six people, use:

- $1\frac{1}{2}$ lbs. boned veal, either top round, round, or sirloin
- 1 lb. 3 oz. field or cultivated mushrooms
- $1\frac{1}{2}$ C. veal stock
- 1 C. good white wine
- 7 oz. pork larding fat
- pickled beef tongue
- plain mustard
- salt and pepper

Lard the meat with some seasoned strips of pork fat. Coat all surfaces of the meat with mustard, wrap the meat in thin sheets of pork fat or leaf lard, and let the mustard impregnate the meat for twenty-four hours.

Next day, peel the mushrooms and cut the stems off at cap level.

Put the meat in a stewing kettle and cook it on all surfaces, very slowly, for a few minutes, without browning. Pour in $\frac{1}{3}$ cup of veal stock and $\frac{1}{3}$ cup of wine. Let this liquid reduce, then add the remaining stock and wine and the mushroom stems. Continue to simmer this slowly, with the cover partially on the pan, for one and a half hours, basting frequently. Taste and strengthen the seasoning if necessary.

Cook the mushroom caps separately and brown them under the broiler.

At the last minute, discard what is left of the pork fat and let the meat take on a shiny golden color by browning it in the oven, basting with the cooking liquid.

Arrange the veal on a platter, skim the fat off the cooking juices, strain, and coat the top of the meat with a little of this sauce. Garnish with the cooked mushroom caps and with some tiny cut-outs or slivers of pickled beef tongue.

Serve, sending along at the same time the rest of the sauce in a sauceboat.

GOULACH DE VEAU

Veal Goulash

For five people, use:

- 2 lbs. veal, preferably lean
- 1 C. cream
- 4 T. white wine
- 4 T. butter
- 2 T. lard
- 2 T. meat juice
- salt
- paprika
- lemon juice

Mince the onions and brown them in a saucepan with the butter and lard. Add the meat cut into two-inch cubes. Add the meat juice, season with salt and paprika and simmer for one hour.

Ten minutes before serving, add the wine, then the cream, which has been soured with a little lemon juice; heat everything up without boiling, taste for seasoning, and serve, sending along, at the same time, a dish of noodles or a dish of rice.

Pork goulash can be made in the same way, but one would add cumin and marjoram.

Pork goulash is generally served with sauerkraut.

One may also make chicken goulash.

This is prepared in the same way as veal goulash, but after having cut up the chicken add one-fifth of its weight of freshened salt pork, diced.

This dish, which in Hungary is called *porckel*, is served with rice.

For eight people, use:

6 cups veal stock
1 lb. 3 oz. top round of veal
1 lb. 3 oz. pork tenderloin
1 lb. or 2 cans okra
1¼ cups thick tomato purée

KALALOU À LA PARISIENNE

The *kalalou* is a Creole dish. It is a ragoût of meat and vegetables, among which the most unusual is okra. It is almost impossible, in France, to make a real Creole *kalalou*, but thanks to the excellent canned okra that one can purchase at all times of the year it is easy to prepare a dish which is reminiscent of the original.

Put the okra in a colander and rinse in cold water.

Cut the pork and veal into large dice and brown them in butter. Add all but ¾ cup of the veal stock and cook for three hours. Now, add half the okra and the tomato purée and continue to cook for thirty minutes, making sure that the okra does not stick to the bottom of the pan. During the cooking, taste and complete the seasoning with cayenne, salt, and pepper

At the same time, heat in a double boiler the rest of the okra in the remaining veal stock so that they soak up the broth but still remain whole. Those that have cooked in the stew will have more or less disintegrated and flavored and thickened the sauce.

At serving time add the whole okra to the stew along with the rest of the veal stock. Serve, sending along, in a vegetable dish, some rice sautéed in butter.

One could also serve the sautéed rice molded in a ring mold. The *kalalou* would then be spooned into the center of the ring.

For five people, use:

2 lbs. shoulder or round of veal
1⅓ C. seasoned tomato purée
4 T. lard
4 T. meat juice
2 heads of garlic separated into cloves
1 T. dry, sifted breadcrumbs
salt and pepper

AILLADE[1] DE VEAU

Garlic Veal

In the Midi they love *aillades* and, in particular, veal with garlic. Here is the recipe for *aillade de Casteljaloux*.

Cut the meat into two-inch cubes and brown them in the lard, in a saucepan. Add the breadcrumbs, garlic, tomato purée, meat juice, and season with salt and pepper. Let this all simmer for one hour. Remove the garlic cloves if you do not like to serve them and send along at the same time a dish of sautéed rice.

Aillade of lamb may be prepared in the same way.

NOTE

1. In the literal sense of the term, *aillade* is a garlic sauce (*ail*

being the French word for garlic); however, in the Midi the term extends to those dishes which contain a large amount of garlic.

QUENELLES FOURRÉES

Stuffed Quenelles

For eight people, use:

1. *For the quenelles:*

1 lb. top round raw veal, without skin or sinews
1/2 lb. potato *panade* (see recipe index)
1/4 C. thick, cold Béchamel sauce
2 tsp. salt
pepper to taste
a grating nutmeg
4 egg yolks
2 whole eggs

2. *For the stuffing:*

12 oz. good sausage meat
truffles
madeira wine
brandy
dry, sifted breadcrumbs

Prepare a quenelle forcemeat as in the master recipe for quenelles in the seafood chapter.

Brush, wash, peel, and chop the truffles. Mix this hash with the sausage meat and moisten with a little madeira and brandy to taste.

Mince the truffle trimmings.

Mold 16 quenelles weighing about three ounces each and insert into the center of each one-sixteenth of the truffled sausage meat. Shape them like small sausages.

Mix the truffle trimmings with some dry, sifted breadcrumbs and bread the quenelles with this mixture. Cook them in a frying pan in clarified butter.

Serve them with a *velouté* sauce or some good meat juice.

Other stuffed quenelles may be prepared in the same way by varying the meat and the ingredients of the stuffing.

GALETTES DE VEAU À LA MOELLE DE BOEUF

Veal Patties with Beef Marrow

For six people, use:

10 oz. top round of veal, ground
4 oz. smoked ham, ground
3 oz. beef marrow
3/4 C. dry, sifted breadcrumbs
3 fresh eggs
butter
milk
breadcrumbs
salt

Poach the beef marrow in salted water.

Mix the veal, ham, marrow, 2 whole eggs, breadcrumbs moistened in milk and pressed dry, and salt. Mix this well and shape into 6 flat cakes or patties. Brush them with the yolk of the remaining egg, roll them in breadcrumbs, and cook them in butter in a frying pan.

Cover the pan and the patties will swell. Turn them, and, when they are a lovely golden color on all sides, serve them.

These patties are excellent. They should be served with tomatoes stuffed with broiled mushrooms, or a sorrel purée, or even a tomato sauce, or a *velouté* sauce made with meat broth.

For six people, use:

2 C. jellied veal or chicken stock
3 T. butter
3 T. clarified butter
4 T. flour

To prepare a meat-based *velouté* sauce, or a *velouté*, proceed as follows.

Melt the clarified butter and stir in the flour without browning. Stir in the melted stock until it thickens and comes to a boil. Then place the pan on an asbestos rack and simmer very gently for one hour. At the last minute, whisk the cut-up fresh butter into the sauce. Taste for seasoning.

For eight people, use:

1. *For the pastry crust:*

3 C. hard wheat flour
10 T. butter
1/3 C. (approx.) water
1 T. salt
2 egg yolks

2. *For the body of the pâté:*

14 oz. lean veal
14 oz. ham, either smoked or not, according to taste
1/2 lb. pork fat cut into very thin sheets
7 T. brandy
pinch *quatre épices*
1 egg yolk
salt

3. *For the stuffing:*

1/2 lb. calf's liver
1/2 lb. lean fresh bacon
1/2 lb. mushrooms
5 oz. raw ham
4 T. butter
5 shallots
few grains black pepper
1 bay leaf
1 sprig thyme

4. *For the jelly:*

1 lb. bottom round of beef
1 lb. calf's knuckle or shin bone
1 C. white wine
2 carrots
3 oz. pork rind
3 inch piece of stalk celery
2 qts. water
2 egg whites
1 chicken gizzard
1 calf's foot
1 leek (white part only)
1 onion stuck with a clove
pork bones
madeira
salt, *quatre épices,* **cayenne to taste**

PÂTÉ DE VEAU ET JAMBON EN CROÛTE

Veal and Ham Pâté in Crust

One may prepare *pâtés* in molds or without molds. The former are prettier; the latter, however, allow for the use of a type of dough which gives a better crust, though it is difficult to pour jelly into them—and so the jelly is served as a garnish around the *pâté*.

Here is an excellent recipe for a *pâté* without a mold.

In the brandy, marinate the veal and ham for the body of the *pâté*. Season with salt, pepper and *quatre épices* to taste.

Preparing the dough: Make a smooth dough with the listed ingredients. Let it rest for at least three hours before using.

Preparing the forcemeat: Chop the mushrooms, shallots, thyme, and bay leaf. Cook these together in the butter. Grind the liver, the fresh bacon, and the raw ham. Rub these through a sieve, add the pepper, brandy from the marinade, and the minced mushrooms. Mix everything thoroughly.

Preparing the jelly: Cut up the beef, the calf's shin or knuckle, and the calf's foot, and cook them in a little fat along with the chicken gizzard.

Break up the beef, veal, and pork bones.

In a little fat, brown the carrots, celery, leek, and onion. Let these get lightly browned.

Put the pork rind in the bottom of a large kettle, on top place the cut-up bones, the meats, and the vegetables minus the cooking fat. Season with salt, pepper, and *quatre épices* and add the water and wine. Cook these for six hours, skimming off the grease as it cooks. Reduce the liquid to one-third. A little before the meat is ready, add a little madeira to taste. Once the cooking is finished, clarify the broth with the egg whites.

Forming the pâté: Mix the dough and roll it out on a floured cloth. On this spread a layer of forcemeat, on top arrange some ham which has been larded with strips of fat pork, then another layer of forcemeat, then the veal which has also been larded. Finish off with a layer of forcemeat.

Fold the dough over the above to form a *pâté* and make two or three small openings for the escape of steam. Brush with egg yolk.

Cooking: In a hot oven for forty to fifty minutes.

Finishing: Pour some partially set jelly into the *pâté* with a funnel. Let it cool.

Arrange the *pâté* on a platter, surround it with the rest of the jelly, which has been chilled, and then cut out into diamond shapes and serve.

1 lb. flour
5 oz. (10 T.) butter
7 T. (approx.) water
3 tsp. salt
3 egg yolks

To make the *pâté* in a mold, one would prepare a little bit stiffer dough than the preceding one—by using, for example:

The dough is mixed as above, rolled out, and used to line the mold. This would then be filled as in the preceding recipe, but the cooking time would be longer.

GRILLADE DE PRÉ-SALÉ

Broiled Lamb

To make little *grillades* of lamb, cut some one-and-a-half-inch-thick slices of lamb from the top round and grill or broil them *under* a charcoal fire.

First sear them quickly on one side, then continue cooking under a hot fire for about seven minutes. Turn the meat and do the same with the other side. When the meat is cooked, salt and pepper both sides of the little *grillades* and serve at once, with a watercress garnish.

These small *grillades* made from very young lamb are delicious.

One may also broil or grill, in the same way, some slices of tenderloin or "mutton chops" of equal thickness; but it would then be preferable to tie the meat before cooking it so that it will not lose its shape. Remove the strings before serving.

A refinement of this recipe consists in inserting into the "mutton chops" a trimmed lamb kidney.

CARRÉ DE MOUTON RÔTI

Lamb Rib Roast

Take a trimmed rib section of lamb which is ready for cutting into lamb chops. Remove the chine bone and trim off the top of the rib bones as one would do for chops. Wrap the trimmed meat in a thin sheet of pork fat and roast the rib section thus prepared.

When the roast is done, arrange it on a platter, garnish with a paper frill on the end of each rib bone, and serve. Send along, at the same time, the skimmed cooking juices, in a sauceboat.

All the usual vegetables which accompany chops, saddle, or rack of lamb are perfectly suitable for the rib roast.

Rib of very young lamb is generally broiled rather than roasted.

BROCHETTES DÉ PRE-SALÉ

Skewered Lamb

For four people, use:

- 3 oz. very thin, lean and fat, fresh bacon, cut into 12 small slices
- 1 eight-rib section of lamb
- 1 thin sheet of pork fat
- béarnaise sauce (see recipe)
- curry
- salt and pepper

Use only the rib eye meat,[1] that is, cut away all the bone. Salt and pepper the meat, wrap it in the sheet of pork fat, and slice it into eight little steaks or *noisettes*.

Prepare a béarnaise sauce and season it with curry.

Thread two *noisettes* onto a skewer, separated by three slices of the pork fat. Prepare four such skewers and broil them for about ten minutes.

Serve these little *brochettes* on a hot platter and pass the béarnaise in a sauceboat.

NOTE

1. The rest of the *carré* (rib section) can be used for a ragoût.

CHACHLIK À LA PARISIENNE

For six people, use:

- 18 lamb *noisettes* (medallions) cut from rib eye meat about 1/2-inch thick
- 18 slices bacon, 1/4 inch thick, same size as lamb pieces
- 18 mushrooms or morels having caps the same approximate size as the lamb *noisettes*
- olive oil
- butter
- dry, sifted breadcrumbs
- salt and pepper

Chachlik is a Caucasian dish which is made up of skewered pieces of mutton, alternating with pieces of freshened salt pork and mushrooms, which one broils, basting with mutton fat.

Here is a recipe which is slightly different from the original preparation but is more delicate.

Peel the mushrooms or clean the morels.

Marinate the lamb, bacon, mushroom caps, or morels in the olive oil. Season with salt and pepper and leave these all together for thirty minutes.

Thread these three ingredients alternately on six skewers or *brochettes*. Roll them in the breadcrumbs, butter them lightly, and broil them, preferably over a very slow wood fire, basting them with melted butter as they cook.

Arrange these *brochettes* on a bed of rice pilaf, either plain or with Parmesan, and serve.

This is an excellent dish which differs completely from other lamb preparations.

FILET DE PRÉ-SALÉ AU BACON ET AU ROGNON DE VEAU, SAUCE MOUTARDE

Lamb Tenderloin with Bacon, Veal Kidneys and Mustard Sauce

For six people, use:

- 1 lb. bacon
- 1/4 lb. butter
- 1 qt. consommé
- 2 veal kidneys
- 1 saddle of lamb
- vegetables
- flour
- mustard
- salt and pepper

Cut off the lamb tenderloins and set aside the trimmings.

Peel the vegetables, cut them up, and sauté them in some of the butter. Sprinkle on the flour, then stir in the consommé. Add the bacon and the reserved meat trimmings and bones.

Remove the bacon as soon as it is cooked and keep it warm.
Strain the sauce, reduce it to a good consistency, keep it hot.
Slice the veal kidneys and cook them in the rest of the butter. Season them with salt and pepper.
Roast the lamb tenderloins and keep them pink. Season.
Cut the bacon and lamb into equal slices.
Arrange the tenderloins on a platter, kept warm over an alcohol lamp or similar heating device, and re-form the tenderloins, putting alternate slices of bacon between each slice of lamb. Arrange the slices of kidney around the lamb and coat everything with the sauce, which has been flavored with mustard to taste. Serve, sending along at the same time some croquettes made from Duchesse potatoes or some baked spinach, for instance.

GIGOT DE MOUTON MARINÉ

Marinated Leg of Lamb

For eight people, use:

1. *For the meat:*

1 large leg of lamb
pork fat for larding
salt and pepper

2. *For the marinade:*

6 C. red wine
1 C. red wine vinegar
14 T. oil
1 medium sliced onion
1 medium sliced carrot
10 shallots
1 stalk celery
1 T. sugar
4 cloves garlic
6 sprigs parsley
2 tsp. salt
½ tsp. peppercorns
½ tsp. juniper berries
10 rosemary leaves
¼ tsp. sage
4 leaves basil
¼ tsp. *quatre épices*
½ bay leaf
few leaves thyme
1 clove
few grains cayenne

3. *For the sauce:*

8 T. butter
7 T. meat glaze
4 tsp. flour

Skin the meat and remove any sinews, remove the flat blade bone, and save the trimmings. Cut the bacon into thin strips, season with salt and pepper, and lard the leg of lamb with them, using a larding needle or skewer.
Prepare a marinade: Cook the onion in the oil, along with the carrot, celery, shallots, and garlic. Add the wine, vinegar, salt, sugar, parsley, spices, and aromatics. Cook these for ten minutes.
Cool the marinade, skim off the fat, and put in the leg of lamb, along with the trimmings, and marinate from two to seven days, according to the weather (less time in warm weather).
Remove the leg of lamb from the marinade, dry it, and roast it on a spit over a hot fire for fifteen minutes per pound.
At the same time, prepare the sauce:
Brown the flour lightly in three tablespoons of the butter, stir in the marinade, and add the lamb trimmings. Let this all cook together for one hour. Then add the meat glaze, skim the sauce, and let it simmer for about thirty minutes. Whisk in the rest of the butter.
This sauce is known as *sauce marinade*.
By adding cream to the above sauce one would obtain a *sauce marinade à la russe*.
By adding to the *sauce marinade* a teaspoon of currant jelly, one would obtain a *sauce venaison* (venison sauce).
Last, one could make various *sauces poivrades*, by spiking the *sauce marinade* with either freshly ground pepper, some cayenne or paprika.
Whatever sauce you have chosen, serve the leg of lamb separately and the sauce in a sauceboat.

Marinated leg of lamb has a taste remarkably like that of venison, and it is greatly enjoyed when there is a lack of game. It is even better cold than hot.

One may also prepare, in this way, a leg of spring lamb, baby goat, or mature goat. The last of these is a good facsimile of venison.

GIGOT DE MOUTON AU FOUR, AVEC DES POMMES DE TERRE

Baked Leg of Lamb with Potatoes

This dish may be prepared in several ways:

1. Braise the leg of lamb with potatoes in some kind of meat juice, without any other seasoning except for salt and pepper.
2. Cook the leg of lamb and the potatoes without any liquid but with plain butter (use about ½ cup of butter for 1 leg of lamb and 2 pounds of potatoes). This is known as leg of lamb *à la boulangère* (baker's wife's style).
3. Arrange the potatoes in a pan with some butter and lay the leg of lamb on a rack above them. This will taste somewhat like broiled lamb.

One could prepare, in the same way, a pork tenderloin or a thick slice of fresh ham. But, in this case, the pork fat will suffice: no butter is needed.

These are excellent family dishes.

GIGOT DE MOUTON POCHÉ, SAUCE TOMATE ALLIACÉE AU MIREPOIX

Poached Leg of Lamb with Tomato Garlic Sauce

For six people, use:

1 C. consommé
1 C. thick tomato purée
3 oz. salted, un-smoked ham
3 oz. veal top round
7 T. butter
2 T. coarse salt
12 cloves garlic
½ medium carrot
½ medium onion
4 tsp. flour
5 qts. water
1 5-lb. leg of lamb
bouquet garni
salt and pepper

Make slits and stud the lamb with five of the garlic cloves. Rub the outside with garlic.

Put the water and the salt into a large kettle and bring it to a boil. Drop in the leg of lamb and let it cook for one hour and fifteen minutes, or about fifteen minutes per pound.

The sauce is a tomato sauce seasoned with a *mirepoix* made with veal, ham, onion, carrot, and *bouquet garni* and flavored with garlic, which is prepared in the following manner:

Cut up the veal and ham into tiny pieces.

Chop the onion and carrot.

In a saucepan, put 3 tablespoons of butter and in it cook the veal, ham, and vegetables, sprinkle them with flour, add the *bouquet garni*, the rest of the garlic (in whole cloves), season with salt and pepper, and stir in the consommé. Cook these together for one and a half hours; then add the tomato purée and reduce the sauce. Just before serving, add the rest of the butter cut up into small pieces. Taste and complete the seasoning, if necessary.

Remove the leg of lamb from the kettle and serve it, sending along the sauce in a sauceboat.

Fresh white beans or string beans are a good accompaniment for this dish. If they are not available one could serve spaghetti.

Mutton chops may be poached in this way, but it is better not to stud them with garlic. One would only rub them with a little garlic and drop them into the boiling water.

For mutton chops weighing approximately seven ounces, about ten minutes of cooking would be sufficient.

Pork chops can also be prepared as above.

ÉPAULE DE PRÉ-SALÉ AU RISOTTO

Lamb Shoulder with Risotto

For six people, use:

3 lbs. boned and sliced shoulder of lamb
6 C. bouillon
1 C. raw rice
1 C. seasoned tomato purée
7 T. butter
2/3 C. grated Parmesan
2/3 C. grated Gruyère
1 T. chopped onion
paprika
salt

Put the lamb in a large kettle with the cold bouillon. Place the pan over the heat and bring it rapidly to a boil, then simmer it very slowly for about one and a half hours.

Remove the meat, keep it warm, and reserve the broth.

At the same time, prepare the risotto. Wash the rice, let it soak for one hour in cold water, and dry it in a cloth.

In a saucepan, put the butter and the onion, cook without browning, then strain out the onion. Add the rice, spreading it out on the bottom of the pan, and pour a few spoonfuls of bouillon over it. Heat this up in the open saucepan.

When the bouillon has been absorbed, shake the pan so as to keep the rice from sticking, then moisten again with a little bouillon and continue doing this until all the liquid has been absorbed. While it is cooking, season with salt and the paprika and only add the salt after having tasted it, because the seasoning in the bouillon may be sufficient. Last, add the tomato purée and the cheeses. Cook this for another few minutes.

The rice must be cooked, but the grains should remain whole and the rice should not be pasty.

On a platter, arrange alternating layers of risotto and lamb, ending with a layer of risotto. Serve.

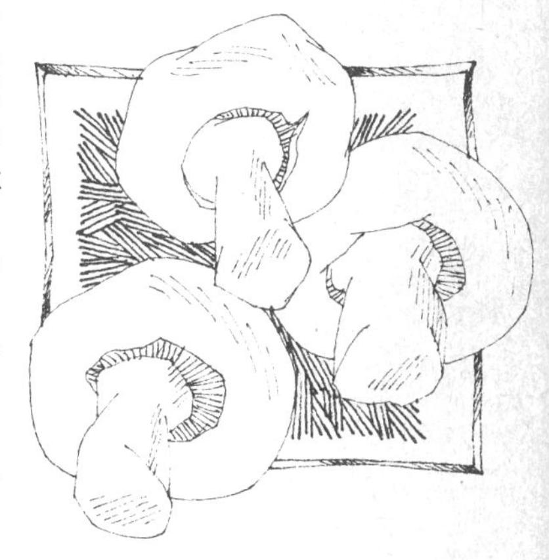

For variation, one could set aside some of the cheeses and sprinkle them on the top layer of risotto and brown the dish in the oven.

This dish, browned or not, is completely different from the ragoût of lamb shoulder with rice and the lamb pilaf.

The meat, which is not browned beforehand, boiled in bouillon, has a very special taste. The rice, flavored with tomato and paprika and enriched with butter, cheese, and meat juice, accompanies this marvelously well; and the whole makes a delicious dish which can be further enriched by adding slivers of truffle cooked in madeira to the rice.

CÔTELETTES DE MOUTON BRAISÉES

Braised Mutton Chops

For six people, use:

1 C. bouillon
7 oz. veal knuckle
2 large sliced carrots
1 large sliced onion
3 oz. pork belly fat for larding
2 T. butter
6 mutton or lamb chops, trimmed, weighing about 1½ lbs. together
3 cloves
2 thin slices of pork belly fat, weighing about 3½ oz. together
1 bay leaf
thyme
quatre épices
salt and pepper

Cut the pork for larding into thin strips and season with salt, pepper, and *quatre épices*.

Run the strips of fat through the chops with a larding needle. Cook the chops lightly in the butter without browning. In the bottom of a saucepan put one of the thin slices of pork fat, on top arrange the lamb chops, veal knuckle, carrots, onions, seasonings, salt and pepper to taste. Add the bouillon and cover with the second sheet of pork fat. Let this all simmer in a closed saucepan for two hours.

Remove the chops, arrange them on a platter, strain the cooking liquid, skim off the fat, reduce it, taste, complete the seasoning if necessary, coat the chops with this sauce, and serve.

Suitable accompaniments for these chops would be either a purée of onions with cream, a purée of white beans, or even a dish of baked white beans.

GIGOT DE MOUTON BRAISÉ, AUX HARICOTS

Braised Leg of Lamb with Beans

For six people, use:

6 C. fresh haricot beans
6 C. good broth or consommé
1 leg of lamb
bouquet garni
butter
garlic, onion, shallot to taste
salt and pepper

Put the leg of lamb in an ovenproof casserole, arrange the beans around it. Season it with salt and pepper, add the *bouquet garni*, garlic, onion, and shallot to taste, and pour in the consommé. Cook the lamb in the oven for fifteen minutes per pound, basting the meat from the moment the liquid no longer covers the meat. When the pan liquids are almost completely absorbed, add some butter in small quantities—as much butter as the beans can absorb.

Serve in the same dish.

One could prepare this dish with dried beans, but it would not be as delicate—on top of which one would have to scald the beans beforehand, and cook them somewhat, before adding them to the lamb, so that they could finish cooking at the same time as the meat.

ÉPAULE DE PRÉ-SALÉ FARCIE, BRAISÉE AU MADÈRE

Braised (Stuffed) Shoulder of Lamb with Madeira

For six people, use:

- 4 lbs. untrimmed shoulder of lamb
- 1¾ C. madeira
- ½ lb. raw smoked ham
- 7 T. butter
- 1 large carrot
- 1 medium onion
- 4 T. meat glaze
- 2 T. brandy
- 1 small clove garlic
- bouillon
- pork caul
- salt and pepper

Trim the shoulder, bone it and set aside the trimmings.

Chop or grind the ham; add 2 teaspoons of chopped onion and a sliver of minced garlic. Sprinkle this with a little pepper and stuff the mixture into the boned shoulder.

Cover the part of the meat which has no skin, then tie it up and stud it with the rest of the garlic. Brown the meat for a half hour in the butter, then flame with the brandy, add the meat trimmings, the sliced carrot, and the rest of the onion, sliced. Let these get golden brown, add the madeira, the bouillon in which you have dissolved the meat glaze, cover the pot, and braise in a moderate oven for two hours, basting from time to time with the pan juices. When the meat is done, remove it to a platter, skim the fat off the pan juice, strain, taste for seasoning and correct if necessary. Remove the strings, the caul fat, and the garlic slivers. Arrange the shoulder on a platter, coat it with the sauce, and serve.

This is a very nice family dish.

DOLMA OU WARACK MALFOUFF À LA PARISIENNE

Stuffed Cabbage Leaves

For six people, use:

- 2 lbs. tenderloin of lamb with bone
- 1⅓ C. thick tomato purée
- 1 C. raw rice
- ½ C. butter
- 4 cloves garlic
- 2 tsp. salt
- paprika to taste
- freshly ground black pepper to taste
- 1 qt. consommé
- 12 whole white leaves of curly cabbage without tears
- nutmeg

This dish, which belongs to Oriental cuisine, is called "dolma" in Turkey and *"warack malfouff"* in Algeria.

Bone the tenderloin without removing the fat. Grind the meat and fat and set aside the bones. To this hash add the raw rice, the butter, salt, pepper, paprika, and nutmeg to taste. Mix well and divide the mixture into twelve portions, which you will roll into sausage shapes.

Blanch the cabbage leaves for three minutes in boiling water. Trim the large ribs and roll the sausages in the cabbage leaves.

In the bottom of a large saucepan, put the bones and garlic, arrange the dolmas on top, coat with the tomato purée, then add enough consommé so that everything is covered with liquid. Cover with a plate which is smaller than the pan which will serve to keep the *warack* from floating to the surface; then cover the pan with the lid.

Cook this over a hot flame for thirty minutes; continue to simmer gently for four hours. The liquid must have been reduced substantially.

Remove the *warack* with care so as not to damage them, arrange them on a hot platter, pour the well-skimmed pan liquid over them, and serve immediately.

The above recipe differs from the Oriental version by the quality of the lamb, the delicacy of the pan juices, and the seasoning, where the paprika takes the place of cayenne, which is hard for many stomachs to tolerate.

ÉPAULE DE MOUTON MARINÉE, BRAISÉE À LA CRÈME

Marinated Lamb Shoulder Braised in Cream

For four people, use:

3 lbs. boned and rolled lamb shoulder
4 C. heavy cream
2 T. butter
4 tsp. flour
½ recipe marinade used in the recipe for *Gigot de Mouton Mariné*
salt and pepper

Prepared a marinade as in the recipe cited, put the lamb shoulder in it, and leave it for forty-eight hours.

Remove the meat from the marinade, dry it off, brown it in butter, sprinkle on the flour, then stir in the strained marinade. Braise this over low heat until it is half cooked, turning the meat several times.

Now add the cream and continue to simmer the meat. Taste the sauce and complete the seasoning with salt and pepper if necessary.

Serve, accompanied by rice with mushrooms (or boletus or morels).

SALMIS DE PRÉ-SALÉ, SAUCE PIQUANTE

Lamb with Piquante Sauce

For six people, use:

4 lbs. lamb: leg, saddle, or shoulder
2 C. strong consommé
1¾ C. white wine
3 T. meat glaze
½ C. chopped sour pickle
3 T. chopped shallots
5 tsp. butter
3 T. flour
1 T. vinegar
1 clove garlic
freshly ground black pepper
cayenne

Cook the shallots and garlic in butter, then stir in the flour and let it brown lightly. Stir in the vinegar and the wine and, last, add the consommé. Let this boil for twenty minutes, strain; add the meat glaze, pepper, and cayenne to taste. Put the sauce back on the fire for about forty-five minutes, skimming it carefully.

At the same time, roast the meat, and keep it just underdone.

Skim the fat off the pan juices from the meat and add the juices to the sauce.

Slice the meat, which you will arrange in an ovenproof dish, pour the strained sauce over it and heat in the oven for fifteen minutes without letting it boil. At the last minute, add the pickles. Serve in the same dish.

At the same time, serve some rice sautéed in butter, in a vegetable dish.

This *salmis* is completely different in taste from all other lamb recipes.

The sauce is delicate and velvety smooth and the rice makes an excellent accompaniment.

Sauce piquante, enriched with tomato sauce, chopped lean ham, mushrooms, capers, and chopped *fines herbes*, makes what is known as *sauce hachée*.

ÉPAULE DE MOUTON AUX NAVETS

Lamb Shoulder with Turnips

For four people, use:

3 lbs. boned and rolled lamb shoulder
3 lbs. turnips
7 T. butter
2 T. brandy
4 C. strong bouillon
granulated sugar
salt and pepper

Brown the meat in 2 tablespoons of the butter, pour off the cooking fat, flame with brandy, then add the bouillon, salt and pepper it, and let this all cook for about two hours (with tender young lamb one and three-quarter hours would be sufficient; for firmer mutton a little over two hours would be needed).

At the same time, peel the turnips, roll them in granulated sugar, and put them in a frying pan with the rest of the butter and brown them over a hot fire, making sure they do not burn.

If you are using very young turnips, add them to the lamb only thirty minutes before serving; but if the turnips are old they may need to cook at least one hour.

Needless to say, this dish is particularly good when prepared with baby lamb and new turnips.

ÉPAULE DE MOUTON AU RIZ

Lamb Shoulder with Rice

For four people, use:

3 lbs. boned and rolled lamb shoulder
1 C. rice
2 T. butter
2 T. brandy
4 C. strong bouillon
salt and pepper

Brown the meat in the butter, pour off the cooking fat, flame with brandy, add the bouillon, season with salt and pepper and let the meat cook for about two hours.

Blanch the rice for fifteen minutes in 3 quarts of salted water, rinse it with cold water, and add it to the lamb about fifteen minutes before serving. The rice will absorb the cooking liquid from the lamb. Taste, correct the seasoning if necessary, and serve.

This is a very nice family dish.

For variation, one could, in season, mix in some peas with the rice. One would use the preceding recipe ingredients plus two pounds of unshelled peas. One would start by preparing the dish as above, and one hour before serving one would add the shelled peas to the lamb and then finish the dish as above.

For another variation, you could add tomato to the rice.

ÉPAULE DE MOUTON À L'AIL

Lamb Shoulder with Garlic

Lard[1] a lamb shoulder with strips of seasoned pork fat and insert chips of garlic.[2]

Brown it on all sides in butter, flame with cognac, then add carrots, turnips, celery, some port wine, a little brandy, salt, spices, and a *bouquet garni*, and simmer the meat in a covered pot for two hours. Then add 20 garlic cloves which have been blanched in boiling water and drained and continue cooking for about one more hour. Remove the lamb to a hot platter. Boil the sauce down rapidly and strain. Serve the lamb on the platter and the sauce in a sauceboat.

Buttered white beans go well with this.

NOTES

1. See glossary of cooking terms and procedures for information on how to "lard" and what type of fat to use.

2. Make small gashes all over the surface of the meat at about three-inch intervals and put tiny slivers or chips of garlic in each, pressing them in well with your fingers.

RAGOÛT DE MOUTON AUX POMMES DE TERRE OU AUX NAVETS

Lamb Stew with Potatoes or Turnips

For six people, use:

3 lbs. lamb[1]
4 C. bouillon
2 lbs. potatoes
4 oz. diced freshened[2] bacon
1 medium onion
4 T. butter
3 T. pork fat
5 tsp. salt
freshly ground pepper to taste
3 T. flour
bouquet garni **(parsley, thyme, bay leaf)**
1 small clove garlic

Ragoût of lamb is essentially a family dish. Some people try to make it a fancy dish by using choicer cuts, such as leg of lamb or loin chops. The best pieces for ragoût are the shoulder and breast (top part of the chops), to which may be added several rib chops.

The ragoût may be prepared with potatoes or with turnips. The following recipe is one for ragoût with potatoes.

Remove any skin from the pieces of lamb and put the pieces of meat into a heavy skillet. Cook them rapidly over high heat to eliminate as much fat as possible.

Sauté the diced bacon in the pork fat until crisp.

In a heavy kettle, put the onions and butter and cook them together. The onions may be browned or not, according to taste. Remove the onions and add the flour. Cook and stir to brown the flour lightly. Add the bouillon, put back the onions, and add the meat, the browned bacon dice, the *bouquet garni*, the garlic, salt, and pepper.

Cook briskly for thirty minutes, making sure that there is enough liquid to cover the meat. At this point, add the peeled potatoes and cook for another thirty minutes, adding more liquid if necessary. About fifteen minutes before serving, start skimming the grease off the top. Remove the meat and keep it hot while boiling down the liquid rapidly. Strain it before serving. Have hot plates ready.

For ragoût of lamb with potatoes or turnips I prefer breast of lamb, which gives the dish a very special flavor and also blends well with the vegetables in the dish. The only problem is that breast of lamb is fairly fat; but this can be remedied by removing as much fat as possible at the very beginning. Rib chops and lamb shoulder are fleshier.

The pork fat used is generally pleasing to the taste, and the fairly strong spices used are also quite pleasing.

Last, the potatoes which accompany the meat give the dish a homey character, which is nice for a family meal and readily enjoyed.

Ragoût of lamb may also be prepared with turnips.

It is prepared just like the ragoût with potatoes except for the following: the turnips, having been peeled, are rolled in granulated sugar, then tossed in hot butter until golden. They are then added to the ragoût, but the cooking must take about an hour more, especially if the turnips are firm. Everything else remains the same.

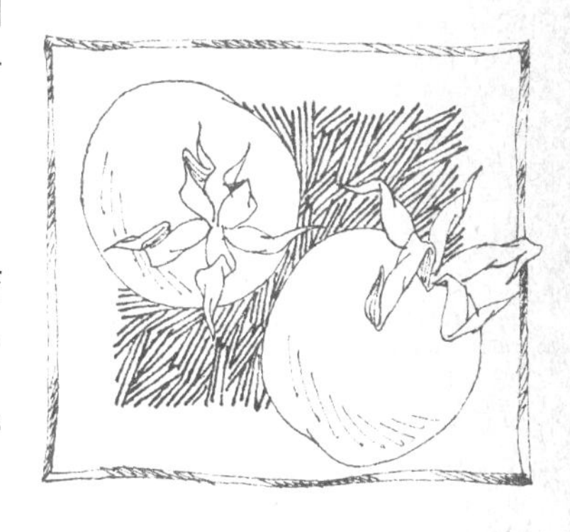

NOTES

1. Here one can use lean breast of lamb; equal quantities of breast and shoulder, mixed; equal parts of breast and sirloin chops. In every case the meat must be cut into serving pieces.

2. See glossary for easiest method of freshening bacon so its flavor will not dominate the dish.

RAGOÛT DE MOUTON À L'ORIENTALE

Lamb Stew à l'Orientale

For six people, use:

2 lbs. breast of lamb
1 lb. 3 oz. boned lamb shoulder
1 C. rice
1/4 lb. tiny onions
4 T. butter
4 T. flour
4 C. bouillon[1]
2 tomatoes
1 eggplant
bouquet garni
powdered saffron
red pepper
salt and pepper

Cut the meat into serving pieces and brown it in a frying pan. Strain off the fat.

Blanch the eggplant in salted water and cut it into lengthwise slices without peeling it. Brown the slices in a little butter.

Blanch the whole onions, then brown them lightly in butter.

Scald the tomatoes, peel and cut them crosswise in two, and remove the seeds.

In a *cocotte* or stewing kettle, put the browned lamb, the eggplant, the tomatoes, onions, the rest of the butter, the *bouquet garni*, salt, pepper, red pepper, and saffron to taste. Sprinkle on the flour and stir in the bouillon. Let this all cook together for about one hour.

About twenty minutes before serving, remove the *bouquet*, and add the blanched and drained rice, so it will cook and absorb some of the liquid.

Spoon the ragoût into a serving dish and serve.

One could also cook the rice entirely separately. One would then arrange the ragoût in a serving dish and pass the rice in a vegetable dish at the same time.

NOTE

1. The Orientals happily use lamb broth.

GIGOT D'AGNEAU RÔTI

Roast Leg of Lamb

For three people, use:

1/2 lb. veal knuckle
4 oz. raw, smoked ham
3 oz. lean bacon
2 oz. mushrooms
1 small carrot
3 T. madeira, port, or sherry wine
3 T. butter
1 small onion
1 stalk celery
salt, paprika, pepper
1 tiny leg of lamb weighing about 2 lbs.
1/2 foot calf's foot
bouquet garni
quatre épices

Cut the smoked ham into strips to lard the lamb with. Save the trimmings. Trim the leg of lamb and either bone it or not. Lard it with the ham strips.

In a little butter, cook the onion, carrot, celery, bacon, the cut-up veal knuckle and the half a calf's foot, *bouquet garni*, ham trimmings, salt, and sufficient water. Cook these all together for three hours. Reduce the cooking liquid so as to have about three-quarters to one cup left. Skim off the fat and strain. Taste and add salt if necessary.

Spread the rest of the butter on the leg of lamb and place the meat on a rack in a roasting pan. Add the above cooking juices, the madeira, port, or sherry, season with paprika, pepper, and a little of the *quatre épices* to taste. Roast it in the oven, basting frequently, for about forty-five minutes. Or, if you prefer, roast it on a spit.

Arrange the lamb on a platter, skim the fat off the cooking juices, and reduce them. Coat the meat with this sauce.

Serve, sending along, at the same time in a vegetable dish, either a mushroom purée, a purée of bulbous chervil, a purée of chestnuts, or a lentil purée.

One may also substitute, for the madeira, port, or sherry, some white wine—chablis for instance—but one would have to use more of it.

GIGOT D'AGNEAU DE LAIT À L'ANANAS, BRAISÉ AU PORTO

Leg of Baby Lamb with Pineapple Braised in Port Wine

Take a nice small leg of baby lamb, bone it, trim it, and, with a nonmetal utensil, lift the skin and insert some slices of fresh pineapple between the flesh and the rind.

Put it in a saucepan with some butter, carrots, and a little onion and let it brown lightly. Then arrange everything in a braising kettle. Moisten with some white port, season with salt and pepper, and let this simmer for about two hours, basting frequently.

Arrange the lamb leg on a platter, pour the sauce over it, and serve it with some dry rice or some risotto.

This is an unusual dish which provides an unusual taste sensation.

PORC RÔTI, SAUCE DIABLE TOMATÉE

Roast Pork with Tomato Sauce Diable

For six to eight people, use:

1¾ C. veal stock or good consommé
1 C. white wine
5 T. vinegar
5 T. thick tomato purée
4 T. heavy cream
2 T. butter
½ tsp. peppercorns
3 shallots
pork loin roast
bouquet garni
paprika
cayenne
quatre épices

Roast the pork slowly in the oven, basting frequently.

At the same time, prepare the sauce. Made a reduction with the wine, vinegar, shallots, and peppercorns. Then add the veal stock or the consommé, the *bouquet garni*, paprika, and a little *quatre épices* to taste. Let this cook down for twenty minutes. Reduce it sufficiently, then add the cream and let this simmer, stirring, until the sauce is very smooth. Thicken it, if necessary, with a little potato starch, then strain it.

Blend the sauce into the tomato purée, add the juices from the meat (from which the fat has been removed). Season with cayenne and, finally, whisk in the butter.

Arrange the pork on a serving platter and surround it with sour pickles. Serve, sending along separately in a sauceboat the sauce and in a vegetable dish some tiny *pommes de terre duchesse* with cheese.

This *sauce diable tomatée* is also a good accompaniment for veal, roast lamb, and bland fish dishes.

FILETS MIGNONS DE PORC PANÉS, GRILLÉS, SAUCE ROBERT[1]

Broiled Breaded Pork Tenderloin Steaks with Sauce Robert

For six people, use:

1⅓ C. demi-glace sauce[2]
1 C. chablis or pouilly sec
3 T. butter
12 trimmed pork tenderloin steaks (filets mignons)
1 medium onion
pork fat for larding
dry, sifted breadcrumbs
mustard
cayenne
paprika
salt and pepper

Lard the tenderloin steaks with thin strips of seasoned pork fat. Roll them first in 5 teaspoons of the lukewarm melted butter, then in the fine, dry breadcrumbs.

Prepare the sauce: Mince the onions and cook them gently in the rest of the butter, add the wine and reduce the liquid to one-fourth of its volume, then add the demi-glace sauce. Let these ingredients simmer for about thirty minutes. Strain the sauce through a fine sieve or cloth; season, off the heat, with mustard, cayenne, and paprika to taste. Blend well. Keep the sauce hot in a double boiler.

Broil the tenderloins, arrange them on a platter, surround them with 12 tomatoes stuffed with broiled mushrooms and serve. Send along the sauce in a sauceboat.

For variation, one could serve these tenderloins with a *sauce charcutière*, which is *sauce Robert* in which the mustard, cayenne, or paprika have been replaced with minced mushrooms.

One could also prepare this *sauce Robert* for fish by substituting, for the demi-glace sauce, some very rich, thick fish stock.

NOTES

1. *Sauce Robert* was already known under Charles VI. The modern versions of this sauce are quite different from the primitive one.
2. See recipe for *Filet de Boeuf Truffé, Sauce Demi-Glace.*

For four people, use:

1 lb. 3 oz. leeks, white part only
7 T. butter
3 T. meat juice or strong broth
4 tsp. flour
4 pork chops, breaded
salt and pepper

CÔTELETTES DE PORC GRILLÉES, À LA PURÉE DE POIREAUX

Broiled Pork Chops with Leek Purée

Cook the leeks in 3 quarts of salted water, using about 1 tablespoon of coarse salt per quart. Cook them until soft. Pour off the water and press the leeks to remove all excess liquid. Chop the leeks; dry them out in a saucepan on low heat or on the back of the stove for about one hour. Then purée them and set aside 2 tablespoonfuls for the sauce.

To the rest of the purée add 5 tablespoons of butter; season with salt and pepper, adding, for instance, 1 teaspoon of salt and a few grains of black pepper.

Make a roux with the rest of the butter and the flour, stir in the meat juice or broth, season with ½ teaspoon of salt and a pinch of pepper, if the meat juice is not either too salty or peppery. Blend in the 2 tablespoons of reserved leek purée.

While doing this, broil the chops, as they are, and season them.

Arrange the chops on top of the leek purée and serve the sauce separately.

Leek purée here replaces the classic onion purée and the leek sauce is used instead of *sauce Soubise.*[1]

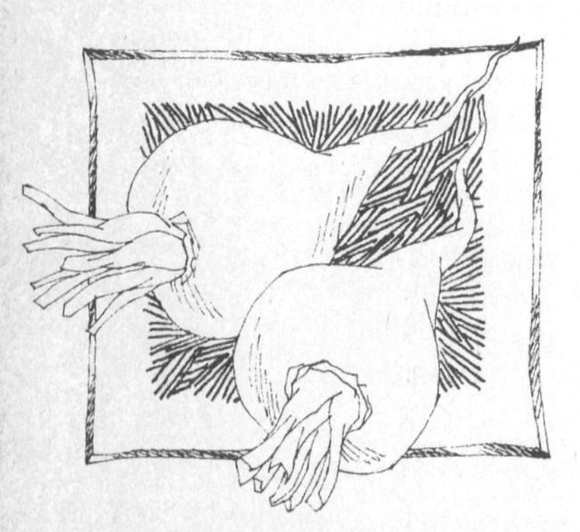

NOTE

1. *Sauce Soubise* is a sauce made with meat juice and onion purée.

PAUPIETTES DE PORC RÔTIES

Roasted Pork Rolls

For four people, use:

$1\frac{1}{2}$ lbs. pork tenderloin or fresh ham in 4 trimmed slices
$\frac{2}{3}$ C. cream
mustard
4 thin sheets of leaf lard
dry, sifted breadcrumbs
lemon juice
salt, pepper, paprika

Spread mustard on each side of each piece of meat. Sprinkle with breadcrumbs; roll them up, wrap them in the leaf lard, and tie them. Chill them for twenty-four hours, then roast them on a spit, basting them with the cream which has been acidulated with lemon juice and seasoned with salt, pepper, and paprika to taste.

Skim the fat off the pan juices (or sauce); remove the strings and the leaf lard from the paupiettes.

Serve with an accompaniment of plain sauerkraut.

JAMBON EN CROÛTE

Ham in Crust

For twelve people, use

1.

7 oz. onions
7 oz. carrot
several large sprigs parsley
thyme
1 bottle white wine
madeira, sherry or marsala as desired
6 shallots
4 bay leaves
2 cloves garlic
1 ham weighing approximately 8 lbs.

2. For the crust:

6 C. flour
2 C. milk
$\frac{1}{2}$ lb. butter
4 tsp. salt
2 eggs

Cook the ham until it is three-fourths done. To accomplish this, put the ham in a large kettle with water and bring it to a boil. As soon as it boils, pour off the water to remove any extra salt. Cover it again with boiling water, add the white wine, the vegetables and the aromatics, then continue cooking it for the remaining time necessary, which should be calculated at fifteen minutes per pound of ham.

Let the ham cool in the liquid.

Lift out the ham, trim it, and remove the rind.

Prepare a dough with the ingredients indicated above. Wrap the ham in the dough, trying to maintain its normal shape. Decorate the surface and bake it in the oven for one and a half hours.

Serve with spinach or asparagus tips and send along, at the same time, either a madeira, sherry, or marsala sauce.[1]

1. For the sauce:

4 C. consommé
$1\frac{3}{4}$ C. madeira, sherry or marsala
4 T. butter
8 tsp. meat glaze
6 T. flour
pepper

Dissolve the meat glaze in the wine, pepper it to taste, and reduce it by half.

Make a roux with the butter and the flour, stir in the consommé, add the reduced wine, and reduce it further, skimming it until it becomes thick enough to coat a spoon.

MOUSSES ET MOUSSELINES DE JAMBON, CHAUDES

Hot Mousses and Mousselines of Ham

Use 1 pound of lean, raw ham, 3 cups of fresh, heavy cream, a little pepper, and 2 egg whites. Dice the ham, then pound it in a mortar or put it three times through the finest blade of a meat grinder. Add the pepper and egg whites, little by little. Force the mixture through a fine sieve or purée it. Put this purée in a bowl

For six people, use:

1 lb. 3 oz. lean, raw ham without sinews
1½ C. thick cream (or 1 C. of cream and 7 T. of cold Béchamel sauce)
6 stiffly beaten egg whites
salt, pepper and spices

over ice, smooth it with a spatula, and chill it for two hours. Then, little by little, incorporate the half-whipped cream, in small quantities, working very carefully. Taste; add salt if necessary and paprika. This forcemeat must have a lovely pink color.

Generously butter a charlotte mold; fill it with this forcemeat, cover it, and cook it in a hot water bath filled with barely boiling water, for forty to forty-five minutes. When it is done, the contents of the mold should have swollen and started to rise. Remove the mold from the hot water bath, wait a few minutes for it to settle, then turn it out onto a platter. Do not lift the mold off until two or three minutes later.

This forcemeat may be used to make simple mousselines or mousselines stuffed with ham hash, foie gras, and truffles, thickened with velouté. These could be decorated with cooked ham and truffles cut out into fancy shapes.

This would be served with a *sauce périgueux* (see recipe).

For six people, use:

1 lb. 7 oz. very lean cooked ham
1¼ C. cold Béchamel sauce
7 egg whites
5 egg yolks

SOUFFLÉS DE JAMBON

Ham Soufflés

Ham soufflés may be made with either raw or cooked meat.

To prepare a soufflé with raw meat:

Pound the ham in a mortar or grind it to a purée. Then add the cream or cream and Béchamel sauce, in small quantities. Season to taste, strain the purée through a fine sieve, then little by little fold in the whites of egg without deflating them.

Spoon this mixture into a buttered mold or deep pan and cook it in a hot water bath in a slow oven for thirty-five to forty minutes.

If, on the other hand, you use cooked ham:

Pound or grind the ham with 4 tablespoons of the Béchamel sauce. Strain through a fine sieve and little by little add the egg yolks, which have been blended with the rest of the Béchamel. Then, fold in, little by little, the stiffly beaten egg whites. Taste for seasoning.

Spoon into a well-buttered mold or deep pan and cook in a slow oven as above.

For variation, one may add to the above soufflé mixtures 7 to 10 tablespoons of grated Parmesan cheese.

These soufflés may be accompanied by the following sauce: demi-glace made with either port, madeira, or sherry (see recipe in Beef section).

PORC AUX CHOUX

Pork with Cabbage

For four people, use:

3 lbs. coarsely shredded cabbage
1 lb. 3 oz. lean pork, cut up
7 oz. coarse salt
2 oz. dried mushrooms
3 T. butter
3 T. white wine
2 T. flour
freshly ground pepper to taste

Put the cabbage in a bowl with the salt and keep it in a cool place for thirty-six hours. Then remove the cabbage and rinse it rapidly under cold running water.

Put the pork and cabbage in a saucepan, heat it up, mix it together; then add the white wine and season with pepper. Let this simmer together for seven hours.

Reheat the whole dish the following day.

Soak the mushrooms and cut them up. Add them to the cabbage and pork after they have been reheating for one hour. Continue cooking for another two hours.

Fifteen minutes before serving, make a roux with the butter and flour, stir it into the contents of the saucepan and serve.

CRÉPINETTES DE PORC

Pork Sausages

To make ten sausages, use:

1 lb. lean, fresh pork, without sinews
1 lb. fresh pork fat without rind
2 T. brandy
1 T. salt
3 T. chopped parsley
pepper
2 fresh eggs
leaf lard or pork caul
nutmeg or *quatre épices* **to taste**

Soak the leaf lard or pork caul in cold running water.

Grind the pork and the pork fat. Mix in the salt, pepper, and the nutmeg or *quatre épices*, the parsley, brandy, and eggs. You now have some good sausage meat. Divide this mixture into ten parts. Wrap each portion in a piece of pork fat five by six inches in size. Give the *crépinettes* a rectangular shape.

Broil them after having sprinkled or brushed them with melted butter. Serve with mashed potatoes.

One may, of course, add truffles to these *crépinettes*. One adds the truffles to the hash; and one decorates the little *crépines* by inserting pieces of truffle underneath the fat.

One could substitute, for the brandy, some wine: madeira, port, sherry, chablis, graves, or champagne. A whole gamut of different tasting *crépinettes* are therefore possible.

SAUCISSES AU VIN BLANC

Sausages in White Wine

For six people, use:

1 lb. (or 1 dozen) long, thin sausages
1¾ C. white wine
7 T. butter
1 medium onion
8 tsp. meat glaze
4 tsp. seasoned tomato purée
4 tsp. flour
bread

Put 5 tablespoons of the butter in a frying pan, add the sausages and the chopped onion, and let these cook together over low heat for about ten minutes. Remove the sausages and keep them hot.

Stir in the flour and add the white wine and reduce it somewhat. Now add the meat glaze and the tomato purée and let this all cook and reduce still more. Last, strain the sauce and whisk in the rest of the butter.

Arrange the sausages on some canapés made with slices of white bread which have been sautéed in butter and arranged on a platter. Coat with the sauce.

BOULETTES AU JAMBON

Ham Balls

For three people, use:

1/2 lb. (8 slices) white or brown bread
14 T. butter
2/3 C. milk
5 oz. raw ham
2 T. chopped herbs, mixture of equal parts of chervil, chives, and parsley
2 eggs
breadcrumbs
flour
salt and pepper

Scald the milk.

Dice the slices of bread, sauté the cubes in 7 tablespoons of the butter; then add them to the scalded milk and let them soak. Mash the bread up in the milk; then add the eggs, one at a time, working them well to get a very smooth paste.

In 3 tablespoons of the butter, sauté the diced ham along with the herbs. Mix these into the bread and milk paste. Taste and complete the seasoning, if necessary, with salt and pepper.

Roll this mixture into balls the size of apricots. Roll these in flour and plunge them for five minutes into boiling, salted water.

Drain them, arrange them on a platter, and coat them with the breadcrumbs which have been sautéed in the rest of the butter.

Serve, sending along, at the same time, a sauceboat with some meat juice and a bowl of grated Gruyère or Parmesan cheese.

For variation, one could fry these ham *boulettes* in fat and serve them with tomato sauce, for instance.

RILLONS

For five or six people, use:

3 lbs. fresh pork belly, not too fat
4 tsp. salt
freshly ground black pepper
sage (powdered)
quatre épices

For more delicate rillons, *use:*

3 lbs. larded pork
1/2 C. dry white wine
2 T. brandy
4 tsp. salt
freshly ground black pepper to taste
powdered sage
quatre épices
1 chopped shallot (optional)

Rillons are made of cubes of larded pork, cooked in their own fat.

Cut the pork into two-and-one-third-inch cubes. Remove all bones.

In a kettle, brown the pieces of pork on all sides over low heat. This should take about a half hour. Drain off the fat; season the meat with salt, pepper, a little sage and *quatre épices*. Cover the kettle and cook very slowly for an hour to an hour and a half. Uncover the kettle, raise the heat so as to dry out the *rillons*. Remove them; put them on a platter and let them cool.

Cook the pork as above. Drain off the grease, flame with brandy, add the wine, and complete the recipe as above.

Rillons are served as an hors-d'oeuvre.

POULTRY

POUSSINS GRILLÉS, SAUCE DIABLE

Broiled Squab Chicken, Sauce Diable

Split the chickens lengthwise down the back into two pieces. Flatten each half with a mallet, season the halves with salt, pepper, and cayenne and cook them under a broiler or on a grill for about five minutes per side.

Roll each of the halves in some breadcrumbs and put them back on the grill and let them cook for another five minutes per side. During the whole cooking time baste them with two tablespoons of melted butter.

Serve with a *sauce diable* which you have prepared in the following manner:

Reduce to a glaze the wine and vinegar with the chopped shal-

For four people, use:

7 T. veal stock
7 T. white wine
3 T. butter
2 T. vinegar
5 chopped shallots
1 T. meat glaze
4 tsp. flour
1 tsp. salt
2 tsp. chopped parsley
freshly ground black pepper to taste
cayenne to taste
2 squab chickens
dry sifted breadcrumbs

lots. Make a roux with the rest of the butter and the flour, stir in the veal stock in which you have dissolved the meat glaze, add the wine and vinegar mixture, the rest of the salt, and pepper and cayenne to taste. Strain through a fine sieve or cloth, sprinkle with chopped parsley and serve.

Large chickens may also be prepared in the same way, but the cooking time will be half an hour instead of twenty minutes.

One good-sized broiler or fryer will serve four people.

NOTE

1. Quantities for pepper and cayenne must be judged individually, according to how hot one wishes the dish to be.

For four people, use:

2/3 C. white wine
4 T. parsley
1 T. table salt
3 shallots
freshly ground black pepper to taste
paprika to taste
2 squab chickens[1]
2 eggs
flour
breadcrumbs

FRITURE DE POUSSINS

Fried Squab Chicken

Quarter the chickens and put the pieces in the white wine with the pepper, shallots, half the salt, and half the parsley. Marinate them for one hour and drain. Dry them.

Break the eggs and beat them with the rest of the salt and the paprika, as for an omelet.

Roll the chicken quarters in flour, then dip them in the beaten eggs, and, last, coat them with the breadcrumbs. Plunge them into boiling hot fat and cook them for fifteen minutes. Drain them in paper.

Arrange them in a pyramid on a hot platter, and decorate them with fried parsley and lemon wedges. Serve, accompanied by a tomato sauce.

Squab pigeons may also be prepared in this way.

NOTE

1. Cornish game hens could also be used in this recipe, but they should only be cut in half rather than quartered.

For four people, use:

1/4 lb. pork fat
7 T. butter
1 medium onion
1/3 C. madeira wine
3 T. meat glaze (or chicken glaze)[1]
2 T. white wine
1 tsp. salt
pepper to taste
quatre épices to taste
3 artichokes
1 chicken weighing 2 1/2 lbs.
1 small bunch (1 lb.) asparagus

POULET EN COCOTTE

Chicken en Cocotte

Put two slices of onion inside the chicken, two teaspoons of butter, the salt, pepper and the *quatre épices* to taste. Truss the chicken, then brown it lightly on all sides in two tablespoons of butter.

Cut the pork fat into dice and brown in the same butter in which the chicken was browned.

In a round or oval casserole with cover, put the rest of the butter, the chicken, the pork fat, and the rest of the onion. Lay a piece of heavy buttered paper between the top and the casserole to seal it hermetically, and bake the chicken in a slow oven for thirty minutes.

At the same time, blanch the asparagus tips and the artichokes in boiling salted water for a few minutes.

Remove all the outer leaves of the artichokes and trim the hearts. Cut each heart into quarters and remove the choke.

After the thirty minutes of cooking, remove the chicken from the casserole, along with the pork fat and the onion. Untruss the chicken and strain the cooking liquid.

Put the chicken back in the *cocotte* with the pork fat and the juices, and add the artichoke hearts, the asparagus tips, the meat glaze, and moisten with the madeira and white wine. Taste for seasoning, correct if necessary, then cook for approximately another thirty minutes, very slowly. Serve.

This chicken is very tender and savory.

For variation, different vegetables could be added to this dish: potatoes, turnips, turnip-rooted chervil, etc. However, I prefer the above recipe, provided that one can obtain fresh asparagus and fresh artichokes.

Finally, as a very luxurious variation, I can mention chicken *en cocotte* with morels and truffles.

"Chicken pie" is an English variation of chicken *en cocotte*. The casserole or *cocotte* (sometimes spelled *cocote*) is sealed with pastry crust.

English chicken pie generally contains chicken, veal, bacon, and halved hard-boiled eggs, the whole seasoned with salt, pepper, *fines herbes* sautéed in butter and moistened with chicken broth.

One may also add mushrooms, olives, and a little madeira.

POULET SAUTÉ AU NATUREL

Plain Chicken Sauté

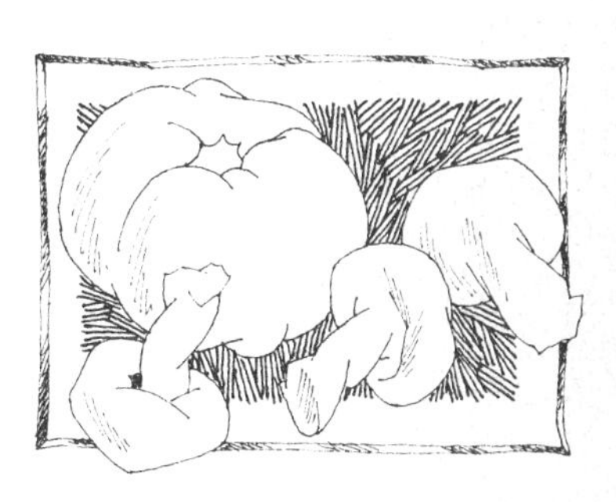

For four people use a medium-sized chicken, tender and plump. Cut it up in the following manner: cut off the wings and thighs close to the body, separate the drumsticks from the thighs and the wingtips from the upper wings. Cut off the whole breast section and cut it in two. Cut the rest of the carcass into two or three pieces. If the feet have been left on the bird, clean and scrape them, trim them, and remove the claws.

Put some clarified butter in a suitable pan and heat it. Arrange the pieces of chicken in the frying pan and season them with salt and pepper. Brown the chicken quickly on all sides. Flame with 1 tablespoon of brandy. Now cover the frying pan or skillet and finish the cooking in a moderate oven, which should take four to five minutes for the more tender parts such as wings and breast and double that time for the thighs.

Remove the pieces of chicken as they are cooked and keep them hot and covered. Drain off the cooking fat and deglaze the cooking pan with 7 tablespoons of white wine and 7 tablespoons of chicken broth, or with 3 tablespoons of fortified wine such as madeira, port, or sherry, etc., and 10 tablespoons of chicken stock. Let this all cook together.

Put back the firmer pieces of chicken, along with the carcass and the feet, and let this simmer for five or six minutes. Reduce the sauce, which should be fairly thick. Put back the other pieces of chicken but do not let this boil.

Arrange the chicken pieces in a deep serving dish, carcass, feet, and wingtips on the bottom, the breast, wing tops, and legs on top. Coat with the sauce and serve.

For variation, one may prepare sautéed chicken *à blanc*, that is, one may cook it in the butter at first without browning it at all. In this recipe the liquid used for deglazing the pan must be white and the sauce must remain light colored and would be enriched with cream.

Sautéed chicken, with or without garnish, may be used in numerous combinations.

POULET SAUTÉ AUX CÈPES FRAIS

Sautéed Chicken with Fresh Boletus Mushrooms

For three people, use:

7 T. butter
6 large fresh boletus mushrooms
1 plump chicken
parsley
lemon juice
salt and pepper

Clean the mushrooms, peel them, and cut them up.

Cut up the chicken as for a fricassee and brown it in two tablespoons of butter.

In a skillet put four tablespoons of butter, the browned chicken, the mushrooms, and season with salt and pepper. Cook these over a hot fire at first and then reduce the heat.

The whole cooking time should take about a half hour.

At serving time add the lemon juice and chopped parsley blended into the rest of the butter.

This dish is absolutely delicious if you are using freshly picked boletus mushrooms.

One could also prepare, in this same way, chicken sautéed with either morels or field mushrooms.

POULET SAUTÉ AU VIN BLANC

Sautéed Chicken with White Wine

For three people, use:

1 C. dry white wine
1/4 lb. field mushrooms
1 large tomato weighing 4 oz.
4 T. butter
2 T. meat glaze dissolved in bouillon
or
4 T. meat juice
4 tsp. brandy
2 tsp. salt
parsley
1 sliver garlic
freshly ground black pepper to taste
cayenne to taste
1 chicken (young tender hen), weighing about 1 lb. 10 oz. without giblets
lemon juice

Cut up the little chicken as for a fricassee.

Put the butter in a saucepan, bring it to a nut-brown color, then, over a hot fire, brown the pieces of chicken. Then add the peeled mushrooms which have been rolled in lemon juice, and the peeled, seeded, and diced tomato. Cook everything together for about five minutes, then add the wine, brandy, and meat juice, season with salt, pepper, and cayenne. Continue cooking for about fifteen minutes.

Arrange the pieces of chicken on a hot platter, skim the fat off the pan juices, add the chopped parsley and garlic, reduce the sauce until it is fairly consistent, and spoon over the chicken.

Thus prepared, sautéed chicken is very eupeptic.

This is generally served accompanied by vegetables.

POULET SAUTÉ À LA CRÈME ET À L'ARMAGNAC

Chicken Sautéed with Cream and Armagnac

For four people, use:

1 1/3 C. cream
3 T. butter
3 T. armagnac
5 shallots
1 T. minced onion
4 tsp. olive oil
4 tsp. flour
1 plump chicken with giblets
vegetables as for *pot-au-feu*
lemon juice
salt and pepper

Clean, gut, flame, and cut up the chicken.

Prepare a broth with the giblets, vegetables, water, salt, and pepper. Boil it down to concentrate it, and strain.

In a big frying pan melt the butter and oil. When this mixture is very hot put in the pieces of chicken, which have been rolled in flour, the shallots, and onion, and brown everything over a hot fire for about ten minutes. Reduce the fire and sauté the chicken for another twenty minutes. Remove the pieces of chicken and keep them hot.

Deglaze the cooking pan with the strained chicken broth, and add the cream and armagnac. Boil these down to make a fairly thick sauce. Season to taste with lemon juice and add salt and pepper if necessary. Strain the sauce, then put back the pieces of chicken and simmer everything together over a very low fire without letting it boil.

Serve with rice with mushrooms or with a purée of truffles.

For variation, one could substitute, for the armagnac, some *fine champagne* (a type of brandy), and one would add to the sauce some mushrooms dipped in lemon juice and cooked in butter, or some truffles cooked in madeira. In the latter case, one would add to the sauce a little of the truffle cooking liquid, but without letting the madeira flavor become dominant.

Sautéed chicken with cream and armagnac or with brandy is worthy of the finest tables.

POULET SAUTÉ À L'ESTRAGON

Sautéed Chicken with Tarragon

Cut up a young chicken, brown it in 4 tablespoons of butter, season with salt and pepper, and then add a bouquet made up of tarragon, along with several spoonfuls of veal or chicken stock. Cover and let this cook for about twenty minutes, shaking the pan occasionally.

Arrange the chicken on a platter, deglaze the cooking pan with some velouté sauce made with veal and chicken broth, strain the sauce, add a little chopped tarragon, spoon the sauce over the chicken, and serve.

For variation, one could garnish the platter with artichoke hearts and eggplants, either sliced or turned (cut up into cork shapes), rolled in flour, then fried in oil and well drained, and then arranged around the platter alternately.

POULET SAUTÉ À L'INDIENNE

Indian Sautéed Chicken

For three people, use:

2 large tomatoes
3 oz. dried mushrooms
7 T. butter
3 T. meat glaze
½ medium onion
1 T. olive oil
1 tsp. salt
1 shallot
1 sliver garlic
curry powder to taste
few threads saffron
1 pinch ginger
freshly ground black pepper to taste
few grains cayenne
1 tender young chicken without its giblets, weighing about 1 lb. 10 oz.
bouillon

Soak the dried mushrooms in water for several hours.

Cut up the chicken.

Heat the oil and the butter in a saucepan until they are a nice nut-brown color. Put in the pieces of chicken and let them brown until they are golden. Then add the chopped onions, shallots, garlic, and the tomatoes, which have been peeled, seeded, and diced. Sauté these all together for five minutes, then add the bouillon in which you have dissolved the meat glaze. Season with salt, pepper, cayenne, ginger, saffron, and curry.

Wash the dried mushrooms in several waters, wipe them off, cut them up, and add them to the ragoût. Continue cooking over a fairly hot fire in a covered saucepan.

Prepare some dry rice, arrange it on a platter, make a slight hollow in the center, and in this arrange the pieces of chicken. Serve, sending the sauce along separately in a sauceboat.

Sautéed chicken, Indian style, is truly a highly seasoned dish.

However, thanks to the blending of all the condiments in suitable proportions, there is no harsh note, and this is generally suitable even for delicate stomachs.

POULET SAUTÉ AU CITRON

Chicken Sautéed with Lemon

For three people, use:

1 C. bouillon
4 T. butter
3 T. meat glaze
4 tsp. flour
2 lemons
1 young chicken without giblets, weighing about 1 lb. 10 oz.
bouquet garni **(1 T. parsley, 1 sprig thyme, a piece of bay leaf)**
caramel
salt and pepper

Cut up the chicken and brown it in the butter, then remove it. Stir in the flour to make a roux. Let it rest a minute then strain off any liquid butter. Stir in the bouillon in which you have dissolved the meat glaze. When these are well blended add the chicken, the bouquet, 3 lemon slices which have been seeded and cut into 5 segments each, salt and pepper to taste.

Let these all cook together for a few moments in a covered saucepan. Give a little color with some caramel. Finish cooking. A half hour in all should be sufficient.

Arrange the pieces of chicken on a platter, remove the bouquet, taste the sauce, and complete the seasoning with a little lemon or caramel to taste, so that the sauce is slightly acid. Coat the chicken with the sauce, leaving the pieces of lemon in the sauce.

Decorate the platter with slices of the second lemon and serve.

POULET SAUTÉ AU PARMESAN

Sautéed Chicken with Parmesan

For three people, use:

2/3 C. cream
1/2 C. butter
5 T. grated Parmesan
2 T. flour
1 1/2 tsp. salt
3 eggs
1 young, tender chicken
breadcrumbs

Cut up the chicken. Brown the pieces for twenty minutes in 4 teaspoons of butter and sprinkle on a little salt.

Cook the flour in the rest of the butter without browning. Stir in the cream, 2 teaspoons of Parmesan, the rest of the salt, and stir these together over a low fire. Finish thickening the sauce with the eggyolks.

In a fireproof dish sprinkle 6 teaspoons of the Parmesan on the bottom, arrange the chicken pieces on this, coat with the sauce, and put in the oven for five minutes. Sprinkle on the remaining Parmesan along with the breadcrumbs and brown for another minute or two in the oven and serve.

POULET SAUTÉ À L'ESPAGNOLE

Spanish Sautéed Chicken

This is one of the better dishes of Spanish cuisine. Here I give a recipe which differs from the original in that in Spain they use water for the liquid, which entails the use of a larger proportion of fat and oil, and therefore makes the dish less delicate.

For six people, use:

2 lbs. unshelled peas
½ lb. lean, smoked ham
½ lb. raw rice
½ lb. tomatoes
3 T. lard
1 T. olive oil
1 tsp. salt
few grains cayenne
1 qt. veal stock
2 green Spanish peppers
1 chicken
1 large Spanish onion
1 large artichoke heart
½ clove garlic

In a skillet or frying pan put the lard, the oil, the cut-up chicken, the diced ham, and season lightly. Sauté for a half hour. Remove the chicken and the ham and set aside.

At the same time cook the shelled peas in some veal broth until they are about three-fourths cooked.

In the fat in which the chicken was cooked, brown the chopped onion, garlic, and peppers, adding the rice which has been blanched in boiling water and cooled under running water. Add the liquid in which the peas were cooked, then add the peeled, seeded, and chopped tomatoes, the chopped artichoke heart, the peas, chicken, and ham. Season well and let everything cook together for a half hour. Off the fire taste for seasoning, arrange on a platter and serve.

Spanish-American countries have this dish in a modified version, by successive additions of ingredients. They have arrived at a mixture which deserves a special designation; it could be referred to as Spanish-American sautéed chicken, although the role of the chicken has been somewhat diminished.

To give an idea I will list the ingredients and their proportions.

For ten people, use:

The same ingredients used in the first version of the Spanish chicken sauté, plus those listed opposite.

½ lb. fresh pork
½ lb. fish filets (sole, whiting, or cod)
¼ lb. shrimps
40 mussels
10 small sausages
2 potatoes
2 hard-boiled eggs
saffron

Cut up the pork; sauté it and the sausages along with the chicken and the ham. Remove the sausages after four or five minutes and keep them hot.

Cook the mussels as usual, as well as the shrimp. Steam the potatoes and fry the fish filets. Keep all these different ingredients hot.

Shell the shrimp and reserve the tail meat.

The whole procedure will be just as in the preceding recipe. Saffron, to taste, should be added at the same time as the rice.

Ten minutes before serving add the cut-up potatoes, the fried fish filets, three-fourths of the mussels, and shrimp tails. Mix everything well.

At serving time decorate the platter with sliced hard-boiled eggs, the sausages, the rest of the mussels and shrimp tails.

It is customary to drink some anisette, as a digestive, after this dish.

POULET À LA JUIVE

Jewish Chicken
(Alsatian Style)

For four people, use:

3 T. chicken fat (raw), or fat from roast chicken; or, alternatively, veal kidney suet
3 T. butter
7 shallots
2 T. flour
1 clove garlic
1 T. chopped parsley
1 chicken
vegetables for *pot-au-feu* (see recipe)
salt and pepper

Cut the chicken up as for fricassee and reserve the giblets.

Prepare about 1¾ cups of broth by cooking the giblets and vegetables in salted water for a long time.

Heat up whatever fat you are using in a large saucepan, add the pieces of chicken, and brown them very lightly. Add the shallots and garlic and stir and cook for a few minutes. Then stir in the flour and let it brown lightly. Add the broth which you have made, salt and pepper everything, and continue cooking in a closed saucepan, over a moderate fire, for one to one and a half hours according to the size of the chicken.

Skim the fat off the sauce, enrich it with butter, taste for seasoning (which must be fairly sharp and peppery), sprinkle with parsley, and serve.

POULET GRATINÉ

Oven-Browned Chicken

Cut up a small chicken and brown it lightly in butter, then cook it gently over a low flame.

Blend a little flour into some cream, salt it, and let this cook without boiling. Off the fire add two whole eggs and two egg yolks and mix well.

Arrange the chicken pieces on an ovenproof platter, coat them with the sauce, sprinkle it with grated Parmesan and dry-sifted breadcrumbs, and put it in the oven to brown for a few minutes.

One may, according to taste, substitute Gruyère for the Parmesan, or even mix the two cheeses.

FRICASSÉE DE POULET

Chicken Fricassee

For four people, use:

2½ C. veal and chicken stock
½ lb. small mushrooms
10 T. dry white wine
7 T. thick cream
7 T. butter
3 scant T. flour
2 egg yolks
2 onions
1 plump tender chicken
1 carrot
lemon juice
parsley
quatre épices
salt and pepper

Cut up the chicken as though to sauté it, then soak the pieces in in cold water or not, as desired.

Peel the mushrooms, cut off the stems at cap level, and set aside.

In a saucepan put three tablespoons of butter and the pieces of chicken. Cook these until stiffened but not brown. Cover the saucepan for a few minutes to let them sweat, then sprinkle on the flour and slowly stir in the wine and the stock. Stir constantly as you do this to avoid lumps. Season with salt and pepper, add the carrot, the onions, the mushrooms stems, the *bouquet garni* and *quatre épices* to taste. Let this all cook for about a half hour.

Cook the mushroom caps in the rest of the butter with some lemon juice and a little salt. Keep them very white.

Remove the chicken pieces and keep them hot in a covered dish.

Boil the cooking liquid down to reduce it, thicken with the egg-yolks, and whisk in the cream.

Arrange the chicken pieces in a serving dish, surround with the mushroom caps, coat everything with the strained sauce, sprinkle with the chopped, blanched parsley, and serve.

Veal fricassee may be prepared in the same way.

POULARDE DEMI-DEUIL

Chicken in Half-Mourning

For six people, use:

1.

1 young hen
veal stock
truffles[1] to taste (optional)
madeira wine
bouquet garni

2.

1½ lbs. veal round
½ lb. ham
14 T. butter
10 T. heavy cream
½ lb. mushrooms
8 T. flour
1 qt. consommé
3 medium carrots
2 medium onions
bouquet garni
celery
salt and pepper

Cook separately: on the one hand the truffles in madeira, and on the other hand the chicken, for one hour in the veal stock along with the *bouquet garni.* Skim off the fat and boil down the cooking liquid.

At the same time prepare a good Béchamel sauce as follows: in the butter cook the coarsely cut-up veal and ham, the minced onions, carrots, and celery; stir in the flour and cook for five minutes. Add the consommé, the minced mushrooms, the *bouquet garni*, some salt, some pepper, and bring this all to the boiling point, then continue to simmer for about two hours. Remove any scum, skim off the fat, and strain the sauce. Whisk in the heavy cream and heat it up without boiling, but keep cooking until the mixture coats the spoon.

Cut up the chicken, arrange the pieces on a platter, coat with the Béchamel sauce to which you have added any liquid from the chicken pan and one minced truffle. Decorate by arranging a slice of truffle on each piece of chicken and serve.

For variation, one could substitute for the Béchamel sauce a *sauce Régence*, prepared in the following manner.

Mix equal quantities of Alsatian wine (Riesling or Riquewihr) or some Rhine wine with some mushroom and truffle broth. Reduce this by half, then add an equal quantity of *sauce allemande* (see recipe) and the reduced cooking liquid from the chicken. Strain through a cloth or fine sieve.

POULARDE BRAISÉE À L'ESTRAGON

Braised Chicken with Tarragon

Truss a nice plump young hen.

Prepare a good broth with the chicken giblets, some extra giblets, some veal bones, vegetables, water, some salt, some pepper, and some aromatic herbs. Skim off the fat and strain it.

In four tablespoons of butter brown the chicken lightly, then finish cooking it in the broth you have made along with a good quantity of tarragon (two tablespoons of dried; double that if it is fresh). Let this simmer for an hour and a half to two hours according to the size of the bird.

Reduce the cooking liquid, thicken it, strain it, and add some fresh, chopped tarragon leaves.

Carve the chicken, arrange it on a platter as much as possible in its normal shape, decorate with some slightly blanched tarragon leaves, coat with the sauce, and serve. Send the rest of the sauce along in a sauceboat.

POULE AU RIZ

Chicken with Rice

For six people use:

2 cups minus 2 T. rice
1½ C. grated Gruyère cheese
1 qt. bouillon
1 young, tender chicken[1]
bouquet garni **(parsley, thyme bay leaf)**
butter
salt and pepper

Put the chicken in a large kettle with the *bouquet*, season to taste, add enough bouillon to come half way up the chicken, cover with a piece of buttered paper, and let this cook in a moderate oven for an hour and a half. Remove the *bouquet*.

Cook the rice for ten minutes in some salted water. Drain it, run cold water over it, then finish cooking it in the chicken broth, which it will absorb.

Cook the rice just long enough to be cooked but with the grains still remaining whole and not mushy. Then add the grated Gruyère and, if necessary, some butter, which would be allowed to melt.

Arrange the rice on a platter, the chicken on top, and serve.

For variation, one could put with the rice, instead of the cheese, ¼ pound of mushrooms or morels; or 2 ounces of dried mushrooms soaked, sliced and sautéed in butter; or even some bacon dice, small sausages, etc.

Last, during the season one could substitute for the cheese some green peas which would be cooked with the chicken.

NOTE

1. If one were using an old hen the cooking time would take three or four hours or even more, and the dish would not be nearly as good.

COQ AU VIN

This dish goes back to the sixteenth century. It was known at that time under the clarionlike name of *coq au vin*, and it was prepared very rapidly, in the presence of numerous guests, in front of a huge crackling wood fire, in the old "Hostelleries" of France. But, since

For four people, use:

4 oz. diced unsmoked bacon
4 oz. fresh mushrooms (in season)
1/2 C. wine (preferably dry white wine)
4 T. butter
3 T. brandy
2 cloves minced garlic
6 small onions
4 small shallots
1 young tender chicken
bouquet garni **(parsley, thyme, bay leaf)**
carrot
parsley
salt and pepper

it can perfectly well be prepared with a young hen, as well as with a young rooster, and since, in the long run, it is a ragoût, it would be preferable to call it *"ragoût de poulet au vin"* (ragoût of chicken with wine, or chicken stew with wine).

Cut the chicken up as for a fricassee.

In 3 tablespoons of butter brown the bacon, onions, shallots, and a few slices of carrot. Remove these and set aside and in their place put the chicken pieces which you will season with salt, pepper, and garlic. Brown these over a hot fire. Put back the bacon, carrot, onions, shallots, flame the dish with brandy, sprinkle on the flour, and stir for a few minutes. Then add the peeled mushrooms, pour in the wine, cover and cook over a hot fire for about fifteen minutes.

At the last minute put the pieces of chicken and bacon in a hot serving dish, skim the fat off the sauce, strain it, whisk in the rest of the butter, and pour the sauce over the chicken and serve.

SOUFFLÉS DE VOLAILLE

Chicken Soufflé

For chicken soufflés one can either use raw or cooked chicken meat.

If you are using raw chicken—

For six people, use:

1 1/4 lb. raw chicken meat, without skin or sinews
1 3/4 C. thick, heavy cream
1 T. salt
6 egg whites
pepper

Pound the chicken in a mortar[1] with two egg whites, then add to it, little by little, the semi-whipped cream, salt and pepper to taste. Force this purée through a sieve and chill it for one hour. Then add, in small quantities, so as not to deflate them, the rest of the stiffly beaten egg whites.

Spoon the mixture into a mold or timbale and cook in a hot water bath in a slow oven for thirty-five to forty minutes.

If you use cooked chicken—

For six people, use:

1 1/4 lb. chicken breast meat
1 C. cold, thick Béchamel sauce
4 T. butter
6 whole eggs
salt and pepper

Break the eggs, separating the whites from the yolks. Beat the whites until stiff.

Pound the chicken breast meat[1] with the Béchamel added little by little. Force through a sieve. Catch the purée in a saucepan, heat it up without boiling, whisk in 3 tablespoons of butter and the egg yolks. Taste, add salt and pepper if necessary, remove the pan from the fire, then slowly fold in the stiffly beaten egg whites.

Butter a mold or timbale with the rest of the butter, spoon in the soufflé mixture, and cook in a slow oven in a hot water bath.

One can also add truffles to the above mixture.

These soufflés may be served with any one of the following sauces: *velouté, suprême* or *demi-glace* (see recipes).

NOTE

1. For a quicker and easier way see note under recipe for quenelles.

GALANTINES

The word galantines was once used to denote dishes which were made up of chopped meat or fish wrapped up in a fish, a young animal such as a lamb or suckling pig, a fowl or a piece of game. Today, one rarely prepares anything but galantines of fowl or game.

The method of preparation of a galantine differs a little according to the size of the animal involved.

If you use a large fowl such as a large hen or a turkey, etc., bone it first, trim it, and remove the sinews. Set aside the bones and trimmings. Then cut off the thigh and breast meat and chop it. Using the chopped thigh meat line any parts of the bird where the flesh has been torn. Put the breast meat to marinate in brandy and madeira, along with either all or a mixture of a few of the following ingredients, to taste: slices of pickled tongue, lean ham, salt pork, veal tenderloin, tiny dice of foie gras and truffles, etc. Season with salt, pepper, and spices.

Prepare a fine forcemeat with veal, fresh pork, the trimmings from the bird, and the truffle trimmings. Season and add some ground pistachio nuts.

Line the skin of the bird with alternating layers of the marinated meats and the forcemeat which has been bound with eggs, or with a mixture of the marinated ingredients, some of the marinade, and the forcemeat thickened with eggs.

Roll this all up into the shape of a long cylinder. Wrap this galantine, thus rolled, first in a thin layer of pork fat, then in a piece of cloth which will be sewn up to keep its shape. This will then be cooked in some veal and chicken stock, at a constant simmer. The cooking time should be calculated at about fifteen minutes per pound of galantine.

Partially cool the galantine in the liquid, then lift it out, tighten the wrapping cloth, and sew it up again, tie it up with string and let it cool with a slight weight on it.

Skim the fat off the cooking liquid and clarify it.

Unwrap the galantine, coat it with the clarified cooking liquid so as to have a half-inch-thick layer of jelly on it. Arrange it on a platter. Decorate with some chopped jelly and some jelly cut into fancy shapes.

If you are dealing with small game, pluck it, flame it, bone it, trim it, and set aside the bones and trimmings.

Make a forcemeat with a second piece of game or with another type of game, some salt pork, pickled tongue, truffles, pistachios, and brandy. Season the stuffing, bind it with eggs, and spoon into the boned bird.

Roll it, wrap it in pork fat, then wrap it in the cloth and cook it in some strong veal stock seasoned with game stock.

Let this cool, press it down, unwrap it, as above, and serve it with a *chaud-froid* sauce (see recipe) prepared with the cooking broth.

CANETON RÔTI, SAUCE À L'ORANGE

Roast Duckling with Orange Sauce

For four people, use:

1/2 C. veal stock (with the duck giblets)
4 T. white Curaçao
2 T. butter
4 tsp. meat glaze
2 T. flour
1 tsp. salt
pepper
2 oranges
1 duckling

Peel one of the oranges, cut up the pulp, and put it inside the duckling. Sliver the zest (thin outer rind) and reserve.

Roast the duckling on a spit for about a half hour, season it with salt and pepper.

At the same time, prepare the sauce.

Blanch the slivered orange peel for ten minutes in boiling water. Drain it and mash it in a mortar along with the duck liver. Mix in the Curaçao.

Heat the veal stock, add the meat glaze, and the butter and flour mashed together, the mashed liver and orange zest, the skimmed cooking juices from the roasting pan; bring this to a boil and strain.

Remove the pieces of orange pulp from the inside of the duck, arrange it on a platter, decorate the platter with the second orange, sliced, and serve. Send the sauce along separately in a sauceboat.

Young guinea fowl may be prepared in this same way.

CANETON AUX NAVETS NOUVEAUX

Duckling with New Turnips

For six people, use:

14 T. butter
1/2 onion
2 T. flour
4 tsp. sugar
30 tiny new turnips
1 plump duckling
1 carrot
1 leek
small *bouquet garni*
salt and pepper

Clean and flame the duckling.

With the duckling giblets, the carrot, leek, *bouquet,* water, and salt, prepare a strong bouillon, reducing it to about one cup. Strain.

Brown the duckling in four tablespoons of butter, season it with salt and pepper, add the onions, and let this simmer for three-quarters to one hour.

Peel the turnips, wipe them, steam them in a saucepan with a half cup of butter. This should take about one-half hour. Ten minutes before they are done, sprinkle them with the sugar and let them brown lightly.

Make a roux with the rest of the butter and the flour, stir in the bouillon, add the duckling along with its strained cooking juices and the turnips. Taste and complete the seasoning if necessary, and let this all simmer for another ten minutes. Skim the fat off the liquid.

Arrange the duckling on a platter with the turnips around it, and coat it with the sauce. Serve.

For variation, the duckling could be roasted on a spit, and the turnips cooked in a strong duck broth.

CANARD AUX OLIVES

Duck with Olives

For six people, use:

1 lb. olives
1 C. madeira wine
7 T. butter
3 T. flour
1 plump duck
extra set of duck giblets
1 carrot
1 onion
bouquet garni
salt and pepper

Truss the duck.

Soak the pitted olives to remove any salt.

Prepare a bouillon with the duck giblets, carrot, onion, *bouquet garni*, water, salt, and pepper. Skim it and strain.

Brown the duck in a saucepan in 3 tablespoons of butter.

Make a roux with the rest of the butter and the flour, stir in the broth and the madeira, add the browned duck and let it braise over a low fire for an hour and a half.

One half hour before it is cooked add the olives, taste and correct the seasoning, if necessary.

Arrange the duck on a platter, olives around it; mask with the sauce which has been skimmed of fat and strained. Serve.

If you are using a young duckling it is best to roast it. The preparation of the sauce and the olives remains the same.

Duck, olives, and madeira are a good combination.

CANARD FROID, EN GELÉE

Cold Duck in Aspic

For six people, use:

7 oz. ham
1 C. veal stock
1 C. madeira
4 T. butter
3 T. meat glaze
1 duck
salt, pepper, *quatre épices*

Cut the ham up into tiny pieces.

Brown the duck and the ham in the butter, then add the veal stock and madeira, the meat glaze, salt, pepper, and a little *quatre épices.*

Cover with a piece of buttered paper and let this all simmer over a low flame for two hours.

Strain the cooking juices, skim them of fat, boil them down, taste for seasoning, mask the duck with this sauce, and let it set.

FOIE GRAS DE CANARD AU NATUREL

Plain Foie Gras of Duck

Use a nice duck liver[1]; they are at their best at the beginning of winter during the first cold spell.

After salting it lightly put it in a tin-lined copper saucepan, or in a stainless steel one, which has been previously coated with a few drops of good olive oil and heated slightly.

Now put the saucepan over a hot fire and shake it constantly to avoid having the liver stick to the pan.

After twelve to fifteen minutes the duck liver should have taken on a slightly golden color and it ought to be just right.

Serve immediately on hot plates.

Foie gras of duck, just plain, is eaten as is, or sprinkled with a little lemon juice. This is how I prefer it.

Prepared in this way, duck *foie gras* is food worthy of the gods. It presents itself under the guise of a pink jelly, perfumed, appetizing. It charms the sight, the smell, the taste, and even the most delicate stomachs are pleased with its easy digestibility.

NOTE

1. The best duck *foie gras* (duck livers) come from mallard ducks.

For four people, use:

3 lbs. unshelled peas
4 oz. lean bacon
2 T. butter
6 tiny onions
2 young pigeons[1]
2 or 3 new carrots
1 heart of lettuce
salt

PIGEONS AUX PETITS POIS

Pigeons with Peas

Clean out, singe, and truss the pigeons. Cut the bacon into tiny dice and brown the pigeons and bacon together for twenty minutes in the butter. Then add the shelled peas, the whole onions, the coarsely chopped lettuce and the cut-up carrots. If the peas are not sweet enough on their own add a pinch of sugar. Cover the pan and let everything cook together over a slow fire for an hour. Skim the fat off the cooking juices, taste, and season with a little salt, if necessary, before serving.

If, at the opening of the hunting season, one can obtain fresh peas, one would prepare partridges, which are far superior to pigeons, in the same way.

One could also prepare duckling with peas. The procedure is the same but it needs an extra half hour of cooking.

Despite the very long-standing reputation that pigeons with peas have, I am not loath to say that I find duckling with peas far superior.

For variation, one may roast the pigeons, partridges or ducklings. They would be served with peas which have been cooked in good stock to which one has added the cooking juices from the roasting pan.

People who have a preference for roast rather than braised meats will prepare them this way.

NOTE

1. Pigeons must never be bled.

GAME

Ortolans[1]

Buntings

The ortolan is a small bird native to central and southern Europe. It is common in the Midi.

Ortolans are captured in nets, as are beccaficcos. They are then caged, fattened, and, last, they are smothered (suffocated) to death. After having been scalded, they are plucked.

Ortolans, like beccaficcos, are most often just roasted, without any preliminary preparation. This is, on the whole, the best way of preparing them. They can also be cooked in a *cocotte*.

NOTE

1. Ortolans are really a type of European bunting, *Emberiza hortulana*. In Britain they are often referred to as wheatear and in

the United States as bobolink. Since the word *hortulana* refers to garden, they might best be called garden bunting.

For twelve people, use:

$1^{3}/_{4}$ C. veal broth
7 oz. purée of foie gras
$^{1}/_{3}$ C. madeira or white port wine
$^{1}/_{4}$ C. *mirepoix*
12 fattened ortolans (recently smothered in aged cognac)
12 large Perigord truffles
3 thrushes
quatre épices **to taste**
salt and pepper

ORTOLANS EN SARCOPHAGES

Garden Buntings in Sarcophagi

Bone the ortolans and stuff them with the purée of foie gras.

Hollow out the truffles, setting aside a round plug to serve as a cork. Season with salt and pepper.

Roast the thrushes; crush them in a meat press. To their juices, add the veal broth, wine, and *mirepoix*, and heat everything up together. Put the ortolans into this mixture and cook them for five minutes, then remove them.

Boil down the mixture, skim off any grease and strain.

Insert an ortolan into each truffle and cork them up. Wrap each truffle in strips of larding fat.

Cook them by any recipe suitable for truffles, preferably *à la maréchale*.[1]

Remove the remains of the larding fat, when they are cooked, and arrange them on a napkin-covered platter. Serve the clarified sauce at the same time.

This dish, also known under the descriptive title of "ortolans in caskets," while a little macabre, is nevertheless one of the more sophisticated concoctions of modern cooking.

A dry champagne is a delightful accompaniment.

NOTE

1. Truffles cooked *à la maréchale* are generally barded with fat, as above, then individually wrapped in paper and cooked in hot wood ashes for an hour. They are then served with butter, salt, and pepper.

ALOUETTES EN LINCEUIL

Larks in Shrouds

Peel and hollow out some large baking potatoes and save pieces of pulp to fashion corks from.

Pluck, flame, and bone the larks. Season them and stuff them with a mixture of game and foie gras with or without truffles. Insert each lark inside a hollowed-out potato and seal with the corks.

Put these stuffed potatoes in a casserole. Use enough strong stock made with feathered game to cover the potatoes and cook them in the oven, basting frequently.

When the potatoes are no longer covered with liquid, add small pieces of butter and finish the cooking.

The potatoes should be golden brown and crusty.

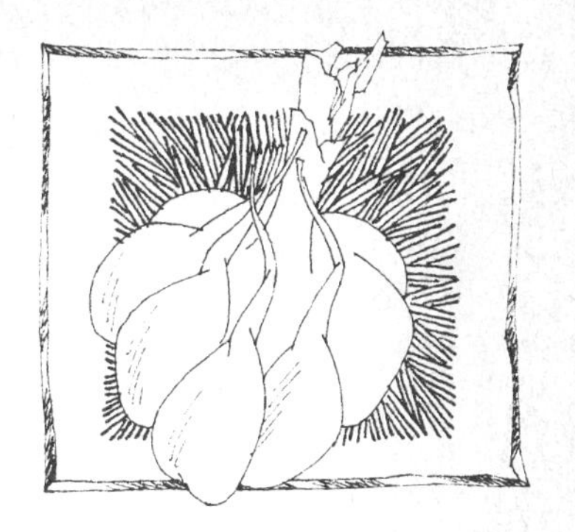

PERDREAUX À LA COQUE

Poached Partridges

Pluck some nice fresh partridges, draw them, and stuff them with a mixture of truffles and foie gras cooked in madeira and seasoned with salt and pepper. Sew up all the openings and wrap them in pork caul which has been thoroughly cleaned. Thus dressed, plunge them into boiling water and let them cook for about thirty minutes.

Remove them from the water, remove the caul, let them cool, and remove the string.

Serve the partridges cold, as is, without any sauce.

This is a choice dish for breakfast and particularly in the morning before going out hunting. An old Burgundy wine is the perfect complement to this dish.

Young doves may also be prepared this way, as may wild ducklings and turtle-doves.

Grouse

The English designate under the name "grouse" the Scottish lagopede commonly called *petit coq de bruyère* in France. This is a wild bird which lives in the north of England. Its flesh is very delicate.

The grouse is common in Scotland in the heather-covered mountains. It is especially good from August to October.

Very young birds, after having been wrapped in fat, are roasted on a spit. Cooking time is twelve to fifteen minutes.

In England they are served with a sort of game sauce made with grouse stock, seasoned with pepper, cloves, and cinnamon, flavored with orange peel and port wine, and sweetened with currant jelly. This sauce is commonly known under the name *sauce Victoria*.

The less young and tender birds are braised in a good, strong stock flavored with white wine or they are braised in cream. In the first instance, they are served with sauerkraut and a sauce made with the concentrated cooking juices. This is a recipe known as *à la norvégienne* (Norwegian style). In the latter instance, the procedure is as follows: Clean the bird, wash out the inside with

a little milk, and throw out the milk. Place the bird in a bowl and pour ½ cup of milk over it. Leave it that way for at least one hour, turning it often.

Drain the bird, truss it, wrap it in fat, and put it in a saucepan with 2 tablespoons of butter and cook it on all sides for about fifteen minutes. Pour the fat out of the pan, season the bird with salt and pepper, add ⅔ cup of heavy cream, and let it simmer for twenty minutes.

Five minutes before serving, add the juice of half a lemon, taste, and correct seasoning if necessary.

Older birds are used for making *pâtés*.

In all these recipes one must use only freshly killed birds, and it is advisable to wash them in milk several times before cooking them.

Tétras

Tétras or *coqs de bruyère* are large gallinaceous birds from the same family as the *gelinottes* and lagopedes. They may attain the size of a large turkey. Their plummage is black and dark green and they have a white underside. They are found in France in high, wooded mountains. Their flesh is very choice, and, as is the case with the *gelinottes* and the lagopedes, their flesh has a slightly resinous flavor.

Generally they are roasted on a spit but they may also be used in *salmis, pâtés, chaud-froids*, etc.

All the birds of the Tetraonidae family which are to be served roasted must only be cooked long enough to give a pink tint to the flesh.

The choicest part—and the only one which is served, usually—is the breast. The rest of the bird is used for making stock.

FRICASSÉE DE BÉCASSES

Fricassée of Woodcock

For four people, use:

3 C. red or white burgundy wine
7 oz. bacon (salted but not smoked)
½ C. butter
½ medium onion
6 shallots
4 T. flour
4 cloves garlic
2 woodcocks
8 juniper berries
2 cloves
bouquet garni
olive oil
salt and pepper

Pluck, singe, and draw the woodcocks. Cut them up and reserve the innards minus the gizzard.

In a little butter, cook the diced bacon and the chopped shallots and onion.

With the rest of the butter and the flour, make a roux. Stir in the wine, add the bacon, shallots, and onion, the woodcocks, garlic, *bouquet garni*, cloves, and the crushed juniper berries. Season with salt and pepper and cook for thirty minutes.

Remove the woodcocks, keep them hot, and strain the cooking juices.

Mash the innards with a little olive oil, add this to the strained cooking juices and mix thoroughly. Heat up the sauce until it is thick enough to coat the spoon. Taste, complete the seasoning, if necessary, with salt and pepper; then skim off any fat.

Arrange pieces of woodcock on a platter, pour the sauce over them, and serve.

FAISAN BRAISÉ À LA CRÈME

Pheasant Braised in Cream

For four people, use:

1 3/4 C. cream
1/2 C. veal, chicken, or game stock
2 T. brandy
2 T. vinegar
2 T. grated horseradish
5 tsp. butter
5 shallots
1 pheasant
1 thin sheet leaf lard
salt and pepper

Pluck the pheasant, draw it, singe it, and wrap in the leaf lard.

Brown the pheasant and shallots in a *cocotte.* Flame with the brandy and season with salt and pepper. Add the stock and cook the pheasant in the oven for thirty minutes, basting often with the pan juices. Add the cream, vinegar, and horseradish, and let it cook for another fifteen or twenty minutes, depending on the size of the bird, basting continually.

Shortly before serving, taste for seasoning. When ready, arrange the pheasant on a platter and serve.

Rice *à l'indienne*, rice sautéed in butter, *petits pois,* tiny mushrooms, truffles carved like olives, or potatoes *noisette* make good accompaniments for pheasant.

HALBRAN RÔTI

Roast Wild Duckling

An *halbran* is a young wild duck which has not yet grown its August plumage. Those killed during the second half of July are perfect. They are hardly any larger than partridges; and their flesh is delicate because they have not yet eaten fish, having been nourished exclusively on cereals.

The best way of preparing them is to roast them, wrapped in a thin sheet of leaf lard.

Served hot, with a green salad and the cooking juices skimmed of fat, they are delicious. They are no less delicious cold, accompanied by a sauce made with olive oil, grated lemon rind, lemon juice, tarragon mustard, salt, and pepper.

Although my opinion may seem daring, I declare that three- or four-month-old *halbrans* may favorably be compared with the most delicate partridge.

Pigeons may be prepared this same way.

The unusual sauce made with lemon rind which I have just mentioned above is equally good with other cold meats.

CANARD SAUVAGE AUX OLIVES FARCIE D'ANCHOIS

Wild Duck with Anchovy-Stuffed Olives

The main thought behind the creation of this recipe was to recall the aquatic nature of the duck by marrying its flesh with that of fish.

When one has a tiny duckling, the best method of cooking it is to roast it. When one only has a mature duck, which is tender, however, the best thing to do is to braise it. As to very old wild ducks, they are generally too tough to be edible.

Whatever duck one has, the first thing is to stuff the olives.

Use enough olives, about a half a pound, for instance, for a duckling, and one pound for a plump, full-grown duck. Soak them to remove the salt, and pit them. Stuff them with pieces of freshened anchovy filets of the same length as the olives.

Draw the bird (duck or duckling); remove the heart and gizzard and in their place put the stuffed olives.

Clean the removed organs and set them aside.

If you are dealing with a duckling, wrap it in a thin layer of pork fat and roast it for twenty minutes, seasoning it only with salt and pepper.

Chop the liver, heart, and gizzard, pepper them, and cook them separately in a little butter.

Remove the barding fat from the roast duckling, chop it up, and add it, along with some anchovy butter, to the above hash and mix well.

Prepare a thin slice of bread, long and large enough to accommodate the duckling. Cover it with the above hash and serve the duckling arranged on this canapé.

Serve the cooking juices, skimmed of fat, separately, in a sauceboat.

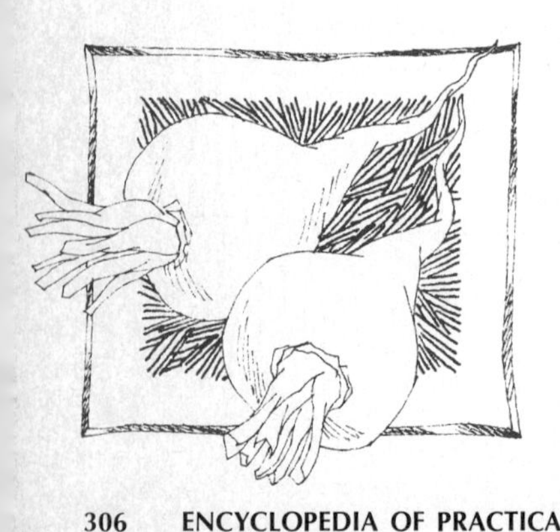

If you are dealing with a full-grown duck, prepare 2½ to 3 cups of strong duck stock, made with 2 duck giblets, minus the livers, which should be reserved, but do not add salt.

Brown the duck in some butter, season with pepper, and set it aside. In its place put 2½ tablespoons of flour and stir for a few minutes, then add the duck stock and stir until smooth. Put the browned duck back in the pan and let it simmer for about an hour. Taste, complete the seasoning if necessary, skim the fat off the sauce, boil it down, and thicken it by adding the reserved liver which has been mashed.

Arrange the duck on a platter and serve coated with the sauce.

This method of preparation is applicable to teal, widgeon, and all water fowl.

RÂBLES DE LAPEREAUX DE GARENNE À LA MOUTARDE

Saddle of Wild Rabbit with Mustard

For four people, use:

1 C. cream
2 young, wild rabbits
2 thin sheets leaf lard
vegetables
white wine
plain mustard
salt and pepper

Skin, draw, and dress the rabbits. Carve off the saddles as high as possible, coat them with mustard on all surfaces and let them macerate for twenty-four hours.

With the trimmings from the young rabbits and the vegetables, white wine, a little water, salt, and pepper, prepare a stock and strain it.

Cut the leaf lard sheets into strips; wrap the saddles like mummies, using these strips; then place them in a buttered casserole and cook them in the oven for about thirty minutes.

Remove the rabbits, skim the fat off the pan juices, add the rabbit stock and the cream, and heat the sauce up without letting it boil. Taste for seasoning.

Arrange the saddles on a platter; coat them with the sauce and serve. For vegetables, send along at the same time either some beets in Béchamel sauce, some mashed, boiled potatoes, or some dry rice.

The mustard has completely disappeared.

This dish is unusual and very pleasant.

Domestic rabbit may be prepared in the same way.

FILETS DE LAPEREAU AU JAMBON, GRATINÉS

Baked Tenderloin of Young Wild Rabbit with Ham

For three people, use:

7 oz. pork fat
1/4 lb. raw, cured ham
1/2 C. cream
3 T. butter
3/4 C. grated Parmesan cheese
1 young wild rabbit
1 medium beet
pot-au-feu **vegetables**
salt and pepper

Skin, draw, and dress the rabbit. Remove the tenderloins and flatten them. Slice the thigh meat, set it aside, and save the trimmings.

Bake the beet in the oven; peel and slice it.

With the rabbit trimmings, some vegetables, water, salt, and pepper, prepare a stock, which should be reduced to several spoonfuls.

Cut the ham into 2 thin slices, blanch it and then cook it in butter. Take it out of the pan, add the rabbit filets, the sliced thigh meat, and the pork fat cut into thin strips. Let these all cook together.

In the cream, gently heat the sliced beet, the pieces of rabbit, and the pork. In a casserole, arrange the slices of ham, and on top of these place the rabbit filets, sprinkle with Parmesan, and brown in the oven.

After removing the pan from the oven, coat the rabbit with the few spoonfuls of rabbit stock and serve in the same pan. Send along, at the same time, the beet, rabbit, and pork mixture, in a vegetable dish.

CIVET DE LAPIN DE GARENNE OU DE LAPIN DOMESTIQUE

Jugged Wild Rabbit or Domestic Rabbit

For four people, use:

1¼ C. strong stock
1 C. good red wine
4 oz. salt pork
7 T. rabbit or pork blood
6 T. butter
4 T. brandy
1 small chopped onion
1 chopped shallots
5 tsp. flour
pepper
quatre épices
1 rabbit, weighing 2 to 2½ lbs. cleaned
bouquet garni **(parsley, thyme, bay leaf)**
fat
salt

Cut up the rabbit; reserve the liver and the blood.

Cook, on the one hand, the meat in a frying pan with 2 tablespoons of butter; on the other hand, the sliced or diced salt pork, in another frying pan with a little fat.

Make a roux with the rest of the butter and the flour, add the onion and shallots, and stir until they have browned slightly; then add the meat from the other pan, flame with the brandy, pour in the wine and stock, and, last, add the *bouquet garni*, the browned salt pork, pepper, *quatre épices*, and 1 or 2 teaspoons of salt, according to how salty the salt pork is. Let this all cook over fairly high heat for as long as necessary, depending on the age of the rabbit, and to reduce the pan liquids so as to have a fairly thick sauce.

Five minutes before serving, add the reserved liver.

Arrange the meat and the salt pork on a platter and keep it hot. Remove the saucepan from the fire, pour the blood into the sauce, cook it for a few moments to thicken it, strain the sauce over the meat, and serve.

Jugged hare may be prepared this same way.

LEVRAUT SAUTÉ

Sautéed Leveret

For four people, use:

1 C. consommé
1 C. dry, white wine
10 T. butter
4 oz. salt pork
4 oz. mushrooms
4 tsp. flour
1 T. chopped parsley
1 leveret
1 minced onion
salt and pepper

Skin, draw and dress the leveret. Disjoint it and brown the pieces, with the diced salt pork, in 7 tablespoons of butter. This part of the procedure takes from fifteen to twenty minutes and must be stopped as soon as the meat is cooked.

Take the leveret and salt pork out of the pan and keep them hot.

Cook the flour in 2 tablespoons of butter until it is lightly browned. Add the minced onion and stir around for a few minutes to let the onion brown slightly. Stir in the consommé and white wine, add the washed and peeled mushrooms, season with salt and pepper, and let this all cook together for ten minutes at the most.

Enrich the sauce with the rest of the butter, put back the pieces of leveret and the salt pork, sprinkle with parsley, heat up for three minutes, and serve.

Needless to say, it is indispensable to use a very young and tender animal for this dish to be as it should be.

FILETS DE LEVRAUT SAUTÉS, SAUCE BÉARNAISE

Sautéed Leveret Tenderloins with Béarnaise Sauce

For two people, use:

9 T. butter
2 oz. port fat for larding
2 T. wine vinegar
2 tsp. cold water
1 leveret
1 egg yolk
1 small shallot
tarragon
salt and pepper

Skin, draw, and dress the leveret and then cut off the filets or tenderloins which lie on either side of the backbone. Lard the pieces with pork fat which has been cut into thin strips and seasoned with salt and pepper.

Cook the vinegar and shallot together; reduce and strain.

Sauté the leveret tenderloins for fifteen minutes in 3 tablespoons of butter. Season with salt and pepper to taste.

At the same time prepare a hollandaise sauce with the rest of the butter, the egg yolk, water, salt, and pepper, and add the strained vinegar and some chopped tarragon. You will then have a béarnaise sauce.

Arrange the leveret tenderloins on a hot platter and serve. Pass the sauce separately in a sauceboat.

RÂBLE DE LIÈVRE RÔTI, SAUCE AU VIN ROUGE

Roast Saddle of Hare with Red Wine Sauce

For six people, use:

1⅓ C. red wine
1¼ C. bouillon
4 oz. port fat for larding
7 T. butter
1 small onion
2 T. flour
1 T. vinegar
1 hare[1]
bouquet garni
nutmeg
salt and pepper

Skin, draw, and dress the animal. Remove the saddle,[2] reserve the liver and the blood, and cook the rest of the animal in the bouillon so as to get about ½ cup of concentrated stock.

Remove the sinews from the saddle, lard it with strips of pork fat which have been seasoned with salt and pepper, and roast it on a spit without any other preparation. While it is cooking, baste it with 3 tablespoons of melted butter and season with salt. Cooking time for a good-sized saddle of hare should take about one hour.

Prepare the sauce. Make a roux with 2 tablespoons of butter and the flour, add the minced onion and brown it lightly, then stir in the wine, the concentrated stock, and the vinegar, and add the *bouquet garni*, some nutmeg, salt, and pepper to taste. Boil these together for one hour. Remove the *bouquet* and reduce the sauce.

Mash the liver, mix it with the blood, and pour the mixture into the sauce. Heat it up but do not boil. Strain the sauce through a fine sieve, using a potato masher to force it through. Keep it hot.

At the last minute, whisk in the rest of the butter, add the skimmed juices from the roasting pan, and blend well.

Arrange the saddle on a hot platter and serve. Send the sauce along, at the same time, in a sauceboat.

NOTES

1. The best hares are those which feed on aromatic herbs such as wild thyme, marjoram, etc.

Hare must never be gamey, and those destined to be spit roasted must be young.

2. The saddle consists of the back of the hare from the nape of the neck to the tail. Certain people use the term saddle just for the part of the animal which is located between the shoulders and the hips. I prefer to use the term filet for this particular piece.

CIVET DE LIÈVRE MARINÉ[1]

Marinated Jugged Hare

For eight people, use:

4 oz. salt pork
7 T. consommé
½ C. good red wine
5 T. butter
4 T. flour
2 tsp. olive oil
1 (medium-sized) adult hare
salt and pepper

For the marinade:

1 C. wine
3 T. vinegar
3 T. olive oil
1 onion
bouquet garni **(parsley, thyme, and bay leaf)**
salt and pepper

The day before you wish to prepare the civet prepare the marinade. Gently brown the sliced onion in the oil, add the wine, vinegar, *bouquet garni*, salt, and pepper, and let this cook for a few minutes, then cool.

Skin, draw, and dress the hare and reserve the liver and the blood.

Put the hare to marinate for one day, turning it frequently in the marinade.

The following day, in a large saucepan, put the butter and olive oil, add the hare and the cut-up salt pork. Let these brown slowly for twenty minutes. Sprinkle on the flour and let this cook for about twenty-five minutes, stirring often, then pour in the consommé and the wine, and season with salt and pepper to taste. Continue cooking for another forty minutes. Strain the cooking liquid and the marinade and combine them. Skim off any fat, reduce the sauce, and thicken it with the mashed liver and the blood. Heat without boiling, taste, complete the seasoning if necessary, and serve.

NOTE

1. The flesh of a nice, fresh hare, which is delicate and without too strong an aroma, does not need to be marinated. The recipe for marinated hare which I give here is intended for an old hare.

Venison Roasts

All venison roasts, such as legs, shoulders, and tenderloins—except for those of extremely young animals—must be marinated.

I have already spoken about marinades. The recipe for marinated leg of lamb is perfectly suitable for venison; however, when it comes to the boar, whose flesh is firm and strongly flavored, there is no reason not to increase the proportion of vinegar.

The length of time the meat should remain in the marinade depends a great deal on the following conditions: the moisture content of the air, the temperature, the age and condition of the game, when it was killed, etc.

In a general way, boar must be marinated longer than either deer or roebuck. One may lard the meat before marinating it or lard it afterward. It will progress faster in the former than in the latter case.

Marinade may be used either cooked or uncooked: at the same temperature the cooked marinade works faster.

Whether one uses cooked or uncooked marinade, it is always preferable to have it at room temperature; but there may be cases when one would like to have it work fast. I will therefore describe a fast procedure, allowing one to eat a leg of boar the same night the animal was killed. This method consists in injecting into the meat the hot, cooked marinade, using a hypodermic syringe.

This having been said, I have nothing to add as far as the roasting part, which is not particularly complicated. The best accompaniments to venison roasts are semi-sweet purées such as purée of chestnuts, bulbous chervil, or a mixture of potatoes and celery. As to sauce, one would choose a *sauce marinade, sauce poivrade,* or *sauce venaison,* the latter being the most recommended.

One would increase the smoothness of all these sauces by adding varying quantities of truffled foie gras, cooked in a *cocotte* and pounded smooth. One would finish the sauces by whisking in some fresh butter once the sauce was off the fire.

SELLE DE FAON GRILLEÉ

Broiled Saddle of Fawn

Bone the saddle, remove the tenderloins, and trim the sinews away.

Season the tenderloins with salt and pepper, then wrap each filet in a sheet of pork fat, putting a few tarragon leaves between the meat and the fat.

Roast them on a grill or under a broiler for about twenty minutes. Use the type of grill or broiler which collects the falling juices and fat.

Prepare a *sauce suprême*, add to it some cut-up chicken livers, and let them cook in the sauce. Then add the fawn kidneys which have been broiled and sliced, a little sorrel which has been cooked, drained, and puréed, and, last, add some chopped tarragon leaves.

Arrange the pieces of saddle on a platter and serve, sending along the sauce in a sauceboat.

Saddle of fawn may be accompanied by chestnut purée, a purée of potatoes and bulbous chervil, a purée of potatoes and celery, or of red kidney beans and wine, or even a purée of lentils with salt pork.

Saddle of deer or roebuck may also be prepared this way, but it is best, before proceeding, to marinate the filets in some wine with onions, carrots, a *bouquet garni*, and some salt and pepper.

One may prepare, this same way, a saddle of lamb or mutton, or even a saddle of hare. But, in the case of the hare, one would use thyme instead of tarragon and one would add the mashed hare liver to the sauce.

The cooking time would depend on the size of the piece of meat one is using.

PASTA, DRIED VEGETABLES, AND GREEN VEGETABLES

PÂTES ALIMENTAITRES ITALIENNES

Italian Pasta

One designates, under the generic term of Italian pasta, those pastas made with flour and which are made in different shapes: tubular macaroni, noodles in narrow ribbons, lasagne in wide strips, shells, etc. As to tubular macaroni, one can list, in decreasing order of size: *cannelloni*, which are meant to be stuffed and which can be very large in diameter; *maccheroni*, which are quite small in diameter (five millimeters, or a little more than an eighth of an inch), varieties of which, going from the largest to the smallest, are: *ziti*, *mezzani* and *maccheroncelli*. Of the baguette types of macaroni, one can list: *spaghetti* from Naples, which are about two millimeters in diameter; *vermicelli* from Sicily, which measure one and a half millimeters in diameter; and the true *vermicelli*, whose diameter does not exceed one millimeter, the most delicate of which are the *capellini* from Sicily.

All pastas differ in quality, depending on their composition. It is therefore preferable to prepare them oneself, especially when it comes to those simple in shape, such as noodles and lasagne, rather than buying them all made. Their taste, in any given dish, differs not only because of the way in which they are prepared, but also on account of their shape.

A good noodle dough consists mainly of hard wheat flour and eggs. Optionally, one may add varying quantities of butter.

3½ C. flour
4 tsp. butter
1 T. salt
10 egg yolks
2 egg whites

The egg white binds the dough and gives it firmness, the yolk gives it delicacy and color and makes it more nourishing. A medium quality all-purpose noodle dough is obtained by mixing the following ingredients in the following proportions: ¾ cup of flour for each egg, along with ½ teaspoon of salt. One may, however, increase the quantity of egg yolk. The ingredients opposite make a very good dough.

3⅓ C. flour
4 tsp. butter
1 T. salt
18 egg yolks

One could even completely omit the egg whites and use as many yolks as the flour can absorb. Using the ingredients listed opposite one can make an absolutely exquisite noodle dough of incomparable delicacy.

These quantities can serve eight to ten people.

Whichever recipe you use, the preparation of the dough remains the same. Here is how to proceed:

Mix all the ingredients so as to have a very homogeneous mixture. Let the dough rest for several hours. For easier handling divide the dough into four parts and roll out each part with a rolling pin until it is very, very thin but without any tears in it. Sprinkle these sheets of dough with flour, roll them up and slice them into quarter-inch strips to make noodles and one-inch-wide strips to make lasagne. When the dough is prepared a little ahead of time and the sheets of dough have been well floured, the noodles or lasagne unroll easily.

All Italian pastas may be used either in soups, or as an accompaniment for meats, or even as a vegetable course.

NOUILLES SAUTÉES

Sautéd Noodles

For four people, use:

½ lb. freshly made noodles
½ C. grated Parmesan cheese
2 T. butter
2 tsp. coarse salt
black pepper to taste
2 qts. water

Put the water, salt, and pepper in a large saucepan and bring it to a boil. Add the noodles and shake the pan gently to keep them from sticking together. Let them cook for five or six minutes,[1] drain them, then sauté them in a skillet with butter and sprinkle them with the Parmesan. Mix everything together thoroughly without breaking up the noodles and serve.

NOTE

1. Dried noodles would take a little more time.

NOUILLES SAUTÉES, PANÉES

Breaded Sautéed Noodles

For four people, use:

½ lb. noodles
8 T. butter
3 oz. bread
1 C. grated Parmesan cheese
1 C. grated Gruyère cheese
2 T. salt
black pepper to taste
2 qts. water

Cook the noodles in the water with the salt and pepper and drain them.

Dry out and toast the bread in the oven. Make some breadcrumbs and sift them.

Put the butter in a skillet and let it brown lightly. Add first the breadcrumbs, then the noodles, mix well and sauté everything together.

Serve, sending along, at the same time, the cheeses mixed together.

Prepared in this way, noodles are part of Slavic cuisine and are known as noodles *à la polonaise*.

NOUILLES MI-SAUTÉES, MI-FRITES

Fried and Sautéed Noodles

Sauté three-quarters of the quantity of noodles as in the recipe for Sautéed Noodles.

Fry the remaining noodles in melted butter. After several minutes they will become very crisp. Remove them.

Spoon the sautéed noodles in a serving dish, arrange the fried noodles on top, and serve.

The contrast between the two types of noodles provides a new and agreeable sensation.

NOUILLES À LA CRÈME

Creamed Noodles

For four people, use:

½ lb. dried noodles[1]
1 C. heavy cream
3 T. butter
2 tsp. coarse salt
freshly ground black pepper to taste
2 qts. water

Put the salt and pepper in the water, bring it to a boil and throw in the noodles. Let them cook for ten minutes over high heat then poach them at a simmer for forty-five minutes.

Drain the noodles, spoon them into a casserole, and add the butter cut into tiny pieces, along with the cream. Heat everything up without boiling. Serve in the same dish.

Creamed noodles, which make an excellent vegetable course, are also an excellent accompaniment for light meats.

NOTE

1. If, instead of using dried noodles, one uses freshly made noodles, the cooking would be the same but poaching them would be unnecessary. The quantity of butter would remain the same but only about half the amount of cream would be use.

Using the same quantity of fresh noodles, by weight, would yield fewer portions.

For six people, use:

1 lb. spinach
1¾ C. meat stock
½ lb. lasagne
1¼ C. grated Parmesan cheese
5 T. coarse salt
5 tsp. butter
pepper to taste
5 qts. water

LAZAGNES GRATINÉES, AUX ÉPINARDS

Baked Lasagne with Spinach

Blanch the spinach in 3 quarts of water to which you have added 3 tablespoons of coarse salt and then refreshed under cold running water.

Add the pepper and salt to two quarts of water; throw in the lasagne and let them cook for ten minutes.[1]

Arrange the lasagne and the well-drained spinach in a saucepan; add the meat stock and let them cook together for fifteen minutes. Now add the butter and the cheese and brown in the oven for about ten minutes.

Lasagne thus prepared makes a very nice vegetable course, and one which is a bit unusual.

NOTE

1. This cooking time applies to dry lasagne, but if it is freshly made five or six minutes would be sufficient.

For six people, use:

½ lb. noodles
6 oz. slivered ham
½ C. veal stock
½ C. grated Parmesan cheese
5 tsp. butter
1 tsp. coarse salt
pepper to taste
2 qts. water

NOUILLES AU JAMBON

Noodles with Ham

Boil the salted and peppered water, throw in the noodles, cook them and drain them.

In a skillet, put the veal stock and in it heat up the ham, then remove it. Into the skillet spoon alternating layers of noodles, ham, and cheese, until they are all used up. Sauté these all together, then add the cut-up butter, sauté just long enough to melt the butter, and serve.

Truffled noodles would be prepared in the same way, but

instead of using slivers of ham one would use slivers of truffle cooked in madeira. Two ounces of truffles to a half-pound of noodles would be sufficient. Naturally, the proportion of truffles would vary according to taste.

VERMICELLI À LA SICILIENNE

Sicilian-Style Vermicelli

For six people, use

½ lb. Palermo-type vermicelli
10 T. tomato purée
5 oz. ground meat (ham, veal, or chicken)
2 C. grated Parmesan cheese
4 T. butter
2 T. coarse salt
pepper to taste
2 qts. water
1 eggplant
olive oil

Cook the vermicelli in boiling salted-and-peppered water. Drain them.

Put the butter and the tomato purée in a saucepan and heat them up. Add the vermicelli, along with ½ cup of grated Parmesan cheese, and mix well.

Slice the eggplant, fry it in olive oil, and cover the slices with the hot, ground meat.

Arrange the vermicelli on a platter, put the slices of eggplant and meat on top, sprinkle with the remaining grated Parmesan, and brown the dish in the oven for a minute or two just before serving.

TURBAN DE MACARONI AUX CHAMPIGNONS FARCIS, SAUCE TOMATE

Macaroni Ring with Stuffed Mushrooms and Tomato Sauce

For six people, use:

½ lb. macaroni
1 C. tomato purée
½ lb. shredded Gruyère cheese
10 T. butter
1½ C. shredded Parmesan cheese
¼ lb. mushrooms
1 T. coarse salt
3 tsp. flour
a grating nutmeg
1 qt. milk
12 small, uniform mushrooms
6 large, round mushrooms
1 egg yolk
dry, sifted breadcrumbs
meat broth
chopped parsley
lemon juice
curry
salt and pepper

Break the macaroni into four-inch lengths.

Bring the milk to a boil, add the coarse salt, nutmeg, and macaroni. Boil up once or twice, then keep the pan hot enough for as long as necessary to cook the macaroni, which should absorb all the milk and swell up. About one hour is generally sufficient.

Drain the macaroni without letting it cool. At once add the shredded Gruyère and Parmesan, reserving 4 tablespoons of each. When the cheese has melted enough to be stringy, spoon the macaroni into a lightly buttered ring mold; keep the mold warm in a hot water bath.

At the same time, prepare a thick tomato sauce: melt 2½ tablespoons of butter, stir in the flour, let it cook for five minutes without browning; then add the tomato purée, a little of the meat juice, salt, pepper, and mix well. Continue cooking for another fifteen minutes. Finish the sauce by adding about 4 teaspoons of butter cut into tiny pieces.

Peel the mushrooms; roll them in lemon juice; remove the stems of the large mushrooms and reserve the caps. Also, set aside the 12 tiny mushrooms.

Chop the rest of the mushrooms along with the stems from the large mushrooms. Add to them some breadcrumbs soaked in meat stock, some chopped parsley, 2 tablespoons of butter, the egg yolk, salt, pepper, and curry powder to taste. Mix well.

With this mixture stuff the large mushroom caps and arrange them, stuffing up, in an ovenproof casserole, buttered with 1 tablespoon of butter. Sprinkle on a little lemon juice and the rest of the mixed cheeses, dot with 1 tablespoon of butter, and bake in a slow oven for about twenty minutes.

Cook the 12 tiny mushrooms in the rest of the butter and some lemon juice and add them to the tomato sauce.

Unmold the macaroni ring onto a serving platter, fill the center with the tomato sauce, arrange the large stuffed mushrooms around the outside of the ring, and serve.

This is pleasant and pretty dish.

MACARONI AU GRATIN

A. MACARONI AU GRATIN WITHOUT CREAM:

For five people, use:

1/2 lb. macaroni
5 T. butter
3/4 C. grated Gruyère cheese
3/4 C. grated Parmesan cheese
7 T. coarse salt
3 qts. water

Boil the water; throw in the macaroni and the boiling will stop. Add the salt, let it boil up a couple of times, then set the pan over very low heat so that the water remains very hot without boiling. Let the macaroni poach only long enough to cook it perfectly, which should take anywhere from forty minutes to one hour depending on the freshness and the thickness of the macaroni. Drain it. In a buttered casserole arrange layers of macaroni, grated cheese, and butter, ending with butter.

Brown in the oven.

Macaroni prepared this way is very crisp.

B. MACARONI AU GRATIN WITH CREAM:

For six people, use:

1/2 lb. macaroni
1 C. heavy cream
4 T. butter
3/4 C. grated Gruyère cheese
3/4 C. grated Parmesan cheese
3 T. coarse salt
3 T. flour
3 qts. water
2 cloves
1 onion
nutmeg to taste

In the water put the onion stuck with the two cloves and wrapped in cheesecloth, add the salt and bring it to a boil. Throw in the macaroni and let it cook as in the preceding recipe.

Melt half the butter and stir in the flour. Season with nutmeg to taste, add the cream, all the Gruyère, and half the Parmesan cheese. Stir these together well and heat up without boiling.

Butter a casserole with 1 tablespoon of butter and in it arrange alternating layers of macaroni and sauce. Top with the rest of the Parmesan and the rest of the butter and brown in the oven.

This macaroni is soft and creamy under a browned crust and differs completely from the preceding recipe.

Cannelloni

Cannelloni are generally made out of noodle dough and they can be either large or small.

To prepare them, start by blanching them until they are three-fourths cooked, in either salted water or bouillon. They are then drained and cooled under cold, running water and dried in a cloth. Then they are stuffed—but take care not to break them, using either a paper cone or a pastry bag, or, simpler yet, split them lengthwise and roll them up around the stuffing. Thus stuffed, they are arranged side by side in a casserole and they are cooked, without boiling, in an appropriate sauce, which should complement the stuffing. They may also be arranged in a buttered casserole, sprinkled with breadcrumbs and Parmesan mixed, covered with melted butter, and browned in the oven for fifteen minutes.

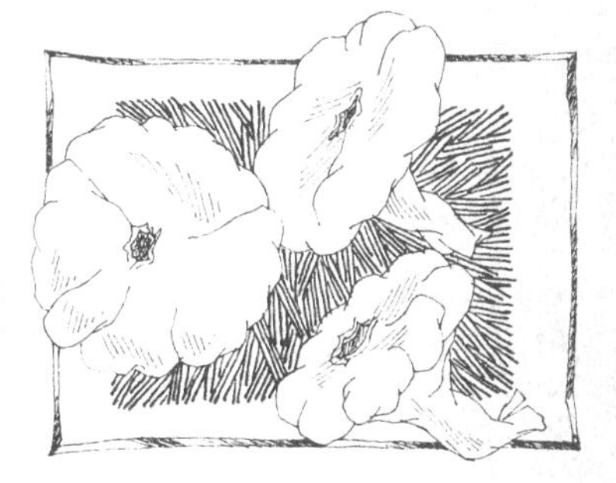

Stuffings for *cannelloni* may be made with or without meat. They may contain shellfish, fish, fish roes, or fish livers; red meat, pork, brains, sweetbreads (veal or lamb); chicken, chicken livers, or foie gras; feathered or furred game; vegetables; mushrooms, morels, or truffles. All these stuffings must be made with the basic ingredients precooked and must be bound with egg yolks. They may also consist of hashes or purées.

One can also prepare *cannelloni* out of semi-puff pastry, which are called *cannelons.*[1] The dough is cut into strips six to eight inches long and about one and a quarter inches wide, which are then rolled spiral fashion on conical cylinders or wooden dowels, taking care to make sure that the edges of the pastry are well sealed by moistening. They should be glazed with egg yolk and baked in a moderate oven for about fifteen minutes. These are then filled with very thick hashes or very stiff purées so that the stuffing does not fall out. They are served on a napkin-covered platter. Here are some examples of different types of *cannelon* stuffings.

MEATLESS

Salpicons (hashes):

- Mussels, shrimp, oysters, mushrooms with *sauce matelote*;
- Scallops, mussels, oysters, mushrooms with *sauce Mornay*;
- Pike, crayfish, mushrooms with *sauce Cardinal*;
- Whiting, crayfish, truffles with *sauce Nantua*;
- Filets of sole, mushrooms, truffles with *sauce normande*;
- Filets of sole, shrimp, mushrooms with *sauce homard*;
- Filets of brill, shrimp, oysters with a meatless tomato sauce;

Purées:

Shrimp, mushrooms, truffles with meatless *sauce veloutée;*
Pike, crayfish, morels with meatless *sauce Béchamel* made with crayfish butter;
Creamed lobster;
Carp roes, truffles poached in wine, with Parmesan;
Soft roes (milts), fish livers, shrimp with *sauce italienne;*

WITH MEAT

Salpicons (hashes):

Veal or lamb sweetbreads, brains, morels, asparagus tips, with *sauce demi-glace;*
Financière with madeira sauce;
White meat of chicken, pickled beef tongue, foie gras, with *sauce suprême;*
White meat of chicken, chicken livers, ham, truffles with *sauce suprême* made with Parmesan cheese;
Feathered game with truffles or not, with *sauce salmis;*

Purées:

Brains, crayfish with hollandaise sauce made with crayfish butter;
Chicken, pickled tongue, truffles with *sauce veloutée;*
Foie gras, truffles with madeira sauce;
Baked larks with port wine;
Pheasant, woodcook with *sauce périgueux;*
Woodcock with *sauce salmis;*
Gratin of hare with *sauce marinade;*

VEGETABLE

Salpicons:

Printanier with cream sauce;
Celery, cardoons *au jus* with tomato sauce;
Spinach, mushrooms with *sauce Mornay;*
Chicory with chicken velouté;
Asparagus tips, truffles with creamy Béchamel sauce;

Purées:

Mushrooms with *sauce Mornay* made with Chester cheese;
Morels with *sauce demi-glace;*
Truffles with *sauce perigueux.*

All these stuffings may be used for *barquettes, bouchées,* and raviolis, and also for filling tartlet shells.

NOTE

1. One may also prepare these *cannelons* using sweetened semi-puff pastry. These would be filled with custards, purées, and chopped fruits. They would be served as sweet desserts.

PÂTES À LA POCHE

Dropped Noodles

For six people, use:

$2\frac{1}{2}$ C. grated Parmesan cheese
1 C. very strong veal or chicken broth
6 eggs
flour
milk
salt

Break the eggs into a bowl and add as much flour as they can absorb. Salt lightly, moisten with some milk, and work the mixture so as to obtain a fairly soft dough. Put this into a noodle maker with medium-sized holes—or in a colander, through which you will drop threads of dough, about four inches long, into a kettle containing boiling broth or some slightly salted water.

As soon as the noodles are cooked they will rise to the surface of the liquid.

Remove them with a skimmer or slotted spoon, drain them well, and arrange them in a casserole in layers, alternating with the cheese and ending up with the cheese. Pour the veal and chicken broth over the noodles and brown them in the oven. Serve right from the casserole.

These noodles are delicious.

For variation, one could serve these dropped noodles with plain melted butter or sautéed in some butter along with some dry, sifted breadcrumbs.

Ravioli

For six people, use:

1. FOR THE DOUGH:

$1\frac{3}{4}$ C. hard wheat flour
7 T. milk
1 tsp. salt
1 egg
1 egg yolk

2. FOR THE STUFFING:

4 oz. chopped roast chicken breast
4 oz. chopped ham
4 oz. veal sweetbreads cooked in butter and chopped
3 T. heavy cream
2 truffles cooked in madeira and chopped
2 egg yolks
salt and pepper

3. COOKING AND ASSEMBLING:

bouillon
butter
grated Parmesan cheese
tomato sauce
meat broth

Ravioli are squares of dough containing a stuffing. Here is a good recipe for ravioli.

Pour the flour onto a board in the shape of a cone, break an egg into the top of the "crater," add the yolk, milk, and salt, and work the mixture into a very smooth dough. Let this rest for an hour at least, then roll it out to a quarter-inch thick. With a cookie cutter cut out forty-eight two-and-a-half-inch circles.

Prepare a stuffing using the chicken, ham, sweetbreads, truffles, salt, and pepper, and bind with the egg yolks.

Divide the dough into forty-eight little balls.

Place one little ball of stuffing in the middle of each round of dough, moisten the edges and fold them over into crescent shapes, and seal the edges with a crimping wheel.

Bring the broth to a boil, throw in the ravioli, and let them cook for about ten minutes. Take the pan off the high heat and put it to simmer very gently to poach the ravioli for another ten minutes. Drain them.

Arrange the ravioli in a serving dish, pour over them some butter which has been melted and heated until it is a nut-brown color. Sprinkle with grated Parmesan cheese and serve. Send along, at the same time, in a sauceboat, some tomato sauce to which you have added a little meat broth.

Ravioli which are to be served in soups are made half this size.

Tortellini, which are a Bolognese specialty, are ravioli which contain a less delicate stuffing; sometimes they are filled with a simple vegetable stuffing, and their main characteristic is that they are twisted over on themselves.

GNOCCHI

For six people, use:

1. *For the dough:*

1 C. all-purpose flour
2 C. grated Parmesan cheese
4 tsp. butter
1 tsp. coarse salt
black pepper to taste
1 qt. milk
2 C. water
3 eggs

2. *For the sauce:*

7 T. heavy cream
½ C. grated Parmesan cheese
3 T. butter
3 T. flour
1 tsp. coarse salt

Gnocchi are pastas using Parmesan cheese.

Here is a recipe which makes a good vegetable course for a family meal:

Preparing the dough.

In a saucepan, put the butter, water, salt and pepper and bring to a boil. Drop the flour in, all at once, stir, add the Parmesan, and mix with a wooden spoon for about one minute. Remove the pan from the heat and, stirring all the while, add the eggs, one by one, making sure each one is absorbed before adding the next.

Divide the dough into tiny marbles. Bring the milk to a boil and drop in these little dough marbles. The boiling will stop immediately. Take the pan off the high heat and leave the pan in a spot where the water will stay very hot without boiling. Let these cook like this for five minutes, then drain.

Strain the milk, which should have reduced by half, and reserve it.

Preparing the sauce.

In a saucepan, put 2 tablespoons of butter and the flour and let these cook together without browning; stir in the milk, add the cream and salt, and continue simmering another ten minutes.

Assembling.

With the rest of the butter, butter a casserole. In this arrange alternating layers of the little *gnocchi,* the sauce and the grated Parmesan, ending up with cheese.

Brown in the oven.

As a beverage, Meursault Goutte-d'Or, it seems to me, would be indicated.

GNOCCHI À LA SEMOULE

Gnocchi with Semolina

For six people, use:

2 C. hard wheat flour
14 T. butter
2 C. grated Parmesan cheese
1 tsp. salt
1 qt. milk
3 eggs

Bring the milk to a boil, drop in the semolina, then add 7 tablespoons of the butter and the salt. Let these cook, stirring often. Remove the pan from the heat, add 1 1/2 cups of grated Parmesan and the beaten eggs. Finish cooking without boiling.

Butter a marble surface or a baking sheet and spread the semolina mixture on it in a one-inch-thick layer. Let it cool.

Cut the cooled semolina into rectangular and heart-shaped pieces. Arrange these in alternating layers in a buttered casserole, sprinkle each layer with Parmesan cheese, add the rest of the butter, and brown the casserole in a hot oven.

Serve in the same dish set onto a cold platter for easier handling.

Gnocchi may be served alone as a vegetable course or as an accompaniment for meat. They are particularly good with veal cutlets and ham.

The same type of gnocchi may be made with cornmeal.

Polenta

Polenta, which is an Italian national dish, is a type of cornmeal mush.

Just cooked in water it is a rather coarse food.

It can be made much tastier by adding butter, grated Parmesan cheese, and sometimes some tomato sauce.

For sweet desserts this mush is prepared with milk.

Polenta generally accompanies dishes which have a sauce, such as ragoûts, *salmis,* civets, etc., but sometimes it is served alone. It can also be made into *croustades*, fritters, or soufflés, which are very popular in Italy.

KOLDUNY

For kolduny, use:

1. For the dough:

6 cups hard wheat flour
3 T. butter
3 tsp. salt
2 eggs
enough water to make a fairly stiff dough

2. For the stuffing:

2 lbs. juicy rump steak
1 lb. beef kidney suet
4 tsp. butter
4 tsp. salt
2 1/2 tsp. powdered marjoram
1 tsp. black pepper
1 onion

Kolduny, of Tartar origin, are, like ravioli (of which they were the precursors), squares of dough containing a filling or stuffing. But here the dough is less delicate and the stuffing is very simply poached at the same time as the dough in which it is wrapped. It consists of raw meats and fats.

With the dough ingredients, prepare a fairly elastic dough. Knead it and roll it out very thin, and cut it into three-inch diameter circles.

Chop the meat very, very fine (I recommend cutting the meat rather than putting it through a grinder, so as to avoid any loss of meat juice), and chop the suet.

Mince the onion and cook it in the butter without letting it brown.

Mix the meat, suet, onion, and butter from the pan, and the salt, pepper, and marjoram, so as to obtain a fairly soft, smooth stuffing.[1]

Prepare little balls of stuffing, arrange these on the pastry circles, then close these *kolduny* as you did the ravioli, leaving enough space inside so that the stuffings may swell without bursting their wrapping as they cook.

To cook the *kolduny*, plunge them into a large kettle of boiling, salted water in such a way that they do not touch each other. At first they will fall to the bottom of the pan and then they will rise to the surface. When they have risen, wait a few minutes, remove them, drain them, and serve them at once, very hot, on hot plates.

Kolduny must be eaten with a spoon. They give off an aromatic juice which perfumes the mouth. This sensation would be lost if they were cut into with a fork.

Kolduny, very popular in Lithuania, are thought to be a little heavy. But those who like them and have a robust stomach are enthusiastic about them, and the proportions indicated above would hardly be sufficient for two moderate Lithuanian appetites.

In Lithuania, *kolduny* are served at the beginning of a meal, almost like an hors-d'oeuvre. Each guest immediately drinks a glass of old brandy *(starka)*; then comes some very hot borscht; and then one attacks the main courses.

Kolduny may also be cooked in a boiling hot fry-bath made with fresh suet, for a few minutes.

NOTE

1. If the stuffing is not soft enough add some meat juice or stock to it.

KOLDUNY AU GRATIN

Put the raw *kolduny* in a skillet with some butter and let them brown without allowing them to stick.

Arrange them in an ovenproof casserole, cover them with a good quantity of cream, and coat them with a heavy layer of grated Parmesan cheese and breadcrumbs which have been browned in butter. Put them in a hot oven for twenty minutes and serve.

YORKSHIRE PUDDING

For six people, use:

2 C. flour
5 T. beef or veal kidney suet or a mixture of both
3 tsp. salt
4 eggs
fat from roast or lard
nutmeg

Yorkshire pudding is very popular in England as an accompaniment for roast beef, especially roast sirloin.

Beat together all the ingredients except for the roast beef fat or lard. Pour it into a flat baking dish containing the smoking hot fat and bake it in the oven for about twenty-five minutes. Then put the pudding into the roasting pan with the meat so that it can absorb the juices from the roast.

At serving time cut this pudding into squares, triangles or diamond shapes and arrange them around the meat.

Yorkshire pudding may also be served alone as a vegetable course.

BOULETTES AU FROMAGE BLANC

Cheese Balls

For four people, use:

1 lb. very well drained cottage or farmer cheese
10 T. butter
¾ C. dry, sifted breadcrumbs
⅓ C. wholewheat flour
1 T. table salt
3 eggs
2 egg whites

In a bowl put the cheese, flour, salt, egg yolks, and egg whites. Mix well. Add 3 tablespoons of butter, melted in a double boiler, and work the mixture so as to get a very smooth, semi-fluid mixture without lumps.

Boil the salted water, using 3 teaspoons of salt per quart, spoon up the dough with either a soup or dessert spoon, and plunge it into the boiling, salted water. Each spoonful will form a little ball.

Remove these balls as they rise to the surface, drain them in a colander, and separate them from each other. Roll them in breadcrumbs.

Heat the rest of the butter in a heatproof casserole, spoon in the little balls, and brown them on all sides and serve them in the casserole.

These little balls, properly prepared, should be very crisp outside and soft inside. They can take the place of a vegetable course.

For variation, one could first dip these little balls in a mixture of egg white and grated cheese (either Gruyère or Parmesan) and then in the dry, sifted breadcrumbs. The procedure would be exactly the same as in the first part of the preceding recipe; but, once the little balls have been rolled in the egg white and cheese and then in the breadcrumbs, they would be fried in a deep, hot fry-bath.

They should be served with tomato sauce.

These preparations are known in Poland as *kluski*.

One could add bacon or ham which has been blanched, coarsely chopped and sautéed in butter, to the dough; but in that case one would use less salt.

These *kluski* are very tasty.

GOUGÈRE BOURGUIGNONNE

Cheese Puff

For eight people, use:

5 C. water
5 1/3 C. flour
1 C. butter
8 oz. Gruyère cheese
8 eggs
salt

Dice the cheese into half-inch squares. Do not grate it. In a saucepan put the water, butter, and salt and bring to a boil. Throw in the flour and stir with a wooden spoon. Continue cooking and stirring over moderate heat until the floury taste has disappeared, which should take about a half hour.

Take the pan off the heat, let the dough cool a little, then break the eggs in, one by one, stirring well until each is absorbed before adding the next one. As soon as the temperature of the dough allows, knead it by hand. The dough must be very smooth but not too heavy. Only then add the cheese and mix once more.

Spoon the dough onto a baking sheet, in a ring. Bake it for forty-five minutes. It is essential not to open the oven door until the dough has risen completely—otherwise it will deflate. The success of this dish depends on that.

Gougère may be served either hot or cold.

Quiches

Quiches are types of pies or tortes or flans which are very popular in Lorraine, where they are served as entrées.

One uses, to make the crust, either bread dough, flaky pastry, puff or semi-puff pastry, or even a pastry made with potato starch.

One makes quiches with *crème fraîche* and eggs; with cream and onions and poppy seeds; with cream, eggs, and bacon or ham seasoned with nutmeg, etc.

One may also prepare quiches for dessert: quiche with cream, flavored with orange-flower water; quiche with noodles and cream, flavored with vanilla; quiche with rice, flavored with vanilla. etc.

QUICHE AU FROMAGE ET AU BACON

Quiche with Cheese and Bacon

Here is an interesting quiche: The crust is made of pre-baked puff pastry. The filling is made up of thin slices of bacon (blanched to remove any excess salt), fried in butter, alternating in the quiche with thinly shredded Gruyère cheese—all these drowned in a Mornay sauce and browned in the oven.

RIZ SEC[1]

Dry Rice

Which is the best rice?

Opinions are divided. Rice from Novara is excellent, those of Charleston and Calcutta are equally very good, and the rest follow.

In France rice is not very popular because it is often poorly prepared. Indeed, it is not uncommon to be served, under the name of rice, a glutinous, colloidal mass, which has nothing appetizing about it.

Here is how it should be prepared:

First, wash the rice in tepid water without soaking it. Then rain the rice into a large saucepan, three-fourths full of boiling, salted water (3 quarts of water and 2 tablespoons of coarse salt for a half-pound of rice).

The rice must be cooked in an open saucepan and the cooking should last from ten to twenty-five minutes according to the type of rice used (Piedmont rice is one of those which cooks the quickest). The water must boil rapidly enough during the whole cooking time to keep the grains of rice agitated so as to keep them from sticking to one another or adhering to the saucepan. To recognize the psychological moment when the rice is just perfect, one must, as the cooking progresses (especially during the last few minutes), take, from time to time, a few grains of rice on a spoon and bite into it. This will soon make it possible to gauge the cooking time necessary to obtain perfect rice.

When the rice is cooked—that is, when it is tender but still firm and not hard—drain it quickly and spread it out on a platter or baking sheet in a layer no thicker than one inch. Let it dry in front of the open oven, stirring it once or twice to make sure that all the grains are drying out.

The rice should be dry, not crisp, which might happen if it is left too long. Two or three minutes more or less can make the difference.

Lightly spoon the rice onto a platter, in a pyramid, using a wooden spatula which you slide underneath the grains so as to lift them without crushing.

Rice thus prepared is a good accompaniment for dishes which have a sauce.

NOTE

1. Another name for this is *riz à l'indienne* or Indian-style rice.

For six people, use:

2 C. water
1/2 C. Carolina rice
10 T. butter
salt and pepper

RIZ CRÉOLE

Creole Rice

Wash the rice, drain it, put it in a saucepan with the water, 5 tablespoons of butter, salt, and pepper. Let it cook over high heat for eighteen to twenty minutes. Separate the rice grains, add the rest of the butter, heat up for a moment to melt the butter, and mix well.

One may substitute lard for the butter or even chicken or goose fat.

For six people, use:

4 1/2 C. strong beef or veal stock
1/2 lb. rice
8 T. butter
5 oz. beef marrow
2/3 C. grated Gruyère cheese (opt.)
2 medium shallots
1 medium onion
salt and pepper

RIZ AU GRAS

Rice with Meat Broth

Chop the shallots and onion.

Wash the rice and let it soak in cold water for one hour. Drain it and dry it in a towel.

In a saucepan, put the butter, marrow, shallots, and onion. Let these cook together without browning, strain through a sieve, add the rice to the butter, and mix well. Spread the rice out in a saucepan, sprinkle it with several spoonfuls of broth, and heat it up in the uncovered pan.

As soon as the broth has been absorbed, shake the pan so as to separate the grains of rice which might have stuck to the bottom of the pan. Moisten again with broth and continue doing this until all the stock has been absorbed.

While it is cooking, add the salt and pepper—only after having tasted it, because the seasoning needed depends on that in the broth. At the last minute add the grated cheese, mix well, and serve.

For four people, use:

1/2 lb. rice
7 T. butter
3 T. coarse salt
3 qts. water
lemon juice (optional)
table salt and pepper

RIZ AU BEURRE CLARIFIÉ, À L'ÉTOUFFÉE

Rice Smothered in Clarified Butter

Wash the rice in cold water and blanch it for ten minutes in the water salted with the coarse salt and flavored or not with lemon juice. Run it under cold water and drain it.

Melt the butter in a saucepan, skim off the foam, and decant the clear butter. Put it back on the heat, add the rice, season with salt and pepper to taste, and finish cooking it in a moderate oven in a closed pan. This will take about twenty-five minutes.

Thus prepared, the rice should have separate grains, slightly swollen but not browned.

Rice smothered in clarified butter may be served alone or as a garnish. It is one of the best accompaniments for pan-broiled steak.

RIZ SAUTÉ AU BEURRE NOISETTE

Rice Sautéed in Nut-Brown Butter

For six people, use:

1⅓ C. rice
1 C. butter
3 T. coarse salt
3 qts. water
table salt and pepper

Wash the rice without soaking it. Blanch it for ten minutes in water and coarse salt. Run it under cold water and drain it.

Put the butter in a frying pan, let it melt and brown lightly. Add the rice, the table salt and pepper to taste, and sauté it for about ten minutes. All the butter must have been absorbed.

Rice sautéed in *noisette* butter has grains which are not swollen; they are firm but not crisp, and they are shiny and golden colored because of the butter.

It is excellent.

Steamed Rice

Steamed rice is prepared in a special two-part steamer. The top part of the steamer has holes in the bottom and it fits snugly over the bottom part.

In the bottom part put well-seasoned consommé and some red meat and some chicken which has been cut into pieces and pre-browned. The top section gets the rice which has been rinsed in cold water and drained. Moisten with either melted butter or some good melted roast beef fat, color with a little saffron and put the cover on tight. The rice will cook in the steam from the liquid below for about an hour.

Serve, at the same time, but separately, the rice from the top part and the ragoût from the bottom part.

Risotto

Risotto is an Italian rice dish which is prepared more or less in the same way as one prepares rice in meat stock, but the cheese which is used in this case is always Parmesan.

All combinations listed under the recipe for Leg of Lamb with Risotto are applicable.

Risotto *à la milanaise* is a risotto flavored with saffron and to which mushrooms have been added.

Risotto à *la napolitaine* is a risotto with tomato purée (1 cup of tomato purée for 1/2 pound of rice).

Risotto à *la piémontaise* is a risotto made with Piedmont truffles.

PILAF

For six people, use:

2 C. well seasoned beef, lamb, and chicken broth
1/2 lb. long-grain rice
3/4 C. butter

Pilaf is a recipe of rice cooked in meat stock, of Egyptian origin, which went from Egypt to Persia and then was introduced into Europe by the Turks.

Primitive pilaf was prepared with mutton broth and mutton fat. This is how it is prepared by the peoples from the Balkan peninsula.

In more elaborate cuisine, butter is substituted for the mutton fat and beef, lamb, or chicken broth is used instead of mutton broth. The rice used is generally long-grain Egyptian rice.

Here is a precise recipe for preparing a simple pilaf:

Wash the rice several times in hot water (long-grain Egyptian rice is generally dirty), dry it in a towel, then brown it lightly in butter.

Bring the broth to a boil, rain in the rice, and let it cook only until the liquid has absorbed, without letting the rice stick to the pan.

Melt the rest of the butter, let it brown lightly, pour it over the rice, cover, and keep the saucepan over moderate heat for twenty minutes or so. Stir it from time to time to avoid having the rice grains stick together. Serve.

The grains must be separate as are grains of sand.

One may also add to pilaf either eggplant, tomatoes, okra, *petits pois*, sweet green peppers, garlic, raisins, etc.

Pilaf is often served with dark meats, especially lamb, or with chicken, game or shellfish.

When it is served with meat, one uses less butter than when it is to be served alone.

PILAF AU CURRY

For six people, use:

2 C. water or chicken broth, lightly salted
1 C. rice
10 T. butter
2 onions
4 tsp. salt
pepper
spices to taste
curry

Peel and chop the onions and cook them in four tablespoons of the butter. Add the water or broth and salt and let them cook.

Wash the rice, drain it, dry it in a cloth, and cook it in the rest of the butter until lightly browned; then pour the onion broth over it, through a sieve. Add the pepper, some spices, and curry to taste.

Cook it for twenty minutes over fairly high heat, making sure that the rice does not stick together.

To this rice one may add green pepper, prawns, scallops, etc.
One serves *pilaf au curry* as an accompaniment to fish, eggs, and fowl.

POMMES DE TERRE FRITES

Fried Potatoes

The best frying potatoes are the so-called Holland potatoes.

After having peeled the potatoes, they are cut according to choice either in wedges (large or small), or thick or thin slices, or julienne strips of varying sizes (straw potatoes being the smallest), or very, very thin slices (potato chips). They are then washed, dried in a towel, and plunged into a large hot fry-bath, containing either suet or oil. After several minutes of cooking, one shakes the fry-bath to even up the temperature. As soon as the potatoes float to the surface, they are ready. They should have acquired a golden color. They are then removed with a skimmer, sprinkled with salt, and served immediately.

Cooking time varies from eight to twelve minutes, according to how they are cut and whether one likes them very crisp or not.

Fried potatoes may be served alone, with or without sauce, or they can be served as a garnish.

POMMES DE TERRE CHIP

Potato Chips

Peel the potatoes on a vegetable slicer, making the thinnest possible slices. Wash them under running water, stirring and washing until the water becomes completely clear.

Drain them, dry them in a towel, plunge them—ten to twelve slices at a time, no more—into a large boiling hot fry-bath. They should cook almost instantly and become crisp without turning brown.

Using a skimmer, remove them from the fry-bath, sprinkle them with salt, and serve immediately.

Because of their thinness and because they have been washed, these potato chips have lost a large proportion of their starch, and the little that remains has been transformed into dextrine or soluble starch, which makes them easy to digest.

Potato chips have an exquisite taste and they are a pretty garnish for all types of meats.

This is an ideal food for diabetics.

For four people, use:

1¼ lb. peeled and evenly sliced potatoes
10 oz. blanched white part of leek
9 T. butter
4 oz. fresh suet
2 tsp. coarse salt
1 tsp. table salt
1 T. chopped parsley

POMMES DE TERRE SAUTÉES

Sautéed or Pan-Fried Potatoes

The methods used for preparing sautéed potatoes may be grouped according to whether one uses cooked or raw potatoes. When one uses cooked potatoes, either boiled or steamed, it is preferable to sauté them while they are hot because they absorb the fat better.

One may sauté raw or cooked potatoes either in butter, oil, or fat; either alone or with other substances, notably onions *(pommes de terre à la lyonnaise)*, mushrooms, truffles, etc.

Here is a recipe for potatoes sautéed in fat, with leeks:

Wash the potatoes, slice them into thin slices on a vegetable slicer, and put them in a towel with the coarse salt. Shake them lightly and leave them in contact with the salt for ten minutes or so, in order for them to render any excess water; then dry them.

Melt the pork fat in a frying pan or skillet, over low heat. Strain the fat. Raise the heat, and when the fat is very hot add the potatoes and sauté them so as to get them browned evenly and soft to the touch. The time needed to achieve this is about twenty minutes, during which the potatoes should be shaken up and turned six times.

Brown the leeks in 7 tablespoons of butter so as to give them the same color as the potatoes.

Mix the leeks and potatoes; the latter must not wait.

For three people, use:

1 lb. tiny, peeled, new potatoes
½ C. (8 T.) butter
salt

POMMES DE TERRE RISSOLÉES AU BEURRE

Slowly Pan-Fried Potatoes

Pommes de terre rissolées are potatoes which have been sautéed over very, very low heat.

Use a large enough skillet so that the potatoes may lie in it in a single layer. Put in the butter, and when it is hot add the potatoes, letting them simmer for one hour in the open skillet without letting the butter brown. Shake the pan frequently. Salt them when they are cooked.

After one hour all the butter must have been absorbed. Serve at once.

These potatoes, soaked with butter, crusty on the outside and soft on the inside, are delicious.

POMMES DE TERRE SAUTÉES OU POMMES DE TERRE RISSOLÉES, À LA SAUCE

Sautéed or Slowly Pan-Fried Potatoes with Sauce

For six people, use:

2 lbs. potatoes
1 C. butter
1 C. heavy cream
1 T. wine vinegar
2 T. chopped *fines herbes*
2 tsp. table salt
garlic

Sauté or rissolé the potatoes in 10 tablespoons of butter, but do not salt them.

At the same time, prepare the sauce.

Put the rest of the butter in a saucepan, let it melt, add minced garlic to taste, heat it gently for a few moments, and strain. Then, to this herb butter, add the cream, vinegar, chopped *fines herbes*, and salt. Heat up once more, mix well and pour this sauce over the potatoes. Spoon everything into a serving dish.

Sautéed artichoke hearts, Jerusalem artichokes, celeriac, and salsify may be served this same way.

POMMES DE TERRE ANNA

Potatoes Anna

For six people, use:

2 lbs. potatoes
1¾ C. butter
4 tsp. table salt
black pepper to taste

Potatoes Anna are potatoes which are steam-baked or "smothered" in butter.

Peel the potatoes; slice them very thin on a vegetable slicer or with a vegetable knife. Wash them in cold water, drain them, and dry them in a towel.

Melt the butter and clarify it by skimming off the foam.

Take a thick, round, copper casserole six inches in diameter and three inches high, butter it with a brush, fit a circle of parchment paper in the bottom, and butter it well. This will help in the unmolding. Arrange the potato slices on the bottom of the pan in a circular, overlapping pattern (as you would apples for a tart). Arrange the bottom layer, then use vertical slices around the edge and, last, fill in the center. Pour butter over the potatoes as you go, using three-fourths of the clarified butter, and season each layer as you go, with salt, and pepper.

Cover the pan with its cover and put it in a slow oven. When the contents has flattened slightly, add the rest of the butter in several times[1] until the potatoes are cooked. This should take one hour. Unmold, remove the paper and serve.

Potatoes Anna should have the appearance of a rather firm cake, golden on the outside, tender and melting on the inside. It makes a very good vegetable course and may also be served as an accompaniment to roast beef, saddle of lamb, leg of lamb, etc.

By substituting, for the sliced potatoes, some straw-cut potatoes,

one would have an even crustier cake, which has been named *pommes de terre Champs-Élysées.*

By adding some grated cheese to *Pommes de Terre Anna*, one would have *pommes de terre Voisin.*

By mixing into the *pommes de terre Champs-Élysées* a julienne of truffles, one would have what is called *pommes de terre des gourmands.*

NOTE

1. It is best to add the butter in small quantities at a time; otherwise it might overflow during the cooking.

POMMES DE TERRE GEORGETTE

Georgette Potatoes

Potatoes Georgette are potatoes stuffed with a meatless stuffing.

Take some large baking potatoes, peel, wash, and wipe them, and bake them in the oven until done.

Cut a slice off—lengthwise and about one-fourth of their width—to form a cover. Hollow out the potatoes, leaving only a thin layer of pulp. Fill the hollow with a hash made of crayfish tails, oysters, mushrooms, and truffles, bound with a thick Nantua sauce. Put on the cover, arrange the potatoes on a napkin-covered platter and serve.

This is a lovely hot hors-d'oeuvre.

POMMES DE TERRE AU GRATIN

Potatoes au Gratin

For three people, use:

1 lb. peeled and sliced potatoes
1¾ C. bouillon
2½ C. shredded Gruyère cheese
5 T. butter
1 tsp. salt
pepper to taste
breadcrumbs

Here are three very different recipes for potatoes *au gratin*:

First with bouillon:

Butter a casserole; in it arrange alternating layers of sliced, raw potatoes, slivers of Gruyère cheese, and tiny dots of butter. Season each layer with salt and pepper and end up with a layer of cheese.

Moisten with the bouillon without covering the top layer of cheese. Sprinkle on some breadcrumbs and bake the dish in a slow oven until all the liquid is absorbed. This should take about one hour. This is known as *gratin savoyard.*

Second, with cream:

Steam the potatoes.

Peel the onions and chop them. Cook them gently in three tablespoons of butter, stir in the flour, and let this all brown lightly. Now add the cream, meat glaze, salt, and pepper, and simmer for five minutes.

When the potatoes are cooked, slice them, arrange them in a buttered casserole, separating each layer of potatoes with a little grated Parmesan and some of the onion sauce. End up with a layer of cheese. Sprinkle on the breadcrumbs, dot with the remaining butter, and brown the casserole in the oven for about twenty minutes.

For three people, use:

1 lb. peeled potatoes
1 C. cream
5 T. butter
½ C. grated Parmesan cheese
1 small onion
2 T. meat glaze
2 T. flour
1 tsp. salt
1 T. chopped parsley
pepper to taste
dry, sifted breadcrumbs

Third, with eggs:

Scald the milk.

Butter a casserole, arrange the potatoes in it in layers. Dot each layer with butter and season with salt and pepper. Pour in the milk and bake the casserole in a slow oven until the liquid has been completely absorbed.

Beat the eggs with the cream and pour the mixture over the potatoes. Finish cooking in a slow oven.

Serve in the casserole.

To make *gratin dauphinois,* one cooks the potatoes with the milk into which the eggs have been beaten.

For three people, use:

1 lb. peeled and uniformly sliced potatoes
1⅓ C. milk
½ C. cream
5 T. butter
2 tsp. salt
pepper to taste
3 eggs

POMMES DE TERRE DUCHESSE

Duchesse Potatoes

For four people, use:

2 lbs. potatoes
1⅓ C. butter
4 T. heavy cream
4 egg yolks
salt and pepper

Duchesse potatoes are excellent potato croquettes.

Peel the potatoes, cut them up, and cook them in salted water without allowing them to get mushy and fall apart. Drain them, dry them out, and rice them or mash them. Add to them 5 tablespoons of butter, the cream, and the egg yolks. Season with salt and pepper to taste, and mix well.

With this mixture, mold some little balls the size of a walnut, which you will cook in the rest of the butter so as to obtain crusty, golden brown potato balls.

For variation, one could add, to the above mixture, ½ to ¾ cup of grated cheese: Gruyère, Parmesan, or Chester.

One would then have *pommes de terre Duchesse au fromage.*

For another variation, one could, to the above mixture for Duchesse potatoes, add about 1 cup of thick, red tomato purée for each 2 pounds of potatoes. These would then be known as *pommes de terre Marquise.*

These croquettes should be forced through a pastry bag onto a buttered baking sheet in the shape of a meringue or an oval. They should be baked in the oven.

Potatoes Duchesse are served either as a vegetable course or as a garnish.

They make a good accompaniment for roasted meats and dishes which have a sauce.

BEIGNETS DE POMMES DE TERRE

Potato Fritters

Peel and grate the potatoes. Drain the pulp, then add chopped parsley, salt, and pepper.

Prepare a light fritter batter (1/2 cup of batter per pound of drained potato pulp). Mix this well with the grated potatoes.

Make some tiny balls of the mixture with a potato cutter. Throw them into a boiling hot fry-bath and let them cook for about ten minutes. Remove the little balls with a skimmer, arrange them on a napkin-covered platter, surround with a ring of fried parsley, and serve.

These fritters make an excellent vegetable course and a very good accompaniment for roasted or broiled meats.

PURÉE DE POMMES DE TERRE

Mashed Potatoes

For three people, use:

1 lb. peeled, floury-type potatoes
1 lb. butter
2 tsp. salt

The best way of preparing mashed potatoes is to my mind the following:

Sprinkle the potatoes with salt, steam them, put them through a ricer or mash them in a hot saucepan, add the butter, mix well, taste, add salt if necessary and serve immediately.

For three people, use:

1 lb. peeled, floury-type potatoes
1 C. milk
10 T. butter
2 tsp. salt

For variation, one could prepare mashed potatoes which would be a little less costly, but also very good.

Steam the potatoes as above, put them in a saucepan over low heat, and mash them with a fork, adding the butter as you go. Then, little by little, add the scalded milk, beating the purée until it is absolutely smooth and lumpless. Taste, season again if necessary, and serve.

PATATE

Sweet Potatoes

The sweet potato, which originally came from India, is today an important crop in all the tropical countries and even in France in the Mediterranean region.

It is a tuber of the Convolvulaceae family, having tender and slightly sweet flesh. There are several varieties: red, white, yellow, and lavender.

All the recipes for potatoes may be applied to the sweet potato. The red and purple varieties are especially suitable for sweet desserts.

Jerusalem Artichokes

Jerusalem artichokes originally came from South America. They belong to the Compositae family, and are closely related to the sunflower.

In cooking, one uses the tuberous rootstocks, which have a taste reminiscent of the artichoke.

The cooking method most recommended for the Jerusalem artichoke is baking, which removes the excess water.

They may be prepared with butter, cream, or bouillon, or served with Béchamel, hollandaise or mousseline sauce. They may be puréed, fried, or made into soups, etc.

PURÉE DE MARRONS

Chestnut Purée

For six people, use:

1 1/2 lbs. chestnuts
2/3 C. heavy cream
1/2 C. butter
1 T. salt
1 qt. milk or water (to taste)

Scald the chestnuts, peel them, and cook them in either milk or water, with some salt. Cooking time is generally about thirty minutes. Put them through a ricer or vegetable mill into a hot saucepan. Add the butter and cream, little by little, stirring constantly, without boiling. Taste and serve.

Chestnut purée is a good accompaniment for light meats such as very young lamb, veal, goose, and game.

FÈVES FRAÎCHES

Fresh Favas

Favas are an excellent vegetable which may be served:

1. *As an hors-d'oeuvre.* Very young, raw, freshly hulled, served with fresh butter.

2. À l'anglaise *(English style).* Freshly hulled, cooked in salted water, drained and served as is, under a napkin, as one would do with new potatoes. Butter as an accompaniment.

3. *In butter.* Hulled, skins removed just at serving time, they

are cooked in salted water flavored with a little savory. When they are done, they are well drained, and butter is added and barely allowed to melt. They are served sprinkled with minced savory.

4. *With cream.* Having cooked the favas as above and having drained them well, one adds heavy cream instead of butter and then sprinkles them with the chopped savory.

5. *Puréed.* After having cooked them in salted water seasoned with savory, they are prepared like mashed potatoes.

PETITS POIS

Green Peas

The classic recipes for preparing peas are the following: *à l'anglaise* (English style), with melted butter; *à la française* (French style), cooked with onions in salted water, then sweetened and served with a thickened butter sauce; *aux laitues* (with lettuce), thickened with cream and egg yolks; *au lard* (with salt pork); *à l'étouffée* (smothered), with butter, as in *potée fermière.*

Here are two new and delicious ways of preparing them:

For four people, use:

4 lbs. young, fresh, unhulled, good quality peas, yielding about 1 qt. shelled
1/2 lb. peeled carrots (red part only)
1/2 C. butter
1/2 C. cream
1 tsp. table salt
1 chopped heart of lettuce
1 onion
1 bunch parsley
granulated sugar

Hull the peas, setting aside a handful of the hulls, selecting tender ones without spots. Remove the tough inner lining and both ends.

In a saucepan, put the butter and the diced carrots, the trimmed pea hulls, cover, and cook over low heat for fifteen minutes.

Now add the peas, lettuce, onion, bunch of parsley, salt, and sugar to taste, and continue cooking over low heat for an hour.

Remove the onion and the bunch of parsley, thicken the sauce with cream, and serve.

When the peas are of top quality, the carrots and shells are generally enough to sweeten them.

For four people, use:

1/2 lb. carrots
1 C. cream
1/2 C. butter
1 tsp. salt
1 qt. freshly hulled peas
2 small bunches asparagus tips
1 onion
1 bunch parsley
granulated sugar

In a saucepan, put the butter, the coarsely cut-up carrots, cover and cook over low heat for fifteen minutes. Then, add the peas, the onion, the parsley, and salt and sugar to taste, and continue cooking over low heat for one hour.

At the same time, cook the asparagus tips in salted water, drain them, and mash them.

Remove the carrot, onion, and parsley bunch from the saucepan. Mix the asparagus purée and the cream with the peas; heat without boiling; then pour into a vegetable dish.

POIS CHICHES AUX ÉPINARDS

Chick Peas with Spinach

Put the chick peas to soak for twenty-four hours in a large quantity of salted water. Drain them. Then, after having put them in some fresh, cold, salted water, bring the water to a boil and let them simmer.

Cook the chopped tomato, garlic, and parsley in the olive oil. Pour this mixture into the saucepan with the chick peas.

Pound or grind the nuts with the hard-boiled egg yolk, add the saffron or cinnamon and pepper or paprika to taste. Chop the egg white and add it to the chick peas along with the pounded mixture and finish cooking everything together.

Drain the cooking liquid off the chick peas, and in it cook the spinach. Drain it and boil down the cooking liquid.

In a serving dish, arrange alternate layers of chick peas and spinach and sprinkle over a little of the concentrated cooking liquid. Serve.

For four people, use:

1 lb. chick peas
1 lb. spinach
8 almonds or hazel nuts
1 large tomato
1 hard-boiled egg
olive oil
garlic
parsley
saffron or cinnamon
pepper or paprika
salt

One could brown the dish in the oven. All that would be necessary would be to sprinkle the top with dry, sifted breadcrumbs or with a mixture of crumbs and grated Gruyère cheese, dot the top with butter, and then brown in the oven.

Green Stringbeans

The classic preparations for stringbeans are the following: *à l'anglaise* (English style), with melted butter; *sautés au beurre* (sautéed in butter), either rissoléed or not, after having been blanched in boiling, salted water; *à la poulette*; *au jus* (with meat stock); *à l'étouffée* (smothered), in butter, as in *potée fermière*; in salad.

HARICOTS VERTS À LA CRÈME

Creamed Green Stringbeans

Creamed stringbeans may be prepared in different ways.

A. WITH SWEET CREAM:

Cook the beans in an open pan, in 3 quarts of water and 1 tablespoon of coarse salt. Remove them as soon as they are flexible and drain them.

In the saucepan, put the butter, the beans, the cream, the parsley, salt, and pepper, and heat up. Mix well and serve.

For four people, use:
1 lb. young, tender, green stringbeans
10 T. sweet cream
4 T. butter
1 T. chopped parsley
1 tsp. table salt
to taste pepper

B. WITH SOURED CREAM:

In the recipe above, substitute some slightly soured cream for the fresh sweet cream and add some meat glaze.

For four people, use:

1 lb. young, green stringbeans
3/4 C. bouillon
1/2 C. cream
6 T. butter
1 T. flour
1 T. minced parsley
salt and pepper

C. À LA CRÈME, À L'ÉTOUFFÉE (BRAISED IN CREAM):

In a porcelain casserole, put 4 tablespoons of butter, the beans, parsley, and onion. Mix well. Cover the casserole tightly and bake in the oven for fifteen minutes. Then, pour in the bouillon, season with salt and pepper, being careful to take into account the saltiness of the bouillon. Continue cooking very slowly for an hour and a half. Work the softened butter and the flour together with a fork or fingers, add this mixture to the beans, and cook for another half hour. A few minutes before serving add the cream and serve.

Italian green beans may be prepared this same way.

HARICOTS ÉCOSSÉS

Hulled Haricot Beans

Haricot beans—white, red, mottled, etc.—and limas are used either fresh or dried. When fresh, they are cooked directly in seasoned and flavored boiling water. If they are dried, they must be soaked several hours in cold water, then drained and put in more cold water and cooked.

There are numerous ways of preparing these beans: plain with butter; with cream; *à la maître d'hôtel*; they are first sautéed in butter, then more butter is added along with chopped parsley and lemon juice; *au jus* (with meat broth); *au velouté* (with velouté sauce); with fat or salt pork; *au maigre* (meatless), with onions, tomatoes, white sauce; with tomatoes and salt pork; *à la lyonnaise,* with minced onions and cooked in butter; *à la bretonne,* with minced onions cooked to a glaze, meat broth or meat juice, and parsley; *à la provençal,* with oil, garlic, and mashed anchovies; *à la moutarde,* with thickened meat broth, butter, and mustard; *à l'étuvée* (steamed); *au gratin*; in croquettes; in salad.

For six people, use:

10 oz. saddle of lamb, trimmed of fat and boned
1/2 lb. bacon
1 1/4 C. good red wine
2 large peeled carrots
1/2 C. (1 stick) butter
1 peeled onion
1 peeled turnip
3 T. flour
1 T. coarse salt
4 peeled shallots
freshly ground black pepper to taste
1 qt. fresh, hulled red beans
bouquet garni **(parsley, thyme, bay leaf)**
quatre épices

HARICOTS ROUGES À L'ÉTUVÉE

Steam-Cooked Red Beans

In a *cocotte* put 4 tablespoons of butter and the flour. Cook until lightly browned. Then, add the carrots, turnip, onion, shallots, and *bouquet garni*. Stir until they take on color, then add the pepper and pour in the wine. Let this mixture simmer for about three-quarters of an hour.

At the same time, cook the beans in 2 quarts of water salted with the coarse salt. Stop the cooking as soon as they feel tender to the touch, so as to be sure and keep the beans whole.

Keep everything hot.

Slice the bacon very thin, or dice it, as desired. Blanch it for two minutes in boiling water to remove any excess salt, dry it in a towel, then cook it in the rest of the butter.

Either broil or braise the saddle of lamb and slice it into six servings.

Remove the carrots, turnip, onion, shallots, and *bouquet* from the *cocotte*. In their place put the drained beans, add about 1 cup of the bean cooking liquid, the bacon and its pan juices, the lamb and its cooking juices skimmed of fat, and a little *quatre épices* to taste. Let this all simmer very slowly for one hour. Serve.

PURÉE DE HARICOTS ROUGES AU VIN

Red Bean Purée with Wine

For six people, use:

1½ lbs. dried red kidney beans
2 C. red wine
13 oz. lightly salted, unsmoked bacon
10 T. butter
3 T. flour
1 carrot
1 onion
bouquet garni
salt and pepper

Soak the beans in water for twelve hours; then cook them in a sufficient quantity of water to cover them; season with salt and pepper. When they are done, remove them and mash them.

Cook the wine, carrot, onion, and *bouquet garni* together until the wine has reduced somewhat. Strain.

Slice the bacon and fry it in a little butter in a frying pan.

Make a roux with some butter and flour, stir in the reduced wine, add the mashed beans, the cooking juices from the bacon pan, and a suitable quantity of bean liquid. Mix well. At the last minute add the rest of the butter and let it barely melt.

Spoon the purée into a serving dish, garnish with the fried bacon, and serve.

Mashed red beans may be served as a vegetable course or as an accompaniment to broiled meats, particularly game.

When red beans are to be served with broiled game, one should first cook the meat trimmings in the wine and, if the meat has been marinated, add the marinade to the wine, adjusting the overall quantity of wine according to the recipe. No more than 2 cups of wine should be used for 1½ lbs. of beans. The rest of the recipe remains the same.

SOJA AU JUS

Soya Bean Sprouts with Meat Broth

For four people, use:

2 lbs. soya bean sprouts
veal or chicken broth
3 T. butter
3 T. white wine
salt and pepper

Wash the bean sprouts in cold water and drain them.

Melt the butter in a saucepan and throw in the sprouts, stirring them for a few minutes. Add the broth, the white wine, and season to taste with salt and pepper. Let them simmer for about twenty minutes.

Serve.

Lentils

Lentils may be prepared like beans. All recipes for beans are perfectly suitable for lentils.

For four people, use:
1 lb. large lentils
1 lb. ham
1/2 lb. sausage (long, flat, or *chipolatas*)
2 large carrots
2 small onions
1 small turnip
bouquet garni
salt and pepper

LENTILLES AUX SAUCISSES

Lentils with Sausages

Carefully pick over the lentils and remove any stones. Wash them.

Put the lentils in a saucepan with cold water, bring it to a boil, add the carrots, onions, turnip, *bouquet garni*, salt, and pepper. Cook these together.

At the same time, braise the ham, which has been seasoned with salt and pepper, and purée it.[1]

Remove the carrots, onions, turnip, and *bouquet garni*. Drain the lentils. Mix them with the ham purée and its cooking liquid. Let these simmer together for thirty minutes.

Broil the sausages.

Spoon the lentils onto a platter, garnish with the sausages, and serve.

Lentils may also be prepared the same way but using wild boar.

NOTE

1. The ham can be puréed several ways: Put it three times through the finest blade of a food grinder, then sieve it, if necessary; blend it in a food blender; or grind it in an electric Moulinex.

For four people, use:

2 lbs. winter spinach[1]
1/2 lb. sorrel
1/4 lb. butter
1/2 C. cream
salt and pepper

ÉPINARDS À LA CRÈME

Creamed Spinach

Trim the spinach and sorrel by removing the stems and any hard parts. Wash them in several waters and cook them in a large, uncovered kettle with 4 quarts of boiling, salted water (2 teaspoons of coarse salt per quart). Skim the surface as foam forms and cook for ten to twenty minutes.[2]

As soon as they are tender, remove them, drain through a colander, cool under running water, press the vegetables hard to remove all excess water, then purée them or chop them coarsely, as desired.

Put the vegetables in a saucepan with 5 tablespoons of butter and let them simmer for fifteen minutes. Salt and pepper them to taste. Five minutes before serving, add the cream and the rest of the butter cut into tiny pieces.

Cooked spinach may be reheated, provided more cream and butter are added each time.

Those who like spinach with a lot of butterfat can manage to use about 1 cup of butter and 3/4 cup of heavy cream per pound of spinach.

Spinach is generally served garnished with fried croûtons.

Chicory may be prepared this same way.

NOTES

1. If one is using young, tender spinach, which contains more water, it will absorb less butter for an equal amount by weight, and there would be a smaller quantity after it was cooked. Therefore, one should use a larger quantity of spinach for the same number of people.

2. Young spinach is generally fully cooked in one or two minutes.

ÉPINARDS ET CHAMPIGNONS GRATINÉS

Oven-Browned Spinach and Mushrooms

For six people, use:

4 lbs. spinach
1/2 lb. mushrooms
1 C. butter
2 1/2 C. grated Gruyère cheese
salt and pepper

Trim and wash the spinach. Blanch it in boiling, salted water. Cool it under cold running water. Press it out and then cook it over high heat in 1/2 cup of butter, to dry it out thoroughly.

Peel the mushrooms, cut them up, put them in a saucepan with 3 tablespoons of butter, season with salt and pepper, and let them cook.

Mix the spinach, the mushrooms, 1 1/4 cups of grated cheese, and 3 tablespoons of butter. Spoon this mixture into a casserole buttered with the remaining butter, sprinkle with the remaining cheese, and brown it quickly. Serve in the same dish.

This spinach dish may be served as a vegetable course, but it is also a very good accompaniment for veal and lamb.

ÉPINARDS, LAITUES, ET CHAMPIGNONS GRATINÉS

Oven-Browned Spinach, Lettuce, and Mushrooms

For four people, use:

2 lbs. spinach
2 lbs. lettuce
1/2 lb. mushrooms
1/4 lb (8 T.) butter
1/2 C. mornay sauce made with Parmesan cheese
4 T. strong meat stock
lemon juice
nutmeg
salt and pepper

Cook the spinach and lettuce in salted water. Cool them under cold, running water, press them dry, and chop them.

In a saucepan, put 7 tablespoons of butter, the spinach, and the lettuce, and heat them up together. Add the stock, season with salt, pepper, and nutmeg, all to taste. Mix well and finish cooking.

Peel the mushrooms, cook them in the remaining butter with a little lemon juice, and slice them.

In a casserole, spoon the spinach–lettuce mixture, lay on them the slices of mushroom, spoon on the Mornay sauce, and brown the dish in the oven.

This is an excellent vegetable course.

SOUFFLÉ AUX ÉPINARDS

Spinach Soufflé

For five people, use:

2 C. Béchamel sauce
1 lb. spinach
1¼ C. grated Parmesan cheese
5 eggs
butter
salt and pepper

Trim the spinach, cook it in boiling, salted water, and drain it. Purée it through a food mill.

Separate the yolks from the whites of the eggs and beat the whites until stiff.

Thoroughly mix the spinach, first, with the Béchamel sauce, then with the egg yolks and cheese. Season well with salt and pepper and then fold in the egg whites.

Butter a soufflé dish, fill it three-fourths full of the above mixture, and bake it in a hot oven ten to twelve minutes.

Spinach soufflé, served alone, is an excellent vegetable course.

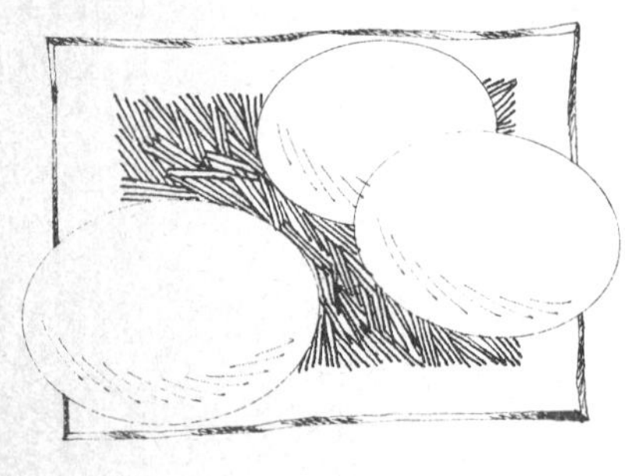

One may prepare, either with or without cheese, a whole gamut of vegetable soufflés: chicory, potato, sorrel, cauliflower, cooked lettuce, etc.

OSEILLE

Sorrel

Sorrel may be prepared with or without meat broth.

WITHOUT MEAT BROTH

For six people, use:

4 lbs. sorrel
½ C. butter
3 T. heavy cream
3 egg yolks
salt and pepper

Trim the sorrel, cut off all the stems, wash it carefully in several changes of cold water, and drain it. Now put it in a saucepan with the water clinging to it and wilt it, if it is young. Or, if it is more mature, blanch it in boiling, salted water. Let it boil up two or three times, then drop it into a colander to drain.

In the saucepan, melt 7 tablespoons of butter, add the drained sorrel, let it simmer for thirty minutes, then add the rest of the butter cut into tiny pieces. Let the butter barely melt and season to taste with salt and pepper.[1]

In a bowl, mix the beaten egg yolks with the cream, blend this mixture into the sorrel, heat it up without boiling for about five minutes, and serve.

WITH MEAT BROTH

For six people, use:

4 lbs. sorrel
1/2 C. strong meat stock
7 T. butter
3 T. cream
2 T. flour
3 egg yolks
salt and pepper

Start this recipe like the one above. While the drained sorrel is simmering in the butter, cook the flour for three minutes in 4 tablespoons of butter; then stir in the stock, add all this to the sorrel, season it with salt and pepper, and continue to cook for another fifteen minutes. Last, bind with the cream and egg yolks.

Here the flour is almost indispensable for giving some body to the dish because of the larger quantity of liquid.

Sorrel is served either as a vegetable course or as a garnish.

As a vegetable course it is generally garnished with fried croûtons or with bits of puff pastry.

As a garnish it is an excellent accompaniment for hard-boiled eggs, fried eggs, poached or shirred eggs. It also goes very well with veal.

NOTE

1. Those people who find sorrel a little too acid for their taste may add a little granulated sugar.

PURÉE DE CRESSON

Watercress Purée

For six people, use:

1 C. heavy cream
7 T. butter
2 tsp. flour
10 bunches watercress
salt and pepper

This recipe requires two separate procedures:

First, the day before you wish to serve this dish, trim the watercress, removing any coarse stems. Wash it several times, drain it, and blanch it for about twelve minutes in boiling, salted water. Cool it under cold running water and then purée it in a vegetable mill. Let this purée rest until the next day. It will render quite a bit of water which you can pour off.

Second, the following day, when it is time to prepare the dish, in a saucepan, melt the butter, add the flour, and cook these together a little without browning. Add the well-drained watercress purée and the cream. Season to taste and heat up over very low heat, stirring as you go, just long enough for everything to be well blended and thickened.

This purée is excellent with veal or lamb.

If served alone, it should be garnished with croûtons fried in butter.

For four people, use:

2 lbs. endive
10 T. butter
1 tsp. salt
black pepper to taste

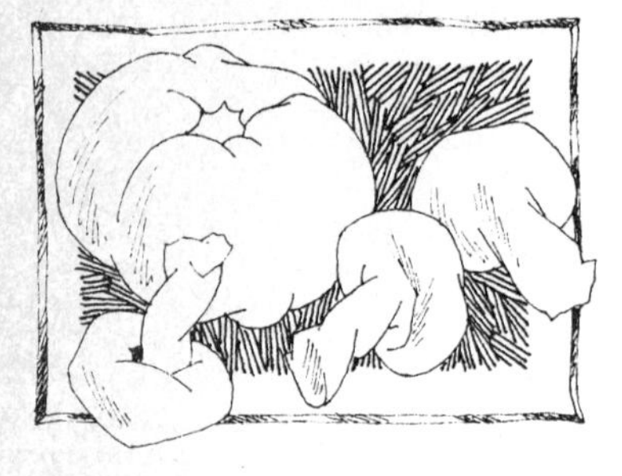

ENDIVES AU BEURRE

Endives with Butter

Trim the endive and, if they are fairly sand-free, do not wash them, merely wipe them. Otherwise, wash them rapidly without soaking them, so they won't become bitter. Dry them in a linen towel before cooking them.

Melt the butter is a saucepan, add the endive, season with salt and pepper, and lay a piece of buttered paper over them. Let the endive simmer in the open pan over very low heat for two hours.

This method of preparing endive is especially recommended for young endive, at the beginning of the season.

Lettuce and escarole may be prepared the same way.

LAITUES BRAISÉES

Braised Lettuce

Peel and slice some Spanish onions.

Cut up some tomatoes and remove the seeds.

Cook the onions and tomatoes in butter and purée them in a food mill.

Blanch some trimmed and well-washed lettuce for a few minutes in boiling, salted water. Drain it.

Spoon the onion and tomato purée into a casserole, arrange the lettuce on top, spoon some veal stock over all, and braise slowly in the oven for two hours.

CHICORÉE AU JUS

Chicory in Meat Stock

Select very green, curly, healthy, and fresh-looking chicory. Trim it carefully, leaf by leaf, so as to make sure that there are no worms, straw or wilted parts. Wash it carefully in a lot of water, several times, and then cook it in boiling, salted water for twenty to twenty-five minutes.

Cool the chicory under cold, running water, drain well, press dry, and chop coarsely.

Cook some flour in butter until lightly browned. Stir in some strong stock, preferably veal and chicken stock, and let this cook for a few minutes. Add the chicory, mix well, cover with buttered paper, and bake in a slow oven.

After thirty minutes, taste, season with salt and pepper if necessary, and flavor with nutmeg if desired. Add some fresh butter cut into tiny pieces just before serving and let it barely melt.

Serve with or without fried croûtons.

Chicory with meat stock is one of the best accompaniments for light meats.

Spinach and escarole may also be prepared this way.

PAIN DE CHICORÉE

Chicory Loaf

For eight people, use:

- 3 C. heavy cream
- 1 C. butter
- 4 tsp. flour
- 6 large heads winter chicory, yielding about 4 lbs.
- 4 eggs
- salt and pepper

Trim the chicory; wash it carefully in cold water.

Cook it in boiling, salted water; drain it; cool it under cold, running water; then put it in a strong linen towel and wring it out to remove all excess water. Chop it.

In a saucepan, put 4 tablespoons of butter and the chicory, cook these for five minutes, pour in ½ cup of cream, stir, add another 4 tablespoons of butter and another ½ cup of cream, little by little. Continue stirring but do not let it boil. This whole procedure should take about fifteen or twenty minutes.

Take the pan off the heat, break in the eggs, season with salt and pepper, and mix well.

Butter a mold, especially on the bottom (use about 3 tablespoons of butter), spoon in the chicory, and cook it in a hot water bath for an hour and a half.

Serve with a sauce prepared in the following way: in a saucepan put the rest of the butter and the flour. Stir without browning, add 1 cup of cream and blend well. As soon as the sauce begins to thicken, add more cream, salt, and pepper, and simmer for a half hour stirring constantly. Before serving, if the sauce is too thick, add all or part of the remaining cream.

FENOUIL

Fennel

Fennel is an aromatic plant of the Umbelliferae family.

Little used in French cuisine, it is, however, extensively used in other countries. In Slavic countries it is the chopped leaves that are most used, as a condiment for soups and other dishes—somewhat as parsley is used in France. In Italy, under the name of *finocchi*, they use the bulbous part of the fennel, either raw or in salad or as an hors-d'oeuvre, or cooked in butter or stock as a vegetable. Fennel can also be baked, in which case it is served either with a cream or tomato sauce.

Finocchi often accompany a piece of veal.
Here are three recipes for preparing it:

A. With Meat Stock. Cut up the bulbous part into two or four pieces, lengthwise. Blanch the pieces for fifteen minutes in boiling, salted water, then finish cooking them in strong stock. One needs about 2 cups of stock for 6 bulbs of fennel. Arrange the fennel on a platter, reduce the cooking liquid, taste for seasoning, and pour over the *finocchi.*

B. Baked in Cream Sauce. Cut up and blanch the fennel. Prepare a white sauce with cream. In a casserole, arrange layers of fennel, sauce, and grated Parmesan cheese, ending up with cheese (1/2 cup of cheese for 6 fennel bulbs). Finish by baking in the oven.

C. Baked with Tomato Sauce. Prepare the fennel as in the preceding recipe but substitute tomato sauce for the cream sauce.

Celery may be prepared in the same way.

ARTICHAUTS FARCIS

Stuffed Artichokes

For six people, use:

2 1/2 C. stock
2 1/2 C. white wine
1 lb. tomatoes
1/2 lb. mushrooms
1/2 lb. white meat of roast chicken
1/2 lb. pork rind
5 small carrots
1/4 lb. smoked ham
8 T. (1/2 C.) meat glaze
8 T. (1/2 C.) butter
2 small onions
2 T. brandy
3 shallots
2 tsp. flour
parsley
6 medium artichokes
6 pieces pork belly fat cut into circles same diameter as artichokes
bouquet garni **(parsley, thyme, bay leaf)**
salt, pepper, paprika

Trim the artichokes, wash them, blanch them just enough to make it possible to pull out the center leaves, and remove the choke with a spoon. Leave all the large outer leaves on.

Make a hash with the white meat of chicken and the ham and season it.

Separately, chop the shallots, mushrooms, and parsley.

Peel, seed, and chop the tomatoes.

Prepare a duxelle mixture as follows: put 3 1/2 tablespoons of butter in a saucepan, heat it up, throw in the chopped shallots and mushrooms, and let these cook together until all the water given off by the mushrooms has evaporated. Sprinkle on the minced parsley and season with salt, pepper, and paprika. To this mixture add the tomatoes, the chicken and ham hash, and the flour blended into 1 tablespoon of butter; mix everything together until it forms a fairly consistent stuffing.

Fill the artichokes with the stuffing and cover each one with a circle of pork fat.

Line the bottom of a pan with the pork rind, put in the sliced or chopped carrots and onions, the *bouquet garni*, and 4 tablespoons of butter, and let these cook together until everything almost adheres to the bottom of the pan. Add the artichokes, then pour in the wine, brandy, and stock into which you have dissolved the meat glaze. The artichokes must bathe in the liquid half way up.

Braise these in a slow oven for one hour.

Remove the artichokes, arrange them on a hot platter, boil down the sauce, and skim it. Coat the artichokes with the sauce and serve.

These artichokes are very delicate.

Artichoke hearts may be stuffed in the same way. The dish is not quite as pretty to look at, but it has the advantage of being easier to eat.

One may also stuff artichokes without any meat, using tiny peas for instance, or fresh string beans, favas, etc., and using them either whole or puréed and coated with a meatless Béchamel or a very thick Mornay sauce.

ARTICHAUTS FROIDS, À L'HUILE

Cold Artichokes with Oil

For six people, use:

1¾ C. water
1⅓ C. olive oil
4 tsp. salt
pepper to taste
6 young, tender artichokes
3 onions
1 lemon
bouquet garni

Wash the artichokes, remove the tough outer leaves, and cut off the tips of the others.

In a saucepan, put the water, oil, lemon juice and a little rind, the onion, salt, pepper, and the *bouquet garni*. Bring these to a boil. Put in the artichokes, cover, and continue cooking until the water has evaporated—a phenomenon which will be noted by a whistling noise.

Let them cool.

ASPERGES, SAUCE MOUSSELINE

Asparagus with Mousseline Sauce

For six people, use:

½ lb. butter
4 T. whipped cream
1 T. cold water
8 egg yolks
salt

Scrape the asparagus, wash them, and cook them in boiling, salted water just until they are barely tender. Drain them and arrange them on a napkin-covered platter.

Serve, sending along, at the same time, a sauceboat with mousseline sauce.

Mousseline sauce is a variation on hollandaise sauce. Here is how it is prepared: start by making a hollandaise sauce, keeping it a little thicker than usual by doubling the number of egg yolks used. Then, off the heat, add some whipped cream.

Adding the whipped cream gives the sauce an especially velvety texture.

Asparagus may also be served with other sauces, particularly with a hollandaise flavored with the juice of a blood orange spiked with a little lemon juice.

ASPERGES VERTES À LA CRÈME

Creamed Green Asparagus

For six people, use:

2 lbs. tender parts of tiny green asparagus
1 C. cream
4 T. coarse salt
3 T. butter
3 T. flour
freshly ground black pepper to taste
2 qts. water

Cut the asparagus into one-inch lengths and cook them in water to which you have added 3 tablespoons of coarse salt. Cook only until the asparagus is barely tender. Ten minutes are generally enough for the stem parts and five for the tips.

Melt the butter, stir in the flour; add the cream, the rest of the salt, and some pepper; and cook over very low heat. Just before serving add the asparagus, cook a moment or two, and serve.

Creamed asparagus is a very good accompaniment for light meats and fowl.

AUBERGINES

Eggplant

Peel the eggplant and slice it lengthwise into uniform slices. Sprinkle the slices with coarse salt and let them render their water for an hour, then season the slices with pepper.

The eggplant may be fried in butter, fat, or oil. If you are frying them in either butter or fat, first coat them with flour; if you are frying them in oil, dip them first in egg white and then coat them with dry, sifted breadcrumbs.

Arrange the slices of fried eggplant in a vegetable dish, one on top of the other, without pressing them down, and serve.

Summer and Italian squash may also prepared this same way.

AUBERGINE ET TOMATES GRATINÉES

Baked Eggplant and Tomatoes

For four people, use:

2 lbs. tomatoes
1 lb. eggplant
1½ C. grated Gruyère cheese
½ C. butter
4 T. breadcrumbs
4 tsp. table salt
freshly ground black pepper to taste

Peel the eggplant and tomatoes, slice them, and remove the seeds.

Using 3 tablespoons of butter, grease a casserole. In it arrange alternating layers of eggplant and tomatoes, sprinkling each layer with grated cheese, salt, and pepper. End up with a layer of cheese.

Sprinkle on the breadcrumbs, dot with the rest of the butter, and bake in a slow oven for one hour.

This dish, baked to a nice, golden brown, is an excellent dish for a simple meal.

MOUSSAKA

For four people, use:

1 lb. eggplant
½ lb. tomatoes
½ lb. leg or tenderloin of lamb or top round of beef
1 C. (½ lb.) butter
2 oz. veal kidney suet
4 T. bouillon
1 onion (chopped)
1 tsp. table salt
freshly ground black pepper to taste
paprika to taste
flour
coarsesalt

Moussaka is a Mideastern eggplant dish.

Peel the eggplant, make slices about as thick as a silver dollar, sprinkle them with coarse salt, and let them render their water for one hour.

Grind together the lamb or beef and the veal kidney suet.

Mince the onion.

Do the four following procedures simultaneously:

Put the cut-up tomatoes in a saucepan, let them soften over low heat, then strain them through a sieve.

Brown the onion in 3 tablespoons of butter, add the bouillon, and cook until they are almost dry.

In 5 tablespoons of butter brown the ground meat, season with salt, pepper, and paprika, put the pan in the oven and let this cook for about ten minutes. Then add the chopped onion and mix well.

Wash off the eggplant slices several times in cold water, coat them with flour, and brown them in the remaining butter.

In a casserole, arrange alternate layers of eggplant and meat. Moisten with the juice from the tomatoes, put the dish in the oven and continue cooking in a slow oven until the liquid has evaporated. This will take at least one hour.

The top must be brown and crusty and the inside soft.

AUBERGINES AUX TOMATES, FROIDES

Cold Eggplant and Tomatoes

For six people, use:

1½ lbs. tomatoes
1 C. veal stock
3 T. butter
6 medium eggplants
4 medium cloves of garlic
olive oil
parsley
salt and pepper

Partially peel the eggplants, leaving on some strips of skin.

Sliver the garlic, set aside about one-eighth, and stud the eggplants with the rest.

Cook the tomatoes in the butter with the remaining garlic slivers and a little parsley. Strain the pulp and keep the purée hot.

Cook the eggplants in olive oil, and when they are nicely browned on all sides drain them and arrange them in a casserole. Season with salt and pepper, add the veal stock and tomato purée, cover, and bake for forty-five minutes.

Arrange the eggplants on a platter, coat with their cooking liquid, and cool.

For five people, use:

5 T. olive oil
5 eggplants with few seeds
4 large onions
3 large tomatoes
2 garlic cloves
salt and pepper

AUBERGINES FARCIES FROIDES

Cold Stuffed Eggplant

Remove three wide lengthwise pieces of peel from each eggplant. This will keep them from totally losing their shape. Cut the stems without detaching them completely and make some deep, longitudinal incisions.

Heat the oil in a skillet and when it begins to sizzle throw in the minced onion and garlic. Let these brown lightly, then add the peeled, seeded, and sliced tomatoes. Continue cooking for two minutes. Season with salt and pepper, mix well, and spoon this mixture into the incisions in the eggplant.

Arrange the stuffed eggplants in a skillet, cover with water, and let them cook until all the water has evaporated. Remove them to a platter and let them cool thoroughly.

This dish, which belongs to Byzantine cuisine, is known in Constantinople (Istanbul) under the picturesque name of *Iman bayeldi*—which literally means "the Iman belched"! Was it really to display his satisfaction in a delicate and expressive way, as fanatics of the dish claim, or was not this reaction induced by an excessive quantity of garlic, onion, and oil? This fact of history will probably long be obscure.

Nevertheless, the dish unquestionably has a very original character and is worth mentioning for this reason.

CHAYOTES

Chayotes are cucurbits (cucumber family) from Central America, whose fleshy fruits are somewhat ovoid. The edible *chayote* known as *Sechium edule*, native of Mexico, is cultivated in the Antilles. These fruits may attain a diameter of four inches at their largest circumference. The so-called French *chayote—Sechium americanum*—is cultivated in Algeria. The fruit is much smaller, hardly bigger than a turkey egg.

The *chayotes*, very much in favor with the Creoles, have an agreeable flavor. Their taste is reminiscent of, but more delicate than, summer squash. They are imported into Paris from October to the end of February.

Chayotes are prepared with the following sauces: *demi-glace* with or without tomato, hollandaise, mousseline, *italienne*, Bordelaise, Béchamel, Mornay, etc. They can be prepared with cream or stock. They may be sautéed or stuffed. They may be glazed like turnips or they may even become part of a mixed salad.

Chayotes are served as a vegetable course.

Here is an example of such a dish.

Peel the *chayotes*, slice them uniformly, cook them in salted water, and drain them.

Spoon some thick Béchamel sauce made with meat stock and thickened with heavy cream into a casserole. On this arrange the slices of *chayote*, sprinkle with grated Parmesan cheese, pour on a little melted butter, and brown in the oven.

If one would like a richer dish, each slice of *chayote* could be covered with a slice of truffle cooked in broth.

This is a very pretty dish.

COURGETTES FARCIES, AU MAIGRE

Squash with Meatless Stuffing

For six people, use:

1 lb. mushrooms
1 C. milk
8 T. butter
1 large carrot
1 small chopped onion
6 T. flour
1 small turnip
6 medium summer squash or zucchini
4 eggs
dry, sifted breadcrumbs
bouquet garni **(parsley, thyme, bay leaf)**
nutmeg
salt and pepper

Peel the carrot and turnip, cut them into small pieces, and cook them, along with the *bouquet garni*, in the milk to flavor it. Strain.

Peel the mushrooms, chop them, and cook them in the milk.

Peel the zucchini if you are using it; do not peel young summer squash. Cut the squash in two, lengthwise, scoop out the pulp, reserve and chop it. Blanch the squash halves in lightly salted and peppered water.

Brown the chopped onion in 6 tablespoons of butter, sprinkle on the flour, and stir until lightly browned. Add the mushrooms, along with their cooking liquid, add salt, pepper, and nutmeg to taste. Reduce the sauce.

Now add the chopped squash pulp and the egg yolks and mix well. Taste and correct the seasoning if necessary. This is the stuffing.

Arrange the squash halves in a lightly buttered casserole, fill the centers with the stuffing, sprinkle on the breadcrumbs, dot with the rest of the butter, and brown in the oven.

For variation, one could make the stuffing using half mushrooms and half tiny peas.

One could, it goes without saying, substitute for the cultivated mushrooms other types of mushrooms: boletus, Lepiotas, and other types of wild mushrooms.

Other vegetables may be prepared this way: eggplants, green peppers, artichoke hearts, potatoes, etc.

COURGETTES AU FROMAGE, FRITES

Fried Zucchini with Cheese

Select preferably, young, white-fleshed zucchini. Peel and slice them and let them render their water with some coarse salt. Sponge them off, coat them with flour, and fry them in oil.

Unite the slices, two by two, by sticking them one to the other with a mixture of egg yolks and grated Gruyère cheese.

At serving time, coat these double slices with dry, sifted breadcrumbs—or dip them in fritter batter and fry them in deep, hot fat. Remove them with a skimmer and arrange them on a platter garnished with fried parsley.

Eggplants may be prepared this same way.

TOMATES FARCIES DE CHAMPIGNONS GRILLÉS

Tomatoes Stuffed with Broiled Mushrooms

The tomato, or love apple, delicious and poetic vegetable–fruit which plays in cuisine predominately the role of a garniture, deserves all the attention of lovers of good food. It is delicate and pretty to work with. As a result of its qualities, the poor thing must suffer greatly when it feels itself stuffed by barbarians with chopped boiled beef and sausage meat. It really deserves a better fate.

To conserve all the tomato's flavor and in order not to profane its delicate aroma, it is best to blend it only with very distinguished stuffings. One of the best ones, to my mind, is a simple stuffing made with broiled mushrooms.

For six people, use:

1/2 lb. mushrooms
1 1/2 C. butter
2/3 C. thick tomato sauce
2 tsp. salt
freshly ground black pepper to taste
6 large tomatoes
1 egg yolk
lemon juice
dry, sifted breadcrumbs

Here is how it is made:

Scald the tomatoes, peel them, and remove the seeds.

Peel the mushrooms, cut them into small pieces, and dip them in lemon juice to prevent darkening. Cook them in 6 tablespoons of butter until they have rendered their water and have started to brown in the pan. As soon as you can smell the characteristic aroma of the mushrooms, remove them from the heat, add the tomato sauce, the egg yolk, salt, and pepper, and mix everything well.

Stuff the tomatoes with this mixture, sprinkle the top with dry, sifted breadcrumbs, dot with butter (2 teaspoons per tomato), and brown them in the oven.

Prepared this way, stuffed tomatoes are delicious and very perfumed. They are a delight to gourmets.

For variation, one could serve stuffed tomatoes coated with a little reduced veal and chicken stock flavored with tomato.

CONSERVE DE PURÉE DE TOMATES

Tomato Purée

During the tomato season nothing is as good as the fresh fruit in dishes which require tomatoes. But, in winter, one can only use commercially prepared products, which are rarely made with all the necessary care.

Here is a practical recipe allowing one to make, during the season, a lovely, perfectly aromatized purée, which is easily preserved all winter long and which is much superior to most of the commercial preparations.

To prepare about four quarts of purée use twenty pounds of very ripe tomatoes. Wash and dry them and put them in a large copper kettle. Mash them well until all the pulp has separated from the skins, using your hands. Keep doing this until they are too hot to handle. Let them boil for one hour, stirring with a spoon; then force them through a fine sieve so as to eliminate all the seeds. Let this purée rest until the next day. Then carefully remove the water which is floating on top, add 1/8 teaspoon of salicylic acid per quart of purée (this does not give any taste whatsoever and is enough to prevent any future fermentation). Mix well.

Pour this into jars and pour a half-inch of olive oil on top, which will provide an airtight seal. Seal the jars as you wish, to avoid dust, and keep the jars upright in a cool spot.

Carrots

Carrots may be prepared in the following ways: in meat juice (stock); glazed; *à la maître d'hôtel*; with milk or cream; with butter *(à la Vichy)*; with bacon; fried: sliced in julienne strips, dried in a cloth, lightly floured, then plunged into boiling oil; in ragoût, either alone or accompanied by other vegetables (*petits pois*, mushrooms, for instance), with various sauces such as Béchamel, poulette, velouté, hollandaise, etc.

They are also served in purée and pudding.

They are made into soups.

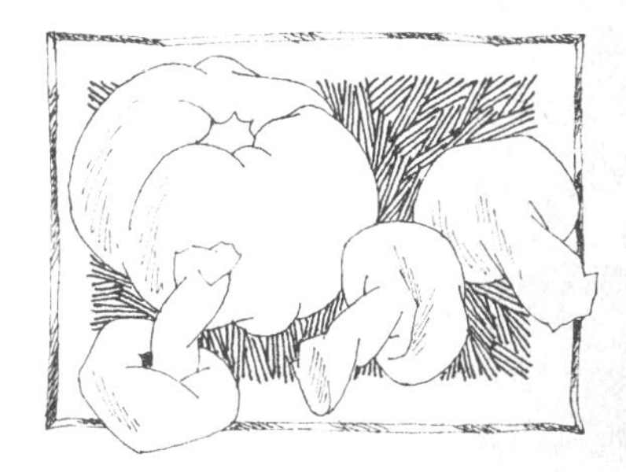

CAROTTES À LA MAÎTRE-D'HÔTEL

Maître-d'Hôtel Carrots

Peel or "turn" (carve into cork shapes) some new tiny carrots. Put them in a skillet with butter, salt, and granulated sugar to taste. Pour some chicken broth over them and let them cook.

Reduce the cooking liquid to a glaze, take the pan off the heat, add some chicken velouté, some butter blended with chopped parsley, and lemon juice or vinegar, heat for a few minutes, and serve.

For four people, use:

2 lbs. new carrots
1¾ C. heavy cream
4 tsp. salt
2 tsp. granulated sugar
water

CAROTTES À LA CRÈME

Creamed Carrots

In a saucepan put enough water so that the carrots may bathe in it; add the salt and sugar and bring it to a boil. Plunge the peeled carrots into the boiling water. Let them cook for thirty to forty minutes, according to size.

Reduce the cooking liquid, add the cream, boil up a couple of times, and serve.

Creamed carrots are particularly good with lamb and veal.

CAROTTES BRAISÉES AU MADÈRE

Carrots Braised in Madeira

Using nice large carrots, peel them and cut them up.

Brown them lightly, in some butter, with a little onion to taste.

At the same time, try out some blanched, diced bacon, add this to the carrots, pour on some bouillon or veal stock, add a *bouquet garni*, a little *quatre épices* and pepper. Let the carrots cook.

Twenty minutes before serving, spike them with some madeira and reduce the cooking liquid. Taste and complete the seasoning if necessary.

Arrange the carrots on a serving dish, decorate with the bacon dice, and coat with the strained sauce.

Turnips may be prepared this way too.

For four people, use:

2 lbs. freshly harvested carrots
1 C. butter
4 T. brandy
2 tsp. granulated sugar
2 tsp. salt

CAROTTES NOUVELLES À LA VICHY

New Carrots à la Vichy

Peel the carrots and slice them very thin.

Melt the butter in a saucepan without letting it brown, add the sugar and salt, mix well, then brown the carrot slices. Add the brandy, cover the saucepan, and cook in a slow oven, without stirring, for one hour. Watch them carefully. At the end of this time the carrots must have absorbed practically all the butter, and the slices must have remained whole and not shriveled.

Turnips

Turnips may be prepared in the following ways: *au jus* (in meat juice or stock); glazed; creamed; stuffed; fried: cut into julienne strips, dried in a towel, floured, and cooked in hot oil; in purée; in soups; etc.

NAVETS GLACÉS

Glazed Turnips

"Turn" (carve to a cork shape) some young turnips. Blanch them in boiling, salted water. Dry them out.

Brown them in butter, sprinkle them with sugar, half cover them with strong beef or chicken stock, and let the liquid boil down to a glaze.

Arrange the turnips on a serving dish, deglaze the pan with some strong stock (meat or chicken), coat the turnips, and serve.

NAVETS FARCIS

Stuffed Turnips

Peel some nice young, round turnips. Hollow them out with a *potato-baller*, put them into a buttered casserole, cover with some strong beef or chicken stock, and bake them in the oven.

At the same time prepare a semolina stuffing, cooked in stock and mixed with grated Parmesan cheese.

Stuff the turnips with this mixture. Dot with butter, put them back in the oven for a few minutes, and serve.

Turnips may also be stuffed with vegetable purées: potato and bulbous chervil, spinach, or asparagus tips, for instance.

NAVETS AU CIDRE

Turnips in Cider

For six people, use:

2 lbs. new, preferably round, turnips
1/2 lb. fresh pork
1 C. veal, duck or goose stock
1 C. cider
4 oz. bacon
2 eggs
1 shallot
butter
tarragon
parsley
thyme
bay leaf
quatre épices
pepper

Peel the turnips; hollow them out with an apple corer if they are the long type or use a potato-baller or knife if they are the round type. Blanch them in boiling water for a few minutes, along with the pulp.

Prepare a stuffing with the fresh pork, bacon, shallot, tarragon, parsley, thyme, and bay leaf to taste. Season with pepper and a little *quatre épices*. Bind with an egg.

Fill the hollow turnips with this stuffing. Brown them in butter;

then simmer them for about an hour in the stock and cider. Fifteen minutes before serving add the puréed pulp.

Boil down the cooking liquid, bind with an egg yolk, and taste and add salt if necessary.

Arrange the turnips on a serving dish, coat with the strained sauce, and serve.

This is very good.

CELERI-RAVE

Celeriac

Celeriac may be prepared in various ways.

1. *Sautéed.* For four people, use a large root weighing about one pound; peel it, slice it very thin, and blanch the slices for five minutes in boiling, salted water. Drain it and then sauté it in a skillet with a quarter of a pound of butter for thirty minutes until it is golden brown. At serving time sprinkle it with chopped green leaves of stalk celery. Sautéed celeriac may be served as is, or it may accompany broiled meat.

2. *Fried.* Slice the peeled root as above and soak the slices for fifteen minutes in cold water with vinegar. Drain them, dip them in a light fritter batter, and cook them in a deep fry-bath of veal kidney suet.

3. *Au Jus* (with meat broth). Cut the peeled root into thick (quarter-inch) slices. Plunge them into boiling, salted water. Let them boil up twice, remove the slices, drain them, and finish cooking them in some good meat stock. Simmer them very slowly for an hour and a half.

4. *À la Béchamel.* Cut the root as in the preceding recipe. Cook the slices for six minutes in boiling, salted water and drain them. Mix them with hot Béchamel sauce made with veal or chicken stock, sprinkle them with chopped, green, celery leaves, and serve them in a vegetable dish.

5. *Au Gratin.* Substitute for the Béchamel sauce in the preceding recipe some Mornay sauce. Put the mixture into a casserole; sprinkle with some dry, sifted breadcrumbs mixed with grated Gruyère cheese (equal quantities). Brown in the oven.

6. *In Salad.* Cut the raw, peeled root into julienne strips. Mari-

nate it for one hour in white Sauterne wine, then season it to taste with oil, vinegar, salt, pepper, mustard, and some chopped green celery leaves. Thus prepared, celeriac is served as an hors-d'oeuvre.

All these recipes are applicable to parsnips, artichoke hearts, and Japanese artichokes.

POTÉE FERMIÈRE

Farmer's Pot

Potée fermière is a mixture of vegetables cooked without water—smothered so to speak. When it is made with freshly harvested vegetables and good butter, it is an exquisite dish. Here is how it is prepared.

In a porcelain casserole with cover, put some butter and some sliced onions and let them brown lightly. Then add some lettuce hearts, tiny peas *(petits pois),* some green beans, carrots, turnips, potatoes, asparagus tips, etc., in whatever proportion you wish. Dot these with butter, about 1/4 pound of butter to each pound of vegetables. Cover the casserole and cook it in a slow oven for two hours. Fifteen minutes before serving, season with salt and pepper, and finish cooking.

It would be difficult to find a better vegetable course.

MACÉDOINE DE LÉGUMES À LA CRÈME

Mixed Creamed Vegetables

For four people, use:

2 C. milk
1 lb. tiny peas (unshelled)
5 large carrots
5 turnips
2 medium potatoes
1/2 lb. stringbeans
1 C. cream
3 T. butter
4 tsp. flour
1 small bunch asparagus tips
salt and pepper

Hull the peas and peel the other vegetables.

Cut the stringbeans and asparagus tips into pieces; cut the carrots and turnips into julienne strips.

Cook the stringbeans and asparagus tips in salted water, the carrots, turnips, and peas in the milk. Steam the potatoes.

When the potatoes are cooked, dice them.

Cook the flour in 5 teaspoons of butter without letting it brown. Stir in the milk left from cooking the vegetables, add the vegetables and the cream, season with salt and pepper, heat up without boiling, and, last, add the rest of the butter and serve.

One could, it goes without saying, use other vegetables than those mentioned above—for example, cabbage, cauliflower, artichoke hearts, etc.

All these *macédoines,* which are excellent as vegetable courses, may be served as garnishes for sautéed or broiled meats.

For six people, use:

2 C. bouillon
10 oz. tomatoes
5 oz. white meat of roast chicken
1/4 lb. mushrooms
1/2 C. rice
1/2 C. strong meat broth
2 oz. fatty ham (smoked type)
1/2 C. grated Gruyère cheese
5 tsp. butter
6 large green peppers
2 egg yolks
lemon juice
paprika
salt and pepper

PIMENTS VERTS FARCIS, BRAISÉS

Braised Stuffed Peppers

Cook the rice in the bouillon until it has absorbed all the liquid and the rice grains still remain whole. Stir in the grated Gruyère.

Chop the chicken.

Peel the mushrooms, dip them in lemon juice, slice them, and cook them in butter.

Remove the seeds and veins from the green peppers, leaving them whole. Blanch them for two minutes in boiling, salted water.

Mix the rice, the chopped chicken, and the mushrooms. Bind with the egg yolk. Season with paprika, salt, and pepper, and taste. Stuff the peppers with this mixture.

Lay the smoked ham in the bottom of a casserole, arrange the peppers on top, moisten with the strong stock, add the mashed tomatoes, and braise for twenty minutes. Reduce the sauce.

Serve the peppers coated with the strained sauce.

Small frying peppers, eggplants, and squash may be prepared in this fashion.

For six people, use:

2 lbs. salsify
1 1/2 C. Béchamel sauce (with or without meat broth)
3 C. grated Gruyère or Parmesan cheese (or a mixture of both)
3 T. butter
1/3 C. dry, sifted breadcrumbs
vinegar
salt

SALSIFIS AU GRATIN

Baked Salsify[1]

Scrape the salsify; put it in water with vinegar to keep them from darkening. Wash, cut up, and cook it in boiling, salted water, and drain it.

Add 1 1/2 cups of the cheese to the Béchamel sauce. Heat up this Mornay sauce.

In a porcelain casserole, spoon some of the sauce, arrange the salsify on top, cover with the rest of the Mornay sauce, sprinkle with the remainder of the mixed cheese and breadcrumbs, dot the top with the butter, and brown in the oven.

Most vegetables can be prepared this way: potatoes, beans (green or dried), peas, lentils, cauliflower, Brussels sprouts, asparagus tips, artichoke hearts, Jerusalem artichokes, celeriac, bulbous chervil, cardoons, endives, beets, carrots, turnips, onions, and mushrooms, as well as rice, pasta, and chestnuts. A great many pleasant dishes are therefore possible.

NOTE

1. Salsify is sometimes sold under the name oyster plant.

OIGNONS FARCIS

Stuffed Onions

Use either large, new round yellow onions or sweet Spanish onions. Remove a thick slice at the top of each to serve as a cap. Hollow out the inside, leaving a layer of shell.

Chop the removed onion pulp.

Cook, on the one hand, the chopped onion pulp with the chopped mushrooms and parsley, in butter; on the other hand, cook some semolina in some veal or chicken stock. Mix everything together and stuff the hollowed-out onions with the mixture.

Arrange the stuffed onions in a casserole, cover them with the caps, pour around some strong veal or chicken stock or some rich meat broth. Cook these for one hour, very slowly, basting frequently.

When the onions are cooked the pan juices should have been reduced to a semi-glaze.

New onions, thus prepared, are an excellent garnish for roast meats.

Stuffed Spanish onions make an excellent vegetable course in themselves.

PURÉE D'OIGNONS À LA CRÈME

Creamed Onion Purée

For four people, use:

2 lbs. peeled onions
1¼ C. butter
1 C. cream
5 T. flour
granulated sugar
salt and pepper

Slice the onions and cook them in one cup of the butter for twenty or thirty minutes, very slowly, without letting them brown. Purée them.

Make a roux with the rest of the butter and the flour, stir in the cream, add the strained purée, sugar, and salt to taste, heat up for a moment, and serve.

This dish is unquestionably better made with new onions, because older onions are apt to be bitter.

This purée is a very good accompaniment for braised pork or braised lamb chops.

BETTERAVES

Beets

To prepare beets as an accompaniment or a garnish (which is one of the best for veal), bake them in the oven, peel them, chop them, or, if you prefer, force them through a coarse sieve.

Thicken with either a Béchamel sauce, or with some kind of cream sauce, or, even simpler, with some heavy cream or butter.

In the latter two cases, sprinkle them with chopped parsley at serving time. Season to taste.

As a vegetable course one can prepare beets with salt pork or bacon.

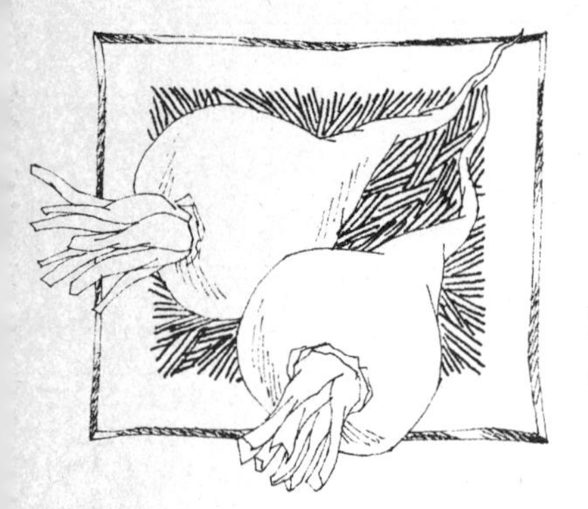

BETTERAVES CONFITES, AU RAIFORT

Beets Pickled with Horseradish

Bake the beets in the oven, peel them, and slice them.

Grate some horseradish root.

In a preserving jar arrange alternate layers of beets and grated horseradish. Drown everything with good tarragon vinegar. This should be ready to eat in a few days.

This is an excellent condiment, particularly with boiled beef.

CONCOMBRES

Cucumbers

Cucumbers are prepared in various ways: white cucumbers are excellent as an hors-d'oeuvre; green cucumbers are very good salted. In certain cases they make a good substitute for pickles.

To prepare cucumbers as an hors-d'oeuvre, select large white cucumbers, peel them, slice them thin, remove the seeds, and sprinkle them with coarse salt and let them render their water. Season the drained cucumbers either with oil, vinegar, salt, and pepper, or cream, vinegar, salt, and pepper—or even with mayonnaise.

These three recipes, which only differ in the use of oil, cream, or mayonnaise, are three very appetizing hors-d'oeuvre, each with its own particular flavor.

To prepare salted cucumbers, select some medium-sized green cucumbers, four or five inches long; brush them, dry them, remove the ends, and cut a cross in each end so that they will not explode as they ferment.

In a deep crock, arrange alternating layers of grape leaves, cherry leaves, horseradish leaves, or, instead, a little grated horseradish, fennel leaves, coarse salt, and some of the prepared cucumbers. Continue these alternating layers of aromatics to within four inches of the top. Drown everything in water and place a little board on top, weighted down with a clean object.

Leave the crock uncovered, with the vegetables well submerged in the liquid, in a cool place. According to the season, the cucumbers will be ready in a minimum of eight days and a maximum of about three weeks. The process must be watched carefully in order to stop it as soon as the cucumbers are ready.

Salted, pickled cucumbers are a good accompaniment for cold meat, especially boiled beef.

CORNICHONS, PETITS MELONS, ET OIGNONS CONFITS AU VINAIGRE

Gherkins, Tiny Melons, and Onions Pickled in Vinegar

Choose, preferably, very tiny, uniform gherkins. Brush them with a stiff brush, cut off the ends, put them in a towel with an equal weight of coarse salt. Mix the salt and gherkins thoroughly, hang the towel by its four corners, and let the gherkins drain over a bowl for twelve hours. Then wipe them, one by one, and arrange them in a pickling jar, on a bed of tarragon branches; add 40 peppercorns, some *samphire* (Crithmum maritimum),[1] and 2 small, hot red peppers per 2 pounds of gherkins. End up with a layer of tarragon. Drown all this with strong wine vinegar, covering everything. Seal the jar airtight. Let them pickle for four or five months.

Pickled gherkins may also be prepared in the following way:

Brush and salt, as above, 4 pounds of gherkins; wipe them. In a porcelain crock put a quantity of tarragon, to taste, a little thyme, a bay leaf, 2 small hot peppers, a small clove of garlic, 5 or 6 tiny, peeled onions, 2 small shallots. On top arrange a layer of gherkins, then 5 little onions, 2 small shallots, and another layer of gherkins. Then on top put 5 little onions, 2 small shallots, and another layer of gherkins. Then on top put 5 little onions, 2 small shallots, another layer of gherkins, ending up with 5 or 6 small onions, a tiny clove of garlic, 2 hot red peppers, 2 cloves, 30 peppercorns, a bay leaf, a little thyme. Cover this with a quantity of tarragon and drown everything in good vinegar.

Let this ferment.

To prepare pickled melons, select tiny melons the size of a walnut. The procedure is the same as for the gherkins.

Onions may prepared in this same way, but they are not salted first.

The onions should be very tiny and carefully peeled.

NOTE

1. *Samphire* is a fleshy European sea coast plant also known as *herbe Saint Pierre*, from whence the name *samphire*.

CHOU-RAVE FARCI

Stuffed Kohlrabi

Select a large kohlrabi. Remove a slice from the top to serve as a cover.

Hollow out the inside; blanch it along with its cover in boiling, salted water. Dry it out in the oven.

Braise some pork tenderloin, and season it with salt, pepper, and other herbs and spices to taste.

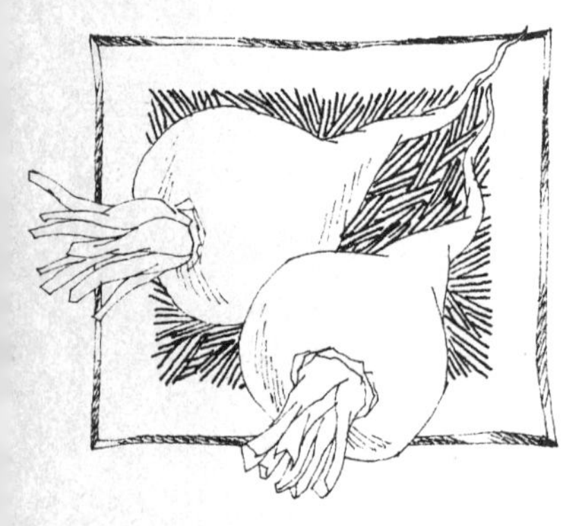

Chop or grind the braised pork, mix it with its pan juices, fill the inside of the kohlrabi with this stuffing, and top with the cover. Finish cooking the kohlrabi in *sauce Soubise*. Serve.

Cauliflower

Cauliflower, after it has been cooked in salted water, can be prepared in many ways. It may be served cold or hot.

The classic procedures for preparing hot cauliflower are the following: in butter; sautéed; with cheese (browned or not); with cheese, wrapped in batter; coated with various sauces: Béchamel, Mornay (browned or not), hollandaise or mousseline, tomato sauce, cream sauces or butter sauces; in souffles; etc.

Cold, it may be presented: plain, on a napkin, with a few of its tender leaves, or in a ring of parsley; as an hors-d'oeuvre, coated with mayonnaise, with mustard sauce or a cream sauce; in salad.

These various recipes are also applicable to broccoli.

CHOU-FLEUR, SAUCE HOLLANDAISE OU SAUCE MOUSSELINE AUX POINTES D'ASPERGES

Cauliflower with Hollandaise Sauce or Mousseline Sauce with Asparagus Tips

Cook the cauliflower in salted water and drain.

Blanch the asparagus tips in salted water for five minutes and drain them. Finish cooking them in butter or cream. Force them through a vegetable mill and keep them hot.

Prepare a hollandaise sauce or a mousseline sauce (see recipe index). Add the asparagus purée to the sauce, complete the seasoning, to taste, with salt, pepper and lemon juice.

Arrange the cauliflower on a platter, coat with the sauce, and serve.

These exquisite sauces may accompany other vegetables: artichoke hearts, celeriac, asparagus, Jerusalem artichokes, etc.

CHOU-FLEUR SAUTÉ

Sautéed Cauliflower

For four people, use:

2 lbs. cauliflower, trimmed and separated into flowerets
3/4 C. butter
salt and pepper

Cook the cauliflower in salted water until it is still a little firm.

In a skillet put the butter and the cauliflower, season to taste with salt and pepper, and sauté it over low heat, very slowly, for twenty or twenty-five minutes so that the little flowerets take on a golden color without burning.

Serve in a vegetable dish.

Sautéed cauliflower, prepared this way, is excellent.

By browning the cauliflower at the last, it would acquire a different taste.

PURÉE GRATINÉE DE CHOU-FLEUR ET DE TOMATE

Baked Purée of Cauliflower and Tomato

For six people, use:

2 lbs. trimmed cauliflower
1 C. well seasoned tomato purée
1 1/2 C. grated Gruyère cheese
6 T. butter
5 tsp. coarse salt
1 tsp. table salt
pepper to taste
1 1/2 qts. water

Boil the water with the coarse salt, throw in the trimmed and washed cauliflower, and let it cook for twenty minutes.

Remove the cauliflower, drain it, and purée it.

Cook the tomato purée with 4 tablespoons of butter for five minutes.

In a saucepan, put the rest of the butter, the cauliflower purée, 2/3 cup of the cheese, the table salt, and the pepper. Heat everything up, then add the tomato purée and mix well.

Spoon everything into a baking dish, sprinkle with the rest of the cheese, and brown in the oven for ten or fifteen minutes.

CHOUX DE BRUXELLES

Brussels Sprouts

Select some nice, tight little Brussels sprouts, trim them, wash them, and blanch them for ten minutes in boiling water. Now, plunge them into another saucepan filled with boiling, salted water in which you will let them cook anywhere from five to fifteen minutes according to the quality of the sprouts. They should cook just long enough so that they are tender but not mushy. Drain them.

Brussels sprouts may be prepared in various ways: coated with melted butter, either covered or not with browned breadcrumbs, seasoned with salt, pepper, and nutmeg to taste; sautéed in butter over high heat for six to eight minutes and served sprinkled with parsley or not; smothered (steamed) in butter; in salad: after they have been cooked, keeping them slightly firm, they are allowed to cool, then they are seasoned to taste with oil, vinegar or lemon juice, salt, and pepper.

CHOUX DE BRUXELLES À LA CRÈME

Creamed Brussels Sprouts

For four people, use:

½ C. heavy cream
3 T. butter
1½ tsp. table salt
1 qt. Brussels sprouts
2 C. milk

Trim the sprouts, blanch them for ten minutes in boiling, salted water, drain them, then put them in a saucepan with the milk and the salt. Let them simmer very slowly for an hour to an hour and a half. Add the butter and the cream, heat for a few minutes without boiling, and serve.

Brussels sprouts, tempered by the milk which they have absorbed, have not the slightest hint of hydrogen sulfide. They are very nourishing and easy to digest.

For variation, one could purée the Brussels sprouts and garnish the purée with croûtons fried in butter.

CHOU BRAISÉ AU MADÉRE

Cabbage Braised in Madeira

For six people, use:

1 lb. sausages (country style)
½ lb. salt pork
1 C. madeira wine
¼ lb. smoked bacon
2 carrots
2 small onions
4 T. butter or roast beef fat
1 large white or curly cabbage
bouquet garni
spices
salt and pepper

Trim and wash the cabbage. Blanch it for ten minutes in boiling water and drain it.

Blanch the salt pork and the bacon to remove any excess salt. Wipe them and chop or grind them up.

Cook this hash in the butter or roast beef fat for a few minutes to brown it lightly.

In a kettle put the cabbage, the browned pork and pan juices, carrots, onions, *bouquet garni*, and season with salt, pepper, and spices to taste. Add the madeira and simmer very slowly in the closed kettle for three to four hours. A little before serving, remove the carrots, onions, and *bouquet garni*, and season to taste with salt, if necessary. Boil down the cooking liquid.

Broil the sausages.

Arrange the cabbage on a platter, garnish with the sausages, and serve.

For variation, one could substitute, for the salt pork, some chicken giblets sautéed in butter and cooked with carrots, onions, *bouquet garni*, salt, pepper, and spices in some strong stock enriched with chicken glaze.

When the pan juices have been reduced to a semi-glaze, one would purée the chicken giblets and the pan juices. One would cook this a little longer with the cabbage and madeira until the cabbage is done.

It would be served as above.

CHOU GARNI

Cabbage Garnished with Ham and Sausages

For six people, use:

2 lbs. cold roast meat (tenderloin, sirloin of beef, leg of lamb, pork tenderloin, saddle of hare, tenderloin of deer or boar, etc.)
2 lbs. pork bones
3 C. white wine
1 lb. smoked ham (cooked in white wine and cooled)
1/2 lb. slightly salted bacon
1/2 lb. apples
1 C. fat from roast chicken or pheasant
1/2 C. butter
3 frankfurters
3 Strasbourg-type sausage[1]
1 cervelas-type sausage[1]
1 large white round cabbage
vinegar
granulated sugar
salt and pepper

Trim the cabbage, wash it, shred it as for sauerkraut, blanch it, and drain it.

Peel the apples, slice them thin, and remove the seeds.

In the chicken fat cook the finely chopped bacon; then add the butter, cabbage, salt and pepper, and mix well for a few minutes.

Arrange the pork bones in the bottom of a porcelain casserole, on top put the bacon and cabbage mixture, pour over the white wine, add the apples, and let this simmer for three hours. Then add the sausages and cook just long enough for the sausages to be cooked, twenty to thirty minutes for the larger ones and ten to fifteen minutes for the smaller ones.

Taste, the dish must have a pleasant, slightly sweet-sour taste. If the wine and the apples have not given this taste, correct the seasoning either with a little sugar or a little vinegar.

Just before serving add the sliced cold meat and ham and just heat up.

Arrange the cabbage on a platter, garnish with the ham, the meat, sausages, and serve.

This dish is completely different from what is known as *Choucroute Garnie* (Garnished Sauerkraut; see recipe index); but it is just as interesting.

NOTE

1. The sausages—either small or large type—used in this dish can vary according to what types are available in each locality. Knackwurst, Smokie link, thuringer, bratwurst, and Polish sausage are among the many types which could be used here.

For four people, use:

1 C. Béchamel sauce made with chicken or veal broth
$^1/_2$ C. butter
$1^1/_2$ C. grated Gruyère cheese
$^1/_3$ C. dry, sifted breadcrumbs
1 trimmed cabbage weighing 4 lbs.
salt and pepper

CHOU À LA BÉCHAMEL, GRATINÉ

Cabbage with Béchamel Sauce Browned in the Oven

Blanch the cabbage in boiling, salted water and drain it.

In a saucepan put 7 tablespoons of butter, heat it up, add the cabbage, season with salt and pepper to taste. Mix well for several minutes then cover the pan and let it bake in the oven, very slowly, for two to three hours.

In a casserole, arrange layers of cabbage, alternately with cheese and Béchamel sauce. End up with sauce. Sprinkle the top with the breadcrumbs, dot with the rest of the butter, and brown in a slow oven for fifteen minutes.

This dish may be served as a vegetable course for a family meal.

CHOU ROUGE CONFIT AU VINAIGRE

Red Cabbage Pickled in Vinegar

Select a nice, large, firm, red cabbage. Cut it into wedges, trim off the large outside leaves and any tough ribs, and shred it as for sauerkraut.

Put it in a bowl with 2 handfuls of coarse salt and let it macerate for twenty-four hours. Keep it in a cool place. Then drain the cabbage.

In a large crock put a few sprigs of parsley and some tarragon leaves, a little thyme, a clove of garlic, 2 hot red peppers, 6 cloves, and 40 peppercorns; then add the cabbage and on top place some parsley, tarragon, and slices of peeled lemon. Drown everything in strong red wine vinegar, cover, and let this pickle for ten days in a warm spot. At the end of that time the cabbage is ready to be used.

Pickled red cabbage is an excellent condiment and is particularly good with boiled beef. It may be served as is or with some olive oil and flavored with cumin.

For four people, use:

2 lbs. sauerkraut
$1^1/_2$ lbs. veal shank
2 C. white wine
$^1/_4$ lb. butter
2 small carrots
2 small turnips
1 leek
1 slice onion
freshly ground black pepper to taste
6 juniper berries

CHOUCROUTE AU NATUREL

Plain Sauerkraut

Prepare 3 cups of veal stock by cooking the veal and vegetables in water.

Wash the sauerkraut and soak out the salt if necessary. Drain it and put it in a porcelain kettle. Season it with pepper, add the butter and juniper berries, pour in the stock and the wine, and start it up over high heat; then let it simmer over low heat for an hour and a half, so that all the liquid is absorbed.

Thus cooked, sauerkraut is white, slightly crispy, and excellent in flavor. It may be served alone or as a garnish.

Garnished with boiled potatoes and frankfurters it is the simplest of the garnished sauerkraut dishes.

CHOUCROUTE GARNIE

Garnished Sauerkraut

For four people, use:

- 2 lbs. sauerkraut
- 2 lbs pork bones
- 3 C. white wine
- 1 C. chicken fat or pork fat (melted)
- 1/2 lb. smoked ham cooked in white wine
- 1/2 lb. sliced, smoked, or pickled tongue
- freshly ground black pepper to taste
- 8 juniper berries
- 8 breaded pork chops
- salt

Freshen and wash the sauerkraut as usual. Then cook it with the bones, pork fat, ham, pepper, juniper berries, and wine for eight to ten hours.

Just before serving, broil the pork chops.

Arrange the sauerkraut on a platter, garnish it with the pork chops, and decorate the platter with the tongue.

For variation, one could substitute for the chicken or pork fat some fat from either feathered or furred game which has been roasted. For the ham, tongue, and pork chops, one could substitute, for instance, slices of wild boar or roasted pheasant.

One would then have a sauerkraut garnished with game with a very delicate flavor and one which is elegant to present for a hunters' luncheon.

MUSHROOMS

Mushrooms may be broiled, sautéed, fried; shirred; braised; prepared with butter, oil, cream, stock; prepared with different sauces whose base could be wine, cream, meat glaze, game stock; served *à la Béchamel, à la poulette, à la sauce Mornay, à la sauce financière, à la sauce suprême*; in stew; stuffed; *au gratin*; prepared in fricassees, in ragoûts, in hashes, in purées. They may go into the preparation of soups, omelets, scrambled eggs, fish dishes, meat dishes, *pâtés*, stuffings; they may also be served in *croustades*, vol-au-vents, custards, tartlets; they can be used as a condiment or as a filling or as a garnish; they can be served as an hors-d'oeuvre; in salad; and, last, they can be preserved or pickled.

Before serving mushrooms, it is wise, in certain species, to remove the skin of the cap (the cuticle), the gills, and the tubes. Sometimes it is also necessary to remove the stems, which can be tough. They are then washed and dried in a towel.

Mushrooms must not be cooked for a long time, because they lose a great deal of their flavor.

Mushrooms with thick flesh such as the Amanita, Tricholoma, Pleurota, Psalliota, Russula, Lactarius, boletus, certain of the Pholiotas and meadow mushrooms, may be broiled whole, directly on a broiler or in a buttered pan and flavored with garlic, shallots, and *fines herbes*. They would be served either with a maître d'hôtel butter or with a snail butter *(à la bourguignonne)*, or with some other sort of flavored butter.

They may be cooked whole in a cooking–serving dish, with butter, chives, garlic or *fines herbes*, salt, pepper, *quatre épices** or nutmeg to taste, then sauced with cream sauce thickened with egg yolks, or with a Béchamel sauce made with or without meat stock, and enriched with butter.

Another way of presenting them in their serving dish is the following: After having lightly salted the mushrooms on the underside, so as to have them render their water, then having wiped them and dried them out in front of an open oven door, they are arranged in a porcelain casserole lined with grape and fennel leaves soaked in oil. They are then flavored with garlic and onion, to taste, and seasoned with salt, pepper, and spices. The caps are decorated with slices of stem and they are then cooked. This recipe is known as *à la génoise*.

All mushrooms may be sautéed. This method of preparing them, however, should be reserved for small mushrooms because they can be kept whole. Naturally, one can sauté large mushrooms, but the procedure is a little more difficult. Thus the Clitocybe, with its sweet or floury aroma, the Laccaria, Hygrophore, Clitopilus, Pholiota, Marasmius, Verpa, and the small meadow mushroom or tiny boletus mushroom may be sautéed in butter or oil with garlic, chopped parsley, salt, pepper, and nutmeg *(à la provençal)*; with shallots, parsley, salt, pepper, and spices and sprinkled with lemon juice *(à la bordelaise)*; with *fines herbes*, salt, and pepper, then moistened with game stock and their pan juices thickened with cream and flavored with lemon juice; or even sautéed with minced truffles and their cooking juices subsequently enriched with light meat glaze or chicken glaze and then thickened with cream.

A butter sauce with chopped almonds or pistachios and lemon juice would be sufficient for many mushroom lovers.

Whole or cut up mushrooms may be sautéed alone or with minced truffles, in plain or flavored butter; and then the cooking would be finished up in madeira, port, or sauterne wine and the cooking juices would be flavored and enriched with game glaze. These sautéed mushrooms could be served in tartlet shells.

Mushrooms may also be sautéed *à la barigoule,* with bacon, butter or oil, pepper, parsley, and shallot.

When one wishes to fry mushrooms one could proceed as follows: After having blanched them for a few minutes in water or milk seasoned with a little lemon rind, they would be fried in very hot fat and could be served either sugared or salted. In the latter case they would be served with a maître d'hôtel or some other sort of flavored butter, or in some good meat broth.

Mushrooms may be prepared in a type of stew with anchovies, parsley, garlic, pepper, white wine, oil, and lemon juice; or with olives, *bouquet garni,* garlic or shallot, salt, pepper, butter, and madeira; or even with tomatoes and some good stock. This method of preparing them, *en daube,* is very suitable for the Clavaria, Hydnum, Entoloma, Polyporus, Cortinarius, Collybia, Paxillus, and Fistulina.

All the large mushrooms with thick flesh—such as the Orange Amanita, Tricholoma, Pleurotus, Lactarius, Russula, Volvariella, Pholiota, Psalliota, boletus, and meadow mushroom—and the large mushrooms with thin flesh—such as the Lepiota, Pluteus, Clitocybe, and Pleziza, as well as the morel—may be stuffed. The stuffing could be without meat, using delicate ingredients such as shellfish, fish, shrimp, crayfish, mushrooms, asparagus, artichokes, etc. These would be cooked in a good fish stock or a good white stock enriched with light meat glaze. The stuffing could also be made with meat, using bacon, ham, or delicate meats such as chicken, partridge, quail, thrush, ortolan. These stuffing ingredients would be cooked in a good beef stock or a good veal or chicken stock, or even a game stock.

To prepare mushrooms *au gratin,* it is generally sufficient to sprinkle the top surface of a great many of the mushroom recipes with dry, sifted breadcrumbs either mixed with some grated Gruyère or Parmesan cheese, or a mixture of both, or not, dot the top with butter and brown in the oven.

One may also make some *au gratin* mushroom dishes using sliced or chopped mushrooms coated with Mornay or Béchamel sauce, made with or without meat stock, or coated with tomato sauce.

When one wishes to prepare fricasseed mushrooms, a good way of proceeding is the following: Cook them in a saucepan with some butter, sprinkle them with flour, and cook and stir for several minutes without letting the flour brown. Season with salt, pepper, some spices, add some chopped parsley, meat, chicken, or game glaze, as desired, thicken with cream and egg yolks, and at the last moment spike the dish with a little vinegar or lemon juice. The Lycoperdon, Bovista, Sparassis, Chanterelle, Coprinus, Helvella, Peziza, Lactarius, Craterellus, Armillaria, Paxillus, Hydnum, Clavaria, and Polyporus may be prepared as above.

Mushrooms with a very delicate flavor must be used as a vegetable dish. The Orange Amanita, Lepiota, Tricholoma, the delicious Lactarius, the Pleurotus, Eryngium, Russula, Chanterelle, Pholiota, Psalliota, Lycoperdon, Boletus, Helvella, Coprinus, the beautiful cultivated mushroom, the morel, prepared with butter, with cream, with Béchamel sauce, *à la poulette*, with Mornay sauce, with suprême sauce, *à la financière, en matelote, en salmis*, etc., are delicious dishes which can be served as is or as a filling for a pastry crust or vol-au-vent.

All mushrooms may be incorporated into meat stews; however, I suggest that one should use mushrooms which have little flavor or dried mushrooms.

Mushrooms with delicate and agreeable flavor may also be used in omelets and scrambled eggs, such as morels, truffles, craterellas, etc.

Small marinated cultivated mushrooms would be served as an hors-d'oeuvre.

The Fistulinus and Lactarius, which are rich in milk, after having been blanched, may be served raw in salad.

The boletus can very advantageously be substituted for cultivated mushrooms in all culinary preparations, and, like many other mushrooms, they may be served as a vegetable course or as a garnish.

Morels give a delicious taste to all the dishes in which they are used, and they are also a superlative vegetable dish.

Truffles, like other fungi, are eaten plain, in stews or in salad. They are very often used as a garnish, and they are used in the finest forcemeats.

One of the best ways of preparing them, a method known as *à la maréchale*, consists, after having seasoned them with salt and pepper, in wrapping them in pork fat, and then individually in paper, and cooking them in hot wood ashes. About one hour would be enough. When they are cooked, one removes all the wrapping, one wipes them and then arranges them on a platter covered with a napkin. The truffles are covered, and they are served as is with butter. These truffles *au naturel* are absolutely exquisite. If no wood ashes are available, the seasoned and wrapped truffles may be cooked on a skewer or in a saucepan.

One may also cook truffles sprinkled with salt, pepper, and herbs, either in plain steam, or steam from wine and brandy. They may also be cooked in butter or even in madeira, port, or Alicante wine, or champagne, basting them with some good strong stock.

They are also be prepared in ragoûts, either oven browned or not. They can be sautéed, either alone or with potatoes. They are served glazed, stuffed, in aspic, in pastry crusts, etc. Truffle *pâtés à la Monglas,* truffled timbales *à la Talleyrand,* turkeys, and truffled capons all belong to classic cuisine.

Gray truffles, which have a peculiar flavor, are suitable for risotto. However, one may, after having sliced them, sauté them in oil and then finish cooking them in chicken stock to which one adds a little lemon juice at the last minute. Finally, they may be served in salad. Rossini loved them thus.

CHAMPIGNONS DE COUCHE FARCIS

Stuffed Cultivated Mushrooms

There are many ways of stuffing mushrooms. Most of the recipes use onion, shallot, or garlic. Here are several which do not contain these, and, for this reason, they may be useful in many cases.

To garnish a dish prepared for six people, use:

5 oz. tiny mushrooms
6 (2 oz. each) large mushrooms
1 egg yolk
butter
meat, chicken or game stock
lemon juice
dry, sifted breadcrumbs
chopped parsley
quatre épices
curry
salt and pepper

Peel the mushrooms; dip them in lemon juice. Remove the stems of the large mushrooms and reserve the caps. Chop the tiny mushrooms along with the large mushroom stems. Prepare a hash with the mushrooms, dry, sifted breadcrumbs soaked in stock, chopped parsley, butter, the egg yolk, and seasonings.

Fill the large mushroom caps with this mixture and arrange them, hollow side up, in a buttered casserole. Sprinkle each mushroom with lemon juice, dot each with a tiny piece of butter, and bake in a slow oven.

CHAMPIGNONS DE COUCHE FARCIS, GRATINÉS

Baked Stuffed Cultivated Mushrooms

For four people, use:

1 lb. largest possible mushrooms
1½ C. strong veal stock
½ lb. shrimp
3 T. butter
⅓ C. grated Gruyère, Parmesan, or Chester cheese
1 tsp. flour
1 small bunch asparagus tips
salt and pepper

Peel the mushrooms, remove the stems, and wash the stems and caps in acidulated water.

Chop the stems and cook them in 3 tablespoons of veal stock.

Cut up the asparagus tips and blanch them in salted water.

Shell the shrimps.

With the shrimp shells and the butter, prepare a shrimp butter.

Chop together the shrimps and asparagus tips, mix with the chopped mushroom stems, taste, and add salt and pepper if necessary. This constitutes the stuffing.

Cook the mushroom caps for a few minutes in the rest of the stock. Arrange them, hollow side up, in a casserole. Fill them with the stuffing, sprinkle on the grated cheese and dot with two-thirds of the shrimp butter. Bake them in the oven and baste them as they cook.

Arrange the stuffed mushrooms on a serving platter and keep them hot.

Blend the flour with the remaining shrimp butter in a small saucepan, stir in the liquid from the mushroom pan, and reduce. Coat the mushrooms with the sauce and serve.

Stuffed mushrooms may be served as a hot hors-d'oeuvre, a vegetable course, or a garnish.

PURÉE DE CHAMPIGNONS

Mushroom Purée

For six people, use:

2 lbs. mushrooms
1¾ C. thick Béchamel sauce made with or without meat stock
10 T. butter
½ C. heavy cream
salt, pepper, nutmeg

Wash the mushrooms, sponge them off, and dry them in a towel. Peel them, chop them coarsely, and force them, raw, through a coarse sieve. Put this purée in a skillet with 4 tablespoons of butter. Let this cook over fairly high heat until all the liquid has evaporated. Now add the Béchamel sauce and the cream and season with salt, pepper, and nutmeg to taste. Heat up over high heat for a moment to thicken the sauce, and, last, off the fire, enrich the purée with the rest of the butter.

Truffle purée may be prepared the same way.

CÈPES GRILLÉS

Broiled Boletus

For six people, use:

½ C. clarified butter
2 tsp. table salt
1 T. chopped parsley
pepper
6 large, firm boletus weighing about 2 lbs. in all
6 large cloves of garlic

Clean the boletus, wipe them, remove the tubes, and cut off the stem at cap level.

Cut each clove of garlic into four, stick each mushroom cap with 4 slivers of garlic, then put them for thirty minutes in the warm, clarified butter.

Arrange the boletus on a heated broiler rack and broil them five minutes per side, seasoning them with salt and pepper, and basting them with the garlic-flavored butter. Remove the garlic slivers.

Arrange the caps on a platter, sprinkle with chopped parsley and serve.

This is a perfect dish.

CÈPES AU CHESTER[1]

Boletus with Chester Cheese

Sauté some tiny, fresh, young boletus in a little olive oil. Then arrange them in a casserole, coat with a little Béchamel sauce made with meat stock into which you have mixed some Chester cheese. Brown in the oven.

Boletus can also be prepared this way with Gruyère cheese, Parmesan cheese, etc.

NOTE

1. This recipe can very well be used for ordinary cultivated mushrooms.

CÈPES À LA BORDELAISE[1]

Boletus à la Bordelaise

For six people, use:

2 lbs. fresh, medium-size, uniform boletus
½ C. olive oil
4 chopped shallots
2 T. chopped parsley
1 large clove grated garlic
1 T. table salt
pepper
lemon juice

Clean the boletus, wipe them, discard the tubes, and reserve the caps.

Peel and chop the stems.

Heat the oil in a skillet, put in the caps, hollow side down. After five minutes of cooking, season with salt and pepper, turn them over and cook them for five more minutes. Salt and pepper again, add the chopped stems, and cook these together for another five minutes. Now add the shallots and cook two minutes, add the garlic and parsley, cook for another minute, and salt and pepper again.

Arrange the mushrooms on a hot platter, pour on the contents of the skillet, sprinkle with lemon juice and serve.

If no fresh boletus are available one could use canned ones. One must, in this case, before using them, drain them well and wash them in boiling water. The rest of the recipe remains the same.

I suggest, for those who do not have a strong stomach, the following modifications: omitting the shallots; replacing the grated garlic with a whole garlic clove, which would be added to the oil along with the mushrooms but which would be removed after ten minutes.

The rest of the recipe remains the same.

Here is a variation which I prefer. Instead of the half-cup of olive oil, I use a mixture consisting of ⅓ cup of clarified butter and 1 tablespoon of olive oil. The procedure remains the same. These are not really boletus *à la bordelaise*, but they are very good anyway.

NOTE

1. This recipe can be used for cultivated mushrooms as well.

CÈPES AU GRATIN

Baked Boletus

For six people, use:

7 T. butter
1 1/4 C. grated Gruyère cheese
2/3 C. dry, sifted breadcrumbs
2 T. olive oil
2 T. milk
3 T. breadcrumbs (fresh)
2 1/2 tsp. salt
1 T. chopped parsley
1 large clove grated garlic
1 tsp. powdered mustard
pepper
nutmeg
6 large boletus, weighing about 2 lbs. together

Clean the boletus, wipe them carefully, and remove the caps. Arrange them on a baking sheet, dark side up, and bake them in a moderate oven for twenty minutes to render any excess water.

Chop the stems, add the garlic, parsley, fresh breadcrumbs soaked in milk, mustard, nutmeg, oil, salt, and pepper. Mix everything thoroughly.

Butter a casserole, spoon in a layer of the stuffing which you have just prepared, sprinkle on some cheese, arrange the boletus caps on top, and on each one put one-sixth of the remaining butter. Sprinkle with Gruyère cheese, cover with the rest of the stuffing, and finish off with the rest of the cheese and the dry breadcrumbs.

Bake in a slow oven for thirty minutes; then raise the heat and brown for fifteen minutes.

CÈPES À LA CRÈME

Boletus with Cream

For six people, use:

2 lbs. tiny, young, fresh boletus
1/2 C. cream
5 T. butter
2 oz. fennel stalks with leaves
2 T. milk
2 T. coarse salt
5 tsp. meat glaze
2 T. flour
1 T. mild wine vinegar
2 tsp. tablesalt
pepper to taste

Wipe the boletus without peeling them. Trim the stems, then plunge them for a few seconds in 2 quarts of boiling water, to which you have added the coarse salt and the vinegar.

Remove them; drain them well in a colander.

In a saucepan put 4 tablespoons of butter, stir in the flour, and then add the milk and 4 tablespoons of cream. Add all but a little of the fennel, and table salt, and the pepper. Heat up, give it one boil, and add the boletus; then cook this until the pan liquids are fairly concentrated, which would be from twenty to thirty minutes.

Arrange the mushrooms in a serving dish, pull out the fennel stalks from the sauce, add the remaining butter, the rest of the cream, and the meat glaze. Heat the sauce up, pour over the mushrooms, sprinkle with the rest of the fennel, chopped, and serve.

Cultivated mushrooms may be prepared the same way.

CÈPES À LA LIMOUSINE

Boletus à la Limousine

For six people, use:

1 lb. bacon
3 oz. swiss chard
1 1/4 C. dry, sifted breadcrumbs
2 T. chopped parsley
6 large, firm boletus, weighing about 1 lb. together
6 potatoes, weighing about 1 lb. together
sheets of pork fat
garlic
nutmeg or *quatre épices**
salt and pepper

Wash the mushrooms, dry them, and discard the tubes. Separate stems and caps and chop the former.

Blanch the bacon to remove any excess salt. Wipe it dry, chop it, and cook it in a skillet.

Blanch the Swiss chard in boiling water and chop it up.

Mix the bacon, chopped mushroom stems, chopped chard, breadcrumbs, and chopped parsley. Add a little chopped garlic and some salt and pepper to taste, and mix well. This is the stuffing.

Peel the potatoes, hollow them out to make room for the stuffing, and fill the cavities with the stuffing.

Force the removed potato pulp through a strainer or purée it in some way; press it hard to remove all excess water; and mix some of this pulp with the stuffing mixture. Season with salt, pepper, nutmeg, or *quatre épices,** and stuff the mushroom caps.

Lay some sheets or strips of pork fat on the bottom of a braising kettle or Dutch oven. On top arrange the potatoes and mushroom caps, hollows up, cover and braise in a slow oven for three hours. Baste often as they cook.

Arrange the potatoes and mushrooms alternately on a serving platter and coat them with the skimmed pan juices.

FRICASSÉE DE CÈPES AU PARMESAN

Fricassee of Boletus with Parmesan

For six people, use:

2 lbs. tiny, fresh, young boletus
1/2 C. butter
4 tsp. meat glaze
1/2 C. grated Parmesan cheese
2 tsp. salt
pepper
quatre épices

Clean and wipe off the boletus and slice them about one-third-inch thick.

In a skillet put the butter, mushrooms, salt, pepper, and *quatre épices* and cook them over high heat for twenty minutes. When the mushroom liquid has evaporated sufficiently add the meat glaze, let it melt; then add the Parmesan, taste, and serve.

Cultivated mushrooms may be prepared the same way.

CHANTERELLES À LA CRÈME

Chanterelles with Cream

For four people, use:

2 lbs. freshly picked chanterelles[1]
3/4 C. cream
3 T. butter
salt and pepper

Peel the chanterelles; wash and drain them.

Put them in a skillet with some salt and pepper and sauté them as is, and they will render their water as they cook. It takes about twenty minutes for all the liquid to disappear. Then add the butter and the cream, taste, complete the seasoning if necessary, let this all simmer for four or five minutes, and serve.

NOTE

1. Chanterelles are commonly known in France as *giroles.*

For four people, use:

2 lbs. fresh chanterelles
1 C. veal and chicken stock
4 T. butter
lemon rind
tarragon
salt and pepper

CHANTERELLES AU JUS

Chanterelles with Meat Broth

Peel the chanterelles; wash and drain them.

Melt the butter in a skillet, add the mushrooms, some lemon rind and tarragon to taste (either chopped or, if whole, wrapped in cheesecloth), season with salt and pepper but taking into account the seasoning in the stock. Sauté until the mushrooms, having rendered their water, become almost dry again. Now add the stock and let this simmer for about a half hour. Discard the cheesecloth bag, if you have used one, and serve the mushrooms.

For variation, one could substitute for the veal and chicken stock some Béchamel sauce made with or without meat stock, a poulette sauce, a Mornay sauce. In the last case, one would put the dish in the oven to brown.

For four people, use:

1 lb. large gray morels
7 T. butter
1 1/2 tsp. salt
pepper
lemon juice

MORILLES AU BEURRE

Morels in Butter

Carefully wash the morels, wipe them, and cut them in half lengthwise. Put them in a saucepan with the butter, salt, pepper, and lemon juice, to taste. Sauté them over a hot fire for fifteen minutes, until the water they have rendered has evaporated.

Morels prepared this way may be served alone or as a garnish for meats.

For four people, use:

1 lb. morels
1 C. cream
1/2 C. bouillon
1/2 C. butter
4 tsp. flour
2 tsp. salt
pepper
juice of a lemon

MORILLES À LA CREME

Creamed Morels

Clean, wash, and dry the morels. Cut them in two lengthwise.

Melt 5 tablespoons of butter in a saucepan, add the mushrooms, salt, and pepper, pour in the stock, and add the lemon juice. Let this all cook for a half hour. At the end of this time almost all of the liquid should have disappeared. Now add the cream, stir in 2 teaspoons of butter blended with the flour, and continue to simmer for ten minutes.

At serving time whisk the rest of the butter into the sauce.

One may serve creamed morels in a large puff pastry case or vol-au-vent, or in a bread case, or just simply with fried croûtons.

MORILLES AU JUS

Morels in Meat Broth

Wash the mushrooms carefully to remove any foreign particles from the honeycomb pits. Drain them, wipe them, and cut them in two lengthwise. Then sauté them in a saucepan with butter, add some strong meat stock or pan juices from a roast and a little lemon juice. Season to taste with salt and pepper and cook very slowly for a half hour, basting often as they cook. Last, bind the sauce with some egg yolks and serve.

This is exquisite.

MORILLES AU VIN

Morels in Wine

For three people, use:

1 lb. morels
3/4 C. veal and chicken stock
1/2 lb. chopped ham
1/3 C. sauterne wine
7 T. butter
2 egg yolks
salt and pepper

First prepare the sauce: In a saucepan put the stock, the wine and the ham. Let this cook and reduce quite a bit. Thicken with the egg yolk, taste, and add salt and pepper if necessary.

Clean, wash, and dry the mushrooms. Cut them in two, season with salt and pepper, and sauté them in the butter until all the water they render has evaporated. This process should take about fifteen minutes.

Arrange them in a serving dish kept hot in a hot water bath or *bain-marie*, spoon on the sauce and leave these together, keeping them hot, for fifteen minutes before serving.

These morels may be served in a puff pastry case or vol-au-vent.

MORILLES FARCIES, EN COCOTTES

Stuffed Morels in Ramekins

For six people, use:

1 lb. large, gray morels
1 C. butter
2 1/2 C. grated Parmesan cheese
2 C. dry, sifted breadcrumbs
1 tsp. salt
pepper to taste

Clean the morels thoroughly and dry them. Remove the stems and chop them along with several of the morels (use the smallest ones), so as to have in all about five ounces of hash.

Put 3/4 cup of butter in a saucepan, let it melt, add the morel hash, the breadcrumbs, 1 1/2 cups of the Parmesan, and the salt and pepper. Mix this all up very well and stuff the morels with this mixture.

Select six small ramekins with covers. Arrange the morels, stuffing side up, in the ramekins. Sprinkle with the rest of the Parmesan, dot with the remaining butter, and seal the covers on with a mixture of flour and water. Bake the mushrooms in their ramekins in a pan of hot water, in the oven, for one hour.

Serve in the ramekins.

CONSERVATION DES CHAMPIGNONS

Preserving Mushrooms

Mushrooms which are to be preserved in some way must be freshly picked, must be harvested in dry weather, and should not have reached full maturity.

There are several ways of preserving mushrooms. First is the hot water bath. After having peeled the mushrooms, one throws them into a large pot full of lightly salted, boiling water, and they are allowed to boil for twenty minutes. They are then drained on a fine hair-sieve and cooled by pouring over them some cooled, boiled water. After having sponged them off thoroughly one places them in canning jars which will then be completely filled up with boiled, salted water which has been cooled (5 teaspoons of salt per quart of water). The jars are hermetically sealed with sterilized tops. The jars are placed in a canning kettle on a rack, the kettle is filled with water to the level of the tops and the jars are boiled for four or five hours, adding water so that the level remains the same. The cooled jars are put under observation for about eight days. If, during that time, there have been no signs of fermentation, the process was successful.

Mushrooms, thus preserved, may be used like fresh ones, as long as they are put first in warm water, after removing from the jars, and then in cold water to stiffen them.

The second method of preservation is in salt. One arranges the mushrooms in a crock, separating the layers of mushrooms with salt. This process only insures preservation for several months.

The third method is preservation in vinegar. Mushrooms may be pickled in vinegar in the same way as cucumbers, but they must first be blanched in boiling water. Pickled mushrooms are served as a condiment or as an hors-d'oeuvre.

Desiccation is the fourth method. Tiny mushrooms may be dried whole. The larger ones must be sliced after having been peeled, and gills, tubes, and stems discarded. The whole or sliced mushrooms are set, a certain distance from each other, on screens placed in the shade in a dry location.

They can be made into chaplets by stringing on heavy thread, making sure they do not touch one another. These garlands should be hung in the shade where they will get plenty of air circulation. According to the type of mushrooms and the humidity of the air, desiccation may take from several days to a few weeks.

One may also dry mushrooms in hot air or in a moderate oven.

Dried mushrooms are kept in cloth or paper bags, which are shaken from time to time, or they are kept in sealed jars in a dry location. When one wishes to use the dried mushrooms, they are first soaked in warm water for one hour, then they are used as though they were fresh.

Mushrooms, dried, as above, may be pounded in a mortar and then sifted. This powder is kept in tightly sealed jars and kept in a dry location.

Another way to preserve mushrooms is in some sort of fat. In the south of France mushrooms are preserved in oil, fat, or butter. After having blanched the mushrooms in boiling water and having dried them in a towel, one puts them into small porcelain crocks, which are then filled with olive oil or melted fat or butter. The level of the fat must be an inch or more over the top of the mushrooms. These jars or crocks are then sealed with corks and these in turn covered with parchment fastened with string.

Un-blanched mushrooms may also be preserved this way, by simply sautéeing them in some sort of fat so as to dehydrate them before putting them in jars or crocks.

These should be kept in a cool, dry spot. Liquefication is still another method. In England, they use a great deal of liquefied mushrooms in a condiment which is called ketchup. Here is how one proceeds to make this: Mushrooms are sliced and placed in a fine hair-sieve. They are sprinkled with table salt. Without pressing them, one lets the juice collect below the sieve. In order to avoid having any deposits, one decants the liquid into small bottles. Space is left for adding some kind of brandy to keep the ketchup from spoiling. The bottles are sealed and kept in a cool spot.

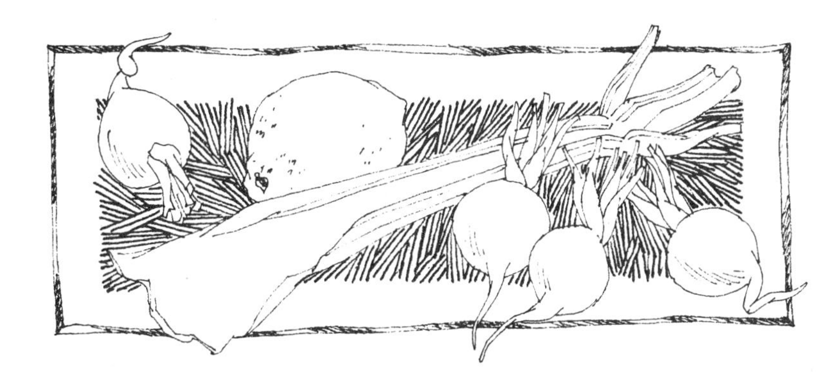

SALADS

SALADES VERTES

Green Salads

Green salads are most often dressed with oil and vinegar. They may also be prepared with cream, which would replace the oil. Their taste depends not only on the nature and the condition of the ingredients used (the freshness of the greens, the quality of the oil and the vinegar), but also on their preliminary preparation. Greens such as lettuce, romaine, escarole, and chicory gain much lightness and delicacy when you remove the tough ribs and when you revive them for a long time in very cold water, if they have not been freshly picked. Needless to say, one must only serve the tender parts of all these greens, to get a really good dish.

The seasoning is prepared, to taste, with oil, vinegar, salt, and pepper, to which one may add a fresh egg yolk. But, the salad must not be mixed until the last minute before serving, and, contrary to the method many people use, it must be very gently and delicately tossed, without bruising it.

NOTE

1. Salads are either cooked or raw foods, served cold, with a sauce whose base contains a fat element and an acid element.

SALADE DE LAITUE À LA CRÈME

Lettuce Salad with Cream

Select some nice lettuce,[1] wash and drain it well.

Prepare, in a salad bowl, a well-blended mixture of cream, lemon juice, or vinegar, sieved hard-boiled egg yolk, salt, and pepper—everything to taste. Add the lettuce and toss it gently until it is evenly coated. Serve at once.

By omitting the hard-boiled egg yolk, and by substituting for regular cream some whipped cream, you would have a salad which some people find a little lighter than the preceding one.

These recipes are applicable to romaine, curly chicory, escarole, Belgian endive, dandelion greens, etc.

NOTE

1. When the French refer to *laitue* (lettuce) they mean Boston-type lettuce, not iceberg.

SALADE DE HARICOTS VERTS ET DE TOMATES

Tomato and Stringbean Salad

For six people, use:

1½ lbs. green stringbeans
1½ lbs. tomatoes
3 T. olive or nut oil
1 T. wine vinegar
1 T. Worcestershire sauce
salt

Remove the strings and the tips of the beans and cook them in salted water.

Scald the tomatoes, peel, seed, and slice them. Let them render their water by sprinkling with coarse salt. Lift the tomatoes out of the rendered liquid and shake them to remove all excess salt.

In a salad bowl mix the oil, vinegar, and Worcestershire sauce; add the stringbeans and tomato slices, mix again, and let these remain together for an hour. Serve. This is a very refreshing salad.

SALADE DE SALSIFIS

Salsify Salad[1]

For six to eight people, use:

1 1/4 lb. peeled salsify
10 oz. peeled celeriac
10 oz. tomatoes
1 C. olive oil
12 walnuts
2 egg yolks
1 lemon
oil
vinegar
salt and pepper

Cut the salisfy into sticks and the celeriac to match. Shell the walnuts and chop them coarsely.

Scald the tomatoes, peel and seed them, and put them to marinate for a half hour in oil, vinegar, salt, and pepper.

Blanch the celery for a few minutes in water with salt and vinegar. Drain and cool. In the same water, cook the salsify, keeping it fairly firm. Drain and cool.

Prepare a mayonnaise with the egg yolks, olive oil, the juice of the lemon, a little salt and pepper, and add to it the salsify, the celeriac, and the nuts. Leave these together for a half hour. At serving time, add the tomatoes along with their marinade; mix well, taste, and complete the seasoning if necessary.

One may prepare, in the same vein, salads of artichoke hearts, Japanese artichokes, soya bean sprouts, etc.

One may also spark the salads with Worcestershire sauce, to taste.

NOTE

1. The salsify is also sold under the name oyster plant. Tender salsify leaves are also used as greens in salads.

SALADE D'ÉPINARDS

Spinach Salad

For six people, use:

3 lbs. fresh spinach
3 T. good quality olive oil
5 tsp. good wine vinegar
4 tsp. prepared mustard
2 tsp. table salt
pepper to taste

Wash and stem the spinach without tearing the leaves. Blanch it quickly in boiling water; drain and cool.

In a salad bowl, put the oil, vinegar, mustard, salt, and pepper. Mix well. Add the spinach leaves and let them marinate, turning frequently for fifteen minutes, being careful not to tear them. Serve.

Spinach salad goes well with cold, light meats, such as veal.

SALADE DE CHOU ROUGE

Red Cabbage Salad

Trim the cabbage, cutting off the large ribs. Wash it, shred it, and blanch it in boiling, salted water. Cool it under running water,

For six people, use:

1 C. heavy cream
4 T. equal proportions of chervil, chives, fennel leaves
6 hard-boiled egg yolks
3 small pickled cucumbers
1 red cabbage, weighing about 2 lbs.
radishes
tarragon vinegar
lemon juice
salt and pepper

drain it, and put it to marinate in tarragon vinegar with salt and pepper. Let these rest together, turning frequently, for about one hour in all. Then remove the cabbage from the marinade and drain it.

Force the egg yolks through a sieve. Mix in the cream; add lemon, salt and pepper to taste, the herb mixture, and the shredded cabbage. Mix well.

Decorate the salad with slices of pickled cucumbers and radishes and serve.

This recipe for red cabbage salad is a little out of the ordinary.

ASPERGES EN SALADE

Asparagus Salad

In boiling salted water, cook on the one hand some large white asparagus, and on the other hand some small green asparagus. Keep the large white asparagus slightly firm. Purée the small green ones. Let everything cool.

Prepare a mayonnaise with lemon juice. Mix into it the green asparagus purée.

Serve the large white asparagus on a platter and pass the mayonnaise in a sauceboat.

You will be delighted.

Other salads may be prepared with this same sauce.

SALADE D'AUBERGINES

Eggplant Salad

For four people, use:

4 medium eggplants
4 long green peppers
oil and vinegar
salt and pepper

Gently broil the peppers and skin them.

Wipe off the eggplants and broil them until soft. Peel them and mash them with a wooden spoon so as to avoid their darkening. Let the purée cool; then season with salt, pepper, oil, and vinegar.

Put this purée on a platter or an hors-d'oeuvre dish; decorate with the peppers and serve.

In the Mideast, this salad is served as an hors-d'oeuvre.

SALADE DE POMMES DE TERRE ET DE CÉLERI

Potato and Celery Salad

For four people, use:

5 oz. celery (leaves and tender stalks washed and drained)
4 T. mild wine vinegar
3 T. olive oil
2 T. water[1]
1 tsp. table salt
1 T. chopped chervil
1 tsp. chopped tarragon
freshly ground black pepper
potatoes

Cook some potatoes, in their skins, in salted water. Peel about 1 pound 3 ounces, while they are still warm, and slice them. Sprinkle them first with the water; then season with 3 tablespoons of vinegar to which you have added the table salt, pepper, and 2 tablespoons of oil. Toss these gently so as not to break up the potato slices. Let them macerate for two hours. Then add the chopped celery and the rest of the oil and vinegar. Mix and let this rest for another fifteen minutes. At the last minute add the chervil and tarragon. Mix again and serve.

NOTE

1. One may, if desired, substitute either bouillon or white wine for the water.

SALADE DE CHOUCROUTE ET DE POMMES DE TERRE

Sauerkraut and Potato Salad

For eight people, use:

2 lbs. potatoes
1 lb. sauerkraut
1 C. white wine
7 oz. tart apples
2/3 C. *sauce douce* **(sweet sauce)**[1]
chopped sour pickles
chopped *fines herbes*
oil
vinegar
salt and pepper

Wash the sauerkraut and drain it well.

Peel the potatoes; steam them and slice them while they are still hot. Pour the white wine over them at once and then mix in the raw sauerkraut.

Peel and dice the apples.

At least two hours before serving, season the potato and sauerkraut mixture with the *sauce douce*, add the apples, *fines herbes*, and pickles and mix again. Taste; complete the seasoning if necessary with oil, vinegar, salt, and pepper. Serve.

This salad is more suitable for robust stomachs.

NOTE

1. To make sauce douce:

For two cups of sauce, use:

3 T. in all mixed chives, tarragon, chervil, and parsley, chopped
1 tsp. granulated sugar
2 hard-boiled egg yolks
oil, vinegar
salt

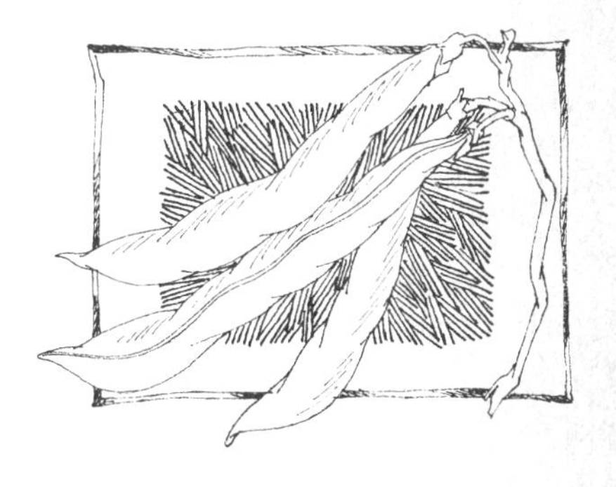

Mash the egg yolks with the herbs, then add the remaining ingredients. Use 1/2 cup of vinegar to 1 1/2 cups of oil, as in regular vinaigrette dressing.

SALADE DE LÉGUMES EN SURPRISE

Surprise Vegetable Salad

This salad is formed into two distinct parts. First is a ring made up of coarsely chopped potato salad mixed with minced celery, the whole seasoned with a very light mayonnaise flavored with hot English mustard. This salad is spooned into a ring mold and thoroughly chilled. Second is a central pyramid made up of cauliflower salad, either in purée or not, seasoned with oil and vinegar and spooned into a charlotte mold and also thoroughly chilled. At serving time it is coated with a very thick, cold, green mayonnaise which gives it the appearance of pistachio ice-cream.

To embellish the platter one may decorate it, on the outside of the ring, with slices of beet, tomato, and red pepper.

This *salade en surprise,* which is very nice tasting, is an amusing culinary joke.

SALADE AUX OEUFS

Egg Salad

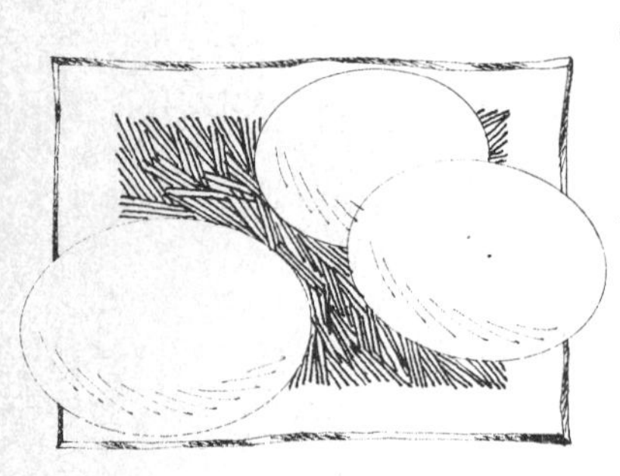

On a platter, arrange in a ring some cooked artichoke hearts. On each heart put either a hard-boiled egg stuffed with a mixture of anchovy and egg yolk, or a coddled egg yolk boiled for three minutes and cooled.

In the center of the ring arrange a small pile of shrimp tails coated with mayonnaise. Garnish the exterior of the ring with seasoned hearts of lettuce and decorate with pickles and capers.

This dish, thus prepared, is quite elegant.

SALADE EXOTIQUE

One may use, in this salad, all or part of the following ingredients: sweet potatoes, yams, Jerusalem artichokes, Japanese artichokes, sorrel, breadfruit, hearts of palm, avocados, okra, coconut, Brazil nuts, pistachio nuts. Use any of these in whatever quantity you wish.

To prepare this salad, cook, either in ashes or in the oven, the sweet potatoes, yams, Jerusalem artichokes, and breadfruit. In salted water, cook the Japanese artichokes, the sorrel, and the okra, keeping them slightly firm and drying them out in front of the open oven door. Cool them.

Cut up the sweet potatoes, yams, Jerusalem artichokes, breadfruit, and sorrel. Put them in a salad bowl, add the Japanese artichokes and okra, either whole or halved, some pitted and sliced avocado, some shredded coconut and a few chopped Brazil and pistachio nuts. Season these with a fairly liquid mayonnaise made with egg yolk, freshly pressed walnut oil or good olive oil, salt, pepper, a little vinegar and some Antilles lemon juice, to taste. One may use *fines herbes* or not, as desired. Mix well and leave them together for twenty minutes before serving.

SALADE RUSSE, À LA FRANCAISE

French-Style Russian Salad

The salad known in France as *Salade Russe* has nothing Russian about it but the name. It is a salad made of a variety of vegetables, such as carrots, artichoke hearts, stringbeans, turnips, tiny peas, asparagus tips, potatoes, small cauliflowerettes, to which one adds capers, truffles, silvers of chicken, pickled tongue—and sometimes also some lobster, anchovy filets, and smoked salmon, the whole is seasoned with mayonnaise or *sauce verte* (green sauce).

SALADE RUSSE

To prepare this salad, use all or part of the ingredients listed in the preceding recipe and add, as to vegetables: salted cucumbers, beets with horseradish, pickled red cabbage, and pickled Russian mushrooms; as to meats: breast of grouse, reindeer tongue, and bear ham; and as to seafood: marinated sterlet, smoked sturgeon, and caviar. All these ingredients are easily available today in Paris and give the salad a right to its name.

Decorate this salad with truffles cooked in champagne and some halved hard-boiled eggs stuffed with caviar.

SALADE DE CHOU-PALMISTE

Hearts of Palm Salad

For six people use one large can of hearts of palm. Open it, drain off the water, and remove the vegetable, which appears in the shape of a cylinder made up of the layers of leaves wrapped around one another. Carefully separate these layers and arrange them in a salad bowl without breaking them.

Prepare a thin mayonnaise made with puréed asparagus tips, which you will add to the palm at serving time.

This salad—which has a faint taste of hazel nut, but has lost a great deal of its original flavor because of the prolonged cooking it has undergone in the canning process—is nevertheless very interesting.

One could add some of the very white leaves of Boston lettuce hearts to give some freshness.

In tropical countries, using fresh heart of palm, this salad is absolutely remarkable. One senses the true flavor of the shoot with all its delicacy. But, in this case, most often one omits the asparagus, and the recipe really needs it. It is only in certain very few areas, where the climate is propitious to the cultivation of the fruits and vegetables from temperate zones as well as those from tropical zones, that one can savor, at its very best, hearts of palm salad with asparagus tips. I had this pleasure at Park Lodge, a charming village setting in the heights above Kingston, in Jamaica, which would be paradise if they only grew truffles. This, in all its simplicity, is the more distinguished of salads; and, if I was not afraid of being accused of exaggeration, I would say that, for epicures, it would be worth the trip.

GASPACHO DE L'ESTRÉMADURE

Gazpacho is a Spanish dish.

It is a sort of salad made with tomatoes and cucumbers, which is very refreshing during hot weather.

It is prepared in various ways. Here is the recipe used in Estremadura.

In a marble mortar pound a clove of garlic, several almonds, some chopped chives, a few dry, sifted breadcrumbs which have been soaked and the liquid pressed out. Season this mixture with salt and pepper to taste and, when the contents of the mortar is very smooth, pour in, drop by drop, some olive oil. Beat as you would for mayonnaise; then, when it has caught and thickened, chill it in a salad bowl. When it is well chilled, sprinkle some dry breadcrumbs over it, add cut-up tomatoes, diced cucumbers which have been peeled and seeded, and some cut up green pepper. Season with tarragon vinegar. Note: A blender is excellent for this procedure and much quicker.

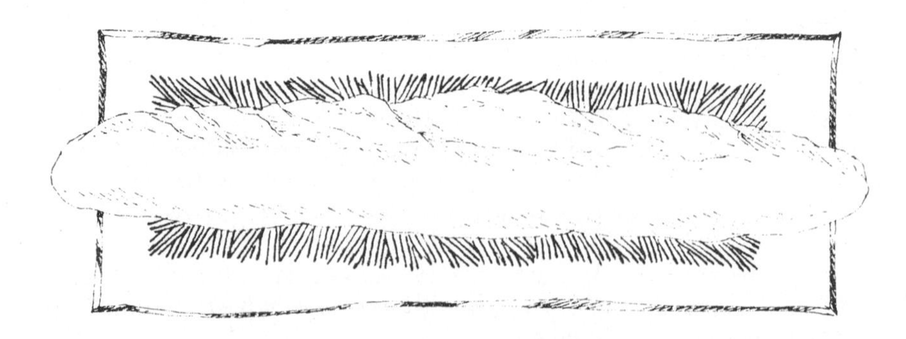

CHEESE

Cheese is a very digestible protein food[1] containing peptones which stimulate the digestion[2] and for this reason cheese is served at the end of a meal.

I feel that I should say a few words about it.

The art of cheese making goes back several thousand years. It was originally the product of individual personal experience, but science is now being applied to the art of cheese making and many well-known specialists have written a great deal on the subject.[3]

Today, a skilled cheese-maker must know how to choose[4] and mix, if necessary, the milks he uses; determine in each case the amount of pressure necessary and the physical and chemical properties within the curing room (temperature, acidity) to insure proper coagulation; drain the curd properly—it contains practically all the milk casein and the major part of the butterfat—in order to obtain a firm, compact, homogeneous, elastic product containing the necessary serum for proper fermentation; see to it that favorable conditions exist in the curing room or cave for the culture of certain types of microorganisms and to inhibit the culture of certain others, so as to avoid disease, since, to date, there has been found no scientific cure for cheese diseases.

All cheese is based on milk curd and may be classified as follows:

1. Fresh, unfermented soft-curd cheeses;
2. Soft-curd cheeses fermented at low temperature and not pressed;
3. Cheeses made from scalded curds, fermented, hard, compressed;
4. Blue mold or marbled cheeses.

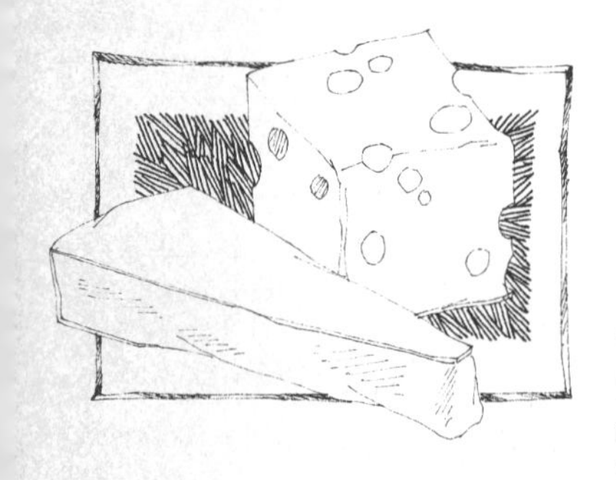

The fresh cheeses include: *fromage blanc* (white cheese), which is just plain, drained, fresh milk curds; *fromage à la crème* and *Petit Suisse* (double cream), which are both cow milk curds beaten with cream, good especially from May to September; Gournay, Bondon de Neufchâtel-en-Bray, which are molded cheeses made from cow and sheep's milk or plain sheep's milk to which cream has been added and which have been treated with a mold (most often *Penicillium candidum*), good from May to October; *fromage demi-sel* (semi-salt cheese), *fromage à la crème légèrement salé* (slightly salted cream cheese), and Vacherin des Alpes, a curd cheese made with cream, which is kept for several days to give it a faintly sourish taste.

The soft, fermented cheeses include: Brie, one of the most renowned of French cheeses, Camembert, Coulommiers, Port-Salut, Livarot, Maroilles, Géromé, Munster, Tomme, Mont-d'Or, Saint-Marcellin, Banon, and Chabichou.

Brie, which is good for five months of the year, from December to April, must be softly ripe but not runny, and be pale yellow in color; cheese from Olivet, near Orléans, which belongs to the brie family, has a great regional reputation. Camembert, whose manufacture is the same as that of brie, differs only by the presence, in the cheese, of a lactic acid ferment known as *Oidium camemberti,* which probably gives it the characteristic taste. The cheese of Monsieur Fromage, manufactured by him, is a variety of Camembert with superlative flavor. Coulommiers[5] is a spring and summer cheese. It is fatty and creamy to the touch; its crust is grayish white. Port-Salut is a summer cheese containing salt, and it is very smooth textured. Livarot and Maroilles, autumn and winter cheeses, have only a limited number of devotees because of their ammoniacal odor. Géromé is a salted cheese mixed with cumin; it is good from October to March. Munster is an excellent-tasting winter cheese, which is usually eaten sprinkled with cumin. Tomme from the Herens valley is aromatic and fatty. Last, Mont-d'Or, Saint-Marcellin, Banon, and Chabichou are excellent goat cheeses. The first of the three is dipped in white wine before cave-ripening.

The hard, fermented cheeses include: Gruyère, a type of cheese which is cooked at 122 to 140 degrees F., of which Emmenthal is a superior quality. This category also includes Cantal, Dutch, Parmesan, Chester, and Stilton. All these cheeses keep well.

A good Gruyère or Emmenthal must have a waxy texture, be pale yellow in color, and have large, not too numerous eyes. Aged Emmenthal, soaked in the cave with white wine for several years, is an incomparable product. Cantal is a salted cow's milk cheese. Dutch cheese is made by heating whole, unskimmed cow's milk to 97 degrees F. It must be a reddish yellow, soft, smooth and unctuous. It is excellent when fresh, in summer. Parmesan, also a cow's milk cheese, is, above all, a seasoning cheese. When it is of good quality and properly aged, it is slightly damp and golden in color. Chester cheese, which is saffroned, and the manufacture of which is similar to that of Dutch cheese, is very popular in England. But the king of English cheeses is Stilton. When it is aged and doused with aged madeira, it is a pure marvel.

Among the blue mold cheeses, we find Roquefort, prepared from ewe's milk. By cultivating a mold on breadcrumbs, known as *Penicillium glaucum,* a greenish marbling is produced. Aging of Roquefort takes place in caves at a constant temperature of 43 to 47 degrees F.

The marbled cheeses also include Bleu d'Auvergne, as well as Gorgonzola, a blue, saffroned cheese very popular in Italy.

Cheese haters are rare. However, some people have the unbelievable idiosyncrasy of not being able to tolerate the slightest bit of food that has come into contact with even the mildest cheese. The plainest macaroni and cheese puts them to flight.

On the other hand, cheese lovers are legion. There are even those fanatic enough to prefer a hunk of dry bread and some cheese to the best dinner served without cheese. One must admit that cheese caps a meal admirably: it completes it if it has not been substantial enough or good enough, and it crowns it if it has been good.

People who are afraid of adding too many calories to their food intake, which in the case of cheese are not negligible, should eat cheese in the following way: they should take only a hazel-nut sized piece of well-ripened, good cheese, and crush it with the tongue against the palate until it has dissolved. They will then get all the taste and aroma and their saliva will discreetly carry its beneficial qualities to the stomach without overloading it.

NOTES

1. Together with bread it provides an almost complete food.
2. It helps in the assimilation of fats and carbohydrates.
3. Several important papers on the subject can be found in the *Annales de l'Institut Pasteur*.
4. The quality of cheeses depends essentially on the quality of the milk from which they are manufactured. The best are obtained from milk coming from animals who feed on good pasture. For a long time this was the only type of milk used for making cheese, and the far-reaching reputation of French cheeses was mainly due to this fact. But recently farmers seem to be attempting to kill the goose that lays the golden eggs by trying to increase the yield, to the detriment of quality, by feeding their livestock grain and fruit residues and beet-root pulp.
5. Coulommiers Double Crème, a luxury cheese, fresh, is prepared at low temperature with freshly drawn milk, the curds of which are mixed with cream.

Cheese Wafers

There are a great number of possible combinations for making cheese wafers. Here are several examples:

CROÛTES AU PARMESAN

Parmesan Wafers

Use:

1 C. flour
1½ C. grated Parmesan cheese
7 T. butter
3 T. water
salt, cayenne

Prepare puff pastry, making eight turns, using the flour, butter, water, salt, and a few grains of cayenne. Each time you give the dough a turn, sprinkle it with the finely grated Parmesan. Let it rest for fifteen minutes. Roll it out to a quarter-inch thick, cut it into diamond shapes, brush with egg, and bake in a hot oven.

Serve on a napkin.

Gruyère wafers may be prepared the same way.

CROÛTES AU CHESTER

Chester Wafers

Use:

1 C. flour
1½ C. grated Chester cheese
6 T. butter
3 T. heavy cream
salt, cayenne

Make a dough, using all the ingredients but do not work it. Let it rest for three hours, then roll it out fairly thin. Cut it with a round two-inch cookie cutter. Brush the uncooked wafers with egg and bake in a hot oven. Assemble them two by two after having coated the surfaces of one of the two circles with a little layer of grated Gruyère and Chester blended with a little butter.

Serve hot, on a napkin.

One may also serve these Chester cheese wafers cold. After having cooked the circles they are allowed to cool, then they are spread with a cheese custard prepared as follows:

Blend 3 egg yolks with 10 tablespoons of heavy cream. Season with salt, cayenne, and rum or whiskey, to taste. Cook this mixture over very low heat; then let it cool almost completely. Add 4 teaspoons of butter and 3/4 cup of grated Chester or a mixture of Chester and Gruyère cheese.

Assemble them two by two, sticking them together.

Arrange on a napkin.

CROÛTES AU ROQUEFORT

Roquefort Wafers

Use:

1 C. flour
7 T. Roquefort
7 T. butter
4 tsp. heavy cream
pinch salt
1 egg yolk
paprika or cayenne

Mix these ingredients without working the dough. Let it rest for about twenty minutes, roll it out quite thin, and cut it into oval shapes. Bake these in a hot oven and cool.

Spread the top of these wafers with a mixture of Roquefort and butter and then join them two by two, filling inside.

Serve on a napkin.

One can also serve these wafers with the following cream.

Blend 3 egg yolks with 2/3 cup of heavy cream. Season with salt, paprika, or cayenne, and set over low heat. Beat in 5 tablespoons of Roquefort cheese and 3 tablespoons of butter. Mix these well and continue cooking and stirring until it thickens. Watch the cream carefully. Take the pan off the heat and flavor with 1/2 teaspoon of kirsch. Let it cool completely.

Sandwich the wafers with cream in between.

Arrange on a napkin.

Hot cheese wafers may be served as an hors-d'oeuvre; cold ones are generally served at the end of the meal, instead of cheese.

SWEET DESSERTS AND PASTRY

BEIGNETS DE POMMES

Apple Fritters

The day before you want to make the fritters, prepare the batter by beating together the flour, egg, beer, brandy, oil, and salt.

The following day, make two marmalades, sweetened to taste. Make one using the first apples and the other using the apricots.

Peel the 2 large apples, cut each one into 6 slices, trim them, poach them in some sugar syrup flavored with the madeira wine and vanilla; and then put them to marinate in the kirsch. Reduce the syrup by boiling it down by half, add the apple and apricot

For six people, use:

1 1/2 lbs. tart apples
1/2 lb. apricots
14 T. kirsch
1 C. plus 3 T. flour
1/2 C. madeira wine
1/2 C. light beer
3 T. brandy
3 T. olive oil
1 tsp. salt
2 (1/2 lb. each) large tart apples
1 egg
vanilla bean (or 1 tsp. vanilla extract)
sugar syrup
cinnamon
granulated sugar

marmalades, the kirsch from the marinade, and some cinnamon. Mix these well and cook until thick.

Dip the apple slices in the batter, plunge them into a clear, hot fry-bath and cook them. Remove them with a skimmer, drain them well, sprinkle them with granulated sugar and caramelize them in the oven.

Spoon the fruit sauce into a crystal bowl, arrange the fritters on top, and serve.

BEIGNETS DE POMMES FOURRÉES

Stuffed Apple Fritters

Select large, tart apples. Remove a plug at the stem end and reserve.

Remove the core and hollow out the apples a little, then marinate them for three hours in sweetened white wine laced with a little brandy and flavored with a little orange-flower water and lemon juice. Drain them and fill them with either custard, jam, or marmalade. Close the openings by sticking the plugs in with beaten egg white.

Dip the stuffed apples in some fritter batter and fry them in plenty of clear, hot fat. Sprinkle them with sugar, glaze them in the oven and serve.

This is a delicious surprise.

For eight people, use:

2 C. flour
1 C. water
4 oz. (8 T.) butter
1 tps. salt
8 eggs
grated orange rind
granulated sugar

BEIGNETS SOUFFLÉS OU PETS DE NONNE

French Crullers

Prepare the batter several hours ahead of time.

In a saucepan put the water, salt, the butter cut into small pieces, and grated orange rind to taste. Bring these to a boil, stirring. Remove the pan from the heat, add the flour all at once, stir vigorously with a wooden spoon, and then dry out the batter over very low heat until it comes away from the sides of the pan.

Let this cool for a few minutes; then beat in the eggs, one by one, making sure each one is fully absorbed before adding the next.

With a spoon, take up a little dough and smooth into a ball, using a second spoon; drop each little ball into clear, hot fat. The balls will swell and turn over. As soon as they have stopped turning, they are cooked.

Remove the crullers, drain them, arrange them in a pyramid, on a napkin-covered platter, sprinkle with sugar, and serve piping hot.

For variation, one may stuff the crullers with jams, jellies, or creams and glaze them in the oven.

Crêpes

Crêpes are sweet desserts. They are made in the shape of thin disks which become crêpey as they cook, from whence their name. They are classic accompaniments to carnival meals.

The ingredients which go into the batter are variable. Most often the batter is flavored with orange-flower water or vanilla, but other flavorings may be used.

INGREDIENTS AND PREPARATION

Here are three examples:

A. To make about forty orange-flower water–flavored crêpes, about nine inches in diameter, medium size, use:

3 C. milk
$3\frac{3}{4}$ C. flour
$\frac{3}{4}$ C. sugar
4 T. brandy
2 T. orange-flower water
1 tsp. coarse salt
1 tsp. dry yeast (or $\frac{1}{3}$ cake of yeast)
8 large eggs
unsalted butter

Prepare the batter twenty-four hours ahead of time in winter, twelve hours in summer.

Break the eggs, separate the yolks from the whites, and beat the whites until stiff.

Mix the flour and egg yolks, add the warm milk in which you have dissolved the sugar, salt, and yeast, add the brandy and orange-flower water, and mix well. Carefully fold in the egg whites thoroughly. You will have a fairly thin batter.

B. To make the same quantity of vanilla crêpes, use:

$3\frac{1}{3}$ C. milk
$3\frac{3}{4}$ C. flour
$\frac{3}{4}$ C. sugar
1 tsp. salt
1 tsp. dry yeast (or use $\frac{1}{3}$ yeast cake)
8 large eggs
vanilla bean or 1 tsp. vanilla extract
unsalted butter

Scald the milk for five minutes with the vanilla bean and cool. Or, if you are using the extract, scald the milk and add the extract when it is cool.

Prepare the batter as above.

C. Finally, here is a third recipe for the batter:

To make ten to twelve crêpes, use:

1 C. plus 9 T. flour
$\frac{1}{2}$ C. warm water
$\frac{1}{2}$ C. beer
1 T. rum
1 T. kirsch
1 tsp. salt
5 eggs
grated orange rind

First mix the flour, eggs, salt and orange rind. Add the water, beer, rum and kirsch, little by little. Beat the dough well, so as to obtain a very smooth and lumpless batter. Let this rest for four hours before using.

COOKING THE CRÊPES

When you are ready to use the batter, beat it again.

The best type of pan for cooking crêpes is a cast-iron griddle, fourteen to sixteen inches in diameter and about one-quarter inch thick. This griddle should be set on a trivet or asbestos plaque placed over a burner. The trivet serves to separate the griddle from the direct heat.

Start by heating the griddle, butter it lightly and evenly with unsalted butter, and remove any excess. Pour a small ladleful of batter onto the griddle; spread the batter rapidly, using a flat wooden spatula. Give the crêpe a circular shape and make it as thin as possible. As soon as one side is cooked, remove it with a spatula, rebutter the pan, and cook the crêpe on the other side. It should brown lightly before you remove it.

Wipe the griddle to remove any particles of batter which might have adhered, then proceed as above, and make the next crêpe.

This method makes it possible to make very thin, light, evenly cooked crêpes. It is easier than using a skillet.

Keep the crêpes hot until serving time.

They are usually served just sprinkled with sugar.

They may be sprinkled with lemon juice, if desired.

Crêpes may be served coated with a butter sauce prepared as follows:

For forty crêpes, use:

1 C. plus 3 T. unsalted butter
1 C. kirsch
7 oz. lump sugar
orange rind from 4 oranges

Rub the pieces of sugar over the orange skins so that they are well flavored, then mash them up in the kirsch.

Melt the butter in a saucepan without letting it brown, then add the sweetened kirsch.

Serve the sauce in a heated bowl and the crêpes separately.

These crêpes, dipped into the sauce, have a delicious flavor.

For variation, one could substitute, for the kirsch, some brandy to which curaçao has been added. One would then ignite it at the last moment. The crêpes would be passed in the flaming sauce.

The crêpes could also be served with a sauce made of some kind of fruit jelly flavored with a liqueur, to taste—apricot jelly flavored with sherry, for instance.

Crêpes are often served spread with honey and rolled up, or stuffed with jams, either as is, or accompanied by a sauce. One can easily conjure up many variations. Here is one, as an example: Fill the crêpes with a mixture of strawberry and pineapple jam flavored with kirsch and Curaçao; roll them; arrange them on a platter and coat them with a Sabayon sauce.

Crêpes could also be filled with tiny pear dice, thinly sliced apples sautéed in butter, or small pineapple bits marinated in some sort of liqueur.

The number of possible combinations is almost limitless. One can get an idea of this from the few examples given here.

Last, one could vary the ingredients in the batter by substituting, for the milk, a mixture of milk, cream and melted, unsalted butter; one could add some macaroon or cookie crumbs soaked in Kümmel, for instance; some orange or tangerine rind cut into fine julienne and soaked in white Curaçao; or even flavor the batter with rum, anisette, maraschino, etc.

Crêpes prepared with these different batters are accompanied by a suitable butter: Butter worked with sugar and fifteen percent champagne, rum, white Curaçao, anisette, Kümmel, maraschino, etc., either mixed, or not, with a boiled custard, so as to obtain a syrupy sauce.

GÂTEAU DE CRÊPES

Crêpe Cake

Crêpes may be presented in the form of a cake. Here are two methods which are easy to vary as you wish. First when you have made the orange flower–water crêpes, arrange then in a high-sided cake pan, one on top of the other, separating the layers with almond paste. Frost the whole thing with thick lemon custard and bake in a slow oven.

Second: if the crêpes are vanilla crêpes, arrange them, as above, in a cake pan, separating the layers with thick vanilla custard. Bake in a slow oven. Serve hot.

BLINY

Bliny are tiny crêpes made of different batters which are much favored in Russia, especially during Shrovetide. Here is the recipe:

For six to eight people, use:

7½ C. flour
3¾ C. buckwheat flour
1¼ C. clarified, unsalted butter
4 T. dry yeast (or 3 yeast cakes)
1 qt. milk
5 eggs
granulated sugar
salt

Mix the two flours thoroughly.

Break the eggs and separate the whites from the yolks.

Dissolve the yeast in the warmed milk.

Prepare a fairly thick batter using the milk and the two flours. The batter should be thicker than one would normally use for ordinary crêpes. Add one-fourth of the warm, clarified butter, the egg yolks, sugar, and salt to taste. Mix well.

Beat the egg whites until firm. Fold them into the batter.

Let the batter rise overnight.

Set out some small, round skillets without handles. They should be about three inches in diameter and three-eighths of an inch deep. Pour a small ladleful of batter into each one and bake them in a baker's oven, with an overhead wood fire, setting them in the oven using a baker's paddle.[1] As they cook sprinkle them with the rest of the butter.

Bliny must be thin, evenly browned on both sides, light, and crusty.

Arrange the bliny on a silver platter and serve them accompanied by clarified butter and sour cream in sauceboats, and with fresh caviar.

For variation, one could make the bliny with wholewheat flour, buckwheat flour, semolina, cream of rice, etc. They may be flavored with lemon or vanilla, and, instead of caviar, clarified butter, and sour cream, one could use syrups, custards, or fruit marmalades.

NOTE

1. Bliny can also be made under a broiler. The taste, of course, would be different.

For six people, use:

2 C. (scant) flour
½ C. milk
2 T. butter
1 T. butter
1 T. orange flower water
3 egg yolks
1 whole egg
granulated sugar
dry, sifted breadcrumbs

CRÈME FRITE

Fried Custard

In a saucepan, melt the butter and stir in the flour. Keeping the pan over low heat gradually add the boiling milk. Sweeten to taste, add the egg yolks, and the orange flower water. Stir well, then bake the custard in a slow oven for one hour, stirring frequently.

Spread the custard on a large platter; let it cool and cut it into diamond shapes. Coat these with flour.

Beat the whole egg, dip the diamonds in it, then coat them with the dry, sifted breadcrumbs and fry them in a clear, hot fry-bath. When they have acquired a golden color, drain them on a napkin-covered platter, and, at serving time, sprinkle them with sugar.

CRÈME D'AMANDES AU RIZ

Almond Cream with Rice

Peel and blanch the almonds, grind them in a mortar,[1] moistening them with a little milk. Force them through a sieve.

Cook the rice in sweetened milk flavored with vanilla or cinnamon, to taste, so as to keep the rice grains whole. Remove the vanilla bean or cinnamon stick, if you have used them.[2]

Mix the rice with the almond paste and some heavy, sweetened cream; add raisins and chill.

NOTES

1. The nuts can be ground much more quickly nowadays in a blender or in a special nut grinder. If they are fine enough they need not be sieved.
2. If you wish to use vanilla extract or ground cinnamon, either of these should only be added when the rice is cool.

Use:

1 C. milk
⅓ C. sugar
3 T. flour
pinch salt
3 egg yolks
vanilla bean or 1 tsp. extract

CRÈME PÂTISSIÈRE

Pastry Cream

Scald the milk with the vanilla bean (if you are using it; or add the extract when cream is cool).

In a saucepan, mix the flour, egg yolks, sugar, and salt. Stir in the scalded milk gradually. Put the pan on the heat, warm it up slowly, stirring constantly, until the custard has thickened.

Pour into a bowl and chill.

CRÈME FRANGIPANE

Macaroon Cream

Use:

2 C. milk
1/3 C. sugar
9 T. flour
2 T. butter
1 oz. macaroon crumbs
pinch salt
3 egg yolks
1 whole egg
vanilla bean or extract (1 tsp.)

Scald the milk with the vanilla bean and remove it. (If you are using the extract add it only when the cream has cooled.)

Mix the flour, sugar, salt, egg, and yolks. Beat these together with a wooden spoon; then gradually stir in the hot milk.

Put the pan on the heat, stir constantly until it comes to a boil. Let it boil one minute. Strain the cream into a bowl and stir in the butter and macaroon crumbs.

CRÈME ANGLAISE VANILLÉE

Vanilla Custard Cream

Use:

2 C. milk
2 2/3 C. sugar
14 egg yolks
vanilla bean or 1 tsp. extract

Scald milk with the vanilla bean. (If you are using extract add it only after the cream has cooled.) Take the pan off the heat and remove the vanilla bean; then gradually beat the hot milk into the beaten egg yolks.

Put the pan over very low heat, in a hot water bath, or in a double boiler and cook it very slowly until thick.

One could prepare, in this same way, custards made with a liqueur, by substituting a liqueur of choice for the vanilla: rum, kirsch, Curaçao, anisette, cassis, Chartreuse, maraschino, etc.; or one could use fortified wines such as: sherry, Chypre, Malvoisie, etc.; but with all fortified wines listed, *in the last instance,* one would have to make the custard a little bit thicker by adding more egg yolks.

One could also make fruit creams: apricot, peach, cherry, strawberry, pineapple, orange, lemon, etc.

CRÈME AU CHOCOLAT

Chocolate Cream

For six people, use:

2 C. milk
4 oz. semi-sweet cooking chocolate
5 T. sugar
pinch salt
4 egg yolks
vanilla bean or 1 tsp. extract

Scald the milk with the sugar, salt, and vanilla bean. (If you are using the extract add it when the cream is cool.) Remove the vanilla bean when the milk has flavored enough.

Grate the chocolate; add it to the hot milk and simmer for about thirty minutes.

Take the pan off the heat. Beat a little of the chocolate mixture into the egg yolks then add them to the pan. Put the pan back over very, very low heat, or in a hot water bath, or use a double boiler. Heat the cream very slowly but do not allow it to boil. Watch this part of the procedure very carefully so as to avoid having the cusard curdle.

Pour the custard through a fine sieve into a serving bowl and chill.

Chocolate cream may be served alone or with wafers, small puff pastry cookies, brioches, etc.

For six people, use:

2 C. milk
4 oz. coarsely ground coffee beans
3/4 C. granulated sugar
pinch salt
5 egg yolks
caramel

CRÈME AU CAFÉ

Coffee Cream

Scald the milk, add the coarsely ground coffee beans, let it boil up a couple of times and then let it infuse for a little while, and strain. Add the sugar, salt, a little caramel for color, and, finally, combine it with the beaten egg yolks. Mix well. Put the mixture back over very low heat, or in a hot water bath, or use a double-boiler, and stir until it has thickened without curdling.

Strain the cream through a fine sieve into a serving dish. Chill.

Cookies, wafers, puff pastries, or other light cakes are a good accompaniment for coffee custard.

For six people, use:

2 C. *crème Chantilly*[1]
1 lb. ripe apricots
1 1/4 C. granulated sugar
1 envelope gelatine
milk

CRÈME AUX ABRICOTS

Apricot Cream

Cut up the apricots and force the pulp through a strainer or food mill.[2]

Remove the almonds from six of the pits, and grind them with a little milk.

Soften the gelatine in a little water, then dissolve it in a small quantity of hot milk.

Gently mix the apricot pulp, almond paste, sugar, gelatine, and *crème Chantilly*. Spoon this mixture into a mold and chill it.

Unmold at serving time.

For variation, one could substitute other fruit for the apricots.

NOTES

1. *Crème Chantilly* is cream which has been whipped with vanilla and sugar. Here is how one prepares it: chill the cream for twenty-four hours before using so that it will become light and frothy when beaten. Remove any water that has separated from the solids, and whip the cream in a bowl set over another bowl filled with crushed ice. Beat in the vanilla flavored sugar as you go.

To make vanilla sugar just place a length of vanilla bean in a jar or canister with granulated sugar. After several days it will start to take on flavor. Vanilla extract may be substituted in recipes calling for vanilla but must only be added to cool ingredients.

2. An electric blender would be very helpful for this step.

CRÈME RENVERSÉE À LA VANILLE

Molded Vanilla Custard

For six people, use:

1¼ C. sugar
pinch salt
1 qt. milk
5 eggs
7 egg yolks
vanilla bean or extract

Scald the milk with the sugar, salt, and vanilla bean. Remove the bean when the milk is well flavored.[1]

Break the whole eggs into a bowl, add the yolks, stir in the milk gradually, and mix well.

Strain the custard through cheesecloth or a fine sieve.

Fill a mold or some small pot-de-crème cups, or even custard cups, with the strained custard and cook in a moderate oven or in a hot water bath. Cool.

At serving time, unmold the custard onto a platter or serve directly from the small cups.

One could prepare, this same way, molded custards flavored with: coffee, tea, caramel, liqueurs, etc. But one should then take into account the quantity of liquid used for flavoring. The quantity of milk should be cut down so that the total volume of liquid remains the same.

NOTE

1. If 2 teaspoons of vanilla extract are used instead of the bean, it should be added just before the custard is poured into molds.

CRÈME GLACÉE

Ice Cream

For eight people, use:

2 C. crème chantilly[1]
1 C. heavy cream
currant–raspberry jelly
anisette, curaçao, or chartreuse

Ice creams are excellent sweet desserts which are easy to prepare. Here is an example:

Whip the two creams together and fill an oiled ice cream mold. Put the cover on the mold with a towel to help seal it hermetically. Place the mold in a mixture of ice and rock salt. Chill it for three hours.

Unmold onto a platter and decorate the top of the ice cream with the currant–raspberry jelly and surround the base with a thickened, cooled syrup prepared with the currant–raspberry jelly which has been flavored with anisette, Chartreuse, or Curaçao.

For variation, one could substitute, for the heavy cream, some thick marmalade or jam, either strawberry or some other fruit. One can easily invent many different combinations by varying the ice cream, the decoration, and the flavoring.

One can also make chestnut ice cream by substituting, for the heavy cream, some thick, vanilla-flavored chestnut purée. The platter would be garnished with *marron glacés* (candied chestnuts).

All these desserts are smooth and velvety. They are served with wafers, cookies, macaroons, *crêpes bretonnes* dried in the oven, etc.

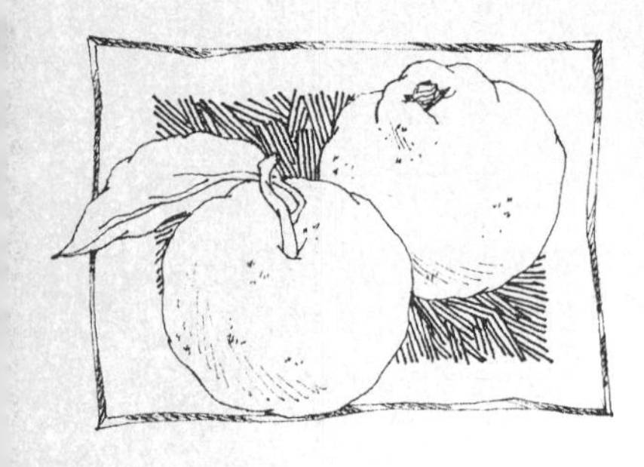

BAVAROIS

Bavarian Creams

Bavarois are sweet, chilled, desserts, made with whipped cream, and gelatine. They can be flavored in many ways: vanilla, anise, rose, violet, orange blossom, carnation, etc.; with liqueurs: mint anisette, Curaçao, kirsch, rum, maraschino, etc.; with punch; with fruit purée or marmalade: apricot, strawberry, raspberry, cherry, red currant, plum, peach, lemon, orange, citron, pineapple, walnut, hazel nut, almond, pistachio, chestnut, etc.; or even with coffee, tea, chocolate, praline, etc.; last, small cakes may be used in their preparation.

Here is an example.

BAVAROIS PRALINÉ

Praline Bavarian Cream

For six people, use:

1½ C. milk
1 C. whipped cream
¾ C. sugar
3 oz. blanched almonds
3 T. kirsch
1 envelope gelatine
pinch salt
3 egg yolks
vanilla bean or extract (1 tsp.)

Prepare the praline. Melt ½ cup of sugar in a skillet with a little water; add the almonds and let them cook until they are golden brown. Put the sugar-coated almonds on an oiled marble slab, without letting them touch each other. Let them cool; then grind them to a paste.

Prepare a vanilla boiled custard or *crème anglaise,* using the milk, egg yolks, sugar, salt, and vanilla.

Soften the gelatine in a little water, add it to the hot custard, and stir until the gelatine is completely dissolved. Strain the custard and let it cool.

To the custard, add the kirsch, the praline, and then fold in the whipped cream.

Oil a Charlotte mold or deep cake pan and spoon the mixture into it. Chill for two hours.

Unmold the Bavarian cream onto a chilled serving plate covered with a napkin. Serve.

OMELETTES SUCRÉES

Sweet Omelets

Sweet omelets make good, easy desserts. They may be served plain or filled.

They are prepared exactly like ordinary omelets, the only difference being that they are seasoned with sugar and very little salt. They are cooked the same way.

Plain dessert omelets are rolled, arranged on a long platter, sprinkled with sugar and flavored to taste with rum, kirsch, cognac, brandy, Armagnac, Calvados, *marc de Bourgogne*, etc., which has been pre-heated and flamed at serving time.

Filled omelets are seasoned and cooked as above, but before being rolled up they are filled with some sort of fruit jam or marmalade. They are then rolled and arranged on a long platter and the top is seared with a hot iron.

One can also make filled omelets which can be flamed with some short of liqueur suitable to the filling.

Here are several examples: omelet filled with cherry jam, flamed with kirsch; omelet filled with pineapple, flamed with *eau-de-vie de châteauneuf-du-Pape;* omelet filled with strawberry jam, flamed with cherry brandy; omelet filled with apricot jam, flamed with marachino; omelet filled with *mirabelle* (a type of plum) jam, flamed with Curaçao; omelet filled with sautéed banana,flamed with rum; omelet filled with applesauce, flamed with Calvados; omelet filled with pear compote, flamed with *eau-de-vie de mirabelles* (plum brandy); omelet filled with cassis–raspberry jelly, flamed with *eau-de-vie de marc* (wine-must brandy); omelet filled with orange jelly, flamed with Curaçao; omelet filled with *quetsches* (type of plum) jam, flamed with kümmel.

Plain *omelettes soufflées* and *omelettes soufflées en surprise* are prepared differently.

OMELETTE SOUFFLÉE

For six people, use:

2/3 C. granulated sugar
1. T. flavoring; kirsch, rum, vanilla, lemon, etc.
pinch salt
6 egg whites
3 egg yolks
butter

Beat the egg yolks until thick and lemon colored with 1/2 cup of sugar and the flavoring.

Beat the egg whites with 1 tablespoon of sugar until they are very stiff. Add the salt when they are half beaten, to keep them from collapsing.

Mix one-fourth of the whites with the yolks, then spoon this mixture over the rest of the beaten whites and fold them in rapidly.

Lightly butter a deep, ovenproof platter, then sprinkle it with sugar. Drop the batter onto the platter all at once. Lift the mixture with a knife as much as possible. Using a thick-bladed knife made a deep slash down the center of the omelet and several small slashes along the sides.

Put the platter in a very hot oven. Have the heat come from below mainly, rather than from the top. Watch the omelet carefully.

After five minutes, turn the platter end to end so that the omelet can cook evenly. Sprinkle with sugar and finish cooking. It should take about ten minutes in all. If, after a few minutes you notice that the oven is too hot and the top is getting too brown, cover with a piece of buttered paper.

Serve immediately after removing it from the oven.

OMELETTE SOUFFLÉE EN SURPRISE

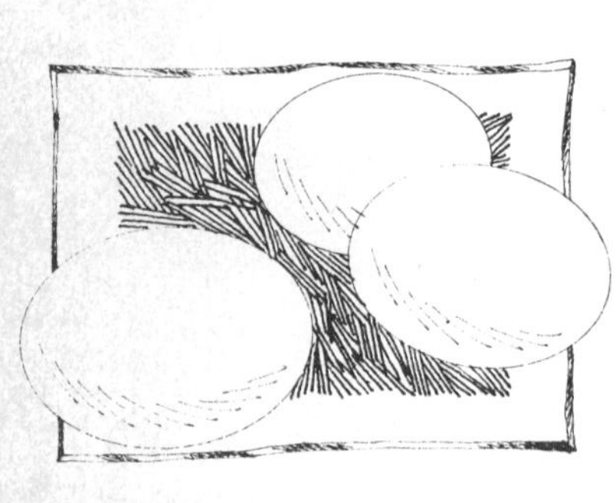

This lovely-looking dessert, paradoxical in appearance, is made of ice cream served inside a piping hot omelet. It is a pretty corollary of the discovery made in 1804, by the eminent American physician, Thomas de Rumfort, that stiffly beaten egg white is a poor heat conductor.

The first gastronomical application of this fact took the form of baked Alaska or meringued ice cream, prepared by covering an ice cream bombe with egg whites whipped stiff with granulated sugar. This was then baked in the oven.

Later on, the idea was conceived of substituting for the egg white, an *omelette soufflée* mixture, which only contains two-thirds white of egg. This was how the *omelette soufflée en surprise* was created.

Here is the technique of the procedure:

First prepare a mixture for *omelette soufflée*. Then, spoon one-fourth of the mixture into an ovenproof casserole. On top gently place some ice cream, either fruit or another flavor, molded the same length and width as the dish you are using, and about one and a half inches thick. Cover with the remaining omelet mixture and smooth the top with a spatula. Place the dish in another larger dish or pan containing crushed ice, and set the whole business under a hot broiler. After five minutes the omelet will have risen. Sprinkle it with a little vanilla-flavored sugar; decorate it quickly with some fruit jelly, using a pastry bag; and serve. It is unnecessary to oil the dish or to make incisions in the mixture, because here the rising is due to the overhead heat.

Those who are afraid of not working fast enough to succeed will be sure to succeed the first time if they increase the insulating layer with lady fingers. Here is how it is done:

Cut the lady fingers lengthwise, so as to reduce their thickness by half. Spoon a quarter of the mixture into the dish, arrange a layer of lady finger halves on this, put the ice cream on, then another·layer of halved lady fingers, and finally the rest of the omelet mixture. Cook as above.

The *omelette soufflée en surprise* prepared with lady fingers is a little less unctuous than the one without them.

One can easily think up a number of different combinations. One could, for instance, put some strawberries and whipped cream on top of the ice cream before covering it with the omelet mixture. I was most interested in describing the principle behind this rather unusual dessert.

SOUFFLÉ À LA CRÈME VANILLÉE

Vanilla Soufflé

For six people, use:

3/4 C. milk
7 T. sugar
5 tsp. unsalted butter
7 tsp. potato starch
pinch salt
6 egg whites
3 egg yolks
vanilla bean or extract (1 tsp.)
confectioner's sugar

Scald the milk with the sugar, salt, and vanilla bean.[1] Remove the vanilla bean and cool the milk.

Blend the starch and butter into the milk; stir as you heat it up. At the first boil, take the pan off the heat. Beat the yolks, add a little of the hot milk to them, then add yolk mixture to the rest of the milk, beating well. When cooled a little, fold in the stiffly beaten egg whites.

Spoon the mixture into a deep soufflé dish, and bake it in a moderate oven for fifteen or twenty minutes at the most. Watch it as it cooks, since the soufflé is apt to fall if it is overcooked.

Before removing the soufflé from the oven, sprinkle it with confectioner's sugar to glaze the top. Serve hot.

A whole gamut of different soufflés can be created by varying the flavoring.

NOTE

1. If using vanilla extract add just before folding in whites.

SOUFFLÉ AU CHOCOLAT

Chocolate Soufflé

For six people, use:

4 oz. semi-sweet cooking chocolate
1/2 C. granulated sugar
2 T. milk
pinch salt
6 egg whites
3 egg yolks

Melt the chocolate in the milk, over low heat. Remove the pan from the heat; add the yolks beaten with 1/3 cup of sugar. Mix well.

Beat the whites until stiff, with the remaining sugar and the salt. Fold into the yolk mixture.

Spoon into a soufflé or Charlotte mold and bake in a moderate oven for fifteen or twenty minutes.

SOUFFLÉ AUX FRUITS CONFITS

Candied Fruit Soufflé

Macerate some candied fruits, either whole if they are small or diced if they are large, in an appropriate liqueur.

Prepare a plain soufflé mixture, flavored to taste. Fold in the macerated fruits and bake as usual.

Garnish the cooked soufflé with assorted fresh fruits.

SOUFFLÉ À L'ORANGE

Orange Soufflé

For four people, use:

7 T. granulated sugar
5 tsp. potato starch
1 T. milk
4 egg whites
2 egg yolks
2 whole oranges
orange rind from 1 orange

Mince the orange rind.

Beat the egg whites until stiff.

Cut the oranges in two, carefully remove the pulp, squeeze out the juice and set aside. Reserve the orange halves.

Mix the potato starch with the milk, add the orange juice and the sugar, and bring to a boil. Take the pan off the fire, add the contents to the beaten egg yolks along with the orange rind (the mixture must be quite thick), then fold in the beaten egg whites.

Fill the orange halves with the soufflé mixture; bake in a fairly hot oven and serve.

SOUFFLÉS EN CROUSTADES

Soufflés Baked in Shells

All soufflés may be baked and served in *croustades* (shells).

Line a well-oiled shallow type pan with brioche dough or flaky pastry. Spoon the soufflé mixture into this and bake as usual.

Unmold with care and serve as is or flame at serving time.

SOUFFLÉ FROID AU CITRON

Cold Lemon Soufflé

For six people, use:

1 C. (scant) granulated sugar
3 T. currant jelly
6 eggs
2 lemons lemon juice

Break the eggs, separate the yolks from the whites, and whip the whites until stiff.

Beat the yolks with the sugar, add the juice of the two lemons, mix well, and heat in a hot water bath or double boiler until the mixture has thickened. Fold the stiffly beaten egg whites into the hot custard and spoon into a glass serving bowl. Let it cool, decorate with currant jelly, and serve with cookies.

One could make, this same way, different kinds of fruit soufflés using assorted jellies.

MERINGUE ORDINAIRE

Plain Meringue

Use:

$2\frac{1}{3}$ C. granulated sugar
pinch salt
12 egg whites

Beat the egg whites until very stiff, adding the sugar and salt as you beat.

Using a pastry tube, drop round or oval mounds of meringue onto an ungreased piece of plain brown paper. The mounds should be about the size of a large egg. Sprinkle on some granulated sugar and shake off any excess. Place the paper on a wet board and bake in a slow oven, leaving the door open.

Unstick the meringues, make a hollow on the flat side (bottom) using a wooden darning egg or other similar gadget, then bake them in a moderate oven to dry them out. They should be crispy.

Fill the inside of the meringue either with *crème Chantilly*, or with whipped cream flavored with either coffee syrup or with a fruit purée (sauce) such as strawberry, cherry, pistachio, etc.—or even fill them with a thick chocolate pudding.

Stick the meringues together two by two on the filling side, and serve.

Plain or Italian meringues are amusing desserts, very light and not filling.

MERINGUE ITALIENNE AU SUCRE CUIT

Italian Meringue Made with Sugar Syrup

Use:

$2\frac{1}{3}$ C. granulated sugar
1 C. minus 2 T. water
pinch salt
10 egg whites

Beat the egg whites until very stiff.

Boil the sugar and water until the thermometer reads 250° F. (between the soft and hard-ball stage). Then add the salt and start pouring the syrup over the egg whites in a very fine stream, beating vigorously the whole time so that the syrup is completely absorbed by the whites.

Italian meringue is used the same way as plain meringue.

GÂTEAU MERINGUÉ

Meringue Cake

Use:

$2\frac{1}{3}$ C. granulated sugar
12 oz. almonds
pinch salt
12 egg whites
6 egg yolks

Prepare the meringue. Beat the egg whites until very firm, adding the sugar and salt as you beat.

Pound the almonds to a paste and mix with the egg yolks. Fold this mixture carefully into the egg whites without deflating them.

Grease a large baking sheet with butter or oil of sweet almonds and flour it lightly. On this spread thin layers of meringue mixture, either in circles or squares, whatever size you wish. Bake in a moderate oven. Cool.

Make the cake by joining the layers of meringue with a filling of praline cream, pistachio cream, mocha or chocolate cream, according to choice. Decorate the top with a frosting which complements the filling, using a pastry bag.

Chill until serving time.

GÂTEAU AU CHOCOLAT

Chocolate Cake

For six people, use:

7 oz. semi-sweet cooking chocolate
1½ sticks (12 T., 6 oz.) butter
½ C. granulated sugar
3 oz. peeled almonds
pinch salt
4 eggs
vanilla extract

Grind or pound the almonds to a paste with the sugar.

Break the eggs, separate yolks from whites, and beat the whites until firm.

Melt 2½ ounces of the chocolate in a little water; then, off the heat, add 5 tablespoons of butter, little by little. Now add the egg yolks one by one, along with the salt, beating the mixture well after each addition. Mix in the almond paste and vanilla to taste. Carefully fold in the egg whites.

Spoon the mixture into a nine-inch cake pan which has been buttered and floured. Bake in a moderate oven for twenty-five minutes. Unmold.

Frost the cake with a chocolate butter-cream made by melting the remaining chocolate and blending it with the rest of the butter. Let cake and frosting cool.

This is a very light, delicate cake.

GÂTEAU AUX AMANDES ET AU CHOCOLAT

Chocolate Almond Cake

For six people, use:

4 oz. semi-sweet cooking chocolate
4 oz. sweet almonds
½ C. granulated sugar
4 oz. (8 T.) butter
4 eggs

Scald the almonds, peel them, and grind them.

Grate the chocolate.

Break the egg, separate the yolks from the whites, and beat the whites until firm.

Put the egg yolks in a bowl and beat them. Then work in the butter (not melted) and the sugar, mixing well. Now add the chocolate and the almonds and work the mixture again vigorously so it is thoroughly blended. Fold in the egg whites.

Butter a Charlotte mold, spoon in the batter, and cook in a *bain-marie* (hot water bath) for two hours.

Unmold the cake onto a hollow platter, let it cool.

At serving time frost the cake with a cold dessert cream flavored with almonds or vanilla, or even frost it with a praline dessert cream.

To make praline cream, use:

1⅔ C. milk
5 oz. almond paste
½ C. granulated sugar
pinch salt
6 egg yolks
rum
vanilla

Pound the almonds in a mortar and force them through a sieve.

Mash the almond paste with the egg yolks and work them together well. The mixture must be slightly frothy. Flavor to taste with rum.

Scald the milk with the sugar, salt, and vanilla. Take the pan off the heat and remove the vanilla bean (if you have used it),[1] then add the milk to the almond mixture, mix well, and heat up gently until thickened. Cool.

The chocolate-almond cake could be served hot, with a Sabayon sauce.

NOTE

1. Vanilla extract could be substituted for the vanilla bean, but should only be added once the cream has cooled slightly. (1 teaspoon would be sufficient.)

GÂTEAU AUX NOIX

Walnut Cake

For six people, use:

1. For the cake:

10 oz. shelled walnuts
1¼ C. granulated sugar
7 eggs
1 lemon

2. For the cream

1¾ C. milk
4 oz. semi-sweet cooking chocolate
5 T. sugar
few grains salt
3 egg yolks
vanilla bean or extract (1 tsp.)

3. For the frosting:

semi-sweet cooking chocolate
granulated sugar

Break the 7 eggs, separate the yolks from the whites, and beat the whites until firm.

Pound or grind the walnuts and work them with the egg yolks and sugar. Fold in the stiffly beaten egg whites, then flavor to taste with grated lemon rind. Mix thoroughly.

Spoon into a nine-inch buttered cake pan and bake in a slow oven for about one hour.

Cool and unmold.

At the same time prepare a chocolate cream following the procedure in the recipe for *crème au chocolat.* Let it cool.

Melt some chocolate and sugar in a very small amount of water, let it cook for a moment, then frost the cake.

Serve the cake and the chocolate cream separately.

One could prepare similar cakes using hazel nuts, almonds, or chestnuts.

All these cakes could be served with a coffee-flavored boiled custard (*crème anglaise au café*). They would then be frosted with coffee frosting.

GÂTEAU GLACÉ AUX FRUITS

Ice-Box Cake with Fruit

Cut some lady fingers in half lengthwise. In a dessert mold placed over crushed ice, arrange a layer of lady finger halves on the bottom. Sprinkle this with maraschino or Curaçao, then add some very ripe, washed cherries which have been dried and cut in two, some seedless Corinth and Malaga raisins,[1] and some diced citron. Cover these with a layer of thick vanilla or pistachio dessert cream and let this freeze on ice or in the refrigerator. Add another layer of lady finger halves, and moisten this layer too with maraschino or Curaçao, sprinkle on some sliced pistachios, some fresh grapes, some diced pineapple simmered in pineapple syrup, cover with a layer of vanilla or pistachio dessert cream, and freeze.

Make four layers of lady fingers and fillings, as above, ending up with a layer of lady finger halves. Freeze.

Unmold at serving time.

NOTE

1. Corinth raisins are known as currants. The Malaga-type raisins grown in California are called muscat.

PRUNEAUX À LA PISTACHE

Prunes with Pistachios

Select some large, plump prunes. Carefully split them in two; remove the pits and in their place put a little pistachio nut paste.[1] Close up the prunes as neatly as possible. Arrange them on a serving dish.

For variation, one could, according to taste, substitute for the pistachio paste some almond, walnut, or hazel nut paste.

One could also stuff very ripe dates, figs, etc., this same way.

NOTE

1. To make nut paste, grind the nuts or pound them with some good brandy, pouring in some sugar syrup which has been cooked to the soft crack state (280° F.), using the following proportions:

1½ to 2 C. sugar
½ lb. nuts
2 T. liqueur of choice (kirsch, Curacao, anisette, rum, maraschino)

PRUNEAUX AU VIN

Prunes in Wine

For six people, use:

3 C. sweet wine (such as Muscatel)
1 lb. large prunes
cinnamon

Boil the wine and cinnamon in a porcelain or glass saucepan, to flavor the wine. Remove the cinnamon stick, then add the prunes to the boiling wine. Take the pan off the heat and let the prunes cool and absorb the liquid.

At the end of three days the prunes will have swollen and become saturated with the wine. They will have acquired a delicious flavor.

For variation, one could prepare these prunes by adding a little lemon rind to the cooking liquid. They would be served cold or chilled with *crème Chantilly*.[1]

These prunes could also be served in a pre-baked pie shell filled with a vanilla custard. The prune liquid should be reduced, cooled, and poured over the prunes and custard.

Serve well chilled.

NOTE

1. *Crème Chantilly* is heavy cream whipped with sugar and vanilla.

PÊCHES FLAMBÉES

Flaming Peaches

For six people, use:

1 C. brandy[1]
5 T. granulated sugar
6 large peaches

Scald the peaches and peel them with a towel. Poach them in a stainless steel, glass, or porcelain saucepan in a light sugar syrup, keeping the pan covered.

Finish cooking the peaches at the table: place the pan with its contents over an alcohol burner; pour in ⅔ cup of brandy, cover, heat up for a few moments, and ignite.

While it is flaming, sprinkle on the sugar, which will caramelize as it hits the flame.

Last, add the rest of the brandy, light again, and serve the peaches flaming.

Other fruits may be prepared in this way: pears or nectarines, which have been cooked in port or sherry and then flamed with brandy.

NOTE

1. Use a brandy such as *eau-de-vie de Châteauneuf-du-Pape*.

For four people, use:

1 lb. strawberries
1 lb. raspberries
1 C. vanilla-flavored sugar[1]
½ C. red port wine
1 qt. white wine
2 C. heavy cream
12 ripe pears (smooth-fleshed variety, not grainy)

POIRES GLACÉES

Chilled Pears

Peel the pears leaving the stem. Cook them in the white wine and let them cool in the liquid.

Crush the strawberries and raspberries and force them through a sieve, reserving the pulp.

In a bowl set over cracked ice, put the cream and sugar. Beat these together, adding the port wine little by little. Chill.

Fill a serving dish with the chilled cream and port wine mixture.

Drain the pears on a napkin, then arrange them on the cream and gently spoon one spoonful of the chilled berry pulp on each pear. Garnish the base of the fruit with the remaining pulp, and serve.

NOTE

1. To make vanilla-flavored sugar, simply add a vanilla bean to a jar full of granulated sugar. After several days the sugar will have become flavored with the vanilla. After each use, add more sugar and just keep the vanilla bean in the jar.

For six people, use:

2 lbs. apricots
1 lb. raspberries
5 T. heavy cream
1 T. gelatine
granulated sugar to taste

ABRICOTINE AUX FRAMBOISES

Apricot Ice Cream with Raspberries

Crush the raw apricots and force them through a sieve. Sweeten the pulp quite heavily.

Soften the gelatine in a little cold water, then dissolve by warming it gently. Whip the cream until stiff. Add the gelatine and cream to the apricot pulp and mix well.

Spoon this mixture into an ice cream mold and put the cover on tightly, using a towel between the mold and top so as to seal it well. Put the mold in a bucket filled with crushed ice and rock salt.[1]

Strain the raspberries through a fine sieve; sweeten the pulp and chill it.

Unmold the apricot ice cream, surround it with the chilled raspberry purée, and serve at once.

NOTE

1. This could also be put in a freezer compartment.

FRAISES AU JUS GLACÉ

Strawberries with Chilled Sauce

One method is as follows:

Select some large, plump, ripe strawberries.[1] Hull them and ar-

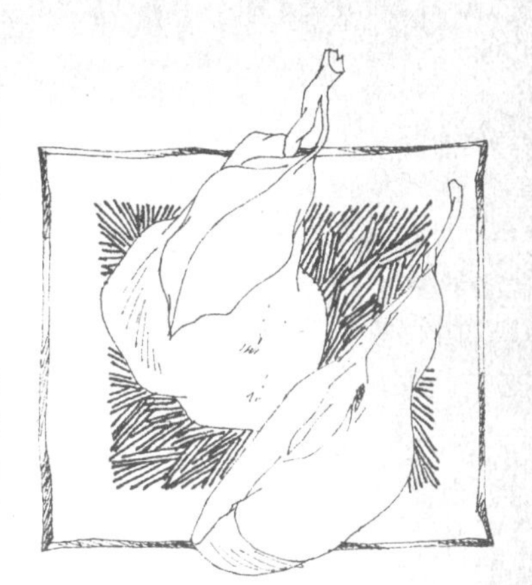

range the best-looking ones in pyramid fashion in a glass serving bowl. With the ones that are not so presentable, make a purée by crushing them and forcing them through a sieve or food mill. Season this purée with an equal quantity of sugar (by weight) and several drops of lemon juice. Chill for one hour.

At serving time, coat the strawberries with the chilled purée.

A second method is:

Select some very large strawberries, hull them, and arrange the best-looking ones in a glass serving bowl. Using any that are left as well as some plain ever-bearing strawberries, make some purée as above. Add an equal quantity (by weight) of granulated sugar and a little orange juice. Chill for one hour.

Coat the strawberries with the chilled purée at serving time.

NOTE

In France one would use a variety known as *fraises Héricart.* In the second recipe above the large strawberries would be a variety known as *fraises ananas* which were originally imported into France from the Americas.

FRAMBOISES AU JUS

Chilled Raspberries

Select some large, ripe, unblemished raspberries. Set aside the largest ones and force the rest through a sieve or food mill.

Cook the resulting pulp with an equal quantity (by weight) of sugar. When this is fairly cool, add the reserved raspberries and chill for an hour.

Arrange them in a bowl at serving time.

All sorts of fruit may be prepared this same way.

ORANGES AU SUCRE

Oranges with Sugar

Select some large, heavy, ripe oranges. Cut them into quarters, peel them, and remove any seeds. Put the fruit in a bowl with some granulated sugar. Cover and leave these together for one to one and a half hours, shaking the bowl from time to time.

Arrange the orange quarters in a glass serving bowl and pour the juice they have rendered over them.

FRUITS RAFRAICHIS

Dessert Fruit Salad

Fruits rafraichis, which are easy to prepare, make an excellent dessert which appeals to everybody.

For six people, use:

2 lbs. large strawberries[1]
2 lbs. raspberries
1 lb. red currants
3/4 C. vanilla-flavored sugar
7 T. kirsch
3 T. maraschino

The number of possible combinations of fruits and liqueurs is considerable. One can make all kinds of *fruits rafraichis.*

First: Here are four recipes:

Crush the raspberries and currants and strain the juice into a bowl that has a cover. Add the sugar, kirsch, and maraschino, and mix well. Put the strawberries on the liquid, cover and freeze for two hours in crushed ice and rock salt.

Serve with sherbet spoons.

Second: Juice some large sweet oranges. Add some pitted cherries to the juice, along with slices of pineapple. Freeze as above.

This combination is quite pleasant.

Third: Select some large strawberries,[3] some lemons and oranges.

Prepare a sugar syrup; flavor it with the juice and grated rind from the lemons and oranges. Add the strawberries and freeze as above.

In this simple but little-known recipe, the flavor of the strawberries is enhanced by the acidity of the citrus fruit.

Fourth: Select some perfectly ripe apricots and cherries. Cut the apricots in half and pit both the apricots and the cherries. Place the cherries in the apricot halves and arrange these on slices of pineapple in a glass serving bowl. Prepare some thick sugar syrup using apricot, cherry, and pineapple pulp. Season to taste with kirsch and Curaçao, coat the fruit, and chill.

MELON

Melon may be served as an hors-d'oeuvre, as a dessert, or as a fruit.

If one serves it, chilled or not, with salt and pepper, it seems to me that it ought to be classed with the hors-d'oeuvre. However, when it is sweetened, it ought to appear as a dessert or fruit.

It is far more digestible when mixed with certain wines or liqueurs: champagne, madeira, sherry, white port, cognac, kirsch, etc. It can then be prepared in three ways: whole, sliced, or puréed, and it can be served cooled, chilled, or candied (preserved).

When you wish to present the melon whole, cut a hole at the stem end so as to form a cork or plug. Scoop the seeds out throught the opening; then put in some vanilla-flavored sugar and 3/4 cup of wine, or 1/2 cup of some sort of liqueur. Plug it tightly and chill the melon in the refrigerator for at least four hours, turning the melon frequently, so that the liquid comes in contact with all of the inside surface.

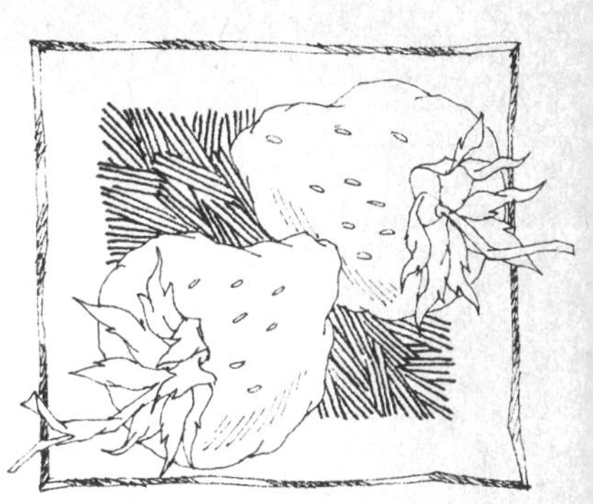

When you wish to serve sliced melon, chill it.

To chill it, as one does other fruits, slice it, discarding all but the edible parts. Strain any juice that might have drained off, and reserve. Roll the slices of melon in granulated sugar, arrange them in a silver vegetable dish, and let them marinate for three hours with some good cognac or some kirsch. At the end of this time most of the liquid should have been absorbed. Baste it with the reserved melon juice and ¾ cup of white port, madeira, or champagne. Cover the dish and put it in a bucket filled with ice and rock salt for two or three hours.

One may serve the slices individually or reform the melon. It is only a question of aesthetics.

To ice the melon, slice it as above, arrange it on a platter set over crushed ice and baste it with sweet wine, a liqueur, or some champagne. When one uses champagne, one could add a little lemon juice also.

To prepare a purée of melon, force the flesh through a sieve or food mill, flavor it to taste with sugar, wine, and liqueurs. You would then have a flavored purée which you would chill and serve in sherbet glasses.

I only mention candied or preserved melon, either whole or sliced, since its preparation is similar to that of other fruits and offers nothing unusual.

Last, one can serve melon as an ice. Here are the proportions for the different ingredients one should use:

For 3 cups of melon purée or pulp, use 3 cups of vanilla-flavored syrup,[1] the juice of 2 oranges and 2 lemons, a little grated orange rind, a few drops of orange-flower water, and 2 tablespoons of kirsch. Mix these ingredients, put them in a mold, and freeze.

All these melon dishes are popular.

NOTE

To make the syrup, dissolve 3 cups of sugar in 2 cups of water, add a vanilla bean (or use vanilla-flavored sugar), bring to a boil, and cool.

WINE

Natural wine is the product of the fermentation of fresh grape juice. Grapevines appeared on the earth during the Tertiary Period. Primitive man made use of the wild grapevines, instinctively seeking strong beverages. He was able to make an alcoholic drink from grapes by simply leaving the crushed grapes to ferment in the sun. As imperfect as this early wine was, it already had such seductive qualities that it was considered a gift from heaven and accorded divine honors. Osiris of Egypt, Bacchus of Greece and India, Saturn of Rome, and Noah of the Hebrews personified the first winegrowers in prehistoric times.

The culture of the grapevine seems to have been introduced to the French Mediterranean coast by the Phoenicians. Little by little, parallel with civilization, more favorable conditions were evolved for its culture, different varieties were developed, the procedure for making wine was perfected, but, unfortunately, scientific means for making it more sophisticated also appeared. One of the effects of Christianity was the improvement of viniculture and vinification (vine-growing and winemaking), since most of the monasteries had their own vineyards and each one manufactured its own wines. Many of today's well-known wines were originally created by monks.

Grapevines actually cover about one-fifteenth of the territorial surface of France. The wine industries employ millions of people and the production of wine is responsible for a great part of the French economy.

I do not intend to go into the rules of enology here, but, rather, I shall say a few words on the chemical composition of wine, the different qualities, which depend on the grape, soil, climate, degree of ripeness of the grapes used, care taken in the manufacture of the wine, and the age of the wine. I will also say a few words on drinking wine, furnish a few details on the principle winemaking regions of France, and, last, I shall speak a little about serving wine and the wine cellar.

CHEMICAL COMPOSITION OF WINES

The chemical composition of wines is fairly variable. In a general way, the most important ingredients, by weight, are water, which goes from 718 to 936 grams per liter; various alcohols, from 45 to 130 grams; glycerine, from 4 to 13 grams; tartrates, from 1 to 3.75 grams; sugar, from 1 to 3 grams (and even more for certain sweet wines such as Malaga, which contains up to 146 grams of sugar per liter); coloring matter, from 0.6 to 3 grams. All other ingredients only amount to from 9 to 13 grams per liter: ethers, essences, aldehydes, pectins, albuminoid substances, gums, dextrines, various acids and salts (iron, magnesium, alumina, etc.), volatile substances, ferments, and fermentable substances.

Extrait sec (dry extract) or *matières extractives* (extractive substances) of wine comprise the total of the nonvolatile substances at a temperature of 100° Centigrade (212° Fahrenheit). The proportion of *extrait sec* generally varies from 14 to 90 grams per liter, except in certain very sweet wines, where it can attain as much as 190 grams per liter. In general, in the better wines of France the *extrait sec* varies from 18 to 26 grams per liter.

Properties and Qualities of Wine

Wine, which poets call the blood of the vine, is a living liquid. It can get sick, it ages, and it dies.

It is considered a food because of the carbohydrates, albuminous (protein) and gelatinous substances, and salts which it contains. It spreads heat throughout the body and stimulates the appetite because of the alcohol and ethers it contains; it is tonic and fortifying, in part because of the iron; it is digestive because of the yeasts. Taken in moderate quantities it is truly beneficial to health.

The young white wines, as well as the white sparkling wines, are more or less laxative because of the carbonic acid; slightly acid white wines have diuretic properties; sparkling wines—principally those from Champagne—tend to soothe irritated mucous membranes.

The prolonged use of wine has certainly contributed to the formation and development of the fundamental characteristics of the French race—cordiality, candor, gayety, wit, and taste—which make the French so different from the beer-drinking peoples.

The principle qualities of wine are: color, taste, and aroma.

From the point of view of color, wines are divided into red and white.

Red wines are the product of the fermentation of black grape must. Their color, which is more or less tinged with purple, according to whether they are heavy or light, varies in shade from pink to brownish red, passing through cinnabar red, which is also known as onion-skin red, and which is characteristic of old wines.

White wines are most often the product of the fermentation of white (i.e., green) grape must. But they can also be produced from black grapes (with the exception of those called *teinturiers* [dyers]) by picking them off the stems and pressing them immediately. Their color varies from a light straw to an amber or golden yellow, characteristic of aged white wines with a larger amount of alcohol.

White wines made from white (i.e., green) grapes have a greenish tint; those made from black grapes have a rosy tone.

Gray wines, which come under the category of white wines, are the product of pink grapes, or white wines which have been tinted by the stem portions of black grapes vines. They can even be obtained by mixing red and white wines.

The color of a wine is often designated by the term *robe* (gown). It is due to the effect of tannins which moderate the action of alcohol on the nervous system. This explains why white wines, which contain less tannins than red wines, are more stimulating.

The special taste called *de terroir* is most often due to the type of soil on which the vine has been grown. Also, it is sometimes due to the type of fertilizers used.

One says that a wine is *fruité* (fruity) when it has the true taste of the grape; it is *équilibré* (balanced) when no single element is dominant and it has a true taste of wine. Perfect balance is a relatively rare quality.

A wine is called *bourru* (unfermented) when it contains a great many solid particles as it comes out of the vat.

A wine is called *dépouillé* (clarified) when the solid particles have come to rest on the bottom and do not affect its limpidity.

A *vin doux* (sweet wine) is a wine which has fermented very little. Only sweet white wines are drunk, as sweetness is a defect in red wine.

A wine is *fort* (strong) or *chaud* (hot) when it is loaded with alcohol; one also says it has *vinosité* ("winy-ness") and *feu* (fire). The wine is *généreux* (generous), when it produces, taken even in small quantities, a sensation of well-being, a tonic effect. It is called *capiteux* (heady) when it goes to the head; all heady wines are rich in alcohol. When a wine is too heady, it is often described as *fumeux* (vaporous—that is, making vapors rise to the head); it is also known as *casse-tête* (literally, head-buster).

A wine is *léger* (light) when it has a relatively low alcohol content; *frais* (fresh) when, at room temperature, because of its slightly acid flavor, it gives an agreeable sensation of freshness to the palate. This is due to the harmony among the alcohol, acid, and mucilages.

A wine is *corsé, étoffé* (strong, full-bodied) when it has a large quantity of alcohol, extract, and coloring matter, which gives a very special "full" sensation. One says that *il emplit la bouche* (it fills the mouth), *il a de la chair* (it has flesh), and *il a de la mache* (it has chew).

A *vin liquoreux* (liquorous wine) is a good wine, more or less heady, which has a velvety, sweet, and agreeable flavor. This term is primarily applicable to white wines such as Château d'Yquem. Sometimes these *vins liquoreux* are known under the name of *vins de paille* (straw wines) because, in their manufacture, one uses grapes in which the sugar has been concentrated by drying them somewhat in the sun, on straw.

Vins de liqueur (liqueur wines), which are red and white, are distinguished from the liquorous wines by a sweetness which is more pronounced, due to having been exposed to stronger sunlight or to cooking of the must; in the latter case they are called cooked or fortified wines; an example of these is Frontignan wine.

A wine is called *vif* (alive) when it makes a quick impression on the palate without any trace of acidity. *Vins vifs* generally have a brilliant hue.

Wine is called *nerveux* (nervous) when it has body and vivacity.

Wine is called *friand* (appetizing) if it is always drunk with pleasure, such as Chablis.

Wine is *moelleux* (rich, mellow) when it flatters the palate and tickles the tastebuds by its melting quality, which is due to the glycerides and gums. One sometimes says of a *moelleux* wine that it is *coulant* (smooth, flowing), that it is *tendre* (tender).

A *moelleux* wine which has body is termed *gras* (fat).

A white wine is *onctueux* (unctuous) when it is both velvety-smooth and sweet. Good Sauternes are very unctuous.

The *arome* (aroma)—that is, the impression it produces on the olfactory sense—is a product of the essences present, as well as of the breaking down and recombination of odorless substances. The aroma of wine is often designated by the term *bouquet* for red wine, and *parfum* (perfume) for white wine.

The *cachet* of a wine is its own individual character (stamp).

The term *sève* (vigor, pith) refers to its vital quality which poets call "the soul of a wine." This quality, which comes from the vine itself, is detected at the back of the palate on first contact. When a wine becomes too old, it loses its vigor, it dies, it is passé.

Wines that are *fin* (fine) are distinguished by the finesse of their vital quality, the pleasantness of their aroma, the crispness of their taste and color.

A wine which is pleasing to the taste and is also delicate is termed *distingué* (distinguished) by the natives of Bordeaux; it is *savoureux* (savory, tasty) when it has an abundant and agreeable *sève*; it is *suave* when it makes a gentle impression and releases an irresistible charm; one says, in that case, that it forms *la queue de paon* (peacock's tail) in the mouth.

A wine that is *velouté* (velvety) is at the same time *fin* and *moelleux* (fine and rich). In Burgundy they say that a *vin velouté* (velvety wine) *a de l'amour* (has love).

Grand vins (great wines) are those in which the sum total of their qualities has an undisputed and undisputable superiority.

One calls a wine *faible, mince*, or *maigre* (weak, thin, or lean) when it is very light, lacking fullness of body, extract, and color. When one drinks a weak wine it virtually seems that there is nothing between the tongue and palate.

A *vin dur* (hard wine) is one that lacks mellowness.

A red wine is *sec* (dry) when it lacks both body and mellowness; the taste of such a wine is slightly astringent; it has often lost some of its extract. Certain red wines become *sec* as they age.

A *sec* (dry) white wine is good when it is not liquorous; it warms the tongue and stimulates the nervous system. A type of good, dry white wine is Chablis.

A wine is *vert* (green) when it has an astringent quality due to lack of maturity of the grapes. Green wines contain an excess of potassium tartrate and tannin.

When a wine is *âpre* (harsh, bitter) it is difficult to swallow; it is called *acerbe* (sharp, acid) when the bitterness or harshness of the taste is characteristic of vegetable acids; it sets the teeth on edge.

A wine is *mou* or *plat* (flabby or flat) when it lacks body and the taste of the mucilaginous substances dominates all the others.

A wine is *lourd* (heavy) when it contains too much coloring matter and extract. Heavy wines contain much too much tannin and they are difficult to digest.

A wine is termed *gros* (coarse) or *bleu* (blue or literally black and blue) when it has too heightened a color, is bitter, and lacks taste.

Petit bleu (little blue) is the name given to the wine of Suresnes.

The term *piccolo* is applied to unpretentious wine.

The best wine years are those which, after a normal winter, the springtime has been bright, dry, and warm, the summer slightly hazy with alternating periods of rain and heat, and the weather has been dry during the grape harvest. However, many wines, once in the bottle, do not live up to what was expected of them when they were young—just as some precocious children do not.

Tasting Wine

One recognizes the different qualities of wines by tasting them, which consists in submitting them to the successive impressions they make on the different organs which are capable of appraising them: the eye, the nose, the tongue, the palate, the throat, and the stomach. For delicate wines one only needs the first five. This is largely sufficient since good wine, taken in moderate quantities, has never hurt anyone.

Here is how one goes about it. After having brought the wine out of the cellar, to a suitable temperature—17 to 18° C. (approximately 63 to 66° F.) for red Bordeaux, 12 to 13°C. (approximately 54 to 56° F.) for the red Burgundies, 10° C. (approximately 50° F.) for the nonsparkling white wines, and 8° C. (approximately 46° F.) or below for the sparkling wines—pour a small quantity into a large, fine crystal goblet[1] and examine the color; then twirl the glass several times to release the aroma and smell the bouquet; now wet the tip of the tongue, which will clearly inform you of certain properties, notably the acidity and astringency. If no perfume or other taste dominates, you may conclude that the wine is balanced. Now take a good mouthful, roll it around in your mouth, and keep it for a moment before swallowing, at the entrance to the pharynx, where certain sensations are particularly acute. This will allow you to note the qualities of *sève* (vigor), *corps* (body), finesse, and *moelleux* (richness, pith) of the beverage. Finally, swallow the liquid slowly, inhaling deeply at the same time; you will then get an impression of ensemble and you will be informed as to the after taste of the wine, which is important. All this is easy. What is less so is to determine, by this test, the vineyard and the age of the wine. Only a few select gourmets, trained by long practice in tasting authentic wines, are capable of resolving this question. Most people, however, even though they may have little taste sense, can at least recognize approximately if the wine is rich in taste, light, dry, sweet, or liquorous, if it is a Burgundy or a Bordeaux, if it is young, old, or passé.

The best practical way of testing ordinary, everyday wines is to taste them and then use them for a certain length of time. If they digest well and do not cause any acidity in the stomach or heaviness of the head, they are decent.

THE BEST WINES OF FRANCE

I deem it sufficient, insofar as the foreign wines are concerned, to have mentioned them in the various chapters dealing with foreign cuisine. So here I will only speak of the best wines of France: wines from Bordeaux, Burgundy, the Beaujolais, the Lyonnais, Champagne, Côtes du Rhône, Jura, Touraine, Anjou, and certain other regions worthy of mention.[2]

Bordeaux Wines

Viniculture, which is very ancient in the Bordelais,[3] received great impetus under the reign of the Emperor Probus. From the Fourteenth century on, the wines from the Médoc were very highly esteemed in Rome.

The reputation of Bordeaux wines began to spread throughout France during the thirteenth century, but for a long time their real value was not properly appreciated. It was only during the reign of Louis XV, after they had been introduced at Court by the Maréchal de Richelieu, that they became popular. Since then, their fame has continually spread; today it is universal.

The good wines of Bordeaux have a lovely color, a rich *sève*, supreme distinction, finesse, suavity, and an exquisite *velouté*; they are well-balanced wines; they are round and mellow; they are generous without being heady; they have a delightful bouquet; they travel well, which is important,[4] and the proportions of alcohol and tannin which they contain allow them to age without becoming desiccated. They are tonic, healthful, and digestive; they are the only wines which are suitable for the elderly and infirm.

The Bordelais soil belongs to the Mesozoic Period. The white (i.e., green) grapes are cultivated on a gravely, nonferruginous soil, which lies over a limestone and clay subsoil; the black grapes are cultivated on alluvial deposits which overlie a reddish, ferruginous limestone base.

The principal black grape is the *cabernet*; the *sémillon* is the principal white (i.e., green) grape.

The wines of Bordeaux may be classified, according to place of origin, into five groups:

1. Wines of the Médoc, on the left bank of the Gironde, to the north of Bordeaux;
2. The wines of Graves and Sauternes, northwest, west, and southeast of the town of Sauternes.
3. The wines of the *côtes* (hills), on the clayey slopes which line the banks of the Gironde and the Dordogne;
4. The wines from the region known as Entre-deux-Mers (between two seas), which lies between the Garonne and the Dordogne (this region provides the good ordinary wines and the blended wines);
5. Les Palus, a region which lies on the alluvial deposits of the valleys of the Dordogne, provides only very ordinary wines and blends.

GRAVES

There is only one great red wine, Château Haut-Brion (Pessac).

The white Graves wines differ from those of the Médoc because of a certain richness and vigor: a few are distinguished wines, but there are no classified Graves white wines.

CÔTES WINES

Wines from the *côtes* which are not classified and whose type is that of the Saint-Emilion deserve a few words.

The region of Saint-Emilion comprises the hills lying parallel to the Dordogne, stretching for seven to eight kilometers in length and three kilometers in width.

Wines of Saint-Émilion are a lovely, dark color, brilliant and velvety, they have body, an agreeable character, generosity, and a special bouquet faintly bordering on the bitter, which pleases the palate. They are often called the *bourgognes* (burgundies) of the Gironde. They are at their best after having been bottled for from ten to twenty years; certain ones may be kept as long as fifty years.

Certain unclassified Bordeaux are designated under the following: *bourgeois, bourgeois du Bas-Médoc, paroisses supérieures, artisans, palus,* and *paysans.* They are sold commercially under the generic names of Médoc, Fronsac, Cistrac, Saint-Estèphe, Saint-Émilion, Saint-Julien, Sauternes, Barsac, etc.

Burgundy Wines

The wines of Burgundy are as ancient as the wines of Bordeaux. Tacitus mentions them. The best vineyards of the area were well known from the third century on, but their real popularity only goes back to the thirteenth century, at the time when the wines of Pommard and Volnay were in great repute. During the fourteenth century the wine of Beaune, which was the only one privileged to appear at the royal table on coronation day, was considered the best in France.

The wines of Burgundy from good vineyards are warm, perfumed, strong, generous, mellow, delicious; they have a very special and agreeable bouquet; they are stimulating; they activate the digestion; they give verve and vivacity of spirit. But they are heady. They are suitable for healthy and active people; people who are nervous, plethoric, ill, or elderly should avoid them.

The wines of Burgundy owe their quality to the soil, to the excellence of the grape, the *pineau,* and to the climate of the region, which is regularly cold in winter and hot in summer. The varied types of soil within the region often lead the vineyard proprietors to make happy mixtures, which in turn have produced a great variety of wines in Burgundy; free classification of these wines (none being official) is much more difficult than that of the Bordeaux. Since the Phylloxera[5] epidemic most of the wines of Burgundy, with the exception of the Hospices de Beaune wines, are *procédé,* that is, sweetened; the proportion of sugar added varies from 5 to 15 kilograms per 228 liter cask.

The soil of Burgundy is fairly chalky and the minerals which seem to affect the quality of the wines are limestone, iron, alumina, and silica.

Burgundy wines may be classified geographically into three zones:

1. Haute-Bourgogne (Côte d'Or);
2. Basse-Bourgogne (Yonne), which is also called the *bouquet de la Bourgogne;*
3. Bourgogne, without any other special designation, com-

prising the département of Saône-et-Loire to the south of Mâcon, just about at the boundary of the commune known as Chapelle-de-Guinchay, where the Jurassic terrain gives way to more primitive terrains and the wine passes from the Burgundy type to the Beaujolais.

RED WINES

The wines of Haute-Bourgogne may be subdivided into three groups which are, by order of importance: those of the Côte de Nuits, from Gevrey to Corgolin; of the Côte de Beaune, from Ladois-Serrigny to Decize (Saône-et-Loire); those of the Côte de Dijon, going from the hills along the left bank of the Ouche, to the far end of the commune of Gevrey-Chambertin.

Côte de Nuits

The wines of the Côte de Nuits are reputedly the best of Burgundy; they are fine and rich and have an exceptional bouquet; they are at their best when they are about twelve years old; one may, however, keep those from the best years for as long as thirty years. Gourmets tend to think that they have an after taste of cassis (black currant).

Côte de Beaune

The wines from the Côte de Beaune have a characteristic perfume which seems to be like a delicious combination of violet and raspberry and a taste which recalls at the same time the peach and the plum. They are true, rich in color, mellow, full of fire and bouquet. They keep for a fairly long time.

Basse-Bourgogne

The wines of Basse-Bourgogne are most often delicate, rich in bouquet, and relatively light. Unfortunately a great number of the ancient vineyards no longer exist.

Bourgogne

Wines which are simply called *de Bourgogne* (Burgundy) comprise those from the Côtes Châlonnaise and Mâconnaise.

WHITE WINES

All the great white wines of Burgundy are produced by the grape known as *chardonnay*. They are extremely stimulating, and, unless one is accustomed to them, one should drink them in moderation.

The principle vineyards are Montrachet and Meursault in the region of Haute-Bourgogne, Chablis in Basse-Bourgogne, and Pouilly in the region known as Bourgogne without any other designation.

Lyonnais Wines

The Lyonnais, which stretches from Burgundy to the Velay and from Auvergne to the Dauphiné, is geographically divided into three regions: the Beaujolais, the Lyonnais proper, and the Forez. Only the first two produce notable wines.

Beaujolais Wines

The Beaujolais region borders on the Mâconnais, but it is completely different from the point of view of geological structure. It comprises a part of the *départements* of Saône and Rhône and a part of the *département* of Saône-et-Loire, as far as the valley of Gien.

The terrain is essentially primitive: granite, gneiss, schist, and feldspar.

The red wines of Beaujolais are reknowned. They are produced from the *gamay* grape, and the vines are located in the communes of Beaujeu and Belleville. These wines are a lovely color; they are fresh, light, very agreeable, with a characteristic taste of soil. They attain their maximum quality after four or five years; but they must not be kept too long, as they fade quite quickly. They do not travel well.

Champagne Wines

The wines of Champagne were known in very early times. The Emperor Probus planted vines in Champagne, as he had done in Burgundy. The first date back to the year A.D. 280.

Saint Rémy, patron saint of Reims, who died in 530, and later on the priests of his diocese, developed some magnificent vineyards in that area.

In 1397 Wenceslas, king of Bohemia and emperor of Germany,

who had come to Reims to negotiate a treaty with Charles VI, developed such a taste for the wines of that region that, when the envoys from the king of France came to fetch him to bring him to their sovereign, they found him dead drunk—which simplified the negotiations no end.

Agnès Sorel,[6] who adored champagne, thought it tasted of peach.

In the sixteenth century, Francois I, Charles V, Leon X of Médici, and Henry VIII of England, acquired vineyards at Ay; and at the coronation of Henri III the wine of champagne took the place of the wine of Beaune.

Only the natural wines of Champagne were known at the time, reds and whites, which combined the character of the Burgundy wines with a great finesse of flavor and a remarkable bouquet. It was only at the end of the seventeenth century, around 1695, that Dom Perignon, who was a monk from the abbey of Hautevillers (near Épernay) and a fine gourmet, got the idea of turning them into sparkling wines. His scientific experiments were completed at last in 1836 by a certain François, chemist from Reims, who established the exact proportions of sugar necessary for obtaining the best sparkling wines.

Today, with the exception of a few red wines, it is scarcely possible to sample any of the natural still wines of Champagne, except in the homes of vineyard proprietors. Most of them are gasified to make sparkling champagne, whose reputation is worldwide.

The soil of Champagne arises from the cretaceous system, and many silica and limestone pebbles are found in the soil of the regional vineyards.

The black grapes come from dark soils, the white (i.e., green) grapes from gray or yellowish terrain.

The black grape varieties are *pineau noir, meunier, vert doré d'Ay* or *morrillon d'Épernay*, and *pineau gris*. Those of the white (i.e., green) grapes are the *gamay, mestier*, and *pineau blanc chardonay d'Avize*.

RED WINES

In Champagne they still manufacture a limited number of vats of red wine, for a very few connoisseurs.

WHITE WINES

White wines are harvested in three regions of the Marne: the Montagne de Reims, the valley of the Marne, and the hills of Avize. The first are fresh and full-bodied; the second ones, all produced from black grapes yielding white wine, are very mellow and have an extraordinary bouquet; the last group are very delicate.

CLASSIFICATION

Any classification of vineyards, by order of merit, is difficult at best and has nothing absolute about it. Most are classified by competent connoisseurs, with serious intent, and that is about all that can be said on the matter.

One may, naturally, "champagnize" all wines (this is a very widespread industry today); but without the vineyards of Champagne it is impossible to produce sparkling wines comparable to those of Champagne proper.[7]

The real wines of Champagne, of an incredible finesse, delicious tasting, fresh, and transparent, are stimulating and digestive. They must be served cool, like all white wine, but not chilled too well,[8] since too much cold affects the delicate aroma. They have the remarkable quality of eliciting gayety, of making one see life through rose-colored glasses. How many invalids owe them their last illusions! The intoxication which they bring on, if abused, is also a gay one; but this abuse unfortunately elevates the blood pressure. They have been responsible for strokes, and most heavy Champagne drinkers have hypertension. One can be poisoned even by beautiful flowers!

From the practical standpoint, the classification of vineyards is relatively unimportant for the ordinary consumer. Each commerical brand has its formulas and dosages; the art of the manufacturer consists in combining the grapes from different vineyards so as to create as harmonious a mixture as possible. It is enough to be able to distinguish brands and years; the taste varies a great deal according to brand; as to years, there are definitely better and lesser ones.

Here too, nothing is infallible, since even in a good year a manufacturer can fail in his mixtures.

One of the best old Champagnes that I have ever tasted was a Cliquot Sec 1869. I tasted it a long time ago, and it was unforgettable.

Most of the wineries classify their products as brut, extra-dry, or dry (which is said to be the English and American taste), sec or demi-sec (which is said to be the French taste). There are also *champagnes doux* (sweet champagnes) and *tisanes* (light champagnes for invalids).

Few vineyards, even in the best years, produce enough natural sugar to make perfect sparkling wines, and, if certain naturally "brut" wines are excellent, they are frequently hard. The different types of champagne are generally produced from more or less heady wines to which have been added a variable proportion of crystallized sugar dissolved in some old champagne, or sometimes in some old *eau-de-vie de champagne* (champagne brandy). These are naturally the dryest wines, those in which there is the least artificial sweetening and those which best conserve the fundamental qualities of the natural wines of Champagne. The sweet wines and the *tisanes* are produced from light wines from lesser vats. As a result, certain Vouvray and Saumur wines are preferable to certain *tisanes* from Champagne.

Wines from the Côtes du Rhône

The parts of the Côtes du Rhône which produce the best wines of the region stretch from north of the Ardèche and the Lez, to the right and left of the Rhône.

The soil is partly granitic and partly calcareous, the latter belonging to the Jurassic system.

The varieties are: *petit syrah* for the dark grapes, *roussanne* for the white (i.e., green) grapes.

Jura Wines

The soil of the Jura is, for the most part, chalky, of the liassic system (part of the Jurassic). The climate is rather hard and humid. Nevertheless, certain Jura wines are interesting.

The varieties which produce the best wines are the *poulsard noir*, the *pineau blanc chardonay*, the *sauvignon blanc*, and the *trousseau*.

In the Jura they also manufacture many sparkling wines called "de l'Étoile" from the names of the vineyards, which are very pleasant, and also a straw wine which has no equal, but whose quantity is unfortunately very limited.

Touraine Wines

The vines which produce the red wines of Touraine are cultivated south of the Loire, in the valleys, upon ancient alluvial deposits, or on chalky hills. Those that produce the white wines are cultivated on sandy or chalky terrain, north of the Loire.

The choice red wines come from a Bordelais grape, the *cabernet franc* or *breton*; they are reminiscent of Bordeaux wines, but, though they have more vivacity and freshness, they are less full-bodied and have less bouquet.

The white wines come from the *pineau blanc*; they are fresh and perfumed, and their perfume is reminiscent of quince.

Anjou Wines

The wines of Anjou are grown on hills where schist predominates.

The reputation of Anjou wines is mainly due to the sparkling wines, which are very sparkly and fresh but which really lack richness and flavor. They can by no means be compared to the wines of Champagne, which their devotees often try to do.

There are a few red and white still wines that are worthy of note.

The best red wines of Anjou come from the *breton* grape, the best whites from the *chenin blanc*.

Alsatian Wines

Alsace mainly produces locally popular white wines, as well as straw wines which are reminiscent of Tokay wine.

Lorraine Wines

Lorraine produces red and white wines.

A Few Interesting Wines from Other Regions

Saint-Pourçain	(Allier)	White, dry, sparkling.
Blanquette de Limous	(Aude)	White, very sweet, much bouquet.
Miserey	(Doubs)	White, exquisite taste, brilliant. Analogous to the white wines of Arbois.
Tavel	(Gard)	Red, little color, strong, very agreeable.
Lunel	(Hérault)	Originally treated as a sweet wine; sold as a natural wine nowadays.
Jurançon	(Basses-Pyrénées)	White, well known locally, slightly pink, heady, faint perfume of truffle.
Banyuls	(Pyrénées-Orientales)	Red liqueur wine, stimulating and tonic.
Rivesaltes	(Pyrénées-Orientales)	White liqueur wine, fine, generous, and perfumed.
Clos des Altesses	(Savoie)	Liquorous and sparkling.

Serving Wines

Volumes have been written on how to serve wine. Certain authors have had the presumption to impose wines from certain vineyards for each different course of a meal. It seems to me that this is going too far, particularly since it is easier said than done. What is certain, is that one must avoid unpleasant clashes. The host who serves Banyuls wine with oysters under the pretext that his Banyuls is very good, a liqueur with game, or a fine Burgundy with a custard blatantly displays his gastronomic ignorance.

Many people feel that madeira, port, etc., should be served after the soup. In my opinion, this is a terrible heresy. Drunk at the beginning of a meal, they make the mouth sticky, and it is impossible to appreciate other wines. A fairly dry Château d'Yquem, a Château Suduiraut, a Barsac, a Montrachet, or a Meursault would be very suitable. Dry white wines are fine with oysters and fish; the red Bordeaux go well with red meats, chicken, and vegetables; the red burgundies and the wines from the Côtes du Rhône should be served with highly seasoned foods, game, and cheese; the liqueurs and sparkling wines go well with desserts. But let it be understood that one can make an excellent meal with just one wine, as long as it is not sweet. I remember an excellent luncheon with champagne and a remarkable dinner accompanied from start to finish by an aged Pontet-Canet wine. However, the tongue does finally get saturated when drinking only one wine.

For a modest gourmet meal, one could get away with, for instance, a Chablis, a Meursault, or a Suduiraut for white wine; a Saint-Émilion, a second or third growth (*cru*) from Bordeaux, a Côte-Rôtie, or a Corton, for red wine.

For a very fine gourmet meal, one could serve some of the pearls in our jewelcase: wines from Haut-Brion, Margaux, Lafite, La Tour, d'Yquem, Ermitage, Romanée-Conti, Clos Vougeot, Musigny Chambertin, Montrachet.

But, whatever the wines, the red burgundies must be served right from the cellar; the red Bordeaux must be at room temperature and be served from carafes; all white wines must be served cool.

As to very ordinary wines: if they are mediocre, I would prefer simply to drink water during the meal and top it off, if I possibly could, with one small glass of good wine, rather than imbide heavy wines or a synthetic wine diluted with water. For a table wine I heartily recommend a small Chablis, a red Beaujolais, or an unclassified Saint-Julien. In the country, many local wines, which generally do not travel well, are very suitable.

The Wine Cellar

Should one create a cellar—that is, buy wine in the barrel, care for it until it is bottled, and let it age—or should one buy it little by little as needed, even though it is more expensive that way?

Unless one is wealthy enough to have a wine steward who knows his business, and supply him with a large enough annual budget and a perfect wine cellar,[9] the simplest and safest is to deal with competent and conscientious suppliers (they do exist) who can deliver, when necessary, good, natural wines, honestly manufactured, which have all the necessary healthful qualities that one has the right to demand of them, and some fine wines, properly aged, from authentic vineyards and specific years.[10] One thus avoids the unpleasantness of losing a whole barrel of wine, and one will then have on hand a choice of impeccable wines—which would otherwise be impossible. The above was suggested to me by the friend who is mentioned in note 10 below. Because of the jolting caused by cars and the heat from fuel burners, he has absolutely given up the idea of having a cellar. I lean on the best authority and on my own personal experience, when I recommend this method as the most suitable for city dwellers. Only those enophiles living in the country can sensibly have a wine cellar.

NOTES

1. Many professional wine-tasters use a shallow silver cup, which, according to them, allows them to better appreciate the color of wine by its reflection. In my opinion, nothing is as nice as a delicate crystal goblet. The only advantage I can see to the shallow, silver wine-taster's cup is that it is portable—which may be important, since they have to move around a lot. Wine-tasters often have to taste so many wines in one morning that they have to eliminate the last part of the ritual, which is not the least agreeable part. Instead of swallowing the wine, they spit it out and rinse their mouth after each taste, for fear of becoming confused.

2. I think that most of my readers agree with my thinking when it comes to the supremacy of French wines; not everyone is of this opinion, however, and I would feel guilty if I did not take note of a completely different opinion expressed by a German *Konnaisseur:* The wines of France," he states, "are wines without thought [?]; ones drinks them because they taste good, but it is only when one drinks Rhine wine that one thinks!"

3. The Bordelais region is formed by the *département* of the Gi-

ronde and by a part of the *arrondissement de Bergerac* (Dordogne).

4. Transportation by water (on a ship) even activates their aging.

5. In 1863 an American louse called Phylloxera was accidentally imported into Europe and large winegrowing areas were devastated as the pest spread.

6. Mistress of King Charles VII of France.

7. To avoid fraud, the law only authorizes the use of the word "Champagne" on the lable and cork of wines harvested and manufactured in Champagne.

8. The habit of serving champagne ice cold or very chilled is only justified if one is dealing with green wines which have been oversweetened, such as the *tisanes*.

9. A wine cellar must, above all, be free from any tremor such as jolting from traffic. The sub-basement of an observatory would be fine. It must be airy but not too much so, with openings only to the north or east. The temperature must be as constant as possible: never below 10° C. (50° F.), nor above 16° C. (61° F.) On the whole it must be dry. All these are very difficult conditions to provide.

If the wine cellar is damp, one must take particular pains in corking to avoid any of the corks becoming mildewed by the dampness.

10. One day when we had an eminent physician and a well-known wine-taster to dinner, I served wines which I had brought from the wine merchant myself and which I had poured into carafes personally, to avoid any possible detection. Without the slightest hesitation or the merest error, our friend spelled out the vineyards and the years.

This experience honors both the wine-taster and wine merchant.

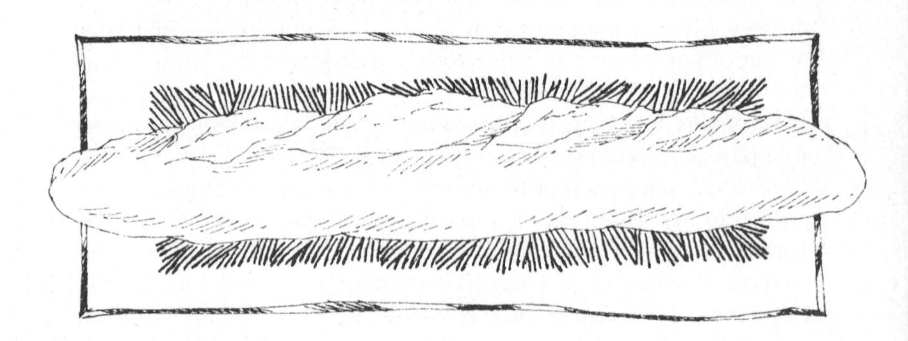

GLOSSARY

[*Note:* In the first part of the book Ali-Bab has gone extensively into culinary nomenclature, so here we will list only certain things which apply specifically to this translation.]

Au Gratin.

Dishes prepared with a sauce and topped with breadcrumbs or breadcrumbs and cheese, then browned in the oven or under a broiler are called *au gratin.*

Bacon.

French bacon is known as *lard maigre fumé*. It is less salty and milder in flavor than American bacon. Because of this, in using American bacon it is advisable to blanch the bacon in boiling water for about ten minutes, then rinse in cold water and dry thoroughly. This removes the saltiness and smoky flavor which would tend to permeate the dish and mask other flavors.

Barding.

This means to wrap foods (usually meats) in a thin sheet of pork fat.

Bouquet Garni.

This term refers to a bunch of herbs which generally consists of bay leaf, thyme, and parsley. These herbs, if fresh, may be tied together, or, if not, they may be wrapped in washed cheesecloth and then dropped into the soups or ragoûts, etc., which they are to flavor. Note that European bay leaves are milder than American ones, so use less if no imported ones are available. Ali-Bab generally specifies the herbs for each bouquet; if he does not, then it is safe to use 1 bay leaf, 3 sprigs of parsley, and 1 sprig of thyme (or some dried, chopped thyme).

Butter.

French butter has a slightly different taste from American butter, since it is made from matured cream and, probably because of this, acquires a pleasant, almost nutlike flavor. It is usually unsalted. Although lightly salted butter is acceptable in most dishes, except for sweet desserts, the original Ali-Bab recipes were most certainly all prepared with unsalted butter. If one is using lightly salted butter, then, the overall salt content of the dish must be taken into account. For this reason we have not specified amounts of salt, preferring to use the phrase "to taste."

The salt in butter has a tendency to fall to the bottom when it is melted, along with any other impurities, and this burns before the butter is hot. Because of this it is preferable to use clarified butter when sautéeing foods.

For clarified butter heat butter in an enamel or glass saucepan very slowly, until it is completely melted. Let it rest a few moments, then skim off the milky foam, or *casein*, which has risen to the surface. Carefully pour off the clear, yellow, liquid butter, leaving any residue which has settled at the bottom of the pan. This residue and milky foam can be saved for flavoring other dishes. For each cup of butter you will get about 3/4 cup of clarified butter.

For *beurre manié*: this is butter which has been worked to a paste with an equal or greater quantity of flour, either using a fork or fingers. Small balls of this paste are used for thickening sauces, etc., at the last minute. One tablespoon will thicken about 3/4 to 1 cup of liquid.

Caramel.

When caramel (for coloring) is called for, it is made by putting sugar into a heavy skillet and stirring with a wooden spoon as it melts, so that it will color evenly without burning. The pan is then removed from the heat and a small amount of water stirred in (keeping a lid partially over the pan to avoid spattering). The liquid should be amber-reddish in color.

Clarifying Stock.

When clarifying stock, make sure that the surface is absolutely free from any fat or grease by careful skimming. Then chop or grind an equal quantity of celery, onion, and carrot, and combine these with unbeaten egg whites. Beat these together until frothy. Pour the lukewarm stock over this mixture and then pour everything into a saucepan. Heat gently, just to the simmering point, agitating the pan slightly. Keep at a simmer without stirring for about twenty minutes. The liquid should very gently bubble up through the crust that has formed at the surface. Pour the stock through a fine strainer lined with damp flannel or several layers of cheesecloth. Sometimes, for enrichment, lean, ground beef is added to the vegetable-egg-white mixture.

Cordon Bleu.

This is the blue ribbon of gastronomy. In France it is conferred on female cooks who are renowned for the excellence of their cooking.

Cream.

French cream is different from American cream in that it is thicker and has acquired a slightly acid flavor from having been gradually fermented or soured at room temperature.

Although heavy whipping cream (if it contains at least thirty percent butterfat) may be used in most recipes, a fair approximation of French heavy cream—which is paradoxically called *crème fraîche*—can easily be made at home, since it is not commercially available in the United States.

Here are three methods for making it:

First: In a saucepan, mix 3 teaspoons of commercial buttermilk with 1 cup of heavy whipping cream. Heat these to lukewarm, then spoon into a jar and let stand at room temperature overnight, or until it has thickened. Stir and refrigerate.

Second: In a jar, mix 1 cup heavy whipping cream with 3 tablespoons of commercial yogurt. Keep in a warm spot overnight (an un-lit, pilot-warmed oven is ideal). Stir and refrigerate.

Third: Repeat the second procedure, using 1 cup heavy whipping cream mixed with 1/3 cup commercial sour cream.

The advantage of using this type of cream (which should contain over thirty percent butterfat) is that it will not curdle when added to hot foods. American commercial sour cream cannot be substituted for this, because it has too low a butterfat content. The term *crème double* refers to cream obtained by centrifugal separation, which contains at least thirty percent butterfat as against ten to twenty percent in cream which has been allowed to rise naturally, known in French as *crème simple* or *fleurette*.

Crème Chantilly: this is cream which has been whipped with sugar and vanilla.

Crème: This term is also applied to dessert creams such as boiled custard and pastry cream, which are generally a mixture of egg yolks and milk, plus flavoring.

Croustade.

This is either a fried bread casing or pastry crust which is used to contain delicately cooked fish, game, ragoûts, hashes, or other entrées.

Croûtons.

Small cubes or slices of firm bread fried in butter.

Deglazing.

This is a very important procedure in French cuisine. It consists of adding some sort of liquid to a pan in which meat has been roasted, broiled, or sautéed, and scraping the bottom of the pan to extract all the flavor of the residues. The proper procedure is to remove the main ingredient, then pour in a liquid such as wine or bouillon, according to the recipe. Next the bottom is scraped with a spoon or spatula, to remove any adhering particles. The sauce can then be flavored, thickened, and enriched.

Fines Herbes.

This term actually applies to a mixture of fresh, aromatic herbs, usually consisting of parsley, chervil, tarragon, and chives. Quite often, however, it is mistakenly applied to just parlsey.

Flour.

The quantities of flour specified in the translation of the Ali-Bab recipes apply to unsifted, all-purpose flour (1 cup = 140 grams).

Forcemeat.

This is a mixture of finely chopped or ground meat or fish, which is usually bound with eggs or other thickening agent. It is seasoned, and often includes other ingredients such as truffles, mushrooms, etc. Forcemeat is used either alone or as a stuffing or garnish. The French word *farce* is best translated as stuffing or filling in English. Forcemeat is a more appropriate term than stuffing, since, although forcemeat is used to stuff meat, fish, poultry, etc., it can also be made into quenelles, *pâtés*, terrines, etc., where it is definitely not a "stuffing."

Garnish, Garniture.

This is just what the name implies. However, in French the word is also used to denote the ingredients which are used to fill something, such as a pastry crust, vol-au-vent, or vegetable, etc. In this sense it is not strictly a garnish but a filling.

Gratin Dish.

This is a heatproof, oven-to-table shallow dish or pan. French gratin dishes, which can be round, oval, or rectangular, are usually heat-resistant enough for stove-top cooking, as well as baking, and they usually have two small handles for easier handling.

Hot Water Bath.

This is basically a hot water bath which could consist of any shape or size pan in which another pan can be set. The water in the bottom pan should come one-half to two-thirds of the way up the pan in which food is to be cooked or kept warm. When cooking such things as delicate sauces, for instance, the water in the bottom pan would be kept at a simmer. To keep foods warm, the water should be below simmering. This type of hot water bath can also be used in the oven for cooking such dishes as custards. Cooking in a *bain-marie* corresponds to cooking in a double boiler, but the water in the *bain-marie* surrounds the food rather than being just underneath. Delicate foods can thus be kept warm without overcooking.

Larding.

This means to run strips of seasoned pork fat through meat with a larding needle or skewer.

Macerate, Marinate.

Both these terms mean to soak food in seasoned liquid. The term marinate generally applies to meats, whereas the word macerate applies most often to fruits soaked in alcohol of some sort.

Pepper.

Unless otherwise specified the word pepper in a recipe refers to ordinary black peppercorns, freshly ground.

Reduce.

This means to reduce a liquid to give it body and concentrate the flavor. Ali-Bab often specifies that a sauce should be reduced either to a half or a third, etc.

Roux.

This is simply fat and flour cooked together, and it is used to thicken sauces. Brown roux is used for brown sauces; white roux is fat (usually butter) and flour cooked together without browning, and is used to make light sauces such as Béchamel, etc.

Simmer.

This means to keep a liquid at below-boiling temperature so that it barely shivers and only very tiny bubbles are occasionally visible.

Terrine.

Technically this is an earthenware container. It could be round, oval, or oblong. It is used for cooking (potting) meats, poultry, fish, game, etc. A terrine often acquires the name of the food which is cooked in it, such as *terrine de lièvre*. Terrines are served cold. An old-fashioned term for such a dish was "potted meat."

ABOUT HENRI BABINSKI

Author of Ali-Bab's Encyclopedia of Practical Gastronomy

Henri Babinski was born in Paris, July 2, 1855. His father was Polish, naturalized French. He died in Paris August 20, 1931. His younger brother, Joseph, also born in Paris, became a famous physician. He was the discoverer of the well-known Babinski syndrome for detecting neurological problems. Henri Babinski entered the École Nationale des Mines (National School of Mines) in 1874. He became a civil mining engineer in 1878 and in 1880 started to travel a great deal in order to study mineral deposits in many different countries. In South America, in the Equatorial region, he lived under very trying and hostile conditions. A couple of years later, enthused by the unusual mining development taking place in the western part of the United States, Babinski took part in prospecting for gold in several of the young western states, where he studied the problems in developing these prospects on a sound financial basis.

In 1887 he returned to French Guiana to study two gold mining areas, both as to ore veins (lodes) and alluvial deposits. At this time he published his first scientific paper. Upon his return to Europe he was immediately called upon to participate in the development of "gold bearing placers" in northern Italy.

His South American assignments were by far his favorites and in 1893 he returned to Chile, to study some coal deposits in the south between Punta Arenas and the Argentine frontier. Audacious and creative, Babinski set up a system for towing the coal barges through the straits of Magellan using coal mined in the area to fuel the tugs.

After this brilliant mission, he went, in 1896, to Brazil to examine some diamond mines in the state of Bahia where he set up the mining venture. After this he undertook many other prospecting missions and his voyages were, for Babinski, not only professional successes but would eventually lead him into his true vocation.

"For my part, I admit having reached the age of twenty-five without having the slightest notion of what culinary art was. And it was only in the course of my first long voyages, as a young engineer, when I was prospecting for mineral deposits in distant lands, that I got a taste for cuisine. My companions and I were reduced to nourishing ourselves by hunting and fishing and the natives would usually boil or broil our bounty, without any other preparation. We had little means of varying our menus except for the few canned goods which we carried, and of which we quickly tired. We had to struggle against lack of appetite and anemia as a result. Therefore, the slightest innovation in the preparation of the food was received with enthusiasm, just because it would give us a gustatory sensation which broke the usual monotony."

This is how Ali-Bab came into being, as he himself states in the Preface to the first edition (1907) of *Gastronomie Pratique, Études Culinaires*, preceded by *Gastronomie a Travers les Ages*, and followed by *Traitement de l'Obésité des Gourmands*.

Other editions followed, totaling for the French-language version (Edition Flammarion) more than 35,000 copies. As soon as it appeared, Ali-Bab received tremendous recognition and Henri Babinski was dubbed the "Brillat-Savarin of the XXth century." His work on the treatment of obesity of gourmands was very well received in medical circles and was reproduced in several medical journals.

On the personal side, those who knew him recognized him as a highly intellectual person, a very enterprising man, who was also kind and very generous.

INDEX

A

B

C

D

E

F

G

H

I

J

K

L

M

N

O

P

S

T

V

NOTES

NOTES

NOTES

NOTES